Successful Writing at Work

EIGHTH EDITION

Successful Writing at Work

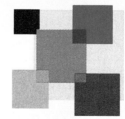

Philip C. Kolin
University of Southern Mississippi

Houghton Mifflin Company
Boston New York

To Kristin, Eric, and Theresa
Evan Philip and Megan Elise
Julie and Loretta
and
MARY

Publisher: Patricia A. Coryell
Editor in Chief: Suzanne Phelps Weir
Senior Sponsoring Editor: Lisa Kimball
Associate Editor: Bruce Cantley
Senior Project Editor: Tracy Patruno
Senior Manufacturing Coordinator: Karen Fawcett
Senior Marketing Manager: Cindy Graff Cohen
Marketing Assistant: Kelly Kunert

Cover image: © Mick Wiggins

Microsoft® Clip Art reprinted by permission from Microsoft® Corporation.

Printed in the U.S.A. UNIVERSITY OF CHICHESTER

Library of Congress Control Number: 2005936528

Instructor's exam copy:
ISBN-13: 978-0-618-69396-2
ISBN-10: 0-618-69396-3

For orders, use student text ISBNs:
ISBN-13: 978-0-618-59370-5
ISBN-10: 0-618-59370-5

3456789-DOC-10 09 08 07 06

CONTENTS

Chapter 10: Summarizing Material

PART IV: Preparing Documents and Visuals

Chapter 11: Designing Clear Visuals

PREFACE

Successful Writing at Work is a comprehensive introductory text for technical, business, professional, and occupational writing courses. As many readers of earlier editions of this popular text have learned, this book can help students develop and master key communication skills essential for career advancement. Writing is a vital part of virtually every job today—and this real-world, practical textbook will guide students to become better writers while they also learn to develop effective workplace documents and visual communications.

The eighth edition offers the most current and extensive application of communication technologies—the Internet, e-mail, computer graphics, presentation software, instant messaging, blogging, digital cameras, electronic files—for writing successfully in the rapidly changing world of work. Equally important, this new edition expands and illustrates the coverage of writing for an international audience at work in the global marketplace.

To do all the above, *Successful Writing at Work* helps students by giving them detailed guidelines for writing and designing clear, well-organized, and readable documents and websites. Effective models are critical in learning new skills, and students will find a wide range of realistic and rhetorically diverse examples (almost all of them annotated and visually varied) drawn from websites, e-mails, student papers and reports, letters and memos, proposals, graphics packages, questionnaires, instructions, minutes, summaries, news releases, company manuals, and magazine and journal articles. These examples—all focusing directly on practical issues in the world of work—portray writers as successful employees.

You'll notice that the trim size for this edition has been enlarged to offer a more open design and accommodate the annotation of sample documents. This new edition is also as versatile as it is comprehensive. Full enough for a 16-week semester, it can also be easily adapted to a shorter 6-, 8-, or 10-week course. Furthermore, this text is designed to go beyond classroom applications: It is a ready reference that students can easily carry with them as they begin or advance in the workplace. As students will quickly find, this edition, like those that preceded it, is rich in practical applications equally as useful to readers with little or no job experience as to those with years of experience in one or several fields.

Viewing the Writer as a Problem Solver

The eighth edition continues to emphasize that writing is a problem-solving activity that helps employees meet the needs of their employers, co-workers, customers, clients, community groups, and vendors worldwide. This edition also emphasizes the most up-to-date technologies to help students become better problem solvers, and hence better writers, by using the varied resources of an evolving, ever more complex workplace that is intertwined with technology. *Successful Writing at Work* presents multiple situations and problems that students writing for the global marketplace will have to address and asks them to consider the rhetorical and technical options available for solving these problems. Another strong feature of the eighth edition is a series of additional case studies showing how writers find resources and develop rhetorical strategies to solve problems in the business world.

Consistent with this overall view of writing as workplace problem solving, the eighth edition expands its coverage of writing as a process for both print and online media. Technology is integrated into its rhetorical applications. Students will find helpful and concise explanations of the *hows* as well as the *whys* of writing for the digital world of work. Accordingly, *Successful Writing at Work* teaches students how to develop the critical skills of brainstorming, researching (through print and online sources), drafting, revising, editing, formatting, and proofreading various business and technical documents—e-mail, correspondence, instructions and procedures, proposals, news releases, short and long reports, websites, and presentations. Through the variety of new case studies and reports, the eighth edition helps students to understand why the mastery of such skills is essential to career advancement.

Emphasis on Audience Analysis and Students as Global Business Professionals

The eighth edition also stresses audience analysis, with greater attention to the writer's obligation to make ethical decisions in meeting the readers' needs and in fulfilling commitments to employers worldwide. This new edition, however, devotes even more space to the legal and ethical use of e-mail, online research, and Web design. Moreover, given the additional Internet applications in this new edition, the concept of audience has been inevitably extended to readers worldwide, whether as co-workers, employers, clients, or representatives of various agencies and organizations. E-mail, letters, websites, instructions, news releases, proposals, and short and long reports are all considered from the points of view of the intended audience(s), again with greater emphasis on the needs of non-native speakers of English, both in this country and abroad.

To engage students more fully in job-related writing, *Successful Writing at Work* addresses them as professionals seeking advancement at different phases of a business career. For example, they are seen as employees who must learn to collaborate as part of a writing team in Chapter 3; as customer relations representatives meeting the needs of employers and customers with specific requests, problems, and complaints in Chapter 6; as job candidates preparing a variety of documents related to a job search in Chapter 7; as researchers who use both primary and secondary sources for company report in Chapter 8; as Web designers developing, constructing, writing, editing, or evaluating sites in Chapter 12; as competitive businesspeople writing a persuasive proposal to win a contract in Chapter 14; as training specialists writing a report on recruiting and retaining a multinational work force in Chapter 16; and as videoconferencing experts making a PowerPoint sales presentation in Chapter 17.

New Material in the Eighth Edition

In addition to its new, more contemporary and open design, the eighth edition has been streamlined and updated to make it a more effective tool for instructors and more useful resource for students both in the classroom and in their jobs. New guidelines, effective and ineffective examples, figures, case studies, model reports, and exercises make the discussion of workplace writing more relevant and current.

The following features are new to the eighth edition:

- **Greatly enhanced coverage of globalization.** New material on thinking and writing globally has been added to this edition to respect and reflect the traditions and communication needs of international audiences. Emphasis is placed on the increasingly international workplace through examples and guidelines.
- **Updated technology coverage.** To keep up with the expanding and ever-changing use of technology in the workplace, coverage of technology has been updated and enhanced, including new material on blogs, instant messaging, online résumés, presentation software, and more.
- **Expanded and updated Tech Notes.** Tech Notes are much more global and better cross-referenced in the text. Those retained from previous editions have been updated, and many new ones have been added. All the Tech Notes in this edition now offer relevant, widely applicable guidelines rather than step-by-step instructions since students use different software and computer platforms.
- **New Chapter 8, "Doing Research for School and on the Job."** This brand new chapter accounts for the multiple research strategies and resources used both for school assignments and in the world of work. Attention is given to both primary research through questionnaires and interviews and secondary research using print and online sources. This chapter also includes new Tech Notes throughout, key annotated models of searches, and practical guidelines on Web searching.
- **Annotated letters and sample documents throughout.** Annotations have been added for almost all sample letters, memos, e-mails, résumés, instructions, procedures, proposals, short and long reports, and the PowerPoint presentation. The annotations highlight rhetorical and stylistic decisions writers have made for effective communication worldwide. Ineffective sample documents are annotated to show students problems to be aware of and how to avoid them.
- **A refocused chapter on "Writing Letters: Some Basics for Audiences Worldwide" (Chapter 5).** This heavily revised chapter provides extensive new information on international business correspondence. Guidelines, information boxes, Tech Notes, and sample letters provide students with valuable materials to research the most effective and culturally acceptable ways to communicate with international readers.
- **More on ethics.** Greater attention has been paid to ethical writing, particularly in sections on writing letters, avoiding sexist language, incorporating and writing about visuals, and researching using the Internet.
- **Revised business report in Chapter 16.** The report on recruiting and retaining a multinational workforce has been revised to change it from a sample research

paper for a school project to an actual report submitted to a manager in the world of work.

An overview of the eighth edition will show how all these new materials have been integrated.

Overview of Part I

Part I deals with the overall writing process. Chapter 1 sets the stage for all occupational writing by describing the needs of the global marketplace, then identifies the basic concepts of audience analysis, purpose, message, persuasion, style, tone, and ethics, and relates these concepts to on-the-job writing.

Chapter 2, on the writing process at work, introduces students to prewriting strategies, drafting, revising, and editing their written work.

Chapter 3 emphasizes the importance of collaborative writing in the world of work and gives students valuable and easy-to-apply guidelines for being productive, cooperative members of a writing team. This chapter also explores some of the major problems writers face when working together and suggests positive, effective strategies for resolving these problems. Three case studies reinforce these points and introduce software programs that aid in the collaborative process.

Overview of Part II

Part II concentrates on global business correspondence. Chapter 4 offers abundant examples of and guidelines for writing memos, faxes, and e-mails in the workplace.

Chapter 5 introduces the nuts and bolts of letter writing and focuses on selecting the appropriate format, language, tone, and content. It also includes major sections on writing for international readers and researching and incorporating their cultural communication protocols into business correspondence.

Chapter 6 examines the rhetorical strategies for producing a variety of business correspondence—inquiry, complaint, adjustment, and sales letters—with additional material on organizational strategies for good-news or bad-news letters, and an expanded discussion, with many new examples, of writing for international readers.

Chapter 7, covering the job search, takes students through the process of preparing a placement file; writing a résumé and organizing it by skill area or chronology, and sending it via the Internet as well as through more conventional means; formatting and organizing online résumés; locating appropriate job openings, through online and print searches; writing a letter of application; interviewing do's and don't's; determining realistic salary expectations; and accepting or declining a job offer. For greater teaching flexibility, instructors will find six application letters and six résumés (print and online versions for one) from applicants with varying degrees of experience—welcome models for new and veteran job seekers alike.

Overview of Part III

Part III, on gathering and summarizing information, occupies a key position in the eighth edition. It helps students acquire the techniques they need to be skilled researchers and accurate writers. Chapter 8, "Doing Research for School and on the

Job," an innovative reconceptualization of the research process as it relates to business writing, is brand new to this edition. The chapter takes a dual approach, simultaneously providing instruction on doing research in an academic context and offering practical advice on how research is prepared and used in the workplace, particularly via questionnaires, surveys, interviews, etc. All of the essential research topics are here—from primary and secondary research to searching periodical databases and doing research on the Internet. The dual focus emphasizes that research is not only a process geared toward writing college papers, but also a skill students will need to master when they enter the world of work.

Chapter 9 is devoted to proper documentation and is based on the most recent methods advocated by the MLA and APA style guides, as well as the *Chicago Manual of Style*. Detailed guidelines show students how to document a variety of print and electronic sources. A revised, updated, and annotated student research paper, "The Advantages of Telecommuting in the Information Age," illustrates how to quote and document print, electronic, and Internet sources, and to import visuals for more effective workplace writing. Greater emphasis is placed on avoiding plagiarism.

In Chapter 10 students learn how to write clear and concise summaries and abstracts, prepare executive summaries for decision makers, and construct cogent and concise news releases for both print and Web readers.

Overview of Part IV

In Part IV students have the opportunity to apply the skills they learned in Part III to more complex writing assignments. The section focuses on key business and technical writing documents—instructions, proposals, and reports.

Chapters 11 and 12 form a unit on the related topics of creating visuals and designing documents and websites. Chapter 11 supplies practical advice on designing and writing about visuals, with emphasis on including visuals in instructions and reports. The chapter discusses and illustrates a variety of visuals, especially from the Web, along with the necessary precautions that students need to take. The chapter offers a greatly expanded and updated section on computer graphics, and concludes with new sections on ethics and visuals and preparing visuals for international readers.

A greatly expanded and updated Chapter 12 stresses the significance of document design and gives students practical advice and pertinent examples for making their work more reader-friendly and visually appealing. The chapter also contains detailed guidelines, with varied models, for preparing websites. In doing so, the chapter emphasizes the differences between a print message and a Web message. Much new material on assessing, designing, and writing websites is included along with new "effective" and "ineffective" sites as examples.

Chapter 13 covers writing accurate instructions and procedures in depth and selecting the most appropriate language and visuals, including an expanded section on the legal considerations and guidelines in writing about protocols and procedures at work.

Chapter 14 explores three common types of proposals: an internal proposal for an employer, a sales proposal (solicited and unsolicited) for customers, and a research proposal for an instructor.

Chapter 15 outlines the principles common to all short reports and then discusses specific types, including sales reports, progress reports, trip/travel reports, test reports, and incident reports. Finally, students are again cautioned about the legal and ethical implications of what they write and are shown how to avoid typical legal pitfalls.

To make it easily accessible to students, Chapter 16, on long reports, has been streamlined for this edition to emphasize the *process* of writing such a report. Students are encouraged to see a long report as the culmination of all their work in the course or on a major project at work. The individual parts of such a report are discussed and illustrated in detail, with a fully annotated and updated model business report from a training specialist to her boss, a human resources manager on the importance of multinational workers in the U.S. work force. This paper, together with the Chapter 9 report on telecommuting and the long report on AIDS and health care workers in the Instructor's Guide, give instructors three complete, documented student research papers from which to teach the long report.

Chapter 17, which stresses the importance of audience analysis in presentations at work, offers commonsense advice for preparing briefings and conferences and on generating, organizing, and delivering formal presentations. This chapter includes a new PowerPoint presentation on the benefits of videoconferencing. It also contains new material on effective telephone use and proper cell phone etiquette.

Supplements

The *Successful Writing at Work,* Eighth Edition, **Online Study Center** (college.hmco .com/pic/kolin8e) provides support directly related to the book. Features include:

- **Revision Checklists** will help students review significant strategies from the text and revise and edit their assignments.
- **ACE Self-Tests** allow students to check their knowledge of important concepts from their reading.
- **Technology Activities** feature software, word processing, e-mail, and Web-based activities that will improve technology skills and knowledge.
- **Web Links** offer relevant websites that expand on topics covered in the text

WriteSpace for *Successful Writing at Work,* Houghton Mifflin's new Blackboard-powered electronic writing program, provides students with an extensive array of writing tutorials and assignments. Students get lots of extra practice and immediate feedback when completing these exercises:

- Expanded technology activities with discussion questions
- Web design tutorial, a step-by-step nontechnical tutorial for designing a website
- Research and documentation tutorial
- Finding an internship or job tutorial
- Collaborative writing tutorial
- Diagnostic tests and exercises

Instructors praise WriteSpace's flexible course management system, with an online gradebook linked to the exercises (so that keeping track of student progress is easy); one convenient environment for course objectives, syllabi, and class information; and the chance to interact with students through live online hours, discussion boards, chat rooms, and an announcement center. Visit *www.eduspace.com* for more information or to sign up for a demo.

The **Student Resource Center** at the Houghton Mifflin website for students provides additional support for coursework.

The *Successful Writing at Work,* Eighth Edition, **Online Teaching Center** (college.hmco.com/pic/kolin8e) extends the book's lessons online, with additional suggestions for in-class exercises and homework assignments.

The *Instructor's Guide,* available at the Online Teaching Center, is updated and revised with five sections. Part 1, "Some Suggestions on How to Teach Job-Related Writing," includes a discussion of writing for international/multicultural readers, guidance on using technology in the writing classroom, collaborative writing, and more. Part II, "Planning a Course with *Successful Writing at Work,*" includes sample syllabi for using the book in short courses, full-semester courses, or online courses. Part III, "Some Teaching-Learning Resources," is an extensive categorized bibliography of resources. Part IV, "Answers to Exercises," includes author comments on the exercises and suggested answers. Part V, "Transparency and Photocopy Masters," includes transparency masters of the exercise answers for class discussion and additional examples of letters, abstracts, visuals, websites, news releases, policy regulations, reports, and case studies.

A new **Blackboard Course Cartridge** and **Web/CT e-pack** provides flexible, efficient, and creative ways for instructors to present materials and manage distance-learning courses. Instructors can use an electronic gradebook, receive papers from students enrolled in the course via the Internet, and track student use of the communication and collaborative functions.

Acknowledgments

In a very real sense, the eighth edition has profited from a collaboration of various reviewers with the author. I am, therefore, honored to thank the following reviewers who have helped me improve the eighth edition significantly:

Nevin Laib, *College of Notre Dame of Maryland*

Tiffany Armand, *State University of West Virginia*

Michael Piotrowski, *University of Toledo*

Erin Herberg, *Rowan University*

Dean Thorpe, *Del Mar College*

Julie Vedder, *West Virginia University*

Nancy Knowles, *Eastern Oregon University*

Maury Maryanow, *Troy State University*

Tina L. Hanlon, *Ferrum College*

Nancy Barron, *Northern Arizona University*

Kyle Bishop, *Southern Utah University*

Mark Smith, *Valdosta State University*

Brenda Aghahowa, *Chicago State University*

Rosemary Golini, *Rhode Island College*

J. Andrew Prall, *University of Saint Francis*

Gary Grund, *Rhode Island College*

Angela K. Rowland, *West Virginia University, Parkersburg; Washington State Community College*

Anne Hendricks Papworth, *BYU-Idaho*

I am also deeply grateful to the following individuals at the University of Southern Mississippi for their help as I prepared the eighth edition. From the Department of English, I thank Deana Holifield, Micah Stack, Ben Butler, Sherry Smith, and William Kuskin; thanks also to Cliff Burgess (Department of Computer Science), Naofumi Tatsumi (Department of Foreign Languages), and Mary Lux (Department of Medical Technology). To the following librarians at Cook Library goes my gratitude for their help—Kay Wall, Mary Beth Applin, Maria Englert, and Irmi Wolfe. I also thank Terri Smith Ruckel at Louisiana State University for her assistance with Chapter 16.

Several individuals from business and industry also gave me valuable assistance, for which I am thankful. They include Joycelyn Woolfolk at the Federal Reserve Bank in Atlanta; Sally Eddy at Georgia Pacific; John Krumpos at Gulf Paper Company; Cathy and Hilary J. Englert at Rice's Potato Chips; Don McCarthy, an independent computer programmer; Russell Dukette at Petro Automotive Group; and Susan Swartwout and Mike Howell from Southeast Missouri State University.

I am also especially grateful to Father Michael Tracey for his counsel and his contributions to Chapter 12 on document design, especially on websites.

I am very grateful to Anna Gibson and Lori Brister for their invaluable help throughout this edition as I updated discussions and Tech Notes on communication technologies and prepared Chapter 8. I am also grateful to Sherry Rankins-Robertson for creating the *Instructor's Guide* that accompanies the text.

My thanks go to my editors at Houghton Mifflin for their assistance, encouragement, and friendship—Michael Gillespie, Bruce Cantley, Lisa Kimball, Julia Casson, and Tracy Patruno, and to Alison Fields at Books By Design.

I deeply thank my extended family—Sister Carmelita Stinn, Mary and Ralph Torrelli, and Margie and Al Parish—for their prayers and love.

Finally, I am grateful to my son Eric, my daughter-in-law Theresa, and my grandson Evan Philip and granddaughter Megan Elise for their love and encouragement. My daughter Kristin merits extraordinary praise for all the times she assisted me throughout this new edition by doing various searches and revisions and by offering practical advice on successful writing at work.

P.C.K.

Successful Writing at Work

PART I

Backgrounds

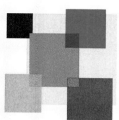

1 Getting Started
Writing and Your Career

2 The Writing Process at Work

**3 Collaborative Writing and
Meetings at Work**

CHAPTER 1

Getting Started
Writing and Your Career

What skills have you learned in school or on the job this year? Perhaps you have learned health care techniques to become a nurse, respiratory therapist, or dental hygienist. Maybe you have received training in law enforcement to work in crime detection or traffic control. Possibly you have studied or worked in software technology, agriculture, computer science, hotel and restaurant management, or forestry. Or maybe you have improved skills that will make you a better marketing specialist, salesperson, office manager, programmer, paralegal, or accountant. Whatever your area of accomplishment, the practical know-how you have acquired is crucial for your career.

Online Study Center

To expand your understanding of writing and your career, take advantage of the ACE quizzes, sample documents, Web links, and exercises at college .hmco.com/pic/ kolin8e

Writing—An Essential Job Skill

Writing is also a part of every job, from your initial letter of application conveying first impressions to the memos, e-mail, business letters, proposals, and reports that will earn you raises and promotions.

The Associated Press reported in a recent survey that "most American businesses say workers need to improve their writing . . . skills." The same report cited a survey of 402 companies that identified writing as "the most valued skill of employees." Still, the employers polled in that survey indicated that 80 percent of their employees need to work on their writing skills. Clearly, then, writing is an essential skill for employers and employees alike. Figure 1.1 is an e-mail from a human resources director offering an incentive to employees to improve their writing skills by taking a college writing course.

As Rowe Pinkerton, the author of that e-mail, realizes, among the most costeffective skills you can offer a prospective employer is your writing ability. Businesses pay a premium price for good writing. According to Don Bagin, a communications consultant, most people need an hour or more to write a typical business letter. If an employer is paying someone $30,000 a year, one letter costs $14 of that employee's time; for someone who earns $50,000 a year, the cost of the average letter jumps to $24. Mistakes in letters are also costly. As David F. Noble cautions in his

Figure 1.1   An employer's view of the importance of writing.

```
Reply        Save        Forward        Print        Delete
```

To: All Employees
From: <rpinkerton@greer.com>
Date: 5/10/2007 8:45 a.m. EST
Subject: New company benefit to improve writing

Stresses the importance of writing

I am pleased to announce a new company benefit approved by the Board at its meeting last week. In its continuing effort to improve writing in the workplace, Greer, Inc. will offer tuition reimbursement to any employee who takes a course in business, technical, or occupational writing, starting this fall.

Three Requirements:
To qualify, employees must do the following:

(1) Submit a two-page proposal on how such a course will improve the employee's job performance here at Greer.

Clearly explains how to take advantage of company offer

(2) Take the class at one of the approved colleges or universities in the Clevand area listed on the attachment to this e-mail.

(3) Provide proof (through a transcript or final grade report) that he or she has successfully completed the course.

To apply, submit your proposal to Dawn Wagner-Lawlor in Human Resources (dwlawlor@greer.com) at least one month before you intend to enroll in the course.

Closes on an upbeat note

Here's to productive writing!

Rowe Pinkerton
Human Resources
781-555-3692
<rpinkerton@greer.com>

book *Gallery of Best Cover Letters*, "the cost of a cover letter (in applying for a job) might be as much as a third of a million dollars—even more—if you figure the amount of income and benefits you don't receive over, say, a 10-year period for a job you don't get because of an error that got you screened out."

The workplace contains numerous reminders of the importance of writing—printers, PCs, disks, monitors, scanners, keyboards, fax machines, and text messaging via smartphones. Business communication also depends on software for PowerPoint presentations, e-mail, Web searches, and graphics. All of this hardware and software is essential. Why? Writing keeps business moving. It allows employees to communicate with one another, with management, and with the customers and clients that the company must serve to stay in business. In your job, you can expect to write e-mail, letters, memos, summaries, instructions, questionnaires, proposals, reports, and much more. This book will show you, step by step, how to write those and other job-related communications easily and competently.

Tech Note

Know Your Computer at Work

A large part of your responsibilities in the workplace will involve writing electronically. To enhance your value as an employee, become knowledgeable about your company's computer system. That includes being familiar with its computer support services, how to report computer problems, the software packages your employer uses, and the location of user manuals. In addition, try to stay informed about new and updated versions of business software packages as they become available. With such knowledge you will increase your opportunities for success.

Chapter 1 gives you some basic information about writing in the global marketplace and offers major questions you can ask yourself to make the writing process easier and the results more effective. It also describes the basic functions of on-the-job writing and introduces you to one of the most important requirements in the business world—writing ethically.

Writing for the Global Marketplace

The Internet, e-mail, express delivery, teleconferencing, and e-commerce have in effect shrunk the world into a global village. It is no longer feasible to think of business in exclusively regional or even national terms. Many companies are multinational corporations with offices throughout the world. In fact, many U.S. businesses are branches of international firms. A large, multinational corporation may have its equipment designed in Japan, built in Bangladesh, and sold in Detroit, Atlanta, and Los Angeles. Its stockholders may be in Mexico City as well as Saudi Arabia—in fact, anywhere. In this global economy, every country is affected by every other one, and all of them are connected by the Internet.

Companies must compete for international sales to stay in business. Every business, whether large or small, has to appeal to diverse international markets to be

Online Study Center

Locate writing and your career globalization exercises at college.hmco .com/pic/kolin8e competitive. Each year a larger share of the U.S. gross national product (GNP) depends on global markets. Some U.S. firms estimate that 30 to 40 percent of their business is conducted outside the United States. Wal-Mart, for example, has opened hundreds of stores in mainland China, and General Electric has plants in fifty countries. If your company has a website, then it is an international business.

To be a successful employee in this highly competitive, global market, you will have to communicate clearly and diplomatically with a host of readers from different cultural backgrounds. Adopting a global perspective on business will help you communicate and build goodwill with the customers you write to, no matter where they live—across town, in another state, or on other continents, miles and time zones away. As a result, don't presume that you will be writing only to native speakers of American English. As a part of your job, you may communicate with readers in Singapore, Malaysia, or India, for example, who speak varieties of English quite different from American English. You will also very likely be writing to readers for whom English is not their first (or native) language. These international readers will have varying degrees of proficiency in English, from a fairly good command to little comprehension without the use of a foreign language dictionary and grammar book to decode your message. These individuals, who may reside either in the United States or in a foreign country, constitute a large and important audience for your work.

See the World Through Their Eyes

Writing to international readers with proper business etiquette means first learning about their cultural values and assumptions—what they esteem and also what they regard as communication taboos. They may not do business exactly the way it is done in the United States, and to think they should is wrong. Your international audience is likely to have different expectations of how they want a letter addressed or written to them, how they prefer a proposal to be submitted, or how they wish a business meeting to be conducted. Their concepts of time, family, money, work, managers, and communication itself may be nothing like those concepts in the United States. If you misunderstand their culture by inadvertently writing or saying something inappropriate, it can cost your company a contract and you your job.

Cultural diversity exists inside as well as outside the company you work for. Don't conclude that your boss or co-workers are all native speakers of English, either, or that they come from the same cultural background that you do. In the next decade, as much as 40 to 50 percent of the U.S. skilled work force may be composed of immigrants who bring their own traditions and languages with them. These are highly educated, multicultural, and multinational individuals who have acquired English as a second language. For the common good of your company, you need to be respectful of these international colleagues. The long report on pages 680–697 describes some ways in which you can both acknowledge and respect the different cultural traditions of these colleagues in the world of work. Businesses want to emphasize their international presence. Figure 1.2 shows how a large corporation like Citibank helps customers worldwide.

But whether these international readers are your customers or co-workers, you will have to adapt your writing to respect their language needs and communication

A company's dedication to globalization.   Figure 1.2

How Citigroup Meets Banking Needs Around the World

WITH A BANKING EMPIRE that spans more than 100 countries, Citigroup is experienced at meeting the diverse financial services needs of businesses, individuals, customers, and governments. The bank is headquartered in New York City but has offices in Africa, Asia, Central and South America, Europe, the Middle East, as well as throughout North America. Live or work in Japan? You can open a checking account at Citigroup's Citibank branch in downtown Tokyo. How about Mexico? Visit a Grupo Financiero Banamex-Accival branch, owned by Citigroup. Citigroup owns European American Bank and has even bought a stake in a Shanghai-based bank with an eye toward attracting more of China's $1 trillion in bank deposits. Between acquisitions and long-established branches, Citigroup covers the globe from the Atlantic to the Pacific and the Indian Oceans.

Many of Citigroup's banking services in other countries are geared toward businesses of all sizes. Small businesses (which the bank calls companies with up to $10 million in

annual sales) not only can use Citigroup's checking and investment accounts, but they also can apply for loans. Retailers and other businesses can have Citigroup process their credit card transactions. The bank also provides more complex financial services for medium-sized and large businesses. For example, a corporation that needs capital can ask Citigroup to arrange for a public offering of its stock or have Citigroup sell bonds on its behalf. Businesses with sizable pension fund portfolios can contract with Citigroup to handle these investments.

Individuals can use Citigroup for all the usual banking services . . . . Personalized service is the hallmark of . . . the bank, which can help prepare customized financial plans for . . . customers, manage their securities trading activities, provide trust services, and much more. What's more, Citigroup is active in communities around the world through philanthropic contributions and grants, financial literacy seminars, volunteerism, and supplier diversity programs. This financial services giant strives for the best of both worlds, wielding its global presence and resources to meet banking needs locally, one customer at a time.

Source: From Pride, Hughes, and Kapoor, *Business,* 8th ed., p. 587. Copyright © 2005 by Houghton Mifflin Company. Used by permission.

protocols. The words, idioms, phrases, and sentences you choose instinctively for U.S. readers may not be appropriate for an audience for whom English is a second, or even third, language. If you find a set of directions accompanying your computer or software package confusing, imagine how much more intimidating such a document would be for a non-native speaker of English. To communicate with non-native speakers, you will have to use "international English," a way of writing that is easily understood, culturally tactful, and diplomatic. International English simply means that your message is clear, straightforward, and appropriate for readers who are not native speakers of English. It is free from complex, hard-to-process sentences as well as from cultural bias. International English is discussed in detail on pages 169–179. Later chapters of this book also give you guidelines on writing e-mail, correspondence, instructions, reports, websites, and other work-related documents for the global marketplace.

■ Four Keys to Effective Writing

Effective writing on the job is carefully planned, thoroughly researched, and clearly presented. Its purpose is always to accomplish a specific goal and be as persuasive as possible. Whether you send a routine e-mail to a co-worker in Cincinnati or in China or a special report to the president of the company, your writing will be more effective if you ask yourself four questions.

1. *Who* will read what I write? (Identify your *audience*.)
2. *Why* should they read what I write? (Establish your *purpose*.)
3. *What* do I have to say to them? (Formulate your *message*.)
4. *How* can I best communicate? (Select your *style* and *tone*.)

The questions *who? why? what?* and *how?* do not function independently; they are all related. You write (1) for a specific audience (2) with a clearly defined purpose in mind (3) about a topic your readers need to understand (4) in language appropriate for the occasion. Once you answer the first question, you are off to a good start toward answering the other three. Now let us examine each of the four questions in detail.

Identifying Your Audience

Knowing *who* makes up your audience is one of your most important responsibilities as a writer. Expect to analyze your audience throughout the composing process.

Look for a minute at the posters in Figures 1.3, 1.4, and 1.5. The main purpose of all three posters is the same: to discourage people from smoking. The essential message in each poster—smoking is dangerous to your health—is also the same. But note how the different details—words, photographs, situations—have been selected to appeal to three different audiences.

The poster in Figure 1.3 is aimed at fathers who smoke. As you can see, it is an image of a father smoking next to his son, who is reaching for his pack of cigarettes. Note how the caption "Will Your Child Follow in Your Steps?" plays on the fact that the father and son are literally sitting on steps, but at the same time the word *steps* implies *footsteps,* as in "following in one's footsteps." The statistic at the bottom

No-smoking poster aimed at fathers who smoke.   **Figure 1.3**

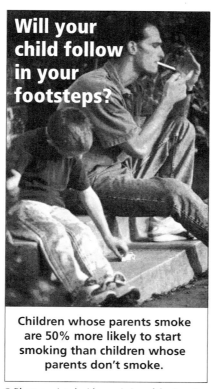

Will your child follow in your footsteps?

Children whose parents smoke are 50% more likely to start smoking than children whose parents don't smoke.

© Photo reprinted with permission of the American Heart Association.

of the poster reinforces both the photo caption and the image, hitting home the point that parental behavior strongly influences children's behavior. Already the child in the photograph is following his father's lead and showing a clear interest in smoking.

The poster in Figure 1.4 is aimed at an audience of pregnant women and appropriately shows a woman with a lit cigarette. The words on the poster appeal to a mother's sense of responsibility as the reason to stop smoking, a reason to which pregnant women would be most likely to respond.

Figure 1.5 is directed toward young athletes. The word *smoke* is aimed directly at their game and their goal. In fact, the ad writers appropriately made the goal the same for the game as for the players' lives. Note, too, how this image is suitable for an international audience.

The copywriters who created these posters have chosen appropriate details—words, pictures, captions, and so on—to convince each audience not to smoke. With their careful choices, they successfully answered the question "How can we best communicate with each audience?" Note that details relevant for one audience (athletes, for example) could not be used as effectively for another audience (such as fathers).

Figure 1.4   No-smoking poster directed at pregnant women.

Photo © 2005 JupiterImages Corporation.

The three messages illustrate some fundamental points you need to keep in mind when identifying your audience.

- Members of each audience differ in backgrounds, experiences, needs, and opinions.
- How you picture your audience will determine what you say to them.
- Viewing something from the audience's perspective will help you to select the most relevant details for that audience.

Some Questions to Ask About Your Audience

You can form a fairly accurate picture of your audience by asking yourself some questions *before* you write. For each audience for whom you write, consider the following questions.

1. **Who is my audience?** What individual(s) will most likely be reading my work?

   If you are writing for individuals at work:

   - What is my reader's job title? Co-worker? Immediate supervisor? Vice president?
   - What kind of job experience, education, and interests does my reader have?

No-smoking poster appealing to young athletes.   Figure 1.5

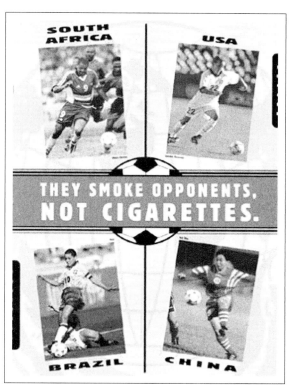

If you are writing for clients or consumers (a very large, sometimes fragmented audience):

- How can I find out about their interest in my product or service?
- How much will this audience know about my company? About me?

2. How many people will make up my audience?

- Will just one individual read what I write (the nurse on the next shift, the production manager) or will many people read it (all the consumers of a product)?
- Will my boss want to see my work (say, a letter to a consumer in response to a complaint) to approve it?
- Will my letter bear someone else's name, not mine?
- Will I be sending my message to a large group of people sharing a similar interest in my topic, such as a listserv?

3. How well does my audience understand English?

- Are all my readers native speakers of English?
- Will I be communicating with people all around the globe?

- Will some of my readers have English as a second or even third language, and so require extra sensitivity on my part to their needs as non-native speakers of English?
- Are my English-speaking readers all located within the United States, or are some from other English-speaking countries, such as England, Australia, Liberia, Ireland, or New Zealand?
- Will some of my readers speak no English, but instead use an English grammar book and foreign language dictionary to understand what I've written?

4. How much does my audience already know about my writing topic?

- Will my audience know as much as I do about the particular problem or issue, or will they need to be briefed or updated?
- Are my readers familiar with, and do they expect me to use, technical terms and descriptions, or will I have to provide easy-to-understand comparisons and nontechnical summaries?
- Will I need to include detailed visuals or maps, or will a photograph or simple drawing be enough?

5. What is my audience's reason for reading my work?

- Is my communication part of their routine duties, or are they looking for information to solve a problem or make a decision?
- Am I writing to describe benefits that another writer or company cannot offer—that is, am I trying to persuade them to buy a product or a service?
- Will my readers expect complete details, or will a short summary be enough for their purpose?
- Are they reading my work to make an important decision affecting a co-worker, a client, or a community?
- Are they reading something I write because they must (a legal notification, for instance)?

6. What are my audience's expectations about my written work?

- Do they want an e-mail or will they expect a formal letter?
- Will they expect me to follow a company format and style?
- Are they looking for a one-page memo or for a comprehensive report?
- Should I use a formal tone or a more relaxed and conversational style?

7. What is my audience's attitude toward me and my work?

- Will I be writing to a group of disgruntled and angry customers or vendors about a sensitive issue (a product recall, a refusal of credit, or a shipment delay)?
- Will I have to be sympathetic while at the same time give firm reasons for my company's (or my) decision?
- Will my readers be skeptical, indifferent, or eager and friendly about what I write?
- Will my readers feel guilty that they have not answered an earlier message of mine, not paid a bill now overdue, or not kept a promise or commitment?

8. What do I want my audience to do after reading my work?

- Do I want my reader to purchase something from me, approve my plan, or send me additional materials?
- Do I simply want my reader to get my message and not respond at all?
- Do I expect my reader to get my message, acknowledge it, save it for future reference, or review it and e-mail it to another individual or office?
- Does my reader have to take immediate action, or does he or she have several days or weeks to respond?

As your answers to these questions will show, you may have to communicate with many different audiences on your job. If you work for a large organization with numerous departments, you may have to write to such diverse readers as accountants, office managers, engineers, public relations specialists, marketing specialists, programmers, and individuals who install, operate, and maintain equipment. On some occasions, you may have to write for multiple audiences at once—a manager, a buyer, and someone in your firm's legal department. In addition, you will need to communicate effectively with customers about your company's products and services. Each group of readers will have different expectations and requirements; you need to understand those audience differences if you want to supply relevant information.

Establishing Your Purpose

By knowing *why* you are writing, you will communicate better and find writing itself to be an easier process. The reader's needs and your goal in communicating will help you to formulate your purpose. It will guide you in determining exactly what you can and must say. With your purpose clearly identified, you are on the right track.

Make sure you follow the most important rule in occupational writing: **Get to the point right away.** At the start of your message, state your goal clearly. Don't feel as if you have to entertain or impress your reader.

> I want new employees to know how to log on to the computer.

Think over what you have written. Rewrite your purpose statement until it states precisely why you are writing and what you want your readers to do or to know.

> I want to teach new employees the security code for logging on to the company computer.

Since your purpose controls the amount and order of information you include, state it clearly at the beginning of every e-mail, memo, letter, and report.

> This e-mail will acquaint new employees with the security measures they must take when logging on to the company computer.

In the opening purpose statement that follows, note how the author clearly informs the reader what the report will and will not cover.

> As you requested at last week's organizational meeting, I have conducted a study of our use of websites to advertise our services. This report describes, but does not evaluate, our current sites.

The following preface to a publication on architectural casework details contains a model statement of purpose suited to a particular audience.

> This publication has been prepared by the Architectural Woodwork Institute to provide a source book of conventional details and uniform detail terminology. For this purpose a series of casework detail drawings, . . . representative of the best industry-wide practice, has been prepared and is presented here. By supplying both architect and woodwork manufacturer with a common authoritative reference, this work will enable architects and woodworkers to communicate in a common technical language. . . . Besides serving as a basic reference for architects and architectural drafters, this guide will be an effective educational tool for the beginning drafter-architect-in-training. It should also be a valuable aid to the project manager in coordinating the work of many drafters on large projects.[1]

After seeing that preface, readers have a clear sense of why they should use this resource and what to do with the material they find in it.

Formulating Your Message

Your message is the sum of *what* facts, responses, and recommendations you put into writing. A message includes the scope and details of your communication.

- The *details* are those key points you think readers need to know to perform their jobs.
- *Scope* refers to how much information you give readers about those key details.

Some messages will consist of one or two sentences: "Do not touch; wet paint." "Order #756 was sent this afternoon by FedEx. It should arrive at your office on March 22." At the other extreme, messages may extend over twenty or thirty pages. Messages may carry good news or bad news. They may deal with routine matters, or they may handle changes in policy, special situations, or problems.

Keep in mind that you will adapt your message to fit your audience. For technical audiences, such as engineers or technicians, you may have to supply a complete report with every detail noted or contained in an appendix. For other readers—busy executives, for example—include only a short discussion or summary of financial or managerial significance.

Consider the message of the following excerpt from a section called "Technology in the Grocery Store" included in a consumer handbook. The message provides factual information and a brief explanation of how a clerk scans an item, informing consumers about how and why they may have to wait longer in line. It also tells readers that the process is not as simple as it looks.

This bar code message is appropriate for consumers who do not need or desire more information. Individuals responsible for entering data into the computer or doing inventory control, however, would need more detailed instructions on how to program the supermarket's computer so it automatically tells the point-of-sale (POS) terminal what price and product match each bar code.

---

[1]Reprinted by permission of Architectural Woodwork Institute.

Bar Code Readers

Every time you check out at the grocery store, many of your purchases are scanned to record the price. The scanner uses a laser beam to read the bar codes, those zebra-striped lines imprinted on packages or canned goods. These codes are fed into the store's computer, which provides the price that matches the product code. The product and its price are then recorded on your receipt.

Scanning an item requires more skill than you might think. To make sure that the scanner accurately reads the bar codes, the clerk has to take into account the following four conditions:

Speed: The clerk has to pass the item across the scanner at a particular speed. If the item moves too slowly, the bars will look too long or too wide and the computer will reject the item. If the item is moved too fast, the scanner cannot identify the code.

Angle: The clerk needs to gauge the exact angle at which to pass the item across the scanner. If the angle is wrong there will be insufficient reflection of the laser beam back to the scanner and so it will not be able to read the code. Since it is best for the item to reflect as much of the laser as possible, the clerk should try to hold the code at right angles to the laser.

Distance: Moving the item too close to the scanner is as unproductive as holding it too far away. Either way the code can be out of focus for the scanner reader. Holding the item about 3–4 inches away is best; holding it out more than 8–9 inches ensures that the scanner will not read the code.

Rotation: The code needs to be facing the scanner so that the lines can be read properly.

Direction in which clerk moves product

If your clerk makes a mistake in any one of these calibrations, your wait in line is sure to be longer.

But technicians responsible for affixing the bar codes at the manufacturer's plant would require much more detailed information than would consumers or store cashiers. These technicians must be familiar with the Universal Product Code (UPC), which specifies bar codes worldwide. They would also have to know about the UPC binary code formulas and how they work—that is, the number of lines, width of spacing, and the framework to indicate to the scanner when to start reading the code and when to stop. Such formulas, technical details, and functions of photoelectric scanners are appropriate for this audience.

Selecting Your Style and Tone

Style

Style is *how* something is written rather than what is written. Style helps to determine how well you communicate with an audience, how well your readers understand and receive your message. It involves the choices you make about

- the construction of your paragraphs
- the length and patterns of your sentences
- your choice of words

You will have to adapt your style to take into account different messages, different purposes, and different audiences. Your words, for example, will certainly vary with your audience. If all your readers are specialists in your field, you may safely use the technical language and symbols of your profession. Nonspecialists, however, will be confused and annoyed if you write to them in the same way. The average consumer, for example, will not know what a *potentiometer* is; by writing "volume control on a radio," you will be using words that the general public can understand. And, as we saw, when you write for an international audience you have to take into account their proficiency in English and choose your words and sentences with their needs in mind (see pp. 169–179).

Tone

Tone in writing, like tone of voice, expresses your attitude toward a topic and toward your audience. Your tone can range from formal and impersonal (a scientific report) to informal and personal (e-mail to a friend or a how-to article for consumers). It can be unprofessionally sarcastic or diplomatically agreeable.

Tone, like style, is indicated in part by the words you choose. For example, saying that someone is "interested in details" conveys a more positive tone than saying the person is a "nitpicker." The word *economical* is more positive than *stingy* or *cheap*.

The tone of your writing is especially important in occupational writing, because it reflects the image you project to your readers and thus determines how they will respond to you, your work, and your company. Depending on your tone, you can appear sincere and intelligent or angry and uninformed. Of course, in all your written work, you need to sound professional and knowledgeable about the topic and genuinely interested in your readers' opinions and problems. The wrong tone in a letter or a proposal might cost you a customer. Sarcastic or hostile language will at once alienate you from your readers, as the letters in Figures 5.5 (p. 156) and 5.6 (p. 157) demonstrate.

A Description of Heparin for Two Different Audiences

To better understand the effects of style and tone on writing, read the following two excerpts. In both, the message is basically the same, but because the audiences differ, so do the style and the tone. The two pieces are descriptions of *heparin*, a drug used to prevent blood clots.

Technical/Scientific Style and Tone

The first description of heparin appears in a reference work for physicians and other health care providers and is written in a highly technical style with an impersonal tone.

> HEPARIN SODIUM INJECTION, USP
> STERILE SOLUTION
> *Description*: Heparin Sodium Injection, USP is a sterile solution of heparin sodium derived from bovine lung tissue, standardized for anticoagulant activity.
>
> Each ml of the 1,000 and 5,000 USP units per ml preparations contains: heparin sodium 1,000 or 5,000 USP units; 9 mg sodium chloride; 9.45 mg benzyl alcohol added as preservative. Each ml of the 10,000 USP units per ml preparations contains: heparin sodium 10,000 units; 9.45 mg benzyl alcohol added as preservative.
>
> When necessary, the pH of Heparin Sodium Injection, USP was adjusted with hydrochloric acid and/or sodium hydroxide. The pH range is 5.0–7.5.
> *Clinical pharmacology*: Heparin inhibits reactions that lead to the clotting of blood and the formation of fibrin clots both *in vitro* and *in vivo*. Heparin acts at multiple sites in the normal coagulation system. Small amounts of heparin in combination with antithrombin III (heparin cofactor) can inhibit thrombosis by inactivating activated Factor X and inhibiting the conversion of prothrombin to thrombin.
> *Dosage and administration*: Heparin sodium is not effective by oral administration and should be given by intermittent intravenous injection, intravenous infusion, or deep subcutaneous (intrafrat, i.e., above the iliac crest or abdominal fat layer) injection. **The intramuscular route of administration should be avoided because of the frequent occurrence of hematoma at the injection site.**[2]

The writer made the appropriate stylistic choices for the audience, the purpose, and the message. Physicians and other health care providers understand and expect the technical vocabulary and the scientific and lengthy explanations to prescribe and/or administer heparin correctly. The author's authoritative, impersonal tone is coldly clinical, which, of course, is also correct because the purpose is to convey the accurate, complete scientific facts about this drug, not the writer's or reader's opinions or beliefs. The author sounds both knowledgeable and appropriately objective.

Nontechnical Style and Tone

The following description of heparin, on the other hand, is written in a nontechnical style and with an informal, caring tone. This description is similar to those found on information cards given to patients about the drugs they are receiving in a hospital.

---

[2]Copyright © *Physicians' Desk Reference*® 45th edition, 1991, published by Medical Economics, Montvale, New Jersey 07645. Reprinted by permission. All rights reserved.

> Your doctor has prescribed a drug called *heparin* for you. This drug will prevent any new blood clots from forming in your body. Since heparin cannot be absorbed from your stomach or intestines, you will not receive it in a capsule or tablet. Instead, it will be given into a vein or the fatty tissue of your abdomen. After several days, when the danger of clotting is past, your dosage of heparin will be gradually reduced. Then another medication you can take by mouth will be started.

The writer of this description also made appropriate choices for nonspecialists such as patients who do not need elaborate descriptions of the origin and composition of the drug. The writer's use of familiar words and personal tone help to win the patients' confidence and explain why they should take the drug.

Characteristics of Job-Related Writing

Job-related writing characteristically serves six basic functions: (1) to provide practical information, (2) to give facts rather than impressions, (3) to provide visuals to clarify and condense information, (4) to give accurate measurements, (5) to state responsibilities precisely, and (6) to persuade and offer recommendations. These six functions tell you what kind of writing you will produce after you successfully answer the *who? why? what?* and *how?*

Providing Practical Information

On-the-job writing requires a practical here's-what-you-need-to-do-or-to-know approach. One such practical approach is *action oriented*. You instruct the reader to do something—assemble a ceiling fan, test for bacteria, perform an audit, create a website. Another practical approach of job-related writing is knowledge oriented: to have someone understand something—why a procedure was changed, what caused a problem or solved it, how much progress was made on a job site, why a new piece of equipment should be purchased. Examples of knowledge-oriented practical writing include a letter from a manufacturer to customers to explain a product recall and an e-mail to employees about changes in their group health insurance.

The following description of Energy Efficiency Ratio combines both the action-oriented and knowledge-oriented approaches of practical writing.

> Whether you are buying window air-conditioning units or a central air-conditioning system, consider the performance factors and efficiency of the various units on the market. Before you buy, determine the Energy Efficiency Ratio (EER) of the units under consideration. The EER is found by dividing the BTUs (units of heat) that the unit removes from the area to be cooled by the watts (amount of electricity) the unit consumes. The result is usually a number between 5 and 12. The higher the number, the more efficiently the unit will use electricity.
>
> You'll note that EER will vary considerably from unit to unit of a given manufacturer, and from brand to brand. As efficiency is increased, you may find the purchase price is higher; however, operating costs will be lower. Remember, a good rule to follow is to choose the equipment with the highest EER. That way you'll get efficient equipment and enjoy operating economy.[3]

---

[3]Reprinted by permission of New Orleans Public Services, Inc.

Giving Facts, Not Impressions

Occupational writing is concerned with what can be seen, heard, felt, tasted, or smelled. The writer uses *concrete language* and specific details. The emphasis is on facts rather than on the writer's feelings or guesses.

The discussion below by a group of scientists about the sources of oil spills and their impact on the environment is an example of writing with objectivity. It describes events and causes without anger or tears. Imagine how much emotion could have been packed into this paragraph by the residents of the coastal states who have watched such spills come ashore.

> The most critical impact results from the escapement of oil into the ecosystem, both crude oil and refined fuel oils, the latter coming from sources such as marine traffic. Major oil spills occur as a result of accidents such as blowout, pipeline breakage, etc. Technological advances coupled with stringent regulations have helped to reduce the chances of such major spills; however, there is a chronic low-level discharge of oil associated with normal drilling and production operations. Waste oils discharged through the river systems and practices associated with tanker transports dump more significant quantities of oils into the ocean, compared to what is introduced by the offshore oil industry. All of this contributes to the chronic low-level discharge of oil into world oceans. The long-range cumulative effect of these discharges is possibly the most significant threat to the ecosystem.[4]

Providing Visuals to Clarify and Condense Information

Visuals are indispensable partners of words in conveying information to your readers. On-the-job writing makes frequent use of visuals such as tables, charts, photographs, flow charts, diagrams, and drawings to clarify and condense information. Thanks to various software packages, you can easily create and insert visuals into your writing. The use of visuals is discussed in detail in Chapters 11 and 12, as well as in PowerPoint presentations in Chapter 17.

Visuals play an important role in the workplace. Note how the drawing in Figure 1.6 from the National Safety Council's booklet *Working Safely with Your Computer* can help computer users better understand and follow the accompanying written guidelines. A visual like this, reproduced in an employee handbook or displayed as a poster, can significantly reduce stress and increase productivity.

Visuals are extremely useful in making detailed relationships clear to readers. The information in Table 1.1 (p. 21) on the world's ten most populous countries in 2000 and those projected for 2050 would be very difficult to discuss and follow if it were not in twin tables. When that information is presented in the two tables, the writer makes it easy for the reader to see and understand relationships quickly. If such information were just written out in prose, it would be much harder to compare, contrast, and summarize.

In addition to the visuals already mentioned, the following graphic devices in your letters, reports, and websites can make your writing easier to read and follow:

---

[4]Source: The Offshore Ecology Investigation. Reprinted by permission of Gulf Universities Research Consortium.

Figure 1.6   Use of a visual to convey information.

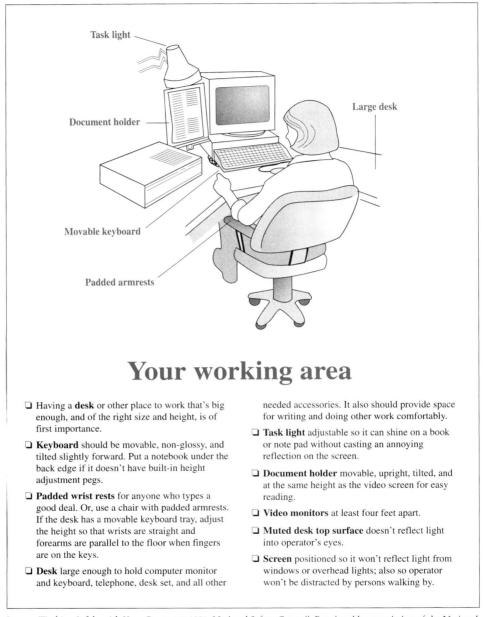

Your working area

❏ Having a **desk** or other place to work that's big enough, and of the right size and height, is of first importance.

❏ **Keyboard** should be movable, non-glossy, and tilted slightly forward. Put a notebook under the back edge if it doesn't have built-in height adjustment pegs.

❏ **Padded wrist rests** for anyone who types a good deal. Or, use a chair with padded armrests. If the desk has a movable keyboard tray, adjust the height so that wrists are straight and forearms are parallel to the floor when fingers are on the keys.

❏ **Desk** large enough to hold computer monitor and keyboard, telephone, desk set, and all other needed accessories. It also should provide space for writing and doing other work comfortably.

❏ **Task light** adjustable so it can shine on a book or note pad without casting an annoying reflection on the screen.

❏ **Document holder** movable, upright, tilted, and at the same height as the video screen for easy reading.

❏ **Video monitors** at least four feet apart.

❏ **Muted desk top surface** doesn't reflect light into operator's eyes.

❏ **Screen** positioned so it won't reflect light from windows or overhead lights; also so operator won't be distracted by persons walking by.

Source: *Working Safely with Your Computer,* 1991, National Safety Council. Reprinted by permission of the National Safety Council.

TABLE 1.1   Ten Most Populous Countries: 2000 vs. Projected 2050

2000		*2050*	
	(Millions)		(Millions)
China	1,262	India	1,620
India	1,014	China	1,470
United States	276	United States	404
Indonesia	225	Indonesia	338
Brazil	173	Nigeria	304
Russia	146	Pakistan	268
Pakistan	142	Brazil	207
Bangladesh	129	Bangladesh	205
Japan	127	Ethiopia	188
Nigeria	123	Kinshasa (Congo)	182

Source: U.S. Census Bureau, March 2000 projections.

- headings, such as **Four Keys to Effective Writing** or **Characteristics of Job-Related Writing**
- subheadings to divide major sections into parts, such as "Providing Practical Information" or "Giving Facts, Not Impressions"
- numbers within a paragraph, or even a line, such as (1) this, (2) this, and (3) also this
- different types of s p a c i n g
- CAPITALIZATION
- *italics* (easily made by a word processing command or indicated in typed copy by <u>underscoring</u>)
- **boldface** (darker print for emphasis)
- icons (visual markers such as →)
- HYPERTEXT (the use of color, shading, or boldface to mark words or icons that indicate links on the Internet)
- asterisks * to * separate * items * or to note key items *
- lists with "bullets" (like those before each entry in this list)

Keep in mind that graphic devices should be used carefully and with moderation, not just for decoration or to dress up a letter or report. Used properly, they can help you to

- organize, arrange, and emphasize your ideas
- make your work easier to read and to recall
- preview and summarize your ideas, for example, headings
- list related items to help readers distinguish, follow, compare, and recall them—as this bulleted list does

Giving Accurate Measurements

Much of your work will depend on measurements—acres, bytes, calories, centimeters, degrees, dollars and cents, grams, percentages, pounds, square feet, units. Numbers are clear and convincing. However, you must be sensitive to which units of measurement you use when writing to international readers. Not every culture computes in dollars or records temperatures in degrees Fahrenheit. See pages 172–173.

The following discussion of mixing colored cement for a basement floor would be useless to readers if it did not supply accurate quantities.

> The inclusion of permanent color in a basement floor is a good selling point. One way of doing this is by incorporating commercially pure mineral pigments in a topping mixture placed to a 1-inch depth over a normal base slab. The topping mix should range in volume between 1 part portland cement, 1¼ parts sand, and 1¼ parts gravel or crushed stone and 1 part portland cement, 2 parts sand, and 2 parts gravel or crushed stone. Maximum size gravel or crushed stone should be ⅜ inch.
>
> Mix cement and pigment before aggregate and water are added and be very thorough to secure uniform dispersion and the full color value of the pigment. The proportion varies from 5 to 10 percent of pigment by weight of cement, depending on the shade desired. If carbon black is used as a pigment to obtain grays or black, a proportion of from ½ to 1 percent will be adequate. Manufacturers' instructions should be followed closely; care in cleanliness, placing, and finishing are also essential. Colored topping mixes are available from some suppliers of ready mixed concrete.[5]

Stating Responsibilities Precisely

Job-related writing, because it is directed to a specific audience, must make absolutely clear what it expects of, or can do for, that audience. Misunderstandings waste time and cost money. Directions on order forms, for example, should indicate how and where information is to be listed and how it is to be routed and acted on. The following three directions show readers how to perform different tasks and/or explain why.

- Enter agency code numbers in the message box.

- Items 1 through 16 of this form should be completed by the injured employee or by someone acting on his or her behalf, whenever an injury is sustained in the performance of duty. The term *injury* includes occupational disease caused by the employment. The form should be given to the employee's official superior within 24 hours following the injury. The official superior is that individual having responsible supervision over the employee.

- What is a **credit report**? A credit report is a record of how you've paid bills with credit grantors such as stores and banks. Credit grantors use credit reports to determine whether or not you will be extended credit. The report identifies you by information such as your name and address, credit accounts, and payment history. Your credit report also includes public record data, such as bankruptcies, court judgments, and tax liens. A list of those who have recently

---

[5]Reprinted by permission from *Concrete Construction Magazine*, World of Concrete Center, 426 South Westgate, Addison, Illinois 60101.

requested a copy of your credit report is also included. A credit report does not contain information on arrest records, specific purchases, or medical records.[6]

Other kinds of job-related writing deal with the writer's responsibilities rather than the reader's, for example, "Tomorrow I will meet with the district sales manager to discuss (1) July's sales, (2) the possibility of expanding our market, and (3) next fall's production schedule. I will e-mail a report of our discussion by August 5, 2007."

Persuading and Offering Recommendations

Persuasion is a vital part of writing on the job. In fact, persuasion is one of the most crucial skills you can learn. It determines how successful you and your company or agency will be. You must make yourself believable by establishing yourself as an authority on the topic. That means being well informed and in command of any factual material. Whether you are writing to someone inside or outside your company, you will have to write persuasively about financial, psychological, and human resources issues. Persuasion is at the heart of the world of work.

Promoting Corporate Image

Much of your writing in the business world is to promote your company's image by persuading customers and clients (a) to buy a product or service or (b) to adopt a plan of action endorsed by your employer. Not only will you have to attract new customers, but you may also have to persuade previous ones to return and purchase your company's product/service again. You will have to convince readers that you (and your company) can save them time and money, increase efficiency, reduce risks, and improve their image, and that you can do this better than your competitors can.

Expect also to be called upon to write convincingly about your company's image, as in the case of product recalls, customer complaints, or damage control after a corporate mistake affecting the environment.

You may also have to convince customers or organizations around the globe that your company respects cultural diversity and that your products and services can appeal to specific ethnic values. The global marketplace is diversity driven.

A large part of persuasion is supporting your claims with evidence. You will have to conduct research, provide logical arguments, supply examples of appropriate data, and, especially important, identify the most relevant information for your particular audience. Notice how the advertisement in Figure 1.7 offers a bulleted list of persuasive reasons—based on cost, time, safety, efficiency, and convenience—to convince correctional officials that they should use General Medical's services rather than those of a hospital or clinic.

Writing Persuasively In-House

Writing for individuals you work for and with also requires you to develop your persuasive skills. In fact, your very first job-related writing will likely be a persuasive letter of application to obtain a job interview with a potential employer.

---

[6]Reprinted by permission of Associated Credit Bureaus, Inc.

Figure 1.7   An advertisement using arguments based on cost, time, efficiency, safety, and convenience to persuade a potential customer to use a service.

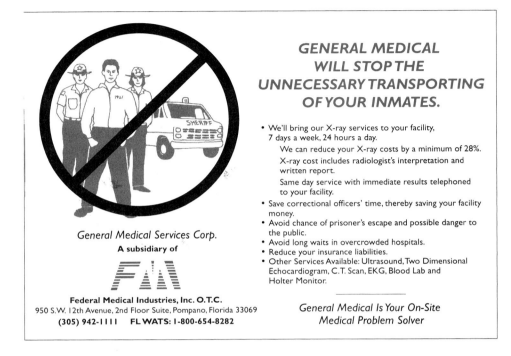

On the job, you will have to evaluate various products or options by studying, analyzing, and deciding on the most relevant one(s) for your boss. Your reader will expect you to offer clear-cut, logical, and convincing reasons for your choice.

The following summary concludes why it is better for a company to lease a truck than to purchase one. Note its persuasive tone and logical presentation.

After studying the pros and cons of buying or leasing a company truck, I recommend that we lease it for the following five reasons.

1. We will not have to expend any of our funds for a down payment, which is being waived.
2. Our monthly payments for leasing the vehicle will be at least $150 less than the payments we would have to make if we purchased the truck on a 3-year contract.
3. All major and minor maintenance (up to 36,000 miles) is included as part of our monthly leasing payment.
4. Insurance (theft and damage) is also part of our monthly leasing payment.
5. We have the option of trading in the truck every 16 months for a newer model or trading up for a more expensive model in the line every 12 months.

A persuasive e-mail from an employee to a business manager.   Figure 1.8

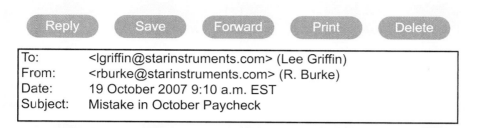

| Reply | Save | Forward | Print | Delete |

To: <lgriffin@starinstruments.com> (Lee Griffin)
From: <rburke@starinstruments.com> (R. Burke)
Date: 19 October 2007 9:10 a.m. EST
Subject: Mistake in October Paycheck

My paycheck for the two-week period ending October 15 was $45.00 short. During this period I should have been paid $525.00. Instead, my check was for only $480.00. I think I know why there may have been a discrepancy. The $45.00 additional pay was the result of my having put in five hours of overtime on October 8 and October 12 (2½ hours each day @ $9.00 per hour). This overtime was not reflected on my current pay stub.

Clearly explains and documents the problem

I have double-checked with my supervisor, Gloria Arrelo, who assured me that she recorded my overtime on the timesheets she sent to your office. She has kindly given me a copy that I have scanned and attached with the e-mail to verify my hours.

Offers further evidence

Thank you for correcting your records and crediting me with the additional $45.00 for my overtime.

Closes politely with request

On the job as well, you will be asked to write memos, e-mail, and even letters to boost the morale of employees, encourage them to be more productive, and compliment them on jobs well done. You can also expect to write about (and explain and solve) problems your company faces, such as when a market has shrunk and your boss wants to know why or when a service or product your company relies on becomes too costly. Finally, you may even have to write persuasively against the merits of a change that you or your collaborative team believe is unnecessary, proposed by a manager or another department in your company's organization.

Figure 1.8 contains a persuasive e-mail from an employee to a business manager to report a payroll mistake and to request a reimbursement. It contains many of the characteristics of job-related writing we have discussed. Note how the writer provides factual, not impressive, information, attaches a time sheet (a type of visual), gives accurate details, identifies his own and his immediate supervisor's responsibilities, and persuasively and diplomatically states his case.

■ Ethical Writing in the Workplace

On-the-job writing involves much more than conveying facts about products, equipment, costs, and the day-to-day operations of a business. Your writing also has to be ethical. Writing ethically means doing what is right and fair and being honest and just with your employer, co-workers, and customers. Your reputation and character plus your employer's corporate image will depend on your following an ethical course of action. Note how proud the Southern Company and its employees are of their ethical commitments to the environment, the community, and the country in the excerpt below from one of their consumer publications.

Our Environmental Responsibility

Southern Company is not only a leader in the energy market, but also a leader in protecting the environment. We believe our environmental initiatives and our strong compliance record will give us a competitive advantage.

The Southern Company's environmental policy spells out each company's commitment to protecting the environment. The first and foremost goal is to meet or exceed all regulatory requirements for domestic and international operations. To do that, we're using a combination of the best technologies and voluntary pollution-prevention programs. We also set aggressive environmental goals and make sure employees are aware of their individual environmental responsibilities. We are good citizens wherever we serve.

As an affiliate of Southern Company, Mississippi Power's environmental issues are business issues. In addition to regulatory obligations, our employees carry out a most active grassroots environmental program. It's this employee involvement and strong environmental commitment that gives our commitment life and promises future generations a healthy environment.

For example, one employee's concern that motor oil is properly discarded led to the founding of a countrywide annual household hazardous waste collection program. Thousands of tons of waste have been collected, including jars of DDT, mercury, paint, batteries, pesticides, and other poisons.

Scores of employees participate in island, beach, and river cleanups throughout Mississippi Power's 23-county service area. More than 30 employees compiled "The Wolf River Environmental Monitoring Program."

This report is the first-ever historical, biological assessment completed on the Wolf River by scientists and engineers. Employees volunteered countless hours to compile the statistical data. Today, Mississippi Power employees continue to support the Wolf River Project by producing photographs and slides as an educational and community awareness project.

Our commitment to the environment goes beyond our business. By sponsoring a variety of programs, we're helping to teach the public, students, and teachers about environmental responsibility.

Reprinted by permission of Mississippi Power Company.

Many of the most significant bywords in the world of business reflect an ethical commitment to honesty and fairness: *accountability*, *public trust*, *equal opportunity employer*, *global citizenship*, *good faith effort*, *truth in lending*, *fair play*, *honest advertising*, *full disclosure*, *high professional standards*, *industry standards*, *community involvement*, *social responsibility*.

Unethical business dealings, on the other hand, are stigmatized in *cover-ups*, *shady deals*, *spin doctors*, *foul play*, *misrepresentations*, *price gouging*, *bias*, and *unfair advantage*. Those are the activities that keep Better Business Bureaus active and make customers angry.

Ethical Requirements on the Job

In the workplace, you will be expected to meet the highest ethical standards by fulfilling the following requirements.

- Supplying honest and up-to-date information about yourself in your résumé and job applications. The résumé (see pp. 248–268) is one key place where most people must make ethical decisions about candor and honesty.
- Respecting co-workers, customers, and suppliers in conduct that avoids bullying, discrimination, or any other unfair and unprofessional action.
- Avoiding language that excludes others on the basis of gender, race, national origin, age, or physical condition (see pp. 177–179).
- Maintaining accurate and current records at work. Remember: "If it isn't written, it didn't happen."
- Complying with all local, state, and federal regulations, especially those ensuring a safe, healthy work environment, products, and/or service, for example, those of the Occupational Safety and Health Administration (OSHA).
- Adhering to your profession's code or standard of ethics, internal audits, licenses, and certificate requirements.
- Following your company's policies and procedures.
- Honoring guarantees and warranties and meeting customer needs impartially.
- Cooperating fairly with your collaborative team.
- Treating international colleagues with respect, as you would any peers.
- Respecting all copyright obligations and privileges.

Following these guidelines may be not only an ethical requirement; it could also be a legal one. For example, doing personal (or outside consulting) work on company time, padding expense accounts, or using company equipment for personal use is unethical and illegal. It would also be neglectful and unethical to allow an unsafe product to stay on the market just to spare your company the expense and embarrassment of a product recall. It would be wrong, legally and ethically, to e-mail information about your employer's patent plans to anyone outside your company.

Computer ethics, especially when using the Internet, are essential in the world of work. Never use a company computer for any activity not directly related to your job. It would be grossly unethical to erase a computer program intentionally, violate a software licensing agreement, or misrepresent (by fabrication or exaggeration) the

Figure 1.9   The Ten Commandments of Computer Ethics.

1. Thou shalt not use a computer to harm other people.

2. Thou shalt not interfere with other people's computer work.

3. Thou shalt not snoop around in other people's computer files.

4. Thou shalt not use a computer to steal.

5. Thou shalt not use a computer to bear false witness.

6. Thou shalt not copy or use proprietary software for which you have not paid.

7. Thou shalt not use other people's computer resources without authorization or proper compensation.

8. Thou shalt not appropriate other people's intellectual output.

9. Thou shalt think about the social consequences of the program you are writing or the system you are designing.

10. Thou shalt always use a computer in ways that insure consideration and respect for your fellow humans.

Computer Ethics Institute, London

scope of a database. Follow the Ten Commandments of Computer Ethics prepared by the Computer Ethics Institute and listed in Figure 1.9.

Writing for the world of multinational corporations places additional ethical demands on you as a writer. You have to make sure you respect the ethics of all the countries where your firm does business. Some behaviors regarded as normal or routine in the United States might be seen as highly unethical elsewhere, or vice versa. In many countries, accepting a gift to initiate or conclude a business agreement is considered not only proper but also honorable. This is not the case in the United States where a "bribe" is bad business. And you should be on your ethical guard not to take advantage of a host country, such as allowing or encouraging poor environmental control because regulatory and inspection procedures are not as strict as those of the United States, or using pesticides or conducting experiments outlawed in the United States.

Some Guidelines to Help You Reach Ethical Decisions

The workplace presents conflicts over who is right and who is wrong, what is best for the company and what is not, and whether a service or product should be changed and why. You will be asked to make a decision and justify it. Here are some guidelines to help you comply with the ethical requirements of your job.

1. **Follow your conscience and "to thine own self be true."** Do not authorize something that you believe is wrong, dangerous, unfair, contradictory, or incomplete. But don't be hasty. Leave plenty of room for diplomacy and for careful ques-

tioning. Recall the story of Chicken Little, who always cried that the sky was falling. Don't blow a small matter out of proportion, but similarly don't overlook something serious just because there is no history of a problem.

2. Be suspicious of convenient (and false) appeals that go against your beliefs. Watch out for these red flags that anyone places in the way of your conscience: "No one will ever know." "It's OK to cut corners every once in a while." "We got away with it last time." "Don't rock the boat." "No one's looking." "As long as the company makes money, who cares?" These excuses are traps you must avoid.

3. Maintain good faith in meeting your obligations to your employer, your co-workers, your customers, and the global community. Examine their reasons for reading your information (see pp. 10–13) and consider how and in what contexts they will use it. It is unethical to lie, exaggerate, or even dodge an issue. Keeping information from a co-worker who needs it, omitting a fact, justifying unnecessary expenses, concealing something risky about a product from an international customer that you otherwise would disclose to a U.S. customer—all are unethical acts, just as cheating on an examination or plagiarizing is unethical in your schoolwork.

4. Take responsibility for your actions. Saying "I do not know" when you do know can constitute a serious ethical violation. Keep your records up-to-date and accurate. Sign and date your work. Never backdate a document to delete information or to fix an error that you committed. Also, do not use someone's password, which is equivalent to his or her electronic signature. If you make a mistake, the other person would be held responsible. Always do what is expected in terms of documentation and notification. Failing to test a set of instructions thoroughly, for example, might endanger readers around the globe.

5. Document your work carefully and honestly. Research what you write and communicate orally. Rely on hard evidence: documentation, testimony, valid precedents. Do your homework by studying code books and agency handbooks; confer with a customer or a co-worker when you are in doubt about a major issue. Familiarize yourself with your company's standard operating procedures (SOPs), specifications, protocols, methods, and materials. Make sure your documents are accurate and comply with appropriate city, state, federal, and international regulations.

6. Weigh all sides before you commit to a conclusion. You may think a particular course of action is right at the time, but don't overlook the possibility that your decision may create a bigger problem in the future. For example, you hear that a co-worker is involved in wrongdoing; you report it to your boss, and a reprimand is placed in that worker's file. Later you learn that what was reported to you was malicious gossip or only a small part of a much larger but very ethical picture. Give people the benefit of the doubt until you have sufficient facts to the contrary. Giving incomplete information on an incident report may temporarily protect you but may falsely incriminate someone else or unfairly increase your company's liability insurance rates.

Ethical Dilemmas

Sometimes in the workplace you will face situations where there is no clear-cut right or wrong choice, even with regard to the six ethical categories described above. You may be involved in an ethical dilemma, or conflict, regarding a decision by your employer, a customer, or a co-worker, or even something you said or did earlier.

Here are a few scenarios, similar to ones in which you may find yourself, that are gray areas, ethically speaking, along with some possible solutions.

- You see an opening for a job in your area but the employer wants someone with a minimum of two years of field experience. You have just completed an internship and had one summer's (12 weeks) experience in the field, which together total almost 7 months. Should you apply for the job, describing yourself as "experienced"?

  Yes, but honestly state the type and the extent of your field experience and the conditions under which you obtained it.

- You work for a company that usually assigns commissions to the salesperson for whom a customer asks. One afternoon a customer visits your store and asks for a salesperson whose name he cannot remember but from whose description you realize is an employee who happens to have the day off. You assist the customer all afternoon, making several long-distance calls to locate a particular model and even arrange to have that item shipped overnight to your store so that the customer can pick it up in the morning. When it comes time to ring up the sale, should you list your employee number for credit (and the commission) or the off-duty employee's number?

  You probably should defer crediting the sale to either number until you speak to the absent employee and suggest a compromise—splitting the commission.

- A piece of computer equipment, scheduled for delivery to your customer the next day, arrives with a damaged part. You decide to replace it at your store before the customer receives it. Should you inform the customer?

  Yes, but assure the customer that the equipment is still under the same warranty and that the replacement part is new and also under the same warranty. If the customer protests, agree to let him or her use the computer until a new unit arrives.

As these brief scenarios suggest, sometimes you have to make concessions and compromises to be ethical in the world of work. But other times you just can't, as the guidelines on page 31 on dealing with a bully point out.

Writing Ethically

Your writing as well as your behavior must be ethical. Words, like actions, have implications and consequences. If you slant your words to conceal the truth or gain an unfair advantage, you are not being ethical. False advertising is false writing. Bias and omission of facts are wrong. Strive to be fair, reliable, and accurate in reporting events, statistics, and trends.

MayoClinic.com
Tools for healthier lives

Dealing with an Office Bully

Bullying isn't just something that happens on the playground in elementary school. It happens at work, too. Bullying is the hurtful and repeated mistreatment of workers by their bosses, a co-worker, or even subordinates. It's a pattern of abusive remarks, arbitrary rages, or attempts to sabotage a person's work.

Examples of bullying work behaviors include

- Talking behind your back
- Interrupting you when you're speaking or working
- Flaunting authority or status
- Acting in a condescending manner
- Belittling your opinions
- Giving you the silent treatment
- Insulting you
- Shouting at you
- Staring at you
- Sending you abusive e-mail

People often react to the bully by:

- Worrying about a specific incident or future interactions
- Losing work time by avoiding the bully
- Being absent or tardy, or leaving early
- Changing jobs

If someone's behavior toward you feels like bullying, consider these steps:

- **Get some support.** Talk with your friends, family, or a counselor. Call your employee assistance program (EAP). Don't suffer in silence.
- **Practice avoidance.** Don't be alone with the bully.
- **Document the behavior in writing.** Be specific. Include how the behavior impacts your productivity and the bottom line. Share this with your supervisor. If your supervisor is the bully, share your documentation with the next supervisor in the chain of command.
- **Check your company's policies.** Many employers know the importance of maintaining a work environment free of violence, coercion, sexual harassment, and hostility. A bully can create an uncomfortable work environment.
- **Confront the bully.** If you're comfortable doing so, let the bully know that his or her behavior bothers you.

© Mayo Foundation for Medical Education and Research, Rochester, MN 55905. Reprinted with permission.

Unethical writing is usually guilty of one or more of the following faults, which can conveniently be listed as the three *M*'s: misquotation, misrepresentation, and manipulation. Here are eight examples:

1. Plagiarism is stealing someone else's words (work) and claiming them as your own. Plagiarism is unethically claiming a co-worker's ideas, input, or report as your contribution. You are guilty of plagiarism in a report if you use another person's words (or even a rough paraphrase) without documenting the source. Do not think that by changing a few words here and there you are not plagiarizing. Copying someone else's software is also an act of plagiarism. Give proper credit to your source, whether in print, in person (through an interview), or online.

The penalties for plagiarism are severe—a reprimand or even the loss of your job. At school, you run the risk of failing the course or, worse, being expelled. See pages 352–353 for advice on how to avoid plagiarism.

2. Selective misquoting deliberately omits damaging or unflattering comments to paint a better (but untruthful) picture of you or your company. By picking and choosing words from a quotation, you unethically misrepresent what the speaker or writer originally intended.

> Full Quotation: I've enjoyed at times our firm's association with Technology, Inc., although I was troubled by the uneven quality of their service. At times, it was excellent while at others it was far less so.
>
> Selective Misquotation: I've enjoyed . . . our firm's association with Technology, Inc. The quality of their service was . . . excellent.

The dots, called *ellipses*, unethically suggest that only extraneous or unimportant details were omitted.

3. Arbitrary embellishment of numbers unethically misrepresents, by increasing or decreasing percentages or other numbers, statistical or other information. It is unethical to stretch the differences between competing plans or proposals to gain an unfair advantage or to express accurate figures in an inaccurate way.

> Embellishment: An overwhelming majority of residents voted for the new plan.
> Ethical: The new plan was passed by a vote of 53 to 49.
>
> Embellishment: Our competitor's sales volume increased by only 10 percent in the preceding year while ours doubled.
> Ethical: Our competitor controls 90 percent of the market, yet we increased our share of that market from 5 percent to 10 percent last year.

4. Manipulation of data or context, closely related to #3, is the misrepresentation of events, usually to "put a good face" on a bad situation. The writer here unethically uses slanted language and intentionally misleading euphemisms to misinterpret events for readers.

> Manipulation: Looking ahead to 2007, the United Funds Group is exceptionally optimistic about its long-term prospects in an expanding global market. We are happy to report steady to moderate activity in an expanding sales

environment last year. The United Funds Group seeks to build on sustaining investment opportunities beneficial to all subscribers.

Ethical: Looking ahead to 2007, the United Funds Group is optimistic about its long-term prospects in an expanding global market. Though the market suffered from inflation this year, the United Funds Group hopes to recoup its losses in the year ahead.

The writer minimizes the negative effects of inflation by calling it "an expanding sales environment."

5. Using fictitious benefits to promote a product or service seemingly promises customers advantages but delivers none.

False Benefit: Our bottled water is naturally hydrogenated from clear underground springs.

Truth: All water is hydrogenated because it contains hydrogen.

6. Unfairly characterizing (by exaggerating or minimizing) hiring or firing conditions is unethical.

Unethical: One of the benefits of working for Spelco is the double pay you earn for overtime.

Truth: Overtime is assigned on the basis of seniority.

Unethical: Our corporate restructuring will create a more efficient and streamlined company, benefiting management and workers alike.

Truth: Downsizing has led to 150 layoffs.

Companies faced with laying off employees want to protect their corporate image and maintain their stockholders' good faith, so they often "put the best face" on such an action.

7. Manipulating international readers by adopting a condescending view of their culture and economy is unethical.

Unethical: Since our product has appealed to U.S. customers for the last sixteen months, there's no doubt that it will be popular in your country as well.

Fair: Please let us know if any changes in product design or construction may be necessary for customers in your country.

8. Misrepresenting through distortion or slanted visuals is one of the most common types of unethical communication. Making a product look bigger, better, or more professional is all too easy with graphics software packages. Making warning or caution statements the same size and type font as ingredients or directions or enlarging advertising hype (Double Your Money Back) is unethical if major points are then reduced to small print. See pages 486–490 of Chapter 11 for guidelines on how to prepare ethical visuals.

In short, ethical writing is clear, accurate, fair, and honest. These are among the most important goals of any work communication. Because ethics are such an important topic in writing for the workplace, they will be emphasized throughout this book. See, for example, pages 352–353.

■ Successful Employees Are Successful Writers

As this chapter has stressed, being a successful employee means being a successful writer at work. The following guidelines, which summarize the key points of this chapter, will help you to be both.

1. Know your job—assignments, roles, responsibilities, goals, what you need to write and what you **shouldn't**.
2. Be prepared to give and to receive feedback.
3. Work toward and meet all deadlines.
4. Analyze your audience's needs, and what they will expect to find in your written work.
5. Respect the cultural diversity and contributions of your customers and co-workers.
6. Write clearly, concisely, and appropriately for readers in the global marketplace. Adapt your message for your audience's background.
7. Document, document, document. Submit everything with clear-cut evidence based on factual details and persuasive, logical interpretations.
8. Include clear visuals to help readers understand your message.
9. Follow your company policy and promote your company's image.
10. Be ethical in what you say, write, and do.

Online Study Center
Access the writing and your career Revision Checklist online at college .hmco.com/pic/ kolin8e

✔ Revision Checklist

At the end of each chapter is a checklist you should review before you submit the final copy of your work, either to your instructor or to your boss. The checklists include the types of research, planning, drafting, editing, and revising you should do to ensure the success of your work. Regard each checklist as a summary of the main ideas in the chapter as well as a handy guide to quality control. You may find it helpful to check each box as you verify that you have performed the necessary revision/review. Effective writers are also careful editors.

☐ Showed respect for and appropriately shaped my message for a global marketplace.
☐ Identified my audience—their background, knowledge of English, reason for reading my work, and likely response to my work and me.
☐ Made it clear what I want my audience to do after reading my work.
☐ Tailored my message to my audience's needs and background, giving them neither too little nor too much information.
☐ Pushed to the main point right away; did not waste my reader's time.
☐ Selected the most appropriate language, technical level, tone, and level of formality.

Continued

Continued

☐ Did not waste my audience's time with unsupported generalizations or opinions; instead gave them accurate measurements, facts, and carefully researched material.

☐ Used appropriate visuals to make my work easier for my audience to follow.

☐ Used persuasive reasons and data to convince my reader to accept my plan or work.

☐ Ensured that my writing is ethical—accurate, fair, honest, a true reflection of the situation or condition I am explaining or describing, for U.S. as well as global audiences.

☐ Followed the Ten Commandments of Computer Ethics.

☐ Gave full and complete credit to any sources I used, including resource people.

☐ Avoided plagiarism and unfair or dishonest use of copyrighted materials, both written and visual, including all electronic media.

Exercises

1. What is your chosen career? Make a list of the types of writing you think you will do, or have already been assigned, on the job.

2. Make a list of the kinds of writing you have done in a history or English class or for a laboratory or shop course.

3. Compare your lists for Exercises 1 and 2. How do the two types of writing differ?

4. Write a memo (see pp. 124–125 for format) addressed to a prospective supervisor to introduce yourself. Your memo should have four headings: **education**—including goals and accomplishments; **job information**—where you have worked and your responsibilities; **community service**—volunteer work, church work, youth groups; and **writing experience**—your strengths and what you would like to see improved.

5. Write a memo in response to Rowe Pinkerton's e-mail in Figure 1.1. Explain how you will use the skills you learn in the company-reimbursed writing course on your job.

6. Bring to class a set of printed instructions, a memo, a sales letter, or a brochure. Comment on how well the printed material answers the following questions.
   a. Who is the audience?
   b. Why was the material written?
   c. What is the message?
   d. Are the style and tone appropriate for the audience, the purpose, and the message? Why?
   e. Discuss the use of color in the document. How does color (or the lack of it) affect an audience's response to the message?

Online Study Center
Find additional writing and your career exercises at college.hmco.com/pic/kolin8e

7. Cut out a newspaper ad that contains a drawing or photograph. Bring it to class together with a paragraph of your own (75–100 words) describing how the message of the ad is directed to a particular audience and commenting on why the illustration was selected for that audience.

8. Pick one of the following topics and write two descriptions of it. In the first description, use technical vocabulary. In the second, use language suitable for the general public.

   a. spark plug
   b. blood pressure cuff
   c. carburetor
   d. computer chip
   e. smartphone
   f. legal contract
   g. electric sander
   h. cyberspace
   i. muscle
   j. protein
   k. SUV
   l. e-mail
   m. bread
   n. money
   o. iPod
   p. soap
   q. blogging
   r. computer virus
   s. AIDS
   t. thermostat
   u. trees
   v. food processor
   w. earthquake
   x. recycling

9. Redo Exercise 8 as a collaborative writing project.

10. Select one article from a newspaper and one article either from a professional journal in your major field or from one of the following journals: *Advertising Age, American Journal of Nursing, Business Marketing, Business Week, Computer, Computer Design, Construction Equipment, Criminal Justice Review, E-Commerce, Food Service Marketing, Journal of Forestry, Journal of Soil and Water Conservation, National Safety News, Nutrition Action, Office Machines, Park Maintenance, Scientific American.* State how the two articles you selected differ in terms of audience, purpose, message, style, and tone.

11. Assume that you work for Appliance Rentals, Inc., a company that rents TVs, microwave ovens, stereo components, and the like. Write a persuasive letter to the members of a campus organization or civic club urging them to rent an appropriate appliance or appliances. Include details in your letter that might have special relevance to members of this specific organization.

12. How do the visuals and the text of the Sodexho advertisement on page 37 stress to current (and potential) employees, customers, and stockholders that the company is committed to human diversity in the workplace? Also explain how the ad illustrates the functions of on-the-job writing defined on pages 18–24.

13. Read the article, "Microwaves," on pages 38–40 and identify its audience (technical or general), purpose, message, style, and tone.

14. Write a letter to an Internet service provider that has mistakenly billed you for caller ID equipment that you never ordered, received, or needed.

15. The following statements contain embellishments, selected misquotations, false benefits, and other types of unethical tactics. Revise each statement to eliminate the unethical aspects.

   a. Hurricane damage done to water filtration plant #3 was minimal. While we had to shut down temporarily, service resumed to meet residents' needs.

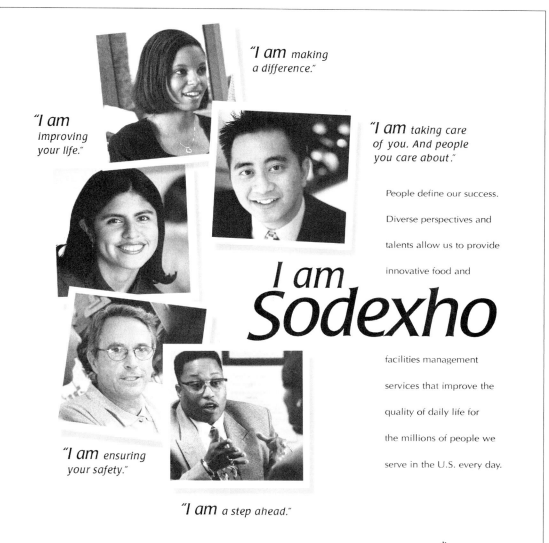

Food Services, Facilities Management, Vending, Catering, Office Refreshment Services, Environmental Services, Landscaping & Grounds Management, Conferencing, Plant Operations & Management

    b. All customers qualify for the maximum discount available.

    c. The service contract . . . on the whole . . . applied to upgrades.

    d. We followed the protocols precisely with test results yielding further opportunities for experimentation.

    e. All our costs were within fair-use guidelines.

    f. Customers' complaints have been held to a minimum.

    g. All the lots we are selling offer easy access to the lake.

16. You work for a large international firm and a co-worker tells you that he has no plans to return to his job after he takes his annual two-week vacation. You know that your department cannot meet its deadline short-handed and that your company will need at least two or three weeks to recruit and hire a qualified replacement. You also know that it is your company's policy not to give paid vacations to employees who do not agree to work for at least three months following a vacation. What should you do? What points would you make in a confidential, ethical memo to your boss (see pp. 26–33)? What points would you make to your co-worker?

17. Your company is regulated and inspected by the Environmental Protection Agency. In ninety days, the EPA will relax a particular regulation about dumping industrial waste. Your company's management is considering cutting costs by relaxing the standard now, before the new, easier regulation is in place. You know that the EPA inspector probably will not return before the ninety-day period elapses. What do you recommend to management?

18. Write a memo to your boss about one of the following unethical activities you have either witnessed or been a victim of in your workplace. Your memo must be carefully documented, fair, and persuasive.

    a. bullying

    b. surfing pornography websites

    c. falsifying compensatory or travel time

    d. telling sexist, off-color jokes

    e. concealing the use of company money for personal gifts (birthdays, anniversaries) for fellow employees

    f. misdating or backdating company records

    g. sharing privileged information with individuals outside your department or company

Microwaves

Much of the world around us is in motion. A wave-like motion. Some waves are big like tidal waves and some are small like the almost unseen footprints of a water-spider on a quiet pond. Other waves can't be seen at all, such as an idling truck sending out vibrations our bodies can feel. Among these are electromagnetic waves. They range from very low frequency sound waves to very high frequency X-rays, gamma rays, and even cosmic rays.

Energy behaves differently as its frequency changes. The start of audible sound—somewhere around 20 cycles per second—covers a segment at the low end of the electromagnetic spectrum. Household electricity operates at 60 hertz (cycles per second). At a somewhat higher frequency we have radio, ranging from short-wave and marine beacons, through the familiar AM broadcast band that lies between 500 and 1600 kilohertz, then to citizen's band, FM, television, and up to the higher frequency police and aviation bands.

Even higher up the scale lies visible light with its array of colors best seen when light is scattered by raindrops to create a rainbow.

Lying between radio waves and visible light is the microwave region—from roughly one gigahertz (a billion cycles per second) up to 3000 gigahertz. In this region the electromagnetic energy behaves in special ways.

Microwaves travel in straight lines, so they can be aimed in a given direction. They can be *reflected* by dense objects so that they send back echoes—this is the basis for radar. They can be *absorbed*, with their energy being converted into heat—the principle behind microwave ovens. Or they can pass *through* some substances that are transparent to the energy—this enables food to be cooked on a paper plate in a microwave oven.

Microwaves for Radar

World War II provided the impetus to harness microwave energy as a means of detecting enemy planes. Early radars were mounted on the Cliffs of Dover to bounce their microwave signals off Nazi bombers that threatened England. The word *radar* itself is an acronym for *RAdio Detection And Ranging.*

Radars grew more sophisticated. Special-purpose systems were developed to detect airplanes, to scan the horizon for enemy ships, to paint finely detailed electronic pictures of harbors to guide ships, and to measure the speeds of targets. These were installed on land and aboard warships. Radar—especially shipboard radar—was surely one of the most significant technological achievements to tip the scales toward an Allied victory in World War II.

Today, few mariners can recall what it was like before radar. It is such an important aid that it was embraced universally as soon as hostilities ended. Now, virtually every commercial vessel in the world has one, and most larger vessels have two radars: one for use on the open sea and one, operating at a higher frequency, to "paint" a more finely detailed picture, for use near shore.

Microwaves are also beamed across the skies to fix the positions of aircraft in flight, obviously an essential aid to controlling the movement of aircraft from city to city across the nation. These radars have also been linked to computers to tell air traffic controllers the altitude of planes in the area and to label them on their screens.

A new kind of radar, phased array, is now being used to search the skies thousands of miles out over the Atlantic and Pacific oceans. Although these advanced radars use microwave energy just as ordinary radars do, they do not depend upon a rotating antenna. Instead, a fixed antenna array, comprising thousands of elements like those of a fly's eye, looks everywhere. It has been said that these radars roll their eyes instead of turning their heads.

High-Speed Cooking

During World War II Raytheon had been selected to work with M.I.T. and British scientists to accelerate the production of magnetrons, the electron tubes that generate microwave energy, in order to speed up the production of radars. While testing some new, higher-powered tubes in a laboratory at Raytheon's Waltham, Massachusetts, plant, Percy L. Spencer and several of his staff engineers observed an interesting phenomenon. If you placed your hand in a beam of microwave energy, your hand would grow pleasantly warm. It was not like putting your hand in a heated oven that might sear the skin. The warmth was deep-heating and uniform.

Spencer and his engineers sent out for some popcorn and some food, then piped the energy into a metal wastebasket. The microwave oven was born.

From these discoveries, some 35 years ago, a new industry was born. In millions of homes around the world, meals are prepared in minutes using microwave ovens. In many processing industries, microwaves are being used to perform difficult heating or drying jobs. Even printing presses use microwaves to speed the drying of ink on paper.

In hospitals, doctors' offices, and athletic training rooms, that deep heat that Percy Spencer noticed is now used in diathermy equipment to ease the discomfort of muscle aches and pains.

Telephones Without Cable

The third characteristic of microwaves—that they pass undistorted through the air—makes them good messengers to carry telephone conversations as well as live television signals—without telephone poles or cables—across town or across the country. The microwave signals are beamed via satellite or by dish reflectors mounted atop buildings and mountaintop towers.

Microwaves take their name from the Greek *mikro* meaning very small. While the waves themselves may be very small, they play an important role in our world today: in defense; in communications; in air, sea, and highway safety; in industrial processing; and in cooking. At Raytheon the applications expand every day.

Reprinted by permission of *Raytheon Magazine*.

CHAPTER 2

The Writing Process at Work

In Chapter 1 you learned about the different functions of writing for the world of work and also explored some basic concepts all writers must master. To be a successful writer, you need to

Online Study Center

To expand your understanding of the writing process, take advantage of the ACE quizzes, sample documents, web links, and exercises at college.hmco.com/pic/kolin8e

- identify your audience's needs
- determine your purpose in writing to that audience
- make sure your message meets your audience's needs
- use the most appropriate style and tone for your message
- format your work so that it clearly reflects your message to your audience

Just as significant to your success is knowing how effective writers actually create their work for their audiences. This chapter gives you some practical information about the strategies and techniques careful writers use when they work. These procedures are a vital part of what is known as the *writing process.* This process involves such matters as how writers gather information, how they transform their ideas into written form, and how they organize and revise what they have written to make it suitable for their audiences.

What Writing Is and Is Not

As you begin your study of writing for the world of work, it might be helpful to identify some notions about what writing is and what it is not.

What Writing Is

- Writing is a fluid process; it is dynamic, not static. It enables you to discover and evaluate your thoughts.
- A piece of writing changes as your thoughts and information change and as your view of the material changes.
- Writing takes time. Some people think that revising and polishing are too time consuming. But poor writing actually takes more time and costs more money

in the end. It can lead to misunderstandings, lost sales, product recalls, and even damage to your reputation and that of your company.

- Writing means making a number of judgment calls.
- Writing grows sometimes in bits and pieces and sometimes in great spurts. It needs many revisions; an early draft is never a final copy.

What Writing Is Not

- **Writing is not something mysterious, created by using a magical formula known only to a few.** Even if you have not written much previously, you can learn to write effectively.
- **Writing is not simply a hit-or-miss affair, left up to chance.** Successful writing requires hard work and thoughtful effort. It is not done well by simply following an ordered set of steps as if you were painting by number. You cannot sit down for fifteen minutes and expect to write the perfect memo, letter, or short report straight through. Writing does not proceed in some predictable way, in which introductions are always written first and conclusions last.
- **Just because you put something on paper or on a computer screen does not mean it is permanent and unchangeable.** Writing means *re*writing, *re*vising, *re*thinking. The better a piece of writing is, the more the writer has reworked it.

█ Researching

Before you start to compose any e-mail, memo, letter, or report, you'll need to do some research. Research is crucial so that you obtain the right information for your audience. Information must be factually correct and intellectually significant. The world of work is based on conveying information—the logical presentation and sensible interpretation of facts.

Don't ever think you are wasting time by not starting to write your report or letter immediately. Actually, you will waste time and risk doing a poor job if you do not find out as much as possible about your topic (and your audience's interest in it). Find out as much as you can about the nature of your assignment and your readers.

Then you can determine the kind of research you must do to gather and interpret the information your audience needs. Your research can include

- interviewing people inside and outside your company
- doing fieldwork or performing lab studies
- preparing for conferences to ask the right questions
- collaborating in person, by e-mail, or instant messaging (IM)
- distributing a questionnaire and conducting a survey
- doing research on the Internet
- searching abstracts, indexes, and other references on the Web or in print
- reading current periodicals, reports, and other documents
- evaluating reports, products, and services

- getting briefings from sales or technical staff
- contacting customers

Keep in mind that research is not confined to the beginning of the writing process; it is an ongoing process. Chapter 8 focuses on these and other types of research you will be expected to do in the workplace and in school.

Case Study: The Writing Process

Office manager Melissa Hill asked Marcus Weekley to recommend ways to improve office efficiency and customer relations. In preparing his report (Figures 2.4 and 2.5, pp. 50 and 52), Weekley knew he had to do research to make his recommendation. To find information about different communication technologies, he searched relevant materials in print and online. As he read articles and explored websites, he learned about the different laser printers on the market.

As he studied the literature about printers from various vendors, he realized that several offered strong benefits for his company. He visited a few dealers in his city and, after seeing some demonstrations, was convinced that purchasing a new laser printer was feasible and economically wise. The results of all his research were reflected in his final report.

Planning

At this stage in the writing process, your goal is to get something—anything—down on paper or on your computer screen. For most writers, many of whom are fearful of writer's block, getting started is the hardest part of the job. But you will feel more comfortable and confident once you begin to see your ideas before your eyes. It is always easier to clarify and criticize something you can see.

Getting started is also easier if you have researched your topic, because you have something to say and to build on. Each part of the process relates to and supports the next. Careful research prepares you to begin writing.

Still, getting started is not easy. Take advantage of a number of widely used strategies to develop, organize, and tailor the right information for your audience. Use one of the following techniques, alone or in combination.

1. Clustering. In the middle of a sheet of paper, write the word or phrase that best describes your topic, then start writing other words or phrases that come to mind. As you write, circle each word or phrase and connect it to the word from which it sprang. Note the clustered grouping in Figure 2.1 for a report encouraging a manager to switch to **flex time,** a system in which employees work on a flexible time schedule within certain limits. The resulting diagram gives the writer a rough sense of some of the major divisions of the topic and where they may belong in the report.

2. Brainstorming. At the top of a sheet of paper or your computer screen, describe your topic in a word or phrase and then list any information you know or found out about that topic—in any order and as quickly as you can. Brainstorming is like thinking aloud except that you are recording your thoughts.

- Don't stop to delete, rearrange, or rewrite anything, and don't dwell on any one item.
- Don't worry about spelling, punctuation, grammar, or whether you are using words and phrases instead of complete sentences.
- Keep the ideas flowing. The result may well be an odd assortment of details, comments, and opinions.
- After ten to fifteen minutes, stop and take a short break. When you come back to your list, you will no doubt want to make some changes. Some of your points will be irrelevant, so strike them.
- Expect to add some ideas or combine or rearrange others as you start to develop them in more detail.

Figure 2.2 shows Marcus Weekley's initial brainstormed list. After he began to revise it, he realized that some items were not relevant for his audience (6, 8, and 13) and that another was pertinent but needed to be adapted for his reader (5). He also recognized that some items were repetitious (1, 2, and 11). Further investigation revealed that his company could purchase a new color laser printer for far less than his initial high guess (17).

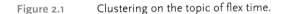

Figure 2.1   Clustering on the topic of flex time.

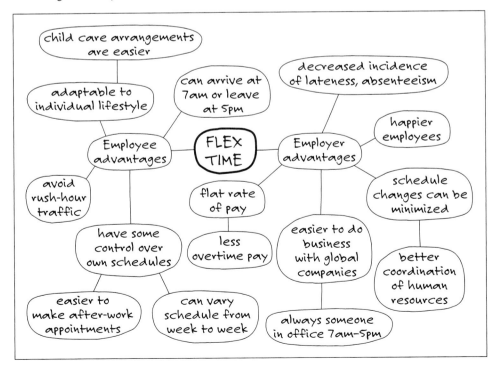

Marcus Weekley's initial, unrevised brainstormed list.   Figure 2.2

1. combines four separate pieces of equip—printer, copier, fax, and scanner

2. more comprehensive than our current configuration of four pieces of equip

3. would coordinate with office furniture

4. energy efficiency increased due to fewer machines being used

5. more scalable fonts

6. one machine interfaces with all others in same-case housing

7. scanner makes photographic-quality pictures

8. print capabilities are a real contribution to technology

9. increase communication abilities through fax machine

10. new scanner picture quality better than current scanner

11. only have to buy one machine as opposed to four

12. speed of fax allows quick response time

13. stock is doing better on Wall Street compared to other stocks

14. reducing our advertising costs through use of color printer

15. increase work area available

16. would help us do our work better

17. top of line models can be bought for $4,500

List is not organized but simply reflects writer's ideas about possible topics

1, 2, and 11 are repetitious

6, 8, and 13 are not relevant

Research will show price is too high

3. Outlining. For most writers, outlining may be the easiest and most comfortable way to begin or to continue planning their report or letter. Outlines can go through stages, so don't worry if your first attempt is brief and messy. It does not have to be formal (with roman and arabic numerals), complete, or pretty. It is intended for no one's eyes but yours. Use your preliminary outline as a quick way to sketch some ideas, a convenient container into which you can put information. You might simply jot down a few major points and identify a few subpoints. Note that Marcus Weekley organized his revised brainstormed list into an outline (Figure 2.3).

Tech Note

Planning on Your Computer

Plan your document by creating either an outline or a brainstorm. Don't jump right into the drafting stage, however tempting a blank computer screen (or piece of paper) might be.

There are several software packages (such as MindManager®, ParaMind, and Visual Mind™) designed specifically to help you brainstorm or cluster your ideas on a computer screen. With them you can then add, delete, rearrange, combine, expand, and organize points into categories and subcategories.

A word processing program can help you create an outline with main points and subpoints that will make it easier to organize your thoughts when you are writing the draft. This is a good way to organize your ideas quickly and efficiently, particularly if you are planning a business document and need to concisely convey a number of points. Most, if not all, word processing programs provide an outline view. The outline view allows you to select the number of levels to display in the outline and to easily change levels in the hierarchy.

Using an outline will help keep you on track during the writing process. You might want to simply list large concepts, as in Figure 2.2, or use complete sentences for your major headings, whichever is easier for you. Leave plenty of space, though, between major parts of the outline so you can fill them in with relevant information, as in Figure 2.3. You might want to insert instructions to yourself, such as "Why is this point important for my audience?" or "What is my purpose here? to inform? persuade?," etc. You might also want to remind yourself after each main idea, "Transition to next idea" so you don't forget to add connecting sentences or transitions.

Be sure to save your outline or brainstorm in a file that you can use when you begin drafting your document.

Anne Stanberry

Marcus Weekley's early outline after revising his brainstormed list.   Figure 2.3

I. Convenience/Capabilities

    A. Would reduce number of machines required to service

    B. Can be configured easily for our network system

    C. Easy to install and operate

    D. 35.6 Kbps fax machine would increase our communication

    E. 2,400 × 1,200 dpi copier means better copy quality

    F. 4,800 × 4,800 dpi scanner means higher quality pictures than current scanner

Outline form helps writer group ideas/ topics and go to next step in revision

II. Time/Efficiency

    A. 50 ppm printer is nearly twice as fast as current printer

    B. 35.6 Kbps speed fax allows quick response time

    C. Greater graphics capability—90 scalable fonts

    D. Scanner compatible with our current PhotoEdit imaging/graphics software

    E. 100,000-page monthly duty cycle means less maintenance

Outline headings correspond to major sections of report

III. Money

    A. Costs less for multitasking printer than combined four machines

    B. Reduced monthly power bill by using one machine rather than four

    C. Included ScanText and WordPort software means not buying new software to network office computers

    D. Save on service costs

    E. Reduced advertising costs through printer 50–1,000% enlargement/ reduction options, which allow for more in-house advertising

Drafting

If you have done your planning carefully, you will find it easier to start your first draft. When you draft, you convert the words and phrases from your outlines, brainstormed lists, or clustered groups into paragraphs. Think of your earlier jottings as the material out of which the basic building blocks (paragraphs) of your drafts will come. During drafting, as elsewhere in the writing process, you will see some overlap as you look back over your lists or outlines to shape your text.

Don't expect to wind up with a polished, complete version of your paper after working on only one draft. In most cases, you will have to work through many drafts, but each draft should be less rough and more acceptable than the preceding one.

Key Questions to Ask as You Draft

As you work on your drafts, ask yourself the following questions about your content and organization.

- Am I giving my readers too much or too little information?
- Is my information too technical for my audience?
- Does this point belong where I have it, or would it more logically follow or precede something else?
- Is this point necessary and relevant?
- Am I repeating myself?
- Have I contradicted myself?
- Have I ended appropriately for my audience?

To answer those questions successfully, you may have to continue researching your topic and reexamining your audience's needs. But in the process new and even better ideas will come to you, and ideas that you once thought were essential may in time appear unworkable or unnecessary.

Guidelines for Successful Drafting

Following are some suggestions to help your drafting go more smoothly and efficiently.

- In an early draft, write the easiest part first, regardless of where in the paper it may finally end up. Some writers feel more comfortable drafting the body (or middle) of their work first.
- As you work on a later draft, write straight through. Do not worry about spelling, punctuation, or the way a word or sentence sounds. Save those concerns for later stages.
- Allow enough time between drafts so you can evaluate your work with fresh eyes and a clear mind.

- Get frequent outside opinions. Show, e-mail, or fax a draft to a fellow student, a co-worker, or maybe a supervisor for comment. A new pair of eyes will see things you missed. Collaboration is essential in the workplace.
- Start considering if visuals would enhance the quality of your work and, if so, where they might best be positioned.

Case Study: Drafting

Figure 2.4 shows one of the several drafts that Marcus Weekley prepared. Because he wisely recognized that his outline was not final, he continued to work on it during the drafting stage. Note that he has added an introduction and a conclusion, which were not part of his original outline (Figure 2.3), to convince Melissa Hill to purchase a new laser printer. Even so, Weekley recognized that his draft was still not ready for his boss to see, so he showed it to a co-worker for suggestions.

Tech Note

Drafting on Your Computer

When you draft your document, try to get some writing on the screen quickly. A word processing program keeps pace with the speed of your thought process and allows you to concentrate on your writing rather than on the more technical aspects of creating a document. Do not stop to check spelling or punctuation; you can return to those tasks later. If you run into a snag on any draft, do not lose momentum by stopping to fix it. Simply flag items to which you want to return or about which you need more information by highlighting or underlining those sections of text.

You can also insert notes to yourself to supply information, qualification, or even documentation, reminding you that your draft is a document in the making. Use the comment tool in your word processing program to add marginal notes or, alternatively, you can add italicized or highlighted comments.

Software enables writers to create and work with multiple drafts. Be prepared to create, expand, delete, move, save, and retrieve different drafts or even portions of one or more of your drafts. That way you can go back to see which version (of a draft) you like best or what might be salvaged from one version and incorporated into another. For that reason, it is best to use the save command after every page or at regular intervals of every two to three minutes. Make sure you use the Save As command if you want to save your draft as a new version rather than completely eliminating the original document. When you save drafts (or revisions), your file names should always clearly reflect their contents (e.g., Draft 1, Works Cited).

Figure 2.4   Intermediate draft of Marcus Weekley's report.

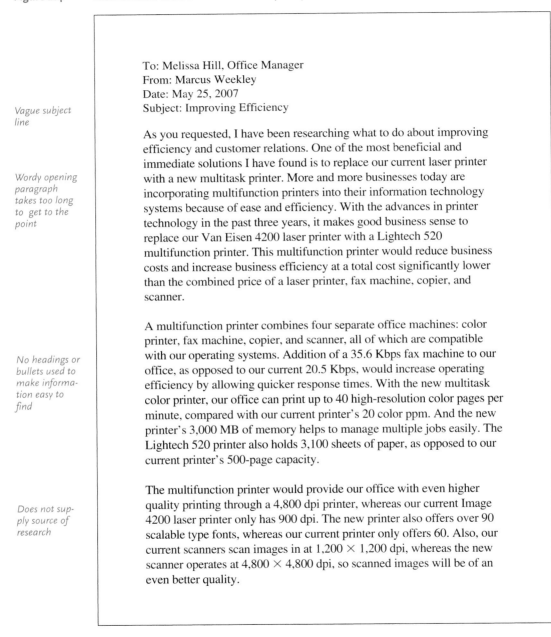

Vague subject line

Wordy opening paragraph takes too long to get to the point

No headings or bullets used to make information easy to find

Does not supply source of research

To: Melissa Hill, Office Manager
From: Marcus Weekley
Date: May 25, 2007
Subject: Improving Efficiency

As you requested, I have been researching what to do about improving efficiency and customer relations. One of the most beneficial and immediate solutions I have found is to replace our current laser printer with a new multitask printer. More and more businesses today are incorporating multifunction printers into their information technology systems because of ease and efficiency. With the advances in printer technology in the past three years, it makes good business sense to replace our Van Eisen 4200 laser printer with a Lightech 520 multifunction printer. This multifunction printer would reduce business costs and increase business efficiency at a total cost significantly lower than the combined price of a laser printer, fax machine, copier, and scanner.

A multifunction printer combines four separate office machines: color printer, fax machine, copier, and scanner, all of which are compatible with our operating systems. Addition of a 35.6 Kbps fax machine to our office, as opposed to our current 20.5 Kbps, would increase operating efficiency by allowing quicker response times. With the new multitask color printer, our office can print up to 40 high-resolution color pages per minute, compared with our current printer's 20 color ppm. And the new printer's 3,000 MB of memory helps to manage multiple jobs easily. The Lightech 520 printer also holds 3,100 sheets of paper, as opposed to our current printer's 500-page capacity.

The multifunction printer would provide our office with even higher quality printing through a 4,800 dpi printer, whereas our current Image 4200 laser printer only has 900 dpi. The new printer also offers over 90 scalable type fonts, whereas our current printer only offers 60. Also, our current scanners scan images in at $1,200 \times 1,200$ dpi, whereas the new scanner operates at $4,800 \times 4,800$ dpi, so scanned images will be of an even better quality.

Continued

(Continued)   Figure 2.4

Page 2

The greatest benefit a multifunction printer would provide our company is monetary. The price of a new multifunctional business printer ranges from $3,000 to $9,000 depending on the model. Lightech's 520 multifunction color laser printer (including 2,400 × 1,200 dpi copier, 4,800 × 4,800 dpi scanner, and 35.6 Kbps fax) costs only $3,175 not including shipping and handling purchased from Computerbuyers.com. This cost nearly equals the price of our own Van Eisen 4200 printer and West 400 scanners, but combines the equipment into one more efficient machine. Purchasing the multifunction printer would not only save our business money on the initial purchase, but use of a multitasking machine that combines four machines into one would also save on subsequent servicing and maintenance, as well as decreasing our monthly electric bill by $50–$150 per month. Use of the multifunction printer's 50–1,000% enlargement/reduction options should also save us an additional $300–$500 each month by using less outside advertising. Computerbuyers.com also offers a two-year warranty on all products sold through its website. What better way to begin improving business efficiency and customer relations than through the purchase of a new multifunction color printer?

Includes most important point for reader— costs—last

Ends with question rather than plan for how to make change

From discussions with his co-worker and after further work on his draft, Weekley realized that he had placed one of the most important considerations for his audience (savings) last. In his final version, shown in Figure 2.5 (pp. 52–54), he moved that section to the beginning of his memo because he realized that Melissa Hill would be most concerned about costs. Weekley thus paid attention to his audience's priorities and needs.

He also added headings and bulleted lists to help his reader find information. The design of his earlier draft in Figure 2.4 did not assist his readers in finding information quickly or reflect a convincing organizational plan.

Figure 2.5   Final version of Marcus Weekley's report.

To: Melissa Hill, Office Manager
From: Marcus Weekley
Date: May 25, 2007
Subject: Purchasing a New Multifunctional Printer

As you requested, I have investigated some ways to improve office efficiency and customer relations. The best solution I have found is to replace our current Van Eisen 4200 laser printer, two Readrite 400 scanners, and XL290 fax machine with a new generation multitask printer.

With advances in printer technology over the previous three years (enclosed is a copy of a review article "New Technology Means Office Efficiency" from *Computer World* [Jan. 2007]: 96–98), it makes good business sense to replace our less-efficient laser printer with a Lightech 520 multifunction printer. Our laser printer does only one task, while the multifunction Lightech will give us higher-resolution color printing, a high-speed fax machine, a copier, and a scanner all in one. This new equipment is economical, more efficient, and will significantly improve the transmission and design of our documents.

Cost
The greatest benefit of the multifunction Lightech 520 is cost. We can purchase this multifunction printer for only $3,175, plus shipping and handling, totaling $3,298 when ordered through **Computerbuyers.com**. Purchasing a Lightech 520 would allow us to recoup that cost easily in just a few months because we would

- realize a savings in the purchase price—one Lightech costs less than the four machines combined
- receive Smartext and WordPort software with the printer
- decrease our monthly electricity bill by $50–$150 by reducing four pieces of office equipment to one

Introduction gets to the point quickly

Documentation shows research on subject

Excellent use of headings and bulleted lists

Continued

(Continued)   **Figure 2.5**

Page 2

- have less maintenance, saving at least $150 per month in service calls
- receive a two-year warranty with guaranteed overnight service, decreasing downtime
- be able to trade in our current printer for $375 and our two scanners for $200 each
- save an additional $300–$500 each month by not having to use outside advertising thanks to Lightech's 50–1,000% enlargement/reduction capabilities

Justification for new purchase clearly laid out

Efficiency

This multitask printer accomplishes all four tasks—printing, faxing, scanning, copying—simultaneously, and each task is compatible with our current networking system. Other key features include

- quicker faxing (3 seconds per page) with 35.6 Kbps and greater storage (600 pages)
- prints twice as fast—40 high-resolution color pages per minute as opposed to our current printer's 20
- enhanced memory of 3,000 MB manages multiple jobs easily
- expanded paper capacity (3,100 sheets) to handle our heavy quarterly mailings easily
- 100,000-page monthly duty cycle means less maintenance
- all four tasks compatible with our PhotoEdit software

Gives reader right amount of detail

Quality

The Lightech 520 prints and processes higher quality and quantity of work because it

- has a 4,800 dpi printer whereas our current printer offers only 900 dpi
- exhibits same color density on the 1,000th copy as on the first; solid ink sticks ensure no toner spills

Contrasts current equipment with new model

Continued

Figure 2.5   (Continued)

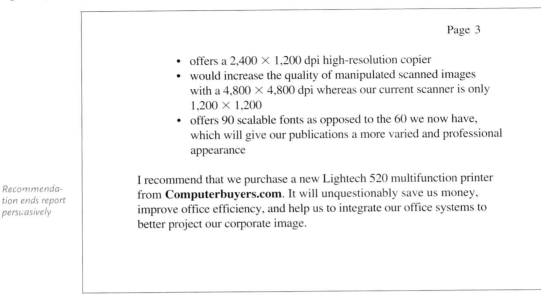

Page 3

- offers a 2,400 × 1,200 dpi high-resolution copier
- would increase the quality of manipulated scanned images with a 4,800 × 4,800 dpi whereas our current scanner is only 1,200 × 1,200
- offers 90 scalable fonts as opposed to the 60 we now have, which will give our publications a more varied and professional appearance

Recommendation ends report persuasively

I recommend that we purchase a new Lightech 520 multifunction printer from **Computerbuyers.com**. It will unquestionably save us money, improve office efficiency, and help us to integrate our office systems to better project our corporate image.

Revising

Revision is an essential stage in the writing process. It requires more than giving your work one more quick glance. Do not be tempted to skip the revision stage just because you have written the required number of words or sections or because you think you have put in too much time already. Revision is done *after* you produce a draft that you think conveys the appropriate message for your audience. The quality of your letter or report depends on the revisions you make now. Revision gives you a second (or third or fourth) chance to get things right for your audience and to clarify your purpose in writing to them, as Marcus Weekley did.

Allow Enough Time to Revise

Like planning or drafting, revision is not done well in one big push. It evolves over a period of time. Allow yourself enough time to do it carefully.

- Avoid drafting and revising in one sitting. If possible, wait at least a day before you start to revise. (In the busy work world, waiting a couple of hours may suffice.)
- Ask a co-worker or friend familiar with your topic to comment on your work, as Marcus Weekley did to make sure his report was convincing.
- Plan to read your revised work more than once.

Revising on Your Computer

Revising online, you can expect to add, delete, qualify, and rearrange words, sentences, and paragraphs, or even transform the appearance of your material. Experimenting with a number of different versions of your work is at the heart of the revision process. Just remember to save what you have done each time.

As you revise your text, use the copy, paste, and move commands to reposition your text the way you want it. At the revision stage, too, insert visuals exactly where you want them and format your document to include headings, different fonts, and other design elements (see Chapters 11 and 12).

Various software packages allow you to split your monitor screen into two or four parts (windows) to view different versions of a text or several pages of the text simultaneously. Or you can view one page while working on another. Moreover, you can go to the print mode and choose print preview to see each page layout. That way you can judge if your document falls under or exceeds the page limits your boss or instructor has set for you. From the broader perspective of your overall document, you will be able to make global revisions, rather than just line changes.

Key Questions to Ask as You Revise

Revision means asking again the questions you have already asked and answered during the planning and drafting stages. By asking and successfully answering the following questions, you can discover gaps, points to change, and errors to correct in your draft.

Content

1. Is it accurate? Are my facts (figures, names, dates, costs, references, statistics) correct?
2. Is it relevant for my audience and purpose? Have I included information that is unnecessary, too technical, not appropriate?
3. Have I given enough evidence to explain things adequately and to persuade my readers? (Too little information will make readers skeptical about what you are describing or proposing.) Have I left anything out?

Organization

1. Have I clearly identified my main points and shown my readers why those points are important?
2. Is everything in the correct, most effective order? Should anything be switched or moved closer to the beginning or the end of my document?

3. Have I spent too much (or too little) effort on one section? Do I repeat myself? What can be cut?
4. Have I grouped related items in the same part of my report or letter, or have I scattered details that really need to appear together in one paragraph or section?

Tone

1. How do I sound to my readers—professional and sincere, or arrogant and unreliable? What attitude do my words or expressions convey?
2. How will my readers think I perceive them—honest and intelligent or unprofessional and uncooperative?

Case Study: A "Before" and "After" Revision

Mary Fonseca, an employee at Seacoast Labs, was asked by her supervisor to prepare a short report for the general public on the lab's most recent experiments. Figures 2.6 and 2.7 show her "before" and "after" revisions.

Figure 2.6   Opening, unorganized paragraphs of Mary Fonseca's draft.

Information hard to follow and not relevant for audience

Drag is an important concept in the world of science and technology. It has many implications. Drag occurs when a ship moves through the water and eddies build up. Ships on the high seas have to fight the eddies, which results in drag. In the same way, an airplane has to fight the winds at various altitudes at which it flies; these winds are very forceful, moving at many knots per hour. All these forces of nature are around us. Sometimes we can feel them, too. We get tired walking against a strong wind. The eddies around a ship are the same thing. These eddies form various barriers around the ship's hull. They come from a combination of different molecules around the ship's hull and exert quite a force. Both types of molecules pull against the ship. This is where the eddies come in.

Scientists at Seacoast Labs are concerned about drag. Dr. Karen Runnels, who joined Seacoast about three years ago, is the chief investigator. She and her team of highly qualified experts have constructed some fascinating multilevel water tunnels. These tunnels should be useful to ship owners. Drag wastes a ship's fuel.

A revision of Mary Fonseca's draft in Figure 2.6.   Figure 2.7

What is drag?

We cannot see or hear many of the forces around us, but we can certainly detect their presence. Walking or running into a strong wind, for example, requires a great deal of effort and often quickly leaves us feeling tired. When a ship sails through the water, it also experiences these opposing forces known as **drag**. Overcoming drag causes a ship to reduce its energy efficiency, which leads to higher fuel costs.

Effective use of definition and headings

How drag works

It is not easy for a ship to fight drag. As the ship moves through the water, it drags the water molecules around its hull at the same rate the ship is moving. Because of the cohesive force of those molecules, other water molecules immediately outside the ship's path get pulled into its way. All the molecules become tangled rather than simply sliding past each other. The result is an eddy, or small circling burst of water around the ship's hull, which intensifies the drag. Dr. Charles Hester, a noted engineer, explains it using an analogy: "When you put a spoon in honey and pull it out, half the honey comes out with the spoon. That's what is happening to ships. The ship is moving and at the same time dragging the ocean with it."

Describes cause and effect of drag

Uses an easy-to-follow analogy

At Seacoast Labs, scientists are working to find ways to reduce drag on ships. Dr. Karen Runnels, the principal investigator, and a team of researchers have constructed water tunnels to simulate the movement of ships at sea. The drag a ship encounters is measured from the tiny air bubbles emitted in the water tunnel. Dr. Runnels's team has also developed the use of polymers, or long carbon chain molecules, to reduce drag. The polymers act like a slimy coating for the ship's hull to help it glide through the water more easily. When asbestos fibers were added to the polymer solutions, the investigators measured a 90 percent reduction in drag. The team has also experimented with an external pump attached to the hull of a ship, which pushes the water away from a ship's path.

Clearly explains the research and its importance

When starting to revise Figure 2.6, Fonseca realized that it lacked focus. It jumped back and forth between drag on ships and drag on an airplane. Since Seacoast Labs did not work on planes, she wisely decided to drop that idea. She also realized that the information on the effects of drag, something Seacoast was working on, was so important it deserved a separate paragraph. In light of this key idea, she realized that her explanation of molecules, eddies, and drag needed to be made more reader-friendly. Researching further, she decided to add a new paragraph on the causes and effects of drag, which became paragraph 2 in Figure 2.7.

Yet by pulling ideas about drag and its effects from her longish first paragraph in Figure 2.6, Fonseca was left with the job of finding an opening for her report. Buried in her original opening paragraph was the idea that we cannot always see the forces of nature but "we can feel them." She thought this analogy of walking against the wind and drag would work better for her audience of nonspecialists than the original wooden remarks she had started with.

Although her original draft organization and ideas were now far better than those in Figure 2.6, she realized she had said very little about her employer, Seacoast Labs. Doing more research, she found information about Seacoast's experiments and why they were so important in saving money. This information was far more important and relevant than saying Dr. Runnels had been at Seacoast for three years.

Through revision and further research, then, Mary Fonseca transformed two poorly organized and incomplete paragraphs into three separate yet logically connected ones that highlighted her employer's work. Thanks to her revision (Figure 2.7), she came up with two very helpful headings—"What is drag?" and "How drag works"—for her nonspecialist readers.

Editing

Editing is quality control for your reader. This last stage in the writing process might be compared to detailing an automobile—the preparation a dealer goes through to ready a new car for prospective buyers. Editing is done only after you are completely satisfied that you have made all the big decisions about content and organization—that you have said what you wanted to, where and how you intended, for your audience.

When you edit, you will check your work for

- sentences
- word choices
- punctuation
- spelling
- grammar and usage
- tone

As with revising, don't skip or rush through the editing process, thinking that once your ideas are down, your work is done. If your work is hard to read or contains mistakes in spelling or punctuation, readers will think that your ideas and your research are also faulty.

The following sections will give you basic guidelines about what to look for when you edit your sentences and words. The appendix, "A Writer's Brief Guide to Paragraphs, Sentences, and Words" (pp. 723–740), contains helpful suggestions on correct spelling and punctuation.

Tech Note

Online Editing

Software programs can help make editing online efficient and easy. These programs flag errors in spelling, punctuation, usage, word choice, and sentence length (readability). Use your spell checker to identify and correct misspelled words. If there are several words that you frequently misspell, add them to your word processor's dictionary. It will be worth the time and effort. Also, include in your dictionary any proper names, brand names, technical terms, or concepts that you use often.

Other programs will, by using the search command, help you eliminate wordiness by deleting excessive words (for example, *due to the fact that*) or by highlighting overused or misused words and suggesting alternatives.

When you edit online, be careful that you do not focus only on the lines you can see on the screen and neglect the larger organization of your document. Scroll or print out the text to check for editing problems throughout the document or to observe how a change in one place affects (contradicts, duplicates, weakens) something earlier or later.

When you finish editing, always make a backup and a hard copy. Your document could be lost because of a power surge, virus, hard disk crash, or problems retrieving the file at a later date.

Editing Guidelines for Writing Lean and Clear Sentences

Here are three of the most frequent complaints readers voice about poorly edited writing in the world of work:

- The sentences are too long. I could not follow the writer's meaning.
- The sentences are too complex. I could not understand what the writer meant the first time I read the work; I had to reread it several times.
- The sentences are unclear. Even after I reread them, I am not sure I understood the writer's message.

Wordy, unclear sentences frustrate readers and waste their time. Writing clear, readable sentences is not always easy. It takes effort, but the time you spend editing will pay off in rich dividends for you and your readers.

If you use the following seven guidelines when you edit your work, you will be better able to write easy-to-read—lean and clear—sentences.

1. *Avoid Needlessly Complex or Lengthy Sentences*
   Do not pile words on top of words. Instead, edit one overly long sentence into two or even three more manageable ones.

Too long:	The planning committee decided that the awards banquet should be held on May 15 at 6:30, since the other two dates (May 7 and May 22) suggested by the hospitality committee conflict with local sports events, even though one of those events could be changed to fit our needs.
Edited for easier reading:	The planning committee has decided to hold the awards banquet on May 15 at 6:30. The other dates suggested by the hospitality committee—May 7 and May 22—conflict with two local sports events. Although the date of one of those sports events could be changed, the planning committee still believes that May 15 is our best choice.

2. *Combine Short, Choppy Sentences*
   Don't shorten long, complex sentences only to turn them into choppy, simplistic ones. A memo, e-mail, or letter written exclusively in short, staccato sentences sounds immature and makes for boring reading.

   When you find yourself looking at a series of short, blunt sentences, as in the following example, combine them where possible and use connective words similar to those italicized in the edited version.

Choppy:	Medical transcriptionists have many responsibilities. Their responsibilities are important. They must be familiar with medical terminology. They must listen to dictation. Sometimes physicians talk very fast. Then the transcriptionist must be quick to transcribe what is heard. Words could be missed. Transcriptionists must also prepare final reports. This will take a great deal of time and concentration. These reports are copied and stored properly for reference.
Edited:	Medical transcriptionists have many important responsibilities. *These include* transcribing physicians' orders using correct medical terminology. *When* physicians talk rapidly, transcriptionists have to keyboard accurately *so that* no words are omitted. *Among the most demanding* of their duties are preparing final transcriptions *and then* making and storing those copies properly for future reference.

3. *Edit Sentences to Tell Who Does What to Whom or What*
   The clearest sentence pattern in English is the subject-verb-object (s-v-o) pattern.

   s   v   o
   Sue mowed the grass.

   s   v   o
   Our website contains a link to key training software programs.

   Readers, both U.S. and international, find this pattern easiest to understand because it provides direct and specific information about the action. Hard-to-read sentences obscure or scramble information about the subject, the verb, or the object. In the following unedited sentence, subjects are hidden in the middle rather than being placed in the most crucial subject position.

> Unclear: The control of the ceiling limits of glycidyl ethers on the part of the employers for the optimal safety of workers in the workplace is necessary. (Who is responsible for taking action? What action must they take? For whom is such action taken?)
>
> Edited: Employers must control the ceiling limits of glycidyl ethers for the workers' safety.

Tech Note

The Writing Process: What Your Computer Can't Do

Use your software to help you increase your writing productivity, improve your writing skills, and design more professional-looking documents. But a computer will not do your writing and thinking for you. *You* still have to plan, draft, revise, and edit. Keep the following points in mind:

- A software package may help you organize your ideas, but *you* must first do research to discover what ideas are relevant and convincing for your audience.
- The computer enables you to produce more writing, but, again, *you* are the one who must select the right words with appropriate tone and put them into readable sentences and logically organized paragraphs.
- A computer cannot tell you what points will please or alienate your audience. *You* must decide what must be changed, modified, retained, or moved, and why and how.
- A software program can tell you that your sentences are too long, but changing every one into a short (ten-word) statement will make your work choppy and less pleasing to read.
- A spell checker will not catch all your mistakes. It may miss things like proper nouns, mistyped words, and homonyms such as *there/their*.
- Finally, never be lulled into thinking that a clear, professionally printed document will hide or make up for incorrect grammar, irrelevant content, or poor organization.

Your computer is an efficient writing tool, not a substitute writer for you.

4. *Use Strong, Active Verbs Rather Than Verb Phrases*

In trying to sound important, many bureaucratic writers avoid using simple, graphic verbs. Instead, these writers use a weak verb phrase (for example, *provide maintenance of* instead of *maintain, work in cooperation with* instead of *cooperate*). Such verb phrases imprison the active verb inside a noun format and slow a reader down. Note how the edited version here rewrites the weak verb phrase.

> Weak: The city provided the employment of two work crews to assist the strengthening of the dam.
>
> Strong: The city employed two work crews to strengthen the dam.

5. *Avoid Piling Modifiers in Front of Nouns*

Putting too many modifiers (words used as adjectives) in the reader's path to the noun will confuse the reader, who cannot decipher how one modifier relates to another modifier or to the noun. To avoid that problem, edit the sentence to place some of the modifiers after or before the nouns they modify.

> Crowded: The vibration noise control heat pump condenser quieter can make your customer happier.
>
> Readable: The quieter on the condenser for the heat pump will make your customer happier by controlling noise and vibrations.

6. *Replace Wordy Phrases or Clauses with One- or Two-Word Synonyms*

> Wordy: The college has parking zones for different areas for people living on campus as well as for those who do not live on campus and who commute to school.
>
> Edited: The college has different parking zones for resident and commuter students. (Twenty words of the original sentence—everything after "areas for"—have been reduced to four words: "resident and commuter students.")

7. *Combine Sentences Beginning with the Same Subject or Ending with an Object That Becomes the Subject of the Next Sentence*

> Wordy: I asked the inspector if she were going to visit the plant this afternoon. I also asked her if she would come alone.
>
> Edited: I asked the inspector if she were going to visit the plant alone this afternoon.

> Wordy: Homeowners want to buy low-maintenance bushes. These low-maintenance bushes include the ever-popular holly and boxwood varieties. These bushes are also inexpensive.
>
> Edited: Homeowners want to buy low-maintenance and inexpensive bushes such as holly and boxwood. (This revision combines three sentences into one, condenses twenty-four words into fourteen, and joins three related thoughts.)

Editing Guidelines for Cutting Out Unnecessary Words

Too many people in business and technology think the more words, the better. Nothing could be more self-defeating. Your readers are busy; unnecessary words slow them down. Make every word work. Cut out any words you can from your sentences. If the sentence still makes sense and reads correctly, you have eliminated wordiness. For example, the phrases on the left should be replaced with the precise words on the right.

Wordy	Concisely Edited
at a slow rate	slowly
at this point in time	now
be in agreement with	agree
due to the fact that	because
for the length of time that	while
for the period of	for
in such a manner that	so that
in the area / case / field of	in
in the neighborhood of	approximately
look something like	resemble
serve the function of	function as
show a tendency to	tend
with reference to	regarding, about
with the result that	so

Another kind of wordiness comes from using redundant expressions—saying the same thing a second time, in different words. "Fellow colleague," "component parts," "corrosive acid," and "free gift" are phrases that contain this kind of double speech; a fellow *is* a colleague, a component *is* a part, acid *is* corrosive, and a gift *is* free. The suggested changes on the right are preferable to the redundant phrases on the left.

Redundant	Concise
absolutely essential	essential
advance reservations	reservations
basic necessities	necessities, needs
close proximity	proximity, nearness
end result	result
final conclusions/final outcome	conclusions/outcome
first and foremost	first
full and complete	full, complete
personal opinion	opinion
tried and true	tried, proven

Watch for repetitious words, phrases, or clauses within a sentence. Sometimes one sentence or one part of a sentence needlessly duplicates another.

> Redundant: To provide more room for employees' cars, the security department is studying ways to expand the employees' parking lot.
>
> Edited: The security department is studying ways to expand the employees' parking lot. (Since the first phrase says nothing that the reader does not know from the independent clause, cut it.)

Adding a prepositional phrase can sometimes contribute to redundancy. The italicized words below are unnecessary. Be on the lookout for the italicized phrases on the next page and delete them.

audible *to the ear*	second *in sequence*	soft *in texture*
bitter *in taste*	short *in duration*	tall *in height*
fly *through the air*	hard *to the touch*	twenty *in number*
orange *in color*	honest *in character*	visible *to the eye*
rectangular *in shape*	light *in weight*	

Figure 2.8 shows an e-mail that Trudy Wallace wants to send to her boss, Lee Chadwick, about issuing cell phones to the entire sales force. Her unedited work is bloated with unnecessary words, expendable phrases, and repetitious ideas.

Figure 2.8   Wordy, unedited e-mail.

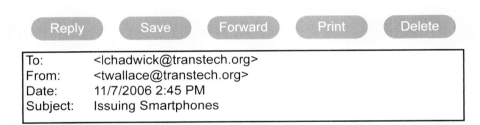

To: <lchadwick@transtech.org>
From: <twallace@transtech.org>
Date: 11/7/2006 2:45 PM
Subject: Issuing Smartphones

One long, unbroken paragraph is hard to follow

Repeats same idea in two or three sentences

Uses awkward and wordy sentences

Does not say what writer will do about problem

Due to the increased reliance on technology, specifically on e-mail and Internet communication, within our company, I believe it would be beneficial to look into the possibility of issuing smartphones to our employees. Issuing smartphones would have a variety of positive implications for efficiency of our company. Unlike normal cell phones, these smartphones have many new features that will help our employees in their daily work, since they combine cellular phone technology with e-mail and document transfer capabilities, as well as many other important features. The employees could increase their efficiency due to the fact that they could constantly keep track of appointments on their schedule for each day. The employees would also benefit from smartphones by having access to their contacts even when they are out on the road traveling, whether they are at local office meetings or on cross-country business trips. By means of smartphones I feel quite certain that our company's correspondence would be dealt with much more speedily, since these devices will allow our employees to access their e-mail at all times. I think it would be absolutely essential for the satisfaction of our customers and to the ongoing operation of our company's business today to respond fully and completely to the possibility such a proposal affords us. It would therefore appear safe to conclude that with reference to the issue of smartphones that every means at our disposal would be brought to bear on issuing such smartphones to our employees.

The e-mail in Figure 2.8 edited for conciseness.   Figure 2.9

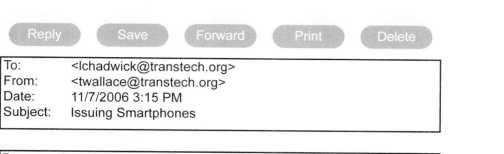

Gets to point quickly

Provides convincing reasons

Closes with plan and request

After careful editing, Wallace streamlined her e-mail to Chadwick. Note how, in Figure 2.9, she pruned wordy expressions and combined sentences to cut out duplication. The revised version is only 81 words, as opposed to the 277 words in the draft. Not only has Wallace shortened her message, she has made it easier to read.

Editing Guidelines to Eliminate Sexist Language

Editing involves far more than just making sure that your sentences are readable. It also reflects your professional style—how you see and characterize the world of work and the individuals in it, not to mention how you want your readers to see you. Your words should reflect a high degree of ethics and honesty, free from bias and offense. They need to be sensitive to your international audience's needs as well.

Sexist language offers a distorted view of our society and discriminates in favor of one sex at the expense of another, usually women. Using sexist language offends and demeans female readers by depriving them of their equal rights. It may cost your company business. Escape displaying gender bias by using inclusive language for women and men alike.

Sexist language is often based on sexist stereotypes that depict men as superior to women. For example, calling politicians *city fathers* or *favorite sons* follows the stereotypical picture of seeing politicians as male. Such phrases discriminate against women who do or could hold public office at all levels of government. Never assume or imply a person's gender based upon his or her profession.

Such language also prejudiciously labels some professions as masculine and others as feminine. For example, sexist phrases assume engineers, physicians, and pilots are male (*he, his,* and *him* are often linked with these professions in descriptions) while social workers, nurses, and secretaries are female (*she, her*), although members of both sexes work in all those professions. Sexist language also wrongly points out gender identities when such roles do not seem to follow biased expectations—*lady lawyer, male nurse, female surgeon,* or *female astronaut.* Such offensive distinctions reflect prejudiced attitudes that you should eliminate from your writing.

Always prune the following sexist phrases: *every man for himself, gal Friday, little woman, lady of the house, old maid, the best man for the job, to man a desk or post, the weaker sex, woman's work, working wives, a manly thing to do,* and *young man on the way up.* Sexist terms will not only offend but also exclude many of the members of the audience you want to reach.

Finally, don't assume all employees are male by writing "All staff members and their wives are invited to attend." Simply say, "All staff members and their guests are invited to attend."

Ways to Avoid Sexist Language

1. *Replace Sexist Words with Neutral Ones*
   Neutral words do *not* refer to a specific sex; they are genderless. The sexist words on the left in the following list can be replaced by the neutral nonsexist substitutes on the right.

Sexist	Neutral
alderman; assemblyman	representative
authoress	writer, author
businessman	businessperson
cameraman	photographer
chairman	chair, chairperson
congressman	representative
craftsman	skilled worker
divorcée	divorced person
fireman	firefighter
foreman	supervisor
janitress	cleaning person
landlord, landlady	owner
maiden name	family name
mailman/postman	mail carrier
man-hours	work-hours
mankind	humanity, human beings
manmade	synthetic, artificial
manpower	strength, power
man to man	candidly
men	human beings, people
policeman	police officer

Sexist	Neutral
repairman	repair person
salesman	salesperson, clerk
spokesman	spokesperson
stewardess	flight attendant
waitress	server
weatherman	meteorologist
woman's intuition	intuition
workman	worker

2. *Watch Masculine Pronouns*

Avoid using the masculine pronouns (*he, his, him*) when referring to a group that includes both men and women.

Every worker must submit his travel expenses by Monday.

Workers may include women as well as men, and to assume that all workers are men is misleading and unfair to women. You can edit such sexist language in several ways.

a. Make the subject of your sentence plural and thus neutral.

Workers must submit their travel expenses by Monday.

b. Replace the pronoun *his* with *the* or *a* or drop it altogether.

Every employee is to submit a travel expense report by Monday.
Every worker must submit travel expenses by Monday.

c. Use *his or her* instead of *his*.

Every worker must submit his or her travel expenses by Monday.

d. Reword the sentence using the passive voice.

All travel expenses must be submitted by Monday.

Moreover, in some contexts exclusive use of the masculine pronoun might invite a lawsuit. For example, you would be violating federal employment laws prohibiting discrimination on the basis of sex if you wrote the following in a help-wanted advertisement for your company.

Each applicant must submit his transcript with his application. He must also supply three letters of recommendation from individuals familiar with his work.

The language of that ad implies that only men can apply for the position.

Your international readers may find these guidelines on using *him/her/his* confusing since many languages (e.g., French, Spanish) follow grammatical instead of natural gender. In French, the word for *doctor* is masculine.

3. *Eliminate Sexist Salutations*

Never use the following salutations when you are unsure of who your readers are:

- Dear Sir
- Gentlemen
- Dear Madam

Any woman in the audience will surely be offended by the first two greetings and may also be unhappy with the pompous and obsolete *madam.* It is usually best to write to a specific individual, but if you cannot do that, direct your letter to a particular department or office: *Dear Warranty Department* or *Dear Selection Committee.*

Be careful, too, about using the titles *Miss, Mr.,* and *Mrs.* Sexist distinctions are unjust and insulting. It would be preferable to write *Dear Ms. McCarty* rather than *Dear Miss or Mrs. McCarty.* A woman's marital status should not be an issue. Try to find out if the person prefers *Ms.* to another courtesy title (e.g., Editor Hawkins, Supervisor Jones). If you are in doubt, write *Dear Indira Kumar.* Chapter 5 shows you acceptable salutations to use in your letters (see pp. 150 and 169).

4. *Never Single Out a Person's Physical Appearance*

The manager is a tall blonde who received her training at Mason Technical Institute.

Such sexist physical references negatively draw attention to a woman's gender. Sexist writers would not describe a male manager that way.

Avoiding Other Types of Stereotypical Language

In addition to sexist language, avoid any references that stereotype an individual because of race, national origin, age, or disability. Not only are such references almost always irrelevant in the workplace (except for Equal Employment Opportunity Commission reports or health care), they are discriminatory, culturally insensitive, and ethically wrong. To eliminate biased language in your workplace writing, follow the guidelines below.

1. Do not single out an individual because of race or national origin or stereotype him or her because of it.

    Wrong: Bill, who is African American, is one of the company's top sales reps.
    Right: Bill is one of the company's top sales reps.

    Wrong: The Chinese computer whiz was able to find the problem.
    Right: The programmer was able to find the problem.

2. Avoid words or phrases that discriminate against an individual because of age. For example, do not use *elderly, up in years, geezer, old timer, over the hill, senior moment,* or the adjectives *spry* or *frail* when they are applied to someone's age: "a spry 67." Similarly, don't refer to employees as *kids, youngsters,* or *wet behind the ears.* Making someone's age an issue is unfair, whatever it may be.

Wrong: Jerry Fox, who will be 57 next month, comes up with obsolete plans from time to time.
Right: Some of Jerry Fox's plans have not been adopted.

Wrong: Our company keeps hiring youngsters who lack experience.
Right: Our firm recruits individuals with little or no experience.

3. Respect individuals who may have a disability by avoiding derogatory words such as *crippled, handicapped, impaired,* or *lame* (physical disabilities) or *retarded* or *slow* (mental disabilities). Stay away from terms such as these because they identify the entire individual rather than just the aspects that the disability affects. Emphasize the individual instead of the physical or mental condition as if it solely determined the person's abilities.

Wrong: Tom suffers from MS.
Right: Tom is a person living with MS.

Wrong: Sarah, who is crippled, still does an excellent job of keyboarding.
Right: Sarah's disability does not prevent her from keyboarding.

Keep in mind that the Americans with Disabilities Act (1990) prohibits employers from asking if a job applicant has a disability.

Online Study Center
Access the writing process Revision Checklist online at college.hmco.com/pic/kolin8e

✔ Revision Checklist

☐ Investigated the research, drafting, revising, and editing benefits available through computer software.
☐ Researched my topic carefully to obtain enough information to answer all my readers' questions—online searches, interviews, questionnaires, personal observations.
☐ Before writing, determined how much and what kind of information are needed to complete writing task.
☐ Spent enough time planning—brainstorming, outlining, clustering, or a combination of those techniques. Produced enough substantial material from which to shape a draft.
☐ Prepared enough drafts to decide on major points in message to readers. Made major changes and deletions if necessary in drafts.
☐ Revised drafts carefully to successfully answer reader questions about content, organization, and tone.
☐ Made time to edit work so that style is clear and concise and sentences are readable and varied. Checked words to make sure they are spelled correctly and appropriate for audience.
☐ Eliminated sexist and other biased language that unfairly stereotypes individuals because of race, ethnicity, or disability.

Exercises

Online Study Center

Find additional writing process exercises at college.hmco.com/ pic/kolin8e

1. Below is a writer's initial brainstormed list on stress in the workplace. Revise the brainstormed list, eliminating repetition and combining related items.

> leads to absenteeism
> high costs for compensation for stress-related illnesses
> proper nutrition
> numerous stress reduction techniques
> good idea to conduct interviews to find out levels, causes, and extent of stress in the workplace
> low morale caused by stress
> higher insurance claims for employees' physical ailments
> myth to see stress leading to greater productivity
> various tapes used to teach relaxation
> environmental factors—too hot? too cold?
> teamwork intensifies stress
> counseling
> work overload
> setting priorities
> wellness campaign
> savings per employee add up to $4,800 per year
> skills to relax
> learning to get along with co-workers
> need for privacy
> interpersonal communication
> employee's need for clear policies on transfers, promotion
> stress management workshops very successful in California
> physical activity to relieve stress
> affects management
> breathing exercises

2. Prepare a suitable outline from your revised list in Exercise 1 for a report to a decision maker on the problems of stress in the workplace and the necessity of creating a stress management program.

3. From the revised brainstormed list in Exercise 1, write a short memo to a decision maker about how the problems of stress negatively affect workplace production.

4. Write a short report (2–3 pages) to the manager of the small company you work for on a topic of your choice. Prepare an outline similar to that on flex time in Figure 2.1 (p. 44). Add, delete, or rearrange anything in this clustered grouping to complete your outline. Submit your final outline along with your report to your instructor.

5. Compare the draft of Marcus Weekley's report in Figure 2.4 (pp. 50–51) with the final copy of his report in Figure 2.5 (pp. 52–54). What kinds of changes did he make? Were they appropriate and effective for his audience and purpose? Why or why not?

6. Assume you have been asked to write a short report (similar to Marcus Weekley's in Figure 2.5) to a decision maker (the manager of a business you work for or have worked for; the director of your campus union, library, or security force; a city official) about one of the following topics.
   a. recruitment of international work force
   b. Internet resources
   c. security lighting
   d. food service
   e. insurance plans
   f. public transportation
   g. sporting events/activities
   h. team building
   i. morale
   j. hiring more part-time student workers

   Do relevant research and planning about one of those topics and the audience for whom it is intended by answering the following questions:

   - What is my precise purpose in writing to my audience?
   - What do I know about the topic?
   - What information will my audience expect me to know?
   - Where can I obtain relevant information about my topic to meet my audience's needs?

7. Using one or more of the planning strategies discussed in this chapter (clustering, brainstorming, outlining), generate a group of ideas for the topic you chose in Exercise 6. Work on your planning activities for about 15–20 minutes or until you have about 10–15 items. At this stage do not worry about how appropriate the ideas are or even if some of them overlap. Just get some thoughts down on paper.

8. Go through the list you prepared in Exercise 7 and eliminate any entries that are inappropriate for your topic or audience or that overlap. Try to see how many of them you might expand or rearrange into categories or subcategories. Then create an outline similar to the one in Figure 2.3 (p. 47).

9. Using your outline in Exercise 8, prepare some drafts of your memo report. Submit at least two drafts to your instructor.

10. Revise your drafts as much as necessary to create the final copy of your report.

11. In a few paragraphs, explain to your instructor the changes you made between your early drafts and your revised drafts. Explain why you made them. Concentrate on major changes—adding and moving paragraphs—as well as matters of style, tone, and even format.

12. In an e-mail—addressed to your instructor—describe any problems that bothered you at various phases of working on your report. Also point out what planning, drafting, and revising strategies worked especially well for you.

13. The following paragraphs are wordy and full of awkward, hard-to-read sentences. Edit these paragraphs to make them more readable by using clear and concise words and sentences.

a. It has been verified conclusively ~~by this writer~~ that our institution must of necessity install more bicycle holding racks for the convenience of students, faculty, and staff. ~~These~~ parking modules should be fastened securely to ~~walls~~ outside strategic locations on the campus. ~~They could be positioned there by work crews or even by the security forces who vigilantly patrol the campus grounds.~~ There are many students in particular who would value the installation of these racks. ~~Their bicycles could be stationed there by them, and they would know that safety~~ measures ~~have been taken to en- sure that none~~ of their bicycles ~~would be apprehended or confiscated ille- gally.~~ Besides the precaution factor, these racks would afford users maximized convenience in utilizing their means of transportation ~~when they have academic business to conduct, whether at the learning resource center or in the instructional~~ facilities.

b. On the basis of preliminary investigations, it would seem reasonable to hy- pothesize ~~that among~~ the situational factors predisposing the Smith family toward showing pronounced psychological identification with the San Fran- cisco Giants is the fact that the Smiths make their domicile in the San Fran- cisco area. In the absence of contrariwise considerations, the Smiths' attitudinal preferences would in this respect interface with earlier behavioral studies. These studies, within acceptable parameters, correlate the fan's domi- cile with athletic allegiance. Yet it would be counterproductive to establish domicility as the sole determining factor for the Smiths' preference. Certain sociometric studies of the Smiths disclose a factor of atypicality which enters into an analysis of their determinations. One of these factors is that a younger Smith sibling is a participant in the athletic organization in question.

14. Following are very early drafts of memos that business people have sent to their bosses or co-workers. Revise and edit each draft, referring to the revising and editing checklists. Turn in your revision and the final, reader-ready copy. As you revise, keep in mind that you may have to delete and add information, rearrange the order of information, and make the tone suitable for the reader. As you edit, make sure your sentences are clear and concise and your words well chosen.

a. TO: All workers
FROM: B.J. Blackwell
DATE: February 3, 2006
RE: Parking

The parking violations around here have gotten very very bad. And the administra- tion is provoked and wants some action taken. I don't blame them. I have been late for meetings several times in the last month because inconsiderate folks from other divisions have parked their cars in our zone. That just is not fair, and so I must not be the only one who is upset. No wonder the management finds things so bad they have asked me to prepare this memo.

A big part of the problem ~~it seems to me is that~~ employees just cannot read signs. They park in the wrong zones. They also park in visitors' spots. The penalties are going to be stiff. The administration, or so I was led to believe, is thinking of fining any employee who does not obey the parking policies. I know for a fact that I saw someone from the research department pull right into a visitor parking area last week just because it was 8:55 and he did not want to be late for work. That gives our business a bad name. People will not want to do business with us if they cannot even find a parking spot in the area that the company has reserved for them.

Ms. Watson has laid the law down to me about all this and told me to let each and every one of you know that things have to improve. One of the other big problems around here is that some employees have even parked their cars in loading zones, and security had to track them down to move.

As part of the administration's new policy, each employee is going to be issued a company parking policy and will have to come in and sign for it verifying that he received it. I think things really have gotten out of hand and that some drastic action has to be taken. We will all have to shape up around here.

b. TO: Betty Cannales-Worth, Director
   FROM: Tom Cranford
   DATE: April 21, 2006
   RE: Vacation request for vacation from June 12–23

I have been a highly productive employee and so I do not think that it is out of line for me to make this request. I have put in overtime and even done others' work in the department while they were away. So, I think that it is fair and just, and I can see no reason why I should not be allowed to take my vacation during the last two weeks of June. *I would like* [handwritten]

Let me explain some of the reasons. I could have others watch my desk and do the work. I have helped them out, too, and they know it. I have been remarkably dependable. I have been readily accessible whenever their vacations have come around, and so I know it can be done. [handwritten: *person*]

I fully realize that this is the busiest time of the year for our company and that vacations are not usually granted during this season. But I do have personal reasons which I think should be honored/respected. Peak business times are major. I understand this, and I do hope an exception will be made in my case. After all, I do have the on-the-job training that other companies would reward. Thanks very much. [handwritten: *you*]

c. TO: All Employees
   FROM: George Holmes
   DATE: October 20, 2007
   RE: Travel

Every company has its policies regarding travel and vouchers. Ours strike me as important and fairly straightforward. Yet for the life of me I cannot fathom why they are being ignored. It is in everyone's best interest. When you travel, you are on company time, company business. Respect that, won't you. Explain your purpose, keep your receipts, document your visits, keep track of meals.

If you see more than one client per day, it should not be too hard or too much to ask you to keep a log of each, separate, individual visit. After all, our business does depend on these people, and we will never know your true contributions on company trips unless you inform us (please!) of whom you see, where, why, and how much it costs you. That way we can keep our books straight and know that everything is going according to company policy.

Please review the appropriate pages (I think they are pages 23–25) about travel procedures. Thanks. If you have questions, give me a call, but check your procedures book or with your office/section manager, first. That will save everyone more time. Good luck.

15. Find a piece of writing—e-mail, memo, letter, brochure, short report, or website—that you believe was not carefully drafted or revised. In a short memo or e-mail, point out to your instructor what is wrong with the piece of writing—for example, not logically organized, inappropriate tone, incomplete or too technical information. Attach a copy of the poor example to your e-mail or memo.

16. Revise the piece of poor writing you analyzed in Exercise 15. Submit your improved version to your instructor.

17. The following sentences contain sexist and other biased language. Edit them to remove these errors.
    a. Every intern had to record his readings daily for the spokesman.
    b. Although Marcel's right hand was crippled, he still could use it to hunt and peck at the keyboard.
    c. She saw a woman doctor, who told her to take an aspirin every day.
    d. Our agency was founded to help mankind.
    e. John, who is a diabetic, has an excellent attendance record.
    f. Every social worker found her schedule taxing—not enough days in the week to help out man to man.
    g. The company golf league never had an African American player before this month.
    h. To be a policeman, each applicant had to pass a rigorous physical and prove himself in the manly art of self-defense.
    i. It's a wise man who can rise to the top in this cutthroat, volatile stock market.
    j. Sandy Frain, a woman, called this morning wanting an appointment about the new policies on travel reimbursement.
    k. As long as his medication is adjusted just right, George Smith performs as well as the next man in this company.
    l. He made his PowerPoint presentation as emphatically as an Italian opera singer on stage.

CHAPTER 3

Collaborative Writing and Meetings at Work

In the workplace you will not always have to write alone, isolated from co-workers or managers. In fact, much of your business writing time may be spent working as part of a team. You will prepare a document with other employees or managers who will collaborate or, at the very least, review your work and revise it. One survey estimates that in the world of work 90 percent of all business people spend some time writing as part of a collaborative team. *Collaborative writing* occurs when a group of individuals—as few as two to as many as seven or more—

- combine their efforts to prepare a single document
- share authorship
- work together for the common good, maybe even the survival, of your department, company, or agency

Keep in mind that teamwork must always take into consideration your employer's corporate image, goals, and politics. As a member of a group, you have to be guided by those issues and directives crucial to corporate success. Your employer determines the content that your group will discuss and the format(s) in which that content appears. Moreover, everything the team does is subject to review and revision by your employer. Viewing collaboration in this broader corporate context will get you off to a good start in the world of work.

Online Study Center

To expand your understanding of collaborative writing, take advantage of the ACE quizzes, sample documents, Web links, and exercises at college.hmco.com/pic/kolin8e

Teamwork Is Crucial to Business Success

Teamwork is essential, then, for success within the world of work. Being a part of a writing team is a major responsibility in a world where each employee is connected to co-workers and managers as well as to customers in the worldwide marketplace of the Internet. Collaboration is networking, and collaborative writing is a vital part of the global network in which individuals depend on each other's expertise, experience, and viewpoints.

Figure 3.1   A collaborating team at work.

© Royalty-Free/CORBIS

Successful collaboration hinges on being a team player, one of the most highly valued skills in the workplace. Being a team player means you

- interact successfully on an interpersonal level
- talk to people to get information
- provide feedback and participation
- give and take constructive criticism
- raise important and relevant questions
- get assistance from resource experts in other departments and fields
- put the good of your company above your ego
- contribute to customer service and satisfaction

Collaboration builds teamwork as it helps get writing done more easily and more efficiently. Figure 3.1 shows a collaborating team at work, planning and interacting on a company project.

Collaboration takes place in preparing many types of writing, from brochures to technical manuals, from proposals to long reports to websites. Collaboration can be done in a variety of ways—face to face, over the telephone, or via e-mail. Several companies market software packages, called *groupware*, that facilitate collaborative writing efforts through electronic conferencing.

This chapter introduces you to successful ways to collaborate with co-workers in your office as well as people with whom you do business around the globe. You'll receive practical advice on how to write in and for a group and how to solve communication problems within a group setting. It takes much work and skillful negotiation to be a member of an effective collaborative writing group, but the energy is worth the effort.

Advantages of Collaborative Writing

Collaborative writing teams benefit both employers and employees. Specific advantages of collaboration include the following, many of them highlighted in Lee Booker's report on his team's interaction at Keeton Pharmaceuticals in Figure 3.2.

1. **It builds on collective talents.** Many heads are better than one. Because no one individual has all the answers, a writing team profits from the diverse backgrounds and skills of its individual members. Collaboration joins individuals from diverse disciplines in the corporate world—scientists, lawyers, designers, security experts—who collectively better ensure that the group will benefit from the most current resources available.

2. **It provides productive feedback.** A company wins by pooling the diverse viewpoints, constructive criticism, and immediate feedback from its work force.

3. **Team members can helpfully critique each other's suggestions, drafts, and revisions.** Playing the role of a devil's advocate, a member can also help a team uncover flaws, inconsistencies, and problems in time to correct them and improve the corporate image.

Tech Note

Instant Messaging

Instant messaging allows two or more individuals to communicate in real time. With e-mail, users experience a lag time while they wait for the recipient to read and to return a message. Thanks to instant messaging, individuals can have a real-time, online conversation. It is the ideal method for electronically conveying time-sensitive information.

Instant messaging is important in the business world, not only for its instantaneous exchange of information, but for its flexibility and convenience. Businesses realize how convenient it is for virtual conferences and collaborative projects. Users can create their own customized chat rooms, share important links with co-workers, and view images and files stored in each others' computers. The only drawback is a lack of security. While most instant messaging programs do provide encryption for the messages and connection information stored on their servers, the technology may not be considered secure enough for conveying confidential information. For more information on instant messaging, see the article in the Exercises section of Chapter 10 (pp. 440–442).

Deana Holifield

Figure 3.2   The advantages of collaboration in the workplace: A manager's notes.

Keeton Pharmaceuticals

KP

———————————— Notes for Human Resources File ————————————

Collaborative writing is essential to the success and morale of the Environmental Testing Lab at Keeton Pharmaceuticals. I supervise four microbiologists, each of whom is responsible for testing a specific area of our plant. We routinely test the environment in production areas throughout the plant by sampling the air, water, and surfaces (e.g., belts, floors, vents). When we find unacceptable ranges of bacteria, we have to investigate and report our findings to management and, ultimately, to the FDA. The report that emerges is the collaborative effort of microbiologists and production personnel, as well as management.

The protocols for such collaboration are as follows. When an unacceptable limit is found, the microbiologist for that area first interviews the production supervisor as well as line personnel to find potential causes of contamination. From such interviews the microbiologist can obtain honest, objective feedback about what happened. Then the microbiologist prepares a memo report in collaboration with the other three microbiologists, who offer helpful and constructive suggestions on how such unacceptable ranges could be eliminated or reduced. This collective brainstorming helps our lab not to overlook key information, strengthens professional communication, and improves team spirit.

After drafting the memo, the microbiologist for that area of the plant sends it to me as the Lab Supervisor and to my boss, the Quality Lab Section Manager, for our response. We confer with the microbiologist and production staff, as necessary, and make any revisions to ensure that the report follows all company guidelines.

Continued

(Continued)   Figure 3.2

Page 2

The report is then forwarded to the Quality Control Manager and, finally, to the plant manager for their approval and signatures. After their review and approval, the report is placed in the plant repository—the Document Center—where it is subject to periodical FDA inspections.

The collaborative efforts of production personnel, microbiologists, and management guarantee that the report will be a model of clear, precise, and ethical writing. In the last three years, management has frequently commended the labs and production staff for our helpful spirit of cooperation.

Lee Booker
Lab Supervisor

4. It increases productivity and saves time. When a group has planned its strategies carefully, collaboration actually cuts down on the number of meetings and conferences, saving a company time and employees travel. See how videoconferencing assists a company in doing this in Figure 17.3 (pp. 708–710).

5. It ensures overall writing effectiveness. The more people there are involved in developing a document, the greater the chances are for thoroughness and cohesion. Guided by the shared principles of company style, documentation, and mission, a collaborative team can better guarantee uniformity and consistency of a piece of writing than can one or two individuals, each writing a different section of a document in isolation.

6. It accelerates decision-making time. A group investigating problems and offering pertinent solutions can cut down considerably on the time it takes to communicate various viewpoints and reach a decision about them.

7. It can offer psychological benefits. Collaboration contributes significantly to employee confidence and morale. Working as part of a team relieves an individual of some job stress because he or she is not solely responsible for planning, drafting, and revising a document. A team, therefore, provides a safety net by assuring individual members that they can always talk over problems and they will have help in meeting deadlines.

8. It contributes to customer service and satisfaction. By pooling their knowledge of an audience's needs, including those of a regulatory government agency such as the FDA cited in Figure 3.2, a collaborative writing team is much more likely—through discussions, interactions, even disagreements—to anticipate a customer's/agency's requests and complaints and thereby respond to or solve them.

9. It affords a greater opportunity to understand global perspectives. By working with a multinational work force, such as that described in the long report in Chapter 16 (pp. 680–697), individuals can develop greater sensitivity to and appreciation of the needs and problems of an international audience.

Collaborative Writing and the Writing Process

The writing process described in Chapter 2 also applies to collaborative writing. Groups use the same strategies and confront the same problems that individual writers do. Writing teams brainstorm, plan, research, draft, revise, and edit. Like the individual writer, too, a team moves through the writing process only by identifying its audience, following a common purpose, defining the problem, and deciding on the best ways to solve that problem.

Group writing also demands planning, scheduling, and coordination to avoid the unnecessary duplication of labor and the unequal distribution of work.

Effective collaborative writing merges with individual writing at times. That is, although collaboration involves group interaction, it also allows for independent time so individual members can perform tasks on their own that will contribute to the team's success.

Below is a brief rundown of how groups move through the writing process.

1. Groups must plan before they can write. The planning phase includes brainstorming on the group scale with each member contributing to the overall discussion. Members should be encouraged to express ideas freely and without fear of criticism at an early planning session. Groups will perform outlining at this stage as well. (Review pp. 43–47.) During planning, the group, like the individual writer, should identify its audience and purpose in preparing the document. In this early phase, the group must also establish the ground rules by which it will operate, including making individual assignments, establishing schedules, and selecting a facilitator.

2. Groups do research. Researching entails more than chitchat or a casual pooling of undocumented opinions. It requires searching, interviewing, and reading. Some tasks may be undertaken by individuals working alone to prepare for the next group session. Or each member may be assigned to research one part of a subject, but all will be expected to contribute to the overall research process.

Never hoard information; always share for the benefit of the group. As a team member, you may even be called on to report on an interview you conducted.

3. Groups prepare drafts. While it is possible for a group to draft a document together, requiring everyone to sit down together and write word for word is not always feasible or justifiable. Individuals are more likely to draft sections of a document on their own and then present their work for group discussion and revision.

4. Groups revise and edit. Group interaction can spot and resolve problems—omissions, difficulties in organization (a section out of order), length, inconsistencies in content, and so on. Discussion also helps groups agree on final style and document design. It often makes sense to appoint someone who has more writing ability to give the group document a final editing for style.

Each stage of the writing process just outlined can be modified to account for group activities. Flexibility is as important to a group of writers as it is to an individual writer.

Case Study: Collaborative Editing

Figure 3.3 contains an e-mail written by Tara Barber, the Documentation Manager of CText, Inc., a large firm in Ann Arbor, Michigan, that develops software for the publishing industry. Barber describes the writing process followed by her team of collaborative writers. Based on many years of experience in corporate writing, Barber's approach sheds light on the practical, day-to-day process of group writing and editing. Group harmony means documents are completed successfully and on time.

Study Barber's approach. She effectively works *with* and *not against* her staff. She manages the collaborative effort without being heavy-handed or suppressing individual creativity. Her strategy offers a good model to follow.

Guidelines for Successful Group Writing

The success of a team-written document depends on (1) the cooperation of team members, (2) the information the team gathers, and (3) the ability of the team to adapt that information to shape the document and meet the reader's needs.

Following the ten guidelines below will increase your chances of success when you write in a group.

1. Know the individuals in your group. Establish rapport with your team. If you do not know them, introduce yourself before you start working on a document. Learn as much as you can about their schedules, backgrounds, special competencies, experiences within your organization, and even their pet peeves. By being concerned and friendly, you create an environment that enhances productivity.

2. Do not regard one person on the team as more important than another. Favoritism leads to hard feelings and decreases the group's productivity. Instead, adopt the attitude that the group succeeds or fails as a whole. Think collectively. Everyone's input is necessary to group effort and success. A unified team accomplishes more than a collection of disgruntled individuals.

3. Set up a preliminary meeting to establish guidelines. Unless members share the same vision and objectives, they may work at cross-purposes and head in different directions. At an introductory meeting, the group should discuss the objectives,

Figure 3.3   Collaborative editing: Advice from a pro.

Reply	Save	Forward	Print	Delete

Newsgroups:	bit.listserv.techwr-1
From:	<tara.barber@ctext.com>
Date:	1 Mar 2006 13:35:15–0600
Subject:	Collaborative Writing/Editing

I would like to describe some ways to edit constructively to help new writers improve.

I agree that the more projects you make collaborative, the better results you will get. Here's how we do it in my department. Although all my writers are experienced, they come from such different backgrounds that some of the ways I have coordinated editing activities are similar to how I would interact with new writers. It's my job to make sure all the pieces fit.

When I first took this job, there were several documentation styles being used for the company's manuals. But the department at that time was very small and so the senior writer and I sat down and prepared a cohesive and consistent style manual. We experienced some tension, but by compromising, we were able to iron out our differences. We developed a style guide and a set of manual conventions that gave new writers precise and helpful guidelines and procedures to follow from the start. The new manual assisted us to eliminate glaring editing problems. That way we do not worry about inconsistencies in spelling, capitalization, formats, headings, or documentation.

But the department has grown since that time, and on at least two occasions all of us have sat down as a department to reassess the style guide and manual. By doing this, we are able to get input from everyone and to allow for new ideas. When a problem arises now, we are comfortable addressing it as a group.

In addition to the usual subject-matter expert reviews, all of us review each other's materials. This review helps us to become familiar with each other's projects, homogenizes our writing styles, and keeps our documentation consistent. It's also a great way to get a good "clean-eyes edit." And, happily, a team member will offer an original idea about how to approach a problem that eliminates a potential editing dilemma. We all win.

Continued

(Continued)   Figure 3.3

In my role as documentation manager, I try to edit early and late, but not in the middle. Our materials usually go through several edits before they're ready. I try to look over early material in the form of outlines and first drafts, to make sure everything looks on track and follows our house style and procedures. I always edit final drafts because I am responsible for the output of my department. But I try not to do too much in the middle unless there is a problem. Peer review works best during this intermediate phase, and I don't want to step on individual creativity.

If I have to make comments, I make them at various levels. And here I'm not talking about catching grammar mistakes, spelling errors, typos, mis-numberings, etc. Instead,

a) I point out problems, or sections that seem confusing, but let the writer suggest fixes.
b) I make suggestions and provide examples—more than one if I can.
c) I actively work with the writer to develop ways around a problem. Sometimes this means coming up with a whole new way of approaching the documentation, which is then addressed at our next style meeting. Sometimes such interaction also gets the rest of the department involved in a brainstorming session.
d) If nothing else works, I play the heavy manager and say, "Do it this way because I say so." I try to avoid this, however, if I possibly can.

Working as a constructive team, we rarely have editing problems that we can't solve, with the result that everyone is happy with the comments and the final document. And our customers find the documents usable and valuable. You can't really ask for more than that.

Tara Barber
Documentation Manager
CText, Inc.
<tara.barber@ctext.com>

Reprinted with the permission of Tara Barber.

audience, scope, format, importance of the document, and, most important, the deadline. It is helpful at the first meeting to identify and discuss any directions and/or directives from management and to set up priorities.

4. **Agree on the group's organization.** Here are some questions to consider.

- Is the group to appoint a leader? If so, how is that person to be chosen?
- Will the leader be the most experienced or skilled writer? The member who has been with the company longest?
- What are the leader's responsibilities?
- Will the leader have the authority to settle disputes, break deadlocks, or make final decisions?

An effective group leader must be skillful at initiating discussions, encouraging team members, compromising for the sake of consensus, and generally presiding over meetings. The leader is the group's moderator.

The group must also consider how to communicate with management and decide whether its work should be shared with individuals outside the group (such as co-workers from another department). As Lee Booker points out in Figure 3.2, management also plays a role in giving feedback.

5. **Identify each member's responsibilities, but allow for individual talents and skills.** Members should be aware of one another's strengths—in writing, document design, graphics, software, marketing, editing. Assign each member a task appropriate for his or her background. Don't underestimate or overestimate the time necessary for each member's (or the entire group's) tasks.

6. **Establish the times, places, and length of group meetings.** The group must decide on a calendar of scheduled meetings and ensure that each member has a copy. Various software programs can help the group to schedule meetings (see p. 109).

7. **Follow an agreed-on timetable, but leave room for flexibility.** The group should estimate a realistic time necessary to complete the various stages of their work—when drafts are due or when editing must be concluded, for example. A project schedule based on that estimate should then be prepared. The group's timetable, with major **milestones** (dates when key parts are to be completed) bold-faced or highlighted, should be sent to each member. **But remember: Projects always take longer than initially planned.** Prepare for a possible delay at any one stage. The group may have to submit progress reports (see pp. 638–644) to its members as well as to management.

8. **Provide clear and precise feedback to members.** Feedback is the most essential ingredient in group dynamics; it should be relevant, intelligent, and timely. Participation in sharing and reviewing is essential for group success. Don't come to a meeting without having done your homework. Come with new ideas and reactions to previously stated ideas. Gather facts, supply evidence, factor in opposing points of view. Think of advantages or disadvantages of group drafts or revisions. Nothing frustrates a writer more than having a reader offer superficial concluding comments—for example, "needs improvement," "lacks focus," "does not flow." Be ready to offer detailed advice on where and how to fix shortcomings.

9. **Be an active listener.** Good listeners are active participants in a group discussion, not passive observers. Listen to what members say and resist the temptation to interrupt. Develop what some communication consultants call a "third ear," listening to the meanings and feelings behind a person's words as well as to the words themselves. Try to see the big picture, as Lee Booker points out in Figure 3.2.

10. **Use a standard reference guide for matters of style, documentation, and format.** Establishing guidelines about style (spelling, abbreviations, capitalizations), documentation, format, graphics, and so forth makes the group's task easier. Many large companies have policy or style manuals that their teams must use, as Tara Barber notes in Figure 3.3. If such a document is not available, your group should select a manual or other reference work to which members should adhere, such as the American Psychological Association (APA) guide or *The Chicago Manual of Style.*

▌ Sources of Conflict in Group Dynamics and How to Solve Them

The success of collaborative writing depends on how well the team interacts. Discussion and criticism are essential to discover ideas, results, and solutions. Members must build on one another's strengths and eliminate or downplay weaknesses. Inevitably, members have different perspectives or viewpoints out of which conflicts will arise.

But "conflict" in the sense of conflicting opinions—a healthy give-and-take—can be positive if it alerts the group to problems (inconsistencies, redundancies, incompleteness) and provides ways to resolve them. A conflict can even help the group generate and refine ideas, thus leading to a better organized and written document.

Establishing Group Rules

When conflict translates into ego tripping and personal attacks, however, nothing productive emerges. Everyone in the group must agree beforehand on three ironclad working policies of group dynamics: (1) Individuals must seek and adhere to group consensus; (2) compromise may be advisable, even necessary, to meet a deadline; and (3) if the group decides to accept compromise, the group leader's final decision on resolving conflicts must be accepted.

Following are some common problems in group dynamics, with suggestions on how to avoid or solve them. (See the box on p. 86 for tips on negotiating.)

Common Problems; Practical Solutions

1. **Resisting constructive criticism.** No one likes to be criticized, yet criticism can be vital to the group effort. Collaboration requires being open to suggestions. But when an individual responds to criticism with anger and threatens to disrupt a meeting, serious miscommunication results. Individuals who insist on "their way or no way" can become hostile to any change or revision, no matter how small.

Good and Poor Negotiators

A *good* negotiator

- Is assertive
- Is diplomatic
- Keeps details of negotiations confidential
- Remembers that everything has a price and clearly defines the exchange rate for any concession to be offered
- Works for incentives that appeal to the opponent
- Does not "dumb down" his or her behavior for the benefit of the opponent
- Abandons persuasion when talks reach the negotiation point
- Enables the opponent to save face

A *poor* negotiator

- Has a negative attitude
- Is argumentative
- Dismisses his or her own statements with self-deprecating laughs
- Criticizes freely
- Is rude
- Whines
- Attempts to buy off the opposition by conceding a point without defining what is expected in return
- Expresses statements of fact as if they were questions by raising the voice at the end of sentences
- Discusses personal issues
- Presses for an admission of error
- Fails to allow the opponent to save face

Reprinted from the March 1999 issue of *Occupational Hazards* magazine. Copyright © 1999 by Penton Media, Inc. Used by permission.

Solution: When emotions become too heated, the group leader may wisely move the discussion to another section of the document or to another issue and allow some cooling-off time. Negotiation is an essential skill.

   2. Failing to give constructive criticism. Just as it is counterproductive to reject criticism, it is also tiresome to saturate a meeting with nothing but negatives. You will block communication if you start criticizing with words such as "Why don't you try . . . ," "What you need is . . . ," "Don't you realize that . . . ," or "If you don't. . . ."
   Solutions: When you criticize an idea, link your reaction to the team's overall goals. Diplomatically remind the individual of those goals and point to ways in which revision (criticism) furthers them. Identify a specific section in the document, explain the problem, and offer a helpful revision. Never attack an individual.

Mutual respect is everyone's right and obligation. Take a "let's work on this together" attitude rather than disrupt group harmony. Be objective, constructive, and cooperative.

3. Refusing to participate. This is a lethal problem in group dynamics. Withholding your opinions hurts the group efforts; identify what you believe are major problems and give the group a chance to consider them.

Solutions: The project leader may be forced to say, "Even though you have not expressed your preference, we need you to make a choice anyway." If you don't feel sure of yourself or your points, talk to another member of the group before a meeting to "test" your ideas or to see if he or she reacts the same way. Or, the leader may ask such a team member to write down his or her ideas or suggestions before a meeting and to share them with the group in this way.

4. Interrupting with incessant questions. Some people interrupt a meeting so many times with questions that all group work stops. The individual may simply be trying to exercise his or her control of the group.

Solutions: When that happens, a group leader can turn the tables on the person by remarking, "We appreciate your interest, but would you try an experiment, please, and attempt to answer your own questions?" If the person claims not to know, the leader might then say, "If you can't come up with an answer now, why don't you think about it for a while and then get back to us?" If that tactic fails, the leader may have to confront the disrupter privately after the meeting.

5. Inflating small details out of proportion. Some individuals waste valuable discussion and revision time by dwelling on relatively insignificant points—the choice of a single word, an optional comma—and overlook larger problems in content and organization. Nitpickers can derail the group.

Solution: If there is consensus about a matter, leave it alone and turn to more important issues. Bring the group back to the big picture.

6. Dominating a meeting. Developing interpersonal skills means sharing and responding, not taking over. Sometimes a group member is so aggressive, territorial, and focused on individual achievement that he or she seems to occupy the floor every minute.

Solutions: The leader may say, "We've been hearing from primarily one or two people; now we need to hear from the rest of the group." The leader may even have to take the person aside to remind him or her of the others' right to speak. Some groups operate democratically with the "one-minute rule." Each member has one minute to voice objections, suggest revisions, report on progress, and so on, and does not get the floor again until everyone else has had a chance to speak.

7. Being too deferential to avoid conflict. This problem is the opposite of that described in #1. You will not help your group by being a "yes person" simply to appease a strong-willed member of the group. Saying that an idea or a plan is excellent when you know that it is flawed and contradictory will only increase your team's workload. Being too deferential is as counterproductive as being too aggressive.

Solution: Feel free to express your opinions politely; if tempers begin to flare, call in the group leader or seek the opinions of others on the team.

8. Not finishing on time or submitting an incomplete document. Meeting established deadlines is the group's most important obligation to one another and to the company. When some members are not involved in the planning stages or when they skip meetings, deadlines are invariably missed. If you miss a meeting, get briefed by an individual who was there. A deadline can also be jeopardized when a member does not clearly understand his or her assignment and therefore risks duplicating or delaying what someone else in the group has been asked to do.

Solution: The group leader can institute networking through e-mail to announce meetings, keep members updated, or provide for ongoing communication and questions. (See Figure 3.11 on pp. 105–108.)

Models for Collaboration

There are as many types of collaborative writing activities and methods as there are companies. Writers interact with other writers, editors, and outside specialists in a variety of ways. The process can range from relatively simple phone calls or e-mail to a much more extensive network of checks and balances, revisions and refinements.

The scope, size, and complexity of your document as well as your company's organization will determine what type of (and how much) collaboration is necessary. A shorter assignment (say, a memo) will not require the same type of group structure and participation as would a policy handbook, a technical proposal, or a long report. At some large companies, for example, a staff of professional editors (such as Tara Barber's team in Figure 3.3) revises the final draft prepared by a departmental team. The more important and more complex a document is, the more extensive collaboration will be.

The following sections describe five possible models for collaboration that are used in the world of work.

Cooperative Model

The cooperative collaborative model is one of the simplest and most expedient ways to write in the business world. An individual writer is given an assignment and then goes through the writing process (see Chapter 2) to complete it. Along the way, he or she may show a draft to a peer to get feedback or to a supervisor for a critique. That is what Randy Taylor did in Figure 3.4. He shared a draft of a letter with a potential client to his boss, Felicia Krumpholtz, who made changes in content, wording, and format and then sent it back to Taylor. Following his boss's suggestions, Taylor then created the revised letter in Figure 3.5.

If Taylor had sent his first draft, the customer would hardly have been impressed with the company's professionalism and might have reconsidered placing an order. But thanks to Krumpholtz's revisions, Taylor made his letter much more effective. Careful writers always benefit from constructive criticism. Even though Felicia Krumpholtz helped Randy Taylor improve his work, strictly speaking it

A draft of Randy Taylor's letter edited by his supervisor, Felicia Krumpholtz.   Figure 3.4

servitron
40E3 randolph street
houston, tx 77016
(713) 555-6761

November 15, 2006

Terry Tatum
Manager
Consolidated Solutions
Houston, TX   *add zip code*

Dear ~~Sir,~~ *Terry Tatum:*

Thank you for asking
~~I am taking the opportunity of answering your request~~ for a price list of Servitron
products. Servitron has been in business in the Houston area for more than ~~twenty-~~
22 ~~two~~ years and we offer unparalleled equipment and service to ~~any customer.~~
Using a Servitron product will give you both efficiency and economy.   *Consolidated*
can   boldface   Solutions
                                                boldface
Whatever Servitron model you choose carries with it a full one-year warranty on
all parts and labor. After the expiration date of your warranty ~~you should~~ purchase
our service contract for $75,000 a year.   *might*

~~Here are the models Servitron offers~~

Model Name	*Number*	*Price*
Zephyr	81072	$459.95 — *wrong price*
Colt	86085	$629.95
Meteor	88096	$769.95

Depending on your needs, one of these models should be right for you.

If I might be of further assistance to you, please call on me. I am also enclosing a
brochure giving you more information, including specifications, on those Servitron
products.

~~Truly,~~ *Sincerely yours,*   *add phone number and e-mail*   *reverse the order of these two sentences*

Servitron — *leave 4 spaces*
Randy Taylor — *sign your name*
Sales Associate

● www.servitron.com

Figure 3.5   The edited, final copy of Figure 3.4.

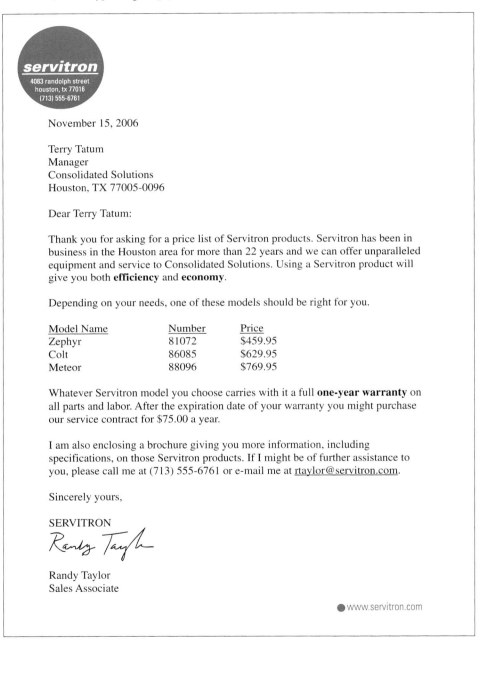

November 15, 2006

Terry Tatum
Manager
Consolidated Solutions
Houston, TX 77005-0096

Dear Terry Tatum:

Thank you for asking for a price list of Servitron products. Servitron has been in business in the Houston area for more than 22 years and we can offer unparalleled equipment and service to Consolidated Solutions. Using a Servitron product will give you both **efficiency** and **economy**.

Depending on your needs, one of these models should be right for you.

Model Name	Number	Price
Zephyr	81072	$459.95
Colt	86085	$629.95
Meteor	88096	$769.95

Whatever Servitron model you choose carries with it a full **one-year warranty** on all parts and labor. After the expiration date of your warranty you might purchase our service contract for $75.00 a year.

I am also enclosing a brochure giving you more information, including specifications, on those Servitron products. If I might be of further assistance to you, please call me at (713) 555-6761 or e-mail me at rtaylor@servitron.com.

Sincerely yours,

SERVITRON

Randy Taylor

Randy Taylor
Sales Associate

www.servitron.com

was not a case of group writing. Although the two interacted, they did not share the final responsibility for creating the letter.

In preparing a longer, more detailed piece of work, a writer may interview technical experts and lawyers, write an early draft and show it to co-workers to gather their opinions, and then submit the document to a mid-level supervisor who may further revise it, as described in Figure 3.2.

Sequential Model

In the sequential model, each individual in a group is assigned a specific, nonoverlapping responsibility—from brainstorming to revising—for a section of a proposal, report, or other document. There is a clear-cut, rigid division of labor. If four people are on the team, each will be responsible for his or her part of the document. For example, one employee may write the introduction, another the body of the report, another the conclusions, and the fourth, the group's recommendation.

Team members may discuss their individual progress and even choose a coordinator to oversee the progress of their work. They may even exchange their work for group review and commentary. When each team member finishes his or her section, the coordinator then assembles the individual parts to form the report.

Functional Model

The division of labor in the functional collaborative model is assigned not according to parts of a document but by skill or job function of the members. For example, a four-person team may be organized as follows:

- The **leader** schedules and conducts meetings, assists team members, issues progress reports to management, solves problems by proposing alternatives, and generally coordinates everyone's efforts to keep the project on schedule.
- The **researcher** collects data, conducts interviews, searches the literature, administers tests, classifies the information, and then prepares notes on the work.
- The **designated writer/editor,** who receives the researcher's notes, prepares outlines and drafts and circulates them for corrections and revisions.
- The **graphics expert** obtains and prepares all visuals, specifying why, how, and where visuals should be placed, and might even suggest that visuals replace certain sections of text; the graphics expert may also be responsible for the design (layout) and production of the document.

This organizational scheme fosters much more group interaction than does the sequential model.

Figure 3.6 illustrates the workings of a functional model. It describes the behind-the-scenes joint effort that went into Joycelyn Woolfolk's proposal for her boss to authorize a new journal, which would incorporate a newsletter her office currently prepares. A publications coordinator for a large, regional health maintenance organization (HMO), Woolfolk supervises a small staff and reports directly to the public affairs manager, who in turn is responsible to the vice president of the regional office.

Figure 3.6   Joycelyn Woolfolk's account of how one proposal originated and was collaboratively prepared following a functional model.

Status Report: Coordinating Regional Magazine Project

The idea to start a regional magazine was first expressed in passing by our vice president, who is interested in getting more and higher-level visibility for our regional office. Several other regional offices in our company have created fairly attractive magazines, and one office in particular has earned a lot of good publicity for its online publication.

The public affairs manager (my boss) and I quickly picked up on the vice president's hint and began to formulate ways to investigate the need for such a publication and ways to substantiate our recommendation. For several weeks the public affairs manager and I had a number of conversations addressing specific points, such as the kind of documentation our proposal would need, what our resources for researching the question were, what our capabilities would be for producing such a publication, and so on. We were guided by the twofold goal of getting the vice president's approval and, ideally, meeting a genuine market need.

After discussions with my boss, I met with members of my staff to ask them to do the following tasks:

1. review existing HMO publications and report on whether there was already a regional magazine for the Northwest
2. develop, administer, and analyze a readership survey for current subscribers to our newsletter, which would potentially be incorporated into the new magazine
3. formulate general design concepts for the magazine in print and online that we can implement without increasing staff, while still producing the quality magazine the vice president wants
4. prepare a detailed budget for projected costs
5. consult with experts on our staff (actuaries, physicians, nurses) about topics of interest
6. confer with our Web experts about online designs and problems

---

Continued

Page 2

I requested e-mail, Web sources, and other written documentation from my staff members about most of these tasks, and then I used that information to draft the proposal that eventually would go to the vice president, and perhaps even to the president's office. And I communicated with my staff often, through e-mail, blogs, personal meetings, and group sessions.

After I revised my draft several times, I asked my staff to look over each draft for feedback and proofreading. Based on their comments, I made further revisions and did careful editing. My boss reviewed my proposal, revising and editing it in minor ways innumerable times. Ultimately, the proposal will go out as a memo from me to my boss, who will then send it under her name to the vice president.

The copy of my proposal may be further revised in response to the vice president's comments when she gets it. She may use some portion or all of it in another report from her to the president, or she may write her own proposal to the president supporting her argument with the specifics from my proposal. The vice president will word the proposal to fit the expressed values and mission of our regional office as well as provide information that addresses budgetary and policy concerns for which her readers (our company president and board members) have final responsibility.

This is how a proposal started and where it will eventually end.

As you will see from Woolfolk's scenario, she assigned specific duties to the members of her team. Then, based on their initial research and documentation, she drafted a document for her staff and her boss to read. As Woolfolk's functional approach shows, collaboration can move up and down the chain of command, with participation at all levels.

Woolfolk's plan is a common one in business. Often, individual employees will pull together information from their separate functional areas (such as finance, information systems, marketing, and sales), and someone else will put that information into a draft that others read and revise until the document is ready to send to the boss. By the time the boss reviews the document, it has been edited and revised many times and by many individuals.

Integrated Model

In the integrated model, all members of the team are engaged in planning, researching, and revising. Each shares the responsibility of producing the document. Members participate in every stage of the document's creation and design, and the group goes back to each stage as often as needed. This model offers intense group interaction. Even though individual writers on the team may be asked to draft different sections of the document, all share in revising and editing that document. Depending on the scope of the document and company policy, the group may also go outside the team to solicit reviews and evaluations from experts.

Co-Writing Model

According to the co-writing model, everyone on the team actually drafts the document together, word for word. Each person may work at a different computer terminal, but all their efforts are focused on the same section of the document at the same time. This model offers the highest degree of collaboration and might be compared to a committee, in which everyone has a direct say (or hand) in every phase of the document.

While co-writing may work for a relatively short document such as a memo, it is rarely used in business because it is neither cost-effective nor practical. Co-writing collaboration is extremely labor intensive, because it ties up all members of the team to draft the document.

■ Evolution of a Collaboratively Written Document

Figures 3.7, 3.8, and 3.9 show the evolution of a memo that follows an integrated model of collaboration. This memo informed employees that their company was enhancing a recycling program. Alice Schuster, the vice president of Fenton Companies, an appliance manufacturing company, asked two employees in the human resources department—Abigail Chappel and Manuel Garcia—to prepare a memo ("a few paragraphs" is how Schuster put it) to be sent to all Fenton employees.

Schuster had an initial conference with Chappel and Garcia, at which she stressed that their memo had to convey Fenton's renewed commitment to conservation and that, as part of that commitment, the employees had to intensify their recycling efforts. Chappel and Garcia thus shared the responsibility of convincing co-workers of the importance of recycling and educating them about practicing it.

Chappel and Garcia also had the difficult job of writing for several audiences simultaneously—the boss, whose name would not appear on the memo, other managers at Fenton, and the Fenton work force itself.

First Draft

Figure 3.7 is the first draft that Chappel and Garcia collaborated on and then presented to the manager of the human resources department—Wells McCraw—for

Early draft of the Chappel and Garcia collaborative memo, with revisions   Figure 3.7
suggested by Wells McCraw.

FENTON COMPANIES

TO: All Employees
FROM: Abigail Chappel; Manuel Garcia
DATE: February 10, 2006
RE: Improving Our Recycling Program

This ¶ is too long. Too many topics — costs, protecting the environment Keep it short — say what we are doing and why

An in-house study has shown that Fenton sends approximately 26,000 pounds of paper to the landfill. The landfill charge for this runs about $2,240, which we could save by recycling. Fenton Companies is conscious of our responsibility to save and protect the environment. Accordingly, starting March 1 we will begin a more intensive paper recycling program. Our program, like many others nationwide, will use the latest degradable technology to safeguard the air, trees, and water in our community. It has been estimated that of the 250 million tons of solid waste, three-quarters of goes to landfills. These landfills across the country are becoming dangerously overcrowded. Such a practice wastes our natural resources and endangers our air and drinking water. For example, it takes 10 trees to make 1 ton of paper, or roughly the amount of paper Fenton uses in four weeks. If we could recycle that amount of paper, we could save those trees. Recycling old paper into new paper involves less energy than making paper from new trees. Moreover, waste sent to landfills can, once broken down, leach, seep into our water supply, and contaminate it. The dangers are great.

Start off with this key idea

Check your facts; I think it is closer to 16–17

Word "it" left out

Delete — not relevant to our purpose

No cap

By enhancing our recycling, we will not be sending so much to the Springfield Landfill and so help alleviate a dangerous condition there. We will keep it from overflowing. Fenton will also be contributing to transforming waste products into valuable reusable materials. Recycling paper in our own office shows that we are concerned about the environmental clutter. By having an improved paper recycling program, we will establish our company's reputation as an environmentally conscious industry and enhance our company's image.

Add the fact about our saving trees in this ¶

Delete — makes us look bad

Start ¶ with this point

Fenton is primarily concerned with recycling paper. The 200 old phone books that otherwise would be tossed away can get our recycling program off to a good start.

When? How? Implications for saving/costs?

Give some examples

We encourage you to start thinking about the additional kinds of paper around your office/workspace that needs to be earmarked for recycling. When you start to think about it, you will see how much paper we as a company use.

Continued

Figure 3.7   (Continued)

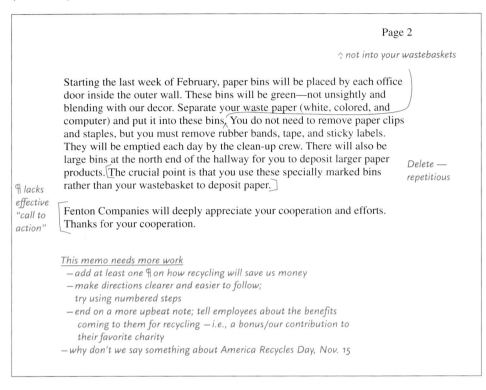

Page 2

↑ *not into your wastebaskets*

¶ lacks effective "call to action"

Starting the last week of February, paper bins will be placed by each office door inside the outer wall. These bins will be green—not unsightly and blending with our decor. Separate your waste paper (white, colored, and computer) and put it into these bins. You do not need to remove paper clips and staples, but you must remove rubber bands, tape, and sticky labels. They will be emptied each day by the clean-up crew. There will also be large bins at the north end of the hallway for you to deposit larger paper products. The crucial point is that you use these specially marked bins rather than your wastebasket to deposit paper.

Delete — repetitious

Fenton Companies will deeply appreciate your cooperation and efforts. Thanks for your cooperation.

This memo needs more work
 —add at least one ¶ on how recycling will save us money
 —make directions clearer and easier to follow;
   try using numbered steps
 —end on a more upbeat note; tell employees about the benefits
   coming to them for recycling —i.e., a bonus/our contribution to
   their favorite charity
 —why don't we say something about America Recycles Day, Nov. 15

his comments and revisions. As you can see from McCraw's remarks, written in ink, he was not especially pleased with their first attempt and asked them to make a number of revisions. As a careful reader (conscious of the document's audience), McCraw found Chappel and Garcia's paragraphs to be rambling and repetitious—the writers were unable to stick to the point. Specifically, he pointed out that they included too much information in one paragraph and not enough in others.

As a good editor, McCraw also directed their attention to factual mistakes, irrelevant and even contradictory comments, and essential information they had omitted. Finally, McCraw offered some advice on using visual devices (see Chapter 1, pp. 19–21) to make their information more accessible to readers.

Subsequent Drafts

Figure 3.8 shows the next stage in the collaboration. In this version of the memo, prepared through several revisions over a two-day period, the authors incorporated McCraw's suggestions as well as several changes of their own. It was this revision

Revision of the Chappel and Garcia memo with changes suggested by   **Figure 3.8**
Vice President Schuster.

FENTON COMPANIES

TO: All Employees
FROM: Abigail Chappel; Manuel Garcia
DATE: February 10, 2006
RE: Improving Our Recycling Program

To save money and protect our environment, Fenton Companies will begin a more intensive waste paper recycling program on March 1. Recycling continues to be an environmental necessity. It has been estimated that three-quarters of the 250 million tons of solid waste dumped annually in America could be recycled. Our program will still use the latest recycling technology to safeguard trees, air, and water. *Say strengthen or continue*

¶ needs more information This new program will ~~establish~~ Fenton's reputation as an environmentally conscious company. Fenton now uses one ton of paper every four weeks. This represents 17 trees that can be saved just by recycling our paper waste. Recycling also means we will send less waste to the landfill, alleviating problems of overfill and reducing the potential for contamination of the water supply. Waste sent to large landfills can leach and seep into water systems. By recycling paper, Fenton will also reduce the risk of long-term environmental pollution. *Add that we no longer use Styrofoam and that our suppliers use only biodegradable products*

Indicate how much we save Recycling saves us money. Right now Fenton pays $180 per month to dump 2,000 pounds (one ton) of paper waste at the landfill. However, scrap paper is worth $100 per ton. Recycling will generate $100 each month in new revenue while eliminating the $180 dumping expense.

This sentence more logically goes in ¶ 3 Ultimately, the success of our project depends on renewed awareness of the variety of office paper suitable for recycling. Paper products that can be recycled include newspapers, scrap paper, computer printouts, letters, envelopes (without windows), shipping cartons, old phone books, and uncoated paper cups. *Put in itemized bulleted list to stand out better*

Do not start new ¶ here; keep as part of previous ¶ Recycling 200 or so old phone books each year alone will save 22 cubic yards of landfill space (or close to $100) and will generate $25 in scrap paper income for our company. The old 2005 phone books, which will be replaced by new 2006 ones on March 1, will give us an excellent opportunity to intensify our recycling.

Continued

Figure 3.8   (Continued)

Page 2

Here are some easy-to-follow directions to make our recycling efforts even more effective:

Boldface these words 1. Starting the last week in February, paper bins will be placed inside each office door. Put all waste paper into these bins, which will be emptied by maintenance.
2. Place larger paper products—such as cartons or phone books—in the green bigger paper bins at the end of each main corridor.
3. Put white, colored, computer printout, and newspapers into separate marked bins. Remove all rubber bands, tape, and sticky notes.

Thanks for your cooperation. To show our appreciation for your help, 50 percent of all proceeds from the recycled paper will go toward employee bonuses and the other 50 percent will be given to the office's favorite charity. The benefits of our new recycling program will more than outweigh the inconvenience it may cause. We will conduct another study in time for America Recycles Day on November 15 to determine how our company has improved in this area.

Add another sentence to this ¶ on how a safer environment will benefit our company and the employees, too

that they submitted to Vice President Schuster, who also made some comments on the memo. Schuster's suggestions—all valid—show how different readers can help writing teams meet their objectives.

Note that in the process of revising their memo Chappel and Garcia had to make major changes from the first draft in Figure 3.7 through several versions to the document in Figure 3.8. Those changes—shortening and expanding paragraphs, adding and deleting information, and refocusing their approach to meet the needs of their audience—are the essential revisions a collaborative writing team, like an individual writer, would expect to make.

Final Copy

With McCraw's further input and continuing to revise the memo on their own, Chappel and Garcia submitted the final, revised memo found in Figure 3.9 to the vice president a few days later. This final copy received Schuster's approval and was then routed to the Fenton staff.

Final copy of the memo prepared by Chappel and Garcia using an   Figure 3.9
integrated model of collaboration.

FENTON COMPANIES

TO: All Employees
FROM: Abigail Chappel; Manuel Garcia
DATE: February 10, 2006
RE: Improving Our Recycling Program

To save additional money and to protect the environment, Fenton will begin a more intensive waste paper recycling program on March 1. For the new program to succeed, we need to increase our paper recycling efforts. Recycling continues to be an environmental necessity. It has been estimated that three-quarters of the 250 million tons of solid waste dumped annually in America is still not being recycled. Our program will continue to rely on the latest recycling technology to safeguard trees, air, and water.

Recycling has already saved us money. Right now Fenton pays $180 per month to dump 2,000 pounds (one ton) of paper waste at the landfill, compared to $360 last year. However, scrap paper is worth $100 per ton. Increased recycling will generate $100 each month in revenue while eliminating the $180 dumping expense.

This new, more intensive program will also strengthen Fenton's reputation as an environmentally conscious company. Three years ago, we stopped using Styrofoam products and asked suppliers to use biodegradable materials for all our shipping containers. Our efforts have proved successful, but Fenton still uses one ton of paper every four weeks. This paper represents 17 trees that can be saved just by recycling our paper waste. We need to send even less waste to the landfill, alleviating problems of overfill and reducing the potential for contamination of the water supply. Waste sent to large landfills can leach and seep into water systems.

Ultimately, the success of this project depends on our being aware of the variety of office paper suitable for recycling. An expanded list of paper products that can be recycled includes:

- newspapers
- letters
- envelopes (without cellophane windows)
- phone books
- uncoated paper cups
- scrap paper
- computer printouts
- junk mail (only black print on white paper)
- shipping cartons

Continued

Figure 3.9   (Continued)

Page 2

The old 2005 phone books, which will be replaced by new 2006 ones on March 1, will give us an excellent opportunity to launch our intensified recycling program.

Here are some easy-to-follow directions to make our recycling efforts even more effective:

1. Starting the last week in February, put all waste paper into the **paper bins** that will be placed **inside each office door.** These bins will be emptied by maintenance.
2. Place **larger paper products**—such as bulky cartons—in the **green bigger paper bins** at the end of the main corridor.
3. Remove all rubber bands, tape, and sticky notes and put white, colored, computer printout, and newspapers into separate marked bins.

Thanks for your cooperation. To show our appreciation for your increased efforts, 50 percent of all proceeds from the recycled paper will go into an annual employee bonus fund and the other 50 percent will be given to the office's favorite charity. We will conduct another study in time for America Recycles Day on November 15 to determine how our company has improved in this area. The benefits of our new recycling program will more than outweigh the inconvenience it may cause. A safer environment—and a more cost-effective way to run our company—benefits us all.

Thanks to an integrated model of collaboration and careful critiques by McCraw and Schuster, Chappel and Garcia successfully revised their work. Effective team effort and shared responsibility were at the heart of Chappel and Garcia's assignment.

Collaborating Online

Collaborating online takes writers into a far more extensive communication environment. Collaborative software, called **groupware**, keeps information flowing within, from, and to your company. Figure 3.10 shows some of the collaborative tasks that one software system supplies through e-mail, instant messaging, websites, and company databases such as those found on an intranet. Using groupware, a collaborative team can track projects, share documents, set up meetings, contact experts, search pertinent company files, and even create their own website.

Such software, of course, does not completely eliminate the need for a group to meet in person to discuss thorny issues, to clarify subtleties, or to build group harmony. But face-to-face communications, though essential, are frequently supplemented with online collaboration.

An advertisement for a groupware product that supports collaboration. **Figure 3.10**

Provide your teams with collaborative tools for enhanced productivity

IBM Workplace Team Collaboration 2.5

Highlights

- *Provides integrated presence awareness, business instant messaging, Web conferencing and team spaces*

- *Lets user know who is available to collaborate, share information and take action*

- *Provides Web conferencing capabilities so team members can share files in real time*

- *Provides a centralized location to post and share documents, and built-in methods for tracking feedback from team members*

- *Allows users to create browser-based forums and members to engage in threaded discussions*

- *Define and control access and participation to team spaces and Web conferences*

- *Lets authorized members search team spaces and Web conferences*

- *Allows authorized members to read, edit and delete documents, and organize information in folders*

To help you and your teams succeed in today's ever-changing business environment, IBM Workplace™ Team Collaboration 2.5 software gives you the access you need—both to critical information and to critical people and experts. As a member of the IBM Workplace family, IBM Workplace Team Collaboration software offers a single, collaborative foundation that integrates business instant messaging, presence awareness, Web conferencing and team space capabilities into a scalable offering, rich with security features, that's designed to help enterprise teams be more productive.

These capabilities can help you give users immediate access to the right people and the right information. They can help you to foster a sense of community and minimize geographical and organizational boundaries. Since you can extend these capabilities to your entire value chain, your extended teams are in a position to make more effective and more efficient decisions.

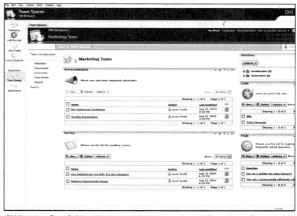

IBM Workplace Team Collaboration gives people a place and the tools they need to collaborate, share documents and work together.

Advantages of Collaborating Online

Collaboration via groupware offers significant advantages to employers and workers. As you develop your online communication skills, here are some benefits you can count on:

1. Generating more information through sharing online exchanges. Writers have increased opportunities to ask questions, to share data, to make suggestions, and to raise and solve job-related issues with one another.

2. Expanding the range of participation in the collaborative process. E-mail encourages the most flexible and extensive group organization possible. Supervisors within a writer's department and from related departments as well as customers and vendors can join in the discussion and revision to improve the quality and service a company provides.

3. Increasing feedback/response rate. Groupware helps team members read, edit, and amplify each other's work quickly and efficiently.

Tech Note

Smartphones

Handheld computers, or smartphones, such as PalmOne and BlackBerry (known as personal organizers), combine a miniature PC, a cell phone, and a Web browser. They are equipped with basic software packages that make them as powerful as many laptops, but are more convenient and smaller—about the size of a cell phone.

Businesses use smartphones to make collaborative writing, editing, and meetings more efficient. Smartphones allow one team member to beam information to another. Writing team members can thereby transmit their address books, calendars, business and travel expenses, ongoing projects, and texts to each other.

With a smartphone you can accomplish the following collaborative writing tasks:

- send, forward, and check your e-mail as well as browse websites
- monitor and share your date book and "to do" lists
- write, add, or edit documents using a stylus
- send files such as PowerPoint presentations, Excel spreadsheets, and Word documents for review by other team members
- view photos or video clips
- ensure privacy and security for yourself and your team with the option to send and receive messages through a choice of encryption symbols

Maureen Curley

4. Removing geographic limitations. Team members can be in different cities all over the globe, which benefits international firms that want to involve overseas offices in decision-making processes.

5. Minimizing the possibility of misunderstanding that likely creeps into verbal face-to-face meetings. Written e-mails provide a precise written record that can be saved or forwarded.

6. Allowing team members to work on a project with less stress. Collaborating via e-mail can make criticism easier to take and to give without being face to face with a difficult colleague.

Methods of Collaborating Online

There are many methods of collaborating online. The method you use will be determined by the group, your company's needs, and the groupware package in use. E-mail technology, however, is essential to groupware. Make sure you follow the guidelines in the Tech Note on page 104. Here are two commonly used ways that a group can create and edit a document. The first is basically the **integrated** model of collaboration (p. 94), while the second follows the **sequential** model discussed on page 91.

Creating and Revising One Draft

1. All members of the group work on the same draft, developing, expanding, revising, and editing it. The original draft is saved so that it is accessible to all team members who will work on it.
2. Each member of the team e-mails his or her edits to every other member of the group. All edits—adding or deleting information, moving text, making stylistic or formatting changes—often appear as highlighted text so that the group sees revised versions of the same document.
3. Each team member looks at these individual highlighted revisions of the draft submitted by the group and accepts, changes, or rejects these revisions.
4. The team then decides on which version or versions of the draft should be included and thereby creates the final edited version. The final copy sent to the boss may be a compilation of various suggestions by the team after members communicate and negotiate with each other.

Dividing One Draft into Parts: Chunking

1. Each member of the team is responsible for drafting only his or her assigned section of the document.
2. Each writer then e-mails that section to everyone in the group for review and revision.
3. All members of the group then edit these individual sections of the draft—again appearing as highlighted text—and e-mail their revisions to the original author of that section of the document.
4. Each writer then revises his or her section based on the group's comments and sends the revised version to a team leader.

5. The leader then reviews each section to make sure that all of the group's edits have been made and that the style and format of each section are consistent with company policy.

6. The team leader merges the individual revised sections (files) into the final document for submission.

Tech Note

Tips on Eliminating Problems with Online Collaboration

Regardless of the online collaborative method your team uses, it must establish ground rules by which documents are created, shared, posted, protected, and submitted. By following the guidelines listed here, your team can avoid common problems in its online collaboration:

■ Be sure that every authorized team member has access to and can share all versions of the document that the team is considering. Team members cannot give input if they cannot open, edit, save, or share a document. To do this, every team member must use the same software and have the correct current password(s).

■ Make sure each team member can search for and access relevant documents within an organization's intranet to make necessary and relevant changes in a document (see the Tech Note on Intranets on p. 296).

■ Verify that you and your team members are all working on the same (and correct) version of the document at the same time. Problems result when a team member wastes time and delays a deadline by editing an earlier, discarded, or otherwise incorrect version. As in a printed draft, be sure all members have access to the latest graphics inserted in each version.

■ Save the most recent versions of the document as well as earlier ones in separate files in case the team needs to return to these earlier copies to verify that changes have been made. Software packages allow authors to open more than one document at the same time in multiple windows and to arrange them in sequential order.

■ Link each revision with the individual who made them.

■ Track each contributor's changes by having an identifying color code for each one's suggested revisions or by using initials to identify who has made any changes.

■ Protect the document from unauthorized users or changes by issuing team members a password that might change daily or weekly.

■ Require every team member to authorize or sign off on the final versions submitted to the boss, agency, or customer.

■ Maintain document confidentiality by asking team members not to share a document unless authorized by management to do so.

Case Study: Collaborating via E-Mail

The series of e-mail exchanges in Figure 3.11 were sent among a team collaboratively writing a single document, a report on expanding a hospital parking facility. They essentially followed the integrated model of collaboration. In these exchanges you will see the dynamics of collaboration through e-mail. As you read the participants' comments, identify each person's concerns and how other team members react to them. Who is leading this collaborative effort? Which ideas most influence the final report? Who raises an ethical issue and what is it? In broad terms, how will the revised document differ from the first draft?

Four online collaborative writers write and revise a report via e-mail.   **Figure 3.11**

To:	<Ramon_Calderez@citymed.org>, <Alex_Latriere@citymed.org>, <Loretta_Bartel@citymed.org>
From:	<Nicole_Goings@citymed.org>
Date:	Wed. 7 April 2007 16:55:00EST
Subject:	Report on Expanded Hospital Parking

Now that we have a pretty clear outline and a first draft of the report before us, I think we all need to try to flesh it out. Thanks for reviewing the attached document to see how it hangs together. My initial reaction is that the draft needs reorganization and more attention to detail.

To:	<Nicole_Goings@citymed.org>, <Alex_Latriere@citymed.org>, <Loretta_Bartel@citymed.org>
From:	<Ramon_Calderez@citymed.org>
Date:	Wed. 7 April 2007 18:01:00EST
Subject:	Report on Expanded Hospital Parking

Thanks for the draft. Our opening is not very strong or convincing. There is too little sense of the overall reason for the hospital investing $3.2 million in expanded parking facilities. I have rewritten the opening, as you will see, and tried to link the currently inadequate parking facilities (a detriment) to the overall growth of patient care (our strong point). Then I tried to emphasize how responsive Bloomington Memorial has been to the needs of visitors and the patients they have come to see.

Let me know what you all think.

To:	<Nicole_Goings@citymed.org>, <Alex_Latriere@citymed.org>, <Ramon_Calderez@citymed.org>
From:	<Loretta_Bartel@citymed.org>
Date:	Thurs. 8 April 2007 8:23:00EST
Subject:	Report on Expanded Hospital Parking

I agree with Ramon and think the revised introduction will work much better, but aren't we being too dramatic and not very pro–Bloomington Memorial by using the last sentence of his in the second paragraph—"new parking facilities will prevent visitors from walking long, bone-soaking distances in the rain." I cut it and used a different closing sentence.

Continued

Figure 3.11   (Continued)

To:	<Nicole_Goings@citymed.org>, <Ramon_Calderez@citymed.org>, <Loretta_Bartel@citymed.org>
From:	<Alex_Latriere@citymed.org>
Date:	Thurs. 8 April 2007 8:54:00EST
Subject:	Report on Expanded Hospital Parking

Loretta's change is OK, but I want to point out two much more important revisions we need to make. One, it is unfair to say we are adding 500 new parking spaces. The exact number is 417. I am more comfortable with saying "more than 400" or just giving the exact number. Two, we should add another paragraph under the section now labeled "Increased Traffic Flow" and devote it entirely to Wentworth Avenue becoming a one-way street.

I inserted one or two points at the end of that section that I think would make a coherent paragraph.

To:	<Alex_Latriere@citymed.org>, <Ramon_Calderez@citymed.org>, <Loretta_Bartel@citymed.org>
From:	<Nicole_Goings@citymed.org>
Date:	Thurs. 8 April 2007 11:08:00EST
Subject:	Report on Expanded Hospital Parking

Alex, all right, bravo—I am happy that you have drafted a new paragraph on Wentworth and have also done some slight editing to make the transition to this topic a little smoother. What do the rest of you think?

To:	<Nicole_Goings@citymed.org>, <Ramon_Calderez@citymed.org>, <Alex_Latriere@citymed.org>
From:	<Loretta_Bartel@citymed.org>
Date:	Thurs. 8 April 2007 13:45:00EST
Subject:	Report on Expanded Hospital Parking

Alex's suggestion and Nicole's additional paragraph work very well together. Great!

To:	<Nicole_Goings@citymed.org>, <Alex_Latriere@citymed.org>, <Loretta_Bartel@citymed.org>
From:	<Ramon_Calderez@citymed.org>
Date:	Thurs. 8 April 2007 14:23:00EST
Subject:	Report on Expanded Hospital Parking

Yes, a good job. The more I looked at the section on "Entry Points" the more I was troubled by including the topic of special needs under this heading. Given the fact that the new parking facility will also involve widening the entrance to the ER, thus making 11 additional special needs spots available, is, in my mind, worthy of a separate section in the report. Accordingly, I think we should take special needs out of the "Entry Points" section and create a new, even if small, section on "Special Needs."

Continued

(Continued)   Figure 3.11

To:	<Ramon_Calderez@citymed.org>, <Nicole_Goings@citymed.org>, <Alex_Latriere@citymed.org>
From:	<Loretta_Bartel@citymed.org>
Date:	Thurs. 8 April 2007 17:17:00EST
Subject:	Report on Expanded Hospital Parking

We should emphasize the new technology behind this facility, but since the report is going to the board of directors and to other general readers, we need to cut back on the technical descriptions.

Eliminate—or at least tone down—the details on stress points, pre-cast concrete, and the low slope vehicular access ramps. Still include some information about the safety and engineering benefits, but since we are also making the architect's site plans available, couldn't we tighten and shorten this section? I have tried to take some details out. Have I taken out too much? Not enough? Let me hear from you!

To:	<Loretta_Bartel@citymed.org>, <Ramon_Calderez@citymed.org>, <Alex_Latriere@citymed.org>
From:	<Nicole_Goings@citymed.org>
Date:	Fri. 9 April 2007 9:49:00EST
Subject:	Report on Expanded Hospital Parking

Thanks and more thanks, Loretta. I spoke with Lee Bukowski, the hospital architect, last evening about your changes. You are on target and so I have let your revisions stand. BUT . . . I do think we need to retain some information about the access ramps and covered areas surrounding them.

To:	<Loretta_Bartel@citymed.org>, <Nicole_Goings@citymed.org>, <Alex_Latriere@citymed.org>
From:	<Ramon_Calderez@citymed.org>
Date:	Mon. 12 April 2007 10:23:00EST
Subject:	Report on Expanded Hospital Parking

We must have a visual about the hospital's efforts. I e-mailed the archives earlier this morning and they found the photograph of an aerial view of the hospital's original parking lot in 1971. Let's incorporate that somewhere in the introduction and then use the artist's drawing of what the new parking lot will look like to begin the section "Expanded Parking Facilities Planned." I have scanned (and now attach) both documents to give you an idea of what I have in mind.

Continued

Figure 3.11   (Continued)

To:	<Ramon_Calderez@citymed.org>, <Alex_Latriere@citymed.org>, <Loretta_Bartel@citymed.org>
From:	<Nicole_Goings@citymed.org>
Date:	Mon. 12 April 2007 14:04:00EST
Subject:	Report on Expanded Hospital Parking

Ramon, you deserve a pat on the back. Yes, the visuals definitely work.

I think we have done a careful job in revising and editing the report. I want to give it to Christine Fernandez tomorrow for her approval before it goes to the Board.

Let me know before 4:30 today if you have any further suggestions or revisions.

Thanks for all your help. I'm going to acknowledge each of you for your excellent work in my cover letter to Director Fernandez.

 Meetings

One of the most frequent ways to collaborate is through meetings, which can take the form of small group discussions (chat rooms on the Internet) or large, formal conferences. Whether it is regularly scheduled (a weekly staff meeting) or a special, unscheduled one, a meeting requires teamwork. Collective energy and goodwill will bear much fruit. Although videoconferencing is used frequently in the workplace, that technology will never take the place of face-to-face meetings. The guidelines on collaborative writing (pp. 81–82) also apply to group interactions at meetings. Basically, you need to know how to plan a meeting, create an agenda, and write minutes.

Planning a Meeting

You will have to schedule a time, a place, and a date, and then notify the people who are to attend. Software such as the IBM Workplace Team Collaboration (see Figure 3.10) contains a Calendar option to help you reach the people who need to attend the meeting. If someone on your team cannot attend and you cannot reschedule the meeting, try to get that person's input through e-mail.

To prepare for the meeting, jot down the main ideas you (and your group) must cover. Collect any data (test results, reports, client communications, statistics) the group will discuss. If you are using graphics such as PowerPoint (see pp. 707–710), make sure you prepare them ahead of time. Careful planning leads to a careful agenda.

Scheduling a Meeting with Groupware

Some groupware will automatically schedule meetings for those listed in your group directory. It will notify each group member of the date, time, and place of the meeting; automatically set up an appointment in their calendars; and alert you about any conflicts. The program also provides an alarm to remind group members 10 minutes, 30 minutes, or even a day or two in advance of the meeting. Other options you can choose include specifying whether the meeting is confidential or if visitors have been invited. Such a program eliminates the need for phone calls, memos, or e-mail messages and speeds up the process of group communication.

Make sure that copies of any documents you plan to discuss are available for the group to review.

Creating an Agenda

Out of your planning will come your *agenda,* or the topics to be covered at the meeting. An agenda is a one-, sometimes two-page outline of the main, pertinent points. The agenda should list only those items that your group, based on its work and interaction, regards as most crucial. Prioritize your action items so that the most important ones come first. An agenda might also include short reports or presentations for which one or two members of your group are responsible. Always distribute the agenda ahead of time (at least a day or two) so that your team will be prepared and better able to contribute.

Writing the Minutes

The *minutes* are a summary of what happened at the meeting. Transmit copies of the minutes to the team members to help them recall what happened at the meeting and to help them prepare for the next one. Copies of minutes are kept on file—they are the official record of the group's deliberations and are regarded as legal documents. Accordingly, minutes must be clear, accurate, and impartial. (Keep the minutes free from your own opinions of how well or poorly the meeting went; for example, "Ms. Saunders customarily offered the right solutions" and "Once more Hicks got off the topic" are not appropriate comments.) Because the person chairing a meeting cannot take minutes and preside at the same time, another member of the group designated as the secretary should prepare the minutes. Minutes are transmitted usually within twenty-four to forty-eight hours after the meeting has adjourned.

Minutes of a meeting should include the following information:

- date, time, and place of meeting
- name of the group holding the meeting and why
- name of the person chairing the meeting
- names of those present and those absent
- the approval or amendment of the minutes of the previous meeting
- for each major point—the action items—indicate what was done:
  - who said what
  - what was discussed/suggested/proposed
  - what was decided and the vote, including abstentions
  - what was continued (tabled) for a subsequent study, report, or meeting
  - time of next meeting
  - time the meeting officially concluded

To be effective, minutes must be concise and to the point. Here are a few guidelines to help you.

- Make sure of your facts; spell all names, products, tests correctly.
- Concentrate on the major facts surrounding action items. Save the reader's time and your own by condensing lengthy discussions, debates, and reports given at the meeting.
- Do not report verbatim what everyone said; readers will be more interested in what the group did.
- List each motion (or item voted on) exactly as it is worded and in its final form.
- Avoid words that interpret (negatively or positively) what the group or anyone in the group did or did not do.

Figure 3.12 shows how these parts fit together.

Taking Notes

Minutes are crucial to the day-to-day operation and long-range planning of a business. Some meetings are held in a company office for a small group such as the Environmental Safety Committee in Figure 3.12. Others take place online as indicated in Figure 3.11. Still others are held off site where, because of time and location, you may be the only member of your team attending and will have to share your notes with co-workers.

Again, a variety of software packages can help you to share your notes via e-mail. Take your laptop to the meeting to help you. As you take notes, include only major issues that have top priority for your audience. Don't get bogged down in recording minor details. Inform your team or boss about important issues affecting new dates, revised schedules, different prices, amended policies or regulations, changes in operations, service, key decisions, and other important business matters. Anticipate the questions your team or boss may have about the meeting and then supply the answers through your notes. Figure 10.8 (pp. 427–428) contains a short summary from the notes two employees made of the major topics covered at a conference they attended.

Minutes from a business meeting.   Figure 3.12

NewTech Solutions

Minutes for Environmental Safety Committee (ESC) meeting on February 2, 2007, in Room 203 of Lab Annex Building at 1:10 p.m. E.S.T.

Members Present:

Thomas Baldanza, Grace Corlee (**President**), Virginia Downey, Victor Johnson, Roberta Koos, Kent Leviche (**Secretary**), Ralph Nowicki, Barbara Poe-Smith, Williard Ralston, Morgan Tachiashi, Asah Rashid, and Carlos Zandrillia

Members Absent:

Paul Gordon (sick leave); Marty Wagner

Old Business:

The minutes from the previous meeting on January 6, 2007, were approved as read.

Reports:

(1) Morgan Tachiashi reported on the progress the Site Inspection Committee was making in getting the plant ready for the March 29 visit of the State Board of Examiners. All preparations are on schedule.

(2) The proposal to study the use of biometric identification in place of employee ID badges was nearly complete, according to Asah Rashid, Chair of the Proposal Committee, and will be presented at next month's meeting for approval.

New Business:

(1) Virginia Downey and Ralph Nowicki expressed concern about a computer virus that may strike the plant—Monkey. Disguised as a familiar e-mail, the virus is contained in an attachment that destroys files. A motion was made by Barbara Poe-Smith, seconded by Virginia Downey, that management upgrade its antivirus protection software. Objecting to this expense, Williard Ralston thought the current software was sufficient. The vote carried by 9 to 3.

Supplies essential information on attendance, date, and place of meeting

Summarizes progress on ongoing business

Records only main points of discussion and votes

Continued

Figure 3.12   (Continued)

Page 2

Sticks to basic facts and re-sults of vote

(2) Thomas Baldanza believed that cross-training should be accelerated, especially in safety areas, to meet the target date of August 9, which the ESC had set in December 2006. Agreeing, Roberta Koos stressed that, without cross-training, some departments would be vulnerable to safety violations. Victor Johnson, on the other hand, found that such cross-training could not feasibly be accomplished in the original time frame since several departments could not spare employees to participate. He moved that the target date motion be amended and pushed to November 15. The vote to amend was defeated 10–2.

Calling attention to the importance of the target date, Grace Corlee will ask Zandria Pickens, Plant Training Coordinator, to come to the next ESC meeting to discuss the current status of the training program and to offer suggestions for its speedy implementation.

Includes other business to be continued

(3) Kent Leviche calculated computer downtime in the plant during the month of January—4 outages totaling 7.5 lost working hours—and asked the ESC to address this problem. After discussion, the ESC unanimously agreed to appoint a subcommittee to investigate the outages and determine solutions. Roberta Koos and Thomas Baldanza will chair the subcommittee and present a survey report at next month's meeting.

(4) Personnel in the Environmental Testing Lab were commended for their extra effort in ensuring that their department maintained the highest professional standards during the month of January. A letter of commendation was sent to Emily Lu, Lab Supervisor, and her staff.

Signals end of meeting and date of next one

(5) Grace Corlee adjourned the meeting at 3:41 p.m.

<u>Next Meeting:</u>

The next meeting of the ESC will be on March 8 at 1:00 p.m. in Room 203 of the Lab Annex Building.

✔ Revision Checklist

- ☐ Tried to be a team player by putting the success of my group over the needs of my own ego.
- ☐ Followed necessary steps of the writing process to take advantage of team effort and feedback.
- ☐ Attended all group meetings and understood and agreed to responsibilities of the group and my own obligations.
- ☐ Finished research, planning, and drafting expected of me.
- ☐ Conducted necessary interviews and conferences to gather and verify information.
- ☐ Shared my research, ideas, and suggestions for revision through constructive criticism.
- ☐ Participated honestly and politely in discussions with colleagues.
- ☐ Treated members of my team with respect and courtesy.
- ☐ Was open to criticism and suggestions for change.
- ☐ Read colleagues' work and gave specific and helpful criticism and suggestions.
- ☐ Kept matters in proper perspective by not being a nitpicker and by not interrupting with extraneous points or unnecessary questions.
- ☐ Sought help when appropriate from relevant subject matter experts and from co-workers.
- ☐ Secured responses and approval from management.
- ☐ Took advantage of e-mail, smartphones, and instant messaging technology such as groupware to communicate with my collaborative team.
- ☐ E-mailed messages in clear, diplomatic, and correct sentences.
- ☐ Attached pertinent documents in e-mail to collaborative team.
- ☐ Answered e-mail questions and responded to requests promptly.
- ☐ Prepared agenda for meetings clearly and distributed ahead of time.
- ☐ Wrote minutes that objectively reported what happened.
- ☐ Took notes that highlighted main points of a meeting for my collaborative team and boss.

Exercises

1. Assume you belong to a three- or four-person editing team that functions the way Tara Barber's does in Figure 3.3. Each member of your team should bring in four copies of a paper written for this course or for another one. Exchange copies with the other members of your team so that each team member has everyone else's papers to review and revise. For each paper you receive, comment on the style, organization, tone, and discussion of ideas as Wells McCraw did in Figure 3.7.

Online Study Center
Access the collaborative writing Revision Checklist online at college .hmco.com/pic/ kolin8e

Online Study Center
Find additional collaborative writing exercises at college.hmco .com/pic/kolin8e

2. With members of your collaborative team (selected by your teacher or self-appointed) select four different brands of the same leading product (such as a software package, a Web browser, a smartphone, a microwave, a DVD player, a power tool, or other item). Each member of your team should select one of the brands and prepare a two-page memo report (see pp. 120–127), evaluating it for your instructor according to the following criteria:

   - convenience
   - performance
   - technical capabilities/capacities
   - appearance
   - adaptability
   - price
   - weaknesses/strengths compared with competitors' models

   Each team member should then submit a draft to the other members of the team to review. At a subsequent group meeting, the group should evaluate the four brands based on the team's drafts and then together prepare one final recommendation report for your instructor.

3. Your company is planning to construct a new office, and you, together with other employees from your company, have been asked to serve on a committee to make sure that plans for the new building adhere precisely to the Americans with Disabilities Act, passed in 1990. According to that act, it is against the law to discriminate against anyone with disabilities that limit "major life activities"—walking, seeing, speaking, working.

   The law is expressly designed to remove architectural and physical barriers and to make sure that plans are modified to accommodate those protected by the law (for example, wider hallways to accommodate individuals in wheelchairs). Other considerations include choosing appropriate nonstick floor surfaces (reducing the danger of slipping), placing water fountains low enough for use by individuals in wheelchairs, and installing doors that require minimal pressure to open and close.

   After studying the plans for the new building, you and your team members find several problem areas. Prepare a group-written report advising management of the problems and what must be done to correct them to comply with the law. Divide your written work according to areas that need alteration—doors, floors, water fountains, restroom facilities. Each team member should bring in his or her section, which the group will edit and revise. The group should then prepare the final report for management.

4. A new president will be coming to your college in the next month, and you and five other students have been asked to serve on a committee that will submit a report about campus safety problems and what should be done to solve them. You and your team must establish priorities and propose guidelines that you want the new administration to put into practice. After two very heated meetings, you realize that what you and two other students have considered solu-

tions, the other half of your committee regards as the problems. Here is a run-down of the leading conflicts dividing your committee:

- **Speed bumps.** Half the committee likes the way they slow traffic down on campus, but the other half says they are a menace because they jar car CD players.
- **Sound pollution.** Half your team wants Campus Security to enforce a noise policy preventing students from playing loud music while driving on campus, but the other half insists that would violate students' rights.
- **Van and sport utility vehicle parking.** Half the committee demands that vans and sport utility vehicles park in specially designated places because they block the view of traffic for any vehicle parked next to them; the other members protest that people who drive these vehicles will be singled out for less desirable parking places on campus.

Clearly your committee has reached a deadlock and will be unproductive as long as those conflicts go unresolved. Based on the above scenario, do the following:

  a. Have each student on the committee write (or e-mail, if available) the other five students suggesting a specific plan on how to proceed—how the group can resolve their conflicts. Prepare your e-mail message and send it to the other five committee members and to your instructor. What's your plan to get the committee moving toward writing the report to the incoming president?

  b. Assume that you have been asked to convince the other half of the committee to accept your half's views on the three areas of speed bumps, noise control, and parking. Send the three opposition students a memo or e-mail persuading them to your way of thinking. Keep in mind that your message must assure them that you respect their point of view.

  c. Assume that the committee members reach a compromise after seeing your plan put forth in (a). Collaboratively draft a three-page report to the new president.

  d. Collaboratively draft a letter to the editor of your student newspaper defending your recommendations to the student body and explaining how the group resolved its difficulty. This is a public statement that the group felt it was important to write; you will have to choose your words carefully to win campuswide support.

5. You work for a hospital laboratory, and your lab manager, under pressure from management to save money, insists that you and the three other med-techs switch to a different brand of vacuum blood-drawing tubes. You and your colleagues much prefer the brand of tubes you have been using for years. Moreover, the price difference between the two brands is small. As a group project, prepare a memo to the business manager of the hospital explaining why the switch is unnecessary, unwise, and unpopular. Then prepare another collaboratively written memo to your lab manager. Be sensitive to each reader's needs as you diplomatically explain the group's position.

PART II

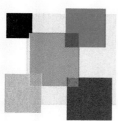

Correspondence

CHAPTER 4

Writing Memos, Faxes, and E-Mail

Memos, faxes, and e-mail messages are the types of writing you can expect to prepare most frequently on the job. These three forms of business correspondence are quick, easy, and effective ways for a company to communicate internally as well as externally with customers. You will find yourself preparing one or more of these types of writing each day to send to co-workers in your department, colleagues in other departments and divisions of your company, and decision makers at all levels.

What Memos, Faxes, and E-Mail Have in Common

These messages have several things in common.

1. Each of these forms of writing is streamlined for the busy world of work. Memos are far less formal in tone than letters; e-mail can be even more informal than a memo. Memos, faxes, and e-mail also require you to follow different formats than you do for letters.

2. They give busy readers information fast. While these messages can be about any topic in the world of work, most often they focus on the day-to-day activities and operations at your company—sales and product information, policy and schedule changes, progress reports, orders, personnel decisions, and so on.

3. Even though routine, they still demand a great deal of thought and time. Which one you use—memo, fax, or e-mail—depends on your company policy, the nature of your message, and your audience's needs and expectations. While some individuals believe we are moving toward a paperless office, most companies still want to see a paper or electronic trail documenting what has been done when and by whom. Your success as an employee can depend as much on your preparing an effective memo, fax, or e-mail as it will on your technical expertise.

Memos

Memorandum, usually shortened to *memo*, is a Latin word for "something to be remembered." The Latin meaning points to the memo's chief function: to record information of immediate importance and interest in the busy world of work. **Memos** are brief in-house correspondence sent up and down the corporate ladder. Employees send memos to their supervisors, and workers send memos to one another. Figure 4.1 shows a memo sent from one worker to another. Figure 4.2 illustrates a memo sent from the top down; Figure 4.3 shows a memo sent from an employee to management. Memos can also be sent to customers and others outside your company.

Figure 4.1   Standard memo format.

Header

Memo parts

Introduction

Preview

Body: Numbered list helps readers follow information quickly

Conclusion: Asks for comments

MEMO

TO: Lucy
FROM: Roger
DATE: November 12, 2007
SUBJECT: Review of Successful Website Seminar

As you know, I attended the "How to Build a Successful Website" seminar on November 7 and learned the "rules and tools" we will need to redesign our own site.

Here is a review of the major topics covered by the director, Jackie Chen:

1. Keep your website content-based—hit your target audience.
2. Visualize and "map out" your site's ad links.
3. Design your website to look the way you envision it—make it aesthetically pleasing.
4. Make your site easy to navigate.
5. Maintain your page outline; make changes when necessary.
6. Create hot links and image maps to move users from page to page.
7. Complete your site with appropriate sound and animation.

Could we meet in the next day or two to discuss recreating our own website in light of these guidelines? I would really like your suggestions about this project. Thanks.

Memo with a clear introduction, discussion, and conclusion.   Figure 4.2

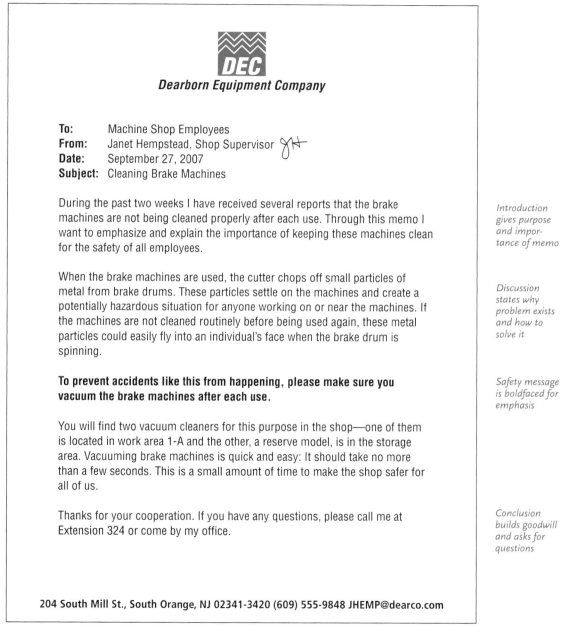

Dearborn Equipment Company

To: Machine Shop Employees
From: Janet Hempstead, Shop Supervisor
Date: September 27, 2007
Subject: Cleaning Brake Machines

During the past two weeks I have received several reports that the brake machines are not being cleaned properly after each use. Through this memo I want to emphasize and explain the importance of keeping these machines clean for the safety of all employees.

When the brake machines are used, the cutter chops off small particles of metal from brake drums. These particles settle on the machines and create a potentially hazardous situation for anyone working on or near the machines. If the machines are not cleaned routinely before being used again, these metal particles could easily fly into an individual's face when the brake drum is spinning.

To prevent accidents like this from happening, please make sure you vacuum the brake machines after each use.

You will find two vacuum cleaners for this purpose in the shop—one of them is located in work area 1-A and the other, a reserve model, is in the storage area. Vacuuming brake machines is quick and easy: It should take no more than a few seconds. This is a small amount of time to make the shop safer for all of us.

Thanks for your cooperation. If you have any questions, please call me at Extension 324 or come by my office.

204 South Mill St., South Orange, NJ 02341-3420 (609) 555-9848 JHEMP@dearco.com

Introduction gives purpose and importance of memo

Discussion states why problem exists and how to solve it

Safety message is boldfaced for emphasis

Conclusion builds goodwill and asks for questions

Memos are not as formal as letters and contain the terms and abbreviations familiar to employees of your company. Increasingly, e-mail is replacing the memo as a quick means of communication, but most companies continue to circulate hard copy memos, so it remains vitally important that you know about the format and uses of memos.

Memo Protocol and Company Politics

Memos reflect a company's image—its politics, policies, and organization. Memos are used for official internal announcements. Note how Janet Hempstead's memo in Figure 4.2 reminds workers about a crucial safety policy at Dearborn Equipment Company. A company's logo may even appear on the top, as in Figures 4.2 and 4.3. Memos reflect the company's identity and leadership skills and the ways in which it builds employee morale and encourages productivity.

Regardless of where you work, your employer will expect memos to be timely (don't wait until the day of the meeting to announce it), professional, and tactful. Just because a memo is sent as an informal in-house communication does not mean you can be gruff, curt, or bossy. Politeness and diplomacy count a lot at work. Memos need to be accurate, complete, and clear. Unclear or inaccurate memos can cost your company money and time, and cause personnel problems. Learning effective memo writing is vital to your success in any organization.

Most companies have their own memo *protocol*—accepted ways in which in-house communications are organized, written, formatted, and routed. In fact, some companies offer protocol seminars on how employees are to prepare communications. In the corporate world, protocol determines where your memo will go. Don't send copies of your memos (or your e-mail for that matter) to individuals who don't need them, however. You will only increase the paper inflation or electronic traffic in your company. For example, it would be presumptuous to send copies of all your memos to the vice president. You would offend your immediate supervisor, who might think that you are trying to avoid going through proper channels.

Functions of Memos

Memos serve a variety of functions, including

- announcing a company policy or plan
- changing a policy or procedure
- confirming a conversation
- offering information (FYI)
- making a request
- explaining a procedure or giving instructions
- clarifying or summarizing an issue
- alerting readers to a problem or a deadline

A memo that uses headings to highlight organization.   Figure 4.3

RAMCO INDUSTRIES

Where Technology Shapes Tomorrow
ramco@gem.com   http://www.Ramcogem.com

Company logo

TO: Rachel Mohler, Vice President
             Harrison Fontentot, Public Relations
FROM: Mike Gonzalez MG
SUBJECT: Ways to Increase Ramco's Community Involvement
DATE: March 2, 2007

At our planning session in early February, our division managers stressed the need to generate favorable publicity for our new Ramco facility in Mayfield. Knowing that such publicity will highlight Ramco's visibility in Mayfield, I think the company's image might be enhanced in the following ways.

Introduction supplies background and rationale

CREATE A SCHOLARSHIP FUND

Ramco would receive favorable publicity by creating a scholarship at Mayfield Community College for any student interested in a career in technology. A one-year scholarship would cost $4,800. The scholarship could be awarded by a committee composed of Ramco executives and staff. Such a scholarship would emphasize Ramco's support for technical education at a local college.

Headings reflect organization

OFFER SITE TOURS

Guided tours of the Mayfield facility would introduce the community to Ramco's innovative technology. The tours might be organized for community and civic groups. Individuals would see the care we take in production and equipment choices and the speed with which we ship our products. Of special interest to visitors would be Ramco's use of industrial robots alongside its employees. Since these tours would be scheduled well in advance, they should not conflict with our production schedules.

Body offers concrete evidence (costs, personnel, location) that plan can work

PROVIDE GUEST SPEAKERS

Many of our employees would be excellent guest speakers at civic and educational meetings in the Mayfield area. Possible topics include the technological advances Ramco has made in designing and engineering and how these advances have helped consumers and the local economy.

Thanks for giving me your comments as soon as possible. If we are going to put one or more of the suggestions into practice before the facility opens, we'll need to act before the end of the month.

Closing requests feedback and authorization

- confirming the outcome of a conversation
- delegating responsibility
- calling a meeting
- providing explanations necessary for business
- offering suggestions or recommendations
- requesting information
- documenting, for your own protection, something you did or did not do
- summarizing a long report or proposal

Memos are valuable written records used for a variety of purposes. They are used for a number of short reports; see Chapter 15 for examples of periodic, progress, and trip reports in memo format. Many internal proposals (pp. 602–610) also are written as memos. In fact, the memo in Figure 4.3 is an example of such a proposal. They can also be used to transmit a long report.

Memo Format

Memos vary in format and the way they are sent. Some companies use standard, printed forms (Figure 4.1), while others (as in Figure 4.2) have their names (letterhead) printed on their memos. You can also make a memo by including the necessary parts in an e-mail, as in Figures 4.4 and 4.5 on pages 129 and 130.

As you can see from looking at Figures 4.1 through 4.3, memos look different from letters, and they are less formal. Because they are often sent to individuals within your company, memos do not need the formalities necessary in business letters, such as an inside address, salutation, complimentary close, or signature line, as we will see in Chapter 5 (see pp. 145–152).

Basically, the memo consists of two parts: the header, or the identifying information at the top, and the message itself. The header includes these easily recognized parts: **To, From, Date,** and **Subject** lines.

TO: Aileen Kelly, Chief Computer Analyst
FROM: Stacy Kaufman, Operator, Level II
DATE: January 30, 2006
SUBJECT: Progress report on the fall schedule

Or you can use a memo template in your word processing program that will list these headings, as follows, to save time.

TO:
FROM: Linda Cowan
DATE: October 4, 2006
RE: (Enter subject here.)

On the **To** line, write the name and job title of the individual(s) who will receive your memo or a copy of it. If you are sending your memo to more than one reader, make sure you list your readers in the order of their status in your company or agency, as Mike Gonzalez does in Figure 4.3 (according to company policy the vice president's name appears before that of the public relations director). If you are on a first-name basis with the reader, use just his or her first name, as in Figure 4.1. Otherwise, include the reader's first and last names. Don't leave anyone who needs the information out of the loop.

On the **From** line, insert your name (use your first name only if your reader refers to you by it) and your job title (unless it is unnecessary for your reader). Some writers handwrite their initials after their typed name to verify that the message comes from them, as in Figures 4.2 and 4.3.

On the **Subject** line, write the purpose of your memo. The subject line serves as the title of your memo; it summarizes your message. Vague subject lines, such as "New Policy," "Operating Difficulties," or "Shareware," do not identify your message precisely and may suggest that your message is not carefully restricted or developed. "Shareware," for example, does not tell readers if your memo will discuss new equipment, corporate arrangements, or vendors; offer additional or fewer benefits; or warn employees about abusing the system. Note how Mike Gonzalez's subject line in Figure 4.3 is so much more precise than just saying "Ramco's Community Involvement."

On the **Date** line, do not simply name the day of the week—Friday. Give the full calendar date—June 1, 2007.

Memo Style and Tone

The style and tone of your memos will be controlled by the audience within your company or agency. When writing to a co-worker whom you know well, you can adopt a more casual tone. You want to be seen as friendly and cooperative. In fact, to do otherwise would make you look self-important, stuffy, or hard to work with. Consider the friendly tone appropriate for one colleague writing to another in Roger's memo to Lucy in Figure 4.1. Note how he ends in a polite but informal way.

When writing a memo to a manager, though, you want to use a more formal tone than when communicating with a co-worker or peer. Your boss will expect you to show a more respectful, even official, posture. See how formal yet conversationally persuasive Mike Gonzalez's memo to his bosses is in Figure 4.3. His tone and style are a reflection of his hard work as well as his courtesy to his employer. Here are two ways of expressing the same message, the first more suitable when writing to a co-worker and the second more appropriate for a memo to the boss.

Co-worker: I think we should go ahead with Marisol's plan for reorganization. It seems like a safe option to me, and I don't think we can lose.

Boss: I think that we should adopt the organizational plan developed by Marisol Vega. Her recommendations are carefully researched and persuasively answer all the questions our department has about solving the problem.

When a boss writes to workers informing them about policies or procedures, as Janet Hempstead does in Figure 4.2, the tone of the memo is official and straightforward. Yet even so, Hempstead takes into account her readers' feelings (she does not blame) and safety, which are at the forefront of her rhetorical purpose.

Finally, remember that your employer and co-workers deserve the same clear and concise writing and attention to the "you attitude" (see Chapter 5, pp. 153–160) that your customers do. Memos require the same care and should follow the same rules of effective writing as letters do.

Strategies for Organizing a Memo

Don't just dash your memo off. Take a few minutes to outline and draft what you need to say and to decide in what order it needs to be presented. Organize your memos so that readers can find information quickly and act on it promptly. For longer, more complex communications, such as the memos in Figures 4.2 and 4.3, your message might be divided into three parts: (1) introduction, (2) discussion, and (3) conclusion. Regardless of how short or long your memo is, recall the three P's for success—*plan* what you are going to say; *polish* what you wrote before you send it; and *proofread* everything.

Introduction

The introduction of your memo should do the following:

- Tell readers clearly about the problem, procedure, question, or policy that prompted you to write.
- Explain briefly any background information the reader needs to know.
- Be specific about what you are going to accomplish in your memo.

Do not hesitate to come right out and say, "This memo explains new e-mail security procedures" or "This memo summarizes the action taken in Evansville to reduce air pollution."

Discussion

In the discussion section (the body) of your memo, help readers in these ways:

- State why a problem or procedure is important, who will be affected by it, and what caused it and why.
- Indicate why and what changes are necessary.
- Give precise dates, times, locations, and costs.

See how Janet Hempstead's memo in Figure 4.2 carefully describes an existing problem and explains the proper procedure for cleaning the brake machines, and how Mike Gonzalez in Figure 4.3 offers carefully researched evidence on how Ramco can increase its favorable publicity in the community.

Conclusion

In your conclusion, state specifically how you want the reader to respond to your memo. To get readers to act appropriately, you can do one or more of the following:

- Ask readers to call you if they have any questions, as in Figure 4.2.
- Request a reply—in writing, over the telephone, via e-mail, or in person—by a specific date, as in Figures 4.2 and 4.3.
- Provide a list of recommendations that the readers are to accept, revise, or reject, as in Figures 4.1 and 4.3.

Organizational Markers

Throughout your memo use the following organizational markers, where appropriate:

- **Headings** organize your work and make information easy for readers to follow, as in Figure 4.3.
- **Numbered** or **bulleted lists** help readers see comparisons and contrasts readily and thereby comprehend your ideas more quickly, as in Figure 4.1.
- **Underlining** or **boldfacing** emphasizes key points (see Figure 4.2). Do not overuse this technique; draw attention only to main points and those that contain summaries or draw conclusions.

Organizational markers are not limited to memos; you will find them in e-mail, letters, and reports as well. (See Chapter 12.)

Faxes

Even though you may use e-mail extensively, fax (facsimile) machines are still in widespread use in the world of work. A fax machine sends copies of original letters, memos, reports, graphs, blueprints, and artwork over ordinary phone lines. You also can send graphics that resemble actual photos. Send a fax when your reader needs an exact copy of an original document, for example, a contract, letter, proposal, or map. A fax does not take the place of the original, which you may later need to send via snail, certified, or express mail.

Faxes are especially effective if you have to make a few changes in a detailed document (for example, a contract or a boilerplate) and do not want to rekey or transmit the entire work. Unlike e-mail, faxes provide a signature authorization and give recipients a hard copy. You might also need to send a fax if your recipient's e-mail server is down.

When you send a fax, be sure to use a fax cover sheet, which lists the persons sending and receiving the fax; their addresses and phone and fax numbers; and the total number of pages being faxed. This last information is essential so that the recipient will know when the transmission is complete and can alert the sender of any interruption or omission during transmission.

Be aware that, unless the recipient has her or his own secured fax machine, your confidentiality is not easily protected when communicating by fax. If your fax is sent to a machine available to the entire office staff, anyone can read it.

Fax Guidelines

When you send a fax, observe the following guidelines:

1. Because the type size of a document generally is reduced during transmission, print your fax message in a larger point size (12 or 14).
2. Avoid writing any comments at the very top or bottom of a fax. Your notes might be cut off or blurred in transmission.

Tech Note

E-Mail and Your Faxes

You can use your computer as a fax machine. You simply need a modem, which converts information from the way your computer handles it to the way the telephone lines handle it; nearly all computers now come with modems already installed. To send a fax, you tell the computer to print your document, and then, instead of choosing the printer normally connected to your computer, you choose FAX.

Also, you can have an Internet-based company, such as j2.com (*http://www .j2.com*) or eFax.com (*http://www.efax.com*), direct faxes to your electronic mailbox (e-mail). Because the services are Internet-based, you do not need to purchase a special computer program, and you can access your account from anywhere.

3. Make sure the document you are faxing is clear, but always include your phone and fax numbers in case the recipient needs to verify your message.
4. Be careful about sending anything longer than three or four pages. You might tie up the recipient's phone line. For a longer document, call before you fax to see whether the recipient will allow you to fax it.

E-Mail

E-mail is the most common workplace communication. It is the lifeblood of every business or organization because it expedites communications within your firm as well as communications with those outside of it. Professionals in the world of work may receive hundreds of e-mails a day from supervisors, colleagues, clients, and vendors. Moreover, you can send a variety of documents via e-mail, including pictures; video clips; soundbites; and various tables, lists, and statistical files. As we saw, e-mail can also substitute for paper memos.

Business E-Mail Versus Personal E-Mail

E-mail is the most informal, relaxed type of business correspondence, far more so than a printed memo, letter, short report, or proposal. (However, e-mail should never be sent in place of a formal letter.) Think of business e-mail as a polite, informative, and professional phone conversation—friendly, to the point, and always accessible. Yet, even though business e-mail is basically informal and casual, sending it does not mean you can forget about your responsibilities as an informed, cautious, and courteous writer.

The e-mail you write on the job will require more from you as a writer than your personal e-mail will. You cannot be sloppy or unorganized. Proofread and, if necessary, revise your e-mail before you send it. You need to follow all the rules of proper spelling, capitalization, punctuation, and word choice, plus the e-mail guidelines in the following section. The **tone** (see pp. 125–126) of your business e-mail should be much more professional than the instant messaging you may do with friends or your conversations in a chat room. You cannot write to your employer or a customer the way you would to an old friend.

Unlike your personal e-mail, your business e-mail must consider the impact it will have on your company and on your career. When you send a business e-mail, you are representing more than just yourself and your preferences, as in a personal e-mail. You are speaking on behalf of your employer. Since your e-mail must reflect your company's best image, make sure it is businesslike, carefully researched, and polite. Sarcasm, slang, and aggressive name calling do not belong in a company e-mail. Figures 4.4 and 4.5 are examples of effectively written business e-mails. Notice that e-mail can be cordial without being unprofessional. But at the same time, contrast the conversational tone of these e-mails with the more formal, straightforward tone of the memo in Figure 4.3.

An example of an effectively written business e-mail.   **Figure 4.4**

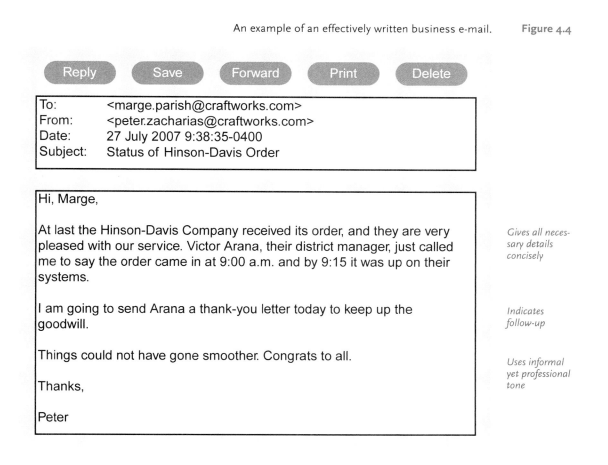

| Reply | Save | Forward | Print | Delete |

To: <marge.parish@craftworks.com>
From: <peter.zacharias@craftworks.com>
Date: 27 July 2007 9:38:35-0400
Subject: Status of Hinson-Davis Order

Hi, Marge,

At last the Hinson-Davis Company received its order, and they are very pleased with our service. Victor Arana, their district manager, just called me to say the order came in at 9:00 a.m. and by 9:15 it was up on their systems.

Gives all necessary details concisely

I am going to send Arana a thank-you letter today to keep up the goodwill.

Indicates follow-up

Things could not have gone smoother. Congrats to all.

Thanks,

Peter

Uses informal yet professional tone

Figure 4.5   E-mail sent to a distribution list of co-workers.

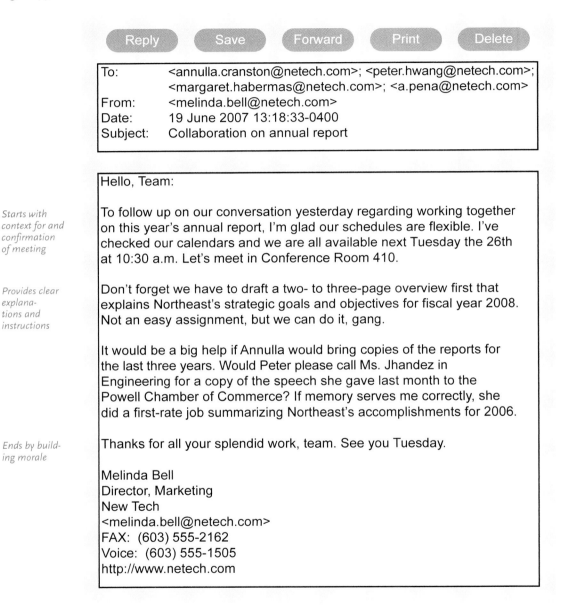

To:	\<annulla.cranston@netech.com\>; \<peter.hwang@netech.com\>; \<margaret.habermas@netech.com\>; \<a.pena@netech.com\>
From:	\<melinda.bell@netech.com\>
Date:	19 June 2007 13:18:33-0400
Subject:	Collaboration on annual report

Hello, Team:

To follow up on our conversation yesterday regarding working together on this year's annual report, I'm glad our schedules are flexible. I've checked our calendars and we are all available next Tuesday the 26th at 10:30 a.m. Let's meet in Conference Room 410.

Don't forget we have to draft a two- to three-page overview first that explains Northeast's strategic goals and objectives for fiscal year 2008. Not an easy assignment, but we can do it, gang.

It would be a big help if Annulla would bring copies of the reports for the last three years. Would Peter please call Ms. Jhandez in Engineering for a copy of the speech she gave last month to the Powell Chamber of Commerce? If memory serves me correctly, she did a first-rate job summarizing Northeast's accomplishments for 2006.

Thanks for all your splendid work, team. See you Tuesday.

Melinda Bell
Director, Marketing
New Tech
\<melinda.bell@netech.com\>
FAX: (603) 555-2162
Voice: (603) 555-1505
http://www.netech.com

Starts with context for and confirmation of meeting

Provides clear explanations and instructions

Ends by building morale

E-Mails Are Legal Records

The workplace has rules that govern what you can put in an e-mail and to whom you can send it. Employers own their internal e-mail systems and thus have the right to monitor what you write and to whom. Any e-mail at work on the company's server can be saved, stored, forwarded, and, most significantly, intercepted. You can be fired for writing an angry or abusive e-mail. Keep in mind your e-mail can easily be converted into an electronic paper trail. You never know who will receive and then forward your e-mail—to your boss, an attorney, or a licensing agency. Your e-mail could be forwarded to people you did not intend to see it. Many companies include disclaimers protecting themselves from legal action against them because of an employee's offensive behavior in a company e-mail.

Here are some good rules to follow about your company's e-mail:

- Do not use it for your personal messages. Use it only for appropriate company business, and make sure you are professional and conscientious.
- Never write an e-mail to discuss a confidential subject—to discuss a raise, to file a grievance, or to complain about a co-worker. Meet with your supervisor in person instead.
- Make sure of your facts before sending an e-mail to customers. If it gives them wrong or misleading information about prices, warranties, or safety features, your company can be legally liable.

Guidelines for Using E-Mail

Using e-mail technology at work obligates you to prepare and organize your messages carefully with your specific reader's needs in mind as well as those of his or her company and your own organization. Following the guidelines below will help you to write effective business e-mail messages.

1. **Make sure your e-mail is confidential and ethical.**
   a. Do not send or forward chain letters, political ads, cartoons, etc.
   b. Do not reply to spam, which will only multiply the amount you will receive. Some businesses estimate that 40 percent of their e-mails come from spammers. Use a spam blocker for protection.
   c. Never attack your employer, a colleague, a customer, or any firm.
   d. Do not spread gossip.
   e. Avoid *flaming*, that is, using strong, angry language that mocks, attacks, or insults your reader, as in Figure 4.6 (p. 137). Abusive, obscene, or racially offensive language in an e-mail constitutes grounds for dismissal.
   f. Send nothing through e-mail that you would not want to see on your company's website, intranet, or on the front page of your newspaper.
   g. Be cautious when you choose Reply All, so that you do not send something that is embarrassing or illegal.
2. **Observe all of the proprietary requirements when using e-mail.**
   a. Use quotation marks to indicate words that are not yours and always give a source.

    b. Do not forward a co-worker's or boss's e-mail without that person's approval.

    c. Never disclose (forward) someone's personal or private e-mail address without permission.

    d. Do not refer readers to another document and ask them to copy it without the writer's permission.

    e. Be careful not to change the wording of a message that you are expected simply to read and then forward.

    f. Print e-mails that are necessary for use in a presentation or report, or those that contain directions you may need to refer to again.

    g. Copy yourself on e-mails where you have to establish or maintain a paper trail.

    h. Establish electronic files organized by client or company name, case number, or date.

3. Use an acceptable format.

Since most e-mail is read online rather than in hard copy, consider how your message will look on a screen and the needs of your online reader. It is always more difficult to read a message on a screen than on a printed page.

    a. Make your e-mail easy to read.

- Do not send e-mail in all capital letters. It's hard to read, unprofessional, and looks as if you are shouting. Conversely, don't write in all lowercase letters.
- Keep your messages to one computer screen. Don't make readers scroll through a long message. Do not exceed 12 to 14 lines.
- Use no more than 65 characters per line and format your e-mail so that it wraps the text, preventing your e-mail from looking like a poem.
- Break your message into paragraphs. A screen filled with one long, unbroken paragraph is intimidating. Consider numbering your paragraphs.
- Watch the length of your paragraphs. Keep them to three or four lines and double-space between them.
- Avoid using boldface, asterisks, italics, and underlining, which may not be translatable by your recipient's e-mail system and garble or distort your message.

    b. Make your e-mail easy to process.

- Include all parts of your message—correct address, subject line, date, and so on.
- Include a concise (three- or four-word) subject line that helps readers sort out and identify your message quickly. Your reader may receive a lot of e-mail from listservs and may miss yours if it is not properly identified.
- Avoid vague one-word subjects. A subject line like "Bill" would leave your reader wondering if your e-mail is about a person, an unpaid account, or a notice just sent.
- Don't use highly emotional words like "Urgent," "Important," "Read at Once" in your subject line. They will turn your readers off.

- Get to the point right away. Because your readers receive vast amounts of e-mail, they may look only at the first few lines you write. Put the most important part of your message first.
- Refer to any relevant previous e-mail to give busy readers necessary background and context information quickly.
- Include a *signature block* with your name, company affiliation, title, address, and phone numbers, especially on e-mail sent outside your company.

Marsala Cooper
Senior Sales Rep.
RTS Technologies
Mcooper@RTS.com
Voice (708) 555-1970
Fax (708) 555-1997

- If your e-mail exchanges are simply adding questions to other questions, consider picking up the phone or meeting face to face to discuss an issue.

4. **Follow all of the rules of "netiquette" when answering e-mail.**
   a. Respond promptly to your e-mail.
      - Check your mail several times each day—don't let it build up in your in-box.

Tech Note

Using an E-Mail Address Book

The most convenient place to store names and addresses for easy retrieval is an e-mail address book. Address books are available in most software office packages and are fully integrated with Web browsers and e-mail programs. Internet-based e-mail services, such as Hotmail® and Yahoo!, also provide address books and calendars to access Internet directory services. The benefits of an address book are many.

- Address books allow you to store phone numbers and e-mail, street, and Web addresses.
- If you need to know someone's address or phone number, a variety of Internet-based directories will locate the information for you. From those services you can create mailing lists.
- By printing all or part of your address book, you have a hard copy to take with you, if necessary.
- Most address books allow you to import and export from other address books so you can combine information from several address books.

Always make sure you update your address book regularly.

- Reply the same day, if possible. Let correspondents know you received their messages and when you will respond if you cannot do so immediately.
- If you receive a lot of messages, prioritize them so that you reply to your boss first and to others later.
- If you expect a delay in getting information, tell the correspondent how long it will be before you can respond.
- If you are offline, use your e-mail software's **auto-reply feature** to send back a message to that effect (and indicate when you will return) to each correspondent.
- Keep your address book up-to-date.

b. Identify your audience correctly.
- Send your e-mail to the right address (is it an individual or a group?).
- Verify if your reader wants unsolicited mail. Never e-mail an advertisement, story, or joke unless the recipient welcomes it.
- Learn all you can about your reader to shape the tone of your mail to his or her needs; judge how much information the reader needs.
- Do not inflate your distribution list by clicking on Reply All with each e-mail. Send messages only to readers who need them (e.g., scheduling a meeting, as in Figure 4.5). Managers dislike being included on unnecessary distribution lists because it wastes their time.

c. Be courteous to your reader.
- Avoid sending e-mails with a delivery receipt notation that many readers see as a discourtesy.
- Don't send the same message over and over (just as you would not send hard copies or faxes of the same information repeatedly).
- Respect the cultural traditions of non-native speakers of English. (See Chapter 5, pp. 169–179.) Do not use first names unless the reader approves, and stay away from jokes and slang. Avoid including abbreviations, monetary units, and measurements that your reader may not use or know. Consider any time zone differences between you and your reader. For example, it might be 2 a.m. when your e-mail arrives, so don't expect an immediate reply.
- Delete long strings of previously answered messages when you reply so that the reader won't waste time scrolling to find your answer. Put your message first if you are forwarding an e-mail.
- Choose the New Message option to avoid sending old news again and again.
- Do not send long attachments or graphics files without obtaining recipients' permission. Such messages may be difficult to read onscreen or use a lot of memory. If your message is long, send it as an attachment.
- Always acknowledge a business gift or courtesy by sending a handwritten note of thanks rather than just dashing off an e-mail. International readers, in particular, will expect this.

5. **Adopt a professional style.**
   a. Use a salutation (greeting) or complimentary close (farewell), but always follow your company's policy:
      - to a colleague—Hi, Hello; Bye, Thanks
      - to a customer—Dear Ms. Pietz, Dear Bio Tech; Sincerely
   b. Keep your message concise.
      - Cut wordy phrases. See how many words you can eliminate without distorting your message.
      - Don't turn your e-mail into a telegram. "Report immediately: need for meeting" makes you sound discourteous and demanding. Likewise, responding with only a "Yes" or "No" is discourteous. Save "Yeah," "Nope," and "Huh" for your personal e-mails.
      - Send only the information needed to answer the reader's questions or concerns. Exclude nonessential details and chatter.

Tech Note

Sending an E-Mail Attachment

Your e-mail program will tell you whether an attachment has been sent, but attachments may arrive in an unusable or partly usable form if the sender's and the receiver's software are different. You need to use the same or compatible software as the person to whom you are sending the attachment in order to open and manipulate each other's documents, especially if the files contain graphics, databases, or spreadsheets. Even simple word processed documents may arrive mangled if the sender and the receiver use different operating systems or incompatible programs. To effectively attach a document to an e-mail:

- Consult the Help files of your software for information about attaching and translating various kinds of files.
- Send a test document and ask the recipient to send you one in return.
- If this experiment fails with a word processed document, start your word processor and save the document again, this time as a text file. Although some formatting may be lost (italics, boldface, indents), text files can be read by most word processing programs.
- When sending image files (such as .jpg or .bmp), try to keep the size of the file as small as possible. Most e-mail programs have specifications as to the size limit attachments cannot exceed; be aware of these limits. If an image attachment is too large, try saving it as another type of file in your imaging software before sending it again.
- Consider adding translation software to your computer system, to let you cross platforms (Windows, Macintosh, Unix) or programs.

    c. Don't reply to a message by including your response at the end of a long string of previous messages.

    d. Avoid abbreviations (e.g., BAK, back at keyboard; OTOH, on the other hand), catchwords, or phrases people outside your office might not understand or appreciate.

    e. Do not use jargon unless it is appropriate for the context and your audience.

    f. Be careful about including **emoticons** (e.g., happy [☺], or sad [☹] faces) made with punctuation marks and letters to indicate the emotional response you want to convey to the reader. When you use such notations, you run the risk of the reader not understanding your humor or not approving of it.

    g. End your message politely. Let the reader know you appreciate and welcome his or her help.

6. Ensure that your e-mail is safe and secure.

    a. Use various e-mail protection services and software (see the Tech Note on E-Mail Protection Services and Software on p. 139).

    b. Avoid obtaining e-mail viruses by deleting unopened, unsolicited e-mail attachments. If you do receive an e-mail virus, don't forward an infected e-mail to anyone else.

    c. Don't be a victim of identity theft e-mail. "Phishing" is a type of identity theft in which someone claiming to be a legitimate company and imitating its logo tells you there is a problem with your account and asks for personal information, such as your bank account or social security numbers. Legitimate companies will not contact you via e-mail for such information.

    d. Do not give out your e-mail address unless you know how it's going to be used.

    e. Do not reply to spam (junk) e-mail, because, in doing so, you are letting the spammers know that they have reached a legitimate e-mail address, which they may sell to other spammers.

    f. Create passwords that aren't easy to guess or obvious. In this way, hackers will not easily be able to access your personal or company information.

    g. Never provide personal or company financial information unless you are sure the information will be relayed over a safe connection. Check with your boss before providing company financial information.

    h. Back up important files on disk. A hacker or a computer virus obtained over e-mail could result in your losing valuable hard drive files.

Figure 4.6 shows an example of a poorly written e-mail that violates many of the preceding guidelines. Figure 4.7 contains an effective revision that reflects the professional and courteous way the writer and his company do business.

A poorly written e-mail, with annotations.   Figure 4.6

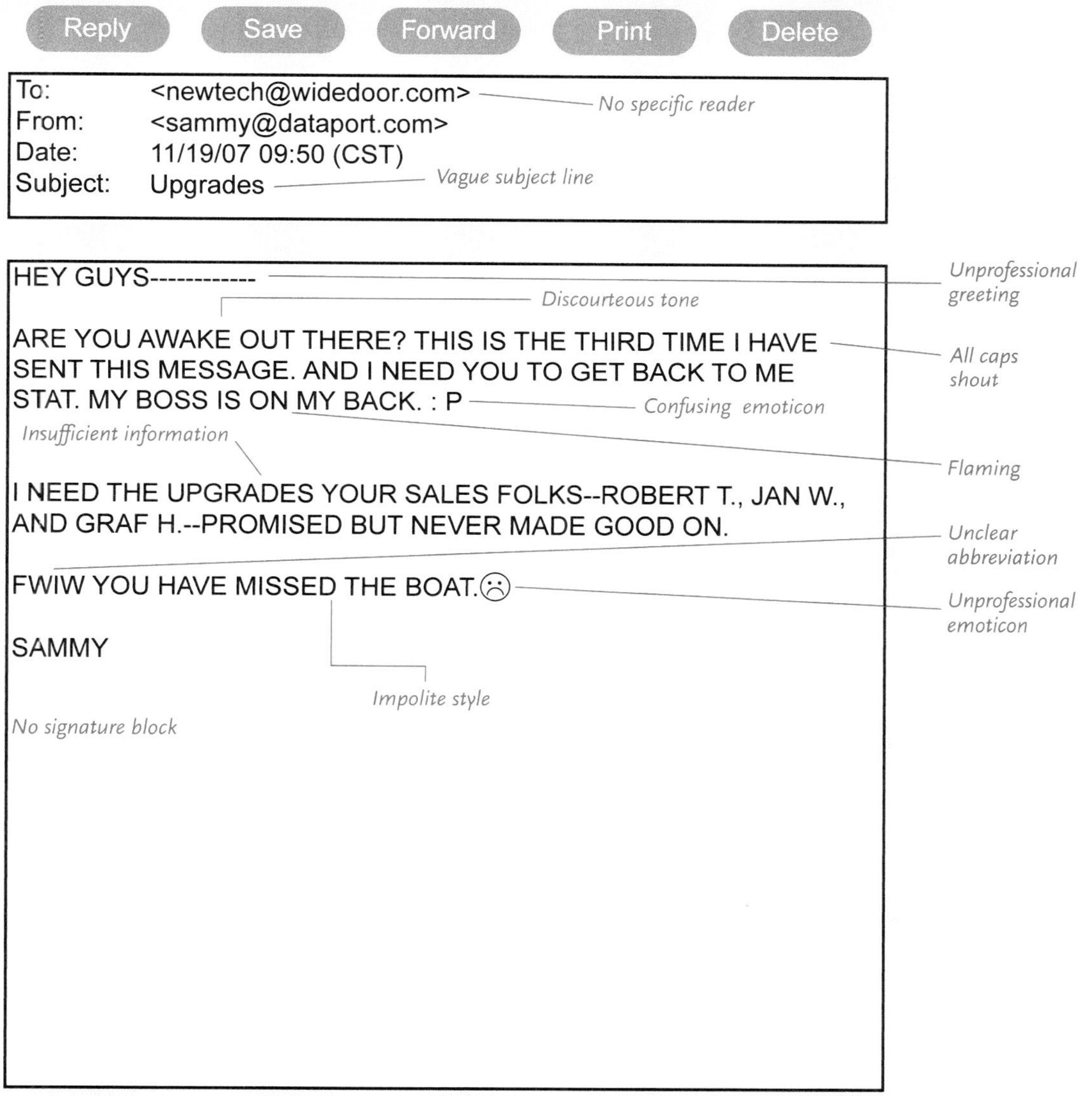

Reply   Save   Forward   Print   Delete

To:	<newtech@widedoor.com>	— No specific reader
From:	<sammy@dataport.com>	
Date:	11/19/07 09:50 (CST)	
Subject:	Upgrades	— Vague subject line

HEY GUYS------------ — Unprofessional greeting

— Discourteous tone

ARE YOU AWAKE OUT THERE? THIS IS THE THIRD TIME I HAVE — All caps shout
SENT THIS MESSAGE. AND I NEED YOU TO GET BACK TO ME
STAT. MY BOSS IS ON MY BACK. : P — Confusing emoticon

Insufficient information — Flaming

I NEED THE UPGRADES YOUR SALES FOLKS--ROBERT T., JAN W.,
AND GRAF H.--PROMISED BUT NEVER MADE GOOD ON. — Unclear abbreviation

FWIW YOU HAVE MISSED THE BOAT.☹ — Unprofessional emoticon

SAMMY

Impolite style

No signature block

Figure 4.7   A revised, effective version of the poor e-mail in Figure 4.6.

Specific e-mail address

Precise subject

Polite salutation

Gets to the point concisely

Provides explanation and documentation

Ends with clear-cut directions

Professional close

| Reply | Save | Forward | Print | Delete |

```
To:        <MWood@widedoor.com>
From:      <sammy@dataport.com>
Date:      11/19/07
Subject:   Upgrades for service contract #4552
```

Hello, Mary:

I would appreciate your delivering the upgrades for our service contract #4552 by Thursday afternoon, the 22nd of November, if at all possible.

We need to proceed to the next phase of our operation and the upgrades are crucial to that task.

I am attaching a copy of our service agreement with Wide Door for your convenience.

If you run into any problem with the delivery date, please give me a call this afternoon or e-mail me.

Thanks,

Sammy

Samuel Atherton
Operations Assistant
Data Port
4300 Morales Highway
San Padre, CA 95620-0326
Voice mail: 723-555-1298
http://dataport.com

E-Mail Protection Services and Software

Privacy protection is absolutely essential in the world of work. You don't want your name and e-mail address sold to unprofessional mailing lists or your messages intercepted. If you make financial transactions over the Internet, you certainly don't want your checking account or credit card numbers stolen.

The following types of protection are available:

- Most e-mail service providers protect their subscribers' privacy. Before signing up for an e-mail account, make sure the provider has a legally binding statement concerning your personal information and whether it will distribute your information to marketing companies. Most service providers (such as Hotmail or Yahoo!) include this information in the statement they require new users to "sign."
- All e-mail programs require their users to input an individualized password to prevent unauthorized access. Do not tell others your password. Change your password frequently.
- More sophisticated programs involving the use of "virtual IDs" and "digital IDs" allow you to prove your identity in electronic transactions with an electronic identity card. Such IDs, which involve a complicated series of codes, are issued through independent certifying authorities. Different classes of IDs provide different levels of security. With the use of a virtual or digital ID, your financial transactions on the Internet can be made even more secure.
- Many computer programs have e-mail security options that function automatically, or that you can activate by consulting the Help resources of your computer, and then searching under Security or E-Mail Security. These options call up windows to ask whether you are certain you want to proceed with your action, whether it is e-mail or financial. These prompts allow you to monitor not only what you are sending out, but also what you are importing, which is important for professionalism.
- Privacy seal programs and user rating programs offer businesses and consumers a way to trust that an Internet business is engaged in ethical online practices. Seals of approval are awarded to businesses that carry a privacy policy that clearly tells consumers what information is being collected and how it will be used. User rating systems allow former customers to rate a business's quality of service to illustrate that business's professionalism to other consumers. These programs can help you decide if you want to transact business and share information with an organization.

TABLE 4.1   The Uses of E-Mail Versus Memos or Letters

	E-Mail	Memo	Letter
Brief messages	X	X	
Informal	X	X	
Formal			X
Legal record		X	X
Relaxed tone	X	X	
Confidential material		X	X
Secure site		X	X
Multiple pages			X
Reports		X	X
In-house messages	X	X	
Proofreading	X	X	X

E-Mail Versus Other Types of Business Communications

Online Study Center

Access the memos, faxes, and e-mail Revision Checklist online at college .hmco.com/pic/ kolin8e

Table 4.1 compares and contrasts the function, scope, and format of e-mail with memos and letters. Note that e-mails are brief, informal, and to-the-point messages that are the workhorses in the world of business. They should never take the place of far more formal and official documents. Keep this table in mind as you learn more about various types of letters, including business letters and job application letters, in the following three chapters, and reports, covered in Chapters 15 and 16.

✓ Revision Checklist

Memos
☐ Used appropriate and consistent format.
☐ Announced purpose of memo early and clearly.
☐ Organized memo according to reader's need for information, with main ideas up front; supplied clear conclusion.
☐ Wrote concise and clear memo suitable for audience.
☐ Included bullets, lists, underscoring where necessary to reflect logic and organization of memo and made it easier to read.
☐ Refrained from overloading reader with unnecessary details.

Continued

Faxes

☐ Verified reader's fax number.

☐ Sent cover sheet with number of pages faxed and phone number to call in the event of transmission trouble.

☐ Enlarged font to minimize reduction of type in transmission.

☐ Excluded anything confidential or sensitive if reader's fax machine is not secure.

☐ Promptly returned any calls regarding transmission difficulties with fax.

E-Mail

☐ Did not send unsolicited or confidential mail.

☐ Sent to reader's correct address.

☐ Formatted e-mail with acceptable margins and spacing.

☐ Observed netiquette, especially by avoiding flaming.

☐ Wrote a separate message rather than returning sender's message with a short reply.

☐ Kept paragraphs short but used full—not telegraphic—sentences.

☐ Avoided unfamiliar abbreviations or terms that would cause reader confusion.

☐ Received permission to repeat or incorporate another person's e-mail.

☐ Observed all legal obligations in using e-mail.

☐ Safeguarded employer's confidentiality and security by excluding sensitive or privileged information.

☐ Included enough information and documentation for reader's purpose.

☐ Honored reader by observing proper courtesy.

☐ Began with friendly greeting; ended politely.

☐ Considered needs of international audience.

☐ Used antivirus program.

☐ Did not forward or reply to spam.

Exercises

Online Study Center
Find additional memos, faxes, and e-mail exercises at college .hmco.com/pic/ kolin8e

1. Write a memo to your boss saying that you will be out of town two days next week and three days the following week for **one** of the following reasons: (a) to inspect some land your firm is thinking of buying, (b) to investigate some claims, (c) to look at some new office space for a branch your firm is thinking of opening in a city five hundred miles away, (d) to attend a conference sponsored by a professional society, or (e) to pay calls on customers. In your memo, be specific about dates, places, times, and reasons.

2. Write a memo to two or three of your co-workers on the same subject you chose for Exercise 1.

3. Send a memo to your public relations department informing it that you are completing a degree or work for a certificate. Indicate how the information could be useful for your firm's publicity campaign.

4. Write a memo to the human resources department notifying it that there is a mistake in an insurance claim you filed. Explain exactly what the error is and give precise figures.

5. You are the manager of a major art museum. Write a memo to various department heads at your museum in which you put the following information into proper memo format.

> **Old hours:** Mon.–Fri. 9–5; closed Sat. except during July and August, when you are open 9–12
> **New hours:** Mon.–Th. 8:30–4:30; Fri.–Sat. 9–9
> **Old rates:** Adults $3.00; senior citizens $1.00; children under 12 free
> **New rates:** Adults $4.50; senior citizens $1.00; children under 12 free but must be accompanied by an adult
> **Added features:** Paintings by Thora Horne, local artist; sculpture from West Indies in display area all summer; guided tours available for parties of six or more; lounge areas will offer patrons sandwiches and soft drinks during May, June, July, and August

6. Select some change (in policy, schedule, or personnel assignment) you encountered in a job you held in the last two or three years and write an appropriate memo describing that change. Write the memo from the perspective of your former employer explaining the change to employees.

7. How would any of the memos in Exercises 1–6 have to be rewritten to make it suitable as an e-mail message? Rewrite one of them as an e-mail.

8. Bring five or six examples of a company's or an organization's e-mail to class. As a group activity evaluate them for style, tone, layout, and preciseness of message.

9. Send a fax to a company or an organization requesting information about the products or services it offers. Include an appropriate cover sheet.

10. Write an e-mail to a business that provides daily or weekly information to interested customers and submit its response along with your e-mail request to your instructor. Choose one of the following:
    a. an airline: an up-to-date schedule along a certain route and information about any bonus-mile or discount programs
    b. a catalog order company: information about any specials for Internet users
    c. a stock brokerage firm: free quotes or research about a particular stock
    d. a resort: special rates for a given week

11. Write an e-mail with one of the following messages, observing the guidelines discussed in this chapter.
    a. You have just made a big sale and you want to inform your boss.
    b. You have just lost a big sale and you have to inform your boss.
    c. Tell a co-worker about a union or national sales meeting.

d. Notify a company to cancel your subscription to one of its publications because you find it to be dated and no longer useful in your profession.

e. Request help from a listserv about research for a major report you are preparing for your employer.

f. Advise your district manager to discontinue marketing one of the company's products because of poor customer acceptance.

g. Send a short article (about two hundred words) to your company newsletter about some accomplishment your office, department, or section achieved in the last month.

h. Write to a friend studying finance at a German, Korean, or South American university about the biggest financial news in your town or neighborhood in the last month.

12. Rewrite the following e-mail to your boss to make it more professional.

Hi--

This new territory is a pain. Lots of stops; no sales. Ughhhh. People out here resistant to change. Could get hit by a boulder and still no change. Giant companies ought to be up on charges. Will sub. reports asap as long as you care rec.

The long and short of it is that market is down. No news=bad news.

13. As a collaborative venture, join with three or four classmates to prepare one or more of the e-mail messages for Exercise 11. Send each other drafts of your messages for revision. Submit the final copy of the group's effort.

14. Assume you have received permission to repost in an e-mail all or part of the article on microwaves (pp. 38–40) or virtual reality and law enforcement (pp. 415–419). Prepare an e-mail message to a listserv or Usenet group containing part of the article you have chosen.

15. Send your instructor an e-mail message about a project you are now working on for class, outlining your progress and describing any difficulties you are having.

16. You have just missed work or a class meeting. E-mail your employer or your instructor explaining the reason and telling how you intend to make up the work.

CHAPTER 5

Writing Letters

Some Basics for Audiences Worldwide

Letters are among the most important writing you will do on your job. Businesses worldwide take letter writing very seriously, and employers will expect you to prepare and respond to your correspondence effectively. Your signature on a letter tells readers that you are accountable for everything in it. The higher up the corporate ladder you climb, the more letters you will be expected to write. Because letter writing is so significant to your career, this chapter introduces you to the entire process, provides guidelines and problem-solving strategies, and shows you how to prepare the most frequently written types of business letters. It also shows you how to write for international readers.

Letters in the Age of the Internet

Even in this age of the Internet, hard copy letters are by no means obsolete. As you will see from the following list of reasons, letters carry great weight in the international world of work. They are formal, permanent, confidential, and bear a company's official seal of approval.

1. **Letters represent your company's public image and your competence.** A firm's corporate image is on the line when it sends a letter. Carefully written letters can create goodwill; poorly written letters can anger customers, cost your company business, and project an unfavorable image of you.

2. **Letters are far more formal—in tone and structure—than any other type of business communication.** Memos and e-mail are the least formal communications.

3. **A hard copy letter has the look and feel of an official document, commanding the reader's respect and attention.** A professional-looking letter is one of the most significant and ceremonious symbols in the world of work. It is the acknowledged way a company makes important announcements.

4. **Letters constitute an official legal record of an agreement.** They state, modify, or respond to a business commitment. When sent to a customer, a signed letter constitutes a legally binding contract. Be absolutely sure that what you put in a let-

144

ter about prices, guarantees, warranties, equipment, delivery or due dates, and other issues is accurate. Your reader can legally hold you and your company to such written commitments.

5. Unlike e-mail, many businesses require letters to be routed through certain channels before they are sent out. Because they convey how a company looks and what it offers to customers, letters often must be approved at a variety of corporate levels.

6. Letters are more permanent than e-mails. They provide a documented hard copy. Unlike e-mail that can be erased, letters are often logged in, filed, and bear a written, authorized signature; they are also far more confidential.

7. A letter is the official and expected medium through which important documents and attachments (contracts, specifications, proposals) are sent to readers. Sending such attachments via e-mail or with a memo lacks the formality and respect readers deserve.

8. A letter is the most formal and approved way to conduct business with many international audiences. These readers see a letter as more polite and honorable than an e-mail for initial contacts and even for subsequent business communications.

9. A hard copy letter is confidential. It is more likely to be delivered to the proper recipient with care in its sealed envelope and less likely to be forwarded to unintended readers, as an e-mail might be.

Letter Formats

Letter format refers to the way in which you print a letter—where you indent and where you place certain kinds of information. Several letter formats exist. Two of the most frequently used business letter formats are full block and modified block.

Full Block Format

In the full block format all information is flush against the left margin, with spaces between paragraphs. Figure 5.1 shows a full block letter. Use this format only when your letter is on **letterhead stationery** (specially printed paper giving a company's name and logo, business and Web addresses, fax and telephone numbers, and sometimes the names of its executives).

Modified Block Format

In the modified block style (Figure 5.2) the writer's address (if it is not imprinted on a letterhead), date, complimentary close, and signature are positioned at the center point and then keyed toward the right side of the letter. The date aligns with the complimentary close, and notations of any enclosures with the letter are flush left below the signature. Paragraphs in the modified style can be indented, as in the figure, or not.

Figure 5.1   Full block letter format.

All printing
lined up
against the
left-hand
margin

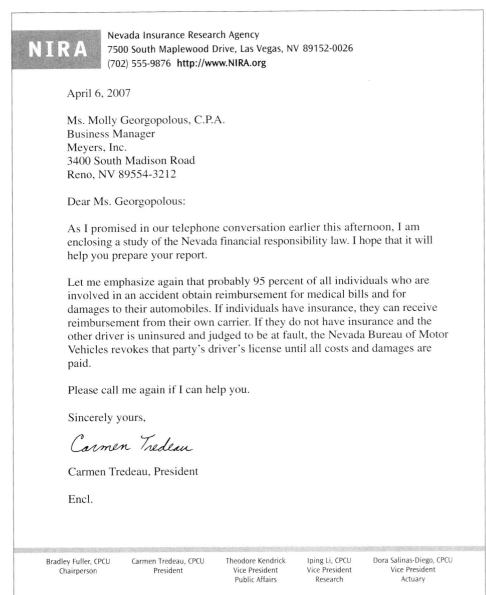

NIRA

Nevada Insurance Research Agency
7500 South Maplewood Drive, Las Vegas, NV 89152-0026
(702) 555-9876 http://www.NIRA.org

April 6, 2007

Ms. Molly Georgopolous, C.P.A.
Business Manager
Meyers, Inc.
3400 South Madison Road
Reno, NV 89554-3212

Dear Ms. Georgopolous:

As I promised in our telephone conversation earlier this afternoon, I am
enclosing a study of the Nevada financial responsibility law. I hope that it will
help you prepare your report.

Let me emphasize again that probably 95 percent of all individuals who are
involved in an accident obtain reimbursement for medical bills and for
damages to their automobiles. If individuals have insurance, they can receive
reimbursement from their own carrier. If they do not have insurance and the
other driver is uninsured and judged to be at fault, the Nevada Bureau of Motor
Vehicles revokes that party's driver's license until all costs and damages are
paid.

Please call me again if I can help you.

Sincerely yours,

Carmen Tredeau

Carmen Tredeau, President

Encl.

Bradley Fuller, CPCU	Carmen Tredeau, CPCU	Theodore Kendrick	Iping Li, CPCU	Dora Salinas-Diego, CPCU
Chairperson	President	Vice President	Vice President	Vice President
		Public Affairs	Research	Actuary

Modified block letter format with indented paragraphs. Figure 5.2

7239 East Daphne Street
Mobile, AL 36608-1012

September 28, 2007

*Date is
indented*

Mr. Travis Boykin, Manager
Scandia Gifts
703 Hardy St.
Hattiesburg, MS 39401-4633

Dear Mr. Boykin:

   I would appreciate knowing if you currently stock the Crescent pattern of model 5678 and how much you charge per model number. I would also like to know if you have special prices per box order.

*Paragraphs
can be
indented or
not indented*

   The name of your store is listed on the Crescent website as the closest distributor of Copenhagen products in my area. Would you please give me directions to your shop from Mobile and the hours you are open?

   I look forward to hearing from you.

   Sincerely yours,

Arthur T. McCormack

*Complimen-
tary close and
writer's name
are indented*

Continuing Pages

To indicate subsequent pages if your letter runs beyond one page, use one of these two conventions. Note the use of the recipient's name.

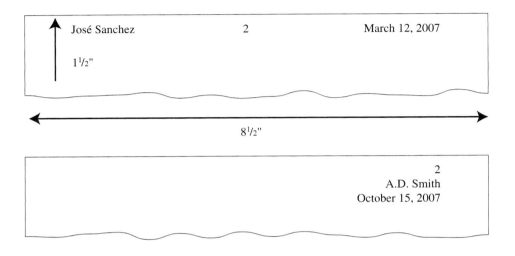

■ Parts of a Letter

A letter contains many parts, each of which contributes to your overall message. The parts and their placement in your letter form the basic conventions of effective letter writing. Readers look for certain information in key places.

In the following sections, those parts of a letter marked with an asterisk (*) should appear in every letter you write. Figure 5.3 is a sample letter containing all the parts discussed here. Note where each part is placed in the letter. Also see the tech note on pages 152–153.

*Date Line

Spell out the name of the month in full—"September" or "March" rather than "Sept." or "Mar." The date line is usually keyboarded this way: November 12, 2007. However, see page 172 on listing dates for international readers.

*Inside Address

The inside address, the same address as you put on the envelope, is always placed against the left margin, two lines below the date line. It contains the name, title (if any), company, street address, city, state, and ZIP code of the person to whom you are writing.

A sample letter, full block format, with all parts labeled.   Figure 5.3

Madison and Moore, Inc.
Professional Architects

7900 South Manheim Road
Crystal Springs, NE 71003-0092
Phone 402-555-2300   **http://www.MMI.com**

March 12, 2007

Ms. Paula Jordan
Systems Consultant
Broadacres Development Corp.
12 East River Street
Detroit, MI 48001-0422

Dear Ms. Jordan:

Thank you for your letter of March 6, 2007. I have discussed your request
with the staff in our planning department and have learned that the design
modules we used are no longer available.

In searching through my files, however, I have come across the enclosed
catalog from a California firm that might be helpful to you. This firm,
California Concepts, offers plans very similar to the ones you are interested
in, as you can tell from the design I checked on page 23 of their catalog.

I hope this will help you and I wish you every success in your project.

Sincerely yours,

MADISON AND MOORE, INC.

William Newhouse

William Newhouse
Office Manager

Encl.: Catalog
cc: Planning Department

Letterhead

Date line

Inside address

Salutation

Body of letter

*Complimen-
tary close*
*Company
name*
Signature
*Writer's name
and title*

Enclosure
Copy to

Make sure that you use the company's exact name consistently: not Hi-Tech, Inc. in one place and Hi Tech Corp. in another. Include the company's full name. If it is Sidow and Lewis, don't write just Sidow Co. Single-space the inside address and do not use any punctuation at the end of the lines.

Dr. Mary Petro
Director of Research
Midwest Laboratories
1700 Oak Drive
Rapid City, SD 56213-3406

Always try to write to a specific person rather than just "Sales Manager" or "President." To find out the person's name, check previous correspondence, e-mail lists, the company's or individual's website, or call the company. Always use an abbreviated courtesy title (Ms., Mr., Dr., Prof.) before the recipient's name for the inside address (e.g., Capt. María Torres; Mr. A. T. Ricks; Rev. Siam Tau). Use Ms. when writing to a woman unless she has expressly asked to be called Miss or Mrs.

The last line of the inside address contains the city, state, and ZIP code. (For guidelines on using correct addresses for international readers, see pp. 168–169.)

✻Salutation

Begin with *Dear,* and then follow with a courtesy title, the reader's last name, and a colon (Dear Mr. Brown:). **Never use a comma for a formal letter.** Avoid the sexist "Dear Sir," "Gentlemen," or "Dear Madam," as well as the stilted "Ladies and Gentlemen" or "Dear Sir/Madam." (For a discussion of sexist language and how to eliminate it, see Chapter 2, pp. 66–68.)

Sometimes you may not be sure of the sex of the reader. There are women named Stacy, Robin, and Lee, and men named Leslie, Kim, and Kelly. If you aren't certain, you can use the reader's full name: "Dear Terry Banks." If you know the person's title, you might write "Dear Credit Manager Banks."

Avoid casual salutations such as "Hello," "Good Morning, "Greetings," or "Happy Tuesday"; these are best reserved for your e-mail. And never begin a letter with "To Whom It May Concern," which is old fashioned, impersonal, and trite.

✻Body of the Letter

The body of the letter contains your message. Some of your letters will be only a few lines long, while others may extend to three or more paragraphs. Keep your sentences short and try to hold your paragraphs to under six or seven lines.

✻Complimentary Close

A close is the equivalent of a formal good bye. For most business correspondence, use one of these standard closes:

Sincerely,
Respectfully,

Sincerely yours,

Yours sincerely,

Capitalize only the first word. The entire close is followed by a comma. If you and your reader know each other well, you can use

Cordially,

Best wishes,

Regards,

But avoid flowery closes, such as

Forever yours,

Devotedly yours,

Faithfully yours,

Admiringly yours,

These belong in a romance novel, not in a business letter.

*Signature

Allow four line spaces so that your signature will not look squeezed in. Always sign your name in ink. An unsigned letter indicates carelessness or, worse, indifference toward your reader. A stamped signature tells readers you could not give them personal attention.

　　Some firms prefer using their company name along with the employee's name in the signature section. If so, type the company name in capital letters two line spaces below the complimentary close and then sign your name. Add your title underneath your typed name. Here is an example:

Sincerely yours,

THE FINELLI COMPANY

Helen Stravopoulos

Helen Stravopoulos
Cover Coordinator

*Enclosure(s) Line

The enclosure line informs the reader that additional materials (such as brochures, diagrams, forms, contracts, a proposal) accompany your letter.

Enclosure (only one item is enclosed)

Enclosures (2)

Encl.: 2006 Sales Report

*Copy Notation

The abbreviation *cc:* informs your reader that a copy of your letter has been sent to one or more individuals.

cc: Service Dept.

cc: Janice Tukopolous
    Ivor Vas

Letters are copied and sent to third parties for two reasons: (a) to document a paper trail and (b) to indicate to other readers who else is involved. Professional courtesy dictates that you tell the reader if others will receive a copy of your letter.

Tech Note

Advantages of and Cautions with Using Wizards

Most word processing programs, such as Microsoft Office or Corel Word Perfect, have letter wizards to help you format and design your letters. These wizards provide templates that automatically position your address, the current date, the recipient's address, greeting, paragraphs, and complimentary close. Using these wizards, all you do is enter the relevant information within a template and select from full or modified block format in addition to other options.

With letter wizards, you can also choose the overall style of your letter—contemporary, traditional, plain, elegant, and so on—by selecting the font and type size. (See pp. 513–516.) For example, when you choose a contemporary look for your letter, the font might be that of an upbeat, faddish electronic magazine, or e-zine, while the traditional choice features characters that look more like basic typewriter letters, as in Figures 5.1, 5.2, and 5.3.

These programs will also help you select a letterhead. You can choose from a list of several predesigned letterheads and then customize any one of them by inserting your, or your company's, name and address. Or you can create an original letterhead.

Although these wizards can create letter formats for you, do not rely on them too heavily. Keep the following precautions in mind:

- Wizards do not create text for you; they merely set up the layout of the letter and provide space to enter your own text.
- Although letter wizards provide standard formal, informal, and business salutations and closings, be careful about which option you choose. Some may be inappropriate for business correspondence because they look too informal, such as "Hi There."

Continued

- Some organizations may prefer not to use standard letter formatting. Always check with your company before using a letter wizard.
- Do not rely exclusively on generic letterhead templates provided by word processing software, since they may be seen as unimaginative by your readers.
- Wizards include parts of a letter you may not need (e.g., copy notation) or that your company does not use (e.g., attention lines).

Organizing a Standard Business Letter

Like the memo in Figure 4.3, a standard business letter can be divided into an introduction, a body, and a conclusion, each section responding to or clarifying a specific issue for your recipient. These three sections can each be one paragraph long, as in Figures 5.1, 5.2, and 5.3, or the body of your letter may be two or more paragraphs, as in Figure 5.4.

To help readers grasp your message clearly and concisely, follow this simple plan for organizing your business letters:

- In your first paragraph tell readers why you are writing and why your letter is important to them. Acknowledge any relevant previous meetings, correspondence, or telephone calls early in the paragraph (as in Figures 5.1, 5.3, and 5.4).
- Put the most significant point of each paragraph first to make it easier for the reader to find. Never bury important ideas in the middle or at the end of your paragraph.
- In the second (or subsequent) paragraph of your letter, develop the body of your message with factual support, the key details and descriptions readers need. For instance, note how in Figure 5.4 Cheryl Hu refers to specific changes her reader wanted.
- In your last paragraph, thank readers and be very clear and precise about what you want them to do or what you will do for them. Let them know what will happen next, what they can expect (Figure 5.4), or any combination of these messages. Don't leave your readers hanging. End cordially and professionally.

Making a Good Impression on Your Reader

You have just learned about formatting and printing your letters. Now we will turn to the content of your letter—what you say and how you say it. Writing letters means communicating to influence your readers, not to alienate or antagonize them. Keep in mind that writers of effective letters are like successful diplomats in that they represent both their company and themselves. You want readers to see you as courteous, credible, and professional.

Figure 5.4   Organization of a business letter.

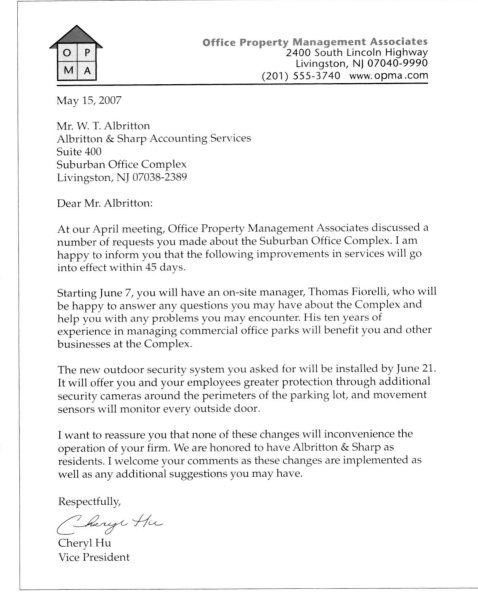

Office Property Management Associates
2400 South Lincoln Highway
Livingston, NJ 07040-9990
(201) 555-3740   www.opma.com

May 15, 2007

Mr. W. T. Albritton
Albritton & Sharp Accounting Services
Suite 400
Suburban Office Complex
Livingston, NJ 07038-2389

Dear Mr. Albritton:

Introduction comes to point quickly, cordially by referencing reader's earlier request

At our April meeting, Office Property Management Associates discussed a number of requests you made about the Suburban Office Complex. I am happy to inform you that the following improvements in services will go into effect within 45 days.

Starting June 7, you will have an on-site manager, Thomas Fiorelli, who will be happy to answer any questions you may have about the Complex and help you with any problems you may encounter. His ten years of experience in managing commercial office parks will benefit you and other businesses at the Complex.

Body describes changes with specific details

The new outdoor security system you asked for will be installed by June 21. It will offer you and your employees greater protection through additional security cameras around the perimeters of the parking lot, and movement sensors will monitor every outside door.

I want to reassure you that none of these changes will inconvenience the operation of your firm. We are honored to have Albritton & Sharp as residents. I welcome your comments as these changes are implemented as well as any additional suggestions you may have.

Conclusion builds goodwill by promising reader what will be done and how

Respectfully,

Cheryl Hu

Cheryl Hu
Vice President

First, put yourself in the reader's position. What kinds of letters do you like to receive? Letters that are vague, impersonal, sarcastic, pushy, and condescending, or polite, businesslike, and considerate? If you have questions, you want them answered honestly, courteously, and fully. You do not want someone to waste your time with a long, puffy letter when a few sentences would suffice.

To send such effective letters, adopt the **"you attitude"**; in other words, signal to readers that they and their needs are of utmost importance. Incorporating the "you attitude" means you should be able to answer "Yes" to these two questions:

1. Will my readers receive a positive image of me?
2. Have I chosen words that convey both my respect for the readers and my concern for their questions and comments?

The first question deals with your overall view of readers. Do your letters paint them as clever or stupid, practical managers or spendthrifts? The second question concerns the language and tone conveying your view of the reader. Words can burn or soothe. Choose them carefully. As you revise your letters, you will become more aware of and concerned about the ways a reader will respond to you and your message.

Figures 5.5 and 5.6 contain two versions of the same letter. Which one would you rather receive? Why? Note the use of a **watermark** in both figures (see pp. 156–157).

Achieving the "You Attitude": Four Guidelines

As you draft and revise your work, pay special attention to the following four guidelines for making a good impression on your reader.

   1. **Never forget that your reader is a real person.** Avoid writing cold, impersonal letters that sound as if they were form letters or voice mail instructions. Let the readers know that you are writing to them as individuals. The letter below violates every rule of personal and personable communications.

> It has come to our attention that policy number 342q-765r has been delinquent in payment and is in arrears for the sum of $302.35. To keep the policy in force for the duration of its life, a minimum payment of $50.00 must reach this office by the last day of the month. Failure to submit payment will result in the cancellation of the aforementioned policy.

There is no sense of one human being writing to another here, of a customer with a name, personal history, or specific needs. The letter uses cold and stilted language ("delinquent in payment," "in arrears for," "aforementioned policy"). Revised, this letter contains the necessary personal (and human) touch.

> We have not yet received your payment for your insurance policy (#342q-765r). By sending us your check for $50.00 within the next two weeks, you will keep your policy in force and can continue to enjoy the financial benefits and emotional security it offers you. Please call us if you have any questions. Thank you.

The benefits to an individual reader are stressed, and the reader is addressed directly as a valued customer. Using "thank you" and "please," the writer creates goodwill.

Figure 5.5   A letter lacking the "you attitude."

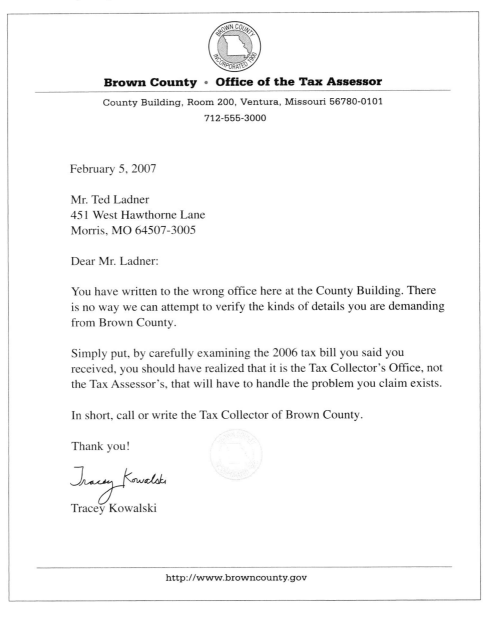

Brown County · Office of the Tax Assessor

County Building, Room 200, Ventura, Missouri 56780-0101
712-555-3000

February 5, 2007

Mr. Ted Ladner
451 West Hawthorne Lane
Morris, MO 64507-3005

Dear Mr. Ladner:

You have written to the wrong office here at the County Building. There is no way we can attempt to verify the kinds of details you are demanding from Brown County.

Simply put, by carefully examining the 2006 tax bill you said you received, you should have realized that it is the Tax Collector's Office, not the Tax Assessor's, that will have to handle the problem you claim exists.

In short, call or write the Tax Collector of Brown County.

Thank you!

Tracey Kowalski
Tracey Kowalski

http://www.browncounty.gov

Tone is sarcastic and uncooperative

Use of "you" alone does not signal a positive image of reader

Insulting and curt ending and close

A you-centered revision of Figure 5.5.   Figure 5.6

Brown County • Office of the Tax Assessor

County Building, Room 200, Ventura, Missouri 56780-0101

712-555-3000

February 5, 2007

Mr. Ted Ladner
451 West Hawthorne Lane
Morris, MO 64507-3005

Dear Mr. Ladner:

Thank you for writing about the difficulties you encountered with your 2006 tax bill. I wish I could help you, but it is the Tax Collector's Office that issues your annual property tax bill. Our office does not prepare individual homeowners' bills.

Thanks reader and gives polite explanation

If you will kindly direct your questions to Paulette Sutton at the Brown County Tax Collector's Office, County Building, Room 100, Ventura, Missouri 56780-0100, I am sure that she will be able to assist you. Should you wish to call her, the number is 458-3455, extension 212.

Helps reader solve problem with specific information

Respectfully,

Tracey Kowalski

Tracey Kowalski

Uses appropriate close

http://www.browncounty.gov

Don't be afraid of using "you," "your," and "yours" in your letters. Readers will feel more friendly toward you and your message. (Of course, no amount of "you's" will help if they appear in a condescending context, such as the letter in Figure 5.5.) In fact, you might even use the reader's name or that of his or her company to create goodwill and to show your sincerity.

2. Keep the reader in the forefront of your letter. Make sure the reader's needs control the tone, message, and organization of your letter—the essence of the "you attitude." Stress the "you," not the "I" or the "we." Here is a paragraph from a letter that forgets about the reader.

I-Centered Draft

```
I think that our rug shampooer is the best on the market.
Our firm has invested a lot of time and money to ensure that
it is the most economical and efficient shampooer available
today. We have found that our customers are very satisfied
with the results of our machine. We have sold thousands of
these shampooers, and we are proud of our accomplishment.
We hope that we can sell you one of our fantastic machines.
```

The draft talks the reader into boredom by spending all its time on the machine, the company, and its sales success. Readers are interested in how *they* can benefit from the machine, not in how much profit the company makes from selling it.

To win the readers' confidence, the writer needs to show how and why they will find the product useful, economical, and worthwhile at home or at work. Here is a reader-centered revision.

You-Centered Revision

```
Our rug shampooer would make cleaning your Comfort Rest Motel
rooms easier for you. It is equipped with a heavy-duty motor
that will handle your 200 rooms with ease. Moreover, that
motor will give frequently used areas, such as the lobby or
hallways, the fresh and clean look you want for your motel.
```

The revision shifts attention away from bragging about how "we have sold thousands" to the benefits the reader gains by purchasing and using the product.

3. Be courteous and tactful. However serious the problem or the degree of your anger at the time, refrain from turning your letter into a punch through the mail. Don't inflame your letter or e-mail readers; review Figures 4.6 and 4.7. Again, when you capture the reader's goodwill, your rewards will be greater. Don't use the following words that can leave a bad taste in the reader's mouth.

it's defective	unprofessional (job, attitude, etc.)
I demand	your failure
I insist	you contend
we reject	you allege
that's no excuse for	you should have known
totally unacceptable	your outlandish claim

Compare the following discourteous sentences with the courteous revisions.

Discourteous	Courteous Revision
We must discontinue your service unless payment is received by the date shown.	Please send us your payment by November 4 so your service will not be interrupted.
The rotten sound card you installed caused all my trouble.	The trouble may be caused by a malfunctioning sound card.
You are sorely mistaken about the contract.	We are sorry to learn about the difficulty you experienced over the service terms in our contract.
The new laptop you sold me is third-rate and you charged first-rate prices.	Since the laptop is still under warranty, I hope you can make the repairs easily and quickly.
It goes without saying that your suggestion is not worth considering.	It was thoughtful of you to send me your suggestion, but unfortunately we are unable to implement it right now.

The last discourteous example begins with a phrase that frequently sets readers on edge. Avoid using *it goes without saying*—it can quickly set up a hostile barrier between you and your reader.

4. Be neither boastful nor meek. Two strategies—one based on pride and the other on humility—often lead inexperienced letter writers into trouble. On the one hand, they believe that a forceful statement will make a good impression on the reader. On the other hand, they assume that a cautious and humble approach will be the least offensive way to earn the reader's respect. Both paths are wrong.

Aggressive letters, filled with boasts, rarely appeal to readers. Letters should let the facts speak directly and pleasantly for themselves. Compare the following boastful sentences with their graceful revisions.

Boastful	Graceful Revision
You will find me the most diplomatic employee you ever hired.	Much of my previous work has been in answering and resolving customer complaints.
The Sun and Sea unqualifyingly promises the nicest rooms on the Coast.	Each room at the Sun and Sea has a refrigerator, microwave, and Internet access.
I have performed that procedure so many times I can do it in my sleep.	I have performed all kinds of IV therapy as part of standard care.
The Debit Card offers you incomparable customer convenience.	The Debit Card gives you a 30 percent discount on all electronic transfer fees.

At the other extreme, some writers stress only their own inadequacy. Their attitude as projected in their letters is "I am the most unworthy person who ever lived." Readers will dismiss such writers as pitiful, unqualified weaklings. Note how the meek sentences on the left are rewritten more positively on the right.

Meek

I know that you have a busy schedule and do not always have time to respond, but I would be appreciative if you could send me your brochure on how to apply Brakelite.

I will be grateful for whatever employment opportunities you could kindly give me.

Positive Revision

Please send me your brochure on how to apply Brakelite.

I will welcome the opportunity to discuss my qualifications with you.

Using the Most Effective Language in Your Letters

How you say something in a letter is just as crucial to your success as *what* you say. An effective letter requires you to pay attention, especially as you revise, to your words and their tone. Three simple suggestions can help. Your letters should be (1) **clear,** (2) **concise,** and (3) **contemporary.** Regard these principles of letter writing as the three C's.

   1. Be clear. Clarity is the most important element in a business letter. If your message cannot be understood easily, you have wasted your reader's time and money. Plan what you are going to say—jot down some questions you want answered or some answers to questions asked of you. Doing that will actually save you time.

   Choose precise details appropriate for your audience to answer the reader's six fundamental questions—*who? what? why? where? when?* and *how?* Supply concrete words, facts, details, numbers. In the following examples the vague sentences on the left will puzzle a reader because necessary details are missing. In the revisions on the right, exact words have replaced unclear ones.

Vague

Please send me some copies of your recent report I can use at work.

You can expect an appraisal in the next few weeks.

One of our New York stores carries that product.

The fee for that service is nominal.

Clear Revision

Please send me 4 copies of your report on the new salt substitute to share with my fellow dietitians.

You will receive an estimate on the installation of a new 50,000-BTU air-conditioning unit no later than July 12.

Our store at 856 Fifth Avenue sells the entire line of Texworld gloves.

The fee for caulking the five windows on the first floor will be $50.00.

   2. Be concise. "Get to the point" is a necessity in the world of work. A concise letter is easy to read and to act on. As you draft and then revise your letter, ask yourself these two questions: (1) What is the main message I want to tell my reader? (2) Does every sentence and paragraph stick to the main point? The secret to concise correspondence is to get to the main point immediately and politely, as in the following examples.

Your order will be delivered by October 26, as you requested.

I am happy to confirm the figures we discussed via e-mail last Wednesday, the 17th.

Please accept our apologies for the damaged Movak shipped to you last week.

Here is the report you asked us to prepare with the projections for the Manchester market.

Many letter writers get off to a deadly slow start by repeating, often word for word, the contents of the letter to which they are responding.

First Draft
I have your letter of March 23 before me in which you ask if our office knows of any all-electric duplexes for rent less than five years old and that would be appropriate for seniors. You also ask if these duplexes are close to shopping and medical facilities.

Revised
Thank you for your letter of March 23. Our office does rent all-electric duplexes suitable for seniors. We have two units, each renting for $375 a month, that are four blocks from the Ortega Clinic and two blocks from the Edgewater Mall.

A concise letter includes only material that is absolutely relevant. For example, in a letter complaining about inadequate or faulty telephone service, mentioning color preferences for picture telephones would be inappropriate. In a request for information on transferring credits from one college to another, do not ask about intramural sports.

You can also make sure your letters are concise by revising them before you print and send them. Review pages 62-65.

3. Be contemporary. Being contemporary does not mean you should use slang expressions ("I had a tire ripped off"; "That rejection was a bummer") or informal language that is inappropriate ("Doing business with Bindex is a hassle"). Nor should you go to the other extreme and become stiff and formal. Write to your reader as if you were carrying on a professional conversation with her or him. A business letter should be reader-friendly, not overbearing.

Don't resort to using phrases that remind readers of "legalese"—language that smells of contracts, deeds, and stuffy rooms. In the following list, the words and phrases on the left are expressions that have crept into letters for years; the ones on the right are contemporary equivalents.

Pompous/Bureaucratic	Contemporary Revision
aforementioned	previously mentioned
as per your request	as you requested
at this present writing	now
I am in receipt of	I have
attached herewith	enclosed

Pompous/Bureaucratic	Contemporary Revision
at your earliest possible convenience	soon
we beg to advise	we believe, we think
endeavor	try
forthwith	at once
henceforth	after this
hereafter, heretofore, hereby	(drop these three "h's" entirely)
immediate future	soon
in lieu of	instead of
kindly advise	let us know

Figure 5.7 is a letter in stilted language written by Brendan T. Mundell to Patricia Lipinski, an executive whose firm has been overcharged for airplane tickets. Mundell's letter overflows with flowery, old-fashioned expressions. The effect is that Mundell's message—offering an apology, a credit, and a promise to correct the situation—is long-winded and pompous. It even sounds insincere. Note how the revision in Figure 5.8, free of such stilted expressions, is shorter, clearer, and far more personable.

▌ Guidelines for Printing Your Letter

Here are some practical tips on printing professional-looking letters.

- Use a letter-quality laser printer. Letters must look crisp, fresh, and businesslike.
- Always check your toner cartridge level. A fuzzy, faint, or messy letter mars your company image and your relationship with your reader.
- Choose a font that is inviting to the eye. Avoid script or other fancy type fonts. See pages 513–514.
- Avoid crowding too much text onto one page by estimating the length of your message. Use the print preview command to view an image of your letter before you print it. Squeezing too many characters on a line makes your letter cramped and hard to read. Don't cram a long letter onto one page; instead, allow your letter to flow to a second page.
- Be careful about lopsided letters. Don't start a brief letter at the top of the page and then leave the lower three-fourths of the page blank. Readers will feel as if you have left them hanging. Start a shorter letter near the center of the page.
- Leave generous margins of approximately 1½ inches all around your message. Set 1-inch margins as the default on your PC. Leave more white space at the top of your letter than at the bottom; watch the right margin in particular, since it is easy to exceed. Shorter letters may require wider margins than longer letters, but don't exceed a margin of 1 inch on the right side.
- Use high-quality white paper and matching standard size business envelopes. Using a heavy bond paper says that your message is important and substantial; thin, lightweight copy paper signals that your message is flimsy. Avoid colored paper, which can look unprofessional.

See the Tech Note on pages 152–153 for information on using wizards for your letters.

A letter written in stilted, old-fashioned language.   **Figure 5.7**

NORTHERN AIRWAYS

July 12, 2006

Ms. Patricia Lipinski
Manager
Lindsay Electronics
4500 South Mahoney Drive
Buffalo, NY 14214-4514

Dear Manager Lipinski:

Please be advised that I am in receipt of yours of July 6th. We are a global air carrier with the interest of our passengers in mind. I would like to take this opportunity to say that we are cognizant of our commitment to good corporate customers like Lindsay and extend our deepest disappointment for the problems your firm has experienced with Northern.

Wordy and pompous

Payment is due your firm, and I hasten to rectify the situation with regard to our error. Forthwith we are adjusting your account #7530, crediting it with the $706.82 you were surcharged. Inasmuch as Northern is such a wonderful company, we are going to enhance the Travel Pass we issue to customers.

Legalese

I would also like to bring to your attention that in an endeavor to correct such billing errors in the immediate future, I have routed copies of your communication to the manager of the billing department, A. T. Padua. I am confident he will take necessary action at his earliest possible convenience to ascertain the full details of your predicament and make the necessary adjustments in our procedures.

Condescending tone

Once again, I want to take the liberty to assure you that Lindsay Electronics is one of our most valued clients. Rest assured that we will take every step imaginable not to jeopardize our long-standing relationship with you. I hope that all the aforementioned problems have now been satisfactorily resolved. Thanking you, I am

Flowery language reeks of insincerity

Faithfully yours,

Brendan T. Mundell

Brendan T. Mundell
General Manager

3000 Airline Highway Tyler, ME 04462-3000 (207) 555-6300 E-MAIL: norair@abc.com
Fly over to our website at www.norair.com

Figure 5.8   A revised version of the stilted and bureaucratic letter in Figure 5.7.

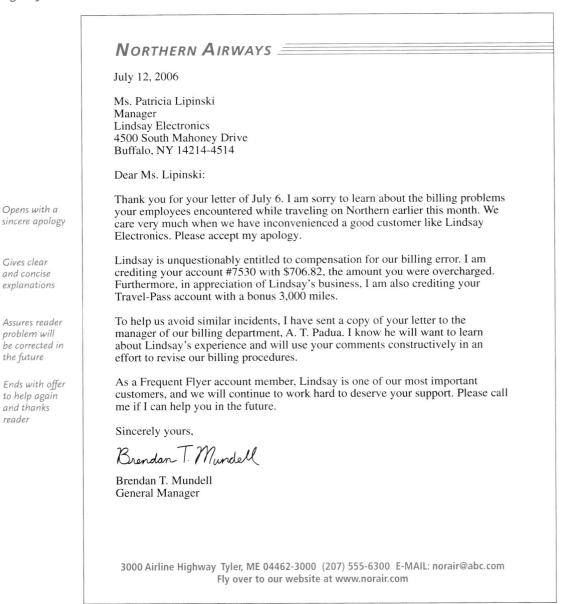

Opens with a sincere apology

Gives clear and concise explanations

Assures reader problem will be corrected in the future

Ends with offer to help again and thanks reader

Envelopes, Labels, Mail Merge, and Watermarks

Envelopes and Labels

Many word processing programs also provide wizards (see pp. 152–153) to help you print mailing labels and envelopes. You can enter your recipient's address, your return address, and the size of your envelope or type of labels, and the wizard helps you print them correctly. Envelopes with printed labels are always more professional looking than those with a handwritten address. Later, you can enter and retrieve one or thousands of addresses using the program's address book, saving you from much tedious keyboarding.

Mail Merge

Use mail merge when you are sending the same letter or e-mail to multiple recipients or creating a page of labels with different addresses. Mail merge will allow you to enter the addresses one by one or to select them from your address book before printing, saving you time. If you are sending the same letter to multiple recipients, you can enter their addresses into mail merge. Then, mail merge will automatically print each letter with a new address at the top. You can then use the addresses to create labels or envelopes with your program's wizard.

Watermarks

Software programs will help you to insert a watermark on your letter. A watermark is any graphic, logo, letterhead, or image that is printed very lightly behind the text typed on the page. Watermarks give your letter the appearance of being printed on expensive and official stationery. (See Figures 5.5 and 5.6.) Images of any kind can be sized, cropped, and otherwise manipulated to fit your needs.

International Business Correspondence

Online Study Center
Locate writing
letters globaliza-
tion exercises at
college.hmco.com/
pic/kolin8e

After e-mails, letters are the most frequent type of communication you are likely to have with international readers. Formal letter writing is a very important skill in the global marketplace. But, as we saw in Chapter 1, you cannot assume that every culture writes letters the way we do in the United States. The conventions of letter writing—formats, inside addresses, salutations, dates, complimentary closes, signature lines—are as diverse as the organization and styles used in writing letters for international audiences. Also, you need to be aware that even though a company is located in the United States, you may need to communicate from an international perspective. For instance, restaurant owner Patrice St. Jacques appeals to the ethnic heritage and pride of a potential customer in an effective sales letter (see Figure 6.4 on p. 200).

Americans are known for their informality, which extends to our relationships at work and is reflected in our letters. Many times we are on a first-name basis with people at work, including the boss as well as some of our customers, after knowing them only a short period of time. However, not all countries condone such informality in the workplace, regardless of how long an employee has been on the job or how much business he or she has conducted with an individual customer.

Some countries are less formal than others:

Less Formal	More Formal
Australia	Germany
Brazil	India
Canada	Japan
Denmark	Poland
United States	Spain

It would be impossible to give you information about how to write letters to each international audience. There are at least 5,000 major languages representing diverse ethnic and cultural communities around the globe. But here are some of the most important culturally sensitive questions you need to ask about writing to readers whose cultures are different from yours:

- What is your status in relationship to the reader (client, vendor, salesperson, or international colleague)?
- How should you format and address your letter?
- What is an appropriate salutation?
- How should you begin and conclude your letter?
- What types and amount of information will you have to give?
- What is the most appropriate tone to use?

To answer these and similar questions about proper letter protocol for your international readers, you need to learn about their culture.

Guides to a Country's Business Writing Culture

The more you know about a particular country and the way its citizens communicate through letters, the better your chances are to build goodwill and establish an international business relationship.

Consult the following resources in addition to those listed on pages 167–168:

- Websites prepared by a country's department of tourism or other reliable references—for example, *http://www.japan-zone.com* discusses customs, dress, business etiquette, important national holidays, and so forth.
- Cultural information officers at the country's embassy or consulate—*http://www.embassyworld.com*, for instance, includes a comprehensive database of every embassy and consulate in the world, as well as an international telephone directory.
- A multinational colleague at work who may be a native speaker from the region or country and who can advise you about proper letter protocols. Note

how Susan DiFusco relied on the assistance of a Korean colleague to prepare her letter in Figure 5.12.

- A foreign language teacher at your school who is familiar with the communication customs of the country.

Internet Guide to a Country's Culture

Here are additional online sources to consult when you cross cultural boundaries. They will give you advice about a country's customs and acceptable business etiquette when communicating with international audiences.

General Information and Travel Search Sites

- *http://www.search-it-all.com* presents an easy set of links for finding government offices, company information, and contact information for individuals and businesses worldwide.
- *http://www.travel.yahoo.com* lets you select the continent or city of your choice, then links you to a variety of country-specific websites, including those dedicated to international business information.
- *http://www.columbusguides.com* claims to be "the most comprehensive and objective guide to the traveler's world, and [one that] has been designed to answer all the questions you will ever need to ask with speed, confidence, and authority." This Internet version of the best-selling *World Travel Guide* contains information about every country in the world, from Afghanistan to Zimbabwe.

Online Chat Groups

Chat groups make it possible for you to ask questions directly to seasoned travelers or citizens of the country where your reader lives.

- *http://www.about.com* is a site where you can choose to chat with expert guides concerning hundreds of human-interest topics.
- *http://www.talkaway.com* provides an exchange of ideas on practically every cultural practice through online group discussions.
- *http://www.executiveplanet.com* offers "valuable tips on business customs, and protocol for doing business worldwide," including advice on such issues as gift giving, proper letter formats and conventions, and acceptable ways of addressing businesswomen. These guides are "authored by experts in international business etiquette, who are available to answer your questions on this discussion board."

U.S. Government Guides to World Cultures

- *http://cia.gov/cia/publications/factbook/index.html*, the online version of the widely consulted and authoritative *CIA World Factbook*, contains maps and statistical, contact, and cultural information for every country in the world, and describes current U.S. relations with each country.

- *http://lcweb2.loc.gov/frd/cs/* is the online version of the *Country Studies* handbooks available from the Library of Congress.
- *http://www.lib.unmich.edu/libhome/Documents.center.foreign.html*, a site organized by the University of Michigan, includes links to background, cultural, and travel information for many countries around the globe.

Organization and Style of an International Letter

Culture plays a major role in how and where you give readers information in your letter and how you word your message, just as it does for good news–bad news letters for U.S. readers (see pp. 206–207). Busy U.S. executives want letters written to them to be concise and to the point, that is, to stick to the facts and not to waste time with flowery compliments or personal details and observations that they regard as irrelevant or extraneous. Readers in the United States want to see any conclusions or recommendations up front, followed by descriptions only of key events that led to the main point.

Readers in other cultures, however, would find this approach to letter writing offensive and very unbusinesslike. A German reader would expect a long letter that unfolded slowly through a highly factual and scrupulously documented narrative of events, all of which would lead to the recommendation at the end of the letter.

A Japanese or Korean reader, on the other hand, would regard a U.S. or German version of a letter as curt, even insulting. These Asian readers would expect the first paragraph or two of a letter to center on the friendship and respect the writer has for them, as in Frank Sims's letter in Figure 5.10 and Susan DiFusco's letter in Figure 5.12. The style of a letter written to a client in East Asia would contain various courtesies and descriptions of, say, the reasons that the letter was written. Readers in other parts of the globe might see these as flattery. Rather than bluntly making a recommendation, the writer to the Japanese reader might phrase such a recommendation in terms that are beneficial to his or her relationship with the reader and include it near the end of the letter.

Guidelines for Letter Conventions

Here are some guidelines for letter conventions you need to take into account when writing for international audiences.

Addresses
Use the correct postal address. Make sure you spell the reader's street, city, state or province, and country correctly and that you include all necessary postal and re-

gional codes with the proper punctuation. Follow the guidelines found in the sources listed on pages 167–168.

Salutations, Closes, and Signature Lines

Find out how individuals in the recipient's culture are formally addressed in a letter. Unless you are expressly asked to switch to his or her first name, always use your reader's full formal surname in your letters, e-mail messages, and memos. Include proper titles and other honorifics (Dr., Don, etc.).

Spanish	German	French	Middle Eastern/East Asian
Señor (Mr.)	Herr (Mr.)	Monsieur (Mr.)	Use Mr. or Ms.
Señora (Mrs.)	Frau (Mrs.)	Madame (Mrs.)	
Señorita (Ms.)	(Avoid Fräulein)	Mademoiselle (Ms.)	

Here are some acceptable salutations by country:

Dear Señor Miguel Portales-Boca:

Dear Frau Irmegard Schultz:

Dear Mademoiselle Gisselle Mornay-Ives:

Dear Mr. Ibrahim Schariff-Azmar:

Dear Mr. Jianquin Zheng:

Never address the reader directly by his or her first name in the text of your letter. Choose an appropriately formal complimentary close. *Respectfully* is acceptable in almost every culture. But before you sign your letter with your name alone, find out the country's custom on using signature lines. Many European businesses list a company or organization name after the complimentary close and then include the writer's name after that, thus giving greater respect and authority to the organization than to the employee.

Guidelines for Communicating with International Readers

The following nine guidelines will help you communicate more successfully with an international audience and significantly reduce the chances of their misunderstanding you.

1. Use common, easily understood vocabulary. Write basic, simplified English. Choose words that are widely understood as opposed to those that are not used or understood by many speakers. Consult helpful dictionaries of basic English such as these:

- *Everyday American English Dictionary,* edited by Richard A. Spears (New York: McGraw Hill–NTC, 2000)
- *NTC's Dictionary of Everyday American English Expressions,* edited by Richard A. Spears, Betty J. Birner, and Stephen Kleinedler (New York: Contemporary Books, 1995)

Whenever you have a choice, use the simpler word; for example, use *stop*, not *refrain*; *prevent*, not *forestall*; *discharge*, not *exude*; *happy*, not *exultant*.

2. Avoid ambiguity. Words that have double meanings force non-native readers to wonder which one you mean. For example, "We fired the engine" would baffle your readers if they were not aware of the multiple meanings of *fire*. Unfamiliar with the context in which *fire* means "start up," a non-native speaker of English might think you're referring to "setting on fire or inflaming," which is not what you intend. Such misinterpretation is likely because most bilingual dictionaries would probably list only those two meanings. Or because *fire* can also mean "dismiss" or "let go," a non-native speaker of English might even suspect the engine was replaced by another model.

Be especially careful of using synonyms just to vary your word choice. For example, do not write *quick* in one sentence and then, referring to the same action, describe it as *rapid*. Your reader may assume you have two different things in mind instead of just one.

3. Be careful about technical vocabulary. While a reader who is a non-native speaker may be more familiar with technical terms than with other English words, make sure the technical word or phrase you include is widely known and not a word or meaning used only at your plant or office. Double-check by consulting the most up-to-date manuals and guides in your field, but steer clear of technical terms in fields other than the one with which your reader is familiar. Be especially careful about using business words and phrases an international reader may not know, such as *lean manufacturing, revolving credit, prime rate, reverse mortgages, leveraging, amortization,* and so forth.

4. Avoid idiomatic expressions. Idioms are the most difficult part of a language for an audience of non-native speakers to master. As with the example of *fire*, the following colorful idiomatic expressions will confuse and may even startle a non-native reader:

I'm all ears	sleep on it
throw cold water on it	burn the midnight oil
hit the nail on the head	give a heads up to
easy come, easy go	land in hot water
get a handle on it	touch and go
go to town	pushed the envelope
right under your nose	cut off your nose to spite your face
check it out	it was a rough go

The meanings of those and similar phrases are not literal but figurative, a reflection of our culture, not necessarily your reader's. A non-native speaker of English will approach such phrases as combinations of the separate meanings of the individual words, not as a collective unit of meaning. By using idioms, you risk confusing or offending your audience.

Imagine the horror a non-native speaker of English—a potential customer in Asia or Africa, for example—might experience if you wrote about a sale concluded at a branch office this way: "Last week we made a killing in our office." Omit the idiomatic expression and substitute a clear, unambiguous translation easily understood in international English. "We made a big sale last week." Or in place of "You hit the nail on the head," write "You have clearly understood what had to be done." For "Sleep on it," you might say, "Please take a week or two to make your decision."

5. Delete sports and gambling metaphors. These metaphors, which are often rooted in U.S. popular culture, do not translate word for word for non-native speakers and so again can interfere with your communication with your readers. In all likelihood, your audience has no equivalent in its culture for U.S. sporting games and events. Moreover, they suggest an aggressive business style frowned upon in many parts of the world. Here are a few examples to avoid:

out in left field	a ballpark figure
struck out	fumbled the ball
go out for a long pass	the bases are loaded
drop the ball	out of bounds
down for the count	made a pass
top of the ninth	beat the odds
long shot	slam-dunked it
hit a home run	scored a touchdown
be in left field	won by a nose

Use a basic English dictionary and your common sense to find nonfigurative translations for those and similar expressions.

6. Don't use abbreviations, acronyms, or contractions. While these shortened forms of words and phrases are a part of U.S. business culture, they might easily be misunderstood by a non-native speaker who is trying to make sense of them in context or by looking them up in a foreign language dictionary. Avoid abbreviations such as pharm., gov., org., pkwy, rec., hdg., hr., mfg., or w/o. The following acronyms can also cause your international reader trouble: ASAP, PDQ, p's and q's, IRA, SUV, RV, DOB, DOT, SSN. If you have to use acronyms, define them. Contractions such as the following might lead readers to mistake them for the English word they look like: I've (ivy), he'll (hell), he'd (held), I'll (ill), we'll (well), can't (cant), won't (wont, want).

7. Watch units of measure. Adapt your references to units of measurement, money, and time to your reader's culture. Do not fall into the cultural trap of assuming that your reader measures distances in miles and feet (instead of kilometers and meters as most of the world does except the United States and Great Britain), buys gallons of gasoline (instead of liters), and spends dollars (rather than pesos, euros, rupees, or yen). Just as not everyone in the world uses 110/220 wiring, keep in mind that not everyone sees the world marketplace solely in terms of the U.S. economy. Adapt your message to the reader's practices.

International Measurements of Distance, Dates, Time, and Temperature

The following guidelines will help you use the proper units of measurement for your international audience.

Metric Versus English Measurements

Most of the international community uses the metric system rather than English units, converting miles into kilometers. In fact, the United States is the only country that has not officially adopted the metric system (except in science and technology). When corresponding with an international reader, use metric units or when writing to multiple audiences in the United States and overseas, display both units. For help converting length, pressure, and volume measurements, consult *http://worldwidemetric.com/ measurements.html*.

Dates

Different cultures express dates in different ways. Most countries, including those in Europe, list the day, month, and then the year; for example, 1-3-06 refers to March 1, 2006. But in the United States, where the month comes first and then day and year, the date above would be read as January 3, 2006. In Japan, a different system is used; the year is listed first, followed by the month and day, 2006.3.1 (or 06/3/1). To avoid any confusion, write out the month and use all the numbers for the year, for example, 2007 rather than 07.

Currency

Even though many European countries now use one currency, the euro, world currencies still vary widely. Always respect the monetary unit your reader uses and include the local symbol for it. But be careful. Don't write $ or "dollars" and think readers will automatically think of the United States. Other areas of the world—Singapore, Hong Kong, Canada—also use dollars. Specify what country or region those dollars belong to: $100 dollars (Hong Kong). To convert U.S. dollar amounts into any international currency based on the present rate of exchange, see *http://www .xe.com/ucc/*. This site also identifies world currencies.

Decimals Versus Commas in Numbers

In many countries, a comma is used instead of a decimal point to separate numbers (expressed in the thousands) and fractions. For example, in the United States 12,001 signifies just over twelve thousand, whereas in Britain the number is written as 12.001. In other countries, however, the comma and decimal point are reversed to express percentages: 82.3% in the United States stands for 82 and 3/10 percent while in Germany or Bolivia the percentage is written as 82,3. Many Latin American and European countries, including Scandinavia, use spaces rather than decimals or commas to visually separate figures, for example, 12 001, 12. But be aware that conventions for numbers can change from country to country. Check the scientific guides and manuals in your discipline to know which practice has international endorsement.

Twenty-Four-Hour Clock

Many countries—including most of those in Europe—use the twenty-four-hour clock, or what is sometimes referred to as "military time" in the United States. Unlike the twelve-hour clock in use in the United States, the twenty-four-hour clock does not use **a.m.** or **p.m.** In Paris, for instance, 13:30 is 1:30 p.m. in New York and 9 **p.m.** in the United States translates to 21:00 in Sweden. Always specify time zones (Eastern Standard Time, Greenwich Mean Time) to help international audiences understand your message more clearly.

Temperature/Season

Most of the world, except the United States and Jamaica, records temperature using the Celsius (represented by C) temperature scale instead of the Fahrenheit scale (represented by F). For this reason, convert Fahrenheit readings to Celsius when writing to international readers. The Celsius scale has a freezing point of 0° and a boiling point of 100°, while on the Fahrenheit scale water freezes at 32° and boils at 212°. Writing to an international reader, accustomed to recording temperatures in degrees Celsius, that it is a pleasant 75 degrees, without noting that the scale is Fahrenheit, may lead to confusion: 75°C is the Fahrenheit equivalent of 120 degrees. To convert Celsius into Fahrenheit, add 40 to Fahrenheit degrees, multiply by 1.8, and subtract 40. Similarly, to convert Fahrenheit to Celsius, add 40, divide by 1.8, and subtract 40.

Be aware of seasonal differences, too. While New York is in the middle of the winter, Australia and Chile are enjoying summer. Be respectful of your readers' cultural (and physical) environment. Thanksgiving is celebrated in the United States in November, but in Canada the holiday is the second Monday in October; elsewhere around the world it may not be a holiday at all.

8. Avoid culture-bound descriptions of place and space. For example, when you tell a reader in Hong Kong about the Sunbelt or a potential client in Africa about the Big Easy, will he or she know what you mean? When you write from California to a non-native speaker in India about the eastern seaboard, meaning the East Coast of the United States, the directional reference may not mean the same thing to your audience as it does to you. Calling February a winter month does not make sense to someone in New Zealand, for whom it is a summer one.

9. Keep your sentences simple and easy to understand. Short, direct sentences will cause a reader whose native language is not English the least amount of trouble. World languages, especially those in Asia, divide information into sentence units far differently from the way English does. A good rule of thumb is that the shorter and less complicated your sentences, the easier and clearer they will be for a reader to process. Long (more than fifteen words) and complex (multiclause) sentences can be so difficult for readers to unravel that they may skip over them or guess at your message. But do not be insultingly childish, as if you were writing for someone in kindergarten. You may offend your international reader, who would find such a style to be condescendingly patronizing.

Always try to avoid the passive voice as well. It is one of the most difficult sentence patterns for a non-native speaker to comprehend. Stick to the common subject-verb-object pattern as often as possible. See pages 60–61 and the appendix (pp. 723–740).

Figure 5.9 is a letter that violates the guidelines for writing to an international reader (pp. 169–174). The writer does not use the correct format in the date line, misspells the reader's city, and leaves out important postal information. The writer also omits part of the reader's surname. The salutation is too informal; the reader's surname should have been used. The letter is filled with U.S. idioms—*drop you a line, ins and outs, give you a ring*—that the reader may not understand. It also uses abbreviations that may trouble the reader, for instance, *prod. eff. quotas*. Moreover, the writer disregards the ways in which the reader records time and temperature—1:30 for an Argentinian reader would signal 1:30 a.m. according to the twenty-four-hour clock he goes by; and the low 80's would hardly be "great weather"; it would mark a scorcher on the Celsius scale used in Buenos Aires. Equally disrespectful of the reader, the writer's overall tone is condescending, using phrases such as "south of the border" and, at the end of the second paragraph, telling the reader that the U.S. company is superior to the Argentinean one.

Note how the letter in Figure 5.10, on the other hand, respects the reader's culture by correctly spelling and punctuating the address, and using a clear date line and appropriate salutation and complimentary close. The opening is clear, courteous, and acknowledges the reader's position of authority in his company. The body of the letter is clearly written in plain international English and carefully informs the reader why and how the merger will affect his relationship with the writer. Above all, the writer respects his audience's culture and role in the business world, and seeks to win the reader's confidence and cooperation, two invaluable assets in the global marketplace.

An inappropriately written letter for an international reader   Figure 5.9

Pro-Tech, Ltd.
452 West Main St. Concord, MA 01742 978-634-2756
www.protech.com

5-8-06

Mr. Antonio Guzman
Canderas
Mercedes Ave.
Bunos Aires, ARG.

Dear Tony,

I wanted to drop you a line before the merger hits and in doing so touch base and give you the lowdown on how our department works here in the good old U.S. of A.

None of us had a clue that Pro-Tech was going to go south of the border but your recent meeting about the Smartboard T-C spoke volumes to the tech people who praised your operations to the hilt. So it looks like you and I both will be getting a new corp. name. Fantastic! I love moving from Pro-Tech, Ltd. to Pro-Tech International. We are so glad we can help you guys out.

At any rate, I'm sending you an e-mail with all the ins and outs of our department struc., layout, employees, and prod. eff. quotas. From this info, I'm hoping you'll be able to see ways for us to streamline, cooperate, and soar in the market. I understand that all of this is in the works that you and I need to have a face-to-face and so I'd appreciate your reciprocating with all the relevant data stat.

Consequently, I guess I'll be flying down your way next month. Before I take off, I would like to give you a ring. How does after lunch next Thursday (say, 1:00–1:30) sound to you? I hope this is doable.

I send you felicitations and want things to go smoothly before the merger is upon us.

We've had a spell of great weather here (can you believe it's in the low 80's today!). So, I guess I'll just sign off, and wait 'til I hear from you further.

Adios,

Frank Sims

Frank Sims

Misleading date line

Incorrect address

Too informal

Culturally condescending

Filled with American idioms

Disregards time differences and reader's 24-hour clock

Ignores Fahrenheit/Celsius temperature scale differences

Sounds insincere

Figure 5.10   An appropriate revision of Figure 5.9.

Pro-Tech, Ltd. 452 West Main St. Concord, MA 01742 978-634-2756
www.protech.com

8 May 2006

Señor Antonio Mosca-Guzman
Director, Quality Assurance
Tecnología Canderas, S.A.
Av. Martin 1285, 4° P.C.
C1174AAB BUENOS AIRES
ARGENTINA

Dear Señor Mosca-Guzman:

As our two companies prepare to merge, I welcome this opportunity to write to you. I am the manager for the quality assurance division at Pro-Tech, a title I believe you have at Tecnología Canderas. I am looking forward to working with you both now and after our companies merge in two months.

Allow me to say that we are very honored that your company is joining ours. Tecnología Canderas has been widely praised for the research and production of your Smartboard T-C systems. I know we have much to learn from you, and we hope you will allow us to share our systems analyses with you. That way everyone in our new company, Pro-Tech International, will benefit from the merger.

Later this week, I will send you a report about how we manage our division. I will describe how our division is structured and the quality assurance inspections we make. I will also give you a brief biography of our staff so that you can learn about their qualifications and responsibilities.

The director of our new company, Dr. Suzanne Nknuma, asked me to meet with you before the merger occurs to discuss the ways we might help each other. I would very much like to travel to Buenos Aires in the next two months to visit with you and take a tour of your company.

Would you please let me know by e-mail when it may be convenient for us to talk on the telephone so we might discuss the agenda for our meeting? I am always in my office from 11:00 to 17:00 your time.

Let me again say that I am looking forward to working with and meeting you.

Respectfully,

Frank Sims
Quality Assurance Manager

Respecting the Cultural Traditions of International Readers

Using simple words and concise sentences certainly will help you to write more effectively and clearly to an international audience. But to avoid even greater troubles, you also must be concerned with respecting the cultural traditions, customs, and preferences of your readers—how they dress, walk, eat, and interact at formal and informal meetings. Cultures differ widely in the way they send and receive information and how they prefer to be addressed, greeted, and informed in a letter. What is acceptable in one culture may be offensive in another.

For example, in Japan you would impress a potential client by bowing rather than shaking hands. But you must learn the protocol involved in bowing—who bows first, for how long, and how deeply. Similarly, Japanese business people are more accustomed to negotiating side by side, unlike U.S. business people, who prefer to sit face to face. Personal space is another key cultural issue. In the United States, individuals are most comfortable by standing 18 inches to 2 feet apart, an arm's length. But such is not the case in other cultures where proximity spells trust. Not all cultures shake hands, palm to palm, to extend a greeting. Moreover, some cultures regard any touch in a business context as disrespectful. In some cultures, sitting with your legs crossed and toes pointed at your audience is rude. Be aware of these physical dimensions of cultural appropriateness as well as verbal ones.

Respecting Your Reader's Nationality and Ethnic/Racial Heritage

Do not risk offending any of your readers, whether they are native speakers of English or not, with language that demeans or stereotypes their nationality or ethnic and racial background. Here are some precautions to take.

   1. **Respect your reader's nationality.** Always spell your reader's name and country properly, which may mean adding diacritical marks (such as accent marks) not used in English. You will insult your reader by omitting the accent from her last name, for example, by spelling her name as Donne rather than Donné. If your reader has a hyphenated last name (e.g., Arana-Sanchez), it would be rude to address him or her by only part of the name (e.g., only Arana or only Sanchez).

   2. **Honor your reader's place in the world economy.** Phrases like "third-world country," "emerging nation," "undeveloped/underprivileged area" are derogatory. Using such phrases signals that you regard your reader's country as inferior. Use the name of your reader's country instead. Saying that someone lives in the Far East implies that the United States, Canada, or Europe is the center of culture, the hub of the business community. It would be better to simply say "East Asia." Never use the word "Oriental," which is insulting. Residents of Hong Kong want to be known not as Chinese but as Hong Kongers.

   3. **Avoid stereotypes.** Expressions such as "oil-rich Arabs," "time-relaxed Latinos," and "aggressive foreigners" unfairly characterize particular groups. Similarly,

Some Guides to Cultural Diversity

Ferraro, Gary P. *The Cultural Dimension of International Business.* 4th ed. Upper Saddle River, NJ: Prentice Hall, 2001.

Harris, Phillip R., and Robert T. Moran. *Managing Cultural Differences: Leadership Strategies for a New World of Business.* Houston: Gulf Professional Publishing, 2000.

Hofstede, Geert. *Culture's Consequences: Comparing Values, Behaviors, Institutions and Organizations Across Nations.* 2nd ed. Thousand Oaks, CA: Sage Publications, 2003.

Morrison, Terri, Wayne A. Conaway, and George A. Borden. *Kiss, Bow, and Shake Hands.* Avon, MA: Adams, 1995.

Rosen, Robert H., and Carl Phillips. *Global Literacies: Lessons on Business Leadership and National Cultures.* New York: Simon & Schuster, 2000.

Walker, Danielle Medina, and Thomas Walker. *Doing Business Internationally: The Guide to Cross-Cultural Success.* 2nd ed. New York: McGraw-Hill, 2002.

prune from your communications any stereotypical phrase that insults one group or singles it out for praise at the expense of another—"Mexican standoff," "Russian roulette," "Chinaman's change," "Irish wake," "Dutch treat," "Indian giver." The word *Indian* refers to someone from India; use *Native American* to refer to the indigenous people of North America, who want to be known by their tribal affiliations (e.g., the Sioux).

4. Be visually sensitive to colors and symbols. Colors carry much cultural symbolism. Do not offend your audience by using colors in a context that would be offensive. Purple in Mexico, Brazil, and Argentina symbolizes bad luck, death, and funerals. Green and orange have a strong political context in Ireland. In Egypt and Saudi Arabia, green is the color of Islam and considered sacred. But in China, green can symbolize infertility or adultery. In China white does not symbolize purity and weddings but mourning and funerals. Similarly, in India if a married woman wears all white, she is inviting widowhood.

Several years ago, Air Canada opened new routes to East Asia and painted their planes black. But because black represents bad luck in that region of the world, Air Canada had to repaint its planes. A signature or a note written in red would signify anger to an Indonesian reader or death to a Chinese audience. And a Saudi audience would be highly offended to see pictures of individuals in short-sleeve shirts or bathing suits in any sales literature sent to them. Respecting the cultural practices of your readers can have far more impact on them than boasting about the price and quality of your product or service.

5. Be careful, too, about the symbols you use for international readers. Triangles are associated with anything negative in Hong Kong, Korea, and Taiwan. Political symbols, too, may have controversial implications (e.g., hammer and sickle, a crescent). Avoid using the flag of a country as part of your logo or letterhead for global audiences. Many countries see this as a sign of disrespect, especially Saudi Arabia, whose flag features the name of Allah.

Tech Note

Finding and Using International Letters and Symbols

To spell names or other proper nouns correctly for global audiences, you may have to use characters (letters, symbols, diacritical marks such as accents) that aren't available on a standard U.S. keyboard. The website *http://www.unicode.org* is the homepage for Unicode, a coding language that has been adopted by most major computer software companies (including Microsoft, Apple, HP, and IBM) that allows you to access the characters you need so that they can be recognized by any computer.

Most word processors also come equipped with a standard database of characters and symbols that you can adapt for your international correspondence. The following shortcut might also help: Press ALT plus a number that will give you the characters. For example, holding the ALT key and pressing the numbers 130 on the number pad (rather than on the numbered keys preceded by F at the top of the keyboard) usually produces *é* on most computers. With Microsoft Office (including Microsoft Word and Outlook, its e-mail software), you can access these symbols by clicking on Insert and then on Symbol.

Keep in mind that you may also have to adjust the font of your letter for international readers to account for the fact that your message may require more space for such changes.

Case Study: Writing to a Client from a Different Culture

Let's assume that you have to write a sales letter to an Asian business executive. You will have to employ a very different strategy in writing to an Asian executive as opposed to an American executive. For an American reader, the best strategy is to take a direct approach—fast, hard-hitting, to the point, and stressing your product's strengths versus the opposition's weaknesses. Businesses in the United States thrive on the battle of the brands, the tactics of confrontation symbolized in the sports metaphors on page 171. So a sales letter to an American reader would be polite but direct.

But such a strategy would be counterproductive in a sales letter to an Asian reader. Business in East Asia is associated with religion and friendship and is wrapped up in a great many social courtesies. The Asian way of doing business, including writing and receiving letters, is far more subtle, indirect, and complimentary than it is in the United States. The U.S. style of directness and forcefulness would be perceived as rude or unfair in, say, Japan, China, Malaysia, or Korea. A hard-sell letter to an Asian reader would be a sign of arrogance, and arrogance suggests inequality for the reader.

Courtesy for an Asian reader would be of paramount importance, more persuasive than a thorough description of a product or service. A sales letter to an Asian reader, therefore, should establish a friendship, a relationship in which trust is established first and business details are dealt with later. It is standard in Japanese companies, for example, to have executives meet three or four times just to socialize before they begin business negotiations. Trust and personal ties are crucial to conducting business.

Two Versions of a Sales Letter

To better understand the differences between communicating with a U.S. reader and an Asian one, study the two versions of the sales letter in Figures 5.11 and 5.12. The letters, written by Susan DiFusco for Starbrook Electronics, sell the same product, but Figure 5.11 is addressed to a U.S. executive, while Figure 5.12 adapts the same message for a business person in Seoul. The two letters differ not only in content but also in the way each is printed.

Format.   The full block style of the letter to the U.S. reader signals a no-nonsense, all-business approach. Everything is lined up in neat, orderly fashion. For the Korean reader, however, DiFusco wisely chose the more varied pattern of indenting her paragraphs. For Asian readers the visual effect suggests a much more relaxed and friendly, yet respectful communication. Note the different typefaces, too.

Opening.   Pay special attention to how the U.S. letter in Figure 5.11 starts off politely but much more directly, an opening the Korean reader would regard as blunt and discourteous. The sales letter written to the Korean audience (Figure 5.12) starts not with business talk but with a compliment to the reader and his company, praising them for trustworthiness and wishing them much prosperity in the future. Susan DiFusco sought the advice of a Korean co-worker, and from him she included the Korean greeting that opens the letter. She knew that when addressing the Korean administrator she should not get to the bottom line right away but instead used the introductory paragraph to show respect for the company and the reader—the equivalent of Japanese business executives socializing before any mention of business is made.

The Body.   Compare the second and third paragraphs of the letters in Figures 5.11 and 5.12. While the letter to the U.S. reader launches an aggressive campaign to get the reader's business, the letter to the Korean reader avoids the hard sell of U.S. business tactics. Susan DiFusco knew that for her Korean reader she must not promote too strenuously. The more she boasted about Starbrook's work, the less likely it was that she would make a sale. She recognized from discussions with other Asian

Sales letter to a native English speaker in a U.S. firm.   **Figure 5.11**

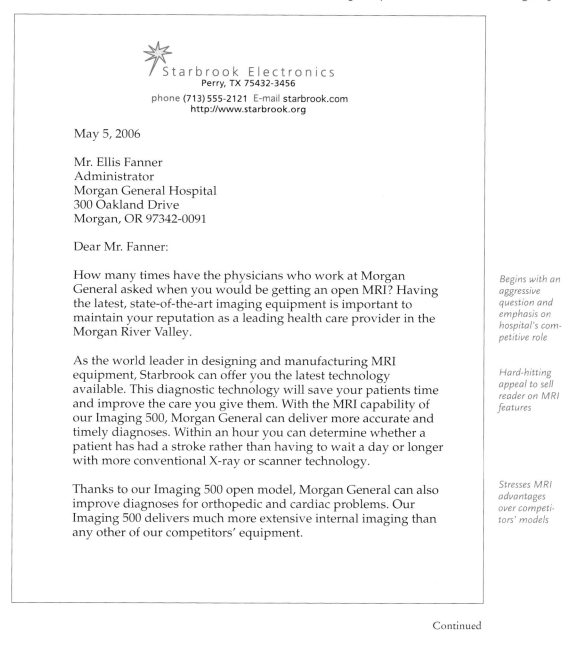

✴ Starbrook Electronics
Perry, TX 75432-3456
phone (713) 555-2121   E-mail starbrook.com
http://www.starbrook.org

May 5, 2006

Mr. Ellis Fanner
Administrator
Morgan General Hospital
300 Oakland Drive
Morgan, OR 97342-0091

Dear Mr. Fanner:

How many times have the physicians who work at Morgan General asked when you would be getting an open MRI? Having the latest, state-of-the-art imaging equipment is important to maintain your reputation as a leading health care provider in the Morgan River Valley.

Begins with an aggressive question and emphasis on hospital's competitive role

As the world leader in designing and manufacturing MRI equipment, Starbrook can offer you the latest technology available. This diagnostic technology will save your patients time and improve the care you give them. With the MRI capability of our Imaging 500, Morgan General can deliver more accurate and timely diagnoses. Within an hour you can determine whether a patient has had a stroke rather than having to wait a day or longer with more conventional X-ray or scanner technology.

Hard-hitting appeal to sell reader on MRI features

Thanks to our Imaging 500 open model, Morgan General can also improve diagnoses for orthopedic and cardiac problems. Our Imaging 500 delivers much more extensive internal imaging than any other of our competitors' equipment.

Stresses MRI advantages over competitors' models

Continued

Figure 5.11   (Continued)

Urges reader to act to surpass competition

Writer praises heer own company

Asks for immediate response from reader

Mr. Ellis Fanner   May 5, 2006   2

By obtaining the Imaging 500, Morgan General will surpass all other health care providers in the Morgan River Valley. No other hospital within a hundred-mile radius has one. By acting now, you, too, will receive Starbrook's unsurpassed guarantee of service and clarity. You are guaranteed one year's free maintenance by our team of experts.

And we will even give you free upgrades to make sure your Imaging 500 continues to be state of the art. Since software updates change so often and so radically, no other MRI vendor dares make such an offer. We deliver what we promise. Ask any of our recent satisfied customers—Tennessee General, Grantsville Uptown Clinic, or Nevada Statewide HMO.

We are hosting a demonstration for hospital administrators on the 4th of June in Portland and would like to see you there. Don't hesitate to call me to arrange for your free showing.

Sincerely yours,

Susan DiFusco

Susan DiFusco
Assistant Manager

---

business people over the years that she had to supply key information—such as the application and the advantages of her product—without overwhelming or pressuring her audience. Yet DiFusco subtly reassures Mr. Kim that her company is honorable and worthy to be recommended to his friends.

View of Competitors.   Observe, too, how the letter to the U.S. executive (Figure 5.11) undermines the competition by stating how much better Starbrook's offer is. For most Asian readers, it would be considered impolite to claim that your product is better than another company's or that your firm is currently doing business with other firms in the reader's country. Asian audiences prefer to avoid anything that hints of impoliteness or assertiveness.

Conclusion.   Finally, contrast the conclusions of the two letters. In the letter to a U.S. audience, DiFusco strongly urges her potential customer to get in touch with

Sales letter to a non-native speaker of English in a foreign firm.   **Figure 5.12**

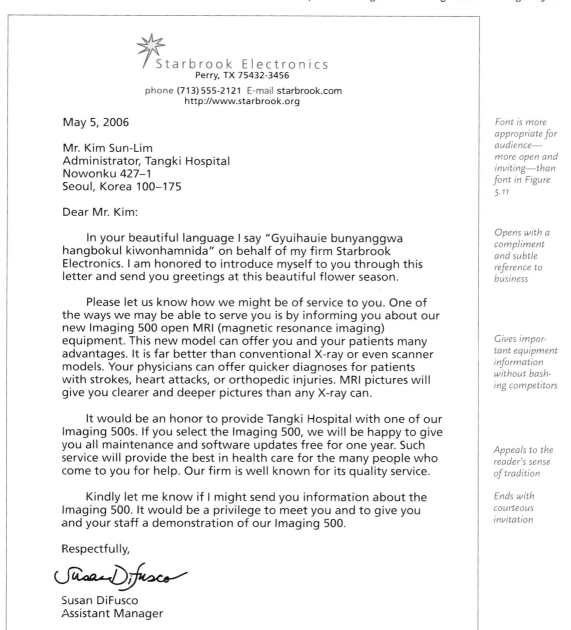

Starbrook Electronics
Perry, TX 75432-3456
phone (713) 555-2121 E-mail starbrook.com
http://www.starbrook.org

May 5, 2006

Mr. Kim Sun-Lim
Administrator, Tangki Hospital
Nowonku 427–1
Seoul, Korea 100–175

Dear Mr. Kim:

    In your beautiful language I say "Gyuihauie bunyanggwa hangbokul kiwonhamnida" on behalf of my firm Starbrook Electronics. I am honored to introduce myself to you through this letter and send you greetings at this beautiful flower season.

    Please let us know how we might be of service to you. One of the ways we may be able to serve you is by informing you about our new Imaging 500 open MRI (magnetic resonance imaging) equipment. This new model can offer you and your patients many advantages. It is far better than conventional X-ray or even scanner models. Your physicians can offer quicker diagnoses for patients with strokes, heart attacks, or orthopedic injuries. MRI pictures will give you clearer and deeper pictures than any X-ray can.

    It would be an honor to provide Tangki Hospital with one of our Imaging 500s. If you select the Imaging 500, we will be happy to give you all maintenance and software updates free for one year. Such service will provide the best in health care for the many people who come to you for help. Our firm is well known for its quality service.

    Kindly let me know if I might send you information about the Imaging 500. It would be a privilege to meet you and to give you and your staff a demonstration of our Imaging 500.

Respectfully,

Susan DiFusco

Susan DiFusco
Assistant Manager

Font is more appropriate for audience—more open and inviting—than font in Figure 5.11

Opens with a compliment and subtle reference to business

Gives important equipment information without bashing competitors

Appeals to the reader's sense of tradition

Ends with courteous invitation

her. Such a call to action is customary in a sales letter to a U.S. firm. But in her concluding paragraph to Mr. Kim, DiFusco adopts a more reserved and personal tone. Her use of such appropriate phrases as "kindly let me know" and "it would be a privilege" expresses the friendly sentiments of respect and esteem that would especially appeal to her reader. Note, too, that DiFusco has chosen a complimentary close ("Respectfully") much more in keeping with Mr. Kim's cultural sensitivities than the "Sincerely yours," which was suitable for the letter in Figure 5.11.

As these two letters show, writers need to know and respect their readers' cultures. In addressing an audience of non-native speakers of English, a writer must consider the readers' communication patterns, use protocols, and cultural (or subcultural) traditions. The same guidelines apply whether you are writing to non-native speakers abroad or in this country. Your message and vocabulary should always be clear, understandable, and appropriate for the intended audience.

Online Study Center

Access the writing letters Revision Checklists online at college.hmco .com/pic/kolin8e

 ## Revision Checklist

Audience Analysis and Research
- [ ] Made sure reader's name and job title are correct.
- [ ] Found out something about my audience—interests and background, well informed or unfamiliar with topic, former clients or new ones.
- [ ] Determined whether audience will be friendly, hostile, or neutral about my message.
- [ ] Did sufficient research—in print, through online sources, in discussions with colleagues—to give audience what they need.
- [ ] Acknowledged previous correspondence.
- [ ] Spent sufficient time drafting and revising letter before printing final copy.

Format/Appearance
- [ ] Followed one letter format (full block, modified block) consistently.
- [ ] Used letter wizards with caution.
- [ ] Left margins wide enough to make my letter look attractive and well proportioned.
- [ ] Included all the necessary parts of a letter.
- [ ] Made sure that my letter looks neat and professional.
- [ ] Printed my letter on company letterhead or quality bond paper.
- [ ] Proofread my letter carefully and made sure each correction was made before final copy was printed.
- [ ] Eliminated any grammatical and spelling errors.
- [ ] Signed my letter legibly in blue or black ink.
- [ ] Sent copies to appropriate parties.
- [ ] Printed envelopes properly.

Continued

Content/Organization

- ☐ Clearly understood my purpose in writing to reader(s).
- ☐ Put most important point first in my letter.
- ☐ Started each paragraph with the central idea of that paragraph.
- ☐ Answered all the reader's questions and concerns.
- ☐ Omitted anything offensive, irrelevant, or repetitious.
- ☐ Stated clearly what I want reader to do.
- ☐ Used last paragraph to summarize and encourage reader to continue cordial relations with me and my company.

Style: Words, Tone, Sentences, Paragraphs

- ☐ Emphasized the "you attitude" by seeing things from reader's perspective.
- ☐ Avoided being too casual or colloquial.
- ☐ Chose words that are clear, precise, and friendly.
- ☐ Cut anything sounding flowery, stuffy, or bureaucratic.
- ☐ Ensured that my sentences are readable, clear, and not too long (less than fifteen to twenty words).
- ☐ Wrote paragraphs that are easy to read and that flow together.

Writing to International Readers

- ☐ Did appropriate research about reader's culture, in print, through online sources, and with native speaker colleagues or teachers, especially about accepted ways of communicating.
- ☐ Adopted a respectful, not condescending, tone.
- ☐ Avoided anything offensive to my reader, especially references to politics, religion, or cultural taboos.
- ☐ Used plain and clear language that my reader would understand.
- ☐ Tested my sentences for length and active voice.
- ☐ Made sure nothing in my letter might be misinterpreted by my reader.
- ☐ Chose colors and symbols culturally appropriate for the context of my message.
- ☐ Selected the right format, salutation, and complimentary close for my reader.
- ☐ Observed the reader's units of measurement for time, temperature, currency, dates, and numbers.

Exercises

1. Find two business letters and bring them to class. Be prepared to identify the various parts of a letter discussed in this chapter.

2. Find a form letter that is addressed to "Dear Customer," "Postal Patron," or "Dear Resident" and rewrite it to make it more personal.

Online Study Center

Find additional writing letters exercises at college.hmco.com/ pic/kolin8e

3. Correct the following inside addresses:
   a. Dr. Ann Clark, M.D.
      1730 East Jefferson
      Jackson, MI. 46759
   b. To: Tommy Jones
      Secretary to Mrs. Franks
      Donlevey labs
      Cleveland, O. 45362
   c. Debbie Hinkle
      432 Parkway
      N. Y. C. 10054
   d. Mr. Charles Howe, Acme Pro.
      P.O. Box 675
      1234 S. e. Boulevard
      Gainesville, Flor. 32601
   e. Alex Goings, man.
      Pittfield Industries
      Longview, TEXAS 76450
   f. ATTENTION: G. Yancy (Mrs.)
      Police Academy
      1329 Tucker
      N. O., La. 3410-70122
   g. David and Mahenny
      Lawyers
      Dobbs Build.
      L.A. 94756
   h. Barry Fahwd
      Man., Peninsular, Ltd.
      Arabia

4. Write appropriate inside addresses and salutations to (a) a woman who has not specified her marital status; (b) an officer in the armed forces; (c) a professor at your school; (d) an assistant manager at your local bank; (e) a member of the clergy; (f) your congressperson.

5. Rewrite the following sentences to make them more personal.
   a. It becomes incumbent upon this office to cancel order #2394.
   b. Management has suggested the curtailment of parking privileges.
   c. ALL USERS OF HYDROPLEX: Desist from ordering replacement valves during the period of Dec. ?? -30.
   d. The request for a new catalog has been honored; it will be shipped to same address soon.
   e. Perseverance and attention to detail have made this writer important to company in-house work.
   f. The Director of Nurses hereby notifies staff that a general meeting will be held Monday afternoon at 3:00 p.m. sharp. Attendance is mandatory.
   g. Reports will be filed by appropriate personnel no later than the scheduled plans allow.

6. The following sentences taken from letters are discourteous, boastful, excessively humble, vague, or lacking the "you attitude." Rewrite them to correct those mistakes.
   a. Something is obviously wrong in your head office. They have once more sent me the wrong model number. Can they ever get things straight?
   b. My instructor wants me to do a term paper on safety regulations at a small factory. Since you are the manager of a small factory, send me all the information I need at once. My grade depends heavily on all this.
   c. It is apparent that you are in business to rip off the public.
   d. I was wondering if you could possibly see your way into sending me the local chapter president's name and address, if you have the time, that is.
   e. I have waited for my confirmation for two weeks now. Do you expect me to wait forever or can I get some action?

f. Although I have never attempted to catalog books before, and really do not know my way around the library, I would very much like to be considered ~~at some later date convenient to you~~ for ~~the~~ a part-time afternoon position. *I hope you will consider me.*

g. ~~It goes without saying that we~~ cannot honor your request. *we are sorry, but we*

h. May I take just a moment of your valuable time to point out that our hours for the next three weeks will change and ~~we trust and pray~~ that no one in your agency will be terribly inconvenienced by this. *We would like to notify you of our hours*

i. Your application has been received and will be kept on file for six months. ~~If we are interested in you, we~~ will notify you. ~~If you do not hear from us, please do not write us again. The soaring costs of correspondence and the large number of applicants make the burden of answering pointless letters extremely heavy.~~ *we will not do anything further notify you.*

j. My past performance as a medical technologist has left nothing to be desired. *A real body My career as a medical technologist I feel I accomplished a lot*

k. Credit means a lot to some people. ~~But obviously you do not care about yours. If you did, you would have sent us the $249.95 you rightfully owe us three months ago. What's wrong with you?~~ *send us $249.95 at your earliest convenience. We are notifying you to please remember credit is important.*

7. The following letter, filled with musty expressions and in old-fashioned language (legalese), buries key ideas. Rewrite and reorganize it to make it shorter, clearer, and more reader-centered.

Dear Ms. Granedi:

This is in response to your firm's letter of recent date inquiring about the types of additional services that may be available to business customers of the First National Bank of Bentonville. The question of a possible time frame for the implementation of said services was also raised in the aforementioned letter. Pursuant to these queries, the following answers, this office trusts, will prove helpful.

Please be advised that the Board of Directors at First National Bank has a continuing reputation for servicing the needs of the Bentonville community, especially the business community. For the last fifty years—half of a century—First National Bank has provided the funds necessary for the growth, success, and expansion of many local firms, yours included. This financial support has bestowed many opportunities on a multitude of business owners, residents of Bentonville, and even residents of surrounding local communities.

The Board is at this present writing currently deliberating, with its characteristic caution, over a variety of options suggested to us by our patrons, including your firm. These options, if the Board decides to act upon them, would enhance the business opportunities for financial transactions at First National Bank. Among the two options receiv-

```
ing attention by the Board at this point in time are the
creation of a branch office in the rapidly growing north
side of Bentonville. This area has many customers who rely
on the services of First National Bank. The Board may also
place a business loan department in the new branch.

If this office of the First National Bank of Bentonville
might be of further helpful assistance, please advise. Re-
member, banking with First National Bank is a community
privilege.

Soundly yours,


M. T. Watkins
Public Relations Director
```

8. Either individually or in a small group, write a business letter to one of the following individuals and submit an appropriate envelope with your letter.
   a. your mayor, asking for an appointment and explaining why you need one
   b. your college president, stressing the need for more parking spaces or for additional computer terminals in a library
   c. the local water department, asking for information about fluoride supplements
   d. an editor of a weekly magazine, asking permission to reprint an article in a school newspaper
   e. the author of an article you have read recently, telling why you agree or disagree with the views presented
   f. a disc jockey at a local radio station, asking for more songs by a certain group
   g. a computer dealer, asking about costs and availability of software packages and explaining your company's special needs

9. Rewrite the following letters, making them appropriate for a reader whose native language is not English. As you revise the letters, pay attention to the words, measurements, and sentence constructions you employ. Be sure to consider the reader's cultural traditions by omitting any cultural insensitivity.

```
   a. Dear Chum,

      Our stateside boss hit the ceiling earlier today when she
      learned that our sales quota for this quarter fell pre-
      cipitously short. Ouch! Were I in her spot, I would have
      exploded too. Numerous missives to her underlings warned
      them to get off the dime and on the stick, but they were
      oblivious to such. These are the breaks in our business,
      right? We can't all bat 1000.

      Let's hope that next quarter's sales take a turn for the
      best by 12-1-06. If they are as disastrous, we all may
```

be in hot water. Until then, we will have to watch our p's and q's around here. We're freezing here—20° today.

Cheers,

b. Dear Mr. Wong,

It's not every day that you have the chance to get in on the ground floor of a deal so good you can actually taste it. But Off-Wall Street Mutual can make the difference in your financial future. Give me a moment to convince you.

By becoming a member of our international investing group for just under $250, you can just about ensure your success. We know all the ins and outs of long-term investing and can save you a bundle. Our analysts are the hot shots of the business and always look long and hard for the most propitious business deals. The stocks we select with your interests in mind are as safe as a bank and not nearly so costly for you. Unlike any of your undertrained local agents, we can save you money by investing your money. We are penny pinchers with our clients' initial investments, but we are King Midas when it comes to transforming those investments into pure gold.

I am enclosing a brochure for you to study, and I really hope you will examine it carefully. You would be foolish to let a deal like Off-Wall Street Mutual pass you by. Go for it. Call me by 3:00 today.

Hurriedly,

c. Dear Mr. Bafaloukos,

My firm is taking a survey of businesses in your part of the world to see if there is any likelihood of getting you on board our international computer network and so I thought I would see if you might like to take the chance. In today's uncertain world, business events can change overnight and without the proper scoop you could be left out in the cold. We can alleviate that mess.

Not only do we interface with major exchanges all around the globe but we make sure that we get the facts to you pronto. We do not sit on our hands here at Intertel. Check out our website on who and how we serve and I have no doubts that you will e-mail or ring us up to find out about joining up.

```
One last point: Can you really risk going out on a limb
without first knowing that you have all the facts at your
fingertips about worldwide business events? Intertel is
there to save you.

Fondly,
```

10. Interview a student at your school or a co-worker who was born and raised in a non-English-speaking country about the proper etiquette in writing a business letter to someone from his or her country. Collaborate with that student to write a letter (for example, a sales letter or a letter asking for information) to an executive from that country.

11. In a letter to your instructor, describe the kinds of adaptations you had to make for the international reader you wrote to in Exercise 10.

12. Assume you work for a large international corporation that has just opened new offices in the following cities:
   a. Dar es Salaam, Tanzania
   b. Istanbul, Turkey
   c. Caracas, Venezuela
   d. Manila, Philippines
   e. Kyiv, Ukraine
   f. Beijing, China
   g. Warsaw, Poland
   h. Mexico City, Mexico
   i. Amman, Jordan
   j. Perth, Australia
   k. Lagos, Nigeria
   l. Prague, Czech Republic

   Using the resources mentioned on pages 167–168, write a short report on the main points of letter etiquette that your boss will have to observe in communicating with the non-native speaker of English who is the manager at one of the nine new offices.

13. As a collaborative project, team up with three other students in your class to write separate letters tailored to executives in each of the following cities:
   a. Riyadh, Saudi Arabia
   b. Tokyo, Japan
   c. Munich, Germany
   d. Nairobi, Kenya

   Assume you are selling the same product or service to each reader but you will have to adapt your communication to the culture represented by the reader.

   Turn in the four letters and explain to your instructor in an accompanying memo how you met the needs of those diverse cultural audiences in terms of style, tone, level of content, format, and sales tactics. Describe the research tools you used to find out about your reader's particular culture (and communication protocols) and how you benefited from using those sources.

Types of Business Letters

As we saw in Chapter 5, letters can be the lifeblood of any company or organization. In this chapter, you will learn to write a variety of letters for different workplace occasions. But regardless of your message, every letter you send needs to

- establish or maintain good rapport with the reader
- protect and promote your company's and your own professional image
- continue or increase business sales, relationships, and opportunities

Letters can help or hurt your company and your career. You want to write letters that lead to promotions, not reprimands.

Writing such letters can be challenging. Business correspondence places a great demand on your ability to formulate and organize a suitable message for your readers. You have to identify your audience, your purpose in writing to them, and their needs in wanting to hear from you. To communicate with them effectively, you have to determine

- what to say
- how to say it
- where to say it

The second and third points are just as important as the first. In fact, they may be even more crucial to your success as a letter writer. The tone and organization of your letter will determine how your message is received. In the process of drafting and revising your letter, consider whether your reader will bristle at or welcome the words you use. Review pages 155–160 on the "You Attitude." You will also have to select the best communication strategy (see pp. 206–207), which means taking into account where and how you give readers information. Some messages need to be direct and clear-cut; others require being indirect, holding off a bad news message until you prepare the reader for it. Remember also from Chapter 1 (pp. 8–18) that tone and audience play a crucial role in letter writing. Consider the following two versions of a letter that sends the same message:

Online Study Center

To expand your understanding of writing letters, take advantage of the ACE quizzes, sample documents, Web links, and exercises at college.hmco.com/pic/kolin8e

Insensitive Version
Your job is being outsourced next quarter. Corporate knows of your twelve years with the firm but downsizing mandates this decision. The firm will try to place you in another job, but expect no guarantees.

Respectful Version
Thank you for your twelve years of excellent work. We appreciate your many contributions. Unfortunately, downsizing means that your position, like several others in the department, will be outsourced. However, I will try to arrange a transfer for you. I may not succeed, but I know you will in your career because of your skills and dedication.

Clearly, the first letter has no respect for the reader's feelings or contributions, while the second is a model of respect and sincerity.

To be a skilled letter writer means that you will have to play several key roles, sometimes all at once. Among them are

- researcher
- problem solver
- decision maker
- honest and ethical spokesperson
- ambassador of goodwill

These are the assets of a valued employee and the characteristics that employers want in job applicants (see pp. 248–249). In fulfilling these roles through your business letters, you demonstrate that you can work well with people, are sensitive to their needs, and represent your company with integrity.

Keep in mind the audience for your letters is not just your customer. It includes the people you work for and with. See letter writing as fulfilling your responsibility to your employer as well. Although it is more likely that you will collaborate on longer documents, you still can expect to work with others on certain letters. For instance, you may be asked to confer with specialists in other divisions of your company to answer a complaint about one of your company's products. You may meet with individuals in your company's law or marketing department when drafting a sales letter. Possibly you may need to get your letter approved by your boss, who may edit your letter (see pp. 94–100) before you send it. Or you may be asked to write a letter for another person's signature, as in Figure 3.6.

This chapter gives you guidelines and strategies to help you become an effective letter writer. It will also show you how *not* to write business letters, an equally valuable lesson worth learning about the world of work.

■ Types of Letters

This chapter discusses the most common types of business correspondence that you will be expected to write on the job:

1. inquiry letters
2. special request letters
3. sales letters
4. customer relations letters

These letter types involve a variety of formats, writing strategies, and techniques. Business letters can be classified as **positive, neutral,** or **negative,** depending on their message and the anticipated reactions of your audience. Inquiry and special request letters are examples of neutral letters. They carry neither good nor bad news; they simply inform, responding to routine correspondence.

- Neutral letters request information about a product or service, place an order, or respond to some action or question.
- Sales letters promoting a product carry good news, according to the companies that spend millions of dollars a year preparing them.
- Customer relations letters can be **positive** (responding favorably to a writer's request or complaint) or **negative** (refusing a request, saying "No" to an adjustment, denying credit, seeking payment, critiquing poor performance, or announcing a product recall).

Inquiry Letters

An inquiry letter asks for information about a product, service, or procedure. Businesses frequently exchange such letters. As a customer, you, too, have occasion to ask in a letter about a special line of products, the price, the size, the color, and delivery arrangements. The clearer your letter, the quicker and more helpful your answers are likely to be.

Figure 6.1 illustrates a letter of inquiry from Michael Ortega to a real-estate office managing a large number of apartment complexes. Note that it follows these five rules for an effective inquiry letter:

- states exactly what information the writer wants
- indicates clearly why the writer must have the information
- keeps questions short and to the point
- specifies when the writer must have the information
- thanks the reader

Had Michael Ortega simply written the following very brief letter to Acme, he would not have received the information he needed about size, location, and price of apartments: "Please send me some information on housing in Roanoke. My family and I plan to move there soon."

Special Request Letters

Special request letters make a special demand, not a routine inquiry. For example, these letters can ask a company for information that you as a student or an employee will use in a report, an individual for a copy of a speech, or an agency for facts that your company needs to prepare a proposal or sell a product. The person or company being asked for help stands to gain no financial reward for supplying the information; the only reward is the goodwill that a response creates. Figure 6.2 contains a special request letter from a student asking for information to complete a report.

Figure 6.1   A letter of inquiry.

Michael Ortega
403 South Main Street Kingsport, TN 37721-0217
mortega@erols.com

March 1, 2007

Mr. Fred Stonehill
Property Manager
Acme Property Corporation
Main and Broadway
Roanoke, VA 24015-1100

Dear Mr. Stonehill:

States precise request

Please let me know if you will have any two-bedroom furnished apartments available for rent during the months of June, July, and August. I am willing to pay up to $650 a month plus utilities. My wife, one-year-old son, and I will be moving to Roanoke for the summer so I can take classes at Virginia Western Community College.

Explains need for information

Identifies area

If possible, we would like to have an apartment that is within two or three miles of the college. We do not have any pets.

Specifies exact date when a reply is needed

I would appreciate hearing from you within the next two weeks. My e-mail address is mortega@erols.com, or you can call me at home (606-555-8957) any evening from 6–10 p.m.

Offers to confer with reader

If you have any suitable vacancies, we would be happy to drive to Roanoke to look at them and give you a deposit to hold an apartment. Thanks for your help.

Sincerely yours,

Michael Ortega

Michael Ortega

A special request letter.   **Figure 6.2**

1505 West 19th Street
Syracuse, NY 13206

phone 315-555-1214

February 5, 2007

Ms. Sharonda Aimes-Worthington
Research Director
Creative Marketing Associates
198 Madison Ave.
New York, NY 10016-0092

Dear Ms. Aimes-Worthington:

I am a junior at Monroe College in Syracuse, and am writing a report on the topic "Internet Marketing Strategies for the Finger Lakes Region of New York" for my Marketing 340 class. Several of my professors have spoken very highly of Creative Marketing Associates, and from my own research I have learned a great deal from reading your article on Web designs and local economies that you posted on your website four months ago.

Given your extensive experience in using the Internet to promote regional businesses and tourism, I would be most grateful if you would share your responses to the following three questions with me:

1. What have been the most effective ways to design websites for a regional marketplace such as the Finger Lakes?

2. How can area chambers of commerce best provide links to benefit both the local municipalities and businesses in the Finger Lakes area?

3. Which other regional area do you see having the same or very similar marketing goals and challenges as the Finger Lakes?

jkawatsu@webnet.com

Explains reason for letter

Proves writer has done research

Acknowledges reader's expertise

Lists specific questions on the topic

Continued

Figure 6.2   (Continued)

Page 2

As an incentive, offers to share report

Your answers to the above questions would make my report much more authoritative and useful. I would be happy to send you a copy and will, of course, cite you and Creative Marketing Associates in my work.

Indicates when needed

Because my report is due by April 2, I would deeply appreciate having your answers within the next month so that I can include them. Would you kindly send your responses, or any questions you may have, to my e-mail address, *jkawatsu@webnet.com*. Many thanks for your help.

Makes contact easy through e-mail

Sincerely yours,

Julie Kawatsu

Julie Kawatsu

Because your reader is not obliged to respond to your letter, the way you present yourself and your request is crucial to your success. "Why should I help?" is a common question any reader might have. Therefore, try to anticipate and remove any barriers to getting his or her help.

- Convince your reader that you are motivated and hard-working and are not simply asking him or her to research and write your report for you. Asking for information for a report is quite different from asking the reader to research and organize your work for you.
- Make sure what you are asking for is not already (and easily) available in a textbook.
- Stress your industry by showing the reader you have done your homework— for example, by conducting a Web search, reading relevant literature, conferring with an instructor or specialist with whom you work.

To build goodwill and increase the chances that your reader will respond, you must be persuasive. Saying "please" and "thank you" will help you get the information you want. Also offer to share a copy of your report with the reader as a professional courtesy. If the reader supplies you with information for a report you are writing for class, ask for his or her approval before sharing the information with classmates.

Make your request clear and easy to answer. Supply readers with an addressed, postage-paid envelope, an e-mail address, and fax and telephone numbers in case they have questions. But don't ask a company to fax a long document to you. It is discourteous to ask someone else to pay the fax charges for something you need.

When writing a special request letter, follow these eight points:

1. Make sure you address your letter to the right person.
2. State who you are and why you are writing—student researching a paper, employee compiling information for a report, and so on.
3. Indicate clearly your reason for requesting the information. Mention any individuals who may have referred you to write for help and information.
4. Make your questions easy to answer. List, number, and separate them clearly. Keep them to three or four at most.
5. Specify exactly when you need the information. Allow sufficient time—at least three weeks. Be reasonable; don't ask for the impossible.
6. As an incentive for the reader to reply, offer to forward a copy of your report, paper, or survey in gratitude for the help you were given.
7. If you want to reprint or publish the materials you ask for, indicate that you will secure whatever permissions are necessary. State that you will keep the information confidential, if that is appropriate.
8. End by thanking the reader for helping.

Note how Figure 6.2 adheres to these guidelines.

Sales Letters: Some Preliminary Guidelines

A sales letter is written to persuade the reader to buy a product, try a service, support some cause, or participate in some activity. A sales letter can also serve as a method of introducing yourself to potential customers. No matter what profession you have chosen, knowing how to write a sales letter is an invaluable skill. There will always be times when you have to sell a product, a service, an idea, a point of view, or yourself!

You have undoubtedly received numerous sales letters from military recruiters, large companies, local merchants, charitable organizations, and campus groups. Websites (discussed in Chapter 12) and e-mail constitute a special type of sales announcement.

Because of the great volume of sales letters in the business world, the ones you write face a lot of competition. To write an effective sales letter that stands out and does its job, you have to do the following:

1. **Identify and limit your audience.** Determine how many people are in your audience. Sometimes a sales letter is written to just one person (Figures 6.3 and 6.4) or to hundreds of readers (Figure 6.5). However, Cory Soufas's sales letter in Figure 6.5 could also be addressed personally to individual readers if Workwell Software purchased a targeted audience mailing list.

2. **Use reader psychology.** Think like your reader and ask: "What am I trying to do for the customer?" Ask that question before you begin writing and you will be using effective reader psychology. Appeal to readers' health, security, convenience, comfort, or pocketbooks by focusing on the right issues (for instance, inform buyers that your product research involves no animal testing). Patrice St. Jacques appeals to the reader's ethnic and community values in Figure 6.4.

Figure 6.3   A sales letter soliciting a financial contribution.

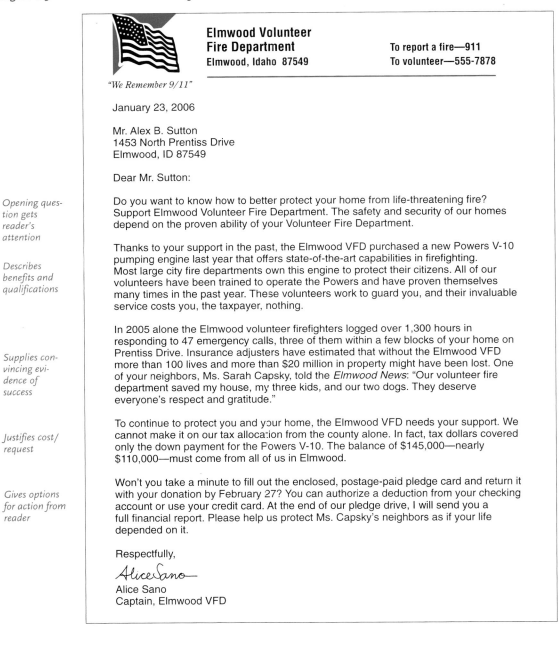

Elmwood Volunteer
Fire Department
Elmwood, Idaho 87549

To report a fire—911
To volunteer—555-7878

"We Remember 9/11"

January 23, 2006

Mr. Alex B. Sutton
1453 North Prentiss Drive
Elmwood, ID 87549

Dear Mr. Sutton:

Opening question gets reader's attention

Do you want to know how to better protect your home from life-threatening fire? Support Elmwood Volunteer Fire Department. The safety and security of our homes depend on the proven ability of your Volunteer Fire Department.

Describes benefits and qualifications

Thanks to your support in the past, the Elmwood VFD purchased a new Powers V-10 pumping engine last year that offers state-of-the-art capabilities in firefighting. Most large city fire departments own this engine to protect their citizens. All of our volunteers have been trained to operate the Powers and have proven themselves many times in the past year. These volunteers work to guard you, and their invaluable service costs you, the taxpayer, nothing.

Supplies convincing evidence of success

In 2005 alone the Elmwood volunteer firefighters logged over 1,300 hours in responding to 47 emergency calls, three of them within a few blocks of your home on Prentiss Drive. Insurance adjusters have estimated that without the Elmwood VFD more than 100 lives and more than $20 million in property might have been lost. One of your neighbors, Ms. Sarah Capsky, told the *Elmwood News*: "Our volunteer fire department saved my house, my three kids, and our two dogs. They deserve everyone's respect and gratitude."

Justifies cost/request

To continue to protect you and your home, the Elmwood VFD needs your support. We cannot make it on our tax allocation from the county alone. In fact, tax dollars covered only the down payment for the Powers V-10. The balance of $145,000—nearly $110,000—must come from all of us in Elmwood.

Gives options for action from reader

Won't you take a minute to fill out the enclosed, postage-paid pledge card and return it with your donation by February 27? You can authorize a deduction from your checking account or use your credit card. At the end of our pledge drive, I will send you a full financial report. Please help us protect Ms. Capsky's neighbors as if your life depended on it.

Respectfully,

Alice Sano

Alice Sano
Captain, Elmwood VFD

3. Don't boast or be a bore. Save elaborate explanations about a product for after the sale. Put detailed documentation in instruction booklets and warranties. Further, do not turn your sales letter into a glowing commendation of your company, or yourself.

4. Use words that appeal to the reader's senses. Use concrete words instead of abstract, vague ones. Choose verbs that are colorful, that put the reader in the picture, so to speak. You will have a greater chance of selling readers if they can hear, see, taste, or touch your product in their mind. That way they can visualize themselves buying or using your product or service. Note how Patrice St. Jacques fills the sales letter in Figure 6.4 with Caribbean sights, sounds, and tastes to appeal to Etienne Abernathy and his company.

5. Be ethical. Avoid untruths, insincere flattery, exaggerations, false comparisons, and unsupported generalizations. Honesty is the best way to make a sale. Never make false claims about the cost, safety, or adaptability of your product or service. You could be prosecuted for mail fraud or sued for misrepresentation. (Review pp. 26–33 in Chapter 1.)

The Four A's of Sales Letters

Successful sales letters follow a time-honored and workable plan; each sales letter follows what can be called the four A's:

1. It gets the reader's *attention.*
2. It highlights the product's *appeal.*
3. It shows the customer the product's *application.*
4. It ends with a specific request for *action.*

Those four goals can be achieved in fewer than four or five paragraphs. Look at Figure 6.5, a one-page letter in which those four parts are labeled. Holding a sales letter down to one page or less will keep the reader's attention. Television commercials and print magazine and webzine ads provide useful models of the fourfold approach to a customer. The next time you see one of these variations of the sales letter, try to identify the four A's.

Getting the Reader's Attention

Your opening sentence is crucial. That first sentence is bait on a hook. If you lose readers there, you will have lost them forever. A typical television commercial has about two to five seconds to catch the viewers' attention and prompt them to keep watching. Keep your opening short, one or two sentences at most. Show a reader how your product or service will make his or her life or job easier, save money, or make him or her safer or happier.

The following six techniques are a few of the many interest-grabbing ways to begin a sales letter. Adapt these techniques to your product or service.

1. Ask a question. Ask a question that your reader(s) will want to see answered. Look, for example, at the opening questions in Figures 6.3 and 6.5. Avoid such general

Figure 6.4   A sales letter that appeals to a specific international audience.

Distinctive, functional letterhead

ISLAND JACQUES
4700 Cyprus Avenue
Philadelphia, PA 19172

6 April 2007

Mr. Etienne Abernathy, President
Seagrove Enterprises
1800 S. Port Haven Road
Philadelphia, PA 19103-1800

Dear Mr. Abernathy:

Compliments reader on award

Congratulations on winning the Hanover Award for Community Service. We in the Port Haven area are proud that a business with Caribbean roots has received such a distinguished honor.

Appeals to reader's ethnic heritage

To celebrate your and Seagrove's success, as well as all your business entertaining needs (annual banquet, monthly meetings, etc.), I invite you to Island Jacques. We are a family-owned business that for 30 years has offered Philadelphia residents the finest Caribbean atmosphere and food west of the Islands. Our black pepper shrimp, reggae or mango chicken, and steak St. Lucie—plus our irresistible beef and pork jerk—are the talk from here to Kingston. You and your guests can also savor our original Caribbean art and enjoy our steel drum music.

Features flexible options to make dining easy, convenient, and enjoyable

Island Jacques can offer Seagrove a variety of dining options; with separate rooms, we are small enough for an intimate party of 4 yet large enough to accommodate a group of 250. We can do early lunches or late dinners, depending on your schedule. And we even cater, if that's your style. Our chefs—Diana Maurier and Emile Danticat—will prepare a special calypso menu just for you. Also a benefit, our prices are generously competitive for the Philadelphia area.

www.islandjacques.netdoor.com
856-555-3295

Continued

Page 2

Please call me soon so you can see Island Jacques's unique hospitality. For your convenience, I am enclosing a copy of this week's menu delights. Check out our website, too, for a taste of Caribbean sound. We would love to feature Seagrove as Island Jacques's "Guest of the Week"!

Gives reader incentive to act soon

Stay Cool, Mon

Patrice St Jacques

Patrice St. Jacques
Manager

questions as "Are you happy?" or "Would you like to make money?" Use more specific questions with concrete language. An ad for Air Force Reserve Nursing asks nurses, "Are you looking for something 30,000 feet out of the ordinary?" Similarly, a sales letter beginning with "Could you use $500?" zeroes in on one particular desire of the reader.

2. Use a how-to statement. This is one of the most frequently used openers in a sales letter. Here are some effective how-to statements: "We can show you how to increase your plant growth up to 91%." "Here is how to save $500 on your next vacation." "This is how to provide nourishing lunches for less than eighty cents a person." Note that the opening sentence of Cory Soufas's sales letter in Figure 6.5 combines both a how-to and a question approach.

3. Compliment your reader. Appeal to the reader's ego. But remember that readers are not naive; they will be suspicious of false praise. Patrice St. Jacques opens the sales letter in Figure 6.4 with fitting and legitimate praise.

4. Offer a gift. Often you can lure readers further into your letter by telling them they can save money or get a second product free or at half price. One realtor tempts customers to see lots for sale with, "Enclosed is a coupon worth $50 in gas after you tour Deer Run Trails Estates."

5. Introduce a comparison. Compare your product or service with conventional or standard products or procedures. For instance, a clothing firm told police officers that if they purchased a particular jacket, they were really getting three coats in one, because the product had a lining for winter and a covering used for greater visibility at night.

6. Announce a change. Link your sales offer to a current event that will positively affect your prospective buyer. When the sales tax on SUVs was about to be increased, a dealer sent sales letters to potential buyers, alerting them to the implications of delaying their purchase: "The sales tax on new cars will jump a WHOPPING 4 percent effective next month. You may not think that 4 percent will mean that much money, but on a new 2007 model that increase could cost you an extra $1,500." The sales letter continued: "Couldn't you use that money for something else, say, those extras you've always wanted, like a DVD player or an extended warranty?"

Highlighting the Product's Appeal

Once you have aroused your reader's attention, introduce your product or service. Make it so attractive, so necessary, and so profitable that the reader will want to buy or use the product or service. Appeal to the reader's intellect or emotions (or both) while introducing the product. In Figure 6.4 the Island Jacques letter zeroes in on the reader's ethnic pride and heritage. In Figure 6.5 Workwell Software's mass mailing letter to office managers appeals to their desire for greater productivity and improved safety. In Figure 6.3 the captain of a volunteer fire department urges citizens to help pay for a piece of fire equipment that might save their lives and property. Here is an emotional appeal by the Gulf Stream Fruit Company:

> Can you, when you bite into an orange, tell where it was grown? If it tastes better than any you have ever eaten . . . full of rich, golden flavor, brimming with juice, sparkling with sunshine . . . then you know it was grown here in our famous Indian River Valley where we have handpicked it, at the very peak of its flavor, just for your order.[1]

Showing the Customer the Product's Application

In the third part of your sales letter supply evidence of the value of what you are selling. You have to be careful, though, that you do not overwhelm readers with facts, statistics, detailed mechanical descriptions, or elaborate arguments. The emphasis is still on the reader's use of the product and not on the company that manufactures or sells it. Shifting the focus from your company to the prospective customer is essential to any sale.

1. Supply the right evidence. What evidence best convinces readers about a product's or service's appeal?

- **Descriptions** that emphasize state-of-the-art design and construction, efficiency, convenience, usefulness, and economy.
- **Special features** or changes that make your product or service more attractive. A greenhouse manufacturer stressed that in addition to using its structure just for growing plants, customers would also find it a "perfect sun room enclosure for year-round 'outdoor' activities, gardening, or leisure health spa."

---

[1]From "Gifts from Gulf Stream," Gulf Stream Fruit Company, Ft. Lauderdale, Fla. Reprinted by permission.

A sales letter sent to a business reader.   Figure 6.5

Workwell Software
3700 Stewart Avenue   Chicago IL 60637-2210
Phone: (312) 555-3720   **Fax:** (312) 555-7601   **E-mail:** sales@workwell.com
http://www.workwell.com

October 1, 2007

Dear Office Manager:

Do you know how much money your company loses from repetitive strain injury? Each year employers spend millions of dollars on employee insurance claims and decreased productivity because of back pains, fatigue, eye strain, and carpal tunnel syndrome.

Gets reader's attention with a question

Workwell can solve your problems with its easy-to-use Exercise Program Software that will automatically monitor the time employees spend at their computers and also measure keyboard activity. After each hour (or the specified number of keystrokes), **Workwell Software** will take your employees through a series of exercises to prevent carpal tunnel syndrome and strains and assure you and them of a safer workplace.

Emphasizes the product's appeal

Workwell's Exercise Program Software will not interfere with busy schedules. Developed by a leading orthopedic surgeon, Dr. Anna Chang, each of the 27 exercises is demonstrated on screen with audio instructions that take less than 3 minutes and can be performed at the employee's workstation.

Shows specific application of the product

You can protect your employees for a fraction of the money you will spend on claims. For $1,499.00, you can provide a networked version of this valuable software to all of your employees. And if you place your order within the next week, **Workwell** will supply you with free upgrades for a year.

Links costs to benefits

To make sure your employees are at the peak of their efficiency in a safe work environment, please call us at 1-800-555-WELL or contact us at **http://www.workwell.com** to order your **Workwell Software** today.

Ends with a call for action

Thank you,

Cory Soufas

Cory Soufas
Sales Manager

- **Testimonials,** or endorsements, from previous customers as well as from specialists. In Figure 6.3 Captain Sano persuasively uses Ms. Capsky's endorsement, and Cory Soufas in Figure 6.5 cites "a leading orthopedic surgeon" by name.
- **Guarantees, warranties, services, or special considerations** that will make your customer's life easier or happier—loaner cars, free home deliveries, ten-day trial period, a year's free Internet access or upgrades, as in Figure 6.5.

2. Do I mention costs? You may be obligated to mention costs in your letter. But postpone them until the reader has been shown how appealing and valuable your product is. Readers will react more favorably to costs after they have seen the reasons why the product or service is useful. Of course, if price is a key selling point, mention it early in the letter. As a general rule, however, do not bluntly state the cost. Note how unobtrusively Patrice St. Jacques handles price at the end of paragraph 3 in Figure 6.4.

Relate prices, charges, or fees to the benefits provided by the services or products to which they apply. A dealer who installs steel shutters did not tell readers the exact price of the product but indicated that they will save money by buying it: "Virtually maintenance free, your Reel Shutters also offer substantial savings in energy costs by reducing your loss through radiation by as much as 65% . . . and that lowers your utility bills by 35%."

Ending with a Specific Request for Action

The last section of your letter is vital. If the reader ignores your request for action, your letter has been written in vain. Tell readers exactly what you want them to do by when. Make it easy for them to

- authorize a deduction (as in Figure 6.3)
- come into your store or business (as in Figure 6.4)
- take a test drive
- participate in a meeting
- fill out a pledge card (as in Figure 6.3)
- respond via the Internet (as in Figure 6.5)
- sign an order blank
- return a form by providing a stamped and addressed envelope

As with price, link the benefits the customers will receive to their responses. "Respond and be rewarded" is the basic message of the last section of your letter. Note that in Figure 6.5 the call to action is made in the last two paragraphs, and urges the reader to act immediately in order to take advantage of the free upgrades and maintenance.

■ Customer Relations Letters

Much business correspondence deals explicitly with establishing and maintaining friendly working relations. Such correspondence, known as **customer relations letters,** sends readers good news or bad news, acceptances or refusals. Good news tells customers that

- you have the product or service they want at a reasonable price
- you agree with them about a problem they brought to your attention
- you are solving their problem exactly the way they want
- you are approving their loan
- you are grateful to them for their business

Thank-you letters, congratulations letters, and adjustment letters saying "Yes" with the above messages are all examples of good news messages.

Bad news messages, however, inform readers that

- you do not like their work or the equipment they sold you
- you do not have the equipment or service they want or you cannot provide it at the price they want to pay
- you are rejecting a proposal they offered
- you are denying someone further use of a facility
- you cannot refund their purchase price or perform a service again as they requested
- you are raising their rent or not renewing their lease
- you want them to pay what they owe you now
- you are downsizing or moving and cannot continue to provide a service

Bad news messages often come to readers through complaint letters, adjustment letters that say "No," and collection letters.

Diplomacy and Reader Psychology

Writing effective customer relations letters requires skill in human relations and reader psychology. Regardless of the news—good or bad—you need to be a diplomatic and persuasive writer. In fact, customer relations letters, like other types of letters, call upon your most effective skills in persuasion (see pp. 23–25). To be at your best persuasively, do some research about your readers—their business needs, their schedules, areas of authority in the chain of command, and even their grievances (if applicable).

Customer relations letters show how you and your company regard the people with whom you do business. The letters should reveal your sensitivity to their needs. The first lesson to learn is that you cannot look at your letter only from your (the writer's) perspective. You have to see the letter from the reader's perspective and anticipate the reader's needs and reactions. What will be their view of you, the writer, and your company?

The Customers Always Write

As you read this section on customer relations letters, keep in mind the two basic principles captured in the pun "the customers always write."

1. Customers will write about how they would like to be or have been treated—to thank, to complain, to request an explanation.
2. Customers have certain rights that you must respect in your correspondence with them. They deserve a prompt and courteous reply, whether or not they

are correct. If you refuse their request, they deserve to know why; if they owe you money, you should give them an opportunity to explain and a chance, up to a point, to set up a payment schedule. Always be ethical in responding—be fair, honest, undeniably legal, and professional. (Review pp. 26–33.)

Planning Your Customer Relations Letters

Whether you are sending good news or bad, determine what to say and how to say it. Construct your letter as if you were building a house—step by step—from laying the foundation (e.g., reader's needs, your purpose, etc.) to painting the trim (polishing and editing). Do some preliminary planning. Outline for a few minutes to find your ideas. Your outline does not have to be formal or even neatly written—a few scribbles sometimes will be enough to get you started. By outlining, you will save (not lose) time, because you can identify your main points, exclude unnecessary or unimportant ones, and avoid the risk of forgetting something essential.

Fortified by your outline, you will feel more confident as you draft your letter. In the process of drafting and revising that letter, consider whether your reader will bristle at or accept the words you use. Your choice of words will determine the success or failure of your letter. You might want to review the discussions on tone and the "you attitude" (pp. 155–160).

Being Direct or Indirect

Your message, tone, and knowledge of your reader are essential ingredients in a successful customer relations letter. But success also involves knowing where and how to start, and, especially, where to present your main point. Not every customer relations letter starts by giving the reader the writer's main point, judgment, conclusion, or reaction. *Where you place your main idea is determined by the type of letter you are writing.* Good news messages require one tactic; bad news, another.

Good News Messages

If you are writing a good news letter, use the direct approach. Start your letter with the welcome, pleasant news that the reader wants to hear. Don't postpone the opportunity to put your reader in the right frame of mind. Then provide any relevant supporting details, explanations, or commentary. Being direct is advantageous when you have good news to convey.

Bad News Messages

If you have bad news to report, do *not* open your letter with it. Be indirect. Prepare your reader for the bad news; keep the tension level down. If you throw the bad news at your reader right away, you jeopardize the goodwill you want to create and sustain. Consider how you would react to a letter that begins with these slaps:

- Your account is in error.
- Your order cannot be filled.

- Your application for a loan has been denied.
- It is our unfortunate duty to report . . .

Having been denied, disappointed, or even offended in the first sentence or paragraph, the reader is not likely to give you his or her attentive cooperation thereafter.

Notice how A. J. Griffin's bad news letter in Figure 6.6 (p. 208) curtly starts off with the bad news of a rent increase. Receiving such a letter, the owner of Flowers by Dan certainly could not be blamed for looking for a new place of business. Or if he did pay the increase, Griffin's letter would hardly ensure that Mr. Sobol would remain a happy tenant. Griffin was too direct when he should have been diplomatically indirect. He did not consider his reader's reaction; all he was concerned about was delivering his message.

Compare the curt version of Griffin's letter in Figure 6.6 with his revised message in Figure 6.7 (p. 209). In the revised version, Griffin begins tactfully with pleasant, positive words designed to put his reader in a good frame of mind about the management of River Road Mall. Then Griffin gives some background information that the owner of Flowers by Dan can relate to. A business person himself, Mr. Sobol doubtless has experienced some recent increases in his own costs. Griffin makes one more attempt to encourage Sobol to recall his good feelings about the Mall—last year they did not raise rents—before introducing the bad news of a rent increase.

Even after giving the bad news, Griffin softens the blow by saying that the Mall knows it is bad news. Griffin's tactic here is to defuse some of the anger that Sobol will inevitably feel. In fact, Griffin words the bad news so that the tenant sees the Mall as acting in the best interest of his flower shop. The Mall will not lower or compromise on the services that the tenant has enjoyed and profited from in the past. Griffin then ends on a positive, upbeat note: a prosperous future for Flowers by Dan.

You will learn more strategies about conveying bad news messages on pages 222–228.

Follow-Up Letters

A follow-up letter is sent by a company after a sale to thank the customer for buying a product or using a service and to encourage the customer to buy more products and services in the future. A follow-up letter is a combination thank-you note and sales letter that resells the reader. The letter in Figure 6.8 is sent to customers soon after they have purchased an appliance and offers them the option of a continued maintenance policy. The letter in Figure 6.9 shows how an income tax preparation service attempts to obtain repeat business. Both letters

1. begin with a brief and sincere expression of gratitude
2. discuss the benefits (advantages) already known to the customer and then transfer the company's dedication to the customer from the product or service to a new or continuing sales area
3. end with a specific request for future business

Figure 6.6   An ineffective bad news letter.

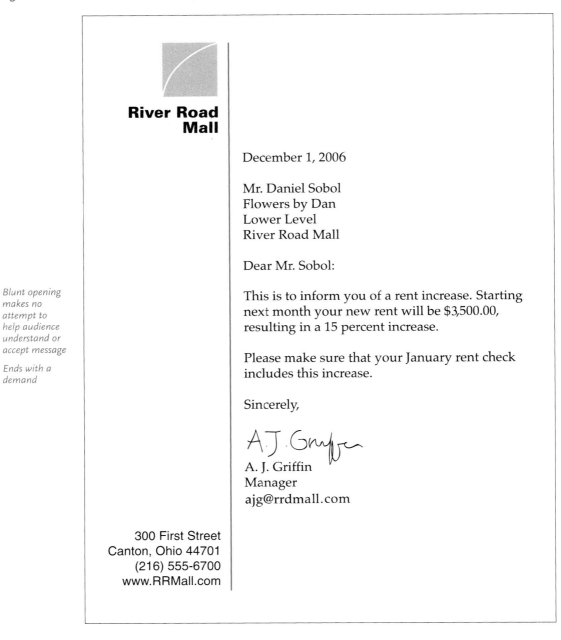

River Road Mall

December 1, 2006

Mr. Daniel Sobol
Flowers by Dan
Lower Level
River Road Mall

Dear Mr. Sobol:

Blunt opening makes no attempt to help audience understand or accept message

This is to inform you of a rent increase. Starting next month your new rent will be $3,500.00, resulting in a 15 percent increase.

Ends with a demand

Please make sure that your January rent check includes this increase.

Sincerely,

A. J. Griffin
Manager
ajg@rrdmall.com

300 First Street
Canton, Ohio 44701
(216) 555-6700
www.RRMall.com

A diplomatic revision of the bad news letter in Figure 6.6.   Figure 6.7

River Road Mall

December 1, 2006

Mr. Daniel Sobol
Flowers by Dan
Lower Level
River Road Mall

Dear Mr. Sobol:

It has been a pleasure to have you as a tenant at the Mall for the past two years, and we look forward to serving you in the future.

Opens with positive association

Over these last two years we have experienced a dramatic increase in costs at River Road Mall for security, maintenance, landscaping, pest control, utilities, insurance, and taxes. Last year we absorbed those increases and so did not have to raise your rent. We wish we could do it again but, unfortunately, we must increase your rent by 15 percent, to $3,500.00, effective January 1.

Prepares reader for bad news to follow

States bad news in most concise, up-beat way

Although no one likes a rent increase, we know that you do not want us to compromise on the quality of service that you and your customers expect and deserve here at River Road Mall.

Links bad news to reader benefits

Please let us know how we can assist you in the future. We wish you a very successful and profitable 2007. If you have any questions, please call or visit my office.

Does not apologize but ends with respectful tone

Cordially,

A.J. Griffin

A. J. Griffin
Manager
ajg@rrdmall.com

300 First Street
Canton, Ohio 44701
(216) 555-6700
www.RRMall.com

Occasionally, a follow-up letter is sent to a good customer who, for some reason, has stopped doing business with the company. Such a follow-up letter should try to find out why the customer has stopped doing business and to persuade that customer to resume business dealings. Study the letter in Figure 6.10, in which Jim Margolis first politely inquires whether Mr. Janeck has experienced a problem and then urges him to come back to the store.

Complaint Letters

Each of us, either as customers or business people, at some time has been frustrated by a defective product, delayed or wrong shipment, unavailable products or parts, inadequate or rude service, or incorrect billing. When we get no satisfaction from calling an 800 number and are routed through a series of menu options, our frustration level goes up. Usually our first response is to write a letter dripping with juicy insults. But a hate letter, like a piece of flaming e-mail (see p. 137), rarely gets positive results. You never know when the company you are attacking may be one of your firm's clients or a prospective employer of yours. A nasty letter will hurt you and give an unfavorable image of your company. In the world of business you do not want to burn bridges.

Reasons for Writing a Complaint Letter

A complaint letter is written for more reasons than just blowing off steam. You want some specific action taken. Register your complaint courteously and tolerantly. Companies want to be fair to you to keep you as a satisfied customer and to correct defective products so that other customers will not be inconvenienced. A complaint letter also gives you and your company a written record (always make a copy) that you reported a problem and that you are notifying the reader about it. Never delay in sending your letter. A product or service warranty or guarantee could expire in the meantime.

An effective complaint letter can be written by an individual consumer or by a company. Figure 6.11 shows Michael Trigg's complaint about a defective fishing reel; Figure 6.12 expresses a restaurant's dissatisfaction with an industrial dishwasher.

Establishing the Right Tone

By adopting the right tone, you increase your chances of getting what you want. A complaint letter is a delicate one to write. Avoid the following:

- name calling
- sarcasm
- insults
- threats
- anger
- unflattering clip art
- intimidating type fonts (e.g., all capital letters)

A follow-up letter to sell a maintenance agreement.   Figure 6.8

Dynamic Appliance Company

100 Walden Parkway
Denver, Colorado 80203-4296
(303) 555-9681
http://www.dac.com

August 9, 2007

Mr. John H. Abbott
3715 Mayview Drive
Cottage Grove, MN 53261-1852

Dear Mr. Abbott:

We are delighted that you have purchased a Dynamic appliance. To help ensure your satisfaction, this appliance is backed by a Dynamic warranty. At the same time, we realize that you bought the appliance to serve you not just for the period covered by the warranty but for many years to come. That's why purchasing a Dynamic Maintenance Agreement now is one of the wisest investments you can make.

A Dynamic Maintenance Agreement provides savings benefits many cost-conscious customers want and look for today. It helps extend the life of your appliance through an annual, on-request maintenance check-up. And if you need service, it gives you as many service calls as necessary for repairs due to normal use—at no extra charge.

All this coverage is now available at a special introductory price of $55 a year. This price includes the warranty coverage you have remaining.

Please act now by visiting our website to sign up for your Dynamic Maintenance Agreement.

Sincerely,

Carole Morrow-Ricks

Carole Morrow-Ricks
Sales Representative

Compliments and persuades reader to protect investment

Explains benefits

Makes warranty cost attractive

Call to action

Figure 6.9   A follow-up letter to encourage repeat business.

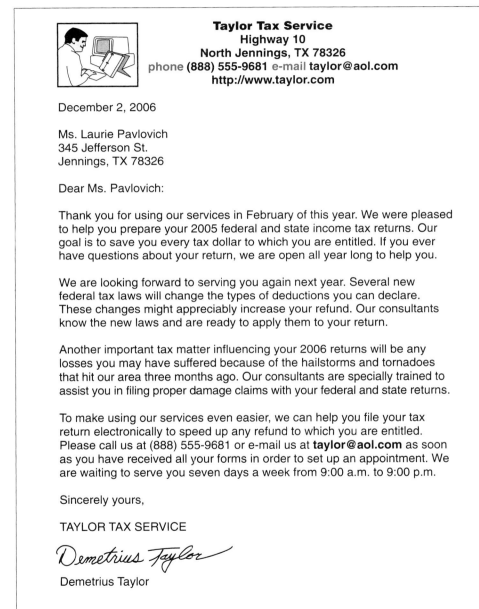

Taylor Tax Service
Highway 10
North Jennings, TX 78326
phone **(888) 555-9681** e-mail **taylor@aol.com**
http://www.taylor.com

December 2, 2006

Ms. Laurie Pavlovich
345 Jefferson St.
Jennings, TX 78326

Dear Ms. Pavlovich:

Thank you for using our services in February of this year. We were pleased to help you prepare your 2005 federal and state income tax returns. Our goal is to save you every tax dollar to which you are entitled. If you ever have questions about your return, we are open all year long to help you.

We are looking forward to serving you again next year. Several new federal tax laws will change the types of deductions you can declare. These changes might appreciably increase your refund. Our consultants know the new laws and are ready to apply them to your return.

Another important tax matter influencing your 2006 returns will be any losses you may have suffered because of the hailstorms and tornadoes that hit our area three months ago. Our consultants are specially trained to assist you in filing proper damage claims with your federal and state returns.

To make using our services even easier, we can help you file your tax return electronically to speed up any refund to which you are entitled. Please call us at (888) 555-9681 or e-mail us at **taylor@aol.com** as soon as you have received all your forms in order to set up an appointment. We are waiting to serve you seven days a week from 9:00 a.m. to 9:00 p.m.

Sincerely yours,

TAYLOR TAX SERVICE

Demetrius Taylor

Demetrius Taylor

Links business goal to customer advantage

Stresses reasons/benefits for customer to return for service

Makes it easy and profitable for customer to act soon

Ends with commitment to customer convenience

A follow-up letter to maintain customer goodwill.   **Figure 6.10**

BROADWAY CLEANERS

April 6, 2007

Mr. Edward Janeck
34 Brompton Lane, Apt. 13
Baltimore, MD 21227-0102

Dear Mr. Janeck:

Thank you for allowing us to take care of your cleaning needs for more than three years now. It has been our pleasure to see you in the store each week and to clean your shirts, slacks, and coats to your satisfaction. Since you have not come in during the last month, we are concerned that in some way we may have disappointed you. We hope not, because you are a valuable customer whose goodwill we do not want to lose.

If there is something wrong, please tell us about it. We welcome any suggestions on how we can serve you better. Our goal is to have a spotless reputation in the eyes of our customers.

The next time you need your garments cleaned, won't you please bring them to us, along with the enclosed coupon worth $10 off your next bill? We look forward to seeing you again—soon.

Cordially,

Jim Margolis

Jim Margolis, Manager

Encl. coupon

Thanks customer and asks for feedback

Expresses concern

Shows goodwill

Offers incentive to resume business dealings

Broadway at Davis Drive   Baltimore, Maryland 21228-6210
(443) 555-1962   broadclean@metdoor.com

Tech Note

Help in Registering Complaints

Several organizations can assist you when you have a problem with a particular company or agency. These organizations will give you valuable advice on how to proceed with your complaint.

- The Better Business Bureau: *http://www.bbb.org/complaints/file.html*
- U.S. Chamber of Commerce: *http://www.uschamber.org*
- International Chamber of Commerce—World Business Organization: *http://www.iccwbo.org*

How you sound is as important as what you say. The better you control your emotions, the more effective your letter will be. The "you attitude" is especially important to maintain the reader's goodwill. Remember that you can disagree without being disagreeable. Be rational, not hostile. Project yourself and your company as professional, fair, and sincere. You might want to write an angry letter—to let off steam—but then tear it up, replacing all the heat with courteous and diplomatic language. See how Figures 6.11 and 6.12 politely make their case.

Writing an Effective Complaint Letter
Your complaint letter needs to answer these questions:

- What's wrong?
- What do you want done?
- Why is your request justified?
- When do you need it?

To increase your chances of receiving a speedy settlement, follow these five steps in writing your letter of complaint. They will help you build your case and answer the key questions.

1. Begin with a detailed description of the product or service. In your opening, give the appropriate model and serial numbers, size, quantity, color, and cost. Specify check and invoice numbers. Indicate when and where (specific address) and how (through a vendor, the Internet, at a store) you purchased it and also the remaining warranty. If you are returning the product to the company, note how you are sending it—U.S. mail, overnight delivery service, through a sales representative, or another way. If you are complaining about a service, give the name of the company, the date of the service, the personnel providing it, and their exact duties.

2. State exactly what is wrong with the product or service. Precise information will enable the reader to understand and act on your complaint.

- How many times did the machine work before it stopped?
- What parts were malfunctioning?

17 Westwood Drive

Magnolia, MA 02171

mtrigg@roof.com

October 10, 2007

Mr. Ralph Montoya
Customer Relations Department
Smith Sports Equipment
P.O. Box 1014
Tulsa, OK 74109-1014

Dear Mr. Montoya:

On September 21, 2007, I purchased a Smith reel, model 191, at the Uni-Mart Store on Marsh Avenue in Magnolia. The reel sold for $84.95 plus tax. The reel is not working effectively, and I am returning it to you under separate cover by first-class mail.

I had made no more than five casts with the reel when it began to malfunction. The button that releases the spool and allows the line to cast will not spring back into position after casting. In addition, the gears make a grinding noise when I try to retrieve the line. Because of these problems, I was unable to continue my participation in the Gloucester Fishing Tournament last week.

I am requesting that a new reel be sent to me free of charge in place of the defective one I returned. I would also like to know what was wrong with the defective reel.

I would appreciate your processing my claim within the next two weeks.

Sincerely yours,

Michael Trigg

Michael Trigg

Documents all relevant details about the product

Explains politely what is wrong

Clearly states what should be done

Specifies an acceptable time frame

- What parts of a job were not done or were done poorly?
- When did all this happen?
- Where and how were you inconvenienced?

Stating that "the brake shoes were defective" tells very little about how long they were on your car, how effectively they may have been installed, or what condition they were in when they ceased functioning safely. Reach some conclusion, even if you qualify your remarks with words like *apparently, possibly,* or *seemingly* when you describe the difficulty.

3. Briefly describe the inconvenience you have experienced. Show that your problems were directly caused by the defective product or service. To justify your complaint, give precise details about the time and money you lost. Don't be vague and say you had "numerous difficulties." If you purchased a calculator and it broke down during a mathematics examination, say so (but do not blame the calculator company if you failed the course). Did you have to pay a mechanic to fix your car when it was stalled on the road? Did you have to take time away from your other responsibilities to clean up a mess made by a leaky new washing machine? Did you have to buy a new printer or recording machine? See how Emily Rashon documents The Loft's inconvenience in paragraph 3 of her letter in Figure 6.12.

Where appropriate, refer to any previous telephone calls, e-mail, or letters. Give the names of the people you have written or spoken to and the dates of your calls or correspondence.

4. Indicate precisely what you want done. Do not simply write that you "want something done," that "adequate measures must be taken," or that "the situation should be corrected." Similarly, just saying you "want a credit" is not enough. Do you want a complete refund, a replacement, a new model, a credit toward your account, or a credit toward the purchase of another product or service? Always state precisely what you want:

- your purchase price refunded in full
- a credit made to your account
- your exact model repaired or replaced
- a completely new repair crew assigned to the job
- an apology from the company for discourteous treatment

If you are asking for damages, state your request in dollars and cents and always include copies of bills documenting your expenses related to the problem. Perhaps you had to rent a car, were forced to pay a janitorial service to clean up, or had to rent equipment at a higher rate because the company did not make its deliveries as promised.

5. Ask for prompt handling of your claim. In your conclusion, ask the reader to answer questions you may have (such as finding out where calls came from that you were billed for but did not make). And ask that your claim be handled as quickly as possible. You might even specify a reasonable time by which you want to hear from the writer or need the problem fixed. Note how the last paragraph in Figure 6.12 effectively does this.

A complaint letter from a business.   Figure 6.12

The Loft

Camerson and Dale, Sunnyside, California 91793-4116   213-555-7500

June 21, 2007

Priscilla Dubrow
Customer Relations Department
Superflex Products
San Diego, CA 93141-0808

Dear Ms. Dubrow:

On September 15, 2006, we purchased a Superflex industrial dishwasher, model 3203876, at the Hillcrest store at 3400 Broadway Drive in Sunnyside, for $5,000. In the last three weeks, our restaurant has had repeated problems with this machine. Three more months of warranty remain on the unit.

The machine does not complete a full cycle; it stops before the final rinsing and thus leaves the dishes dirty. It appears that the cycle regulators are not working properly because they refuse to shift into the next necessary gear. Attempts to repair the machine by the Hillcrest crew on June 4, 11, and 15 have been unsuccessful.

The Loft has been greatly inconvenienced. Our kitchen team has been forced to sort, clean, and sanitize utensils, dishes, pans and pots by hand, resulting in additional overtime. Moreover, our expenses for proper detergents have increased.

We want your main office to send another repair crew at once to fix this machine. If your crew is unable to do this, we want a discount worth the amount of the warranty life on this model to be applied to the purchase of a new Superflex dishwasher. This amount would come to $1,000, or 20 percent of the original purchase price.

So that our business is not further disrupted, we would appreciate your resolving this problem promptly within the next week.

Sincerely yours,

Emily Rashon

Emily Rashon
Co-owner

▼ Browse our menu, which changes daily, at www.theloft.com

Gives all product's facts and warranty information

Describes what's happened and when

Further documents problem and reason for adjustment

Provides clear description of how problem should be solved

Concludes politely with justification for prompt action

Adjustment Letters

Adjustment letters respond to complaint letters by telling customers dissatisfied with a product or service how their claim will be settled. Adjustment letters should reconcile the differences that exist between a customer and a firm and restore the customer's confidence in that firm.

The Importance of Complaint Letters to a Business

Rather than ignoring or quarreling with complaint letters, most companies view answering them as good for business. By writing to complain about a product or service, the customer alerts your company to a problem that can be remedied to avoid similar complaints in the future. Customers who take time to write obviously want and deserve a reply. If you do not answer the customer's letter politely, you may lose a lot of business—not just the customer's business, but also that of his or her friends, family, and associates, who will all have been told about your discourtesy.

How to (and Not to) Write an Adjustment Letter

An effective adjustment letter requires diplomacy. Be prompt, courteous, and decisive; do not brush the complaint aside in hopes that it will be forgotten. Investigate the complaint quickly and determine its validity by checking previous correspondence, warranty statements, guarantees, and your firm's policies on merchandise and service. In some cases you may even have to send returned damaged merchandise to your company's laboratory to determine who is at fault.

A noncommittal letter signals to the customer that you have failed to investigate the claim or are stalling for time. Do not resort to vague statements such as the following:

- We will do what we can to solve your problems as soon as possible.
- A company policy prohibits our returning your purchase price in full.
- Your request, while legitimate, will take time to process.
- We will act on your request with your best interest in mind.
- While we cannot now determine the extent of an adjustment, we will be back in touch with you.

Customers want to be told that they are right; if they cannot get what they request, they will demand to know why, in the most explicit terms. When you comply with a request, a begrudging tone will destroy the goodwill that your refund or replacement would have created. At the other extreme, do not overdo an apology by agreeing that the company is "completely at fault," that "such shoddy merchandise is inexcusable." An expression of regret need not jeopardize all future business. If you make your company look too bad, you risk losing the customer permanently, and saying your company was negligent may result in a lawsuit.

Adjustment Letters That Tell the Customer "Yes"

If investigation reveals the customer's complaint to be valid, write a letter saying, in effect, "Yes, you are right; we will give you what you asked for." Basically, your letter needs to answer four questions:

- How can I comply with the reader's request and reestablish goodwill?
- How do I explain what happened?
- How can I reassure the reader it won't happen again?
- How can I keep the reader as a customer?

It is easy to write a "Yes" letter if you remember a few useful suggestions. As with a good news message, start with the favorable news the customer wants to hear; that will put him or her in a positive frame of mind to read the rest of your letter. Let the customer know that you sincerely agree with him or her—don't sound as if you are reluctantly honoring the request. For example, if your airline lost or misplaced luggage, apologize before you offer a settlement.

The two examples of adjustment letters saying "Yes" show you how to write this kind of correspondence. The first example, Figure 6.13, says "Yes" to Michael Trigg's letter in Figure 6.11. You might want to reread the Trigg complaint letter to see what problems Ralph Montoya faced when he had to write to Mr. Trigg. The second example of an adjustment letter that says "Yes" is in Figure 6.14. It responds to a customer who has complained about an incorrect billing.

You might also want to review the letter in Figure 5.8, which is an adjustment letter saying "Yes."

Writing a "Yes" Letter

The following four steps will help you write a "Yes" adjustment letter.

1. Admit immediately that the customer's complaint is justified and apologize. Briefly state that you are sorry and thank the customer for writing to inform you.

2. State precisely what you are going to do to correct the problem. Let the customer know that you will

- extend warranty coverage
- credit the account with funds, more air miles, or the like
- offer a discount on the next purchase
- cancel a bill
- repair a damaged camera
- repaint a room
- enclose a free pass
- provide a complimentary dinner or lodging
- give the customer credit toward another purchase
- upgrade software

Do not postpone the good news the customer wants to hear. The rest of your letter will be much more appreciated and convincing if the customer is told the good news right away. In Figure 6.13 Michael Trigg is told that he will receive a new reel; in Figure 6.14 Kathryn Brumfield learns she will not be charged for parts or service.

3. Tell customers exactly what happened. They deserve an explanation for the inconvenience they suffered. Note that the explanations in Figures 6.13 and 6.14 give only the essential details; they do not bother the reader with side issues or petty remarks about who was to blame. Assure customers that the mishap is not typical

Figure 6.13   An adjustment letter saying "Yes."

Smith Sports Equipment
P.O. Box 1014   Tulsa, Oklahoma 74109-1014
(918) 555-0164 ■ www.smithsport.com

October 19, 2007

Mr. Michael Trigg
17 Westwood Drive
Magnolia, MA 02171

Dear Mr. Trigg:

Apologizes and announces good news

Thank you for alerting us in your letter of October 10 to the problems you had with one of our model 191 spincast reels. I am sorry for the inconvenience the reel caused you. A new Smith reel is on its way to you.

Explains what happened and why problem will not recur

We have examined your reel and found the problem. It seems that a retaining pin on the button spring was improperly installed by one of our new soldering machines on the assembly line. We have thoroughly inspected, repaired, and cleaned the soldering machine to eliminate the problem from happening again.

Expresses respect for customer

Since we began making quality reels in 1955, we have taken pride in helping loyal customers like you who rely on a Smith reel. We hope that your new Smith reel brings you years of pleasure and many good catches, especially next year at the Gloucester Fishing Tournament.

Closes with friendly offer to help again

Thank you for your business. Please let me know if I can assist you again.

Respectfully,

SMITH SPORTS EQUIPMENT

Ralph Montoya

Ralph Montoya, Manager
Customer Relations Department

An adjustment letter saying "Yes."   Figure 6.14

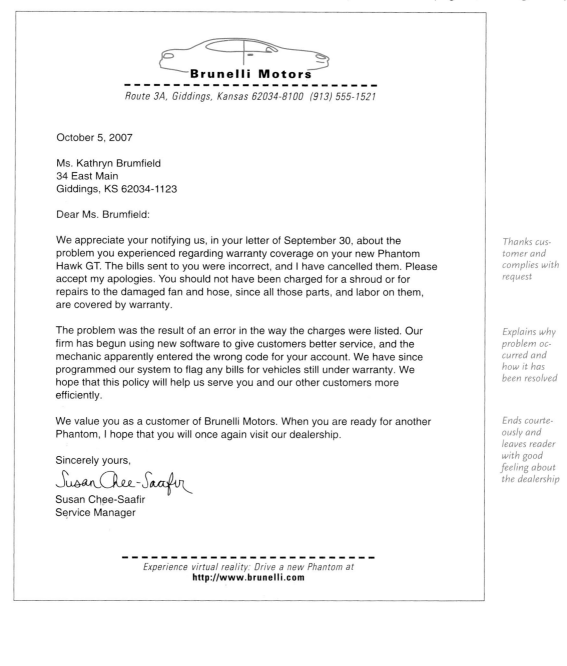

Brunelli Motors
- -
Route 3A, Giddings, Kansas 62034-8100 (913) 555-1521

October 5, 2007

Ms. Kathryn Brumfield
34 East Main
Giddings, KS 62034-1123

Dear Ms. Brumfield:

We appreciate your notifying us, in your letter of September 30, about the problem you experienced regarding warranty coverage on your new Phantom Hawk GT. The bills sent to you were incorrect, and I have cancelled them. Please accept my apologies. You should not have been charged for a shroud or for repairs to the damaged fan and hose, since all those parts, and labor on them, are covered by warranty.

The problem was the result of an error in the way the charges were listed. Our firm has begun using new software to give customers better service, and the mechanic apparently entered the wrong code for your account. We have since programmed our system to flag any bills for vehicles still under warranty. We hope that this policy will help us serve you and our other customers more efficiently.

We value you as a customer of Brunelli Motors. When you are ready for another Phantom, I hope that you will once again visit our dealership.

Sincerely yours,

Susan Chee-Saafir
Susan Chee-Saafir
Service Manager

- -
Experience virtual reality: Drive a new Phantom at
http://www.brunelli.com

Thanks customer and complies with request

Explains why problem occurred and how it has been resolved

Ends courteously and leaves reader with good feeling about the dealership

of your company's operations. While your comments should not shift the blame, your letter should center on the unusual reason or circumstance for the difficulty. Avoid promising, however, that the problem will never recur. Not only is such a guarantee unnecessary, but keeping it may be beyond your control.

4. End on a friendly—and positive—note. Do not remind customers of the trouble they have gone through. Leave them with a good feeling about your company. Say that you are looking forward to seeing them again, that you will gladly work with them on any future orders, or that you can always be reached for questions.

Adjustment Letters That Tell the Customer "No"

Writing to tell customers "No" is obviously more difficult than agreeing with them. You are faced with the sensitive task of conveying bad news, while at the same time convincing the reader that your position is fair, logical, and consistent. Write a letter that is customer-centered. As discussed earlier, do not bluntly start off with a "No." (See pp. 206–207.)

It is not wise to accuse or argue. Avoid remarks that blame, scold, or remind customers of a wrongdoing. Remarks like these are likely to cost you business:

- You obviously did not read the instruction manual.
- Our records show that you purchased the set after the policy went into effect.
- The company policy plainly states that such refunds are not allowed.
- You were negligent in running the machine.
- You claim that our word processor was poorly constructed.
- You must be mistaken about the merchandise.
- As any intelligent person could tell, the switch had to be in the "off" position.
- Your complaint is unjustified.

How to Say "No" Diplomatically—Some Strategies

The following six suggestions will help you say "No" diplomatically. You can find practical applications of them in Figures 6.15, 6.16, and 6.17. You might also want to review pages 205–207 and Figures 6.6 and 6.7.

1. Thank customers for writing. Put your readers in a good frame of mind by opening with a polite, respectful comment that will make the rest of your letter easier to accept. Such a neutral or pleasant opening is called a **buffer,** a way to soften a reader's response before he or she sees your "No." Make sure, though, that your buffer is relevant and sincere, as in Figure 6.7. The letter writers in Figures 6.15 and 6.16 use buffers that thank customers for bringing the matter to their attention and that sympathize with them about their inconvenience.

Telling customers "No" ("we regret to inform you") in the first sentence or two will only make them more angry and put them on the defensive. Avoid these reader-hostile openings:

- I was surprised to learn that you found our product unsatisfactory.
- We have been in business for years and nothing like this has ever happened.
- There is no way we could give you what you demand.

An adjustment letter saying "No."   Figure 6.15

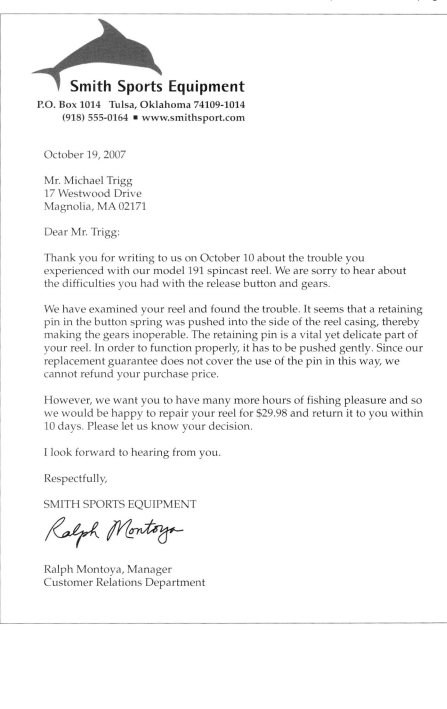

Smith Sports Equipment

P.O. Box 1014   Tulsa, Oklahoma 74109-1014
(918) 555-0164 ■ www.smithsport.com

October 19, 2007

Mr. Michael Trigg
17 Westwood Drive
Magnolia, MA 02171

Dear Mr. Trigg:

Thank you for writing to us on October 10 about the trouble you experienced with our model 191 spincast reel. We are sorry to hear about the difficulties you had with the release button and gears.

We have examined your reel and found the trouble. It seems that a retaining pin in the button spring was pushed into the side of the reel casing, thereby making the gears inoperable. The retaining pin is a vital yet delicate part of your reel. In order to function properly, it has to be pushed gently. Since our replacement guarantee does not cover the use of the pin in this way, we cannot refund your purchase price.

However, we want you to have many more hours of fishing pleasure and so we would be happy to repair your reel for $29.98 and return it to you within 10 days. Please let us know your decision.

I look forward to hearing from you.

Respectfully,

SMITH SPORTS EQUIPMENT

Ralph Montoya

Ralph Montoya, Manager
Customer Relations Department

Buffer—thanks and sympathizes with reader

Explains problem without directly blaming the reader; gives firm decision

Turns a "No" into a "Yes" for customer

Ends politely without any reference to the problem

Figure 6.16   Another adjustment letter saying "No."

*Professional
you-centered
opening*

*Justifies firm
decision by
explaining
causes of prob-
lem and condi-
tions of sale*

*Provides prac-
tical alterna-
tive with an
incentive*

*Ends with
goodwill*

*Health*AIR

4300 Marshall Drive
Salt Lake City, Utah 84113-1521
(801) 555-6028
www.healthair.com

August 20, 2007

Ms. Denise Southby, Director
Bradley General Hospital
Bradley, IL 60610-4615

Dear Director Southby:

Thank you for your letter of August 21 explaining the problems you have encountered with our Puritan MAII ventilator. We were sorry to learn that you were unable to get the high-volume PAO_2 alarm circuit to work.

Our ventilator is a high-volume, low-frequency machine that can deliver up to 40 ml. of water pressure. The ventilator runs with a center of gravity attachment on the right side of the diode. The trouble you had with the high oxygen alarm system is due to an overload on your piped-in oxygen. Our laboratory inspection of the ventilator you returned indicated that the high-pressure system had blown a vital adaptor in the machine. An overload in an oxygen system is a condition that does not apply to warranty coverage of the ventilator, and so we cannot replace it free of charge.

We would, however, be pleased to send you another model of the adaptor, which would be more compatible with your system, as soon as we receive your order. The price of the adaptor is $600, and our service representative will be happy to install it for you at no charge.

Please let me know your decision. I look forward to hearing from you.

Sincerely yours,

R. P. Gifford

R. P. Gifford
Customer Service Department

2. State the problem so that customers realize that you understand their complaint. Let customers know that you have read their letter carefully and that you are responding to it fairly. Reassure them that you are aware of the facts of the situation. You thereby prove that you are not trying to misrepresent or distort what the customer told you or that you are ignoring key details.

3. Explain what happened with the product or service before you give the customer a decision. Provide a factual, respectful explanation to show customers they are being treated fairly. Put the emphasis on the proper or best way to use a product or service rather than focusing on the customer's misunderstanding instructions, failing to observe an agreement or contract, or mishandling equipment.

> Poor: "By reading the instructions on the side of the paint can, you would have avoided the streaking condition that you claim resulted."
>
> Better: "Hi-Gloss Paint requires two applications, four hours apart, for a clear smooth finish."

Note how the writers in Figures 6.15 and 6.16 do not blame customers but politely point out the terms of an agreement that govern the use of a particular piece of equipment, whether it is a fishing reel or an adaptor.

4. Give your decision without hedging. It might seem easier at the time to dangle some hope before the readers that you might say "Yes." But this is not a good strategy for establishing a business relationship. Don't say, "Perhaps some type of restitution could be made later" or "Further proof would have been helpful." Indecision will only infuriate your customers, who believe they have already presented a sound, convincing case.

Arrive at a fair and firm decision, but don't dwell on it. Keep your bad news short and anchor it to an honest explanation, such as those in Figures 6.15 and 6.16. Never apologize for your decision and avoid using words such as *reject, claim,* or *grant. Reject* is harsh and impersonal. *Claim* implies you distrust the customer's complaint. *Grant* signals that you have the power to respond favorably but decline to do so. Instead, use words that reconcile.

5. Turn your "No" into a benefit for readers. Link your firm "No" to an attractive alternative for readers. Your attitude needs to be "Here's what we can do to solve your problem." Find some way to make your "No" more acceptable by supplying a workable alternative to what customers have asked for but did not receive. Surround the bad news with benefits for the reader.

- Offer to repair a part for them (Figure 6.15).
- Send them a replacement and install it for a lower fee (Figure 6.16).
- Encourage readers to see the "No" of a refusal of credit as good for the writer's business (Figure 6.17).

Never promise to do the impossible or go against company policy, but do continue to convince readers you have their needs in mind.

6. Leave the door open for better and continued business. Close with a short, diplomatic sentence or two showing respect for readers and expressing your desire

Figure 6.17   An effective letter refusing credit.

WEST COAST
CREDIT INC.   4800 Ridge Road
Los Angeles, CA 91666
Phone (714) 555-3500
FAX (714) 555-4323

March 19, 2007

Mr. Otto L. King
Sunshine Interiors
8235 Mimosa Highway
Vinedale, CA 92004-0318

Dear Mr. King:

Begins on a positive note

We appreciate your interest in doing business with West Coast Credit. It is always gratifying to see a store like yours open in an expanding community like Vinedale.

Denies credit but explains why

In reviewing your credit application, we checked into the business history and credit references you supplied. We also called your local credit bureau. While we found nothing negative in your credit history, we did determine that for a business of your size you have already reached a maximum level of indebtedness. For that reason, we believe that this would not be the best time to extend your credit line.

Encourages reader to reapply

We would, however, encourage you to visit our website and fill out the credit survey. This site is periodically reviewed and can give you up-to-date information on credit availability. In the meantime, we wish you every success in your new business.

Cordially,

B. Rimes-Assante

B. Rimes-Assante
Supervisor

www.wcredit.com

to do business with them again. Figure 6.15 ends by letting the reader know that the writer is looking forward to hearing from him, and Figure 6.16 graciously thanks the reader for being a valued and loyal customer.

Refusal-of-Credit Letters

A special set of bad news letters deals with a company's refusing credit to an individual or another company. Writing such a letter requires a great deal of sensitivity. You want to be clear and firm about your decision; at the same time, you do not want to alienate the reader and risk losing his or her business in the future.

How to Say "No"

1. Begin on a positive—not a negative—note. Find something to thank the reader for; make the bad news easier to take. Compliment the reader's company or previous

---

Tech Note

Writing Ethical and Legal Refusal-of-Credit and Collection Letters

Various state and federal laws specify how and when a creditor can communicate with individuals who have borrowed money or purchased materials on time. Creditors may not:

- publish a list of those who owe a debt (except to a credit bureau)
- imply that you have committed a crime
- give you insufficient or incorrect information about the amount of your loan or your payment schedule
- falsely imply that they are attorneys or are representing attorneys

Consumers are protected from harassment, threats, and any violations of contract agreements. In fact, companies in the European Union are required to list such contractual terms as liability limits, product histories, and time limits for settling claims. Before you write a collection or refusal-of-credit letter, be sure that you and your company comply with all the city, county, state, federal, and country guidelines dealing with such communications. Below are a few helpful websites that can guide you through such matters:

- *http://www.ftc.gov/bcp/conline/pubs/credit/crdright.htm* (click on "Your debt and debt collectors")
- *http://www.ftc.gov/os/statutes/2summary.htm*
- *http://www.creditcards.com/credit-consumer-rights-article.php*
- *http://www.wvs.state.wv.us/wvag/faq/consumer/debt_collection.html*
- *http://www.pueblo.gsa.gov/cic_text/money/fair-debt/fair-debt.htm*

good credit achievements (if known); certainly express gratitude to the individual for wanting to do business with your company.

2. In a second paragraph provide a clear-cut explanation of why you must refuse the request for credit, but base your explanation on facts, not personal shortcomings or liabilities. Appropriate reasons to cite for a refusal of credit include

- a lack of business experience or prior credit
- the individual or company's being "overextended" or needing more time to pay off existing obligations (Figure 6.17)
- current unfavorable or unstable financial conditions
- an order that is too large to process without some prepayment
- a lack of equipment or personnel for the company to do the business for which they are seeking credit

3. End on a positive note, too. Encourage the reader to reapply when business conditions have improved or when the reader's firm is in a better financial position. Make an attempt to keep the reader as a potential customer, eager to try you again. Figure 6.17 illustrates an effective letter that denies credit, following the organizational plan just discussed.

Writing About Credit to a Non-Native Speaker of English

Writing a letter denying credit to a non-native speaker of English requires double tact. As you saw in Chapter 5, you have to consider the cultural expectations of such an audience and use easily understood international English. Compare the inappropriate refusal letter in Figure 6.18 with the far more diplomatic and more acceptably worded letter in Figure 6.19 (p. 230). The letter in Figure 6.18 is rude, uses words a non-native speaker of English may not understand ("expedited," "herewith"), and does not encourage future business dealings with Consolidated Plastics.

The diplomatic letter in Figure 6.19 follows the guidelines for effective communication with non-native speakers and adheres to the suggestions for denying credit. In Figure 6.19 Emma Corson compliments her reader and his firm, expresses an interest in doing business with Mendson SA, and helps her reader to understand how Consolidated's credit policy might even help Mendson in the future.

Collection Letters

Collection letters require the same tact and fairness as do complaint and adjustment letters. Each nonpayment case should be evaluated separately. A nasty collection letter sent to a customer who is a good credit risk after only one month's nonpayment can drive the customer elsewhere. On the other hand, three easygoing letters to a customer who is a poor credit risk may encourage that individual to postpone payment, perhaps indefinitely.

Many businesses send several letters to customers before turning matters over to a collection agency. Each letter in the series employs a different technique, ranging from giving compliments and offering flexible credit terms to issuing demands for immediate payment and threats of legal consequences. One hospital uses the collection letters illustrated in Figures 6.20 and 6.21 to encourage ex-patients to pay

An inappropriate letter refusing credit to a non-native speaker of English.   Figure 6.18

Consolidated Plastics

May 25, 2007

Mr. Jan Buwalda
Mendson SA
Hoofdstraat 23
Dokkum, The Netherlands 1324 XK

Dear Mr. Buwalda:

I have received herewith your request and news about your company. Thanks.

Curt, begrudging tone

Regarding that request to open a credit account with us, it just cannot be done. I don't know how things are expedited in your country, but in the United States giving credit to a first-time foreign customer is just not standard business practice. As you will understand, your credit rating could be unacceptable as far as we are concerned. You will be expected to pay in cash for your first transaction with us. We'll evaluate the situation thereafter.

Insensitive to reader's needs and cultural heritage

Let me know how you anticipate proceeding.

Sincerely,

Emma Corson

Emma Corson
Accounts Executive

Disrespectful close—no attempt to encourage future business

900 Technology Blvd., Bambrake, NH 03243
Phone (603) 555-7000 ■ Fax (603) 555-4321 ■ conplastics@compuserv.com
www.conplastics.com

Figure 6.19   A diplomatic revision of Figure 6.18, a letter refusing credit to a non-native speaker of English.

Consolidated Plastics

May 25, 2007

Mr. Jan Buwalda
Mendson SA
Hoofdstraat 23
Dokkum, The Netherlands 1324 XK

Dear Mr. Buwalda:

*Expresses grati-
tude to and
interest in
reader's
company*

Thank you very much for your letter inquiring about opening a credit account with our firm. It is always a pleasure to hear from potential customers in Holland. I was most interested to learn about Mendson's diverse activities.

*Welcomes
future business
contact*

We understand and share your company's wish to have a U.S. supplier to work with you. Having Mendson as a customer would be beneficial for Consolidated Plastics, too. Working with you would allow us to enter a new market.

*Politely ex-
plains proce-
dure to ensure
reader's
goodwill*

However, I am sorry that we cannot open any new account on credit. If you would kindly send us your check for the first month's supplies you need, we would rush your shipment to you. This will establish an account with us, and you can charge your second month's supplies on that account.

*Closes with
friendly offer to
help*

Please write or e-mail me if you have any questions. I look forward to serving you and Mendson in the future.

Cordially,

Emma Corson

Emma Corson
Accounts Executive

900 Technology Blvd., Bambrake, NH 03243
Phone (603) 555-7000 ▪ Fax (603) 555-4321 ▪ conplastics@compuserv.com
www.conplastics.com

A first, or early, collection letter.   **Figure 6.20**

SABINE COUNTY HOSPITAL
7200 Medical Blvd.
Sabine, TX 77231
512-555-6734
www.sabine.org

May 15, 2006

Mr. Cal Smith
24 Mulberry Street
Valley, TX 77212

Re: Inpatient Services
Date of Hospitalization: March 11–12, 2006
Balance Due: $4,725.48

Dear Mr. Smith:

We are grateful that we were able to serve your health care needs during your recent stay at Sabine County Hospital. It is our continuing goal to provide the best possible hospital care for residents of Sabine County and its vicinity. To do so we must keep our finances up-to-date.

Links hospital mission to patient's payment

Our records indicate that your account is now overdue, and that we have not received a payment from you for two months. If you have recently sent one in, kindly disregard this letter and accept our thanks.

Polite reminder to pay now

If for any reason you are unable to pay the full amount at this time, we will be happy to set up a payment schedule that is convenient for you. Just fill in the appropriate blanks below, and return this letter to us. That will enable us to avoid billing you on a "Past Due" basis. Thank you for your cooperation.

Offers options to maintain goodwill

Sincerely,

Morris T. Jukes

Morris T. Jukes
Accounts Department

( ) I will pay $ _____ ( ) monthly ( ) quarterly, on my account.

( ) Enclosed is a check for full payment in the amount of $ _____.

Signature

_____

Figure 6.21   A final, collection letter.

SABINE COUNTY HOSPITAL
7200 Medical Blvd.
Sabine, TX 77231
512-555-6734
www.sabine.org

September 21, 2006   Re: Inpatient Services
                                      Date of Hospitalization: March 11–12, 2006
                                      Balance Due: $4,725.48
Mr. Cal Smith
24 Mulberry Street
Valley, TX 77212

Dear Mr. Smith:

Direct opening about history and current status of the account

During the past few months we have written to you several times about your balance of $4,725.48 for services you received on March 11 and 12. Your account is now more than 190 days overdue, and we cannot allow any further extensions in receiving a payment from you.

Reminds patient of goodwill and requests payment

As you will recall, we have tried to help you in any way we could to meet your obligations by offering several options for paying your bill. You could have arranged for installment payments that would be due each month or quarter, whichever would be more convenient. Because you have not replied, we must ask for full payment at this time.

States final option

If we do not hear from you within ten days, we will have no alternative but to turn your account over to our collection agency, which will seriously hurt your credit rating. Neither of us would find this a welcome alternative.

Sincerely,

Morris T. Jukes

Morris T. Jukes
Accounts Department

their bills. Figure 6.20 is a letter sent early in the collection process when a client is only a month or two late. The collection letter in Figure 6.21 is sent much later to a client who has ignored earlier notices.

The tone of Figure 6.20 is cordial and sincere—now is not the time to say "pay up or else." It stresses how valuable the person is and underscores how pleased the hospital is to have provided the care he needed. The last paragraph makes a request for payment, offering (1) a flexible payment schedule and (2) an escape from the inconvenience (or embarrassment) of receiving past due notices. The bottom of the letter conveniently lists payment options available to the patient.

The later collection letter in Figure 6.21, on the other hand, points out that the time for concessions is over, and reminds the patient of all the efforts that the hospital has expended to collect its bills. Then it announces what consequences will result if he still does not pay.

Sending Letter-Quality Messages: Final Advice to Seal Your Success

This chapter has introduced you to different types of letters you can expect to write on the job—inquiry, special request, sales, and a variety of customer relations letters. Although you will send many more e-mail messages and memos than letters, every job will also expect you to write effective, professional letters. Your business letters represent your employer's and your own professional image.

Judging and checking your letters in light of the following guidelines will help you to draft, tailor, and evaluate the various types of business letters you will be called upon to write.

- **Identify your reader:** one individual; a group; a company or agency; a new individual customer or a long-time one; a native or non-native speaker
- **Determine your purpose for writing:** routine or special request; explanation; complaint; apology; sell product/service; build goodwill; express thanks; refuse credit; collect a debt
- **Determine reader's reason for writing:** complaint; request information; approval for a plan; seek credit
- **Organize information:** direct or indirect; begin with good news and save negative message for middle of the letter
- **Include essential information:** schedules and dates; prices and expenses; personnel involved; legal matters; explanation of services, warranties, products; background and need for credit
- **Use right style and tone:** professional and courteous; concise and focused; sensitive to reader's needs, including his or her culture and traditions
- **Test your overall goal:** request or provide information; make a new customer or maintain goodwill with an established one; resolve a customer's complaint or explain why not; encourage reader to extend credit

Planning your letter carefully—its purpose, its organization, its content—will help you to make sure your message begins, continues, and ends professionally and successfully.

✔ Revision Checklist

☐ Planned what I am going to say to my readers. Did necessary homework and double-checking to answer any questions. Proved to my readers that I am knowledgeable about my topic.

☐ Used an appropriate (and consistent) format and page layout for my letters.

☐ Followed acceptable company protocol in format, organization, style, and tone of my letters.

☐ Adapted style and length of my message for my readers.

☐ Organized and, if necessary, highlighted information in my letters in the most effective way for my message and for my readers.

☐ Emphasized the "you attitude" with my readers, whether employer, customer/client, or co-worker.

☐ Conveyed impression of being courteous, professional, and easy to work with.

☐ Used clear and concise language appropriate for my reader.

☐ Began my correspondence with reader-effective strategies. If reporting good news, told the reader right away. If reporting bad news, was diplomatically indirect and considerate of my reader's reactions.

☐ Followed the four A's of effective sales letters. Identified and convinced my target audience.

☐ Wrote complaint letters in a courteous tone. Informed the reader what is wrong, why it is wrong, and how the problem should be corrected.

☐ Wrote adjustment letters that say "Yes" sincerely and to the point. Made those that say "No" fair but did not begin with a "No." Acknowledged reader's point of view and provided clear explanation for my refusal.

☐ Ensured correspondence was timely. Was prompt and reasonable in answering all my correspondence—both from people in my company and from customers.

☐ Took special care to meet the needs of non-native speakers of English in both tone and message.

☐ Tailored collection letters according to audience, time, and circumstances of overdue account; tried to maintain goodwill.

☐ Followed all legal guidelines in informing readers about past due accounts and refusal-of-credit policies.

Online Study Center

Access the writing letters Revision Checklists online at college.hmco .com/pic/kolin8e

Exercises

1. Write a letter of inquiry to a utility company, a safety or health care agency, or a company in your town and ask for a brochure or an annual report describing

its services to the community. Be specific about your reasons for requesting the information.

Online Study Center

Find additional writing letters exercises at college.hmco.com/ pic/kolin8e

2. In which course(s) are you or will you be writing a report? Write to an agency or company that could supply you with helpful information and request its aid. Indicate why you are writing, precisely what information you need, and why you need it. Offer to share your report with the company.

3. Examine an ad in a magazine, a TV commercial, or on a website and then write a one-page assessment in which you identify the four parts of its sales message.

4. Choose one of the following and write a sales letter addressed to an appropriate audience on why they should
   a. major in the same subject you did
   b. live in your neighborhood
   c. be happy taking a vacation where you did last year
   d. dine at a particular restaurant
   e. shop at a store you have worked for
   f. have their cars repaired at a specific garage
   g. give their real-estate business to a particular agency
   h. visit your website

5. Find at least two sales letters you, your family, or your firm has received, and in an e-mail or a memo to your instructor or employer evaluate how well they follow the four parts of a sales letter discussed in this chapter. Attach a copy of the sales letters to your evaluation. If your e-mail or memo is addressed to your boss, indicate how you would improve your competition's sales letters.

6. As a collaborative project, rewrite the following sales letter to make it more effective. Add any details you think are relevant.

Dear Pizza Lovers:

Allow me to introduce myself. My name is Rudy Moore and I am the new manager of Tasty Pizza Parlor in town. The Parlor is located at the intersection of North Miller Parkway and 95th Street. We are open from 10 a.m. to 11 p.m., except on the weekends, when we are open later.

I think you will be as happy as I am to learn that Tasty's will now offer free delivery to an extended service area. As a result, you can get your Tasty Pizza hot when you want it.

Please see your weekly newspapers for our ad. We also are offering customers a coupon. It is a real deal for you.

I know you will enjoy Tasty's and I hope to see you. I am always interested in hearing from you about our service and our fine product. We want to take your order soon. Please come in.

7. Write a sales letter similar to the one in Figure 6.4 from a manager of one of the following ethnic restaurants or one of your choice. Make sure you include relevant details for the particular audience:
   a. Mexican
   b. Indian
   c. Cuban
   d. Soul food
   e. Czech
   f. Turkish
   g. Vietnamese
   h. Thai
   i. Greek
   j. German
   k. Irish
   l. Chinese
   m. Pakistani
   n. Italian
   o. Polish
   p. French
   q. Hawaiian

8. Send a follow-up letter to one of the following individuals:
   a. a customer who informs you that she will no longer do business with your firm because your prices are too high
   b. a family of four who stayed at your motel for a week last summer
   c. a wedding party or professional organization that used your catering services last month
   d. a customer who exchanged a coat for the purchase price
   e. a customer who purchased a used car from you and who has not been happy with warranty service
   f. a company that bought software from you nine months ago, alerting them about updates

9. Write a bad news letter based on an experience at your workplace—rejecting an applicant for a job, a warranty claim, an increase in insurance rates, or a request for funding. If you have already written such a letter, rewrite it by applying the principles you learned in this chapter.

10. Write a bad news letter to an appropriate reader about one of the following:
    a. Your company has to discontinue Saturday deliveries because of rising labor and fuel costs.
    b. You are the manager of an insurance company writing to tell one of your customers that, because of reckless driving, his or her rates will increase.
    c. You have to refuse to send a bonus gift to a customer who sent in an order after the expiration date for qualifying for the gift.
    d. You have discontinued a model that a business customer wants to reorder.
    e. You have to notify residents of a community that a bus route or hours of operation are being discontinued.
    f. You represent the water department and have to tell residents of a community that they cannot water their lawns for the next month because of a serious water shortage in your town.
    g. You cannot send customers a catalog—which your company formerly sent free of charge—unless they first send $10 for the cost of that catalog.
    h. You cannot repair a particular piece of equipment because the customer still owes your company for three previous service visits.

11. Write a good news letter about the opposite of one of the situations listed in Exercise 10.

12. You just found out that a business that applied for credit has missed its last mortgage payment. You have to refuse credit to this local firm, which has been in business successfully for eight years. Write a refusal letter without jeopardizing future business dealings.

13. Write a complaint letter about one of the following:
    a. an error in your utility, telephone, credit card, or Internet provider bill
    b. discourteous service you received on an airplane or bus
    c. a frozen food product of poor quality
    d. a shipment that arrived late and damaged
    e. an insurance payment to you that is $357.00 less than it should be
    f. a public television station's policy of not showing a particular series
    g. junk mail or spam that you are receiving
    h. equipment that arrives with missing parts
    i. misleading representation by a salesperson
    j. incorrect information given at a website

14. This exercise might be done as a collaborative project. You are a section manager at e-Tech. Your company has a service contract with Professional Office Cleaners (POC). However, each morning when you arrive at work you are disappointed with what they've done. POC has overlooked some essential tasks and done a poor job on others. Your staff is also disappointed and has e-mailed or spoken to you about problems with POC. Write the following:
    a. a memo or e-mail to your boss, the vice president, about POC's shoddy work
    b. a complaint letter to POC that the vice president has asked you to write and to sign his name to it
    c. a letter to the vice president from the manager of POC who is responsible for your e-Tech section, apologizing for the problem and offering a solution
    d. a letter from POC to the vice president taking issue with the complaint made against his cleaning company, offering proof that the work was done according to contract specifications
    e. an e-mail you send to your staff about what's happened with POC

15. Write the complaint letter to which the adjustment letter in Figure 6.14 responds.

16. Write the complaint letter to which the adjustment letter in Figure 6.16 responds.

17. Rewrite the following complaint letter to make it more precise, less emotional, and effectively persuasive.

```
Dear Sir:

We recently purchased a machine from your Albany store and
paid a great deal of money for it. This machine, according
to your website, is supposedly the best model in your line
and has caused us nothing but trouble each time we use it.
Really, can't you do any better with your technology?
```

```
We expect you to stand by your products. The warranties you
give with them should make you accountable for shoddy work-
manship. Let us know at once what you intend to do about our
problem. If you cannot or are unwilling to correct the sit-
uation, we will take our business elsewhere, and then you
will be sorry.

Sincerely yours,
```

18. The following story appeared recently in a local newspaper.

Residents concerned about relocation of pet food plant

OCEAN SPRINGS (AP) – Finicky Pet Food is moving its processing plant from Pascagoula to Ocean Springs, a decision that has some residents concerned of possible odor and other problems.

The plant is moving to an industrial area bordering a subdivision of expensive homes.

"The wind doesn't discriminate," said Jo Souers, who lives in the Bienville Place subdivision. "I don't want this in our neighborhood."

City officials said the plant is moving to an area zoned to accommodate it.

"We don't have a lot of control over it," said city planner Donovan Scruggs. "It is a permitted use for this property."

Scruggs said the property was zoned industrial before the subdivision was built. A body shop, cabinet shop, and boat business are located nearby.

The plant will be built in the small industrial area on U.S. 90, directly across the highway from the Super Wal-Mart.

It is moving into a vacant building, the interior of which has been renovated for its new purpose, city officials said.

The plant will process frozen fish and fish parts for bait and pet food. It will employ 10 workers, with that number doubling during fishing season.

Plant manager Dean Niemann said in a statement that the company no longer needed its Pascagoula location near deep water, which was rented from the county.

Scruggs said the city has investigated the possibility that the plant will emit odors.

"We've told Dean (Niemann) from day one, 'You're locating next to a residential area. If you start stinking, action will be taken,'" Scruggs said.

He said the city has a nuisance ordinance that should handle anything that might arise.

"Residents concerned about relocation of pet food plant," The Associated Press, September 27, 2005. Reprinted by permission.

Based upon information in this story, which you may want to supplement, write the following complaint/adjustment letters:
  a. a complaint letter to the city from resident Jo Souers
  b. a complaint letter to Finicky Pet Food from city officials warning about dangers of pollution to the residential area
  c. a letter from plant manager Dean Niemann to the residents of Bienville Place subdivision
  d. a letter from city officials to the residents of Bienville Place subdivision

19. Write an adjustment letter saying "Yes" to the manager of The Loft, whose letter is in Figure 6.12.

20. Write an adjustment letter saying "No" to the customer who received the "Yes" adjustment letter included in Figure 6.14.

21. Rewrite the following ineffective adjustment letter saying "Yes."

    Dear Mr. Smith:

    We are extremely sorry to learn that you found the suit you purchased from us unsatisfactory. The problem obviously stems from the fact that you selected it from the rack marked "Factory Seconds." In all honesty, we have had a lot of problems because of this rack. I guess we should know better than to try to feature inferior merchandise along with the name-brand clothing that we sell. But we originally thought that our customers would accept poorer quality merchandise if it saved them some money. That was our mistake.

    Please accept our apologies. If you will bring your "Factory Second" suit to us, we will see what we can do about honoring your request.

    Sincerely yours,

22. Rewrite the following ineffective adjustment letter saying "No."

    Dear Customer:

    Our company is unwilling to give you a new toaster or to refund your purchase price. After examining the toaster you sent to us, we found that the fault was not ours, as you insist, but yours.

    Let me explain. Our toaster is made to take a lot of punishment. But being dropped on the floor or poked inside with a knife, as you probably did, exceeds all decent treatment. You must be careful if you expect your appliances to last. Your negligence in this case is so bad that the toaster could not be repaired.

    In the future, consider using your appliances according to the guidelines set down in warranty books. That's why they are written.

    Since you are now in the market for a new toaster, let me suggest that you purchase our new heavy-duty model, number 67342, called the Counter-Whiz. I am taking the liberty of sending you some information about this model. I do hope you at least go to see one at your local appliance center.

    Sincerely,

23. You are the manager of a computer software company, and one of your sales-people has just sold a large order to a new customer whose business you have tried to obtain for years. Unfortunately, the salesperson made a mistake writing out the invoice, undercharging the customer $229. At that price, your company would not break even and so you must write a letter explaining the problem so the customer will not assume all future business dealings with your firm will be offered at such "below market" rates. Decide whether you should ask for the $229 or just "write it off" in the interest of keeping a valuable new customer.

   a. Write a letter to the new customer, asking for the $229 and explaining the problem while still projecting an image of your company as accurate, professional, and very competitive.

   b. Write a letter to the new customer, not asking for the $229 but explaining the mistake and emphasizing that your company is both competitive and professional.

   c. Write a letter to your boss explaining why you wrote the letter in (a).

   d. Write a letter to your boss explaining why you wrote the letter in (b).

   e. Write a letter to the salesperson who made the mistake, asking him or her to take appropriate action with regard to the new customer.

24. Write an appropriate collection letter to one of the following:

   a. a loyal customer who has not responded to a first notice letter

   b. a new business customer who placed a large order with you last quarter and paid for it promptly but who has ignored two notices you have already sent about an order filled this quarter

   c. a customer who has just placed an order over the Internet but has not responded so far to any of your notices for payment for previous purchases

   d. a customer who has been continually late but has always paid eventually

   e. an international customer who has sent in only partial payment

CHAPTER 7

How to Get a Job

Résumés, Letters, Applications, and Interviews

Obtaining a job involves a lot of hard work. Before your name is added to a company's payroll, you will have to do more than simply walk into the human resources office and fill out an application form. Finding the *right* job takes time. And finding the right person to fill that job also takes time for the employer.

Online Study Center

To expand your understanding of how to get a job, take advantage of the ACE quizzes, sample documents, Web links, and exercises at college.hmco.com/pic/kolin8e

▌Steps the Employer Takes to Hire

From the employer's viewpoint, the stages in the search for a valuable employee include the following:

1. deciding what duties and responsibilities go with the job and determining the qualifications the future employee should possess
2. advertising the job on the company website, in newspapers, and in professional publications
3. scanning, reading, and evaluating résumés and letters of application
4. having candidates complete application forms
5. requesting further proof of candidates' skills (letters of recommendation, transcripts, portfolios)
6. interviewing selected candidates
7. offering the job to the best-qualified individual

Sometimes the steps are interchangeable, especially steps 4 and 5, but generally speaking, employers go through a long and detailed process to select employees. Step 3, for example, is among the most important for employers (and the most crucial for job candidates). At that stage employers often classify job seekers into one of three groups: those they definitely want to interview, those they may want to interview, and those in whom they have no interest.

▌Steps to Follow to Get Hired

As a job seeker you will have to know how and when to give the employer the kinds of information the preceding seven steps require. You will also have to follow a certain schedule in your search for a job. The following seven procedures will be required of you:

1. analyzing your strengths and restricting your job search
2. looking in the right places for a job
3. preparing a dossier
4. preparing a résumé
5. writing a letter of application
6. filling out a job application
7. going to an interview

Your timetable should match that of your prospective employer. This chapter shows you how to begin your job search and how to prepare an appropriate résumé and letter that are a vital part of your job search.

Analyzing Your Strengths

Before you apply for jobs, analyze your job skills, career goals, and interests. Here are some points to consider as you narrow your career choices and the jobs that are appropriate based on those choices.

1. Make an inventory of your most significant accomplishments in your major and/or on the job. What are your greatest strengths—writing and speaking, working with people in small groups, organizing and problem solving, managing money, speaking a second language, developing software, creating graphics, performing accounting audits?
2. Decide which specialty within your chosen career appeals to you the most. If you are in a nursing program, do you want to work in a large teaching hospital, for a home health or hospice agency, or in a physician's office? What kinds of patients do you prefer to care for—pediatric, geriatric, psychiatric?
3. What are the most rewarding prospects of a job in your profession? What most interests you about a position—travel, international contacts, on-the-job training, helping people, being creative?
4. What are some of the greatest challenges you face in your career today—or may face in five years?
5. Which specific companies or organizations have the best track record in hiring and promoting individuals in your field? What qualifications will such firms insist on from prospective employees?

Once you answer the questions above you can avoid applying for positions for which you are either overqualified or underqualified. If a position requires ten years of related work experience and you are just starting out, you will only waste the employer's time and your own by applying. However, if a job requires a certificate or license and you are in the process of obtaining one, go ahead and apply.

The *Occupational Outlook Handbook* (*http://www.bls.gov/oco/*) can give you valuable career information on job prospects, requirements, and salary ranges.

▉ Looking in the Right Places for a Job

One way to search for a job is simply to send out a batch of letters to companies you want to work for. But how do you know what jobs, if any, those companies have available, what qualifications they are looking for, and what deadlines they might want you to follow? You can avoid these uncertainties by knowing where to look for a job and knowing what a specific job entails. You need to prepare a targeted list of eight to ten employers before you apply for a job. Consult the following resources for a wealth of job-related information.

   1. Networking. Networking pays. It is regarded as the most important strategy to follow. John D. Erdlen and Donald H. Sweet, experts on job searching, cite the following as a primary rule of job hunting: "Don't do anything yourself you can get someone with influence to do for you." Contacts in the business world are invaluable. Let your professors, friends, classmates, alumni associations, neighbors, relatives, and even your clergy know you are looking for a job. They may hear of something and can notify you. Better yet, they may recommend you for the position—with a phone call or a visit to their own company's human resources department. See how the job seekers in Figures 7.11 and 7.12 have successfully networked with people they know. You can also network with people you don't know personally through websites such as

http://www.monster.com

http://www.fastcompany.com/cof/

http://www.guru.com

http://www.groups.yahoo.com

Career counselors also recommend that you attend job fairs, professional and organization meetings, community and civic functions—places where you can meet the right contact people whom you can ask for advice and also for possible follow-up help and recommendations. Network with recruiters at job fairs. Even if they do not have a job for you now, they might tell you when one is likely to be available or may even refer you to another company that does have a relevant position for which you can apply.

   2. The Internet. Prospective employers rely on the Internet to find employees. Companies post job openings and describe precisely what they are looking for in far more detail than in a classified ad. You can learn about jobs by visiting a company's website to see if it has vacancies and what the qualifications are for them. You can also consult the many online job services that list positions and sometimes give advice, including:

- Findajob.com—*http://findajob.com*
- CollegeGrad.com—*http://www.collegegrad.com*
- CareerBuilder—*http://www.careerbuilder.com*
- Spherion—*http://www.spherion.com*

- Monster.com—*http://www.monster.com*
- Riley Guide: Employment Opportunities and Job Resources on the Internet—*http://www.rileyguide.com*
- Yahoo! hotjobs—*http://hotjobs.yahoo.com*

The following are some specialized sites:

- For health care professionals—*http://www.medhunters.com*
- For tech jobs—*http://computerjobs.com*
- For jobs in business: BizWeb—*http://www.bizweb.com*
- For jobs in criminal justice—*http://www.corrections.com*

Make sure you always sign up for job alerts. Also study how to use Internet search engines (pp. 328–334) to find contacts and jobs.

3. Newspapers. Look at local newspapers as well as the Sunday editions of large city papers with a wide circulation, such as the *New York Times Job Market* (*http://www.nytimes.com/pages/jobs/*). The *National Business Employment Weekly* (*http://www.careerjournal.com*), published by the *Wall Street Journal*, also lists jobs in different areas, including technical and managerial positions. You can access job listings found in many large newspapers through careerbuilder.com (*http://www.careerbuilder.com*). Make sure you check every possibly relevant category (for example, jobs for "Computer Programmers" might be listed under "Programmers").

4. Your campus placement office. Counselors keep an online file of available positions and can also tell you when a firm's recruiter will be on campus to conduct interviews. Many placement offices have online recruiting databases, allowing students access to a broad range of recruiting contacts and interview information. They can also help you locate summer and part-time work, both on and off campus, positions that might lead to full-time jobs. Most important, they will give you sound advice on your job search, including strategies for finding the right job, salary ranges, and interview tips. Many placement offices also sponsor career fairs to bring job seekers and employers together in specific professional, technical fields.

5. Federal and state employment offices. The U.S. government is one of the biggest employers in the country. During 2003 and 2004, for instance, the most active career site on the Web was operated by the federal government, with 1.6 million new hires. Counselors at federal and state employment centers also help job seekers find career opportunities. Figure 7.1 shows the homepage of the website for USAJOBS, which helps job seekers find employment opportunities with the U.S. government. Consult the following websites for listings of government jobs:

- America's Job Bank—*http://www.ajb.dni.us*
- Federal Jobs.Net—*http://www.federaljobs.net*
- Studentjobs.gov—*http://www.studentjobs.gov*
- U.S. Office of Personnel Management—*http://www.usajobs.opm.gov*

Many state agencies partner with one another, increasing your pool of possible openings.

USAJOBS website.   Figure 7.1

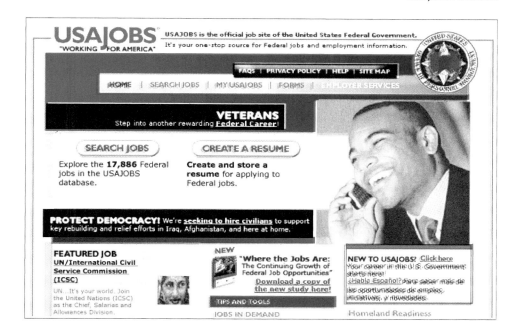

6. **Professional and trade journals and associations in your major.** Identify the most respected periodicals in your field and search their ads. The *American Journal of Nursing*, for example, carries notices of openings arranged by geographic location in each of its monthly issues; and each issue of *Food Technology* features a section called "Professional Placement," a listing of jobs all over the country. Similarly, *CIO Magazine—IT Professional Research Center* (*http://www.cio.com/ research/itcareer/*) can help you find jobs in the computer industry, engineering, and technology. Consult the *Encyclopedia of Associations* (*http://library.dialog .com/bluesheets/html/bl0114.html*) for a list of journals and newsletters for your profession. Many of the journals are also available online.

7. **The human resources department of a company or agency you would like to work for.** Often you will be able to fill out an application even if there is not a current opening. But do not call employers asking about openings; a visit shows a more serious interest.

8. **A résumé database service.** A number of online services will put your résumé in a database and make it available to prospective employers, who scan the database regularly to find suitable job candidates. Figure 7.2 describes a résumé database service offered by one professional organization—the Association for Computing Machinery (ACM)—for its members. Check to see if a professional society to which you belong (or might join) offers a similar service.

Figure 7.2   A description of one résumé database service.

Employers Benefit from ACM Résumé Database

The ACM Résumé Database is composed of résumés of ACM members—high-caliber, information-technology professionals who can bring expertise to your company. All résumés are up-to-date and can be searched according to criteria you provide, in a short period of time and at low rates. Single searches as well as annual subscriptions to the database can be requested from the database administrator, Resume-Link, at 614-529-0429. ACM institutional members get a 10% discount off the cost of the search.

And for ACM members! Our database also is now searchable for internships and co-op positions, as well as for full-time and consultant placements. Use this free career development service and submit your résumé online at **http://www.Resume-Link.com/**.

9. **Professional employment agencies.** Some agencies list two kinds of jobs—those that are applied for free of charge (because the employer pays the fee) and others that charge a stiff fee, usually a percentage of your first year's salary. If you do use an agency, be sure to ask who pays the fee for the service. Because employment agencies often find out about jobs through channels already available to you, speak to your campus career center first.

Whenever you find a relevant job, apply for it as soon as possible. Most jobs are filled in a few weeks, or sooner.

■ Preparing a Dossier

Your *dossier*, French for "bundle of documents," is your personal file stored at your campus placement office. It contains information about you that substantiates and supplements the facts listed on your résumé and letter of application. Basically, your dossier contains these documents:

- letters of recommendation
- letters that awarded you a scholarship, praised your work on the job, or honored you for community service
- your résumé, including job experiences
- your academic transcript(s)

You may ask that your dossier be sent to an employer, or employers may request it themselves if you have listed the placement office address on your résumé.

Individuals You Should Ask for Letters of Recommendation

The most important part of your dossier consists of your letters of recommendation. They can sell you or sink your chances, so select them carefully. Ask the following individuals to write letters describing your work qualifications and habits:

- a previous employer (even for a summer job)
- two or three of your professors who know and like your work, have graded your papers, or have supervised you in fieldwork or laboratory activities
- superiors who evaluated your work in the military
- community leaders or officials with whom you have worked on civic projects

Recommendations from such individuals will be regarded as more objective—and more relevant—than a letter from your clergy or a neighbor. Of course, if you are asked specifically for a character reference, by all means ask a member of the clergy.

Whoever you ask, make sure he or she is a strong supporter of yours, someone who has sincerely and consistently complimented your work and encouraged you in your career. Stay clear of individuals who are lukewarm or might be reluctant to recommend you.

Always Ask for Permission

Ask permission before you list an individual as a reference. You could jeopardize your chances for a job if a prospective employer called someone whom you named but did not ask to be a reference and that person responds that he or she did not even know you were looking for a job or, worse yet, reveals that you did not have the courtesy to ask to use his or her name.

Should You Ask Your Current Boss?

Asking your boss to recommend you for another job can be tricky. Be cautious. If your current employer knows that your education is preparing you for another profession, or if you are a student working at a part-time job, by all means ask for a letter of recommendation to be included in your dossier. However, if you are employed and are looking for professional advancement or a better salary elsewhere, you may not want your current employer to know that you are searching for another job.

You have the right to ask a prospective employer to respect your confidentiality (for instance, not to call you at work) until you become a leading candidate. At that point you may be happy to have your current employer consulted for a reference. On the other hand, if you are not on particularly good terms with your current employer and want to find another, more suitable position, inform the prospective employer as honestly and professionally as you can with the least damage to yourself. Use your best judgment depending on the circumstances of your search.

Should You See Your Letters?

You have a legal right to determine whether you want to see your letters. If you have read them, the fact is noted on the dossier. Some employers believe that if candidates see what is written about them, the references may be less frank and may withhold critical information. If you waive your right to see the letters written about you, you must sign an appropriate form, a copy of which is then given to the individual recommending you. Remember, though, that some individuals may refuse to write a letter that they know you will see; they may prefer absolute confidentiality. Before you make any decision about seeing your letters, get the advice of your instructors and placement counselors.

▇ Preparing a Résumé

The résumé, sometimes called a **data sheet** or **curriculum vitae,** may be the most important document you prepare for your job search. It deserves your utmost attention. Prepare your résumé at least six months before you plan to graduate. You'll need the finished document before writing any application letters. It is a factual and concise summary of your qualifications. A résumé is not your life history or your emotional autobiography. It is a record of results, showing a prospective employer that you have what it takes (in education and experience) to do the job you are applying for.

Résumés Are Persuasive Documents

Regard your résumé as a persuasive ad for your professional qualifications. It is not just a listing of job titles or a transcript of your courses; it should convince employers to interview you. Always customize your résumé, tailoring it for each job.

What you include—your key details, the wording, the ordering of information, and formatting—are all vital to your campaign to sell yourself and land the interview. Know what employers want to see. Basically, they want to get the most crucial details about your qualifications quickly. Accordingly, keep your print résumé short (preferably one page, never longer than two) and hard hitting. Everything you put on your résumé needs to convince an employer you have the very skills and background he or she is looking for. See pages 263–266 for an online résumé.

What Employers Like to See in a Résumé

Prospective employers will judge you and your work by your résumé, their first view of you and your qualifications. They want to see the following seven characteristics in an applicant's résumé.

- **Honesty.** Be truthful about your qualifications—your education, experience, and skills. Distorting, exaggerating, or falsifying information about your education or job experiences on your résumé is unethical and could cost you the job you get. If you were a clerical assistant to an attorney, don't describe yourself as a paralegal. Employers demand trustworthiness.
- **Attractiveness.** The document should be pleasing to the eye with appropriate spacing, fonts, and use of boldface; it shows you have a sense of proportion and document design and that you are neat, professional.

- **Careful organization.** The orderly arrangement of information is easy-to-follow, logical, and consistent; it shows you have the ability to process information and to summarize. Employers prize analytical thinking.
- **Conciseness.** Generally, keep your résumé to one page, as in Figure 7.3. However, depending on your education or job experience, you may want to include a second page. Résumés are written in short sentences that omit "I" and that use action-packed verbs, such as those listed in Table 7.1.
- **Accuracy.** Grammar, spelling, dates, names, titles, and programs are correct; your résumé shows you can communicate effectively. Typos say you are not responsible in small matters and may not be in larger ones as well.
- **Currency.** All information is up-to-date and documented, with no gaps or sketchy areas, and demonstrates your computer literacy and ethics. Missing or incorrect dates or not supplying contact information are flags to reject your résumé.
- **Relevance.** The information is appropriate for the job level, shows that you have the necessary education and experience, and confirms that you can be an effective team player.

Your goal is to prepare a résumé that shows the employer you possess the sought-after job skills. One that is unattractive; difficult to follow; poorly written; filled with typos, inconsistencies, and unexplained gaps; and not relevant for the prospective employer's needs will not make the first cut.

TABLE 7.1   Action Verbs to Use in Your Résumé

accommodated	customized	initiated	researched
accomplished	dealt in	installed	scheduled
achieved	designed	instituted	searched
administered	determined	instructed	selected
analyzed	developed	interpreted	served
arranged	directed	maintained	settled
assembled	drafted	managed	sold
assisted	earned	monitored	solved
attended	elected	motivated	supervised
awarded	established	navigated	taught
built	estimated	negotiated	tested
calculated	evaluated	operated	tracked
coached	expedited	organized	trained
collected	figured	oversaw	translated
communicated	fulfilled	performed	tutored
compiled	guided	planned	updated
completed	handled	prepared	upgraded
composed	headed	programmed	verified
computed	implemented	reappraised	weighed
conducted	improved	reconciled	won
coordinated	increased	reduced	worked
created	informed	reported	wrote

Figure 7.3   Résumé from a student with little job experience.

Anthony H. Jones

73 Allenwood Boulevard • Santa Rosa, California 95401-1074 • 707-555-6390
ajones@plat.com   www.plat.com/users/ajones/resume.html

Website Developer • Designer • Graphic Artist

Offers precise, convincing objective

Career Objective

Full-time position as a layout artist with a commercial publishing house using my knowledge of state-of-the-art design technology.

Starts with most important qualification—education

Education

Santa Rosa Junior College, 2004–2006, A.S. degree to be awarded in 2006
 Dean's List in 2005; GPA 3.45
 Major: Commercial Graphics Illustration, with specialty in design layout
 Related courses included:
 • Digital Photography
 • Graphics Programs: Illustrator, Photoshop
 • Desktop Publishing: QuarkXPress, WordPerfect Suite 8

Stresses job-related activities of apprenticeship

Apprenticeship, 2005–2006, McAdam Publishers
 Major projects included:
 • Assisting layout editors with page composition and importing images.
 • Writing detailed reports on digital photography, designs, and artwork used in *Living in Sonoma County* (www.sonomacounty.com) and *Real Estate in Sonoma County* (www.resc.net) magazines.

Includes part-time work experience

Experience

Salesperson (part-time), **2001–2003**, Buchman's Department Store
 Duties included assisting customers in sporting goods and appliance departments and coordinating sport shop by displaying merchandise.

Computer Skills

Know QuarkXPress, WordPerfect Suite 8.

Demonstrates skills in Web design

Related Activities

Volunteer; designed website and three-fold brohure for the Santa Rosa Humane Society's 2005 fund drive.

Credentials and portfolio emphasize accomplishment in photography and Web design

References

References, college transcripts, and a portfolio of web designs and photographs available upon request.

It might be to your advantage to prepare several versions of your résumé and then adapt each one you send out to the specific job skills a prospective employer is looking for. It pays to customize your résumé. Following the process in the next section will help you prepare any résumé.

The Process of Writing Your Résumé

To write an effective résumé, ask the following important questions:

1. What classes did you excel in?
2. What papers, reports, or presentations earned you your highest grades?
3. What computer skills have you mastered—languages, software knowledge, navigating and developing Internet resources? Knowledge of e-commerce? E-journaling? Ability to design a website?
4. What jobs have you had? For how long and where? What were your primary duties?
5. What technical skills have you acquired?
6. Do you work well with people? What skills do you possess as a member of a team working toward a common job goal (e.g., finishing a report)?
7. Can you organize complicated tasks or identify and solve problems quickly?
8. Have you had experiences/responsibilities managing money—preparing payrolls, conducting nightly audits at a store, advising clients about portfolios and retirement accounts?
9. Have you won any awards or scholarships or received a raise, bonus, commendation, and/or promotion at work?

Pay *special attention* to your four or five most significant, job-worthy strengths and work especially hard on listing them concisely.

Although not everything you have done relates directly to a particular job, indicate how your achievements are relevant to the employer's overall needs. For example, supervising staff in a grocery store points to your ability to perform the same duties in another business context.

Regardless of the job you apply for, keep in mind that all companies and other organizations place a premium on an employee who can excel in one or more of these roles:

- problem solver
- people person
- computer programmer
- Web designer
- money manager
- information analyst

As you prepare your résumé, see how many of your skills and experiences allow you to portray yourself in these roles.

Balancing Education and Experience

If you have years of experience, don't flood your prospective employer with too many details. You cannot possibly include every detail of your job(s) for the last ten or twenty years.

- Emphasize only those skills and positions most likely to earn you the job.
- Eliminate your earliest jobs that do not relate to your present employment search.
- Combine and condense skills acquired over many years and through many jobs.

Figures 7.5 and 7.8 show the résumés of Anna Cassetti and Donald Kitto-Klein, who have a great deal of job experience to offer prospective employers.

Many job candidates who have spent most of their lives in school are faced with the other extreme: not having much job experience to put down. The worst thing to do is to write "None" for experience. Any part-time, summer, or other seasonal jobs, as well as work done for a library or science laboratory, show an employer that you are responsible and knowledgeable about the obligations of being an employee. Figure 7.3 shows a résumé from Anthony Jones, a student with very little job experience; Figure 7.4 shows the résumé of María Lopez, a student with a few years of experience.

What to Exclude from a Résumé

Knowing what to exclude from a résumé is as important as knowing what to include. Since federal employment laws prohibit discrimination on the basis of age, sex, race, national origin, religion, marital status, or disability, do not include such information on your résumé. Here are some other details best left out of your résumé:

- salary demands, expectations, or ranges
- preferences for work schedules, days off, or overtime
- comments about fringe benefits
- travel restrictions
- reasons for leaving your previous job
- your photograph (unless you are applying for a modeling or acting job)
- social security number
- comments about your family, spouse, or children
- height, weight, hair or eye color
- personal information, hobbies, interests (unless relevant to the job you are seeking, in which case put under Related Skills)

Save comments about salary and schedules for your interview. (See pages 275–281.) The résumé should be written appropriately to get you that interview.

Parts of a Résumé

Contact Information

At the top of the page center your name (do not use a nickname); address, including your ZIP code; telephone number; and e-mail address. Avoid unprofessional e-mail addresses such as <Toughguy@netfield.com> or <barbiegirl@techscape.com>. Also, include your website and fax number if you have these for an employer to contact you.

Career Objective

One of the first things a prospective employer reads is your career objective statement that specifies the exact type of job you are looking for and in what ways you

Résumé from a student with some job experience.   Figure 7.4

MARÍA H. LOPEZ
1725 Brooke Street
Miami, Florida 32701-2121
(305) 555-3429   **mlopez@eagle.com**

Provides easy-to-find contact information

Career Objective	Position assisting dentist in providing dental care, counseling, and preventive dental treatments, especially in pedodontics.
Education	A.S. in Dental Hygiene, Miami-Dade Community College, Miami, Florida August 2004–May 2006 Completed courses in oral pathology, dental materials and specialties, periodontics, and community dental health. Experienced with procedures and instruments used with oral prophylaxis techniques. Subject of major project was proper nutrition and dental health for preschoolers.
	Minor: Psychology (twelve hours in child and adolescent psychology) Received excellent evaluations in business writing course. GPA is 3.3. Bilingual: Spanish/English.
	Will take American Dental Assistants' Examination on June 2.
Experience	St. Francis Hospital, Miami Beach, Florida April 2002–July 2004 Full-time clerk on the pediatric floor. Ordered supplies, maintained records, transcribed orders, and greeted and assisted visitors.
	Murphy Construction Company, Miami, Florida June 2001–April 2002 Secretary-receptionist. Did keyboarding, billing, and mailing in small office (three employees).
	City of Hialeah, Florida Summers 1999–2000 Water meter reader
Computer Skills	Microsoft Office, Excel, Health Care spreadsheet
References	Available upon request

Lists course and clinical work required for licensure and job

Calls attention to being bilingual, a benefit for employer and patients

Highlights previous job responsibilities in health care setting

are qualified to hold it. Create an objective that precisely dovetails with the prospective employer's requirements. Such a statement should be the result of your focused self-evaluation and your evaluation of the job market. It will influence everything else you include. Depending on your background and the types of jobs you are qualified for, you might formulate two or three different career or employment objectives to use with different versions of your résumé as you apply for various positions.

To write an effective career objective statement, ask yourself four basic questions:

1. What kind of job do I want?
2. What kind of job am I qualified for?
3. What capabilities do I possess?
4. What kinds of skills do I want to learn?

Avoid trite or vague goals such as "looking for professional advancement" or "want to join a progressive company." Compare the vague objectives on the left with the more precise ones on the right.

Unfocused	Focused
Job in sales to use my aggressive skills in expanding markets.	Regional sales representative using my proven skills in marketing and communication to develop and expand a customer base.
Full-time position as staff nurse.	Full-time position as staff nurse on cardiac step-down unit to offer excellent primary care nursing and patient/family teaching.

Credentials

The order of the next two categories—**Education** and **Experience**—can vary. Generally, if you have lots of work experience, list it first as Anna Cassetti did (see Figure 7.5). However, if you are a recent graduate short on job experience, list education first, as Anthony Jones did (see Figure 7.3). María Lopez (Figure 7.4) also decided to place her education before her job experience because the job she was applying for required the formal training she received at Miami-Dade Community College.

Education

Begin with your most recent education first, then list everything **significant since high school.** Give the name(s) of the school(s); dates attended; and degree, diploma, or certificate earned. Don't overlook military schools or major training programs (EMT, court reporter), institutes, internships, or workshops you have completed. Avoid vague titles such as Science 203 or Nursing IV. Instead, concentrate on describing the kinds of skills you learned.

30 hours in planning and development courses specializing in transportation, land use, and community facilities; 12 hours in field methods of gathering, interpreting, and describing survey data in reports.

Completed 28 hours in major courses in business marketing, management, and materials in addition to 12 hours in information science, including HTML/Web publishing.

Résumé from an individual with ten years' job experience.   Figure 7.5

ANNA C. CASSETTI

6457 Blackstone Avenue   MacMurray Real Estate
Fort Worth, TX 76321-6733   1700 Ross Boulevard
(817) 555-5657   Haltom City, TX 77320-1700
acassetti@netdor.com   (817) 555-7211

OBJECTIVE
Full-time sales position with large real-estate office in the Phoenix or Tucson areas with opportunities to use proven skills in real-estate appraisal and tax counseling.

EXPERIENCE
MacMurray Real Estate, Haltom City, Texas, 2006–present
Real-estate agent. Excelled in small suburban office (five salespersons plus broker) with limited listings; **sold individually over three million dollars in residential property**; appraised both residential and commercial listings.

Dallman Federal Savings and Loan, Inc., Fort Worth, Texas, 1999–2005
Chief Teller. Responsible for supervising, training, and coordinating activities of six full-time and two part-time tellers. Promoted to Chief Teller, March 2000, with bonus.

H&R Block, Westover Hills, Texas, 1999 (Sept.–Dec.)
Tax Consultant. Prepared personal and business returns.

Cruckshank's Hardware Store, Fort Worth, Texas, 1996–1998
Salesperson.

U.S. Navy, 1989–1995
Honorably discharged with rank of Petty Officer, Third Class.
Served as stores manager; earned three recommendations

EDUCATION
Texas Christian University, Fort Worth, Texas, 1998–2004
Awarded B.S. degree in Real-Estate Management. Completed thirty-three hours in business and real-estate courses with a concentration in finance, appraising, and property management. Also took twelve hours in programming and Web designing. Wrote reports on appraisal procedures as part of supervised training program.

H&R Block, Westover Hills, Texas, 1998 (Sept.–Dec.)
Earned diploma in Basic Income Tax Preparation after completing intensive ten-week course.

Provides home and work contact information

Begins with the most important job qualification first— experience

Job history focuses on sales achievements, promotion, and responsibilities

Gives related military experience

Documents education by citing specific areas

Includes computer and communication skills

Continued

Figure 7.5   (Continued)

Cassetti 2

U.S. Naval Base, San Diego, California, 1993–1996
Attended U.S. Navy's Supply Management School.
Applied principles of stores management at Newport Naval Base.

SKILLS AND ACTIVITIES
Licensed Texas Realtor—756a2737
Chair, Financial Committee, Grace Presbyterian Church, Fort Worth.
Adviser, Junior Achievement.

REFERENCES
References available upon request.

Provides necessary license information

List your grade point average (GPA) only if it is 3.0 or above; otherwise, indicate your GPA in just your major or during your last term, again if it is above 3.0.

Experience

Your job history is the key category for many employers. It shows them that you have held jobs before and that you are responsible. Here are some guidelines about listing your experience.

1. Begin with your most recent position and work backward—in reverse chronological order. List the company or agency name, location (city and state), and your title. Do not mention why you left a job.

2. For each job or activity provide short descriptions of your duties and achievements. If you were a work-study student, don't say that you helped an instructor. Emphasize your responsibilities; for example, you helped to set up a chemistry laboratory, you ordered supplies and kept an inventory of them. Rather than saying you were a secretary, indicate that you wrote business letters and contracts, learned various software programs, designed a company website, prepared schedules for part-time help in an office of twenty-five people, or assisted the manager in preparing accounts.

3. In describing your position(s), emphasize any responsibilities that involved handling money (for example, billing customers, filing insurance claims, or preparing payrolls); collaborating with employees; working with customer accounts, services, and programs; or writing letters and reports. Prospective employers are interested in your leadership abilities, financial shrewdness (especially if you saved your company money), tact in dealing with the public, and communications skills. They will also be favorably impressed by promotions you may have earned.

4. If you have been a full-time parent for ten years or a caregiver for a family member or friend, indicate the management skills you developed while running a household and any community or civic service, as Dora Cooper Bolger does in her résumé in Figure 7.6. She skillfully relates her family and community accomplishments to the specific job she seeks. Her volunteer work translates into marketing skills an employer wants.

Related Skills and Achievements
Not every résumé will have this section but the following are all employer-friendly things to include:

- second or third languages you speak or write
- extensive travel
- certificates or licenses you hold
- memberships in professional associations (e.g., American Society of Safety Engineers, Black Student Association, National Hispanic Business Association, Child Development Organization)
- memberships in community groups (e.g., Lions, Red Cross, Elks); list any offices you hold—recorder, secretary, fund drive chairperson

Computer Skills
Knowledge of computer hardware, software, word processing programs, and Web design and search engines is extremely valuable in a job market. Note how Anthony Jones and María Lopez inform prospective employers about their relevant computer competencies in Figures 7.3 and 7.4.

Honors/Awards
List any academic honors you have won (dean's list, department awards, school honors, scholarships, grants, honorable mentions). Memberships in honor societies in your major and professional associations also demonstrate that you are professionally accomplished and active.

References
You can simply say that you will provide references on request or you can list the names, titles, e-mail and street addresses, and telephone numbers of no more than three or four individuals. Be sure to obtain their permission first. List your references only when they are well known in the community or belong to the same profession in which you are seeking employment—you profit from your association with a recognizable name or title.

Asking your boss can be tricky. If your current employer knows that your education is preparing you for another profession, ask her or him. However, if you are employed and are looking for professional advancement or a better salary elsewhere, you may not want your current employer to know you are searching for another job until you become a leading candidate.

In this section of your résumé, you may also indicate that a portfolio of your work is available for review, as Anthony Jones did in Figure 7.3.

Figure 7.6   Dora Cooper Bolger's résumé organized by skill areas.

DORA COOPER BOLGER
1215 Lakeview Avenue
Westhampton, MI 46532
Home: 616-555-4772   Cell: 616-555-4773   dbolger@aol.com

OBJECTIVE

Seek full-time position as public affairs officer in health care, educational, or charitable organization

SKILLS

Organizational Communication
- Delivered 20 presentations to civic groups on educational issues
- Recorded minutes and helped formulate agenda as president of large, local PTA for past $6^1/_2$ years
- Possess excellent computer skills in PeopleSoft and Microsoft Word
- Updated and maintained computerized mailing lists for Teens in Trouble and Foster Parents' Association

Financial
- Spearheaded 3 major fund-raising drives (total of $178,000 collected)
- Prepared and implemented large family budget (3 children, 8 foster children) for 15 years
- Served as financial secretary, Faith Methodist Church, for 4 years

Administrative
- Organized volunteers for American Kidney Fund (last 5 years)
- Established and oversaw neighborhood carpool (17 drivers; more than 60 children) for 7 years
- Coordinated after-school tutoring program for Teens in Trouble; president since 1996

HONORS

"Volunteer of the Year"(2005), Michigan Child Placement Agency

EDUCATION

Metropolitan Community College, A.A., 2001
Mid-Michigan College, B.S., expected 2007; major: public administration; minor: psychology. GPA 3.45

WORK EXPERIENCE

Secretary, 1991–1999 (full- and part-time): Merrymount Plastics; Foley and Wasson; Westhampton Health Dept.; G & K Electric

REFERENCES

Available on request

Aptly features skill areas before education

Links achievements and awards from volunteer and home-based work skills most important to prospective employer

Chooses strong, active verbs to convey image of a results-oriented professional

Places education after experience; includes major and related minor plus strong GPA

Organizing Your Résumé

There are two primary ways to organize your résumé: chronologically or by function or skill area.

Chronologically

The résumés in Figures 7.3, 7.4, and 7.5 are organized chronologically, with most recent listed first. Information about the job applicants is listed year by year under two main categories—education and experience. This is the traditional way to organize a résumé. It is straightforward and easy-to-read, and employers find it acceptable. The chronological sequence works especially well when you can show a clear continuity toward progress in your career through your job(s) and in schoolwork or when you want to apply for a similar job with another company.

A chronological résumé is appropriate for students who want to emphasize recent educational achievements.

By Function or Skill Area

Depending on your experiences and accomplishments, you might organize your résumé according to function or skill area. According to this plan, you would *not* list your information chronologically in the categories "Experience" and "Education." Instead, you would sort your achievements and abilities—whether from course work, jobs, extracurricular activities, or technical skills—into two to four key skill areas, such as "Sales," "Public Relations," "Training," "Management," "Technical Capabilities," "Counseling," "Group Leadership," "Communications," "Network Operations," "Customer Service," "Working with People," "Multicultural Experiences," "Computer Skills," "Problem-Solving Skills."

Under each area you would list three to five points illustrating your achievements in that area. Skills or functional résumés are often called **bullet résumés** because they itemize the candidate's main strengths in bulleted lists. Some employers prefer the bullet résumé because they can more easily skim the candidate's list of qualifications in a few seconds.

Preparing a Skills Résumé

When you prepare a functional or skills résumé, start with your name, address, telephone number, and career objective, just as in a chronological résumé. To find the best two or three functional areas to include, use the prewriting strategies (especially clustering and brainstorming) discussed in Chapter 2. Think of your skills areas as the common denominators that cross job and educational boundaries—the common threads that link your diverse experiences. Note how Donald Kitto-Klein (Figure 7.8) was able to pull together a series of related, marketable skills from the many different jobs he had held over several years.

After you discover and suitably revise the information to be included in your categories, briefly list your educational and work experiences, as Dora Cooper Bolger (Figure 7.6), Anna Cassetti (Figure 7.7), and Donald Kitto-Klein (Figure 7.8) do.

Figure 7.7   Anna Cassetti's résumé organized by function or skill areas.

ANNA C. CASSETTI

Home	**Office**
6457 Blackstone Avenue	MacMurray Real Estate
Fort Worth, TX 76321-6733	1700 Ross Boulevard
(817) 555-5657	Haltom City, TX 77320-1700
acassetti@netdoor.com	(817) 555-7211

Begins with a clear and focused objective

OBJECTIVE   Sales position with real-estate office in the Phoenix or Tucson areas with opportunities to use proven skills in appraisals and tax counseling

Groups accomplishments into the three most relevant and marketable skills for prospective employer

SALES/ FINANCIAL
- Sold over $3 million of residential property in 2 years
- Served as a tax consultant with special interest in real-estate sales/market conditions
- Performed general banking procedures as chief teller
- Responsible for maintaining, purchasing, and ordering supplies for ship's store in U.S. Navy

Uses bullets, strong verbs, and specific examples

PUBLIC RELATIONS
- Helped clients select appropriate property for their needs and income
- Counseled commercial and individual clients about taxes
- Supervised, trained, and coordinated the activities of six bank tellers
- Earned bonus for rapport in assisting customers with their banking needs

Emphasizes written and oral skills

COMMUNICATION
- Prepared standard real-estate appraisals
- Wrote in-depth business reports on appraisal procedures, property management problems, and banking policies affecting real-estate transactions
- Achieved proficiency in CorpSheet and other spreadsheet programs
- Conducted small group training and sales sessions

Stresses educational preparation after skills

EDUCATION   B.S. in Real-Estate Management, 2004
Texas Christian University, Fort Worth, Texas
Advanced course work taken in business, finance, and real estate; minor in data processing

Diploma, Basic Income Tax Preparation, 1998
H&R Block, Westover Hills, Texas

Continued

(Continued)   **Figure 7.7**

Cassetti 2

EMPLOYMENT	MacMurray Real Estate, Haltom City, Texas 2006–present; sales agent
	Dallman Federal Savings and Loan, Inc., Fort Worth, Texas 1999–2005; Chief Teller
	H&R Block, Westover Hills, Texas 1999 Sept.–Dec.; consultant, tax preparer
	Cruckshank's Hardware Store, Fort Worth, Texas 1996–1998; salesperson
	U.S. Navy, San Diego, California (last duty station) 1989–1995; stores manager; honorably discharged with rank of Petty Officer, Third Class
REFERENCES	Available from the Placement Office, Texas Christian University, Fort Worth, TX 76119-6811

Demonstrates professional commitment and successes

Supplies contact information for references

Who Should Use a Functional Résumé?

The following individuals would probably benefit from organizing their résumés by function instead of chronologically:

- nontraditional students who have diverse job experiences
- individuals who are changing their profession because of downsizing or seeking new professional opportunities
- individuals who have changed jobs frequently over the last five to ten years
- individuals who are entering the civilian marketplace after retiring from the military

Note Dora Cooper Bolger's profitable use of a functional résumé format in Figure 7.6. She was out of school because of family commitments, yet she uses the experiences she acquired during those years to her advantage in her résumé organized under "Skills." She successfully translates her many accomplishments in managing a home and working on charitable and community projects into marketable skills of great interest to a prospective employer, and no gap of ten years interrupts a work experience list.

Because a functional résumé clearly emphasizes skills acquired over long periods of time, Donald Kitto-Klein also chose this format for his résumé in Figure 7.8.

Figure 7.8   Functional résumé by a candidate who has held a variety of jobs.

DONALD KITTO-KLEIN

kitto@gar.com   http://www.dkk@opengate.com

56 South Ardmore Way   Garland.Com
Petersburg, NY 15438   Grand Banks, NY 15532
(716) 555-9032   (716) 555-4800, Ext. 5398

Connects writer's technical and administrative skills

Objective	Seek supervisory position in computer maintenance and service to provide network continuity to staff and clients.
Computer Languages	C, C+, C++, Java, Unix
Computer Programs	QuarkXPress, Lotus Notes, Adobe Acrobat, Microsoft Word
Systems Experience	MACHINES: IBM, RS60000, Macintosh, Sun NETWORKS: Novell, Banyan; set up Internet sites

Establishes technical background/qualifications for job

Computer Maintenance/ Service Skills
- Serviced PCs and workstations on a regular basis for $3^{1}/2$ years
- Worked extensively on spreadsheets/database software
- Modified software billing program
- Coordinated maintenance/service activities

Emphasizes the management skills and experiences prospective employer wants

People Skills
- Promoted to Support Services Team Leader
- Supervised Computer Servicing with three technicians
- Worked closely with computer manufacturers and vendors to minimize hardware down time
- Elected to employee benefits committee

Demonstrates ability to be a problem solver, a leader, and a spokesperson for company

Communication Skills
- Collaboratively wrote safety manual for power company road crews
- Taught in-house training sessions on computer maintenance, networking, data security
- Devised routing systems to expedite work orders
- Coordinated small group meetings in systems analysis

Employment	Garland.Com, 2003–present Business Graphics and Computers Store, Salesperson, 1999–2003 U.S. Army, Specialist, 4/E, 1992–1998

Includes relevant military background

Education	B.S., Grand Valley Technical Institute, 2004 U.S. Army schools in computer programs, 1994–1998
References	Available on request.

You might want to prepare two different versions of your résumé—one functional and one chronological—to see which sells your talents better, as Anna Cassetti did in Figures 7.5 and 7.7. Don't hesitate to seek the advice of your instructor or placement counselor about which one will work best for you.

The Online Résumé

In addition to preparing a hard copy of your résumé, expect to send it online. Prospective employers will often want applications sent to their Web addresses or they will scan résumé databases such as **hotjobs.yahoo.com** or **monster.com** as well as databases sponsored by professional societies such as the ACM in Figure 7.2. An online résumé will give you the widest possible exposure to attract prospective employers. It can take many different formats. You can send it by disk, by e-mail, through a database service, or via other posting channels, including your own website.

Tech Note

Developing Your Own Website for Your Job Search

You can create your own website with your résumé, samples of your work, a cover letter, and perhaps scanned copies of awards you have received.

If you include your website address in your correspondence, prospective employers will be able to find a list of your qualifications quickly. Because your e-mail address will appear on your webpage, requests for additional information can be directed to you immediately.

Other advantages of having a résumé linked to your webpage include the following:

- Prospective employers looking for computer-literate employees are impressed by a résumé that includes a Web URL.
- You can change and revise your résumé quickly.
- Posting your résumé online will save you money in printing and postage.
- Posting and revising a résumé through your free homepage allows for more memory size than sites such as monster.com (*http://www.monster.com*) and the Academic Employment Network (*http://www.academploy.com*).
- Having your résumé online increases your job-market accessibility.

The Internet is full of user-friendly places that give simple-to-use instructions for building a webpage. Try the following:

- Designing an Accessible Webpage (*http://www.trace.wisc.edu/world/web/index.html*)
- Web Page Design for Designers (*http://www.wpdfd.com*)
- Yahoo! Geocities (*http://www.geocities.yahoo.com/home*)

Also see Chapter 12 (pp. 521–545) for specific advice on designing a website.

Employers may receive 400 or 500 résumés online for one job, or even more for a series of jobs. Because of such volume, they often scan a résumé in 20 seconds or less to make their first cut. You need to prepare your online résumé so that it reaches and captures the attention of the maximum number of employers. Basically, an online résumé contains the same information found in the kinds of résumés already discussed on pages 248–263. But while the information may be the same, the design of an online résumé is different. If your online résumé is not designed and sent properly, employers will not be able to scan or file it in their database. Figure 7.9 shows an online version of the Anthony Jones résumé from Figure 7.3.

Formatting an Online Résumé

Here are some guidelines to help you make sure your résumé is scannable:

1. Create your résumé as an RTF, HTML, or MS Word file (the most common file formats in the world of work) rather than as a PDF, WordPerfect, or Zip file.
2. Save your résumé properly and consistently—as an ASCII plain text file. Always follow the directions given by the résumé database service or the prospective employer.
3. Avoid underlining, boldface, italics, boxes, or shadowing. Such word processing features garble the text of your résumé, making it unscannable. Use full caps instead of bold or italics for emphasis, and an asterisk (*) or a plus sign (+) in place of a bullet at the beginning of a line, as in Figure 7.9.
4. Do not use hard to read or fancy fonts like script. Instead, choose a font like Courier 12 that is clear and does not mask letters, which makes them unscannable. Use a sans serif font (see p. 514).
5. Make your résumé functional and easy to scroll. Keep in mind that reading a résumé on a screen is different from seeing it on a printed page. Use plenty of white space between sections so that headings are clear and distinct from one another. Put no more than 65 characters on a line to make your résumé easy to read.
6. Design your résumé to be concise. Prospective employers will not have the time or patience to scroll through multiple screens to find information. The equivalent of one printed page is still best.
7. Select the automatic wrapping feature to avoid losing characters at the end of a line. Such a feature will also make sure you do not exceed the limit of 65 characters per line.
8. Align everything flush with the left margin. Do not indent anything or use tabs.
9. Never send your résumé as an e-mail attachment. A prospective employer will not open it because of the risk of contracting a virus. Copy and paste it into your e-mail message.
10. Include a short cover note, placed before your résumé, telling the prospective employer you are sending it in response to a specific job (and name it).
11. Format and save your résumé before you send it to any database service.

An online résumé.   Figure 7.9

Anthony H. Jones
P.O. Box 1074
Santa Rosa, California 95401-1074
Phone: (707) 555-6390
For additional information: Ahjones1@santarosa.career.edu/~dossier

KEYWORDS

Web designer, computer graphics, Illustrator, Photoshop, QuarkXPress,
fundraiser, budgets, sales, Soapscan, WriteNow, virus protection,
team player

OBJECTIVE

A position as layout and Web design editor with commercial publisher

EDUCATION

Santa Rosa Junior College, A.S. degree to be awarded in June 2006.
Commercial Graphics Illustration major. Digital photography minor.
GPA 3.45

COMPUTER SKILLS

Excellent working knowledge of computer graphics: Illustrator,
Photoshop, QuarkXPress, WordPerfect Suite 8, Soapscan, WriteNow

EXPERIENCE

*Intern in layout and design department. Preparing page composition,
importing visuals, manipulating images, McAdam Publishers, 8 Parkway
Heights, Santa Rosa, CA 94211

*Salesperson; display merchandise coordinator, Buchman's Department
Store, Greenview Mall, Santa Rosa

*Volunteer: designed website, brochures, and other artwork for
successful fund drive, Santa Rosa Humane Society

*Web designer, graphic artist, proofreader, Thunder, student
magazine

REFERENCES

Career Center, Santa Rosa Junior College
Portfolio available: Ahjones1@santarosa.career.edu/~dossier

All lines aligned flush with the left margin

Provides keywords for search engine readiness

All caps rather than bold, italic, fancy fonts used to highlight categories

Uses terminology appropriate for position

Uses keyword nouns rather than action verbs to increase employer matches

Asterisks rather than bullets mark beginning of lines

Making Your Online Résumé Search-Engine Ready

The most important part of your online résumé is the kind of keywords you use. Prospective employers scan résumés to find the keywords they most want to see in the job seeker's description of his or her experience, education, and interpersonal skills. The more matches, or hits, they find between appropriate keywords on your résumé and their list, the better your chances are of being interviewed. List keywords at the top of your résumé, as in Figure 7.9, and also include them throughout your résumé in appropriate places. Table 7.2 lists some examples of persuasive keywords employers like to see in a job candidate's résumé highlighting experience, skills, and education.

Here are a few tips to help you select appropriate keywords:

1. Include the keywords found in the employer's ad to increase your chances of securing an interview.
2. Do not be afraid of using shoptalk (or jargon). An employer searching for a specialist will expect you to be aware of current terminology.
3. Use keywords to head and connect sections or categories of your résumé. Keyword headers will help you emphasize your job strengths and make it easy for employers to scroll back to an appropriate section of your résumé.
4. Replace the kind of action verbs found in conventional résumés on the left with keyword nouns on the right. Here are some examples:

Conventional Résumé	Online Résumé
edited company newsletter	newsletter editor
wrote technical report	technical writer
performed laboratory tests	laboratory technician
responsible for managing accounts	accounts manager
won two awards	award winner
solved software problems	software specialist

Testing, Proofing, and Sending Your Online Résumé

1. Test your formatting. Send your résumé to a friend who does not use your Internet provider to be sure your file is readable and formatted correctly.
2. Proofread carefully just as you would a traditional paper résumé.
3. Don't just put *résumé* as the subject of your file to an employer. List your name, or your professional e-mail address, along with *résumé* so that your file is properly credited (**suesmithresume@netscape.com**).
4. Simply posting your résumé online is not enough. Send a scannable hard copy as well as a cover letter to prospective employers. But do not fold or staple your résumé. Put it, along with your cover letter, in a large envelope so an employer can scan and file it easily.
5. Always keep a log of where you have sent your résumé online.

TABLE 7.2   Sample Keywords for an Online Résumé

Job Title	Area of Expertise	Computer Skills	Degrees/ Licenses	Job Interpersonal Skills
Accountant	Accounting	Access	AA	Analytical
Consumer advocate	Automotive repair	Adobe Illustrator	AS	Bilingual
Editor	Budget	DreamWeaver	ASID	Competency based
Environmentalist	Computer support	E-commerce	BA	Competitive
Fitness/wellness	Construction	Excel	BS	Cooperative
Health care	Consumer affairs	Filemaker Pro	CPA	Critical thinking
Hospitality management	Counseling	HTML	EMT	Customer oriented
Intern	Customer service	Adobe InDesign	LAT	Ethical
Law enforcement officer	Engineering	JavaScript	LTC	Experienced
Maintenance expert	Financial affairs	Lotus Notes	LPN	Flexible
Officer	Graphics	Lotus 1-2-3	MAT	Fund raising
Paralegal	Health care	Microsoft Word	MT	Goal oriented
Pharmacy tech	Human resources	Outlook	NAVT	High energy
Planner	Information technology	PageMaker	OT	International
Programmer	Legal	PeopleSoft	PTA	Leadership
Public relations	Management	PhotoShop	PT	Multitasking
Report writer	Marketing	PowerPoint	RN	Speaker/writer
Resident manager	Networking systems	QuarkXPress	RT	Research oriented
Sales associate	Office support	QuickBooks		Results oriented
Technician	Public relations	SPSS		Risk taking
Tutor	Purchasing	WordPerfect		Safety conscious
Underwriter	Recruitment	XML		Self-motivated
Veterinary tech	Safety/security			Strong work ethic
Waitperson	Sales			Studied abroad
Web designer	Technical support			Team player

Tech Note

Cyber-Safe Your Résumé

Whether you use a database service or post your résumé on a website, protect your identity and your current and future jobs. By being careful about revealing personal information, you demonstrate to a prospective employer that you have a high commitment to confidentiality and safety. Here are some guidelines:

- Do not put personal information in your résumé—home or cell phone number and home address, social security number or photograph. Use a post office box if you need a land address.
- Use an anonymous e-mail address rather than your personal one. Consider a generic e-mail address available through an online service but one that includes a word or phrase that might identify your area of expertise, for example, *JosieProgrammer@aol.com*. Or include an e-mail link with a built-in "mailto" on your résumé.
- Never put the names of your references or their addresses online. Simply say, "References available on request."
- Block certain readers from searching your résumé, such as your current employer or firms that you know send out spam.
- Never use your present employer's company name or use a business e-mail address.
- The online résumé is *not* the place to allow readers access to a portfolio of your work.

◼ Letters of Application

Along with your résumé, you must send your prospective employer a letter of application, one of the most important pieces of correspondence you may ever write. Its goal is to get you an interview and ultimately the job. Letters you write in applying for jobs should be **p**ersonable, **p**rofessional, and **p**ersuasive—the three P's. Knowing how the letter of application and résumé work together and how they differ can give you a better idea of how to compose your letter.

How Application Letters and Résumés Differ

The résumé is a persuasive record of dates, your important achievements, skills, names, places, addresses, and jobs. As noted earlier, expect to prepare several different résumés depending on your experience and the job market.

Your letter of application also must be tailor-made for the jobs you want to apply for. You must write a new, original letter to each prospective employer. It should respond precisely to the exact qualifications the employer lists for the job.

The letter of application is a sales letter that emphasizes and applies the most relevant details (of education, experience, and talents) in your résumé. In short, the résumé contains the raw material that the letter of application transforms into a finished and highly marketable product—you.

Résumé Facts to Exclude from Letters of Application

The letter of application should not simply repeat the details listed in your résumé. In fact, the following details that you would include in your résumé should *not* be restated in the letter:

- personal data, including license or certificate numbers
- specific names of courses in your major
- names and addresses of all your references

Duplicating those details in your letter gives no new information that might persuade prospective employers that you are the individual they are seeking.

Writing the Letter of Application

The letter of application can make the difference between your getting an interview and being eliminated early from the competition. Keep in mind that employers receive hundreds of letters and yours will have to compete fiercely for attention. You want your letter to be placed in the "definitely interview" category. Limit your letter to one page. As you prepare your letter, use the following general guidelines.

1. **Follow the standard conventions of letter writing** (see Chapter 5). Print your letter on good-quality, white 8.5" × 11" paper. Proofread meticulously; a spelling error, typo, or grammatical mistake will make you look careless and will ruin your chances of getting the job.

2. **Make sure your letter looks attractive.** Your letter represents you in the eyes of a prospective employer. Make a favorable impression with it. Use wide margins and don't crowd your page. Keep your paragraphs short and readable—four or five sentences (see p. 150 in Chapter 5).

3. **Send your letter to a specific person.** Never address an application letter "To Whom It May Concern," "Dear Sir or Madam," "Director of Human Resources," or "Dear Employer." Try to get an individual's name by double-checking the company's website. If you cannot find the human resources director there, try calling the company's switchboard and be sure to verify the spelling of the person's name and his or her title.

4. **Don't forget the "you attitude"** (see Chapter 5, pp. 155–160). Focus on how your qualifications meet the employer's needs, not the other way around. Employers are not impressed by vain boasts ("I am the most efficient and effective safety engineer"). One applicant spent so much time on the advantages he would get from the job that he forgot the employer entirely: "I have worked with this kind of equipment before, and this experience will give me the edge in running it." Convince

readers that you will be a valuable addition to their organization—a team player, a problem solver, a skilled professional.

5. Don't be tempted to send out your first draft. Write and rewrite your letter of application until you are convinced it presents you in the best possible light. Getting the job may depend on it. A first or even second draft rarely sells your abilities as well as a third, fourth, or even fifth revision does.

The sections that follow give you some suggestions on how to prepare the various parts of an application letter successfully.

Your Opening Paragraph

The first paragraph of your letter of application is your introduction. It must get your audience's attention and get him or her to read the rest of your letter by answering three questions:

1. Why are you writing?
2. Where or how did you learn of the vacancy or the company or the job?
3. What is your most important qualification for the job?

Begin your letter by stating directly that you are writing to apply for a job. And specifically mention the job. The company may have more than one vacancy to fill. Don't say that you "want to apply for the job"; such an opening raises the question, "Why don't you, then?"

Avoid an unconventional or arrogant opening: "Are you looking for a dynamic, young, and talented accountant?" Do not begin with a question; be more positive and professional.

If you learned about the job through a newspaper or journal, make sure you italicize or underscore its title.

> I am applying for the events coordinator position you advertised in the May 10 edition of the *Los Angeles Times* online.

Since many companies announce positions on the Internet, check there first to see if their position is listed online, as Anthony Jones did (Figure 7.10, p. 271).

If you learned of the job from a professor, a friend, or an employee at the firm, state so. Take advantage of a personal contact who is confident that you are qualified for the position, as María Lopez (Figure 7.11, p. 272) and Dora Cooper Bolger (Figure 7.12, p. 274) did. But first confirm that your contact gives you permission to use his or her name.

The Body of Your Letter

The body of your letter, comprising one or two paragraphs, provides the evidence based on information from your résumé to prove you are qualified for the job. You might want to spend one paragraph on your education and one on your experience or combine your accomplishments into one paragraph.

Follow these guidelines for the body of your letter:

1. **Keep your paragraphs short and readable—four or five sentences.** Avoid long, complex sentences. Use the active voice to emphasize yourself as a doer. Review the action verbs in Table 7.1 and keywords in Table 7.2.

Letter of application from Anthony Jones, a recent graduate with little job experience.   **Figure 7.10**

Anthony H. Jones

707.555.6390
ajones@plat.com
www.plat.com/users/ajones/resume.html

Clear, easy-to-follow letterhead

May 24, 2006

Ms. Jocelyn Nogasaki
Human Resources Manager
Megalith Publishing Company
1001 Heathcliff Row
San Francisco, CA 94123-7707

Dear Ms. Nogasaki:

I am applying for the layout editor position advertised on your website, which I accessed on 14 May. Early next month, I will receive an A.S. degree in commercial graphics illustration from Santa Rosa Junior College.

Identifies position and source of ad

With a special interest in the publishing industry, I have successfully completed more than forty credit hours in courses directly related to layout design, where I acquired experience using QuarkXPress as well as Illustrator and Photoshop. You might like to know that many of the design patterns of Megalith publications were used as models in my graphics communications and digital photography classes.

Validates necessary education and applies it directly to employer's business

My studies have also led to practical experience at McAdam Publishers as part of my Santa Rosa apprenticeship program. While working at McAdam, I was responsible for assisting the design department in page composition and importing images. Other related experience I have had includes creating a website for the Santa Rosa Humane Society. As you will note on the enclosed résumé, I have also had experience in displaying merchandise at Buchman's Department Store.

Convincingly cites related job experience

Refers to résumé

I would appreciate the opportunity to discuss with you my qualifications in commercial graphics. My phone number is 707.555.6390. After June 12, I will be available for an interview at any time that is convenient for you.

Asks for an interview and gives contact information

Sincerely yours,

Anthony H. Jones

Anthony H. Jones

Encl. Résumé

Figure 7.11   Letter of application from María Lopez, a recent graduate with some job experience.

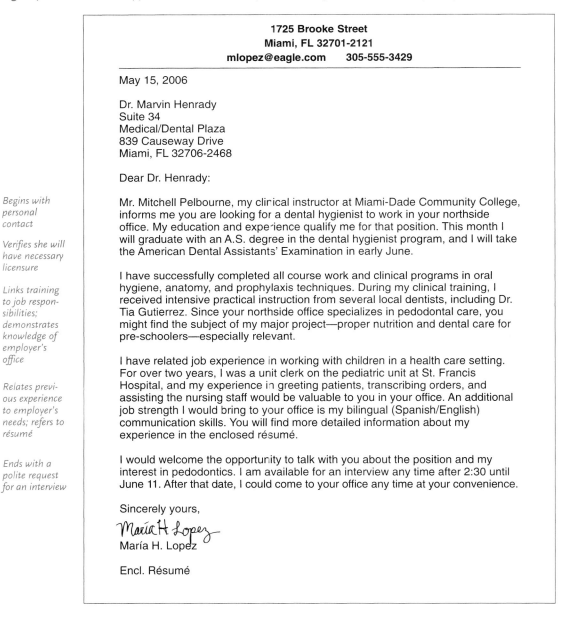

1725 Brooke Street
Miami, FL 32701-2121
mlopez@eagle.com   305-555-3429

May 15, 2006

Dr. Marvin Henrady
Suite 34
Medical/Dental Plaza
839 Causeway Drive
Miami, FL 32706-2468

Dear Dr. Henrady:

Begins with personal contact

Mr. Mitchell Pelbourne, my clinical instructor at Miami-Dade Community College, informs me you are looking for a dental hygienist to work in your northside office. My education and experience qualify me for that position. This month I will graduate with an A.S. degree in the dental hygienist program, and I will take the American Dental Assistants' Examination in early June.

Verifies she will have necessary licensure

Links training to job responsibilities; demonstrates knowledge of employer's office

I have successfully completed all course work and clinical programs in oral hygiene, anatomy, and prophylaxis techniques. During my clinical training, I received intensive practical instruction from several local dentists, including Dr. Tia Gutierrez. Since your northside office specializes in pedodontal care, you might find the subject of my major project—proper nutrition and dental care for pre-schoolers—especially relevant.

Relates previous experience to employer's needs; refers to résumé

I have related job experience in working with children in a health care setting. For over two years, I was a unit clerk on the pediatric unit at St. Francis Hospital, and my experience in greeting patients, transcribing orders, and assisting the nursing staff would be valuable to you in your office. An additional job strength I would bring to your office is my bilingual (Spanish/English) communication skills. You will find more detailed information about my experience in the enclosed résumé.

Ends with a polite request for an interview

I would welcome the opportunity to talk with you about the position and my interest in pedodontics. I am available for an interview any time after 2:30 until June 11. After that date, I could come to your office any time at your convenience.

Sincerely yours,

María H. Lopez
María H. Lopez

Encl. Résumé

2. **Don't begin each sentence with "I."** Vary your sentence structure. Write reader-centered sentences, even those beginning with "I."

3. **Concentrate on seeing yourself as your employer sees you.** Focus on how your education and experience can meet the employer's needs. Prove that you can help an employer's sales and service, promote an organization's mission and goals, and be a reliable team player.

4. **Highlight your qualifications by citing specific accomplishments.** Tell your reader exactly how your schoolwork and job experience qualify you to perform and advance in the job advertised. Don't simply say you are a great salesperson. Demonstrate your accomplishments by stressing that you increased the sales volume in your department by 20 percent within the last 6 months.

5. **Mention you are enclosing your résumé.**

Education.   Emphasize your most significant educational accomplishments— course work, degrees, training—that are relevant for the particular job. Employers want to know which specific skills from your education translate into benefits for them and their company or organization.

Simply saying you will graduate with a degree in criminal justice does not explain how you, unlike all the other graduates of other criminal justice programs, are best suited for a particular job. But when you indicate that you have completed 36 credit hours in software security and have another 12 credit hours in business communications, you show exactly how and where you are qualified. Note how Anthony Jones in Figure 7.10 and María Lopez in Figure 7.11 establish their educational qualifications with specific details about their training.

Experience.   After you discuss your educational qualifications, turn to your job experience. But if your experience is your most valuable and extensive qualification for the job, put it before education, as Donald Kitto-Klein does in Figure 7.13. If you are switching careers or returning to a career after years away from the work force, start the body of your letter with your experience or your community and civic service, as Dora Cooper Bolger does in Figure 7.12. Her volunteer work convincingly demonstrates she has the organizational and communication skills her prospective employer seeks. Never minimize such contributions.

Relate Your Experience/Education to the Job.   Link your education and experience as benefits to the particular job you apply for. Persuasively show a prospective employer how your previous accomplishments have prepared you for future success on the job for him or her. Relate your course work in computer science to being an efficient programmer. Indicate how your summer jobs for a local park district reinforced your skills in providing exemplary customer service. Connect your background to the prospective employer's company. Any homework you can do about the company's history, goals, or structure (see pp. 277–278) will pay off.

- By citing Megalith publications as a model in his courses, Anthony Jones in Figure 7.10 stresses he is ready to start successfully from the first day on the job.

Figure 7.12 Letter of application from Dora Cooper Bolger, a recent graduate with community and civic experience.

Dora Cooper Bolger
1215 Lakeview Avenue
Westhampton, MI 46532
Voice: 616-555-4772   **Cell:** 616-555-4773   **dbolger@aol.com**

February 9, 2007

Dr. Lindsay Bafaloukos
Tanselle Mental Health Agency
4400 West Gallagher Drive
Tanselle, MI 46932-3106

Dear Dr. Bafaloukos:

At a recent meeting of the County Services Council, a member of your staff, Homer Strickland, told me that you will be hiring a public affairs coordinator. Because of my extensive experience in and commitment to community affairs, I would appreciate your considering me for this opening. I expect to receive my B.S. in Public Administration from Mid-Michigan College later this year.

For the past ten years, I have organized community groups with outreach programs similar to Tanselle's. I have held administrative positions in the PTA and the Foster Parents' Association and was president of Teens in Trouble, a volunteer group providing assistance to dysfunctional teens. My responsibilities with Teens have included coordinating our activities with various school programs, scheduling tutorials, and representing the organization before government agencies. I have been commended for my organizational and communication skills. My twenty presentations on foster home care and Teens in Trouble demonstrate that I am an effective speaker, a skill your agency would find valuable.

Because of my work at Mid-Michigan and in Teens and Foster Parents, I have the practical experience in communication and psychology to promote Tanselle's goals. The enclosed résumé provides details of my experience and education.

I would enjoy discussing my work with Teens and the other organizations with you. I am available for an interview any day after 11:00 a.m. Thank you for reaching me at the phone numbers or e-mail address at the top of this letter.

Sincerely yours,

Dora Cooper Bolger

Dora Cooper Bolger

Encl. Résumé

Begins with contact made at professional meeting, highlighting her interests

Relates proven past successes to employer's needs; gives concrete examples of her skills

Encourages reader to see her as best-prepared candidate; includes résumé

Requests interview and gives contact information

- Note how María Lopez in Figure 7.11 uses her knowledge of Dr. Henrady's specialty in pedodontics and her work on a pediatric unit of a hospital to her advantage.
- Dora Cooper Bolger in Figure 7.12 likewise shows her prospective employer that she is familiar with and can contribute to Tanselle's programs in community mental health. Moreover, she frames her public-speaking abilities as an additional asset to her prospective employer.

Your goal is to convince readers in the body of your letter to interview and hire you for the contributions you will make to their company.

Closing

Keep your closing paragraph short—about two or three sentences—but be sure it fulfills the following three important functions:

1. emphasizes once again your major qualifications
2. asks for an interview or a phone call
3. indicates when you are available for an interview

End gracefully and professionally. Be straightforward. Don't leave the reader with a single weak, vague sentence: "I would like to have an interview at your convenience." That does nothing to sell you. Say that you would appreciate talking with the employer further to discuss your qualifications. Then mention your chief talent. You might also express your willingness to relocate if the job requires it.

After indicating your interest in the job, give the times you are available for an interview and specifically tell the reader where you can be reached. If you are going to a professional meeting that the employer might also attend, or if you are visiting the employer's city soon, say so.

The following samples show how *not* to close your letter and why not.

Pushy:	I would like to set up an interview with you. Please phone me to arrange a convenient time. (That's the employer's prerogative, not yours.)
Too Informal:	I do not live far from your office. Let's meet for coffee sometime next week. (Say instead that since you live nearby, you will be available for an interview.)
Introduces New Subject:	I would like to discuss other qualifications you have in mind for the job. (How do you know what the interviewer might have in mind?)

Note that the closing paragraphs in Figures 7.10 through 7.13 avoid these errors.

Going to an Interview

There are various ways for a prospective employer to conduct an interview. It might be a one-on-one meeting—you and the interviewer. Or you may visit with a group of individuals who are trying to decide if you would fit in. Or you might have your interview over the telephone or through a videoconference. If your interview is over the phone, make sure you won't be interrupted during the call. An interview can last thirty minutes or take all day.

Figure 7.13   Letter of application from Donald Kitto-Klein, who has strong work experience.

Designs professional, distinctive letterhead

Identifies specific position and his major qualification

Documents accomplishments in technology, training, and management pertinent to the job

Puts education after experience

Emphatically closes by offering to put his career successes to work for employer and requests an interview

---

DONALD KITTO-KLEIN
■ ■ ■ ■ ■ ■ ■ ■ ■ ■ ■

56 South Ardmore Way
Petersburg, NY 15438
716-555-3177

☎ (716) 555-9032
💻 kitto@gar.com
🌐 http://www.dkk.opengate.com

November 4, 2006

Ms. Michelle Washington
Vice President, Operations
Patterson Corporation
Sun Valley, CA 94356

Dear Ms. Washington:

I am very interested in the position of Director of Computer Services posted on your website 30 Oct. My knowledge of computers and my proven ability to work with people in a large organization such as Patterson qualify me to be a productive member of your management team.

For the last three years, I have been responsible for all phases of computer maintenance and service at Garland.Com. As a regular part of my duties I have serviced and repaired 15 to 20 PCs a month as well as supervised a mainframe. I have successfully coordinated the activities of my department with Garland's other offices and worked closely with vendors and manufacturers. The training programs and in-house conferences I have conducted repeatedly receive high praise from Garland's management. Because I have worked so effectively with management and staff, I was promoted to support services team leader.

My educational achievements include a degree in computer technology from Grand Valley and certificates from U.S. Army schools in computers. The enclosed résumé will give you information about these and my other accomplishments.

I would like to put my ability to motivate personnel and to manage computer services to work for you and Patterson Corporation. I am available for an interview at your convenience. I look forward to hearing from you.

Sincerely yours,

Donald Kitto-Klein

Donald Kitto-Klein

Encl. Résumé

Preparing for the Interview

Before you go to the interview, do the following:

1. Do your homework about the company or organization as outlined below:

   - Is it privately or publicly owned?
   - Is it a for-profit or nonprofit organization?
   - Is it owned by a U.S. corporation or is it part of an international operation?
   - Is it a subsidiary of a larger company or unit or is it locally owned?
   - If it is a government agency, what are its departments, divisions, mission?
   - Who founded the company, when, and why?
   - What are its chief products or services?
   - What are its most profitable areas?
   - How long has it been in business?
   - How many employees does it have?
   - What types of contributions has the company made to the community?
   - Who are its top employees—and why?
   - Who is the CEO or head?
   - Who are its chief clients or customers?
   - Did it show a profit in the last six months? In the last year?

   If the company is listed on the New York Stock Exchange or another stock exchange, check the *Wall Street Journal* to see how its stock is doing the week of your interview. Consult such business reference sources as *Moody's Industries* (*http://www.Moodys.com*) and *Thomas Register* (*http://www.thomasregister.com*). Study the company's website and obtain its annual stockholders' report, if possible.

2. Review the technical skills most relevant for the job. Do some focused Web searching, reread sections of a textbook or manual, study recent journal articles, or talk to an instructor or an employee you know from the company.

3. Prepare a brief (one- or two-minute) review of your qualifications to deliver orally should you be asked about yourself. Think about specific ways to convince the employer that your experience and education are precisely right for the job.

4. Be able to elaborate on what is on your résumé. Always bring extra copies of it with you. You can be sure that its contents will be the subject of many questions. Any extra details or information that bring your résumé up-to-date ("I received my degree"; "I'll get the results of my state board examinations in one week") will be appreciated.

5. Carry a small notepad and pen (or PDA) to jot down only the most essential details about the job. Leave your laptop at home. Keyboarding during an interview is rude.

6. Bring copies of your driver's license, social security card, and any licenses or certificates you may need for the job.

7. Bring your enthusiasm with you. Be upbeat, positive, eager. Express your desire to know more about and to work for the company.

Questions to Expect

The following questions are typical of those you can expect from interviewers, with advice on how to answer them.

- **Why do you want to work for us?** (Bring in your knowledge of the company's goals/mission/successes and indicate how and why your career goals relate to the company's.)
- **What qualifications do you have for the job?** (Mention educational achievements and relevant work experience, especially computer and language skills.)
- **What could you possibly offer us that other candidates do not have?** (Say "enthusiasm," being a team player, having problem-solving abilities, motivating, empowering others.)
- **Why did you attend this school?** (Be honest—location, costs, programs.)
- **Why did you major in "X"?** (Do not simply say financial benefits; concentrate on both practical and professional benefits. Be able to state career objectives.)
- **Why did you get a grade of "C" in a course?** (Don't say that you could have done better if you'd tried. Explain what the trouble was and mention that you corrected it in a course in which you earned a B or an A.)
- **What extracurricular activities did you participate in while in high school or college?** (Indicate any responsibilities you had—managing money, writing memos, coordinating events. If you were unable to participate in such activities, tell the interviewer that a part-time job, community or church activities, or commuting prevented your participation. Such answers sound better than saying that you did not like sports or clubs in school.)
- **Did you learn as much as you wanted from your course work?** (This is a loaded question. Indicate that you learned a great deal but now look forward to the opportunity to gain more practical skill, to put into practice the principles you have learned; say that you will never be through learning.)
- **What is your greatest strength?** (Say being a team player, cooperation, willingness to learn, ability to grasp difficult concepts easily, managing time or money, taking criticism easily, and profiting from criticism.)
- **What is your greatest shortcoming?** (Be honest here and mention it, but then turn to ways in which you are improving. Don't say something deadly like, "I can never seem to finish what I start" or "I hate being criticized." You should neither dwell on your weaknesses nor keep silent about them. Saying "None" to this kind of question is as inadvisable as rattling off a list of faults.)
- **How do you handle conflict with a co-worker, boss, customer?** (Stress your ability to be courteous and honest and to work toward a productive resolu-

tion. State that you avoid language, tone of voice, or gestures that interfere with healthy dialogue.)

- **Why did you leave your last job?** ("I returned to school full-time" or "I moved from Jackson to Springfield." *Never attack your previous employer.* That only makes you look bad.)
- **Why would you leave your current job?** (This is a hard question. Again, never attack an individual or an organization. Say your current job has prepared you for the position you are now applying for. Emphasize your desire to work with and for a new company because of its goals, plans, opportunities.)

What Do I Say About Salary?

Again, do your homework. Find out what the salary range is for your professional level in your area. Consult the U.S. Bureau of Labor Statistics at *http://www.bls.gov.oco* as well as *http://www.salary.co.* Ask your instructors or individuals whom you know who work for the company; or call a professional organization to which you may belong for information. If the issue of salary comes up, you can then ask if the company has established a salary range for the position. Then you will be better able to assess where you stand in relationship to that range. But since many companies set fixed salaries for entry-level positions, it may be unwise to try to negotiate.

If you are asked about what salary you expect for the job, do not give an exact figure. If you do this, you may undercut yourself if the employer has a higher figure in mind for the position. By doing your homework on salary ranges, you will have a better feel for the market when the employer does mention salary. Ask the interviewer what the salary range is for the position and where he or she thinks you may fall in that range. That way you are better able to respond to any specific salary offer that the prospective employer may make.

Keep in mind, too, that the figure you are quoted as an annual or monthly salary is only part of the financial picture. Factor other things into your job equation—health insurance, day care, housing, uniform/clothing allowances, product or service discounts, any retirement plans, and tuition reimbursement. See Figure 1.1 for an example of such a job perk.

Questions You May Ask the Interviewer(s)

You will have a chance to ask the interviewer(s) questions. Watch for appropriate cues and be prepared to say more than "No, I don't have any questions," which suggests either indifference or unpreparedness on your part. Here are some legitimate questions you can ask interviewers:

1. Will there be any safety, security, proficiency requirements I will need to meet?
2. When is the starting date?
3. Is there a probationary period? If so, how long?
4. How will my work be evaluated (monthly, quarterly, semiannually) and by whom (immediate superior, committee)?

5. What types of on-the-job training are offered?
6. Are there any mentoring programs in place?
7. Is there any support for continuing my education to improve my job performance?

What an Interviewer Can't Ask

There are some questions an interviewer may not legally ask you. Questions about your age, marital status, ethnic background, race, or any physical disabilities violate equal opportunity employment laws. Even so, some employers may disguise their interest in those subjects by asking you indirect questions about them. A question such as "Will your husband care if you have to work overtime?" or "How many children do you have?" could probe into your personal life. Confronted with such questions, it is best to answer them positively ("My home life will not interfere with my job," "My family understands that overtime may be required") rather than bristling defensively, "It's none of your business if I have a husband."

Ten Interview Dos and Don'ts

Keep in mind these other interview dos and don'ts.

1. Be on time. In fact, show up about fifteen minutes earlier in case the interviewer wants you to complete some forms.
2. Go to the interview alone. Turn your cell phone off!
3. Dress appropriately for the occasion. Never wear blue jeans. **Men:** Wear a suit and tie. **Women:** Wear a suit (pants or skirt) or equally businesslike attire.
4. Be careful about tattoos. Job counselors warn that visible tattoos can hurt a job seeker's chance for success.
5. Greet the interviewer with a friendly, not vicelike, handshake. Thank your interviewer(s) for inviting you.
6. Don't sit down before the interviewer does. Wait for him or her to invite you to sit and to indicate where.
7. Speak slowly and distinctly; do not nervously hurry to finish your sentences and never interrupt or finish an interviewer's sentences. Avoid one- or two-word answers, which sound unfriendly or unprepared. Do not use slang (e.g., "Right on," "Way to go," "You go, girl") or overly casual language ("Like . . . ," "You know?").
8. Refrain from chewing gum; clicking a ballpoint pen; fidgeting; twirling your hair; or tapping your foot against the floor, a chair, or a desk.
9. Maintain eye contact with the interviewer; do not sheepishly stare at the floor or the desk. If you are interviewed by a group of individuals, make eye contact with each one of them. Body language is equally important. For instance, don't fold your arms—a signal that you are closed to the interviewer's suggestions and comments. Sit up straight; do not slouch.
10. When the interview is over, thank the interviewer for considering you for the job and say you look forward to hearing from him or her.

The Follow-Up Letter

Within a week after the interview, it is wise to send a follow-up letter, not e-mail, thanking the interviewer for his or her time and interest in you. In your letter, you can reemphasize your qualifications for the job by showing how they apply to conditions described by the interviewer; you might also ask for further information to show your interest in the job and the employer. A sample follow-up letter appears in Figure 7.14.

Accepting or Declining a Job Offer

If you accept a job, send the employer a letter within a week of the offer. Accepting verbally on the phone is not enough. Your letter will make your acceptance official and will probably be included in your permanent personnel file. Accepting a job is easy. Make the communication with your new employer a model of clarity and diplomacy.

A sample acceptance letter appears in Figure 7.15 (p. 283). In the first sentence tell the employer that you are accepting the job and refer to the date of the letter offering you the position, the specific job title, and salary. Indicate when you can begin working. Then mention any pleasant associations from your interview or any specific challenges you are anticipating. That should take no more than a paragraph.

In a second paragraph express your plans to fulfill any further requirements for the job—going to the human resources office, taking a physical examination, having a copy of a certificate or license forwarded, sending a final transcript of your college work. A final one-sentence paragraph might state that you look forward to starting your new job.

Refusing a job requires tact. You are obligated to inform an employer why you are not taking the job. A sample refusal letter appears in Figure 7.16 (p. 284).

Do not bluntly begin with the refusal. Instead, prepare the reader for bad news by starting with a complimentary remark about the job, the interview, or the company. Then move to your refusal and supply an honest but not elaborate explanation of why you are not taking the job. Many students cite educational opportunities, work schedules, geographic preference, or more relevant professional opportunities. End on a friendly note, because you may be interested in working for the company in the future and do not want to leave any bad feelings.

Figure 7.14   A follow-up letter.

2739 East Street
Latrobe, PA 17042-0312

610-555-6373
mlb@springboard.com

September 20, 2006

Mr. Jack Fukurai
Manager of Human Resources
Transatlantic Piping Company
1334 Ridge Road N.E.
Pittsburgh, PA 17122-3107

Dear Mr. Fukurai:

Expresses grati-
tude for inter-
view and
singles out
main company
feature

I enjoyed talking with you last Wednesday and learning more about
the security officer position available at Transatlantic Piping. It was
especially helpful to take a tour of the plant's north gate section to
see the challenges it presents for the security officer stationed there.

Reemphasizes
qualifications

As you noted at the interview, my training in surveillance electronics
has prepared me to operate the sophisticated equipment
Transatlantic has installed at the north gate. I was grateful to
Ms. Turner for taking time to demonstrate the equipment.

Asks for
newsletter to
express further
interest

I am looking forward to receiving the handbook about Transatlantic's
employee services. Would it also be possible for you to include a
copy of the newsletter from last year that introduced the new security
equipment to the employees?

Ends politely
by thanking
interviewer

Thank you, again, for considering me for the position and for the
hospitality you showed me. Please let me know if there are any other
questions I can answer for you.

Sincerely yours,

Marcia Le Borde

Marcia Le Borde

• KEVIN DUBINSKI •

73 Park Street
Evansville, WI   53536-1016

Home: 608-555-3173   •   Cell: 608-898-4291
KDubinski@global.net

June 29, 2007

Ms. Melinda Haas, Manager
Weise's Department Store
Janesville Mall
Janesville, WI 53545-1014

Dear Ms. Haas:

I am pleased to accept the position of assistant controller that you offered me at a salary of $29,250 in your letter of June 22. Starting on July 18 will be no problem. I look forward to helping Ms. Meyers in the business office. In the next few months I know that I will learn a great deal about Weise's.

Accepts job and shows willingness to be team member

As you asked, I will make an appointment early next week with the Human Resources Department to discuss travel policies, salary payment schedules, and insurance coverage.

Agrees to conditions

I am eager to start working for Weise's.

Looks forward to starting

Cordially,

Kevin Dubinski

Kevin Dubinski

Figure 7.16   Letter refusing a job.

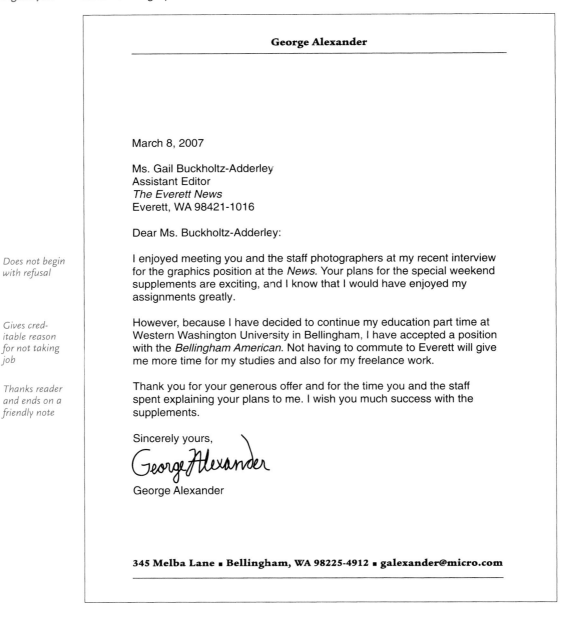

George Alexander

March 8, 2007

Ms. Gail Buckholtz-Adderley
Assistant Editor
The Everett News
Everett, WA 98421-1016

Dear Ms. Buckholtz-Adderley:

Does not begin with refusal

I enjoyed meeting you and the staff photographers at my recent interview for the graphics position at the *News.* Your plans for the special weekend supplements are exciting, and I know that I would have enjoyed my assignments greatly.

Gives creditable reason for not taking job

However, because I have decided to continue my education part time at Western Washington University in Bellingham, I have accepted a position with the *Bellingham American.* Not having to commute to Everett will give me more time for my studies and also for my freelance work.

Thanks reader and ends on a friendly note

Thank you for your generous offer and for the time you and the staff spent explaining your plans to me. I wish you much success with the supplements.

Sincerely yours,

George Alexander

George Alexander

345 Melba Lane ▪ Bellingham, WA 98225-4912 ▪ galexander@micro.com

✔ Revision Checklist

☐ Restricted the types of job(s) for which I am qualified.

☐ Prepared a dossier at school placement office, including letters from professors, employers, and community officials.

☐ Identified places where relevant jobs are advertised.

☐ Notified instructors, friends, relatives, clergy, and individuals who work for the companies I want to join that I am in the job market.

☐ Checked with chamber of commerce, state employment office, and relevant government agencies.

☐ Researched the companies I am interested in—on the Internet, through printed sources, and in networking with current employees I know.

☐ Inventoried my strengths carefully to prepare résumé.

☐ Eliminated weak, irrelevant, repetitious, and dated material from inventory.

☐ Wrote a focused and persuasive career-objective statement.

☐ Determined the most beneficial format of résumé to use—chronological, functional, or both.

☐ Prepared an online résumé to send to prospective employers.

☐ Investigated creating a website for my job search–related documents.

☐ Made résumé attractive and easy to read with logical and persuasive headings and keywords.

☐ Made sure résumé contains neither too much nor too little information.

☐ Proofread résumé to ensure everything is correct, consistent, and accurate.

☐ Wrote letter of application that shows how my specific skills and background apply to and meet an employer's exact needs.

☐ Prepared short oral presentation about myself and my accomplishments for an interview.

☐ Researched prospective employer's company/organization.

☐ Sent prospective employer a follow-up letter within a few days after interview to show interest in position.

☐ Sent prospective employer a polite acceptance or rejection letter.

Online Study Center

Access the how to get a job Revision Checklist online at college.hmco.com/pic/kolin8e

Exercises

1. Make a brainstormed list of your marketable job skills. To do that, first concentrate on the specialized kinds of skills you learned in your major or on your job (for example, giving injections, fingerprinting, preparing specialized menus, learning a computer language, creating a website). List as many skills as you can think of; then organize them into three or four separate categories that reflect your major abilities.

Online Study Center
Find additional
how to get a job
exercises at
college.hmco.com/
pic/kolin8e

2. Translate the list of skills from Exercise 1 into a number of "persuasive, selling clauses," each introduced with a strong action verb such as those in Table 7.1.

3. Compile a list of ten employers for whom you would like to work. Get their names, street and e-mail addresses, phone numbers, and the names of the managers or human resources officers. Then select one company and write a profile about it—locations, services, kinds of products or services offered, number of employees, clients served, types of schedules used, and any other pertinent facts.

4. Write an e-mail message to your instructor describing the resources you used to find three to four jobs in your area that you could apply for upon graduation.

5. Obtain some personal evaluation forms from your placement office. Write a sample letter to a former or current teacher and employer, asking for a recommendation. Tell the individuals what kinds of jobs you will be looking for and politely mention how a strong letter would help you in your job search. Make sure you bring them up-to-date about your educational progress and any employment you have had since you worked for them.

6. Which of the following would belong on your résumé? Which would not belong? Why?
   a. student ID number
   b. social security number
   c. the ZIP codes of your references' addresses
   d. a list of all your English courses in college
   e. section numbers of the courses in your major
   f. statement that you are recently divorced
   g. subscriptions to journals in your field
   h. the titles of any stories or poems you published in a high school literary magazine or newspaper
   i. your GPA
   j. foreign languages you studied
   k. years you attended college
   l. the date you were discharged from the service
   m. names of the neighbors you are using as references
   n. your religion
   o. job titles you held
   p. your summer job washing dishes
   q. your telephone number
   r. the reason you changed schools
   s. your current status with the National Guard
   t. the URL of your website
   u. your volunteer work for the Red Cross
   v. hours a week you spend reading science fiction
   w. the title of your last term paper in your major
   x. the name of the agency or business where you worked last

7. Indicate what is wrong with the following career statements and rewrite them to make them more precise and professional.

- **a.** Job in a dentist's office.
- **b.** Position with a safety emphasis.
- **c.** Desire growth position in a large department store.
- **d.** Am looking for entry position in health sciences with an emphasis on caring for older people.
- **e.** Position in sales with fast promotion rate.
- **f.** Want a job working with semiconductor circuits.
- **g.** I would like a position in fashion, especially one working with modern fashion.
- **h.** Desire a good-paying job, hours: 8–4:30, with double pay for overtime. Would like to stay in the Omaha area.
- **i.** Insurance work.
- **j.** Working with computers.
- **k.** Personal secretary.
- **l.** Job with preschoolers.
- **m.** Full-time position with hospitality chain.
- **n.** I want a career in nursing.
- **o.** Police work, particularly in suburb of large city.
- **p.** A job that lets me be me.
- **q.** Desire fun job selling cosmetics.
- **r.** Any position for a qualified dietitian.
- **s.** Although I have not made up my mind about which area of forestry I shall go into, I am looking for a job that offers me training and rewards based upon my potential.

8. As part of a team or on your own, revise the following poor résumé to make it more precise and persuasive. Include additional details where necessary and exclude any details that would hurt the job seeker's chances. Also correct any inconsistencies.

```
                      RÉSUMÉ OF

                      Powell T. Harrison
                      8604 So. Kirkpatrick St.
                      Ardville, Ohio
                      345 37 8760
                      614 234 4587
                      harrison@gem.com

PERSONAL              Confidential

CAREER                Seek good paying position with progressive
OBJECTIVE             Sunbelt company.

EDUCATION

2005–2007             Will receive degree from Central Tech.
                      Institute in Arch. St. Earned high average
```

	last semester. Took necessary courses for major; interested in systems, plans, and design development.
1999–2000	Attended Ardville High School, Ardville, OH; took all courses required. Served on several student committees.
EXPERIENCE	None, except for numerous part-time jobs and student apprenticeship in the Ardville area. As part of student app. worked with local firm for two months.
HOBBIES	Surfing the Net, playing Gameboys. Member of Junior Achievement.
REFERENCES	Please write for names and addresses.

9. Determine what is wrong with the following sentences in a letter of application. Rewrite them to eliminate any mistakes, to focus on the "you attitude," or to make them more precise.

   a. Even though I have very little actual job experience, I can make up for it in enthusiasm.
   b. My qualifications will prove that I am the best person for your job.
   c. I would enjoy working with your other employees.
   d. This e-mail résumé is my application for any job you now have open or expect to fill in the near future.
   e. Next month, my family and I will be moving to Detroit, and I must get a job in the area. Will you have anything open?
   f. If you are interested in me, then I hope that we make some type of arrangements to interview each other soon.
   g. I have not included a résumé since all pertinent information about me is in this letter.
   h. My GPA is only 2.5, but I did make two B's in my last term.
   i. I hope to take state boards soon.
   j. Your company, or so I have heard through the grapevine, has excellent fringe benefits. That is what I care about most, so I am applying for any position that you may advertise.
   k. I am writing to ask you to kindly consider whether I would be a qualified person for the position you announced in the newspaper.
   l. I have made plans to further my education.
   m. My résumé speaks for itself.
   n. I could not possibly accept a position that required weekend work, and night work is out, too.
   o. In my own estimation, I am a go-getter—an eager beaver, so to speak.
   p. My last employer was dead wrong when he let me go. I think he regrets it now.
   q. When you want to arrange an interview time, give me a call. I am home every afternoon after four.

10. Explain why the following letter of application is ineffective. Rewrite it to make it more precise and appropriate.

Apartment 32
Jeggler Drive
Talcott, Arizona

Monday

Grandt Corporation
Production Supervisor
Capital City, Arizona

Dear Sir:

I am writing to ask you if your company will consider me for the position you announced in the newspaper yesterday. I believe that with my education (I have an associate degree) and experience (I have worked four years as a freight supervisor), I could fill your job.

My schoolwork was done at two junior colleges, and I took more than enough courses in business management and modern technology. In fact, here is a list of some of my courses: Supervision, Materials Management, Work Experience in Management, Business Machines, Safety Tactics, Introduction to Packaging, Art Design, Modern Business Principles, and Small Business Management. In addition, I have worked as a loading dock supervisor for the last two years, and before that I worked in the military in the Quartermaster Corps.

Please let me know if you are interested in me. I would like to have an interview with you at the earliest possible date, since there are some other firms also interested in me, too.

Eagerly yours,

George D. Milhous

---

11. From the Sunday edition of your local newspaper or from one of the other sources discussed on pages 243–246, find notices for two or three jobs you believe you are qualified to fill and then write a letter of application for one of them.

12. Write a chronologically organized résumé to accompany the letter you wrote for Exercise 11.

13. Write a functional résumé for your application letter in Exercise 11.

14. Prepare an online version of the résumé in either Exercise 12 or 13. Use persuasive keywords such as those in Table 7.2.

15. Bring the two résumés you prepared for Exercises 12 and 13 to class to be critiqued by a collaborative writing team. After your résumés are reviewed, revise them.

16. Write an appropriate job application letter to accompany Anna Cassetti's résumés in Figures 7.5 and 7.7.

17. Write a letter to a local business inquiring about summer employment. Indicate that you can work only for one summer and that you will be returning to school by September 1. Include an appropriate résumé.

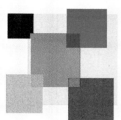

Gathering and Summarizing Information

CHAPTER 8

Doing Research for School and on the Job

Being able to do research is vital for your success on the job and in school. Whether for a school paper or job assignment, research means

- being able to find, summarize, and incorporate and cite sources accurately and concisely
- networking with people you work with and for as well as with a broader audience worldwide
- sifting through a host of studies, suggestions, and alternatives to recommend only those most relevant to your paper or assignment

Online Study Center
To expand your understanding of doing research, take advantage of the ACE quizzes, sample documents, Web links, and exercises at college.hmco.com/pic/kolin8e

Research involves identifying key questions and knowing what types of answers, backed up by the information, you need to supply.

Research in the world of work helps a company keep current, meet the needs of its customers worldwide, stay within a budget, and make a profit. No company can remain in business in today's competitive market without access to the latest research technology and to the vast amounts of information that it provides. Companies, therefore, expect their employees to be able to solve problems based on gathering essential information and then interpreting that information through careful research.

Here are just a few of the areas where employers will expect you to do research to solve problems:

- writing persuasive, diplomatic letters, proposals, and reports for a variety of readers worldwide
- competing successfully against other companies
- launching or upgrading a new product or service
- delivering winning presentations
- knowledgeably conferring with clients, co-workers, government agencies about the ongoing daily, weekly, monthly, quarterly activities on your job
- keeping customers and attracting new ones
- recruiting the most qualified work force
- maintaining or improving operation costs
- providing the most efficient warranties, schedules, product information

Doing research for these assignments keeps a business strong and shows your boss that you are getting the necessary work done.

In terms of academic research, your instructor, like your boss at work, will want you to find the most relevant and current information, to provide accurate descriptions, and to reach logical conclusions. See how much research the writer of the telecommuter paper did in Chapter 9 (see pp. 383–405). Moreover, in school you will want to do your research in your major or on a subject that is very important to help you prepare for the job market. A carefully researched paper done for a class can be an essential document for your job portfolio.

This chapter introduces you to the kinds of research you will be expected to do on the job and for your school reports. It guides you through the following fundamental areas of research:

- following the process of doing research
- using effective research strategies
- knowing the two main types of research
- doing primary research—observing, visiting sites, surveying others' opinions
- conducting secondary research—finding and using a variety of print and online sources and tools
- researching on the Internet—using search engines, finding the most relevant keywords, writing business blogs
- taking notes as you research

The research strategies and sources of research information in Chapter 8 are basic to every type of writing discussed in this book.

The Research Process

Just as there is a process for writing—brainstorming, drafting, revising, editing—there is a process involved in doing research. In research you go through the steps of finding, assessing, and incorporating information into your written work.

Like the writing process, in doing research you may find yourself repeating certain steps. Say, for example, you are writing a business proposal and are incorporating information from several sources you've researched. At this stage of the process, you might think you've gathered enough information. However, as you work on the proposal, you realize that it raises new questions. That may lead you back to revise and further restrict or define your purpose (step 2) or to find more information (step 3). Let's look at the process in more detail:

Step 1. Identify a significant and relevant topic.   The most important part of research is identifying the topic, problem, or issue you are researching and ensuring that it is both timely and worthwhile. This means knowing what constitutes a significant topic and what does not. In business, the topic of your research is often chosen for you—for example, how to attract new customers through a website or retain the ones you have or how a job can be done more efficiently. For a class, your instructor will ask you to choose and restrict a topic. Don't take the obvious—mercury in drinking water is hazardous. Or the impossible—lasers are significant in business—a topic too broad and complex. You need to find a carefully restricted topic, for example, comparing and contrasting mercury level at one local water source or the use of lasers in your library's security systems. If you have to select a topic, find something that really interests you. Do some brainstorming, browsing periodicals or sites online. Get some background information.

Step 2. Know the purpose for your research.   A clear sense of purpose is the first step toward successfully completing your report or paper. The purpose of your research will determine everything you do—from the amount of information you gather to what will be done with it. In business, research helps a business to make informed decisions to solve a problem (upgrade a company's outdated software) or propose a new venture (reach a different customer base). Know what your boss expects from your research—how it will fulfill or complement a company's mission or the specific objectives of your department or job. In both a business report and in a report done for class, you should be able to describe the purpose or mission of your research in a few sentences by answering these questions:

- What do I intend to argue, propose, solve, uncover, change, describe, or compare?
- What evidence or data will I need to support my approach/assignment?
- Why is my research necessary and important for my major, my career portfolio, my department, my company, or community?

Formulating your purpose or mission statement will help you stay on target. It will filter out tangential or irrelevant information and save you from false starts and wasted hours of work. Expect to revise your mission statement as you learn more about your topic.

Step 3. Use a variety of research materials.   Whether you're doing research from your school's library or at your workstation, you should include diverse resources. Not only should those include different sources, but these sources may also be in different media formats: print, online, audio, and video. If you rely on only a single source—a fast Internet search or looking at one or two journals or library books—your research findings will be based on an incomplete understanding of your topic.

Library resources typically include encyclopedias, almanacs, and other reference works; periodicals; bibliographies; and collections of books and other media. In the workplace, researchers may need to consult industry publications; databases; information services (e.g., LexisNexis); and in-house publications, newsletters, reports, customers' files, and vendor contracts accessed via the company's intranet (see page 296). Don't narrow the focus of your search until you've examined resources to determine how and why they might be relevant to your topic. You may also have to do fieldwork such as observing firsthand an activity or interviewing a variety of people.

Step 4. Learn to use research materials.   Once you've identified valuable sources of information, you may need to master some techniques for using those sources. Information can be stored in a variety of formats and systems. A researcher's life would be much easier if information were stored and retrieved the same way for each source. But, just as the navigation of two websites differs, information from

Tech Note

Intranets

To store and share information, diversified companies, government agencies, and large organizations have created **intranets**. As the name suggests, intranets are communication networks modeled after the Internet that use the same tools and procedures—hyperlinks, directories, passwords, and multimedia content. Unlike the Internet, though, an intranet is designed for internal use by the personnel of a particular company or organization. Coordinating the websites of various groups and departments, Web administrators and editors oversee a company's intranet. From a centralized directory, information is sent to, from, and about various divisions within the company—management, engineering, human resources, sales, public relations. Information can be designated "public" or "private," restricting audience and content. Intranets often use firewalls to secure the site so that other businesses or unauthorized individuals cannot gain access.

different academic disciplines and business areas is organized according to different standards. Other reference materials—almanacs, encyclopedias, government documents, and microforms—include pages that explain how information is organized within them. You may also need to learn how to use audiovisual equipment and software that you have not used before.

Step 5. Know how to evaluate sources, both in print and online.   Doing research means more than just repeating information you find. Given the explosion of information of all kinds found online and the continuing expansion of print materials available, it is crucial that you are able to evaluate the content of what you read. Be prepared to evaluate websites and printed sources critically to see if they have a particular agenda or bias that might slant their opinion on certain topics. Whether the source of information is one person's blog (Web log), a local newspaper, or an online academic journal, here are some questions to ask:

- Is the information accurate and reliable?
- Who authored this work and what is this person's experience in the field?
- Is the information current? (If the information appears on a website, when was the site last updated?)
- Is the information complete? What is missing? If the source uses statistics, for example, is the amount of data sufficient to draw the conclusions the author reached?
- Is the information valid? If the source uses statistics, how were those statistics gathered and analyzed?

Step 6. Consult appropriate resource people and experts.   Doing research in the world of work, and often for a class, involves asking individuals who are experts on the topic for information or for different viewpoints of or perspectives on the problem topic you are studying. These can be people from different divisions of your company—technical support, human resources, finance—or co-workers and members of your collaborative team who have previously investigated a similar topic. You might also consult various specialists who work for the local, state, or federal government or teach at your institution. Your research could be as simple as sending an e-mail to ask a brief question or as complex as analyzing a detailed laboratory report. Certainly one of the most important resources is your reference librarian, who is professionally trained to understand how information is stored and retrieved in a wide range of academic disciplines and business fields. You might have a formal interview with such a person, attend a meeting or lecture, or just engage in a short conversation on the phone.

Tech Note

Newsgroups

The Internet provides a number of research services through e-mail and user groups, for example, listservs. Becoming a part of these special-interest discussion groups can greatly enhance the way you obtain information and do research. Some researchers estimate that there are as many as 100,000 newsgroups asking for and providing information on an endless list of specialized subjects. Once you tap into such a network, your possibilities for research expand phenomenally. A helpful, specialized search engine for finding newsgroups on the Usenet network is Google Groups (*http://groups.google.com*).

Step 7. Continue to ask questions.　　Research involves more than gathering information. It also means asking the right questions throughout the process of writing your report or paper. As you read, conduct an interview, send e-mails, or search databases, you may encounter dead ends, contradictions, and even new sources or leads you need to investigate. Research does not always go as smoothly as you might expect it to. Don't get discouraged. See such hurdles as temporary and as opportunities to make sure your work is accurate, complete, and relevant. Investigating your original problem may reveal several others you weren't aware of, or you may discover that there is more than one way to solve a problem. Compare and contrast what you find. Be careful to describe and define the information you gather in terms of your purpose. In fact, periodically refer to your purpose as you ask these key questions at various times during your research:

- Which of my sources will be of the most value—relevant, timely—to my audience and my purpose?
- What is the best way to incorporate my research within my paper or report?
- Does the information I have found raise more questions? If so, what is the best way to research them?
- Do I need to find more information? If so, where and why?

■ Do I agree with the conclusions presented in my sources? Are there major differences of opinion among my sources? How do I determine which, if any, is more appropriate, effective, and economical?

Step 8. Document your sources.   One of the most important steps in the research process is documenting—citing the various sources of information (online, in print, personal interviews with experts) on which your report, paper, or presentation is based. This information may include any ideas, facts, solutions, or recommendations that you did not find yourself, or information not considered common knowledge. Chapter 9 will give you specific guidelines on how to document your sources. Remember, to claim another's works as your own is plagiarism. It will undermine you on the job and in school. It is legally and ethically wrong. Avoid the mistake of "borrowing" information from an authoritative source or omitting the names of co-workers who assisted you with your report. Readers inevitably discover the truth, and then the author is considered unreliable if not downright dishonest. When you are asked to write on an unfamiliar topic, research it and cite as many authoritative sources as the scope and purpose of your project requires. By referring to these experts, your paper or report will carry greater weight.

Step 9. Submit specific recommendations based on your research.   Depending on the directions your instructor or employer gave you, you may be required to give recommendations. These can be informed projections, predictions, alternative measures, specific solutions, or a plan of action. Make sure your recommendations follow from the research you have done and that they are

■ realistic	■ environmentally sound
■ possible	■ ethical
■ technically accurate	■ consistent with your company's policies

Step 10. Adhere to a schedule.   Research for a business report or class paper cannot go on indefinitely. Your boss, or your instructor, will expect you to meet clearly established deadlines. Businesses and classes are run by deadlines, e.g. weekly summaries, monthly surveys, quarterly reports. If you delay, you will jeopardize not only other ongoing business projects that may depend on your research, but also your company's chance for acquiring new business. Budget your time wisely. Plan ahead. Before you go to the library or meet with a librarian, take time to think through the purpose of your research project. Don't start out with a broad, general topic (e.g., daycare). Focus on a specific aspect of your topic (e.g., ways for parents to check on children in daycare via PDAs). Confer with your boss or instructor regularly to chart your progress or to ask questions so that you complete your research and can submit your written work on time.

■ Types of Research

As we have seen, research is vital in every type of business or organization. Just as the reasons for research can vary, so, too, do the methods you use for the type of research that your boss, or instructor, will expect of you. These methods describe how you obtain the information you need. The two types of research conducted most often are primary research and secondary research.

Primary research is original research. It involves the direct gathering of facts not found in books, reports, manuals, or on websites. You generate the information you and your boss or instructor need. When a business wants to investigate how a specific procedure or policy or budget is working out, or what the impact of such a procedure or budget is, it will need to conduct primary research. For instance, the transportation division of a company might need to find ways to cut operating costs and thus gather firsthand information on such areas of investigation as schedules, energy costs, and labor costs to find out where it might make changes. That information comes from studies within the company and from the logs companies keep about repairs, fuel, overtime, and routes. All of this is considered primary research. Or an Internet provider wants to survey its customers about the quality of its services. The provider sends customers a questionnaire; the answers generated are considered primary information. Or your instructor may ask you to incorporate a face-to-face interview or a survey of students and faculty into your research paper. You'll need to generate this information on your own, and then, by taking notes and analyzing the data, prepare your paper.

To conduct **secondary research**, you do not generate the information you need yourself but you rely on the research that someone else—an individual, a government agency, another company—has published or made available to you. For secondary research, you will use—among other resources—a library, reference books, the Internet, and a host of research services that may provide statistical and other types of data—for example, Dow Jones for stock prices; the U.S. Department of Commerce for the number of international visitors to the United States in the month of October; the amount of rainfall in Duluth for the last three years.

Secondary research is essential to the reports and papers you will be asked to write for your instructor, such as the one on telecommuters in Chapter 9 (pp. 383–405). Businesses also rely on secondary research, and you will be expected to cite internal documents such as e-mail correspondence on a particular topic, materials on the company intranet, newsletters, or specialized journals in your discipline. For example, your boss might want you to give a report on the latest techniques in occupational therapy for individuals who have been injured at a particular job site in your company. Or an advertising department might be asked to study industry or trade publications to learn more about how and why a competing firm's product line has won a large share of the market.

Here are some examples of the types of methods and sources you will use for primary and secondary research.

Primary	Secondary
▪ direct observations	▪ Internet searches
▪ on-site inspections	▪ books
▪ experiments/tests	▪ journals/magazines
▪ interviews	▪ encyclopedias/almanacs
▪ networking	▪ product reviews
▪ focus groups	▪ government documents
▪ questionnaires/surveys	▪ trade/professional association studies

Both types of research are used in the world of work and in academia; the long report in Chapter 16 incorporates both methods in the same document. The following sections of Chapter 8 describe each type of research, how you can use it, and provide guidelines on preparing the types of documents based on primary and secondary research.

Primary Research

Sometimes on the job or in academic research you will be faced with questions that require you to conduct original research. You will be expected to uncover answers to questions that may not have been answered before. You won't be able to consult books, databases, or other secondary sources. The purpose of your research may be to obtain customer feedback, to test products, or to take measurements that cannot be calculated in any other way. You will have to gather data firsthand by going directly to the source and observing, testing, experimenting, interviewing, surveying, and providing well-researched conclusions.

The key to such primary research is planning. You can't just set off to study something hoping to find interesting and relevant information. Instead, you will have to follow procedures just as scientists do, formulating hypotheses and deciding how best to research your hypotheses, systematically conducting the research and then compiling and interpreting the information.

There are several methods of doing primary research, including the following:

1. observations/site visits/tests
2. interviews
3. surveys/questionnaires

Observations/Site Visits/Tests

One of the most important ways to gather primary research is by directly observing people, products, companies, events, or sites. A wildlife biologist for the Department of the Interior studying animal life cycles may have to count the numbers of an endangered species and then comment on what changes in the environment need to be made to protect these animals. Observation can involve both quantitative and qualitative assessments, as the preceding example shows. Direct observation includes a variety of activities vital to the world of work—visiting a location or site, observing how individuals perform a task, conducting a marketing campaign, comparing and contrasting different products, or running a test in a laboratory. For example, several of the e-mails, letters, and short reports in this book have been based on the writer's direct observations.

There are many ways to observe people, products, companies, or events. In the workplace, you may be asked by your boss to research your competitors—their products, their service, their image. Let's say, for example, your company manufactures waterproof sunscreens and a competitor has just launched a new product that may hurt your sales. Your boss will want to know if the competitor's new product is cheaper, better, or more attractive than yours. To find out, you may examine the competitor's website, promotional mailings, press releases, and communications to investors. Your job may also require you to investigate how the product is manufactured. This type of primary research requires that you conduct laboratory tests to find out what ingredients make up the competitor's new sunscreen and how packaging, color, and design may affect sales. See, for instance, Figures 15.10 and 15.11.

You will also have to be a keen observer when your job or academic research takes you to an off-site location to report on what you find there. The site you visit could be another department in your company, a prospective customer's office, the place where an incident or accident occurred, or some other place relevant to your paper for a class. Or you may have to access a facility as part of a student internship field trip report, as in Figure 15.7. Regardless of the location, you will have to describe for someone else what you found out firsthand. Note how the writer of the incident report in Figure 15.12 describes in detail what he found at the site of a train derailment.

Similarly, your keen powers of observation would be essential if your company—a chain of dry cleaners—wanted to open a new store and asked you to investigate the most profitable location. Before your company broke ground or signed a lease, you would have to conduct a great deal of primary research based on your observations. First, you would have to identify available locations and find out such things as the volume of pedestrian and automobile traffic, the availability of parking, and whether other area businesses would help to increase your business or would compete with it. The trip report in Figure 15.8 about opening a new restaurant contains all that information. To gauge the overall effect of competitors, you would have to observe nearby dry cleaners and assess the amount of business they do, the quality of their services, the prices they charge, the appearance of their stores, and even the professionalism of their employees.

Regardless of what and where you are called upon to observe, follow these guidelines:

- Always prepare for your visit and observations. Determine what problems you have to solve, what questions your boss or instructor will want answered, and what data you'll have to gather—specimens, maps, sample products—to answer those questions and solve the problem.
- Make careful notes about what you observe. Take a tape recorder, laptop, camera phone, and/or PDA with you. Record results precisely and impartially.
- Conduct any tests or experiments according to the most ethical standards of your discipline and the requirements of your job.

Interviews

Another method of gathering primary research is to interview experts or other resource people about your topic. Interviews can be conducted in person, over the telephone, or even in online chat rooms. Interviews are a useful tool in business and in many other disciplines as well—for example, psychology, health care, criminal justice. Conducting an interview is a much more complex, detailed procedure than you might think. You need to prepare for your interview just as carefully as you did to gather information from direct observation. You cannot go to an interview cold, unprepared. To learn more about the process of interviewing, consult the following sources:

- "Using Interviews in Research" on Rider University's Teaching Clinical Psychology website, *http://www.rider.edu/~suler/interviews.html*
- "General Guidelines for Conducting Interviews" on the Management Assistant Program for Nonprofits website, *http://www.mapnp.org/library/evaluation/interview.htm*
- "A Guide to Interview Guides" on Michigan State University's Teacher Education Doctoral Students' Digital Advisor For Research Projects website, *http://edwe3.educ.msu.edu/digitaladvisor/Research/Files/InterviewGuide.htm*

It is crucial to structure and administer your interview questions carefully. Researchers have found that how questions are worded has a substantial effect on interviewees' responses and the overall success of the interview itself.

To conduct a successful interview, follow these guidelines:

- First determine what level of expertise or kind of experience you need from your interviewee to draw on for your research.
- Ask your boss or instructor to help you identify the experts in your organization, community, or company.
- Gather background information about your resource person and the organization or professional group or society that he or she represents.
- Whether for a personal visit or a phone call, always make an appointment and specify how much time you will need. Be realistic—fifteen minutes may be too short; two hours too long.
- Always prepare your list of questions ahead of time.
- Ask if you can use a tape recorder before you click one on.
- Ask focused, direct questions that will give you the information you need. Don't ask only yes or no questions—"Do you think there is enough security on campus?" Avoid vague, general questions such as, "How can the Internet help businesses today reach customers?" Instead, develop questions that will give you relevant history, and the interviewee's ideas, suggestions, and views on options and alternatives.
- If an interviewee raises a relevant point not on your list of questions, be prepared to ask follow-up questions.
- Stay focused. Don't stray from the topic or delve into personal or confidential matters.
- If the interviewee does not want to answer a question, move to the next question on your list. If the interviewee has no more information to add to one of his or her answers, don't push the point. Be courteous.
- Conclude by thanking your resource person and ask if you might call back with any further questions or to clarify a point.
- Request permission to quote the individual in your report or paper.
- Don't wait too long to listen to and transcribe the interview or to review your notes. Determine how you can incorporate the interviewee's comments, ideas, statistics, or alternatives into your ongoing research.

Surveys/Questionnaires

Questionnaires are a common way to conduct a survey of people's opinions about community or political issues, products or services, television shows, and other topics. No doubt you've been asked to participate in a survey recently. For example, many online vendors ask customers, after a purchase is made, to rate their experience doing business with the company. Online customer feedback provides crucial research in decision making for e-commerce companies. Better surveying leads to increased customer satisfaction online as well as for in-store visits. Note how the survey in Figure 8.1 was designed to help online shoppers. Sometimes companies have contests or offer financial incentives to encourage people to participate in these surveys. Surveys may also be used to conduct primary research for an academic paper, such as finding out what individuals on a campus might think of library service, parking, dining facilities, or security.

The goal of surveys is simple: to collect and quantify information about people's attitudes, beliefs, product loyalty, ideas, knowledge, or opinions. You can survey people in person, by mail, over the telephone, or online. Think of a survey as an interview with a relatively large number of people.

Although surveys can require a very complex method to conduct research, there are some basic steps you need to follow in the survey process:

1. determining the population you want to survey
2. selecting a sample of the population to survey
3. carefully crafting the questions that appear on the questionnaire
4. conducting the survey
5. compiling and analyzing the results

Selecting Your Respondents

Surveys depend on targeting the right audience. Sometimes that audience is easy to reach, for example, all the nurses and technicians who work in an ICU unit at your hospital or a cross section of students and instructors at your college. But more often the group you want to survey—all the nurses who work in the ER in your state—is so large that you could not possibly survey the opinions of such a population, such as the audience for Figure 8.1.

To make your survey valid, you have to gather information from enough people to make judgments about a larger population. In other words, you need a statistically valid sample, a cross section of the group whose views you want to survey. Let's say you want to do a survey on the quality of food in a school cafeteria, or the cost and availability of health benefits at a company. You would need to obtain the opinions of a representative sample of people in that school or company. This is how, for example, Nielsen Media Research (*http://www.nielsenmedia.com/*) rates the popularity of television shows in the United States. Because Nielsen cannot survey all 275 million television viewers, the company selects a representative sample of 5,000 households. You may need to send your questionnaire first to a small segment of your audience to test your questions.

Figure 8.1   An example of an online survey.

Reply   Save   Forward   Print   Delete

To:	\<Carol_Smith@acme.com\>
From:	\<Gregg_Laos@whecomm.com\>
Date:	Thurs. 8 April 2007 9:02:00 EST
Subject:	Survey

Dear Valued WH eComm Customer,

At WH eComm, we are committed to providing our customers with high-quality e-commerce software through an efficient and user-friendly website. Customer feedback is extremely important in helping us continue to improve our website. So that we may best meet your needs, we ask you to take the time to answer a short survey about your experience at WH eComm. You will find the survey on our website by clicking here. Your answers will help us continue to improve WH eComm online and to offer you the service you need.

Provides incentive to reply

To say thank you for filling out this short questionnaire, we would like to offer you a 5 percent discount on your next purchase. When you have completed the survey, your discount will automatically be noted in your WH eComm online account.

Many thanks for your time and business,

Gregg Laos
Manager
WH eComm

WH eComm
revolutionizing e-commerce

1. How many times have you visited our website?
○ First visit   ○ 2–4 times   ○ 5–7 times   ○ more than 7

2. How did you hear about our website?
○ Colleague
○ Advertisement in business journal
○ Another website
○ Search engine
○ Other (please specify)

Fill-in option does not require a lengthy answer

3. Is the website easy to navigate?
○ Very easy   ○ Easy   ○ Somewhat easy   ○ Not easy

Question is not phrased in a leading manner

4. How effective did you find the following sections of WH eComm?

	Extremely effective	Effective	Could be improved	Ineffective	No response
Web features	○	○	○	○	○
Search	○	○	○	○	○
FAQ	○	○	○	○	○
Online check out	○	○	○	○	○

Continued

5. How many times have you purchased our products?
○ 1–2 times   ○ 3–4 times   ○ 5–7 times   ○ 8–9 times   ○ more than 9 (please specify)

```

```

6. What type of product(s) have you purchased from WH eComm? (check as many as apply)
○ E-commerce software
○ Networking software
○ Web design software
○ E-conferencing software

Multiple-choice items clearly differentiated

7. How helpful did you find our customer service?
○ Extremely helpful
○ Helpful
○ Could be improved
○ Not helpful
○ No response

8. How have you most often contacted our customer service office?
○ Phone   ○ E-mail   ○ Fax   ○ Web

9. How soon was your query answered?
○ Same day   ○ Next day   ○ Within 3 days   ○ Within a week   ○ Longer

10. How satisfied were you with the speed and efficiency of our online customer service center?
○ Very satisfied
○ Somewhat satisfied
○ Dissatisfied

11. Please rank, in order of importance, which factors most influence your online purchases.

	Price	Shipping options/time	Returns policy	Website quality
Most important	○	○	○	○
	○	○	○	○
	○	○	○	○
	○	○	○	○
	○	○	○	○
Least important	○	○	○	○

Ranking question supplies all necessary options

12. What would you most like to see changed or improved on our website?

```

```

Provides opportunity for respondent to elaborate

Thank you for taking the time to answer our questions.

Home

To learn more about sampling, look at introductory marketing or statistics text-books such as Charles Henry Brase's *Understandable Statistics*, 8th ed. (Boston: Houghton Mifflin, 2006). You may also want to consult these websites:

- "Questionnaire Design and Surveys Sampling" by Professor Hossein Arsham at the University of Baltimore (*http://homeubalt.edu/ntbarsh/stat-data/Surveys.htm*)
- "Choosing the Sample" on the Marquette University Writing Center website (*http://www.marquette.edu/writingcenter/ChoosingtheSample.htm*)

Asking Respondents to Participate

Don't expect all of your respondents, or even half of them, for that matter, to reply to your questionnaire. Researchers find that a response rate of 12 percent from a statistically chosen sample group is still valid. But to increase your chances of hearing from respondents, do the following:

1. Provide a cover letter or e-mail, as in Figure 8.1, asking them to respond and thanking them in advance for doing so.
2. Make the questionnaire easy and quick to answer—don't use more than ten to fifteen questions, and don't ask for detailed responses or ask respondents to do your research for you. Note how WH eComm in Figure 8.1 asks only twelve key questions.
3. Clearly specify how they are to indicate their responses—clicking on an answer or using check marks or a numerical scale.
4. Indicate whether you would like them to identify themselves or to remain anonymous.
5. Never ask a question about age, gender, religion, or educational level unless it is crucial and relevant to your survey.
6. Offer them some incentive, such as the discount in Figure 8.1.

Types of Questions to Ask

There are many types of questions you can ask, as illustrated in Figure 8.1, including yes or no, ranking, rating, multiple choice, or open ended. Researchers advise asking questions that require the least amount of effort on the part of respondents (yes or no, multiple choice) to increase the chances of their filling out the questionnaire. Accordingly, ask open-ended and rating questions (where respondents have to carefully weigh a range of choices) sparingly.

Here are some guidelines for writing valid and reliable questions:

1. **Phrase questions precisely.**

   Poor: Is there enough open time at the pool? Yes____ No____
   Better: How many hours of open time would you use at the pool?
   1____ 2____ 3____ 4____

2. **Supply respondents with clearly differentiated options in multiple-choice questions.**

Poor: When is the best time to call you to give you a quote?
daytime____
noontime____
weekday____
after work____
evenings____
nights____
Better: When is the best time to call you?
____mornings (8:00 a.m.–noon)
____afternoons (noon–5:00 p.m.)
____evenings (5:00 p.m.–10:00 p.m.)

3. **Supply all necessary options for multiple-choice/ranking questions.**

Which type of beverage do you like best? (1 least; 5 best)
coffee____   soft drinks____   tea____   milk____

This question omits a key option for many readers—bottled water.

4. **Don't write slanted or biased questions.**

Poor: Were you impressed by this award-winning film?
yes____   no____
Better: Did you think this was an award-quality film?
yes____   no____

5. **Ask one question at a time.**

Are there other services you would like the library to offer?
more books____   better hours____   more databases____
faster document delivery____   more study carrels____   other____

Break this question into two or three, one each on schedules, facilities, and collections.

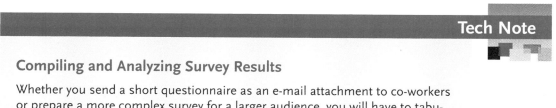

Tech Note

Compiling and Analyzing Survey Results

Whether you send a short questionnaire as an e-mail attachment to co-workers or prepare a more complex survey for a larger audience, you will have to tabulate the results and analyze them for your readers. Here are some guidelines to follow to make sure your results will be accurate and valid:

1. Pretest your questionnaire by sending it to only a few of your respondents to see if they have trouble answering it, find any options contradictory or incomplete, or suggest important topics you neglected to include.

2. Make sure your respondent pool is large enough to provide accurate data. If you don't sample enough respondents, you won't gather the information necessary to arrive at valid conclusions.

Continued

Continued

3. Use a representative sample of respondents to query. For instance, if you are questioning physical therapists about a policy or protocol that affects only this group, don't also include pharmacists as part of your target (or pretest) audience.

4. As your questionnaires are returned, tabulate the responses clearly and systematically. Keep a record of the data in a table or data sheet and enter each response into an appropriate category. Prepare a key ahead of time in which you enter the raw data to keep track of the number of individuals who have responded and what their responses were. Assign each completed questionnaire a number so you can double-check responses and you have a record of completed questionnaires.

5. After you tabulate responses to the individual questions, you have to analyze the data. You need to supply an interpretation that helps readers connect the data you gathered to the recommendations you are making.

6. Decide whether your statistical data (the responses to your questions) support any recommendations or predictions you want to make.
   - If twenty out of twenty-five respondents say they're not satisfied with the performance of your product or service, you cannot ethically say they have written glowingly about it. Falsifying or fabricating data is unethical and will distort and discredit your recommendations.
   - Where respondents are equally divided on an issue, you are obligated to inform your boss about these divided opinions. In some instances, such divided responses may not really affect a product redesign.
   - If respondents skip a question, you cannot count it as a yes or a no or assume anything about their opinions. You must discount it entirely.
   - If a respondent's answer is unclear or ambiguous (answering both "Yes" and "No" to a question), discard their response to that question.

7. Depending on the scope of your survey, consider providing readers with a table tallying the overall responses to key issues. Do not give your reader a table for each question in your survey; rather, prepare one or two tables that show a clear picture of the major conclusions the data suggest.

Statistical sampling can be a very complex process. But a variety of software packages can collect feedback, suggest correlations, and make predictions based on respondents' answers. The software programs SPSS and Excel, for example, can help you generate the categories as well as predict trends, invaluable information for sales and growth projections. Using these software programs, a company can access and improve its evaluations of products and services, thereby increasing its competitive edge. To find out more information, consult

- *http://www.SPSS.com*
- Dennis Hinkle, William Wiersma, and Stephen Jurs, *Applied Statistics for the Behavioral Sciences*, 5th ed. (Boston: Houghton Mifflin, 2003).

Maureen Curley

Secondary Research

As we saw earlier in this chapter, secondary research is using information that has already been made available, unlike primary research, which is generated by you, the researcher. Like primary research, conducting secondary research involves planning and organizing your time. You will need to learn about your library and its various services (both print and online), and about how to effectively use materials available on the Web. Let's start with the library.

The Library

Almost every institution—whether a school or a corporation—maintains a library. Although many large companies have e-libraries, where almost all of their materials may be found online, most businesses, like schools, also have a physical space reserved for accessing, using, and archiving research materials and tools. This space may be a room at the main corporate headquarters or several large buildings at an international firm.

No matter where your research materials are housed, familiarize yourself with your school or company library. There are lots of ways to do it. Get a map, go for an orientation, or make an appointment with a reference librarian.

Libraries are usually divided into the following sections to help you find various tools, books, services, and equipment:

- **circulation desk**—where the library user can check out, return, renew, or recall a book, film, or other library materials.
- **online catalog**—where you gain access to the library's holdings and resources, including materials on the Web or at other libraries. You can generally access your school's or company's online catalog from your home or in the library, provided you have the necessary password.
- **reference collection**—where you can find dictionaries, encyclopedias, almanacs, handbooks, and hard-copy recent issues of some indexes and abstracts. These materials cannot be checked out of the library.
- **the stacks**—where books and other hard-copy materials are shelved and arranged according to either the Library of Congress system (letters followed by numbers) or the Dewey decimal system (primarily numbers).
- **periodicals section**—where journals, magazines, newsletters are found. Current issues of those publications as well as the most recent issues of several newspapers may be arranged here on shelves for browsing and reading. Bound periodicals contain several past issues of one journal (e.g., the fall, winter, spring, and summer issues for one or two years) collected into a book or volume and often stored in the stacks.
- **microform section**—where past issues of newspapers, magazines, and other documents are stored on film or tape and read on a machine that enlarges the images.

Keep in mind that the physical library building houses these departments or divisions and that many companies also include the same areas in their facilities. However, a business may call its periodicals section the trade journals area, and it may provide additional business-specific areas not usually found in a typical school library, e.g., patents, blueprints/specs, and government contracts.

Online Catalogs

Your library's online catalog has replaced the card catalog system. The online catalog lists all materials the library owns, subscribes to, or has access to through its membership in a consortium library network. The catalog is not restricted to books but also lists websites, microforms, encyclopedias, periodical indexes, audio and video recordings, visuals, and the magazines and journals (electronic and print) to which your library subscribes. Many large companies also have online library catalogs. You can access the library's online catalog either on library terminals or from a remote location, such as your office or home computer.

Online catalogs provide you with a wealth of options for accessing material, often providing links to full-text electronic resources such as journal and magazine articles that can be downloaded from the Internet. You can also e-mail search results from an online catalog to yourself to keep track of your research process. In addition to your library's online catalog, comprehensive Web-based catalogs, such as FirstSearch or WorldCat, allow you to search for materials in over 50,000 libraries worldwide, highlighting results found in your own library. From your library's online catalog you can retrieve information about all books relevant to your search from libraries almost anywhere. Web-based catalogs are a crucial part of a global search network.

Accessing the Online Catalog

As you start your research, you should keep the following search strategies in mind:

- **Know your topic.** Start with an encyclopedia or other general reference resource for background information on your topic so that you are aware of the various subtopics involved.
- **Restrict your subject.** When you are searching your library's catalog you may need to narrow your topic in order to find a more manageable amount of information. Suppose you are researching the use of lasers in printing. The online catalog finds every document with *both* the words *lasers* and *printing*, and may include too many resources. To narrow your subject, you might specify exactly what you want *excluded*. For example, searching "lasers NOT military" would help you focus on nonmilitary uses of lasers.
- **Expand your search.** In some cases you may have to expand your search in order to find more information on your subject. For example, if you are looking for information on international businesses based in Asia that export to the United States, your search may be too specific and produce no results. Instead, you might want to expand your search to "international business in Asia."
- **Take advantage of links.** An online catalog will usually provide you with links to related materials that may be even more helpful to your search. Use the previous and next links to navigate through sources in the same subject.

The most significant advantage of starting your research with your library's online catalog is that it makes your search easier because of the powerful search options

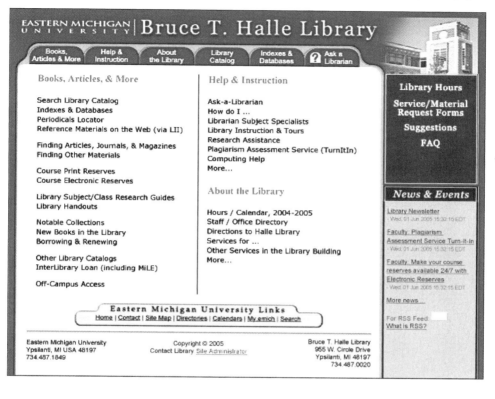

Helpful menu serves as guide to library holdings, locations, and services

Link at top of left column is for searching library catalog

available. Much of the power of library searches comes from being able to filter out unwanted search results. Say, for example, that out of the 4,152 management titles your library holds, you were interested only in books written in Spanish and published after 2000. Using the filters available in the catalog, you would be able to limit your search results to only those works that met these modified criteria.

It's a good idea to get to know the full range of services your library provides. Begin by accessing your library catalog's homepage for directions on how to conduct a search. See Figure 8.2 for an example of a library homepage. All library homepages are organized differently, but every library's homepage should provide a clear link to that library's online catalog, as the Search Library Catalog link in Figure 8.2 does. Clicking on the link to the online catalog will bring up a new screen similar to that in Figure 8.3.

As you can see, you can search your catalog in a variety of ways. Most searches start with more general subject or keyword searches before moving on to author and title searches.

Subject Searches

If you don't have a specific author or title in mind, then subject searches are the best place to begin. Often, looking at the related subject lists will give you ideas

Figure 8.3   Search screen with options.

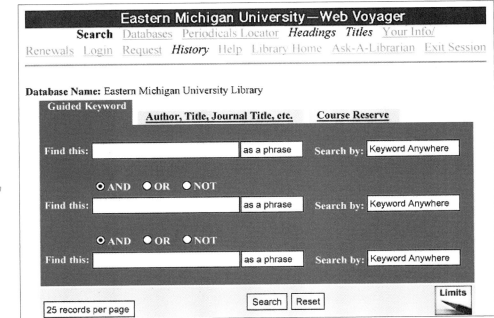

about focusing your topic to limit the scope of your investigation. Keep in mind that this search does not usually retrieve lists of books or library materials. Instead, it lists the subject headings derived from the Library of Congress Subject Headings list (*http://www.loc.gov/catdir/cpso/lcco/lcco.html*). If you search for a subject heading, such as "management," you can then explore similar headings or browse relevant subheadings. Each subject heading will link to a list of materials relating to that topic in your library's holdings.

Keyword Searches

Keyword searches allow you to find keywords that appear in titles, descriptions, or publication information. Keyword searching gives a broader scope of materials because it searches deeper into the individual records for each work. For example, if you entered "Bill Gates" in a keyword search, your results may include materials written by Bill Gates, books and articles about Bill Gates, or materials that mention Bill Gates in the description or table of contents. Keyword searches are particularly useful because they allow you to search for more specific topics than would a subject search. However, a keyword search is much like using an Internet search engine: You may find that some of the results are irrelevant to your subject.

Online catalog entry. Figure 8.4

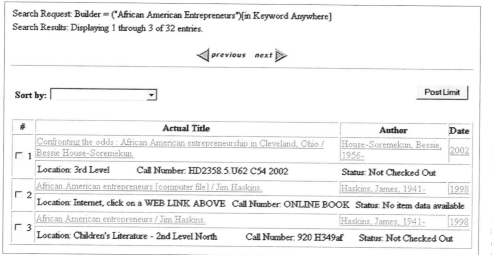

Author, title, and publication date

Library location, call number, and holding status

Author/Title Searches

When you enter the author's name, you will see a screen displaying all of the author's work(s) available through your library. Similarly, if you know only the first part of a title, the online catalog will list all the titles that begin with the words you enter. You can then select the one you are searching for.

Call Numbers

Nearly all searches in an online catalog will give you a call number, which indicates where the book or document is physically located in your library—stacks, reference collection, audio-visual library. If you locate a relevant book in the online catalog through a keyword or subject search, you can choose to do a call number search on many catalogs and browse the **virtual shelves** to find similar books. This search allows you to move backward and forward, so that you can "see" what titles are next to, above, or below your book on the shelves of your library.

Information Found in an Online Catalog Entry

Each online catalog entry contains a great deal of information beyond the author and title. As you search the catalog for the information you need, you will see bibliographic data (descriptive information of the works) displayed on the screen, as in Figure 8.4. You can print, download, or e-mail the information, saving you time and eliminating errors in transcribing. That information can include:

- **call number**—a number indicating the location and subject matter of the work, according to the Dewey Decimal or Library of Congress system of categorizing works. These groupings help researchers find similar works on a topic by browsing a shelf in person or electronically.
- **status of a holding**—whether it can be checked out, if it has been checked out, when it is due back, how you can "recall" it, whether it is on reserve, and for how long.
- **type of work**—what kind of holding it is, for example, a periodical or a government document. If the work is an electronic document, the catalog will provide a link or instructions for downloading it.
- **publishing information**—typically includes the city of publication, the name of the publisher, the edition or number of volumes (when applicable), the specific edition (if not the first), and date of publication.

Periodical Databases

Periodical databases are electronic indexes that allow you to search and retrieve a wealth of data on a variety of subjects. They can guide you to magazine or journal articles, newspaper articles, and other materials available through your library's online catalog or document delivery service. Through databases you can search through thousands of articles published over several years in a matter of minutes. Some indexes include not only abstracts, but also provide the actual text of the articles themselves. However, if you are doing research on articles published before 1988, you may find that the text is available only in printed form.

Many libraries, including those at corporations, subscribe to a group of different databases covering various fields, including:

- **subject databases.** Almost every professional discipline has its own database or collection of databases. For example, there are many business databases, including LexisNexis Business, General BusinessFile ASAP, Business Source Elite, Business & Company Resource Center, and Business Source Premier. Databases such as MEDLINE and Ovid search only medical-related articles, while AGRICOLA is devoted to articles in agriculture. Table 8.1 lists some frequently consulted, subject-specific databases.
- **company databases.** Many large companies have developed their own information databases or research resources for their employees. Intel, for example, has its own searchable resource center, and GlaxoSmithKline, the international pharmaceutical manufacturer, provides a research library for its 120,000 employees in labs and offices around the world.
- **government databases.** A government database such as FirstGov is the gateway or Web portal to all U.S. government information available online. Other government databases search specific government resources from various departments. For example, the Homeland Security Information Center is a gateway to information about security issues, health, preparedness, and response, while Business.gov guides users through government regulations and provides access to government resources for small businesses.

TABLE 8.1   Some Available Databases by Discipline/Field

Database	Contents
ABI/INFORM	Lists business management articles from U.S. and international sources
AGRICOLA	Research materials relating to agriculture
Animal Science	Provides information on animal production and veterinary science
Business & Company Resource Center	Offers a variety of global business topics, company profiles, case studies, and investment information
Business Source Elite	Provides full-text, index, and abstracts of business journals and magazines
CINAHL	Index of over 550 journals of nursing and allied health
Computer Science Index	Abstracts and indexes of over 500 academic journals, professional publications, and other sources on computer science
Contemporary Women's Issues	Women's issues on health and human rights, in over 150 countries
Criminal Justice Abstracts	Covers journals, books, and reports on criminology and related disciplines
EconLit	Includes bibliographic citations, abstracts and journal articles, books, collected essays, and full-text book reviews dealing with economics
Environmental Science & Pollution Management	Journal articles on environmental science and pollution management
FactSearch	Indexes over 1,000 newspapers, periodicals, newsletters, and government documents dealing with criminal justice and legal issues
Facts On File	Provides worldwide news stories from newspapers, periodicals, journals, and online government sources
FirstGov	Official database of the U.S. federal government accessing files, documents, and reports from all government agencies
General BusinessFile ASAP	Covers articles on business and management from over 3,000 publications
Health Source: Nursing/ Academic Edition	Provides full-text articles from over 255 periodicals covering nutrition, medical self-care, drugs, and alcohol
LexisNexis Business	Full range of sources for business information, financial news, international company information, market research, industry reports
MEDLINE	Indexes more than 4,600 journals covering all areas of medicine
Microcomputer Abstracts	Covers popular magazines and professional journals on microcomputing for business, industry, education, and home use
National Criminal Justice Reference Center	Provides information, documents, and reports from the U.S. Department of Justice
NetFirst	Online Computer Library Center (OCLC) database of the Internet
NTIS Homeland Security Information Center	Government resource covering national security concerns, biological and chemical warfare, preparedness and response, and safety training
PsychARTICLES	Full-text journal articles in general and specialized psychology
U.S. Bureau of Consular Affairs	Government resource for international travel information, advice, and warnings
U.S. Department of Treasury	Provides government information on accounting and budget, currency, financial markets, small businesses, and taxes

There are thousands of databases available from different information services. Some of these databases are electronic indexes and abstracts, which list articles available in journals, magazines, newspapers, collections, and conferences. Some indexes include abstracts (see pages 428–431) as well, which summarize each citation. Examples of index and abstract databases are Computer Science Index and Criminal Justice Abstracts. Many other databases allow you to access the entire text of articles from journals, magazines, reports, laws, and other sources. Examples of full-text databases include Regional Business News and Academic Search Premier.

Information Available from a Database

Searching an online database, you can receive the following information crucial for your research either on the job or for school:

- **bibliographic citations**, including author, title, publication information, page numbers, and the language in which the article is written
- **abstracts** summarizing the article's content
- **keywords, subjects**, and **descriptors** to identify the contents of the article and help you locate similar studies
- **full text** of many articles, often including an image or a PDF version of the original document
- **factual information**, ranging from stock quotations to patent numbers, public affairs news, and product and company information

Databases in Your Library

Find out which databases your library subscribes to. Some offer free access, but most are available only by subscription. Ovid, for example, searches over 300 databases specializing in medical and scientific information. Among the most frequently used databases are FirstSearch and NewsBank InfoWeb, which primarily search newspaper articles.

Here are some other widely used services that your school, work, or community library may subscribe to:

1. **EBSCO.** Indexes, abstracts, and gives full text of articles from thousands of popular magazines, professional journals, and newspapers. EBSCOHOST boasts the biggest full-text collection of scholarly materials in the world. Figure 8.5 describes some of the databases you can search through EBSCO.
2. **OCLC FirstSearch.** Available only through libraries, this database is a comprehensive reference collection offering access to dozens of databases and more than 4,000 electronic journals with over 10 million full-text articles, including images. At the heart of FirstSearch is WorldCat, a bibliographic catalog that lists materials available at over 50,000 libraries worldwide.
3. **LexisNexis Academic.** This database is a valuable source for industry information, providing full-text documents from over 5,600 news, business, legal, medical, and reference publications.

4. **NewsBank InfoWeb.** Contains full text of over 70,000 news articles annually from over 500 U.S. and Canadian newspapers. Figure 8.6 shows a basic search screen for NewsBank.
5. **ProQuest.** Indexes more than 7,400 publications, including newspapers and scholarly and general interest sources in business, news, medicine, humanities, social sciences, and science and technology.

Figure 8.6   NewsBank basic search screen.

Search options

NewsBank™ inc.
a world of information
NewsBank NewsFile Collection   *1992-Current*

Home > NewsFile Collection   Help

Search: all categories

for: **Search**   more search options...

Return: Best matches first   from   the past twelve months

Reading Level: ⊙ all   ○ By Lexile:

Limit to: ☐ Newspapers   ☐ Newswires

Search Hints

Connect terms with AND, OR, NOT or other search operators.

Put phrases in quotation marks, e.g., "gun control."

Easy-to-follow icons

Explore NewsFile Collection

Civics, Government and Politics
- news leaks
- political polarization
- U.S. Supreme Court nominations
- ...more

Crime and Law
- USA Patriot Act
- child kidnapping
- capital punishment and mercy
- ...more

$ Economics
- Social Security
- teenage employment
- fraud in the telecommunications industry
- ...more

Education
- high-stakes testing
- intelligent design and evolution
- vending machines in schools
- ...more

Subdivisions help you narrow search

Environment
- hurricanes
- hazardous wastes
- motor vehicle emissions
- ...more

Film and Television
- anime
- trends in reality TV
- film festivals
- ...more

Fine Arts and Architecture
- skylines and architecture
- current art criticism
- museum acquisitions
- ...more

Health
- skin cancer
- morning-after pill
- obesity and public health
- ...more

History
- World War II
- Iraq and history
- Age of Exploration
- ...more

International
- terrorism in London
- Iranian nuclear weapons
- development of Iraq's government
- ...more

Literature
- literary awards
- censorship
- blogs
- ...more

People
- George W. Bush
- Vladimir Putin
- Pope Benedict XVI
- ...more

Other resources:
Tools
- News Headlines
- Maps

Strategies for Searching a Database

With so many databases available, it can be difficult to know where to start your search. When you search a database retrieval service such as those listed on page 315, you will often be presented with a screen such as that of EBSCOHOST in Figure 8.5, which asks you to select the subject databases you want to include in your search. Search those that relate to your topic. You should expect to use several databases in your search. For example, if you are searching for an article on the growth of information technology companies in Asia, you will want to include business as well as international news databases.

You search a database much like you would an online catalog, probably choosing subject or keyword before author or title. Use the same guidelines you would rely on for a catalog search to refine or expand your search. A database will often provide you with a number of advanced search options that help you locate what you are looking for more efficiently. For example, if you are searching for recent developments in the news about computer virus protection, you can choose to limit your search to include only newspaper articles, excluding all journal articles and book citations. Similarly, you could refine your search options to include only newspaper articles published since January 2006 so that your results are current and include up-to-date developments. You can also choose to limit your search to only full-text articles that you can download and print. These strategies for refining your search will help you to retrieve a manageable number of results that are tailored to your needs as a researcher.

Tech Note

Guides to Internet Journals

A variety of sites provide information about online journals. New Jour (*http://gort.ucsd.edu/newjour*) lists new journals and newsletters on the Web. The WWW Virtual Library (*http://vlib.org*) organizes information into major subjects, such as "Business and Economics" or "Communications and Media," and then supplies links to more specific sites, which then list journals in those fields. You can also consult subject-specific sites such as FindLaw (*http://www .findlaw.com/journals*), which locates legal journals and resources, SciCentral (*http://www.scicentral.com*), which gives journal titles and other resources in many scientific areas, and Primary Care Internet Guide (*http://www.uib.no/isf/ guide/journal.htm*), which is a guide to medical journals online.

Case Study: Searching the Databases

Jaime Iglesia has been asked to write a short report on identity theft for his boss, the financial manager of a medium-sized Internet-based company that sells DVDs online at discount prices. Because of so many consumers who had recently been tricked into giving away personal and financial information via e-mail, Jaime's boss wanted to find out how customers of a company such as his would be affected by identity thieves.

Through EBSCOHOST, Iglesia began his search by focusing on only those databases that relate to business news and technology. But knowing he would need to expand his search to cover more subjects, he consulted several databases, such as Academic Search Premier, Business Source Elite, Newspaper Source, and Regional

Business News because those particular databases seem to cover more materials relevant to his boss's needs.

His first attempt searching for the keywords "identity theft" yielded 878 results, everything from real-estate identity theft to stolen passports. Knowing that his search was too broad, Iglesia decided to focus on just identity theft on the Internet, which was more directly related to what his boss requested. Searching the databases for "identity fraud AND online" gave him a much more manageable number of 165 results.

However, some of the titles appeared to be too dated, ranging from 1997 to the present. Iglesia knew his boss wanted him to investigate recent trends in online identity fraud, so he refined his search to include only articles published since 2005. He also decided he wanted to locate only full-text articles that he could download onto his home computer, so he limited his search to full-text results. His final search gave him sixteen articles, many of which appeared in the professional business magazines his boss would find of most value. Searching through the list, he was able to select seven key articles that would form the basis of his report.

Finding Reference Materials

Reference materials include encyclopedias, indexes, guides, dictionaries, and manuals that will give you an up-to-date introduction to or a survey of a topic. Most reference works may *not* be checked out of the library, but many of them are available online, either through your library's homepage or on the Internet. Ask your librarian to direct you to the most important reference works in your field. Here is a brief overview of some helpful reference works you can consult for your reports at school or for work.

Encyclopedias

The word *encyclopedia* comes from the Greek phrase meaning "general education." A general encyclopedia is a great starting point for researchers because it provides introductions to topics, summarizes events or processes, explains key terms, and includes references to related topics, along with lists of further reading. You should be able to access online encyclopedias via your library's subscription to them or use them in their book format. Some popular encyclopedias include

- *Columbia Encyclopedia*
- *Encyclopedia Britannica*
- *Encyclopedia Americana*

Other general encyclopedias covering a wide assortment of topics are available online. These include *Wikipedia* (*http://wikipedia.org/*) and *Encarta Encyclopedia* (*http://encarta.msn.com/*).

Many encyclopedias are devoted to specialized subjects. The following list is only a representative sample:

- *Blackwell Encyclopedia of Management*
- *Encyclopedia of Banking and Finance*

Online version of *Hoover's Handbook of American Business.*   Figure 8.7

Courtesy of Hoover's, Inc.

- *Encyclopedia of Business Information Sources*
- *McGraw-Hill Encyclopedia of Science and Technology*
- *Gale Encyclopedia of Nursing and Allied Health*

Directories

If you are trying to find research information about specific companies, turn to one of the many available industry-specific directories. Often, these directories are named for the companies or agencies that publish them.

- *Hoover's, Inc. (www.hoovers.com)*
- *Minority and Women Business Directory*
- *Standard & Poor's Industry Survey*
- *Thomas Register of American Manufacturers*

Figure 8.7 shows a screen from Hoover's website, where users can find a wealth of secondary research compiled about individual businesses.

Many industry directories are online, although not all of them are available without subscription. Check to see which directories your library subscribes to. The following list is only a small sample of the diverse range of available online directories:

- Agribusiness Online (*http://www.agribusinessonline.com/*)
- Biotechnology Information Directory (*http://www.cato.com/biotech/*)
- Business.com (*http://www.business.com/*)
- eHotelier (*http://www.ehotelier.com/*)
- Retail Source (*http://www.retailsource.com/*)

Dictionaries

In addition to general dictionaries, such as *The American Heritage Dictionary of the English Language*, there are hundreds of specialized dictionaries that define words and phrases that are used in the literature of different professions and industries, such as

- *Dictionary of Architecture and Construction*
- *Illustrated Computer Dictionary*
- *International Dictionary of Business and Finance*
- *The Blackwell Encyclopedic Dictionary of Marketing*

You may also find industry-specific dictionaries available online, including:

- American Institute of Certified Public Accountants' *Glossary of Terms, Acronyms, and Abbreviations* (*http://www.aicpa.org/members/glossary/a.htm*)
- *Glossary of Marketing Definitions* (*http://www.ifla.org/VII/s34/pubs/glossary .htm*)
- *LogisticsWorld Logistics Glossary* (*http://www.logisticsworld.com/logistics/ glossary.htm*)
- *The New York Times Glossary of Financial and Business Terms* (*http://www .nytimes.com/library/financial/glossary/bfglosa.htm*)

Handbooks and Manuals

Handbooks and manuals supply explanations of procedures, definitions of terms and concepts, and overviews of practical and professional issues within a field. If you're doing research about a certain career, start with the *Occupational Outlook Handbook*, produced by the U.S. Bureau of Labor Statistics (*http://www.bls.gov/ oco/*). This online resource, which is updated every other year, "describes what workers do on the job, working conditions, the training and education needed, earnings, and expected job prospects in a wide range of occupations." You may also want to consult more than one manual to compare different perspectives on the same topic.

Among the most useful manuals are *Moody's Manuals*, which provide a wealth of information on the history of companies, descriptions of products and services, and basic financial details (stocks, earnings, and mergers). Many manuals are available online, and your library may also have copies of other popular manuals, such as

- *Handbook of North American Industry*
- *National Forestry Handbook*
- *Standard & Poor's Standard Corporate Descriptions*

Almanacs

Almanacs contain carefully organized statistical information—charts, tables, graphs, price indexes, federal and state budgets—as well as descriptions of events by year and region. Some almanacs are published for specific states, such as the *Texas Al-*

manac (http://www.texasalmanac.com/). As the following list of titles indicates, almanacs are published on a variety of specialized subjects:

- *Almanac of Business and Industrial Financial Ratios*
- *Healthcare Almanac and Yearbook*
- *Plunkett's Almanacs* (covering a wide range of specific fields)
- *The American Almanac of Jobs and Salaries*

Statistics

Statistical resources contain numerical data on a wide range of health care, business, and technology subjects. General statistical resources include LexisNexis Statistical, which you can access via your library's database search. This statistical database provides data from the U.S. government, private agencies, international organizations, and universities. Other statistical references found on the Web include

- FedStats (*http://fedstats.gov*)
- U.S. Bureau of Labor Statistics (*http://www.bls.gov/*)
- National Center for Health Statistics (*http://www.cdc.gov/nchs/*)
- BizStats.com (*http://www.bizstats.com/*)
- GeoHive (*http://www.geohive.com/*)

Government Documents

The U.S. federal government is the largest publisher in the country. Virtually every federal agency and department conducts primary and secondary research and publishes its findings. These publications, collectively referred to as **government documents**, include journal articles, pamphlets, publications, research reports, transcripts of government hearings, speeches, statistical reports, films, maps, and books.

Many government documents are available on the Internet through the website of the department or agency that created them. You can access these websites via FirstGov (*http://www.firstgov.gov*), the official Web portal of the U.S. government, which provides access to information, reports, and publications of any government department or agency. Figure 8.8 shows the FirstGov "Publications from the U.S. Government" page.

The Library of Congress website (*http://www.loc.gov*) is also a valuable research tool for finding government documents, including books, articles, videos, and other media from government departments, private agencies, and individuals. This site allows you to search by keyword, author, title, or subject to find material in the library's online catalog, website, virtual exhibitions, and research centers, such as the Library of Congress Business Reference Service. It is an invaluable source.

The federal government publishes a wealth of periodicals that range from agricultural information to congressional developments. LexisNexis Government Periodicals Universe is the most comprehensive government periodical index, helping you to locate more than 125,000 articles from 1988 to the present. Approximately 10,000 new articles from 160 periodicals are added each year, and LexisNexis

Figure 8.8   FirstGov "Publications from the U.S. Government" page.

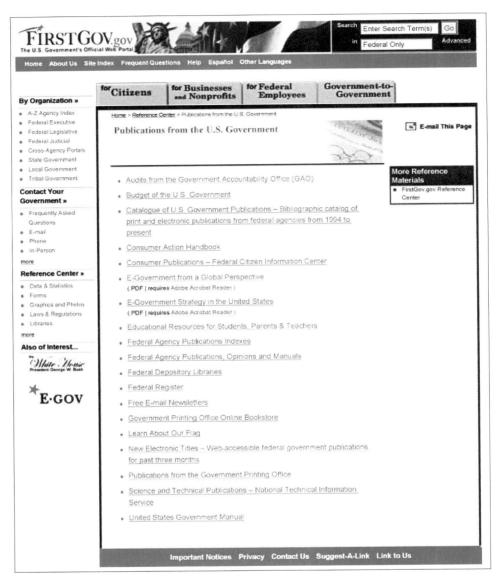

provides links to electronic versions when available. You can access the database via your library's website.

For a catalog of all U.S. government publications, visit the Government Printing Office at *http://www.gpoaccess.gov/cgp/* (see Figure 8.9), which lists some of the titles you can search. You can also access a catalog of all government periodicals

Government Printing Office "Catalog of U.S. Government Publications" main page.   Figure 8.9

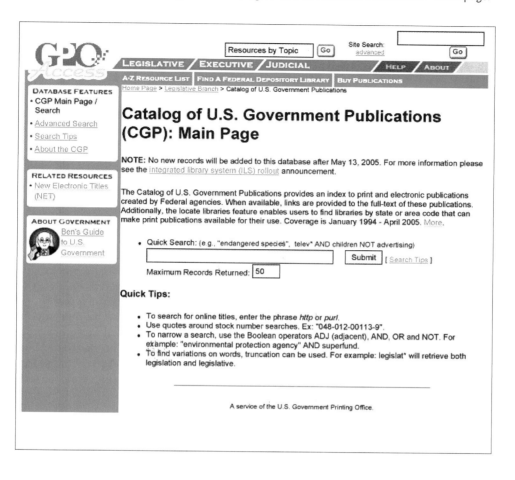

at *http://bookstore.gpo.gov/subscriptions/*, although you will need to use Lexis-Nexis to view the contents of each edition. Electronic access to many government publications is also possible through individual agency websites.

Doing Internet Research

There is an enormous amount of information available on the Internet, and it grows larger every day. Acting as a "network of networks," the Internet gives you access to information from millions of sources. As a research tool, the Internet offers many ways to conduct both primary and secondary research, including e-mail, Usenet newsgroups, instant messaging, Web logs (also known as blogs—see Tech Note, pp. 334–335), and the World Wide Web.

The Web is by far the largest information-sharing medium of the Internet, allowing you access to

- information services and databases
- government information and publications
- encyclopedias, dictionaries, and other reference works
- newsgroups, listservs, and online communities of researchers
- statistical data
- technical manuals
- video and audio files

With more than 8 billion sites from thousands of sources, including governments, corporations, organizations, and individuals, the Web is your key to Internet research.

Searching, Not Surfing, the Web

When you surf the Web, you wander from website to website without any particular goal in mind. However, surfing accomplishes very little when you are researching. Just like conducting library research, your Internet research needs to be carefully planned and focused. You wouldn't wander into a library and browse the stacks until you stumbled across something useful if you were there to do research. Instead, you would consult a database or catalog to locate materials relevant to your topic.

Searching the Web, however, can be more difficult than finding a book in your online library catalog. The Web is much larger and contains much more information. Moreover, there is no single catalog of all the information it holds. To conduct effective research online, you need to use e-libraries, subject directories, and search engines, all of which index webpages like a database, acting as gateways to vast amounts of information.

Tech Note

Punctuation and Structure of a URL

Just as proper punctuation helps you understand the written language better, so understanding the structure and punctuation of URLs can assist you in navigating the Web.

A URL (uniform resource locator) is logically divided into separate parts by slashes. As an example, let's use the website for the Office of Minority Health's Resource Center: *http://www.omhrc.gov/OMHRC/index.htm*. Each piece of information indicates different levels of information particular to the information hierarchy. The first portion, *http://*, indicates the protocol or method of access and type of document being sent. The second, *www*, indicates the host computer and that it is a page on the World Wide Web. The third part, *omhrc.gov*,

Continued

Continued

gives the domain name, which indicates the type of site (for example, *.edu*—an educational institution; *.com*—a commercial enterprise; *.gov*—a government agency; and *.net*—an Internet provider). Fourth, *OMHRC* points to a directory or folder of the domain. Last, *index.htm* is the name of the file being viewed on the Web. The *htm* (or *html*) indicates the page is written in the language of webpages. Together, the entire string of characters serves as a path the computer follows to get you to certain information. URLs are case-sensitive, meaning that you must type in upper- or lowercase letters exactly as they appear.

Knowing the structure can prove useful in at least two ways. First, because natural language is often used to name files and directories, when a source provides an erroneous URL, researchers can often backtrack to the parent directory and search for the relevant file or info. Second, by backtracking, researchers can discover other relevant valuable information.

Liam Kennedy

E-Libraries

Unlike a company or school library catalog that includes print and e-materials, e-libraries search for articles only available electronically via the Internet, filtering out irrelevant websites and focusing on articles and essential Web documents.

These Internet sites can speed your research and help you narrow your search even further, but expect to rely on other searches as well.

- **FindArticles** (*http://www.findarticles.com/*) searches the full text of 5 million articles from topics ranging from business to arts and entertainment to home and garden.
- **FreeFullText** (*http://www.freefulltext.com/*) provides online access to articles from over 7,000 scholarly journals. It allows full-text access to some and document delivery of others.
- **BPubs** (*http://www.bpubs.com/*) looks specifically for business publications.
- **HighBeam** (*http://www.highbeam.com/*) gives you an e-library with over 32 million documents from 2,800 sources, including magazines, journals, and newspapers, and offers free abstracts but charges for access to full-text articles.
- **CEOExpress** (*http://www.ceoexpress.com*) acts as an online information portal for business research, SEC filings, investor information, government research on a variety of topics, and financial market sites.

Subject Directories

Many businesses and groups have created Internet subject directories that easily locate appropriate websites (as opposed to articles, which are located via e-libraries). Subject directories are helpfully organized into logical categories (e.g., Business) and subcategories (e.g., International Business and Trade) for easy navigation. Each subcategory is typically annotated. These directories are also searchable, but the search area is limited to what the directory creators have selected. Think critically when using subject directories, as some subject directories provide more scholarly information than do others. Here are a few examples:

- **Librarians' Index to the Internet** (*http://lii.org*). This index surveys over 14,000 websites, each with a brief explanatory annotation, and is organized into 15 general interest categories (arts and humanities, business, media, science, etc.).
- **Academic Info** (*http://www.academicinfo.net*). As the name indicates, this is an academic subject directory aimed at both undergraduate and graduate students, and is an excellent way to conduct scholarly research.
- **Business.com** (*http://www.business.com/*). This site provides an easy way to locate business websites for news and information on companies, products, services, people, and jobs.
- **Google Directory** (*http://www.google.com/dirhp*). Organized into 16 broad categories (similar to those at the Librarians' Index) and many subcategories, this subject directory provides over 1 million annotated links to websites both academic and commercial.
- **Yahoo! Search** (*http://www.search.yahoo.com*). Very similar to the Google Directory, Yahoo! Search provides well over 1 million annotated links to various sites. It is more useful for popular and commercial topics than for scholarly ones.

Search Engines

When you begin your research, start with a search engine. Search engines are automated tools that use keywords to locate the webpages containing the most relevant information you need. Using computer robots that "crawl" through and "read" pages on the Web, a search engine indexes the information it finds to create a frequently updated database of results.

Search engine software ranks the results of your search using a computer algorithm that records the popularity of websites, their contents, where the keywords appear on the page, and other sites that link to that page, presenting you with the most relevant matches for your keywords. A search engine can find information from a wealth of sources on the Web, including websites, articles, periodicals, indexes, abstracts, summaries, newsgroup posts, message boards, blogs, and other e-documents.

Because there is no single index to or abstract of material on the Web, you should expect to use a wide range of search engines. Given the vastness of the Internet, it only makes sense that multiple search engines are available, as Table 8.2 shows. These include general and metasearch engines (which combine multiple search engines) as well as specialized, subject-specific, newsgroup, and media search engines. Like the Web itself, search engines are constantly expanding as they index more pages in cyberspace each second.

TABLE 8.2   Different Types of Internet Search Engines

Search Engines	Metasearch Engines
AltaVista	Excite
Ask Jeeves	DogPile
Google	Mamma
Lycos	MetaCrawler
Teoma	Profusion
Yahoo!	SavvySearch
	WebCrawler
	Zapmeta

Specialized Search Engines

General

AllSearchEngines (directory of subject-specific search engines)

Search Engine Colossus (an international directory of search engines)

Business.com (a business-only search engine)

Media

AltaVista's MP3/Audio Finder

AltaVista's Image Finder

ClipArt Searcher

Yahoo! Images and Video Finders

Listservs, Discussion Groups, and Newsgroups

EGroups (Yahoo!'s comprehensive listserv directory)

TileNet (directory of lists, Usenet, FTP, and Web design companies)

News

Google News

MoreOver (updates news hourly)

NewsDirectory.com

Newspapers.com (directory of international, national, college, and business papers)

Of course, search engines will vary in coverage and relevance for your project. Some are faster than others, while many incorporate results from multiple engines simultaneously. To some extent, all search engines overlap. For example, searching for "CNN" in any search engine will lead you to CNN's homepage at *http://www.cnn.com*. Moreover, no single search engine is comprehensive. Researchers estimate that almost 40 percent of the Web is not even indexed by the most popular search engines. But by using a variety of search engines to conduct keyword searches (see pp. 330–333), you will access a broader scope of sources and thereby increase your chances of finding the information you need.

Listed below are some frequently used search engines and metasearch engines.

Search Engines

1. **AlltheWeb** (*http://www.alltheweb.com*), one of the largest search engines, accesses over 3 billion documents and features specialized and advanced search options.
2. **AltaVista** (*http://www.altavista.com*) provides one of the most comprehensive searches in over 25 languages and includes audio and video searches, images, directories, and news. It also offers a free webpage translation service, BabelFish.
3. **Ask Jeeves** (*http://www.ask.com*) provides a variety of personalized search options, including MyJeeves, to save and organize your results in folders; view your search history; and share, print, and repeat searches.
4. **Google** (*http://www.google.com*) is currently one of the world's largest and easiest-to-use search engines, indexing over 8 billion pages. Google offers specialized engines such as Google Government, Google University, Google Microsoft (which searches sites only related to Microsoft), Google Apple (which searches Apple/Macintosh-related sites), and Google Local (to search for businesses in your area).
5. **Yahoo!** (*http://www.yahoo.com*), one of the earliest search engines, also includes a human-edited, subject-based directory of the Web. Yahoo! suggests related keywords and allows you to open links in new windows.
6. **Northern Light Business Research Engine** (*http://www.northernlight.com/library.html*) is a subscription service accessing millions of full-text articles from trade journals, business publications, and newspapers as well as specific company websites.

Metasearch Engines

1. **Dogpile** (*http://www.dogpile.com*) searches other engines, including Google, Yahoo!, and Ask Jeeves.
2. **MetaCrawler** (*http://www.metacrawler.com*) searches a variety of the largest search engines, organizing them either by relevance or by search engine. It offers news, image, audio, video, yellow pages, and white pages searches.
3. **WebCrawler** (*http://www.webcrawler.com*) also searches Google, Yahoo!, Ask Jeeves, LookSmart, Overture, and About.com for news, images, audio, video, and yellow pages and white pages directories.
4. **ZapMeta** (*http://www.zapmeta.com*) previews each site on the result page using a "Quick View" tool to make sure you are selecting the most useful search results.

Keyword Searches

To use search engines, online catalogs, and databases effectively, knowing how to conduct a keyword search is crucial to your success. When you enter a keyword into a search engine, it searches through its indexed websites and presents you with those that feature your keyword in the title, heading, meta tags, or text of the page. Your choice of keywords is vital since the results you receive depend on the keywords you plug into the search engine.

Example of a general search that yields too many results.   Figure 8.10

Keyword is too broad

Too many hits

Related links

Reprinted courtesy of Google Inc.

Following the guidelines here will help you to conduct successful keyword searches.

Be Specific

- **Identify your subject.** Although it might be tempting to start off with a broad subject like *computer security*, you may find yourself confronted with millions of hits that range from computer theft to message encryptions. Take a look at Figure 8.10, which shows what occurs from a search that floods you with general results. A search on the words *computer security* yielded over 186 million results. Before you start your search, try to narrow the focus of your subject.
- **Don't be abstract.** Words such as *government, technology, society, health, money,* and *history* are far too general and will yield millions of unrelated results.
- **Use multiple keywords.** Choose at least two or three significant keywords to specify your search. For example, if you key in just the word *virus*, you might receive vast amounts of information on everything from avian flu and the West Nile virus to computer problems. Specify *computer virus* to narrow your search.
- **Don't use prepositions.** Most search engines automatically exclude *of, to, in, from,* and *on.*

Figure 8.11   Example of a more refined Google search.

*Insert quota-
tion marks to
limit search*

*Use multiple
keywords to
restrict search*

*Click on re-
lated links*

Reprinted courtesy of Google Inc.

Adjust Your Keywords

- **Refine your search.** Unlike the vague keywords *computer virus*, specify the type of information you want to receive by refining your topic: Search for *computer virus causes* or *computer virus prevention* to net more precise, pertinent information. Figure 8.11 shows how advanced search options on a search engine can help you narrow your keyword search. Here the search was narrowed by using multiple and more specific search words: *computer security*, *pop-ups*, *phishing*, and *firewalls*.
- **Find relevant synonyms.** Try to locate possible synonyms or alternative keywords that might give you additional pathways to gain information on your topic. Many search engines even suggest ways to refine your search using other keywords. Take advantage of these suggestions.

Use Boolean Connectors

Boolean connectors, such as AND, OR, and NOT, are essential to limit and guide your search by reducing unrelated search results.

- Inserting *AND* between keywords will limit your results to those containing all your keywords. For example, *virus AND computer AND prevention* will produce only records that contain all three terms. Note that some search engines, such as Google, automatically search all keywords and therefore don't require the *AND* command.
- *OR* will produce records containing either or both keywords. *Virus OR computer* will list pages containing either *virus* or *computer* or both words.

- *NOT* as part of your keyword search excludes unwanted pages. *Telecommuting benefits NOT environmental* indicates that you are not concerned with how telecommuting saves energy or reduces pollution. Instead, you are looking for benefits to employers and employees.

Use Delimiters

To refine your search even further, use the following **delimiters**, sometimes called "wild-card characters":

- Quotation marks around a string of keywords limit your term to that particular phrase. For example, Wells Fargo without quotation marks would pull up sites for Wells Engineering; Fargo, North Dakota; and Fargo Wells.
- A plus sign (+) between terms can be used to replace the Boolean AND command, locating results that include all keywords. Similarly, a minus sign (−) can replace the OR command in many search engines.
- An asterisk (*) at the end of a term broadens your search beyond that afforded by a keyword. For example, the term *employ** will return all terms that use *employ* as the stem of a keyword, such as *employment*, *employer*, and *employability*.
- Some search engines, such as Google, allow you to use an asterisk within quotation marks to indicate a missing word. Searching for "*Australian * technology*" will find results including keyword phrases ranging from *Australian medical technology* to *Australian information technology*.

Internet Search Shortcuts

In addition to the keyword search strategies above, there are a number of shortcuts to access frequently requested information quickly and easily on the Internet. Many of these techniques take advantage of advanced search options available on major search engines. Of course, depending on the type of Internet resources available to you, and the constantly changing Web terrain, you will doubtless discover many more shortcuts. But the following ones give you additional ways to access information faster and more efficiently.

- Use Google Alerts by entering your e-mail address and a keyword term into the Alerts system to be notified when your search term appears in the top ten or twenty search results for a Google News or Web search. This service is particularly useful for ongoing business research because it provides constant updates on the latest information relevant to your topic.
- Select the image-only option from AltaVista, Yahoo!, Google, WebCrawler, Dogpile, Ask Jeeves, and MetaCrawler to obtain thumbnails of all indexed images that relate to your keywords.
- Narrow your search to audio or video results at AltaVista, WebCrawler, MetaCrawler, and Dogpile.
- To find a local law firm or delivery service, for example, both Ask Jeeves and Google allow you to search firms by city or ZIP code.
- To help you locate information about and a map of a particular business, simply type in the phone number with area code into Google.

- To find sites in a particular language, file format (Word, PDF, PowerPoint), or date, use advanced search options available on most search engines.
- To obtain frequently sought-after information on weather, flight times, and time zones, just type in such keywords as "Chicago weather" or "time Tokyo" into Ask Jeeves or Yahoo!.
- To receive a selection of Web definitions taken from a variety of respected sources, type in "define:" and then your keyword into Google.
- Choose country-specific search engines, such as those available at Yahoo! or Google, to access information about companies, laws, news, and international relations essential for communicating with international readers.
- Go to FindArticles.com and plug in your question or keywords to find out quickly how other businesses have handled a problem your firm is researching. You will find research studies, articles, and interviews, always valuable for business solutions.
- To locate information on well-known people, Ask Jeeves provides an instant biography with a photo, along with links to encyclopedia articles and official websites.
- Enter advanced delimiters to specify the exact type of domain you want to search. Searching Google for *"internet security" site:gov* will retrieve all *.gov* (government) sites with information on Internet security. Similarly, searching for *"international training" site:edu* will pull up all *.edu* (education) sites with information on international training.

Tech Note

Blogs and Message Boards

A blog, or Web log, is an easy-to-use, electronic, self-published diary of ideas, information, and news. There are now more than 7 million blogs on the Internet. Blogs and message boards are key aspects of interactive information exchange in the business world for disseminating and retrieving information quickly. They provide an inside track to corporate news. Sun Microsystems, Microsoft, Yahoo!, and IBM, for example, offer employees free blogs on their company websites. A large number of CEOs and public relations departments also keep blogs to promote, interpret, and research a corporate image, as shown in Figure 8.12.

Blogs offer the following advantages for business research:

- They provide a fast, informal way to disseminate information on everything from product announcements to organization news, project updates, research results, marketing developments, and industry headlines.

Continued

Continued

■ Because blogs are interactive, readers can write comments and ask questions on the blog posts, allowing for a two-way information exchange—the customer provides feedback and the employee answers vital consumer questions.

■ Blogs allow companies to express their own points of view and respond quickly to media coverage, adding further clarifying information and interpreting news stories for shareholders, customers, and employees.

■ Blogs provide quicker, less intrusive, and more informal sources of information than do newsletters, and they give a face to a corporate image.

■ Blogs help researchers find out information about competing companies—their recruiting needs, markets, developments, and products or services.

Message boards, also called discussion forums, offer another resource to obtain business information:

■ Researchers can access **financial message boards** for every public corporation by name or market symbol, giving investors the chance to assess stock prices, company performance, and future markets. Hosting services such as Yahoo! provide locations for these forums, such as the Hewlett Packard Co. at *http://finance.yahoo.com/q/mb?s=HPQ.*

■ **Community message boards**, such as the Dell Community Forum (*http://forums.us.dell.com/supportforums/*) or the Microsoft Technical Newsgroups forum (*http://www.microsoft.com/communities/newsgroups/*), expedite customer-to-customer and customer-to-expert interaction on technical issues.

■ **Intranet message boards** act as in-house research tools, allowing employees to share vital information across a company network. Intranet message boards enable all company employees to view the same messages, ask and answer questions, and share new developments.

Anna Gibson
Lori Brister

Evaluating Websites

Not everything you find on the Internet will be correct, up-to-date, and useful. Just because something is posted on the Web does not make it accurate—after all, anyone can post practically anything on the Web. Remember, unlike most traditional forms of publishing, much of the information on the Internet is placed there without a review process where facts are checked, sources are qualified, and ideas and opinions are backed up by solid evidence. In short, the quality of information you find on the Internet can range from the very poor, unsupported, or biased to the impartial, authoritative work of experts in the field.

Keep in mind, too, that you cannot use every hit from a search engine, no matter how carefully you restrict your search. One hit may be an individual's webpage,

Figure 8.12   An example of a business blog.

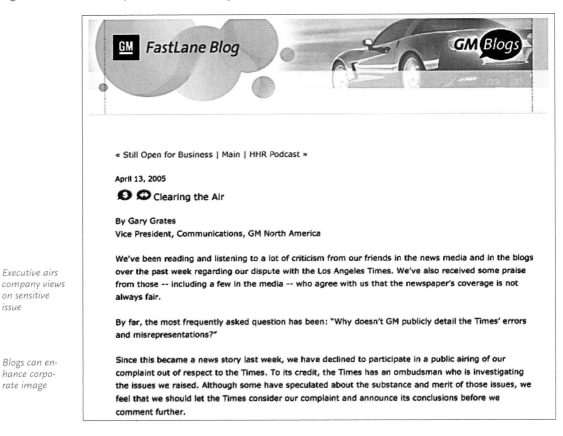

Executive airs company views on sensitive issue

Blogs can enhance corporate image

consisting of his or her thoughts on a subject, and not necessarily authoritative or accurate. Another hit may be a commercial website that may be biased toward a particular company's products or interests. Still another may be slanted by a political agenda. You will have to read, assess, and differentiate carefully the Web material you want to include in your research report or papers. Recall that research requires making critical inquiries (see pp. 297–298). You will have to seek out and test different viewpoints.

Here are some questions to ask as you determine whether websites are credible, accurate, up-to-date, and objective.

Credible

- Is the site maintained or endorsed by a reputable author, professional society, organization, company, or government agency, e.g., the American Society of Women in Sales and Marketing or the Society of Hispanic Professional Engineers?
- What are the author's credentials, degrees, experiences, years on the job, and membership(s) in professional organizations?

- Does the author show that he or she is aware of and refers to the most respected and recent research being done in the field?
- Is the author cited in other studies, including reference works and other highly respected websites?
- Is it possible to contact the author or organization with questions or requests for further help?

Accurate

- How have the data been gathered, recorded, and interpreted? Are they complete, valid, logical, and consistent with the procedures and protocols of your major or job requirements?
- Did you verify facts, dates, and statistical information by comparing them with other independent webpages as well as more traditional research sources such as almanacs or encyclopedias? (See pp. 320–323.) Do not rely on only one website for facts and figures to make a major point in your report.
- Are all visuals relevant and consistent with the information presented, and clear?

Up-to-Date

- When was the site last updated?
- How often has the content been revised? Does it refer to current events, studies, and experiments, or do all the references go back too many years?
- Is the information on the site contradicted, supplemented, or labeled out-of-date on other, more recent websites and reference works?

Ethical/Objective/Unbiased

- Does the site clearly state its purpose? Does it claim to give information, or is it really just trying to sell you something? Read "About Us" links very carefully.
- Is the site legitimate? Check with the National Consumers League (*http://www.nclnet.org*) to verify that it is safe to buy or sell online from the site.
- Does the site use a professional, objective tone or is there unwarranted humor or sarcasm?
- Is the site free from sexist, biased, or other demeaning, stereotypical language and visuals?
- Is the site honest? Does it acknowledge freely and clearly its own limitations, restrictions, and agenda?
- How connected is the site to other sites on the same topic? Could this source be considered part of a reputable online discussion community or is it a platform for one individual's idiosyncratic viewpoints?

Note Taking

Once you have consulted appropriate print and online sources, you need some systematic way to record relevant information from them to use in preparing your outline and draft(s) of your report or paper. But before you can outline or draft, you have to organize and classify the information from your research efficiently.

And even after you start to draft your work, you will probably need to continue your research and take additional notes.

The Importance of Note Taking

Note taking is the crucial link between finding sources, reading them, and writing your paper, report, or proposal, which needs to include information from these sources in just the right place in your work. Never trust your memory to keep all your research facts straight. Taking notes is time well spent.

Take your time. Do not be too quick in getting it done or too eager to begin writing your paper. Careless note taking could lead to serious omissions, inconsistencies, or even contradictions between what different parts of your paper or report say.

Notice how the student paper on telecommuters in Chapter 9 (pp. 383–405) and the business report in Chapter 16 on international employees in the work force incorporate many important facts, interpretations, and even visuals from the sources that the writers consulted. But before these research details could be included in the paper or report, the writers had to take careful notes.

How to Take Effective Notes

Follow these guidelines to make note taking easier and more efficient:

1. Photocopy any print articles, sections of books, reports, and other sources that you consult and mark relevant quotations, statistics, and other information you may incorporate into your work. Use different colors to highlight or underline different types of information or to indicate where such information may go in your work (e.g., background material, methods, visuals, etc.).
2. Record all quotations verbatim, as shown in Figure 8.13.

Figure 8.13   Electronic note containing a direct quotation.

Iona Crandell, "Importance of Internet Medicine," <u>Journal of Emergency Medicine</u> 15 (Sept. 2007): 32.

"The Internet is a primary source of medical information for consumers. CybMed, an Internet marketing firm, estimates that more than 80 million people in 2006 consulted the Web for a variety of health-related information. Most users searched popular sites such as Medscape to look up the signs and symptoms of their medical problems. Consumers also flocked to PharmInfo.net, an FDA website, to find information on new drugs and their possible side effects. These websites are the closest thing to a doctor who makes house calls."

Tech Note

Using Bookmarks

Just as you slip a sheet of paper into a book or turn down the corner of a page of a magazine to mark your place, you can use a Web browser's bookmark feature to keep track of your favorite sites on the Internet and to return quickly to them later. In Netscape Navigator you choose the command Add Bookmark; in America Online's browser you click on a heart-shaped icon in the corner of the webpage. When you want to return to that site later, activate the bookmark, and your Web browser will go online automatically and take you directly to that page.

3. Bookmark any sites on the Internet that you know will be important for your work and that you may be likely to return to.
4. Cut and paste information from online sources directly into your word processing program for reference, being careful to include exact source information.

What to Record

To take effective notes you have to know how to summarize a great deal of information accurately. Study the guidelines on writing summaries in Chapter 10 (pp. 412–414). Here are the types of information you need to record in your notes.

1. Include full bibliographic information for each source—author, title of book, article, report, or Internet site. For *books,* list city of publication, publisher, date of publication, and edition (if not the first). For *journal articles,* include volume number, date. For both books *and* journals, supply page numbers. Keep a record of Internet addresses and the dates you accessed them as well.
2. Copy names, facts, dates, and statistics accurately from the source. Be sure, too, that you record the author's words correctly and from which specific work they come. You may want to quote them verbatim in your paper or report. Always compare what you have written with the original or the copy you may have obtained from an online or Internet search.
3. Distinguish quotations from paraphrases (see pp. 340–342) by placing quotation marks around any word, sentences, or extended quotations you record directly to avoid the risk of plagiarizing (see pp. 352–354).
4. Indicate in your notes why the material you quoted or paraphrased might be significant to your argument or, again, where you might include such information in your report.
5. If you are using two or more works by the same author, make sure you accurately identify from which work a quotation or other material comes.

Electronic Note Taking

Electronic note-taking software offers a fast and convenient way to organize your notes, saving you from worrying about losing note cards or scraps of paper (see Figure 8.14). The following programs will help you keep track of your notes:

- Microsoft OneNote 2003 (*http://www.microsoft.com/office/onenote/*) combines digital organizational tools with the benefits of conventional note taking.
- GoBinder (*http://www.gobinder.com*) helps researchers to organize class and work-related notes.
- EverNote (*http://www.evernote.com*) enables you to store and access all types of notes, from handwritten memos to e-mail, brainstorms, sketches, or documents.

Basically, electronic note-taking software offers a variety of practical tools to help you organize your notes. With these software programs you can

- copy and paste information or images from Web sources. Many note-taking programs will automatically include the URL, helping you to keep track of your sources so that you can easily document them.
- incorporate your own notes as you read Web sources, articles, books, and other materials.
- annotate your notes in different colors and write wherever you want to on the page.
- organize your notes in categories or folders that allow you to retrieve information quickly when you are writing your report or paper.
- quickly search your notes for keywords to locate relevant information.
- type your notes using your computer keyboard or input handwritten notes using a tablet PC or a pen input device connected to your computer.
- save your notes to a disk to make sure you don't lose them.
- print or e-mail your notes or even upload them to a website.
- record audio notes to accompany your written notes (most, not all, programs have this capability).
- instantly incorporate Web content by adding end notes to your Internet browser toolbar, allowing you to select Add to End Notes when you find a particularly useful Web source.

To Quote or Not to Quote

Before recording information from sources, ask yourself three questions:

1. How much should I take down?
2. How often should I copy the author's words verbatim?
3. When should I paraphrase or summarize?

Quote Sparingly

A safe rule to follow is this: Do not be a human scanner. If you write down too many of the author's own words, you will simply be transferring the author's words from the book, article, or website to your paper. That will show that you have read

Electronic note containing a paraphrase.   **Figure 8.14**

> Acid rain
> damage to forests
> (body of report)
>
> Dampier, www.rainenviron.com
>
> Acid rain is as dangerous to the forests as to the lakes. Victims of "premature senescence," the trees become defoliated and die with no new trees taking their place. Without the trees' protection, wildlife vanishes. Although the exact damage is hard to measure, Swedish scientists have observed that in their country forest products decreased by one percent yearly.

the work but not whether you have summarized and evaluated its findings. Do not use direct quotations simply as filler.

Use direct quotations sparingly—save them for when they count most:

- an author has summarized a great deal of significant information concisely into a few well-chosen sentences
- a writer has clarified a difficult concept exceedingly well
- an author's chief statement or thesis

For example, the electronic note in Figure 8.13 contains an important statement by an author. Be careful not to quote verbatim all the evidence leading to that conclusion. The conclusion may be pointedly expressed in two or three sentences; the evidence could cover many pages.

If you are uncertain about exactly how much to quote verbatim, keep in mind that no more than 10 to 15 percent of your paper should be made up of direct quotations. Remember that when you quote someone directly, you are telling your readers that these words are the most important part of the author's work as far as you are concerned. Be a selective filter, not a large funnel.

Using Ellipses

Sometimes a sentence or passage is particularly useful, but you may not want to quote it fully. You may want to delete some words that are not really necessary for your purpose. These omissions are indicated by using an *ellipsis* (three spaced dots within the sentence to indicate where words have been omitted). Here are some examples.

Full Quotation: "Diet and nutrition, which researchers have studied extensively, significantly affect oral health."
Quotation with Ellipsis: "Diet and nutrition . . . significantly affect oral health."

When the omission occurs at the end of the sentence, you must include the end-of-sentence punctuation after the ellipsis. In the following example, note how the shortened sentence ends with four spaced dots: the three dots for the ellipsis and the closing period.

Full Quotation:	"Decisions on how to operate the company should be based on the most accurate and relevant information available from both within the company and from the specific community that the establishment serves."
Quotation with Ellipsis:	"Decisions on how to operate the company should be based on the most accurate and relevant information available. . . ."

At times you may have to insert your own information within a quotation. This addition, known as an **interpolation**, is made by enclosing your clarifying identification or remark in brackets inside the quotation; for example, "It [the new transportation network] has been thoroughly tested and approved." Anything in brackets is not part of the original quotation.

Paraphrasing

Most of your note taking will be devoted to paraphrasing rather than writing down direct quotations. A **paraphrase** is a restatement in your own words of the author's ideas. Even though you are using your own words to translate or restate, you still must document the paraphrase because you are using the author's facts and interpretations. You do not use quotation marks, though. When you include a paraphrase in your paper, you should be careful to do four things:

1. Be faithful to the author's meaning. Do not alter facts or introduce new ideas.
2. Follow the order in which the author presents the information.
3. Include in your paraphrase only what is relevant for your paper. Delete any details not essential for your work.
4. Use paraphrases in your report selectively. You do not want your work to be merely a restatement of someone else's.

Paraphrased material can be introduced in your paper with an appropriate identifying phrase, such as "According to Dampier's study," "To paraphrase Dampier," or "As Dampier observes." The electronic note shown in Figure 8.14 paraphrases the following quotation:

> While the effects of acid rain are felt first in lakes, which act as natural collection points, some scientists fear there may be extensive damage to forests as well. In the process described by one researcher as "premature senescence," trees exposed to acid sprays lose their leaves, wilt, and finally die. New trees may not grow to replace them. Deprived of natural cover, wildlife may flee or die. The extent of the damage to forest lands is extremely difficult to determine, but scientists find the trend worrisome. In Sweden, for example, one estimate calculates that the yield in forest products decreased by about one percent each year. . . .[1]

---

[1]Bill Dampier, "Now Even the Rain Is Dangerous," *International Wildlife* 10 (March–April 1980): 18–19.

◼ Conclusion

This chapter has introduced you to some very basic yet essential strategies and tools to do research for school or on the job. Clearly, you need to rely on a host of resources—print and online reference works, databases, various search engines, websites, and message boards. Relying on these research tools and strategies, you will have the most up-to-date, most thorough, and most relevant answers to the questions you are asked to investigate and the problems you need to solve on the job or for a school assignment. Exploring (and preparing) all of today's potential resources will prepare you to write the types of documents—websites, instructions, short and long reports, proposals—discussed in later chapters.

Online Study Center

Access the doing research Revision Checklist online at college.hmco.com/ pic/kolin8e

✔ Revision Checklist

Process of Research

☐ Identified a significant, timely, and restricted topic.

☐ Formulated a mission statement to develop a clear sense of the purpose of my research.

☐ Consulted a wide variety of research materials.

☐ Conducted database, online catalog, and Internet searches.

☐ Used both primary and secondary research methods as needed.

☐ Evaluated the relevance and validity of my sources.

☐ Met with reference librarians or experts in my field.

☐ Documented sources accurately and completely.

☐ Adhered to a schedule to meet all deadlines.

Primary Research

☐ Conducted, or observed directly, an experiment or visited a site to describe events, places needed for research.

☐ Set up an appointment with an expert on my topic. Prepared a list of appropriate questions beforehand.

☐ Interviewed an expert using prepared questions, and stayed focused on the subject. Asked important follow-up questions.

☐ Created and distributed questionnaire surveys with only valid, accurate questions to ask and then interpreted my respondents' opinions.

☐ Identified a target audience for my questionnaires.

Secondary Research

☐ Searched online catalog(s) for necessary research materials.

☐ Used databases to find relevant articles and other research materials.

Continued

Continued

☐ Obtained full-text of appropriate articles and other materials in hard or electronic copy.

☐ Checked relevant reference materials, such as almanacs, abstracts, encyclopedias.

☐ Located relevant government sources using FirstGov, the Library of Congress, or the U.S. Government Printing Office.

☐ Read and scrutinized periodicals, books, government documents, and websites.

Internet Searches

☐ Searched for pertinent information using at least two search engines.

☐ Used multiple specific, concrete keywords to conduct an Internet search.

☐ Used search strategies such as Boolean connectors or delimiters to narrow and focus my keyword search.

☐ Conducted a directory search or used online-library sources.

☐ Downloaded electronic sources available via my library's online catalog or databases.

☐ Located webpage(s) relating to my topic.

☐ Continued to refine my search using synonyms, alternative keywords, or more specific terms to access only the most useful material for my project.

☐ Joined a newsgroup or surveyed blogs to extend my research.

Taking Notes

☐ Took careful notes and identified precisely the source from which my information came.

☐ Recorded all quotations accurately.

☐ Paraphrased fairly, ethically representing original material.

☐ Distinguished my comments and responses clearly from those of my sources.

☐ Incorporated information from notes into appropriate places in my document.

☐ Used correct punctuation with direct quotations, especially ellipses and brackets for interpolations.

Exercises

Online Study Center
Find additional doing research exercises at college.hmco.com/ pic/kolin8e

1. Choose, define, and restrict a topic based on a problem or issue you might deal with in one of the following divisions of a company:
   a. technology
   b. human resources
   c. security
   d. marketing
   e. accounting
   f. health care
   g. energy/utilities
   h. transportation

Discuss the steps you took to narrow the topic, the audience you are writing for, and the types of questions that audience may have.

2. Based on the problem you identified in Exercise 1, select an expert relevant to that field to interview for primary research. Prepare a list of ten questions for the interview, remembering to stay focused on your topic.

3. Plan a direct observation experiment, selecting either to visit a site or record data in a laboratory, to further investigate the topic you selected in Exercise 1. Construct an outline for this experiment, considering the types of information you expect to record and how it will enhance your research.

4. Construct a questionnaire to gather more information about the topic you selected in Exercise 1 or one of the following:
    a. Internet security
    b. online purchasing
    c. business etiquette
    d. safety in the workplace
    e. global business trends
   Come up with a list of ten questions and vary the format to include multiple-choice, dichotomous (yes or no), ranking, and open-ended questions. Think about how you will select your participants, the type of information you want to gather, and how it will enhance your research.

5. Working in a group, assume you are employed by a company that is marketing a new product or service. Your group is conducting market research into possible competitors. Choose three or four different brands of a product or service that is comparable to yours. Prepare a short report in which your group observes, tests, and analyzes these competing products or services and make recommendations about how the product or service offered by your company can excel in the marketplace.

6. Prepare a list (providing full bibliographic information) of fifteen articles for the restricted topic you selected in Exercise 1. Use at least one of the online databases discussed in this chapter (pp. 314–330).

7. By reviewing the source or title lists in several databases that provide newspaper articles, find a database that accesses your hometown newspaper or a newspaper from a nearby large city. Next, locate a newspaper from a nearby state and one from another country. Print out an article from each newspaper, and in each case identify which database you used. Explain which database you found best for covering local papers, for national news, and for international news.

8. Identify three online databases that would help you in your research at school or on the job. List five periodicals that are indexed on each of the databases. Do not include the same periodical more than once, even though it may appear in more than one database. Be sure to consult a librarian if you need help; he or she may be able to direct you to lists of periodicals indexed on each database.

9. Briefly research the topic "videoconferencing" using the Internet, databases, and your library's online catalog. Compare and contrast the types of information

given by the different sources, for example, definitions, any commercial aspects, or available resources. Describe which sources were the most informative, the most helpful, the most current, and so on, and which sources would be best for particular audiences, such as the general public, businesses, or technical experts. Consider how all three sources could be used together to gather information for a project or report.

10. Using the search strategies explained in this chapter, use the Internet to research recent developments in online credit card fraud. Narrow your topic to a specific aspect of credit card fraud, such as prevention, detection, prosecution, and so on. Find the following:
    a. two recent and reliable Web sources using one of the search engines mentioned on pages 328–330
    b. two government sources (e.g., articles, reports, statistics, handbooks) using FirstGov
    c. two online articles using one of the e-libraries listed on page 327
    d. two online newspaper articles using a news search engine such as Yahoo! News or Google News
    e. one corporate website source using a directory such as those listed on page 328

11. Using the search tools discussed in this chapter, including those on the Internet, locate the following items related to your major. Select titles that are most closely related to your major and explain how they would be useful to you. Prepare a separate bibliographic citation for each title.
    a. an index to periodicals
    b. titles of three important journals that are available in print and online
    c. an abstract of an article appearing in one of the journals
    d. a term in a specialized dictionary
    e. a description or illustration in a specialized encyclopedia
    f. an article in an international newspaper available online
    g. a film or tape recording since 2000
    h. three U.S. government documents
    i. a story in the *New York Times* or one of the newspapers covered by News-Bank that, in the last year, discussed a topic of interest to students in your major
    j. an article in an online magazine or journal

12. Assume you have to write a brochure about one of the following topics, introducing it to an audience of consumers. Using the resources of the Internet and those of a few of the databases discussed in this chapter, prepare a working bibliography of relevant materials that contains at least ten sources. After gathering and reading those sources, prepare the text and a visual for the brochure and submit them with your bibliography to your instructor. This assignment may be done as a collaborative writing exercise.
    a. virtual reality
    b. fiber optics

   c. Internet auctions (e.g., eBay)
   d. interactive television
   e. robotics in medicine
   f. the greenhouse effect
   g. computer dating
   h. laser surgery
   i. globalization
   j. diversity in the workplace
   k. DNA testing
   l. ethics of business blogging
   m. airport security
   n. tablet PCs
   o. any topic your instructor approves

13. Using appropriate references discussed in this chapter, answer any five of the following questions. After your answer, list the specific works you consulted. Supply complete bibliographic information. For books, indicate author or editor, title, edition, place of publication and publisher, date, and volume and page numbers. For journals and magazines, include volume and page numbers; for newspapers, precise date and page numbers. For Internet sites, provide complete URL (e.g., http://www.).
   a. What is nanotechnology?
   b. How many calories are there in an orange?
   c. List three interviews that Condoleezza Rice granted between 2004 and 2005.
   d. What is the boiling point of coal tar?
   e. What was the headline in the *New York Times* the day you were born?
   f. List three publications on outdoor recreation issued by the U.S. Department of the Interior from 2004 to the present.
   g. What was the population of Spokane, Washington, in 2000?
   h. List three articles on the advantages of electronic signatures published between 2005 and 2006.
   i. Who discovered the neutrino?
   j. What is the first recorded (printed) use of the word *ozone*?
   k. Who edited the second edition of the *Encyclopedia of Psychology*, published in 1994?
   l. Give the title, date, page number, and author (if listed) of a story in your local newspaper that focused on child abuse in the past year.
   m. List the title of three articles on the abuse of credit cards that have appeared in professional journals within the past two or three years.
   n. What is a blade server?
   o. Name five plants that have the word *fly* as part of their common name.
   p. What are the names and addresses of all the four-year colleges in the state of South Dakota?
   q. Who is Nigeria's current head of state?
   r. What is the current membership of the American Dental Association?
   s. What are the names of the justices who currently serve on the U.S. Supreme Court?

14. Research the following items in your occupation/major and provide your instructor with complete addresses and citations. Also give your instructor the names and addresses and a brief description of three professional associations/societies in your field/major.
    a. the title and editor of three major journals/magazines/newspapers
    b. the names and locations of two major conferences
    c. four of the most significant terms/concepts along with an article on each one written in the past two years
    d. the five most useful websites for students in your major and the reason for your choices
    e. three major books on key topics in your area
    f. five to seven reviews of one of the books in (e)
    g. three blogs and three message boards or listservs related to your major

15. Write a paraphrase of two of the following paragraphs.
    a. Deep-fat frying is a mainstay of any successful fast-food operation and is one of the most commonly used procedures for the preparation and production of foods in the world. During the deep-frying process, oxidation and hydrolysis take place in the shortening and eventually change its functional, sensory, and nutritional quality. Current fat tests available to food operation managers for determining when used shortening should be discarded typically require identification of a change in some physical attribute of the shortening, such as color, smoke, foam development, etc. However, by the time these changes become evident, a considerable amount of degradation has usually taken place.[1]
    b. E-mail marketing is one of the most effective ways to keep in touch with customers. It is generally cost-effective, and if done properly, can help build brand awareness and loyalty. At a typical cost of only a few cents per message, it's a bargain compared to traditional direct mail at $1 or more per piece. In addition, response rates on e-mail marketing are strong, ranging from 5 to 35% depending on the industry and format. Response rates for traditional mail averages in the 1–3% range.

    One of the benefits of e-mail marketing is the demographic information that customers provide when signing up for your e-mail newsletter. Discovering who your customers really are—based on age, gender, income, and special interests, for example—can help you target your products and services to their needs. Points to consider when creating your e-mail newsletter:

    ▪ HTML vs. plain text: Response rates for HTML newsletters are generally far higher than plain text, and graphics and colors tend to make the publications look far more professional. The downside is that HTML e-mail is slower to download, and some e-mail providers may screen out HTML e-mail.

---

[1]Vincent J. Graziano, "Portable Instrument Rapidly Measures Quality of Frying Fat in Food Service Operations," *Food Technology* 33, page 50. Copyright © by Institute of Food Technologists. Reprinted by permission.

- Provide incentive to subscribe: Advertise the benefits of receiving your newsletter to get customers to sign up for your newsletter, such as helpful tips, informative content, or early notification of special offers or campaigns.
- Don't just sell: Many studies suggest that e-mail newsletters are read far more carefully when they offer information that is useful to the customers' lives rather than merely selling products and services. Helpful tips, engaging content, and humor are often expected to accompany e-mail newsletters.
- Limit questions: As each demographic question you ask may reduce the number of customers signing up, it's best to limit the amount of information you solicit or give customers the option of skipping the questionnaire.

Establishing a Web Presence   Even if you choose not to sell your goods or services online, a business website is a virtual marketing brochure that you can update on demand with little or no cost. Your presence on the Internet can be a useful marketing tool by providing richer pre-sale information or post-sale support and service. This might temporarily differentiate your product or service from your competitors. E-marketing has lessened the disadvantage that small businesses have faced for years when competing with larger businesses.

E-commerce has redefined the marketplace, altered business strategies, and allowed global competition between local businesses. The term *electronic commerce* has evolved from meaning simply electronic shopping to representing all aspects of business and market processes enabled by the Internet and other digital technologies. SBA is preparing to help this new generation of Internet-enabled or eSmall Businesses.

Today's business emphasis is on e-commerce—rapid electronic interactions enabled by the Internet and other connected computer and telephone networks. Rapidly business transactions and unparallelled access to information are changing consumer behavior and expectations. The U.S. Small Business Administration (SBA) is reshaping its programs to better serve small businesses that are taking advantage of the Internet and other emerging technologies.

Many small businesses assume that the Internet has little value to them because they feel that their product or service cannot be easily sold online. But inexpensive information processing and electronic media can help most small businesses provide better, faster customer service and communication.[2]

c. Phishing is a form of identity theft in which victims are tricked into turning over their personal information to criminals through bogus e-mail and websites. Phishing schemes, which rely on spam e-mail, emerged in 2004 as a method of capturing personal information to use in identity theft. In phishing schemes, consumers receive e-mail that purports to convey some urgent message about their financial accounts. Recipients are encouraged to respond promptly by clicking a link in the message to what are imitations of

---

[2]Small Business Administration, Starting Your Own Business. *E-Marketing.* 2005. http://www.sba.gov/starting_business/marketing/emarketing.html.

legitimate, trusted websites. As a result, the online consumer, believing he or she is connected to a legitimate enterprise, divulges personal financial information, which is diverted to the location of the criminal perpetrator. Essentially, phishers have hijacked the trusted brands of well-known banks, credit card issuers, and online retailers, to obtain valuable personal financial information that can be misused or sold to others for the same purpose. Although later phishing attacks have been more generic, they are based on a similar pretext.

Spam e-mail easily reaches thousands if not millions of unsuspecting consumers at a time. With perhaps 5 percent of recipients estimated to divulge personal financial information, the spam scams are lucrative. In November 2004, the Anti-Phishing Working Group (APWG) reported over 1,500 new phishing attacks that month and a 28 percent average monthly growth rate in phishing sites from July through November. The APWG also identified a new form of fraud-based websites that pose as generic e-commerce sites, rather than brand-name sites, and perpetrate loan scams, mortgage frauds, online pharmacy frauds, and other banking frauds. While the United States hosts the largest number of phishing sites, South Korea, China, Russia, the United Kingdom, Mexico, and Taiwan have also been identified as hosts. Federal law enforcement and others work with foreign counterparts to take down offending sites.

Thus, phishing attacks and "spoofed" e-mail afford criminals an easy and cheap means of obtaining sensitive personal information from consumers which can be very lucrative even if the false website is shut down within 48 to 72 hours. Other electronic crimes also pose a danger. For example, the use of spyware, to log a user's keystrokes, is a silent way to obtain account numbers from a customer accessing his banking or brokerage accounts online. Spyware is a rapidly growing threat to consumer confidence in electronic finance and commerce.[3]

---

[3]Anti-Phishing Working Group (APWG), Phishing Attack Trends Report (July 2004). See *http://www.antiphishing.org*. APWG is an industry association focused on eliminating the identity theft and fraud resulting from phishing. It reports regularly on the form and volume of phishing scams.

CHAPTER 9

Documenting Sources

Documentation is at the heart of all the research you will do at school or on the job. To document means to furnish readers with information about the print and electronic sources you have used for the factual support of your statements, including books, journals, newspapers, manuals, reports, and websites, and other resources such as listservs and e-mail. Without proper documentation, you will not be able to persuade a customer to buy your product or service and you will not convince your boss that you are doing your best work.

This chapter gives you practical and precise directions on what to document and how to do it efficiently and consistently. Of the various systems (or formats) of documentation, parenthetical documentation is preferred over documentation through footnotes or endnotes. For that reason, this chapter will emphasize the parenthetical documentation methods advocated by the following two large professional organizations—the Modern Language Association (MLA) and the American Psychological Association (APA). The MLA style is found primarily in the humanities and other related disciplines while the APA style is used in psychology, nursing and allied health, the social sciences, and some technological fields.

> *MLA Handbook for Writers of Research Papers,* edited by Joseph Gibaldi (6th ed., New York: Modern Language Association, 2003), http://www.mla.org
>
> *Publication Manual of the American Psychological Association* (5th ed., Washington, DC: American Psychological Association, 2001), http://www.apastyle.org

The sample research paper about telecommuting at the end of this chapter uses the MLA style of documentation; the long report on international speakers of English in the work force in Chapter 16 (pp. 680–697) follows APA style. This chapter concludes with a review of other types of documentation styles, including *The Chicago Manual of Style,* which you may be asked to use.

Online Study Center

To expand your understanding of documenting sources, take advantage of the ACE quizzes, sample documents, Web links, and exercises at college.hmco.com/pic/kolin8e

The Whys and Hows of Documentation

Before looking at the specific techniques you need to use when you document, it's necessary to understand why documentation is so important and the major role it plays in your writing strategies at school and at work.

Why Is Documentation Important?

Documentation is important for at least three reasons.

1. It demonstrates that you have done your homework by consulting experts on the subject and relying on the most current and authoritative sources to build your case persuasively.
2. It gives proper credit to those sources. Citing works by name is not a simple act of courtesy; it is an ethical requirement and, because so much of the material is protected by copyright, a point of law.
3. It informs readers about specific books, articles, or websites you used so they can find your source and verify your facts or quotations.

The Ethics of Documentation: What Must Be Cited

By documenting your sources, you will avoid being accused of **plagiarism**—stealing someone else's ideas and presenting them as your own (see p. 32 in Chapter 1). Such misrepresentation is unethical and illegal. There are a variety of ways to commit plagiarism. To ensure that your paper or report avoids any type of plagiarism and maintains high ethical standards, follow these guidelines.

- If you use a source and take something from it, document it. Document any direct quotation(s), even a single phrase or keyword.
- Stay away from **patchworking**—using bits and pieces of information and passing them off as your own—which is also an act of plagiarism. Always put quotations marks around anything you take verbatim and document it.

  If any opinions, interpretations, and conclusions expressed verbally or in writing are not your own (e.g., you could not have reached them without the help of another source), document them.
- Even if you do not use an author's exact words but still get an idea, concept, or point of view from that author, document the work in your paper.
- Never alter any original material to have it suit your argument. Twisting someone else's ideas to make them agree (or disagree) with yours is unethical. Changing any information—names, dates, times, test results—is a serious offense.
- Do not misquote or misattribute. Adding a few words—qualifiers, conditions—to a source violates the author's work.

  If you use statistical data you have not compiled yourself, document them.
- Do not use just one source or repeatedly cite the same source. You will not have sufficiently researched and documented your work for the reader.

A cartoon reminding readers that there is no excuse for plagiarism.   **Figure 9.1**

"Really? Someone told me it's
not plagiarism if they're dead."

Always document any visuals—photographs, graphs, tables, charts, images downloaded from the Web (and if you construct a visual based on someone else's data, you must acknowledge that source).

- Never submit the same research paper you wrote for one course for another course without first obtaining permission from the second instructor.
- Be faithful to the rules established by your collaborative writing team. Never submit as your own work that which was done through collaboration.
- Do not delete an author's name when you are citing or forwarding a Web document. You are obligated to give the Web author full credit.
- Document any software programs you did not develop yourself.

The cartoon in Figure 9.1 humorously reminds readers about a very serious matter—there are *no* excuses for plagiarism.

What Does Not Need to Be Cited

Quotations from the Bible, Shakespeare, or any literary text should be identified according to the specific work (*Exodus, Merchant of Venice*) and the exact place in that work (for example, act 3, scene 4, line 23, which would be listed as 3.4.23).

Of course, do not document obvious facts, such as normal body temperature, well-known dates (the first moon landing in 1969), historical information (Ronald Reagan was the fortieth president of the United States), formulas (H_2O; the quadratic formula), the distance to Jupiter, proverbs from folklore ("The hand is quicker than the eye"), or well-known quotations ("We hold these truths to be self-evident . . .").

Documentation in the Writing Process

Documentation is vital to writing a research paper or report. It begins as soon as you start researching your topic and continues as you organize, draft, revise, and even edit your work. You need to keep a careful record of the sources you use and the exact material you take from them (see pp. 356 and 368–370).

Throughout your various drafts be sure to document precisely what you are using and then add every source you refer to in the text of your paper to the Works Cited or Reference list. During revision (and editing) be careful to check and double-check the accuracy of your documentation. That means making sure names, Web addresses and posting and access dates, page numbers, dates, and quotations are correct and that bibliographic information mentioned in the text of your paper matches that on your Works Cited or Reference pages precisely.

Parenthetical Documentation

Numerous formats exist for documenting sources. Two of these formats are *parenthetical documentation* and *footnote documentation*. Most of this chapter will focus on the widely used parenthetical documentation style found in the MLA and APA guides. Basically, both MLA and APA

- do *not* recommend footnotes or endnotes to document sources
- do *not* contain a bibliography of works the writer may have consulted but has not actually cited directly in the paper or report

Instead, the MLA and the APA use **parenthetical**, or **in-text, documentation**. That is, the writer tells readers directly in the text of the paper, at the moment the acknowledgment is necessary, what reference is being cited. MLA style, for example, includes the author's last name in parentheses together with the appropriate page number(s) from which the information is borrowed.

> Creating an effective website was among the top three priorities businesses have had over the last two years (Morgan 205).

The citation (Morgan 205) lets the reader know that the writer has borrowed information from a work by Morgan, specifically from page 205 of that work. Such a source (author's last name and page number) obviously does not provide sufficient

Saving Bibliographic Citations on Your Computer

It is relatively easy to transfer bibliographic information—Works Cited pages and other bibliographic citations—from the Internet or a CD-ROM into your word processing program. If you are using a Web browser, go to the file menu and click on Save as. You will see a box in which you can give the information a file name and save the new file in your word processing program. If you want to incorporate bibliographic information into another document—you may be using many of the same sources—open the document into which you want to incorporate the new material. It is helpful to keep all of your citations in a single document. Many websites provide prewritten citations that you can simply copy and paste into your citations document.

documentation. Instead, the parenthetical reference refers readers to an alphabetical list of works that appears at the end of the paper. The list—called "Works Cited" in MLA or "References" in APA—contains full bibliographic data—titles, dates, websites, publishers, page numbers, and so on—about all the sources cited in the paper.

To provide accurate parenthetical documentation for your readers, you must first carefully prepare a Works Cited list or a Reference list and then include the documentation in the right form and at the right place in your text.

Preparing an MLA Works Cited List

Before you can document your sources parenthetically, you must first establish what those sources are. As noted earlier, just giving an author's name and page number in parentheses *does not* provide readers with adequate publication information. You need to supply that information in a Works Cited list, which will document the information you borrowed from sources to do the research for your paper or report and allow your reader to verify it.

You need to prepare this list *before* you ever start to document. The list tells *you* and your readers what specific sources you have used and where to find them. By keeping this list accurate and complete, you will avoid accidentally omitting a source, and by using this list as a research ruler, you know that you will use only the sources on this list.

This section will show you how to prepare a Works Cited list following the guidelines listed in the *MLA Handbook*. For a model, refer to the Works Cited list within the sample research paper at the end of this chapter (pp. 402–405). According to the MLA, your Works Cited list needs to

1. be at the end of your paper or report, on a separate sheet(s), with the words *Works Cited* at the top.

2. list your sources in alphabetical order according to the author's last name (Fukayama, Jacki, not Jacki Fukayama). Look at the title page for the author's name but do not add an academic (University of Maryland) or business (Microsoft) affiliation. Also, do not include any title, degrees, or certificates.

3. start each entry at the left margin but indent the second and subsequent lines of the entry five spaces (or about one-half inch). See Figure 9.3 (p. 379).

4. include this information in an entry in the following order according to the current MLA style (note that books and journal entries are the most common Works Cited entries; examples of other types of entries appear later in this chapter).

   ▪ **For books:**

   ```
   Author/Editor last name, first name. Book Title. Edition.
         Place of publication: Publishing company, publication
         date.
   ```

   ▪ **For journal articles:**

   ```
   Author last name, first name. "Journal Article Title."
         Periodical Title volume number (Date): page numbers.
   ```

5. separate the main elements in an entry (author, title, publication information) with a period and single space (one space, not two). But use a colon to separate the city of publication from the publisher's name.

6. double-space within and between each entry. Do not insert extra spaces between the entries.

▌Using MLA In-Text Documentation

The MLA Works Cited list does not, of course, tell readers what you actually borrowed from your sources or where that information is located in a source. To give readers that information, you must include documentation in the text of your paper or report.

Citing Sources with MLA: What to Include and Why

As you write and revise your draft(s), make sure that you (1) insert the author's name and appropriate page number(s) for each source that you use; (2) match the information you include parenthetically in the text—names, page numbers, and sometimes short titles—precisely with the information you supply under Works Cited at the end of your paper or report; and (3) begin short titles within parenthetical citations with the first key word used in the title. Remember: If you fail to document in your text, you are guilty of plagiarism. Also, if your documentation is incorrect or incomplete, readers will have trouble finding the source and may doubt the reliability of your work.

How to Document with MLA: Some Guidelines

Parenthetical, or in-text, documentation is relatively simple. Keep your documentation brief and to the point so you do not interrupt the reader's train of thought. In most cases, all you will include is the author's last name and appropriate page number(s) in parentheses, usually at the end of the sentence. For unsigned articles and websites or radio and television programs, use a shortened title in place of an author's name. Note in the following example that no mark of punctuation appears before the citation and that a period follows it. Also, no "page" or "p." or comma appears between the author's name and the page number.

```
About 5 percent of the world's population has diabetes
mellitus, and 25 percent of the world's population acts as
carriers of the disease (Walton 56).
```

Seeing this parenthetical documentation, the reader will expect to find the title and publication information about Walton's study correctly listed under Walton on your Works Cited page.

```
Walton, J. H. Common Diseases of the World. New York:
     Medical Books, 2007.
```

The number after Walton's name in the parenthetical documentation refers to the page number in Walton's book where the information you cite can be found.

You may refer to the same work more than once in your paper or report. For second or subsequent references use the same method of documentation. For the Walton example, you would place Walton's name and the appropriate page number—even if it is the same as in the previous reference(s)—in parentheses following the borrowed information. Of course, if you included Walton's name in the sentence, there would be no need to repeat it in the parentheses; you would need to give only the page number. (The exact placement of the author's name in the sentence is discussed on page 358.)

If you are using a work that has two authors, list both last names parenthetically.

```
Tourism has increased by 14 percent this last quarter,
thanks to individuals passing through our state on their
way to the National Association of Business Leaders
convention (Muscovi and Klein 2-3).
```

If one of the works you use has three or more authors, list just the first author's last name in parentheses followed by et al. (Latin for "and others") and the page number(s). Note that MLA does not use all-inclusive numbers, that is, 345–47, not 345–347 but 307–8, not 307–08.

```
The principles of ergonomics have revolutionized the
design of office furniture (Brodsky et al. 345-47).
```

If the work you are borrowing from has a corporate author, use a shortened version of the name in the parentheses. In the following example, "Commission" replaces "Commission on Wage and Price Control."

```
Salaries for local electricians were at or above the
national average (Commission 145).
```

In the preceding examples, the names of the authors have appeared in parentheses. When you mention the author's name in your text, include only the appropriate page number(s) in parentheses. The following examples show three acceptable ways of citing an author's name in the text.

```
Clausen sees the renovation of downtown areas as one of the
most challenging issues facing city governments today (29).

As Clausen notes, the renovation of downtown areas is one
of the most challenging issues facing city governments
today (29).

The renovation of downtown areas, according to Clausen, is
one of the most challenging issues facing city governments
today (29).
```

Similarly, if you list the title of a reference or an anonymous work in the text of your paper, you need not repeat it for your parenthetical documentation.

```
According to the Encyclopaedia Britannica, Cecil B.
DeMille's King of Kings was seen by nearly 800,000,000
individuals (3:458).
```

The first number in parentheses refers to the volume number of the *Encyclopaedia Britannica*; the second is the page number in that volume. In this case, the writer gives both volume and page numbers to indicate that the information is listed under DeMille and not the title of the film.

If you are citing information from two or more works by the same author, you will have to inform readers clearly from which work a particular fact or opinion comes. In the Works Cited section, these works are alphabetized by title. Let's say you used information from the following works by the same author:

```
Howe, Grace. Networking in the Information Age. New York:
     Business Publications, 2006.

---. "Systems Control for Internet Businesses." The
     E-Workplace 15 (2007): 67–81.
```

You have a number of ways to tell readers from which work by Grace Howe you are borrowing material.

1. Cite the author's name, a short title, and the page number parenthetically.

   ```
   Communication checkpoints are necessary in any business to
   provide a maximum flow of information (Howe, Networking
   132).
   ```

   Use a comma after the author's name but not before the page number.

2. Mention the author's name in your sentence and use a short title and page number in parentheses.

   ```
   Howe thinks communication checkpoints in any business are
   necessary to provide a maximum flow of information
   (Networking 132).
   ```

3. Give the author's name and a shortened title in the text with only the page number included parenthetically.

   ```
   According to Howe's article, "Systems Control," productiv-
   ity increases by at least 20 percent after each training
   session involving communication networking techniques (71).
   ```

Occasionally you will have to cite two sources at the same time to document a point. Include the names of the authors of both sources (alphabetically) just as if you were listing them individually but insert a semicolon between sources.

```
The use of salt domes to store radioactive wastes has
come under severe attack (Jelinek 56-57; McPherson and
Chin 23-26).
```

Be careful, though, that you do not overload readers by including a long string of references in your parenthetical documentation.

```
Wind energy has been successfully used in both rural and
urban settings (Bailey 34; Calderon 78; Henderson 9;
Mankowitz 98-99; Olsen 456-58; Vencenti 23; Walker and
Smith 43).
```

Rather than interrupting the reader and crowding references together, consider revising your sentence to make the subject more precise and the references more restricted.

```
Wind energy has long benefited the agribusiness community
(Calderon 78; Walker and Smith 43). But recent experiments
in New York City have shown the effectiveness of this form
of energy for city dwellers, too (Bailey 34; Henderson 9).
Similar experiments in San Francisco also show how wind
```

```
power helps urban residents (Mankowitz 98-99; Olsen
456—58; Vincenti 23).
```

If you include a quotation, place the parenthetical documentation at the end of the sentence containing the quotation.

```
Pilmer has observed that coffee "is only mildly addictive
in the sense that withdrawal will not harm you or produce
violent symptoms" (16).
```

Note that the period follows the parentheses, not the quotation marks. Even if the quotation is short and appears in the middle of the sentence, place the documentation at the end of the sentence.

```
Alvin Toffler used the phrase "third wave" to characterize
the scientific and computer revolution (34).
```

If the material you quote runs to more than four typed lines, set the quotation apart from the text by indenting it *ten spaces or one inch* on the left side and eliminate the quotation marks. Double-space the quotation. Place the parenthetical documentation after the quotation and outside the period, as in the following example.

```
L. J. Ronsivalli offers this graphic analogy of how radia-
tion can penetrate solid objects:
        One might wonder how an X-ray, a gamma ray, or a
        cosmic ray can penetrate something as solid as a
        brick wall or a piece of wood. We can't see that
        within the atomic structures of the brick wall
        and the wood there are spaces for the radiation
        to enter. If we look at a cloud, we can see its
        shape, but because distance has made them too
        small, we can't see the droplets of moisture out
        of which the cloud is made. Much too small for the
        eyes to see, even with the help of a microscope,
        the atomic structure of solid materials is made of
        very small particles with a lot of space between
        them. In fact, solids are mostly empty spaces.
        (20-21)
```

If you omit anything from a quotation, follow the rules governing ellipses on pages 341–342.

If you take a quotation from any place but the original source (if, for example, the quotation you want to use is included in the book you are citing but originally came from another book or article), you should document that fact by including "qtd. in" ("quoted in") in your parenthetical documentation.

```
The monthly business meeting serves a number of valuable
functions. In fact, perhaps the most important one is that
"chain-of-command meetings provide the opportunity to pass
information up as well as down the administrative ladder"
(qtd. in Munroe 87).
```

This documentation lets readers know that you found the quotation in Munroe, not in the original work from which these words come.

Sample Entries for an MLA Works Cited List

The following examples will give you models for a variety of sources you may include in your MLA Works Cited page(s).

- *Book by One Author*

```
Barth, Steven R. Corporate Ethics: The Business Code of
     Conduct for Ethical Employees. Boston: Aspatore,
     2003.
```

- *Book by Two Authors*

```
Davidson, Marilyn J., and Ronald J. Burke. Women in
     Management Worldwide: Facts, Figures, and Analysis.
     Burlington: Ashgate Press, 2004.
```

- *Book by More Than Three Authors*

```
Perez, Jennifer, et al. Holistic Nursing: Practice for
     Body, Mind, and Soul. 4th ed. Baltimore: Nursing
     Research, 2006.
```

List all authors' full names or list only the first author's name, in reverse order, and add et al. after a comma following the first author's name. Note that when a book has a subtitle, you must include it, too. Separate the title from the subtitle by a colon, as in the Perez entry above. When a book goes into a second or subsequent edition, list that fact after the title, as in the Perez book, but do not underscore the edition or put it in italics.

- *Book by a Corporate Author*

```
Ernst & Young LLP. The Ernst and Young Tax Guide 2005. New
     York: Wiley, 2005.

United Nations. Trade and Development Report 2004: Capital
     Accumulation, Economic Growth, and Structural Change.
     New York: United Nations Publications, 2005.
```

A corporate author refers to an organization, society, association, institution, or government agency that publishes a work under its own name—for example, the Federal Aviation Administration. In the examples on the previous page, the accounting firm of Ernst & Young and the United Nations are considered the authors.

- *Edited Collection of Essays*

> Tyson-Jones, Sandra, ed. The E-Investor: Building
>   Portfolios Online. New York: Merrimack, 2006.

The abbreviation *ed.* for *editor* follows the editor's name, which is listed in reverse order.

- *Work Included in a Collection*

> Rich, Wilbur. "Networking, Career Management, and
>   Diversity in the Public Sector." Diversity and Public
>   Administration: Theory, Issues, and Perspectives. Ed.
>   Mitchell F. Rice. New York: Sharpe, 2005. 139-52.
>
> Waldman, Lila. "International Business Courses: Partnering
>   with Overseas Students." E-World: Virtual Learning,
>   Collaborative Environments, and Future Technologies.
>   Ed. Doris Christopher. Reston: National Business
>   Education Association, 2004.

The name of the author of the article in a collection comes first—in reverse order—and then the title of the article in quotation marks. Next comes the title of the collection underscored or in italics. The editor's name is listed after the title with the abbreviation Ed. (Use "Ed." even when citing more than one editor.) Do not list the editor's name in reverse order. The page numbers on which the essay appears in the collection conclude the entry.

- *Article in a Professional Journal*

> Carter, Jim, and Norman Sheehan. "From Competition to
>   Cooperation: E-Tailing's Integration with Retailing."
>   Business Horizons 47 (2004): 71-78.
>
> Okazaki, Shintaro. "How Do Japanese Consumers Perceive
>   Wireless Ads?" International Journal of Advertising
>   23.4 (2004): 420-54.

Note how a reference to a journal article differs from that of a book in MLA style. The title of the article is in quotation marks, not underscored or italicized; no place of publication is listed. The volume number and issue number (vol. 23, issue 4) immediately follow the title of the journal with no intervening punctuation. And the page number(s) on which the article is found follow the colon that is placed after the publication date, which is given in parentheses.

- *Article in a Magazine*

Dexter, Robert, Wendy Zeller, and Carol Matlock. "China: Let the Retail Wars Begin." <u>Newsweek</u> 17 Jan. 2005: 44–45.

Pearlman, Russell, and Evelyn Ellison Twitchell. "15 Stocks for Under $15." <u>Smart Money</u> Feb. 2005: 71–81.

Unlike scholarly journal articles, popular and widely read magazines (such as *Business Week, Time, U.S. News & World Report*) are listed by date, not by a volume number.

- *Unsigned Magazine Article*

"The Differences in Writing an E-Newsletter." <u>Practical Accountant</u> Jan. 2005: 23.

Unsigned works are always listed according to the first word of their title (disregarding any initial *A, An,* or *The* when you are alphabetizing).

- *Newspaper Article*

Wittington, Delores. "The Dollar May Buy More Vacation Overseas This Year." <u>Springfield Herald</u> 30 Mar. 2007, late ed., sec. 2: 10.

List a newspaper article by day, month, and year, not according to the volume and issue numbers. Identify section, page, and edition information for readers. In the example above, readers know that the story appeared in the late edition in section 2 on page 10. Sometimes the article you cite will not require those details. The next example documents an article found on pages D1 and D10 of a paper that issues only one edition per day.

Tam, Pui-Wing. "New Ways to View Your Digital Pictures." <u>Wall Street Journal</u> 26 Jan. 2005: D1, D10.

- *Encyclopedia Article*

Judd, Deane B., and Jack Lambert. "Colorimetry." <u>McGraw-Hill Encyclopedia of Science and Technology</u>. 9th ed. 2002.

When citing a well-known multivolume, alphabetical work, only the particular edition and year of the encyclopedia have to be listed in the Works Cited. When an encyclopedia article is not signed, alphabetize it under the first word of the title (disregarding any initial *A, An,* or *The*).

Tech Note

How Documentation of an Internet Source Differs from a Print Source

You can expect to document a variety of Web sources—everything from an e-mail to an issue of an online journal to an e-book to a corporate website to a government document to a cartoon (as on p. 353). Citing Internet sources poses challenges for researchers that print sources do not.

1. An Internet site has a URL that uses a different set of symbols and punctuation marks than a print source uses, including angle brackets (< >), dots (...), tildes (~), and slashes (/). Make sure you copy them correctly and consistently in your citations; otherwise, your reader won't be able to find your reference's site (assuming the link to it still exists).
2. A source on the Web does not usually have page numbers, or numbered individual paragraphs.
3. Because Internet sources are often anonymous, you will need to begin your Works Cited entry with the website title rather than an author's name.
4. An Internet source can change its address, or URL.
5. Keep in mind that an Internet source can have many versions—it can change over months, weeks, or even hours (which is why so many sites are frequently "under construction"). Moreover, it can be revised and updated at any time. You can find the most recent version of a webpage by reading the annotated page's Web listing.
6. Since an Internet site can be deleted, always make a hard copy for your records.
7. The date you access a site is usually not the same date the site was posted. Help readers by providing both dates in your documentation where relevant.
8. You may have to hunt for the date of publication or posting. Look for it at the top or bottom of the homepage or at the end of the site in the link labeled "About This Site."
9. Although you can access an Internet site through many different pathways—different access providers, search engines, and so on—keep in mind that search engines often lack completely updated URLs and may sometimes even take you to broken links.

- *Pamphlet or Brochure*

Environmental Protection Agency. <u>Drinking Water and
Health: What You Need to Know</u>. Washington: EPA, 1999.

Document a pamphlet or brochure the same way you would a book. Note here that the corporate author is also the publisher of the book.

- *Editorial*

> Colson, Robert H. "CPA--Codes of Conduct: Scope and Nature
>   of Services." Editorial. CPA Journal Aug. 2004: 80.

- *Published Interview*

> Jones, W. Randall. "CEO to CEO: Point of Difference: An
>   Interview with Peter Scatourru About Citigroup
>   Private Bank." Worth June 2002: 112.
>
> Zeluto, Thomas. "Interview with Former Budget Director Zia
>   Verges." Findlay Magazine Aug. 2006: 3-7.

Begin with the name of the individual conducting the interview, if known, and then indicate the title of the interview and publication information.

- *Unpublished Interview*

> Cilwik, Martin. Personal interview. 7 Feb. 2007.
>
> Lu, Barbara. E-mail interview. 15 May 2006.

Begin with the name of the interviewee—in reverse order—and then indicate how and when the interview was conducted.

- *Cartoon*

> Adams, Scott. "Dilbert." Cartoon. Washington Post 28 Dec.
>   2004: E2.
>
> Beale, Roger. "Funny Business." Cartoon. Financial Times
>   [London] 5/6 Oct. 2001: 36.

- *Lecture/Speech*

> Ricks, Sonya. "How the FLA [Future Lawyers Association]
>   Can Prepare You for the LSAT." Metropolitan Center
>   College, Hartford. 29 Apr. 2006.

- *Film*

> Fire Investigation. Prod. Detrick Lawrence. DVD. Emergency
>   Film Group, 2004.
>
> Targets of Opportunity: Information Security, "The Human
>   Factor". Commonwealth Films, 2004.

- *Corporate Websites*

Association of Professional Landscape Designers. 2005.
     Assoc. of Professional Landscape Designers. 2 Mar.
     2005. <http://www.apld.com/>.

General Electric. "Global Locations." General Electric
     2005. 17 Apr. 2005 <http://www.gepower.com/prod_serv/
     serv/energy_rentals_cc/en/global_locations/index.htm>.

Give the date of publication as well as the date of access. Enclose the URL in angle brackets.

- *Personal Website*

Hoffman, Carrie. The Carrie Hoffman Webpage. 22 Jan. 2005.
     1 Feb. 2005 <http://www.carriehoffman.com>.

- *Blog*

Kennedy, Niall. "Bay Area Technology Events Calendar."
     Niall Kennedy's Weblog. 27 Jan. 2005. 2 Feb. 2005
     <http://www.niallkennedy.com/blog/>.

- *E-Mail*

Even though e-mail messages are regarded as unpublished correspondence like memos or letters, you still need to document them by giving the following information:

- writer's name (last name first)
- title of the message (taken from the subject line), if given
- person or organization to whom the e-mail was sent
- date the e-mail was sent

Jerach-Gordon, Tina. "Hosco Software Version C Updated."
     E-mail to the author. 30 Apr. 2006.

Waddle, Sophia. "Results of Preliminary Staph Tests."
     E-mail to Lab Supervisor Parvan Raz. 7 Oct. 2006.

- *Online Book Available in Print or Online*

Lansdell, Sally. Working Globally. London: John Wiley,
     2002. 31 Jan. 2005 <http://www.ebookmall.com/
     alpha-authors/Sally-Lansdell.htm>.

Heyman, Phillip B. Terrorism and America: A Commonsense
     Strategy for a Democratic Society. Cambridge: MIT,

```
1998. netLibrary. 31 Oct. 2003
<http://www.netlibrary.com/index.asp>.
```

Note that a period separates the publication date from the access date but that no period appears between the access date and the URL (uniform resource locator).

- *Online Book Available Only Online*

```
Institute of Medicine. Telemedicine: A Guide to Assessing
    Telecommunications for Health Care. 18 June 2002
    <http://www.nap.edu/books/0309055318/html/index.html>.
```

```
Kutsher, Martin L. The ADHD e-book. 4 June 2002. Pediatric
    Neurological Associates. 18 June 2002 <http://
    www.pediatricneurology.com/adhd.htm#W>.
```

- *Online Scholarly Article*

```
Char, Sandy. "Instant Messaging in Business: IM Here to
    Stay." Computer Bits 20.5 (2004). 21 Feb. 2005 <http://
    www.computerbits.com/archive/2004/1100/busim.html>.
```

```
Gillespie, Joe. "Adapting Print Design Skills for the
    Web." Web Page Design for Designers 5.2 (2004). 26
    Jan. 2005 <http://www.wpdfd.com/editorial/wpd0804news
    .htm#feature>.
```

- *Online Article in a Magazine*

```
Philipkoski, Kristen. "Will Robots Sail Your Veins?" Wired
    16 Jan. 1999. 1 Feb. 2005 <http://www.wired.com/news/
    print/0.1294.17376.00.html>.
```

- *Electronic Mailing List or Newsgroup Message*

```
Favorito, Rebecca. "Re: Marketing Issues." Online posting.
    20 Jan. 2005. 1 Feb. 2005 <news.timer.international
    .business.general>.
```

- *Article in an Online Encyclopedia, Dictionary, or Other Online Reference Source*

```
"HTML." Webopedia. 2005. 26 Jan. 2005 <http://
    www.webopedia.com/TERM/H/HTML.html>.
```

```
"Magnetic Disks." NASA Thesaurus. 2002. 15 Jan. 2003
    <http://www.sti.nasa.gov/thesaurus/M/word8907.html>.
```

"Marketing Without Spam." <u>Nolo Legal Encyclopedia</u>. 2005.
    26 Jan. 2005 <http://www.nolo.com/lawcenter/ency/
    article.cfm/ObjectID/1B5A1C4B-A0A4-42DB-
    A69463370AA2C5AB/catID/007A76EC-6651-4D6E-
    9C37D5EA3478F109>.

- *Online Radio Program*

Abramson, Larry. "Microsoft Adds Program to Fight
    Spyware." <u>Morning Edition</u>. National Public Radio.
    24 Jan. 2005 <http://www.npr.org/templates/story/
    story.php?storyId=4463541>.

Prakash, Snigdha. "Entrepreneurs Seek More Federal Aid."
    <u>Morning Edition</u>. National Public Radio. 4 Oct.
    2002 <http://www.npr.org/cf/cmn/segment_display
    .cfm?seg1D=151092>.

- *Television Program*

<u>Pompeii: The Last Day</u>. Discovery Channel. 5 Feb. 2005.

- *Online Map*

"Afghanistan." Map. 2006. CNN. 16 March 2006
    <http://www.cnn.com/SPECIALS/2001/trade.center/
    afghan.zoom.html>.

"Rue des Jardins Saint-Paul, Paris 75004." Map. 2006 <u>Yahoo
    Maps</u>. 18 June 2006 <http://maps.yahoo.com/>.

■ Preparing an APA Reference List

In APA style, the sources you cite in your paper are listed on a References page or pages at the end of the paper. As in MLA style, entries are arranged alphabetically by author. The elements in APA entries are listed in this order:

author(s) (last name first, followed by initials)

date

title

edition

publication data

The APA style emphasizes the date of publication, of crucial interest in the dissemination of technical information, and for that reason it is given a prominent place in the citation. Below are some guidelines on documenting your sources for a References page(s). Make sure you list the information for each reference in the order given here. For additional help, look at the sample report using APA style on pages 680–697 and study the examples on pages 373–378 as models, too.

Format

- Begin the reference list on a new page, with the word *References* at the top.
- Arrange all entries in alphabetical order by the author's last name or by the first key word of the title in works not listing an author. When alphabetizing, disregard *A, An,* or *The* at the beginning of a title.
- Start each entry at the left-hand margin and indent the second and subsequent lines of the entry five to seven spaces.
- Separate each major element in an APA citation with a period followed by only one space.
- Double-space between and within each entry.

Author(s)

- List the author's surname first, followed by a comma, and first and middle initials: Jones, T. C. rather than Jones, Tracy C.
- List all authors, up to six, before using *et al.* Reverse the names of all the authors, not just the first one; and use an ampersand (&), not *and,* before the last author's name.

Dates

- For books, and articles in professional journals, list just the date in parentheses; for articles in popular magazines, list the month and the year in parentheses. Dates are found on copyright pages for books and on the masthead (contents) page for journals and magazines. Write out in full the names of months for periodicals.
- Place the date of publication in parentheses immediately after the author's inverted name: Jones, T. C. (2006).

Titles

- Capitalize only the first word in an article or book title (except for proper nouns in the title), e.g., *The problem of soil erosion in southeastern Lancaster County,* and the first word after a colon.
- Cite the full title (including the subtitle), which is found on the title page.
- For periodicals, capitalize every major word of the title of the magazine, journal, or newspaper (e.g., *The St. Louis Post-Dispatch, Journal of Lifelong Learning*).
- Do not put quotation marks around article or magazine titles.
- Italicize the title of a book, journal, newspaper, or magazine.

Publication Data

- Use a shortened name for publishers (e.g., Houghton, not Houghton Mifflin). In general, delete the words *Inc., Publisher,* and *Company.*

- List the city and state (or city and country for publishers outside the U.S.) of publication followed by the publisher (e.g., Springfield, IL: Lincoln Books). Major cities can be listed without the state (e.g., New York: Norton).
- When a book is published by a university press, provide the full name of the press (e.g., Urbana: University of Illinois Press). Do not duplicate location information that already appears in the name of the university (e.g., Illinois).
- Italicize the volume number of all journals and magazine articles, including the commas that separate the elements.

```
Wang, S., Bailey, S. E., & Foxx, W. (2004). Signaling the
     trustworthiness of small online retailers. Journal of
     Interactive Marketing, 18, 53–59.
```

- Put volume numbers for journals in Arabic, not Roman, numerals.
- List page numbers completely (e.g., 79–86; 262–268; not 262–68). Use *p.* or *pp.* in references to newspapers, encyclopedia articles, and chapters in books. Do not italicize page numbers.
- For an article in an encyclopedia, put volume and page numbers in parentheses following the title of the encyclopedia, as in the example below.

```
Tang, A. (2003). Gates, Bill. In The encyclopedia of
     leading U.S. CEOs (Vol. 3, pp. 78–82). Baltimore:
     Redmond.
```

Electronic Sources

Be aware that APA provides updates online to accommodate the fast-changing world of technology, so it is always wise to double-check the APA website (*http://www.apastyle.org/elecref.html*) for the most recent practices. Here are some general rules that will apply to most of the electronic sources you will document.

1. Follow the same order and publication information as for print sources. Note that there is no period at the end of the entry following the URL.

2. Include a retrieval statement that tells the reader when you accessed the source (month, day, and year). This source may be a website or a database such as InfoTrac or EBSCO (see pp. 314–319).

3. Give the URL or other electronic address. Be sure the address is correct.

```
Melka, Mary (2007, February 16). Ergonomically designed
     office eliminates light fixtures to use paper-thin
     diodes. Business Online. Retrieved March 1, 2007,
     from http://buson./com/search/weekly/
```

▌Using APA In-Text Documentation

Like the MLA, the APA uses parenthetical (or in-text) documentation. According to APA style, you provide readers with a brief reference to the sources that you cite in the text and then in your Reference list you supply the full publication information. Only works actually cited in your paper should be listed in your Reference list and vice versa. Here is an example of APA in-text documentation.

```
T. C. Jones (2006) maintains that "as buyers move farther
north, new housing becomes increasingly more expensive"
(p. 13).
```

The reader sees that Jones developed that theory on page 13 of his 2006 work. To find publication information about Jones's work, readers would then turn to an alphabetically arranged Reference list at the end of the paper, report, or article, where, under Jones, they would find a full bibliographic entry. If two works by Jones were cited, references for both would be given. If they were published in the same year, they would be differentiated in the text and in the References by the lowercase letters *a* and *b*. Otherwise, they are arranged by year of publication, ordered from earliest to most recent.

```
The farther north residents move, the more homes will cost
(Jones, 2006a).

A recent study established a demographic pattern for small
cities in the Midwest (Jones, 2006b).
```

In the Reference list, the two works by Jones in the same year would be listed as follows:

```
Jones, T. C. (2006a). The cost of housing on Lincoln's
     north-side. Urban Studies, 72, 10–24.

Jones, T. C. (2006b). Demographic density in three
     Midwestern small cities. Cincinnati: Western Press.
```

As the above examples show, APA style requires a minimum amount of information for in-text documentation, usually author, date, and page number. In this practice, the APA differs from MLA, which does not require a date to be listed with each in-text mention of a reference. Another difference between the two styles is that APA uses p. or pp. to cite a page for a quotation or paraphrase, but MLA does not use an in-text p. or pp. Depending on where you cite information in your sentence, there are a variety of ways to provide APA in-text documentation. Here are some examples of how to employ APA's guidelines:

```
Recent theory asserts that "as buyers move farther north,
new housing becomes increasingly more expensive" (Jones,
2006a, p. 13).
```

In this example the reader sees that Jones developed the theory on page 13 of a work written in 2006, and the documentation immediately follows the quotation as called for by APA.

```
In his book published in 2006, Jones asserts that "as
buyers move farther north, new housing becomes
increasingly more expensive" (p. 13).
```

When the author's name and date of publication are mentioned in the sentence, there is no need to repeat them parenthetically. Just include the page reference.

```
"As buyers move farther north, new housing becomes
increasingly more expensive" (p. 13), according to one of
Jones's major theories (2006).
```

APA stipulates that you put a page reference directly after the quotation, whether it is at the beginning, middle (as above), or end of the sentence, and then provide the date after the author has been identified.

```
The housing market has greatly changed on the north side
of town (Jones, 2006).
```

Since there is no direct quotation—only a paraphrase—simply supply author and date parenthetically.

```
The cost of houses, which "as buyers move farther
north . . . becomes increasingly more expensive"(Jones,
2006, p. 13), is a leading economic barometer in Washington
County.
```

Note that when the quotation is used in the middle of the sentence, as in the subordinate clause above, the author, date, and page documentation immediately follows the quotation rather than falling at the end of the sentence. If your quotation runs to 40 words or more, begin the quotation on a new line and indent all lines of the quotation five spaces from the left margin. Do not use quotation marks.

If the work you are citing includes more than one author, list all authors up to six in the text in your first reference to them, and if more than six, use just the first author and et al., which is not italicized and is followed by a period. For subsequent references to works with more than two authors, use just the name of the first author and et al. For works with just two authors, always list both names.

First Reference:
```
Kendrick, Foo, and Himinez (2007) identified the three
leading causes of pollution.
```

Subsequent References:
```
Three leading causes of pollution include soil erosion,
smoke emission, and landfill abuse (Kendrick et al., 2007).
```

```
Kendrick et al. (2007) determined that soil erosion played
a major role in pollution.
```

APA uses an ampersand between the last two authors when the names are cited parenthetically as we saw on page 369. But spell out *and* when used in the text.

For works by corporate and governmental agencies, simply list the organization's full name followed by the date in your parenthetical citation or in the sentence itself.

```
The Association of Retired Pilots (2007) has a strong
lobby in Washington.

Subsidies to farmers for growing energy-rich fuel crops
are at an all-time high (U.S. Department of Agriculture,
2005).
```

When your source does not have an author, the first words of the reference entry can be given parenthetically.

```
The new marketing strategies have been exceptionally well
received in Europe ("Marketing Euros," p. 17).
```

For a source from the Internet, cite the author and date but do not list the sometimes long and complex Web address (URL) in text.

Wrong:

```
According to Ti Sing (http://www.comtechpro.com/text/
03211/htm, 2007), . . .
```

Right:

```
According to Ti Sing ("Navigating Websites," 2007), . . .
```

Interviews, e-mail messages, bulletins, listserv messages, letters, lectures, and seminars are cited in the text as personal communications but are not included in the Reference list. Give the initials as well as the surname of the communicator and provide a date.

```
Dr. Patavi said that this information came from the
preliminary report submitted last month (V. A. Patavi,
personal communication, September 13, 2007).
```

Sample Entries for an APA Reference List

The following examples will give you some models to document entries according to APA guidelines.

- *Book by One Author*

```
Elliott, G. (2004). Global business information
    technology: An integrated systems approach. New York:
    Addison Wesley.
```

Shen, M. (2004). *How to do business in China.* Pittsburgh, PA: Dorrance.

- *Book by Two Authors*

Evans, D. S., & Schmalensee, R. (2005). *Paying with plastic: The digital revolution in buying and borrowing* (2nd ed.). Boston: MIT Press.

Lauden, K. C., & Traver, C. G. (2004). *E-commerce, business, technology, society.* New York: Addison Wesley.

- *Book by Three or More Authors*

Munro, M. A., Silverman, D. J., & Tyson, E. (2004). *Taxes for dummies 2005.* Hoboken, NJ: Wiley.

- *Book by a Corporate Author*

American Bar Association. (2004). *The American Bar Association guide to wills and estates: Everything you need to know about wills, estates, trusts, and taxes* (2nd ed.). New York: Random House.

American Psychological Association. (2005). *Concise rules of APA style.* Washington, DC: Author.

- *Government Document*

U.S. Congress. House Committee on Small Business. (2004). *Women's entrepreneurship: Successes and challenges. Hearing before the Committee on Small Business, House of Representatives.* Washington, DC: U.S. Government Printing Office.

U.S. Congress. Senate Committee on Small Business and Entrepreneurship. (2004). *Impact of stock option expensing on small businesses: Hearing before the Committee on Small Business and Entrepreneurship.* Washington, DC: U.S. Government Printing Office.

- *Online Report*

United States Department of the Treasury. (2004). *2004 financial report of the United States Government.*

Financial Management Service. Retrieved January 29, 2005, from http://www.fms.treas.gov/fr/04frusg/04frusg.pdf

- *Work in a Collected Edition*

Sharma, S. K. (2004). Socio-economic impacts and influences of e-commerce in a digital economy. In H. Kehal and V. P. Singh (Eds.), *Digital economy: Impacts, influences and challenges* (pp. 1–20). Hershey, PA: Idea Group.

- *Paper Presented at a Conference*

Wagner, F., Wagner, T., & Wolstenholme, P. (2004, May 24–27). *Closing the Gap between Software Modelling and Code.* Paper presented at the 11th IEEE International Conference and Workshop on the Engineering of Computer-Based Systems. Retrieved February 15, 2005, from http://csdl.computer.org/comp/proceedings/ecbs/2004/2125/00/2125toc.htm

Panda, M. K., Venkatesh, T., Sridhar, V., & Singh, Y. N. (2004, October 25–29). *Architecture for a Class of Scalable Optical Cross-Connects.* Paper presented at the IEEE First International Conference on Broadband Networks. Retrieved January 30, 2005, from http://csdl.computer.org/comp/proceedings/broadnets/2004/2221/00/2221toc.htm

- *Article in a Professional Journal*

Decker, R., & Zhao, X. (2004). SME's choice of foreign market entry mode: A normative approach. *International Journal of Business and Economics, 3*(3), 181–200.

Marcotte, C., & Niosi, J. (2005). Small and medium-sized enterprises involved in technology transfer to China: What do their partners learn? *International Small Business Journal, 23*, 27–47.

- *Article in a Monthly Magazine*

Buss, D. (2005, January). Joining forces. *Sales and Marketing Management, 157*(1), 38–42.

- *Newspaper Article*

Kessler, M. (2005, January 27). Net-based phones lure more users. *USA Today*, p. B3.

Lim, P. J. (2005, January 23). Want to invest abroad? Maybe you already have. *The New York Times*, p. B7.

- *Encyclopedia*

Accommodation: Contingency Theory. (2004). In *Encyclopedia of public relations* (Vol. 1, pp. 1–3). Thousand Oaks, CA: Sage.

- *Work in a Series*

E-world: Virtual learning, collaborative environments, and future technologies: National business education yearbook: Vol. 42 (2004). Reston, VA: National Business Education Association.

- *Website*

Business Resource Center. (2005). National Association of Women Business Owners. Retrieved May 2, 2005, from http://www.nawbo.org/resourcecenter/index.php

Global and international business news. (2004). *Business Week Online.* Retrieved February 13, 2005, from http://www.businessweek.com/globalbiz/

- *Online Book*

Abraham, K. G., & Mackie, C. (Eds.). (2005). *Beyond the market: Designing nonmarket accounts for the United States.* Retrieved January 29, 2005, from http://www.nap.edu/books/0309093198/html/

Thierauf, R. J., & Hoctor, J. J. (2003). *Smart business systems for the optimized organization.* Retrieved January 30, 2005, from Questia Online Library: http://www.questia.com/PM.qst?a=o&d=101283703

- *Online Scholarly Journal*

Archer, N., & Wang, S. (2004). Strategic choice of
electronic marketplace functionalities: A
buyer-supplier relationship perspective. *Journal of
Computer-Mediated Communication, 10*(1). Retrieved
January 29, 2005, from http://www.ascusc.org/jcmc/
vol10/issue1/wang_archer.html

Byrd-Blake, M. (2004). Female perspectives on career
advancement. *Advancing Women in Leadership, 15*.
Retrieved December 15, 2004, from http://www
.advancingwomen.com/awl/spring2004/BYRD_BLAKE.html

- *Online Magazine Article*

Kay, J. (2005, January 28). P&G to acquire Gillette for
$57 Billion. *Forbes.com*. Retrieved March 2, 2005,
from http://www.forbes.com/associatedpress/feeds/ap/
2005/01/28/ap1791274.html

Michaels, N. (2004, Winter). Women entrepreneurs growing
in numbers and importance. *Score: Counselors to
America's Small Business*. Retrieved April 12, 2005,
from http://www.score.org/m_pr_20.html

- *Online Encyclopedia*

Poland. (2005). In *Encyclopaedia Britannica Online*.
Retrieved May 10, 2005, from http://www.britannica
.com/eb/article?tocId=9108558

- *Speech*

Otellini, P. (2005, February 25). 3GSM World Congress 2005
keynote address. *Intel Worldwide*. Retrieved March 23,
2005, from http://www.intel.com/pressroom/archive/
speeches/otellini20050225.htm

- *Abstract*

Abell, M., Bauder, D, & Simmons, T. (2004). Universally
designed online assessment: Implications for the
future. *Information Technology and Disabilities,*

10(1). Abstract retrieved November 21, 2004, from
http://www.rit.edu/~easi/itd/itdv10.htm

Luo, X., Sivakumar, K., & Liu, S. S. (2005).
Globalization, marketing resources, and performance:
Evidence from China. *Journal of the Academy of
Marketing Science, 33,* 50–65. Abstract retrieved
July 7, 2005, from http://jam.sagepub.com/cgi/
content/abstract/33/1/50

- *Online Posting*

Beuerlein, R. M. (2004, June 1). Profession at risk. Message
posted to Society of Actuaries forum, archived at
http://forums.soa.org/thread.jspa?messageID=3336

- *Online Map*

Marietta Street, Atlanta, GA 30303. *MapsOnUs.com.*
Retrieved January 29, 2005, from http://mapsonus
.switchboard.com/bin/maps-maponly/usr=~414b1a0d
.2822c.5b63.6/c=10/isredir=1/

◼ The *Chicago* Numbered Note Style of Documentation

Up to now we have focused on the parenthetical style of documentation recommended by the MLA and the APA. Another way to document your research is to use the numbered note system found in *The Chicago Manual of Style* (15th ed., University of Chicago Press, 2003). In this method, you add a slightly raised numeral, called a *superscript*, immediately following the information you wish to document, like this: [1]. These numbers run consecutively throughout your report or paper and are accompanied by corresponding numbered notes that appear either at the bottom of the page on which the number appears (footnotes) or in endnotes (or notes) gathered at the end of your paper. These notes provide full bibliographic information and sometimes additional information about sources. It is critical that the endnotes be numbered correctly, so that a source can be matched accurately with the corresponding material in your paper.

Comparing the Two Methods

Figure 9.2 shows a section of endnotes for sources that have been cited for a paper. The same sources, documented for a paper using parenthetical documentation, are listed in Figure 9.3, which shows the relevant section of a Works Cited page.

An example of an endnotes page showing the documentation of sources.   Figure 9.2

Notes

  1. Julie Teunissen, "Opportunities for Technical Writers," Computer
Outlook 17 (2006): 43.

  2. George Tullos, "Technical Writers and the Importance of Online
Documentation," Journal of e-Operations 8 (2007): 15.

  3. Mary Bronstein, The New Generation of Technical Writers
(San Francisco: FTP Systems, 2005), 107.

Documentation of sources in Figure 9.2 for a Works Cited page.   Figure 9.3

Works Cited

Bronstein, Mary. The New Generation of Technical Writers.
      San Francisco: FTP Systems, 2005.

Teunissen, Julie. "Opportunities for Technical Writers." Computer
      Outlook 17 (2006): 42–45.

Tullos, George. "Technical Writers and the Importance of Online
      Documentation." Journal of e-Operations 8 (2007): 15–21.

Some Basic Guidelines for the *Chicago* Style

Here are some basic rules to observe when documenting your work using endnotes according to the *Chicago* style. Figure 9.4 contains a sample endnote page following the *Chicago* guidelines.

1. Place a raised numeral at the end of a phrase, sentence, paragraph, and after every direct quotation.

2. Do not use more than one note (numeral) in the same place. In other words, don't build up notes after a sentence like this:

Figure 9.4   A sample endnote page using the *Chicago* style of documentation.

Notes

Indent first line five spaces

1. S. Rhinesmith, *A Manager's Guide to Globalization* (New York: McGraw-Hill, 2004), 72.

Separate major elements with commas

2. Tricia Avery, William Fuentes, and Sandra Gleason, "A New Global Marketplace," *World Business* 19 (Fall 2005): 21.

3. Ibid., 29.

Put publication information in parentheses

4. Li Chan, "Adjusting to International Assignments," in *New Issues in International Business,* ed. Ruth El Safir (London: Plume Press, 2007), 181–82.

Use Ibid. for source repeated in two or more consecutive notes

5. Avery, Fuentes, and Gleason, "New Global Marketplace," 18.

6. Rhinesmith, *Manager's Guide,* 61.

7. Ibid., 67.

Do not invert author's name

8. Robert Traynor-Ellis, "Educating Globally Savvy Leaders," *International Management Review* 17 (June 2004): 16.

9. Chan, *International Assignments,* 197.

10. Traynor-Ellis, "Educating," 5.

11. Ibid.

List the website's title and address and the date you accessed it

12. "International Business: FAQ's." [Website] 2006, available at http://businessworld/faq/international/html (accessed March 7, 2006).

13. "Going There: A New Overseas Assignment," editorial, *Journal of Resource Management* 27 (Summer 2005): 18.

List author's last name, short title, and page reference for second and subsequent listings of a source

14. Chan, *International Assignments,* 179.

15. Avery, Fuentes, and Gleason, "New Global Marketplace," 27.

16. Sarah Fingle, "Training for a Career in International Business," *Seattle Post,* July 6, 2007, E1.

```
High Speed Internet connections are changing communication
strategies.1,2,3,4
```

Instead, use only one note that contains all necessary information.

3. Put endnotes on a separate page at the end of your report. Double-space the entire list.

4. Indent the first line of every endnote by five spaces but go back to the left margin for the second and subsequent lines.

5. List the author's full name in normal, not inverted, order (e.g., Paul Yee, not Yee, Paul).

6. If a work has fewer than four authors, list each name in normal order, but if there are more than four authors list only the first author followed by *and others*.

7. Separate each major element (author, title, date, etc.) with a comma, not a period.

8. After the author's name, list the title of a book (in italic) or article title (in quotation marks) followed by the journal or magazine title (in italic).

9. Put publication data for a book (place of publication: publisher, year) in parentheses. For an article, place the volume number after the title of the journal or magazine and follow it with the date in parentheses.

10. List the specific page number on which your source appears, *not* the entire pagination of a book or article.

11. If you repeat a source in two or more subsequent notes, use Ibid. (Latin for "the same"). If page numbers change but the source remains the same in two or more consecutive notes, continue to use Ibid. but with different page numbers for the source.

12. For a second or subsequent listing of a source, you do not have to repeat the bibliographic information. Just list the name(s) of the author(s), an abbreviated title, and a page reference(s).

The *Chicago Manual* advises that when you use the note style you also supply your readers with a bibliography.

Other Ways to Document in Scientific and Technical Writing

The MLA, APA, and numbered note styles are, of course, not the only methods for documenting sources. Numerous other formats exist. Many professions have their own style guide or manual. Here are a few examples.

- American Chemical Society, *ACS Style Guide: A Manual for Authors and Editors*. 2nd ed. Washington, DC: American Chemical Society, 1998. http://www.acs.org

- American Society of Civil Engineers, *The Practice Periodical*. Reston, VA: American Society of Civil Engineers, 2001. http://www.pubs.asce.org/authors/index.html
- Council of Science Editors, *Scientific Style and Format: The CBE Manual for Authors, Editors, and Publishers*. 6th ed. New York: Cambridge University Press, 2000. http://www.councilscienceeditors.org
- *United States Government Printing Office Style Manual*. Washington, DC: U.S. Government Printing Office, 2000. http://www.gpo.gov

Find out what guide your discipline/profession recommends and follow it. Most professions recommend that writers follow the documentation format used in a specific technical or scholarly journal. The way information is listed in these sources is a model for you to follow. Before you write a paper or report, ask your instructor or employer about the format he or she prefers. Note that your employer may have a company or agency documentation guide that you will be expected to follow in preparing memos, reports, proposals, or papers.

▌Sample Research Paper Using MLA In-Text Documentation

The rest of this chapter consists of an annotated research paper on the advantages of telecommuting. Study the paper to see how the student author has successfully used MLA documentation to cite print, CD-ROM, and Internet sources. Compare the references mentioned in the text with the Works Cited page to see how the writer has handled documentation appropriately. The sample long report in Chapter 16 on pages 680–697 follows the APA system of documentation. You might want to compare the two papers to become even more familiar with these two methods of parenthetical documentation.

Henry Holland

Professor Anne McQuin Meyer

Business Writing 301

17 April 2005

The Advantages of Telecommuting

in the Information Age

Telecommuting has transformed the world of work. Perhaps the best definition of telecommuting comes from the New York Telecommuting Advisory Council:

> Telecommuting, also called telework, is using telecommunications technology to replace traditional forms of commuting. Employees work all or part of the time outside the traditional office, at remote work locations, which may include home. The work goes to the worker rather than the worker to the work. People work where they are most effective.

Telecommuters travel to their jobs on the information superhighway. Any individual whose job depends on information technology can be a telecommuter, from skilled professionals such as programmers and analysts, architects, and documentation specialists to telemarketing representatives and travel agents who process information over the Internet or telephone (Steve 37). Telecommuters are represented by international, national, and regional organizations such as the Metro Atlanta Telecommuting Advisory

Start one inch down from top of page

Student name, instructor, course information, and date double-spaced in upper left corner

Title centered

Everything double-spaced

One-inch margins

Long quotation indented ten spaces; no quotation marks

No page reference for Web source

Parenthetically cites author and page

Holland 2

Council, the Telework Coalition, the International
Telework Association, and others.

Telecommuting became a significant part of the
American workplace in 1992 when AT&T's telecommuting
program began with a handful of employees and grew
enormously in the first seven years. This rapid change
Refers to figure; relates it to text reflects a national trend, as Figure 1 shows. Telecommuting has grown steadily each year. "Fifty-seven
percent of all employers now offer their staff a
telecommuting option" (McDavid 7). A survey by
Uses statistics to show importance of paper topic In-Stat/MDR, a Scottsdale, Arizona market research
team, shows that in 2004, "Forty-four million U.S.
employees worked from home at least part-time--a
number that will rise to 55 million by 2008"
Cites author and page (Hendricks 56).

Even more optimistically, Myra Perez-Hoya
believes that by 2010 approximately 75 million workers
will be telecommuting ("Workers" 102). That figure is
Identifies which of two works by same author is cited not unrealistic given the enthusiastic welcome telecommuting has received in Washington in the aftermath
of 9/11, according to the U.S. Office of Personnel
Management ("Status"). While the United States is a
Web source requires only short title world leader in promoting telecommuting, Australia,
Canada, Japan, and Scandinavia have all enthusiasti-
cally endorsed the concept.

But telecommuting is much more than a substi-
Signals that paper is not about just technology but also work policies tution of technology for travel to and from work. The
technology involves important changes in management
policies as well as in the way people work and view
their careers. This paper will survey the growth of

Holland 3

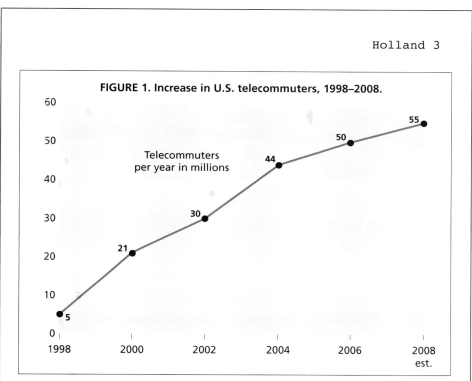

FIGURE 1. Increase in U.S. telecommuters, 1998–2008.

Source: Lewis and Zhang 20.

telecommuting by discussing (1) the ways it differs from the traditional office, (2) the advantages telecommuting has for employers, (3) the benefits it offers employees, and (4) the impact telecommuting will have on the workplace in the twenty-first century.

Telecommuting Transforms the Traditional Office

Telework opens up a whole new world. It uses technology to accommodate business goals and to improve the lives of workers. As society has switched from being an industrial/manufacturing economy to one based on

Holland 4

information, telecommuting becomes the "new world of work in electronic infrastructure" (Perez-Hoya, "Telecommuting" 8). Advances in communication technology in this "new world"--fiber optics, wireless access, broadband cable services, semiconductors, WiFi cards, PDAs, VoIP Primer "Find me/Follow me" phone services (Hendricks 58)--make telecommuting practical and profitable. Thanks to these technological advances, telecommuting is radically altering the traditional idea of work schedules and workplaces.

Traditionally, office operations have functioned on a fixed schedule. From the days of Scrooge in Charles Dickens's A Christmas Carol demanding that Bob Cratchit not be late for work to the child-care issues in the film Nine to Five, the workday has been run on a "ruthless timeclock" ("Learning New Work" 12). Employees often had to stay late or come in early to perform (or keep) their jobs. As one former 9-to-5er put it, "When a big report had to go out, we all worked frantically to beat the clock" (Vint).

Communicating electronically, a telecommuter can conduct business online at any time, day or night, weekends and holidays. No set hours dictate when something must be done. Offering maximum flexibility, telecommuters can do time tradeoffs to make up lost "daytime" hours in the evening hours. Gone are the days when an employee had to take work home. But as an International Telework Association survey revealed, more than 50 percent of the respondents

Gives author's name in reference since not mentioned in sentence

Provides brief historical context

Cites title since no author listed for work

No page number needed for unpublished interview

Uses documentation from primary research

Holland 5

found working at home even during a vacation helpful
because it "reduced the pileups they would face when
they returned [and] . . . enabled them to rejoin the
flow without post-vacation downtime" ("Teleworkers
Still on the Job").

Telecommuting also transforms the traditional
idea of the workplace--a centralized office usually
in a large downtown building where employees are restricted to their cubicles. Telecommuters can work
at home, at remote sites, or while traveling at any
time in the global marketplace. Obviously, telecommuting's flexibility of place is inappropriate for
health care, person-to-person customer service, counseling, or positions requiring specialized equipment
or conditions (U.S. Office of Personnel Management,
"What Is Telework?"; Sullivan). But for millions of
telecommuters, work is accomplished through technologies that are blind to their surroundings. E-mail
or instant messages sent from the central office
to a customer are identical to e-mail or instant
messages sent from a sales representative at an
off-site location.

Telecommuting does not eliminate the need for
a central office, however. A company's server and the
staff to operate and maintain it have to be located
somewhere, and an organization needs an official
mailing address for legal purposes. Telecommuters
typically work at a remote location one to three
days a week but work in an office at other times
(Robertson; Lewis and Zhang 71). Ivor Patel stresses

Uses ellipses for omitted material

Web source cited by title

Cites two works that address this issue and uses title to distinguish two works by same author

Makes an important qualification

Web source with author; distinguishes specific work by Lewis, who is cited for two separate studies

Holland 6

Does not use title or page number to cite e-mail

that, in his company, telecommuters are expected to come to the central workplace "to attend seminars, meet clients, participate in audits, and discuss personnel issues with management." Similarly, In-Stat/MDR estimates that as many as 44 million Americans work from home at least some time during the week and go to the office, plant, or conference center the rest of the week (Hendricks 57).

Advantages of Telecommuting for Employers

Must repeat author's name each time author is cited

Telecommuting offers many dividends for companies whose overriding corporate concern is productivity (Hendricks 57; Lewis 50). Managers have repeatedly acknowledged that the quality and quantity of an employee's work improve with telecommuting. Many managers report as well that, in Bob Steve's words, "telecommuters have more energy working at home and

Does not have to cite author whose name is in text

are more accurate" (37). According to numerous studies, employers further verify that telecommuters have a more positive attitude, which contributes to increased productivity and company loyalty (Bell 10; Steve 39). Employers find telecommuting increases productivity by 15 to 25 percent (Robertson). One

Must cite author's name in this citation

company--America West Vacations--reported greater productivity of up to $50,000--$60,000 per year due to improved employee attendance, retention, and morale ("Telecommuting Case Study").

Many large corporations (AT&T, General Dynamics, GE, Hewlett-Packard) and government agencies (U.S.

Holland 7

Departments of Transportation and Energy) also
happily found that telecommuters took less leave
time. Allowed to work at home, telecommuters can care
for sick children, spouses, or parents, too. Figure 2
shows that employees who are parents are more likely
to telecommute. This trend will continue.

Clearly identifies figure; ties it into text

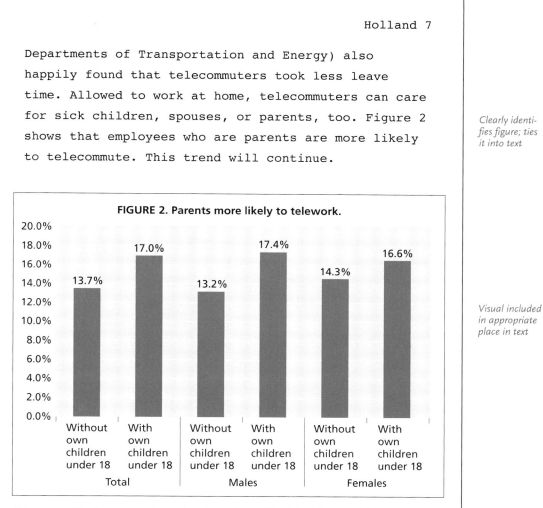

FIGURE 2. Parents more likely to telework.

Visual included in appropriate place in text

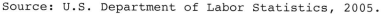

Source: U.S. Department of Labor Statistics, 2005.

Telecommuting also helps companies recruit and
retain valued, skilled employees who, as Perez-Hoya
notes, might otherwise leave due to a spouse's transfer or other change ("Workers" 104). Faced with
a smaller staff turnover, a company will find its

Documents paraphrase

Holland 8

Short quota-
tions are not
indented

Quotation can
be found in
this source

schedules and marketing plans less frequently interrupted or delayed. As one manager of Southwest Cyber-
Systems observed, "Before telecommuting, when we lost
a key person, everything went off center. Highly
qualified people often left not because of salary or
benefits but because of schedules. Switching to
telecommuting was one of our smartest moves" (qtd. in
Lewis and Zhang 53).

Telecommuting saves a business money, too. By
gaining access to a much larger, and increasingly
flexible, work force, even to a global labor market,
as we'll see below, firms escape paying relocation
expenses (Korzeniowski 47). Companies like AT&T and
insurance conglomerates (e.g., WorldLife) with large
numbers of telecommuters recoup a great deal of facilities costs. Fewer employees permanently assigned
to a central workplace means smaller facilities can
suffice.

Includes rele-
vant statistics
to prove point

Ties text and
visual together

Based on her own firm's findings, Agnes Reynolds
believes that companies can reduce their office space
costs by at least $14,000 to $16,000 per telecommuter
(7). Figure 3, below, records the amount of savings an
employer can reap by using teleworkers. The accounting
firm of Ernst & Young cut its annual real-estate budget
by $25 million when it began telecommuting (Bell 9).
And when reduced costs for power, light, security,
and support staff are factored in, telecommuting is,
according to Alicia Lewis, "a bargain worth the time
and energy that go into implementing and coordinating
it" (51).

Holland 9

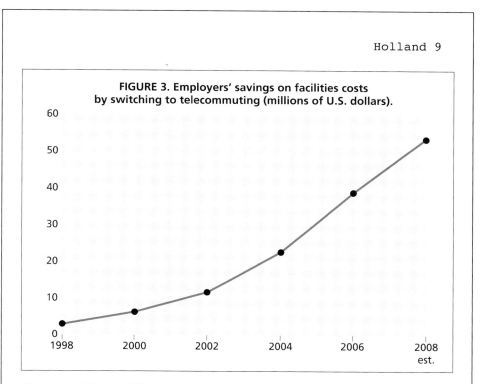

FIGURE 3. Employers' savings on facilities costs
by switching to telecommuting (millions of U.S. dollars).

Source: Steve 10.

Provides clear
title for visual

Documents
source of infor-
mation in
visual

Leaves space
between visual
and text

Telecommuting also helps a company protect the
environment by complying with the 1990 Clean Air
Act. This law, passed to improve air quality in
smog-plagued cities, requires businesses with more
than 100 employees in any one of thirteen specific
areas to curtail work-related vehicle miles traveled
by their employees by at least 25 percent or risk
hefty fines (Nyberg; Perez-Hoya, "Telecommuting" 8).
By encouraging carpooling and permitting telecommuting, a company can adhere to the letter as well as
the spirit of the law while enhancing its public
image. Officials from Detroit's Clean Air Campaign

Cites two
different
sources—Web
and print—for
information

A crucial point
for business
culture

have been especially "encouraged by the rise in numbers of those (like telecommuters) who have tried
some form of alternate commuting" (McDavid 8).
Predictably, telecommuting saves customers travel and
time. "Taxpayers can avoid long commutes into a downtown city by obtaining assistance from staffers at
the IRS, Veterans Affairs, or other agencies where
telecommuting is available" (U.S. Office of Personnel
Management, "Status").

As beneficial as telecommuting can be for the
employer, the practice presents some challenges. As
Lewis points out, employers have feared losing management or supervisory control (42). But such worries
are more potential disadvantages than actual liabilities. By planning telecommuting programs carefully,
employers can avert problems before they occur, and
by exploring different management styles, companies
can improve employees' motivation.

Moreover, when employers supply the broadband
Internet service to their telecommuting employees,
businesses have the right to install monitoring software to check on keyboard and phone activity. But
since employers as well as "office-bound workers have
access to the networked calendars which show phone
calls, appointments, and other activities" of telecommuters, resentments and doubts about who is working and when are eliminated (Hendricks 59). These and
other positive experiences have, for Korzeniowski,
all but removed the management fear that telecommuters will "watch Oprah rather than work" (46).

*Direct quota-
tion from Web
source*

*Transition to
possible prob-
lems of
telecommuting*

*Answers pos-
sible objection
to such
monitoring*

*Citations fit
better at end
than in middle
of sentence*

Holland 11

Benefits of Telecommuting for Employees

Telecommuting employees benefit by not working fixed
hours in a traditional office. Gaining more flexible
work hours and more personal time for self and family
were the chief advantages of telecommuting for
employees cited in a recent survey ("Vast Majority").
Telecommuting saves workers enormous commuting time.
"Bay Area [California] motorists collectively spent
an average of 121,800 hours each day in traffic in
2003" (Nyberg). A veteran telecommuter, Alice Bredin
enthusiastically observes in her widely consulted
Virtual Office Survival Handbook:

> Working at least part time away from a
> traditional work site means you can com-
> plete your job efficiently and still have
> some time left over. It means you can
> drop your kids off a little later at day
> care and pick them up a little earlier.
> You can finally find time to stay in shape
> because you aren't giving a couple of hours
> a day to a commute. It means you can do
> the quality of work you know you are ca-
> pable of because you have interruption-free
> time. (3-4)

Because of flexible schedules and work environments,
Bell reported that telecommuters also experienced
"improved family relationships" and "increased civic
involvement" (10). McDavid maintains that telecommuters are to be commended for finding more time for

Brackets indicate words inserted into quotation

Provides lead-in to indented quotation

Lists page reference after quotation

Author's name not in parenthetical citation because mentioned in sentence

Holland 12

volunteer work and thereby contributing to area development (7).

   An additional advantage of telecommuting is that it saves employees money. Not having to travel back and forth to work each day, five days a week, significantly reduces transportation costs. On the average, an employee travels at least twenty miles a day to work, according to Lewis and Zhang (42). Taking into account expenses for gasoline, parking, and upkeep of a vehicle (or public transportation fees), a telecommuter can save $8,000 or $10,000 a year. Other savings result from reduced costs for food (the telecommuter will eat out less often), office clothes, and dry cleaning. Any expenses incurred by telecommuting are small in comparison to the savings a worker receives. As Myra Perez-Hoya maintains, telecommuters should have minimal overhead in establishing a home office, most often set up in a spare bedroom, since employers frequently pay for additional equipment ("Workers" 106). Moreover, specially developed software such as Citrix System's GoToMyPC or Sprint Business helps telecommuters work efficiently and economically.

   As an employee, the telecommuter reaps rewards. Flexible schedules allow telecommuters to produce at the time most desirable for them. By starting the workday earlier or later than at a traditional office, telecommuters work when their energy levels are the highest, even if that is in the middle of the night. Being at home also lets telecommuters take longer, and perhaps more frequent, breaks without worrying

Holland 13

that "they will have to stay at the office until midnight" to finish the job (Perez-Hoya, "Workers" 103). Bell observes that many telecommuters feel "less affected by a stressful deadline when they can work at home as opposed to a hectic central office" (9).

Another benefit of telecommuting is expansion of the job market to individuals who might otherwise not be able to compete. According to North Carolina's e-NC Authority, "Telecommuting can enable citizens to enjoy a rural lifestyle while working for large corporations and garnering higher salaries as a result." To cite another example, when a paper mill closed in rural New Hampshire, unemployed workers became telecommuters for an international company that sold most of its products over the telephone and the Internet (Lewis, "Business" 46).

Telecommuting also offers employment opportunities to people living with disabilities. Individuals with particular sight and speech needs can, with proper equipment, function superbly as telecommuters. In addition to providing job opportunities for these workers, telecommuting allows individuals recovering from injuries and/or illnesses to return to work more quickly because they can perform their duties at off-site locations. Telecommuting thus keeps employees on the job who might otherwise have to retire on disability (U.S. Office of Personnel Management, "What Is Telework?"). Other types of workers benefit, too. The Best Western Motel chain has successfully hired women incarcerated in a correctional facility as reservation

Carefully inserts quotation into sentence

Transition to related topic

Links two examples

Author's name, title, and page number necessary here

Uses nonstereotypical language to describe another group of telecommuters

takers, offering them job training and the possibility
of rehabilitation (Steve 38).

Although telecommuting is highly productive,
it has some drawbacks. Technical outages or other
glitches are stress-intensive. As Ivor Patel rightly
announces, technology is the lifeline of any company.
Vint fears it can encourage people to overwork when
they are no longer locked into the 9-to-5 routine.
More commonplace, however, is the sense of isolation
that some telecommuters express (Bell 10; Reynolds 7).
As Vint graphically notes, she sometimes "feels
marooned on an island." Yet many of these potential
disadvantages can be reduced, if not eliminated, if
the telecommuter practices time management. Feeling
out of the loop by working alone at home is a normal
reaction telecommuters can overcome by seeing themselves as part of the global village (Sullivan).
Finally, since most firms require telecommuters to
make regular visits to the office, "separation
problems" can be minimized (Hendricks 57-58; Patel).

What the Future Holds for Telecommuting

The future looks even more promising for telecommuting. As Kathy Lynch, spokesperson for the Boston
College Center for Work and Family, points out,
"[Telecommuting is] being taken very seriously. . . .
[Companies] are becoming much more strategic about
telework. . . . It's not going away. It's becoming a
natural part of the way you operate business" (qtd. in

Objectively includes disadvantages

Both authors discuss this issue

Uses informa-tion from pub-lished article and personal interview

Ellipses signal omission of material not necessary

Holland 15

Carlson). At the Spring 2004 Festival of Telecommuting, Agnes Reynolds similarly foresaw many benefits:
"Imagine our big cities with no traffic jams, far less
pollution, happier and more productive workers freed
from undue stress, and a better-informed and more
cohesive society--all these are possible through more
telecommuting" (8). Unquestionably, telecommuting
has far-reaching implications for workers, especially
in terms of collaboration. Sullivan believes that
"telecommuting lends itself to a different model of
a team." She uses a comparison suggested by Edward
Demming: "The analogy to an orchestra . . . is appropriate . . . because each player needs to practice
and periodically be brought together to make sure the
music is in tune . . . " (qtd. in Sullivan).

Technology advances will make the telecommuter's
job even easier. As Carlson again points out, "At
IBM, about one-third of the work force" can operate
outside the office because "e-mail and other data
[can be sent] to any wireless handheld device." Those
numbers will surely increase because communication
technologies are advancing in large leaps. Instant
messaging software, for example, is playing a pivotal
role in telecommuting. "By providing the ability to
hold real-time conversations on the computer, instant
messaging can help employees at home and in the office
connect with one another in a way formal telephone
conversations or time-lapse e-mails do not" (U.S.
Office of Personnel Management, "What Is Telework?").
Improvements in remote computer access also will

*Helpful use
of direct
quotation*

*Indicates quo-
tation included
in a secondary
source that
must be cited*

*Brackets signal
words added
are not part of
original text*

*Quotation
provides illus-
tration and
proof*

Holland 16

encourage corporations to allow more employees to telecommute in the next few years. With thin-client technology, teleworkers can open their computing environment from any workstation--including their home computer or laptop--and be connected to the company network (Carlson; Patel).

Web source and interview—no pages necessary

Even greater expansion of the Internet in the next decade will unquestionably broaden telecommuting. Faster connections to the Net are crucial to the development of the home office because they will provide the same technological resources found at the company's central office. Telework America research in 2004 predicted an increase in telecommuting as access to broadband Internet connections multiplied (Pratt). These predictions were corroborated by an American Interactive Consumer Survey, which found that the number of telecommuters working at home with broadband increased dramatically from 2003 to 2004 ("Work at Home"). The survey found that broadband enhanced productivity, work flexibility, and employee interest in telecommuting.

Uses information based on primary research

Survey included in source

These and other developments in technology will ensure that telecommuters will be a truly global work force. Telecommuters will become better-informed citizens of the world economy by effortlessly gathering critical business data from around the globe ("Learning New Work" 10). They can respond to global markets more quickly and efficiently and thereby reach clients worldwide. Even small home-based businesses will be able to follow the products they sell from design

Cites another future benefit

Holland 17

stage to sales, exchanges, returns, and replacements via Internet outlets (Robertson; McGlinchey). Telecommuting allows an international company to bring its employees together from branches around the globe into a virtual office, communicating as efficiently as they would in a central office. Through increased global collaboration, telecommuters will have colleagues as "intelligent agents," as Perez-Hoya perceptively labels them ("Workers" 105), who collaborate, research, report, and summarize relevant business news along with interpretations over the Internet.

Many distinctions between worker and manager will dissolve because of telecommuting (Lewis and Zhang 80-81). "Rather than being a part of a company's work force fixed on the payroll, telecommuters can operate more like private contractors responding to the most lucrative proposals" (Perez-Hoya, "Telecommuting" 10). The role of managers, too, is undergoing major changes, according to two key experts (Hendricks 57-58; "Learning" 14). A manager may become more like a collaborator than a supervisor, working with teams of individuals functioning as complementary, not subordinate, units, thus eliminating the hierarchies of power. "The roles of telecommuter and manager will merge by the year 2010" (Vint).

Ultimately, the greatest incentive to promote telecommuting comes in light of the events surrounding 9/11 and other more recent acts of terrorism. Rep. Steny Hoyer (Maryland) claimed that government and business have "learned many lessons" from the

Two sources provide validation

Citation necessary here rather than at end of sentence because it refers only to "intelligent agents"

New reference requires citation even though Perez-Hoya is cited earlier in paper

Uses effective short quotation to end paragraph

Last paragraph of this section supplies most important consequence of using telecommuting

Holland 18

September 11 terrorist attacks, chief of which was
that "having telework capabilities in place can be a
major advantage in dealing with any event that dis-
places workers. The ability to continue government
functions and private commerce will make a world of
difference in being able to cope with whatever events
we may confront" (qtd. in Sibert). To combat terrorism, the government has insisted that all of its
agencies have strong telecommuting programs in place
by the end of 2005 (McGlinchey). Playing a vital role
in national defense, telecommuters have become the
new patriots in the ongoing war against terrorism.

Conclusion

*Conclusion
summarizes
key topics and
is proportional
to length of
the paper*

Telecommuting is transforming the world of work and
the way employers and employees think of their jobs.
Presenting a challenging, though profitable, alternative to the traditional office, telecommuting effectively conducts business in the Information Age. As
one telecommuting proponent put it, "Ever since the
introduction of the PC in the early 1980s, the business world has been moving toward the greater flexibility and productivity that telecommuting offers"
(Reynolds 3). Information companies are the biggest
employers. Telecommuters play a major role in this
vibrant economy and provide a powerful means of
defense at times of national crisis, as on 9/11 and
during Hurricane Katrina.

Holland 19

As we have seen, both employers and employees profit professionally and personally from telecommuting. Employers gain a more productive and trusting work force while saving money on office space and protecting the environment. Similarly, telecommuters can work at their most productive times during the day (or night) and still meet family and personal obligations at any remote site. Telecommuting also opens up the world job market to individuals who in the past may have been excluded, allowing employees worldwide to communicate successfully in a virtual office.

Telecommuters and their employers have traveled a long distance on their information superhighways since the 1990s. As technological advances make telecommuting even more attractive and feasible, current limitations or problems will unquestionably be resolved or fade away. The world of business is on the threshold of a vast new frontier because of telecommuting.

Signals author is wrapping up by reviewing

Uses effective connective phrase

Short, final paragraph makes persuasive point

Works Cited

Bell, Allison. "The Telecommuting Workforce: Advice
    for Managing Telecommuters." <u>HR Focus</u> 15 Jan. 2002:
    9-10. CD-ROM. UMI-ProQuest. Mar. 2005.

Bredin, Alice. <u>The Virtual Office Survival Handbook:</u>
    <u>What Telecommuters and Entrepreneurs Need to</u>
    <u>Succeed in Today's Nontraditional Workplace</u>.
    New York: Wiley, 1996.

Carlson, Leah. "Overcoming Telework Tech Challenges."
    <u>Benefit News.com</u> 1 June 2004. Employee Benefit News.
    25 Jan. 2005 <http://www.benefitnews.com/work/
    detail.cfm?id=6020>.

Hendricks, Mark. "Remote Control." <u>Entrepreneur</u>
    Feb. 2005: 56-59.

Korzeniowski, Paul. "Telecommuting--A Driving
    Concern." <u>Business Communications Review</u> 13.2
    (1999): 45-48.

"Learning New Work Technologies." <u>Business Planning</u>
    18.2 (2003): 8-15.

Lewis, Alicia. "The Business of Telecommuting." <u>Journal</u>
    <u>of Contemporary Business</u> 11 (2003): 39-51. 20 Feb.
    2005 <http://www.contempbus.jrn.com>.

Lewis, Alicia, and Tim P. Zhang. <u>Telecommuting</u>
    <u>Practices</u>. New York: Technology P, 2004.

McDavid, Marsalis. "Working at Home." <u>Detroit News</u>
    23 Jan. 2005: 4, 7-8.

Works Cited appears at top of page

Sources listed in alphabetical order by author's last name

Double spacing within and between entries

Unsigned magazine article

Holland 21

McGlinchey, David. "Union Praises Passage of Telework
    Language." <u>GovExec.com</u> 13 Dec. 2004. 27 Jan. 2005
    <http://www.govexec.com/dailyfed/1204/121304d1.htm>.

New York Telecommuting Advisory Council. "What Is
    Telecommuting?" <u>Telecommuting Today</u> 1 Apr. 2004.
    3 Apr. 2005 <http://www.sccsi.com/telecommute/
    ny/html>.

North Carolina e-NC Authority. "e-NC Economic Impact
    Statement." <u>North Carolina's e-NC Authority</u>
    Feb. 2003. 28 Jan. 2005 <http://www.e-nc.org/
    Press%20Kit/econImpact.shtml>.

Nyberg, Justin. "Bay Area Roads Are Less Traveled."
    <u>San Francisco Examiner</u> 7 Jan. 2005. 27 Jan. 2005
    <http://www.sfexaminer.com/article/index.cfm/i/
    010705n_traffic>.

Patel, Ivor. Personal interview. 26. Feb. 2005.

Perez-Hoya, Myra. "Telecommuting and Tomorrow's Work-
    ers." <u>Home Office Journal</u> 3 (2004): 7-10.

- - -. "Workers Become Telecommuters." <u>The Electronic</u>
    <u>Workplace</u> 21.10 (2003): 101-06.

Pratt, Joanne H. "Teleworking Comes of Age with Broad-
    band: A Telework America Research Report of the
    International Telework Association and Council."
    <u>International Telework Association & Council</u>
    Apr. 2003. 26 Jan. 2005 <http://www.telecommute
    .org/pdf/TWA2003_Executive_Summary.pdf>.

*Web source
lists posting
and access
dates*

*Corporate
authors*

*MLA inverts
date here*

*Two works by
same author;
name replaced
by dashes in
second entry*

*Second and
subsequent
lines indented
five spaces*

Holland 22

Reynolds, Agnes. "2004: The Festival of Telecommuting--
    The Most Effective Way of Doing Business." <u>Business</u>
    <u>Strategies Today</u> 19 (2004): 3-8. <u>InfoTrac</u>. CD-ROM.
    Information Access. Apr. 2005.

Robertson, Ken. "How Telework Is Changing the
    Traditional Corporate Office." <u>KLR Consulting</u>
    27 Jan. 2005. 10 Mar. 2005 <http://klr.com/
    article04.htm>.

Sibert, Karen. "Telework Offers Business Benefits."
    <u>PR Newswire</u> 17 Mar. 2002. 29 Mar. 2005 <http://
    web.lexis-nexis.com/universe/>.

Steve, Bob. "Telecommuting: Concepts and Resources."
    <u>Business Credit</u> 7.1 (2004): 36-40.

Sullivan, Sandra. "ITAC Telework Employers' FAQ."
    <u>International Telework Association & Council</u> 2004.
    1 Feb. 2005 <http://www.workingfromanywhere.org/
    resources/faq.htm>.

"Telecommuting Case Study: America West Vacations."
    <u>Valley Metro.org</u> 27 Jan. 2005. 10 Mar. 2005 <http://
    www.valleymetro.org/Rideshare3/9Telework/Resources/
    casestudies/TW%20America%20West%20Vacations.html>.

"Teleworkers Still on the Job over Holidays." <u>Inter-</u>
    <u>national Telework Association & Council</u> 18 Aug.
    2003. 26 Jan. 2005 <www.telecommute.org/news/
    pr081803.htm>.

U.S. Department of Labor. <u>Labor Statistics, 2005.</u>
    Washington, DC: GPO, 2006.

*Authored sec-
tion of website*

*Alphabetizes
by first word of
title when no
author is given*

Holland 23

U.S. Office of Personnel Management. "The Status of
     Telework in the Federal Government: Report to the
     Congress." May 2004. 27 Jan. 2005 <http://
     www.telework.gov/documents/tw_rpt04/rpt.pdf>.

- - -. "What Is Telework?: Telework: A Management Pri-
     ority. A Guide for Managers, Supervisors, and Tele-
     work Coordinators." Working for America Interagency
     Telework May 2003. 26 Jan. 2005 <http://
     www.telework.gov/documents/tw_man03/ch1.asp>.

"Vast Majority of Job Seekers Say Telecommuting Option
     Is Important, According to New TrueCareers Survey."
     TrueCareers.com 8 Nov. 2004. TrueCareers. 28 Jan.
     2005 <http://www.truecareers.com/corporate/pr/
     pr110804.shtml>.

Vint, LaKeshia. "Re: Telecommuting at Pacific Software
     Systems." E-mail to the author. 24 Jan. 2005.

"Work at Home Grows in Past Year." International
     Telework Association & Council 2 Sept. 2004.
     26 Jan. 2005 <http://www.telecommute.org/news/
     pr090204.htm>.

Government documents contain valuable statistics and definitions

Identifies source and purpose of e-mail

✓ Revision Checklist

☐ Gave full and proper credit to sources consulted and those used for the preparation of my work.

☐ Avoided all forms of plagiarism by supplying complete and accurate documentation of all sources quoted, paraphrased, or consulted for the paper or report.

☐ Recorded all direct quotations accurately; included page references where applicable.

☐ Paraphrased information correctly and acknowledged rightful sources.

☐ Double-checked spelling of authors' and publishers' names and accuracy of all pertinent publication information.

☐ Followed MLA, APA, or *Chicago Manual of Style* notes documentation method consistently in preparing Works Cited or Reference lists.

☐ Included all necessary in-text (parenthetical) references; cited each parenthetical reference fully and in correct alphabetical order in Works Cited or Reference lists.

☐ Indicated clearly which work I used when sources included more than one work by same author.

☐ Included only the works referred to in my paper in Works Cited or Reference lists.

☐ Cited all CD-ROM and online database material completely and consistently.

☐ Alphabetized Works Cited and Reference entries correctly.

☐ Documented all Internet sources properly, giving both posting and access dates.

☐ Made sure numbered references in the text exactly corresponded to citations in footnotes or endnotes advocated by *The Chicago Manual of Style* documentation method.

Online Study Center

Access the documenting sources Revision Checklist online at college .hmco.com/pic/ kolin8e

Online Study Center

Find additional documenting sources exercises at college.hmco .com/pic/kolin8e

Exercises

1. Ask a professor in your major what he or she regards as the most widely respected periodical in your field. Find a copy of the periodical and explain its method of documentation (providing examples). How does it differ from the MLA method?

2. Put the following pieces of bibliographic information in proper form according to the MLA method of documentation for Works Cited. Correct errors in formatting, punctuation, and so on.

   a. "American Takes on Travel Web Sites." http://www.forbes.com/business/ 2005/02/01/cx_ld_0201amr.html. Forbes.com. Lisa DiCarlo. Access Date: 4 August 2005. Post date: 1 February 2005.

   b. New York Times. "Sinking Dollar Dominates Davos Debate." Page C1. January 27, 2005. Mark Lander.

   c. Electronic News. Post date: January 27, 2005. Access date 6 March, 2005. Ann Steffora Mutschler. "Special Market Focus: Collaborative Design." http://www.reed-electronics.com/electronicnews/article/CA499446.html

d. Diane Domeyer. <u>Office Pro</u>. January/February 2005. "Admins' Paychecks Enjoy Small Boost." Pages 7-11.

e. "Remarks by Bill Gates." Post date: February 2, 2005. http://www.microsoft .com/billgates/speeches/2005/02-02EuropeGLF.asp. European Government Leaders Forum. Bill Gates. Access date: 20 December 2005.

f. "Savings Incentive Match Plans for Employees of Small Employers: A Small Business Retirement Savings Advantage." http://www.dol.gov/ebsa/ Publications/simple.html. U.S. Department of Labor. Access Date: 3 April 2005. Post Date: 2 February 2005.

g. <u>Inc.com</u>. Access Date: 7 June 2005. Post Date: 31 January 2005. "Manufacturers Go Online to Boost Business." http://www.inc.com/criticalnews/ articles/200501/manufacturers.html. Allen Roberts.

h. "Public Expenditure Accountability in Africa: Progress, Lessons, and Challenges." Pages 179-210. Bill Dorotinsky and Rob Floyd. <u>Building State Capacity in Africa: New Approaches, Emerging Lessons</u>. Published in 2004 by World Bank Publications, Washington D.C.

i. "Market Roll-Out and Retailer Adoption for New Brands." <u>Marketing Science</u>. Bart J. Bronnenberg and Carl F. Mela. Pages 500-518. Volume 23, Number 4. Fall 2004.

j. Volume 27, Number 10. "Regional Diversity and Economic Growth in China." <u>The World Economy</u>. Yuko Arayama and Katsuya Miyoshi. Pages 1583-1607. November 2, 2004.

k. "Portrait of an Entrepreneur." Pages 15-16. Amy Ellis. <u>Dimensions</u>. January/February 2005.

l. "Blind Investment." <u>HRMagazine</u>. Robert J. Grossman. Pages 40-47. January 2005.

m. <u>CA Magazine</u>. January/February 2005. "Private Industry Hazards." Pages 45-47. David B. Wende.

n. <u>Business Ethics Quarterly</u> 15 (1). 2005. "Transnational Corporate Responsibility: A Tri-Dimensional Approach to International CSR Research." Marne Arthaud-Day. Pages 1-22.

o. <u>The International Trade Journal</u>. "Exports and Economic Growth in Bangladesh." Winter 2004. Volume 18, Number 4. Mohammad A. Hossain and Neil Dias Karunaratne. Page 303-334.

p. February 2005. Volume 83, Number 2. <u>Harvard Business Review</u>. "Productive Friction: How Difficult Business Partnerships Can Accelerate Innovation." John Hagel III and John Seely Brown. Pages 82-91.

q. "Best Practices in Action." Joseph Dobrian. Pages 54-64. <u>The Meeting Professional</u>. January 2005.

r. "Steel Partners Make Offer for GenCorp Shares." Page C2. Julie Tamaki. November 12, 2004. <u>Los Angeles Times</u>.

s. Barbara Hagenbaugh. December 15, 2004. Page B1. <u>USA Today</u>. "Fed Boosts Short Term Rates ¼ Point."

t. EH.Net Encyclopedia. Santos, Joseph. http://eh.net/encyclopedia/?article= Santos.futures. "A History of Futures Trading in the United States". Edited by Robert Whaples. Post Date: August 10, 2004. Access Date: 18 February 2005.

u. Jonathan Krim. <u>Washington Post</u>. "Firms Seek Copyright Act Change." Pages E1 and E5. January 6, 2005.

v. "Should You Take This Tax Break?" <u>Business Week</u>. February 7, 2005. Anne Tergesen. 88-89.

3. Put the bibliographic references you listed in MLA format in Exercise 2 into APA format for a Reference list.

4. Convert the bibliographic information given for one article in the periodical you chose for Exercise 1 into the MLA parenthetical style.

5. The following passage contains mistakes in the MLA method of documentation. Find the mistakes and explain how to correct them.

More and more companies are allowing employees to "telecommute" (see Smith; Dawson; Brown; Gura and Keith; and Allen). One expert defines telecommuting as "home-based work" (13). Having terminals in their homes "allows employees to work at a variety of jobs" ("New Employment Opportunities"). It has been estimated that currently 900,000 employees work out of their homes (Pennington, p. 56). That number is sure to increase as computer-based businesses multiply in the late 1990s (Brown). In one of her recent articles on telecommuting, Holcomb (167) found that "in the last year alone 43 companies in the metropolitan Phoenix area made this option available to their employees."

Employees who telecommute cite a variety of benefits for such an arrangement (see in particular articles by Gura, Smith, and Kaplan). One employee of a mail order company whose opinion was quoted observed that "I can save about 15—17 hours a week in driving time" (from Allen). Working at home allows the telecommuting employee to work at his or her optimum times ("The Day Does Not Have to Start at 9:00 a.m."). Also, in articles by Kaplan and Keith the benefits of not having to leave home are emphasized: "A telecommuting parent does not have to worry about child care" (39). Telecommuting may "be here to stay" (quoted in a number of different website sources).

6. Submit your preliminary list of references (your tentative Works Cited page) for a research paper or long report to your instructor.

CHAPTER 10

Summarizing Material

A summary is a brief restatement of the main points of a book, report, website, article, laboratory test, meeting, or convention. A summary saves readers hours of time because they do not have to study the original work or attend a conference. A summary can reduce a report or an article by 85 to 95 percent (or even more) or capture the essential points of a three-day convention in a one-page memo. Moreover, a summary can tell readers whether they should even be concerned about the original; it may be irrelevant for their purposes. Finally, since only the most important points of a work are included in a summary, readers will know they have been given the crucial information they need.

Summaries can be found all around you. Television and radio stations regularly air two-minute broadcasts called "newsbreaks" to summarize in a few sentences the major stories covered in more detail on the evening news and include these summaries on their websites, as, for example, on CBSnews.com. Some newspapers simply offer a column entitled "News Summary" on the first or second page of an issue (in print or online) to condense major news stories. Facts On File News Services provide a helpful reference by summarizing current-events information in their *Facts On File Weekly World News Digest* (*http://www.facts.com*).

Summaries are widely used on Internet websites to encourage users to go further into the subject. A homepage is in essence a summary of the various links to which it is connected. Summaries are also a vital part of the search strategies on the Internet (see pp. 320–334). When search engines retrieve positive "hits," a short summary accompanies each citation to help users determine whether the material is relevant to their needs.

Online Study Center

To expand your understanding of summarizing material, take advantage of the ACE quizzes, sample documents, Web links, and exercises at college.hmco.com/pic/kolin8e

The Importance of Summaries in Business

Summaries are vital in the world of work. They get to the main points—the bottom line—right away for busy readers. New communication technologies such as text messaging and PDAs all require you to summarize information concisely and quickly.

Figure 10.1   A summary of a long report on child-care facilities.

HIGH MARKS FOR ON-SITE CARE

The best place to find high-quality child care may be your workplace, according to a new study by Burud & Associates, a California-based work/life benefits consulting firm. The study of 205 work-site child-care programs found that such centers are eight times more likely than other facilities to meet the high standards set by the National Association for the Education of Young Children (NAEYC).

Forty-one percent of work-site centers open at least two years are NAEYC-accredited—compared to only 5 percent of all child-care centers. Other key findings include:

• Ninety-two percent of work-site centers offer infant care.
• Workplace centers provide "substantially better" employee benefits—which help the centers recruit and retain high-quality caregivers.
• One in four centers is open past seven p.m. and one in seven is open before six a.m. and/or offers weekend care.

Source: First appeared in *Working Mother,* May 1999. Reprinted by permission.

On the job, writing summaries for employers, co-workers, and customers is a regular and important responsibility. Each profession has its own special needs for summaries. Chapter 15 discusses a variety of reports—progress, sales, periodic, trip, test, and incident—whose effectiveness depends on a faithful summary of events. You may be asked to summarize a business trip that lasted a week into one or two pages for your company or agency. You may have to condense a proposal to fit a one-page format for an organization. A busy manager may ask you to read and condense a ninety-page report so she will have a knowledgeable overview of its contents. You may be asked to write a **news release**—another type of summary vital for your organization's image, discussed on pages 431–438—for your employer's website.

Acute-care nurses must write one- or two-page discharge summaries for patients who are being referred to other agencies (home health, nursing home, rehabilitation center). The nurses must read a patient's record carefully and summarize what has happened to the patient since admission to the hospital—surgeries, treatments, diagnoses, and prognoses—and indicate necessary follow-up treatments (medications, office visits, outpatient care, MRIs).

Figure 10.1 is a summary of a long report evaluating child-care facilities. Note how it concisely identifies the main purpose and conclusions of this report.

Contents of a Summary

The chief problem in writing a summary is deciding what to include and what to omit. As we have just seen, a summary is a streamlined review of *only* the most significant points. You will not save your readers time if you simply rephrase large sections of the original and call the new version a summary. That will simply supply readers with another report, not a summary.

Make your summary lean and useful by briefly telling readers the main points: purpose, scope, conclusions, and recommendations. A summary should concisely answer the readers' two most important questions:

1. What findings does the report or meeting offer?
2. How do those findings apply to my business, research, or job?

Note how the summary in Figure 10.1 successfully answered those two questions by indicating to working mothers where the best child care is likely to be found in the workplace and why.

How long should a summary be? While it is hard to set down precise limits about length, effective summaries are generally 5 to 10 percent, or less, of the length of the original. The complexity of the material being summarized and your audience's exact needs can help you to determine an appropriate length. To help you know what is most important for your summary, the following suggestions will guide you on what to include and what to omit.

What to Include in a Summary

  1. Purpose. A summary should indicate why the article or report was written or why a convention or meeting was held. (Often a report is written or a meeting is called to solve a problem or to explore new areas of interest.) Your summary should give the readers a brief introduction (even one sentence will do) indicating the main purpose of the report or conference.

  2. Essential specifics. Include only the names, costs, titles, places, or dates essential to understanding the original.

  3. Conclusions or results. Emphasize what the final vote was, the result of the tests, or the proposed solution to the problem.

  4. Recommendations or implications. Readers will be especially interested in important recommendations—what they are, when they can be carried out, and why they are necessary, or why a plan does not work.

What to Omit from a Summary

  1. Opinion. Avoid injecting opinions—your own, the author's, or a speaker's. You distract readers from grasping main points by saying that the report was too long or missed the main point, that a salesperson from Detroit monopolized the meetings, or that the author digressed to blame the Land Commission for failing to act properly. A later section of this chapter will deal with evaluative summaries.

2. New data.   Stick to the original article, report, book, or meeting. Avoid introducing comparisons with other works or conferences; readers will expect a digest of only the material being summarized.

3. Irrelevant specifics.   Do not include any biographical details about the author of an article that might be included in a section entitled "Notes on Contributors." This information plays no role in the reader's understanding of your summary.

4. Examples.   Illustrations, explanations, and descriptions are unnecessary in a summary. Readers will want to know outcomes, results, and recommendations, not the illustrative details supporting or elaborating on those results.

5. Background.   Material in introductions to articles, reports, and conferences can usually be excluded from a summary. Such "lead-ins" prepare the reader for a discussion of the subject by presenting background information, not the big picture readers expect to see.

6. Jargon.   Technical definitions or jargon in the original may confuse rather than clarify the essential information for the general reader.

7. Reference data.   Exclude information found in footnotes, bibliographies, appendixes, tables, or graphs.

Tech Note

Using Software to Summarize Existing Documents

Your word processing software can help you prepare your summary. Download the material (article, report, technical paper) you need to summarize and then, as you read through it the first time on your screen, cut nonessential material. The first time through, it is easier to cut what you don't want than it is to select exactly what you do want. Using this method of editing, you can delete single sentences or several paragraphs at a time. Also, highlight key points as you read through the material you have downloaded. Highlighting during the first pass can guide you on your second reading as you attempt to include only relevant material for your summary.

Preparing a Summary

To write an effective summary, you need to proceed through a series of steps. Basically, you will have to read the material carefully, making sure that you understand it thoroughly, to identify the major points, and, finally, to put the essence of the material into your own words. Follow these steps to prepare a concise, useful summary:

1. Read the material once in its entirety to get an overall impression of what it is about.   Become familiar with large issues, such as the purpose and organization of the work and the audience for whom it was written. Look at visual cues—headings, subheadings, words in italic or boldface type, sidebars—that will help you to classify main ideas and summarize the work. Also see whether the author has included any mini-summaries in the article or report or whether there is a concluding summary.

2. Reread the material.   Read it a second time or more often if necessary. To locate all and only the main points, underline them. (If the work is a book or in a journal that belongs to your library, work with a photocopy so you can underline.) To spot the main points, pay attention to the key transitional words, which often fall into predictable categories.

- Words that enumerate: *first, second, third, initially, subsequently, finally, next, another*
- Words that express causation: *accordingly, as a result, because, consequently, subsequently, therefore, thus*
- Words that express contrasts and comparisons: *although, by the same token, despite, different from, furthermore, however, in contrast, in comparison, in addition, less than, likewise, more than, more readily, not only . . . but also, on the other hand, the same is true for, similar, unlike*
- Words that signal essentials: *basically, best, central, crucial, foremost, fundamental, indispensable, in general, important, leading, major, obviously, principal, significant*

Pay special attention to the first and last sentences of each paragraph. Often the first sentence of a paragraph contains the topic sentence, and the last sentence summarizes the paragraph or provides a transition to the next paragraph.

Also be alert for words signaling information you do *not* want to include in your summary, such as the following:

- Words announcing opinion or inconclusive findings: *from my personal experience, I feel, I admit, in my opinion, might possibly show, perhaps, personally, may sometimes result in, has little idea about, questionable, presumably, subject to change, open to interpretation*
- Words pointing out examples or explanations: *as noted in, as shown by, circumstances include, explained by, for example, for instance, illustrated by, in terms of, learned through, represented by, such as, specifically in, stated in*

3. Collect your underlined material or notes and organize the information into a draft summary.   At this stage do not be concerned about how your sentences read. Use the language of the original, together with any necessary connective words or phrases of your own. Key the draft into your computer. *Expect to have more material here than will appear in the final version.* Do not worry; you are engaged in a process of selection and exclusion. Your purpose at this stage is to extract the principal ideas from the examples, explanations, and opinions surrounding them.

4. Read through and revise your draft(s) and delete whatever information you can.   As you revise, see how many of your underlined points can be condensed, combined, or eliminated. You may find that you have repeated a point. Check your draft against the original for accuracy and importance. Be sure to be faithful to the original by preserving its emphases and sequence.

5. Now put the revised version into your own words.   Again, make sure that your reworded summary has eliminated nonessential words. Connect your sentences with words that show relationships between ideas in the original (*also, although, because, consequently, however, nevertheless, since*). Compare this version of your summary with the original material to double-check your facts.

6. Do not include remarks that repeatedly call attention to the fact that you are writing a summary.   You may want to indicate initially that you are providing a summary, but avoid such remarks as "The author of this article states that water pollution is a major problem in Baytown"; "On page 13 of the article three examples, not discussed here, are found."

7. Edit your summary to make sure it is clear and concise.   Check to be certain it is coherent, too. Tell the reader how one point flows into another. Also proofread your summary carefully.

8. Identify the source you have just summarized.   Include pertinent bibliographic information in the title of your summary or in a footnote or an endnote. That gives proper credit to the original source and informs your readers where they can find the complete text if they want more details.

Figure 10.2, a 2,500-word article entitled "Virtual Reality: The Future of Law Enforcement Training," appeared in the *FBI Law Enforcement Bulletin* and hence would be of primary interest to individuals in law enforcement administration. Assume you are asked to write a summary of the FBI article for your boss, a police chief in a medium-sized city who might be interested in incorporating virtual reality segments into the police academy training program.

By following the steps outlined above, you would first read the article carefully two or three times, underscoring or highlighting the most important points, signaled by key words. Note what has been underscored in the article. Also study the comments in the margins to see why certain information is to be included or excluded from the summary.

After you have identified the main points, extract them from the article and, still using the language of the article, join them into a coherent working draft sum-

An original article with important points underscored for use in a summary.   **Figure 10.2**

Virtual Reality:
The Future of Law Enforcement Training

By
Jeffrey S. Hormann

A late night police pursuit of a suspected drunk driver winds through abandoned city streets. The short vehicle chase ends in a warehouse district where the suspect abandons his vehicle and continues his flight on foot. Before backup arrives, the rookie patrol officer exits his vehicle and gives chase. A quick run along a loading dock ends at the open door to an apparently unoccupied building. The suspect stops, brandishes a revolver, and fires in the direction of the pursuing officer before disappearing into the building. The officer, shaken but uninjured, radios in his location and follows the suspect into the building.

> *Delete scenario— example of background; an opener*

Did the officer make a good decision? Probably not by most departments' standards. Whether the officer's decision proves right or wrong, the training gained from this experience is immeasurable, that is, provided the officer lives through it. Fortunately for this officer, the scenario occurred in a realistic, high-tech world called virtual reality, where training can have a real-life impact without the accompanying risk.

> *Include important observation*

Traditional Training Limitations

Experience may be the best teacher, but in real life, police officers may not get a chance to learn from their mistakes. To survive, they must receive training that prepares them for most situations they might encounter on the street. However, because many training programs emphasize repetition to produce desired behaviors, they may not achieve the intended results, especially after students leave the training environment. Thus, the more realistic the training, the greater the lessons learned.

> *Major distinction*

Additionally, even some in law enforcement may fall prey to the effects of what has come to be termed "The MTV Generation."[1] As products of this generation, today's young officers purportedly have short attention spans requiring new, non-traditional training methods. The key to teaching this new breed is to provide fast-paced, attention-getting instruction that is clear, concise, and relevant.[2]

> *Delete explanation and example*
>
> *Include significant qualification*

Training with Virtual Reality

Virtual reality can provide the type of training that today's law enforcement officers need. By completely immersing the senses in a computer-generated environment, the artificial world becomes reality to users and greatly enhances their training experiences.

> *Emphasize author's main point*

Although considerable research and development have been conducted in this field, only a limited amount has applied directly to law enforcement. The apparent reason simply is that, for the most part, law enforcement has not asked for it.

> *Important reason for its neglect by law enforcement*

Because virtual reality technology is relatively new, most law enforcement administrators know little about it. They know even less about what it can do for

> *Restatement of main point above*

Continued

Figure 10.2   (Continued)

their agencies. By <u>understanding what virtual reality is, how it works</u>, and <u>how</u> it <u>can benefit them</u>, law enforcement administrators can become significantly involved in the development of this important new technology.

What Is Virtual Reality?

*Include
definition*

<u>Simply stated, virtual reality</u> is <u>high-tech illusion</u>. It is a computer-generated, three-dimensional environment that engulfs the senses of sight, sound, and touch. Once entered, it becomes reality to the user.

*Important
explanation*

Within this virtual world, users travel among, and interact with, objects that are wholly the products of a computer or representations of other participants in the same environment. Thus, the limits of this virtual environment depend on the sophistication and capabilities of the computer and the software that drives the system.

How Does Virtual Reality Work?

*Significant
phrase*

*Delete specific
pieces of
equipment*

Based on data entered by programmers, computers create virtual environments by generating <u>three-dimensional images</u>. Users usually view these images through a head-mounted device, which, for instance, can be a helmet, goggles, or other apparatus that restricts their vision to two small video monitors, one in front of each eye. Each monitor displays a slightly different view of the environment, which gives users a sense of depth.

Delete example

<u>Another device</u>, called a position tracker, monitors users' physical positions and provides input to the computer. This information instructs the computer to change the environment based upon users' actions. <u>For example</u>, when users look over their shoulders, they see what lies behind them.

<u>Because</u> virtual reality users remain stationary, they use a <u>joy stick</u> or trackball to move through the virtual environment. Users <u>also</u> may wear a special glove or use other devices to manipulate objects within the virtual environment. <u>Similarly</u>, they can employ virtual weapons to confront virtual aggressors.

*Delete further
examples*

*Major
conclusion*

To enhance the sense of reality, some researchers are experimenting with tactile feedback devices (TFDs). TFDs transmit pressure, force, or vibration, providing users with a simulated sense of touch.[3] <u>For example</u>, a user might want to open a door or move an object, which in reality, would require the sense of touch. A TFD would simulate this sensation. At present, <u>however</u>, it is important to remember that these devices are <u>crude</u> and somewhat <u>cumbersome to use</u>.

Uses for Virtual Reality

In <u>today's competitive business environment</u>, organizations continuously strive to accomplish tasks faster, better, and inexpensively. This especially holds true in training.

*Major value to
audience of
administrators*

Virtual reality is <u>emerging rapidly</u> as a <u>potentially unlimited</u> method for providing <u>realistic</u>, <u>safe</u>, and <u>cost-effective training</u>. <u>For example</u>, a firefighter can battle the flames of a virtual burning building. A police officer can struggle with virtual shoot/don't shoot dilemmas.[4]

*Emphasize sig-
nificant advan-
tages in training*

Within a virtual environment, <u>students</u> can <u>make decisions</u> and act upon them <u>without risk</u> to themselves or others. By the same token, <u>instructors</u> can critique

Continued

students' actions, enabling students to review and learn from their mistakes. This ability gives virtual reality a great <u>advantage over most conventional training methods</u>.

The Department of Defense <u>(DOD) leads public and private industry</u> in <u>developing virtual reality training</u>. <u>Since</u> the early 1980s, DOD has actively researched, developed, and implemented virtual reality to <u>train members</u> of the <u>armed forces</u> to fight effectively in combat.

<u>DOD's current approach</u> to virtual reality training <u>emphasizes team tactics</u>. Groups of military personnel from around the world engage in combat safely on a virtual battlefield. Combatants never come together physically; <u>rather</u>, simulators located at various sites throughout the world transmit data to a central location, where the virtual battle is controlled. Basically, it costs less to move information than people. Consequently this form of training has proven quite cost-effective.

An <u>additional benefit</u> to this <u>type of training</u> is that <u>battles</u> can be <u>fought under varying conditions</u>.

Virtual battlefields <u>re-create real-world locations</u> with <u>interchangeable characteristics</u>. To explore "what if" scenarios, participants can modify enemy capabilities, terrain, weather, and weapon systems.

Virtual reality <u>also can re-create actual battles</u>. Based on information from participants, the Institute for Defense Analyses re-created the 2nd Armored Cavalry Regiment Offensive conducted in Iraq during Operation Desert Storm. The success of the virtual re-creation became apparent when, upon viewing the simulations, soldiers who had fought in the actual battle reported the extreme accuracy of the event's depiction and the feeling of reliving the battle.[5] <u>Clearly, virtual reality holds great potential</u> for accurate review and analysis of <u>real-world situations</u>, which would be <u>difficult to accomplish</u> by <u>any other method</u>.

Preliminary studies, for instance, show that military units perform better following virtual reality training.[6] <u>Even though</u> virtual environments are only simulations, the complete immersion of the senses literally overwhelms users, totally engrossing them in the action. <u>This realism</u> presumably plays a <u>major role</u> in the <u>program's success</u> and <u>likely</u> will prove positive in future endeavors. <u>In fact</u>, due to its success in training multiple participants in group combat situations, DOD plans to train infantry personnel individually with virtual reality fighting skill simulators.[7]

Law Enforcement Training

While virtual reality has proven its value as a training and planning tool for the military, <u>applications for this technology reach far beyond DOD</u>. In varying but key ways, many military uses can <u>transfer to law enforcement</u>, including training in firearms, stealth tactics, and assault skills.

Unfortunately, few organizations have dedicated resources to developing virtual reality for law enforcement. <u>According</u> to a recently published resource guide, more than <u>100 companies</u> currently are <u>developing and/or selling virtual reality hardware or software</u>. However, <u>none</u> of these firms <u>mentioned law enforcement uses</u>.[8]

<u>Further</u>, a review of relevant literature revealed numerous articles on virtual reality technology, but only a few addressed law enforcement applications. <u>Yet</u>, vir-

Continued

Use only main points relevant to target audience of administrators

Note main military advantage

Delete examples

Major conclusion signaled by key word "clearly"

Omit example

Key word "major" signals relevant idea for audience

Omit military application

Key point

Significant parallel points

Delete statistics

Subordinate idea

Figure 10.2   (Continued)

Restatement of major point

tual reality <u>clearly offers law enforcement benefits</u> in a number of areas, including pursuit driving, firearms training, high-risk incident management, incident re-creation, and crime scene processing.

Pursuit Driving

Include application but omit example

<u>Pursuit driving</u> represents one area in which <u>virtual reality application</u> has become <u>reality for law enforcement</u>. Law enforcement personnel identified a need and provided input to a well-known private corporation that developed a driving simulator equipped with realistic controls.

Delete specific mechanism and explanation of operation of screen mechanism

The simulator provides users with realistic steering wheel feedback, road feel, and other vehicle motions. The screen possesses a 225-degree field of view standard, with 360-degree coverage optional. <u>As noted in demonstrations,</u> simulations can involve one or more drivers, and environments can alternate between city streets, rural back roads, and oval tracks. The vehicle itself can change from a police car to a truck, ambulance, or a number of others.

Note cost efficiency again

Virtual reality driving simulators provide police departments invaluable training at a <u>fraction of the long-term cost of using actual vehicles</u>. In fact, the simulator is being used by a number of police departments around the country.

Include major advantage but exclude specific example

During the past year, for example, the Los Angeles County Sheriff's Office Emergency Vehicle Operations Center (EVOC) has used a four-station version of the driving simulator to train its officers. The simulators help students develop judgment and decision-making skills, while providing an environment free from risk of injury to students or damage to vehicles. Still, as the EVOC supervisor cautions, <u>virtual reality training</u> should <u>complement, not replace,</u> actual behind-the-wheel instruction.[9]

Note major distinction for training purpose

Firearms Training

New subtopic; include advantage but delete examples

In another way, virtual reality could <u>greatly enhance</u> shoot/don't shoot <u>training simulators</u> currently in use, such as the Firearms Training System, a primarily two-dimensional approach that possesses limited interactive capabilities. A <u>virtual reality system</u> would <u>allow officers</u> to enter any <u>three-dimensional environment</u> alone or as a member of a team and confront computer-generated aggressors or other virtual reality users.

Include significant points on advantages

Evaluators could specifically observe the <u>training from any perspective</u>, including that of the officers, or the criminal. The <u>training scenarios</u> could involve actual building floor plans or local city streets, and criteria <u>such as</u> weather, number of participants, or types of weapons could be altered easily.

High-Risk Incident Management

Next three reasons to use virtual reality signaled by key words in addition, also, and likewise

<u>In addition</u> to weapons training, virtual reality <u>could prove invaluable for SWAT team members</u> before <u>high-risk tactical assaults</u>. Floor plans and other known facts about a structure or area could be entered into a computer to create a virtual environment for commanders and team members to analyze prior to action.

Incident Re-creation

Law enforcement agencies could <u>also</u> <u>collect data</u> from victims, witnesses, suspects, and crime scenes <u>to re-create traffic accidents</u>, shootings, and other crimes.

Continued

The virtual environment created from the data could be used to refresh the memories of victims and witnesses, to solve crimes, and ultimately, to prosecute offenders.

Crime Scene Processing

Virtual reality crime scenes could <u>likewise</u> be used to <u>train both detectives and patrol officers</u>. First, students could search the site and retrieve and analyze evidence <u>without ever leaving the station</u>. Then, actual crime scenes could be re-created to add realism to training or to evaluate prior police actions.

Delete examples

Is Virtual Reality Virtually Perfect?

<u>Though</u> virtual reality may appear to be the <u>ideal law enforcement tool</u>, as with any new technology, <u>some drawbacks exist</u>. <u>Currently</u>, areas of concern range from cumbersome equipment to negative physical and psychological effects experienced by some users. Fortunately, <u>however</u>, the <u>field is evolving and improving constantly</u>, and as <u>virtual reality gains widespread use</u>, most <u>major concerns should be dispelled</u>.

Crucial qualification and justification for using virtual reality in law enforcement training

Physical Limitations and Effects

<u>Because</u> computers currently are <u>not fast enough</u> to process large amounts of graphic information in real time, <u>some observers</u> describe virtual environments as "slow-moving."[10] The human eye can process images at a much faster rate than a computer can generate them. In a <u>virtual environment</u>, frames are displayed at a rate of about 7 per second, an extremely slow speed when compared to television, which generates 60 frames per second.[11] Users find the resulting choppy or slow graphics less than appealing.

Delete examples of limitations/effects

Adapted from: *FBI Law Enforcement Bulletin* 64, no. 7: 7–12.

---

mary, as in Figure 10.3 (pp. 420–421). Then shorten and rewrite the working draft in your own words to produce the compact final version of your summary, as shown in Figure 10.4. Only 161 words long, the final summary is 12 percent of the length of the original article and records only major conclusions relevant to the audience for the article.

To further understand the effectiveness of the summary in Figure 10.4 (p. 422), review the wordy and misleading summary of the same article in Figure 10.5 (p. 423). The latter summary not only is too long but also dwells on minor details at the expense of major points. It includes unnecessary examples, statistics, and names; it even adds new information while ignoring crucial points about the applications of virtual reality to law enforcement officials. But even more serious, the summary in Figure 10.5 distorts the meaning and the intention of the original article. The reader concludes that the article says virtual reality is not very valuable for law enforcement administrators and officers—just the opposite of the point the article makes. You can avoid such mistakes by de-emphasizing minor points, by making sure that all parts of your summary agree with the original, and by not letting your own opinions distort the message of the original article.

Figure 10.3   A working draft summary of the "Virtual Reality" article in Figure 10.2.

Law enforcement officers put their lives on the line every day, yet their training does not fully allow them to anticipate what they will find on the streets. Virtual reality will give them realistic, high-tech benefits of encountering criminals without any risks. Traditional training methods, which work through repetition, cannot equal the advantages of virtual reality when it comes to teaching officers the lessons they must learn to survive in the field. This new breed of officers is demanding the attention-getting, highly realistic training that virtual reality affords them. Virtual reality translates the artificial world of the computer into the real world. Yet even though much research has been done on virtual reality, it is new to law enforcement officials. Moreover, manufacturers have not marketed their technology to them. It is essential that these administrators know how virtual reality works and what it can do for them. Virtual reality has been defined as high-tech illusion through the computer user's perceived interaction with the real world. Working through sophisticated software, virtual reality gives users a three-dimensional (hearing, feeling, and seeing) view of the things and people around them. Virtual reality requires specific equipment including goggles/headsets, a tracker, a trackball, and special gloves. But these devices do have problems; at present, they are crude and can be cumbersome. Even so, virtual reality provides cost-effective and life-saving benefits for law enforcement administrators. Thanks to this technology, students will be able to make quicker and better decisions in the field. Virtual reality has already been tried by the Department of Defense; the armed forces have used it to re-create battlefield conditions, helping the troops better understand the enemy and its position. Yet virtual reality holds great appeal for other real-world applications, especially law enforcement. Unfortunately, the 100 companies that manufacture virtual reality equipment have neglected these law enforcement applications. Yet virtual reality easily accommodates law enforcement instruction. Driving simulators help officers prepare for high-speed chases. In Los Angeles

Continued

County, such simulators complement more traditional training. Virtual reality can help officers in a variety of training missions—firearms, high-risk incidents, re-creating crimes, understanding the crime scene. Using virtual reality, officers never have to leave the station. Admittedly, virtual reality has drawbacks, but as this new technology improves, users should face fewer problems.

Executive Summaries

An executive summary, found at the beginning of a formal proposal (Chapter 14) or a long report (Chapter 16), is usually one or two pages (four to six concise paragraphs) and condenses the most important points from the proposal or report for a busy manager—the executive. This boss wants the big picture, not all the technical details. It is written to help the reader reach a major decision based on the report or proposal. Figure 10.6 (p. 424) is an executive summary of a report on software for a safety training program. Managers use executive summaries so they will *not* have to wade through entire reports. An effective executive summary is like a report itself—self-contained and able to stand on its own.

What Managers Want to See in an Executive Summary

Executive readers are most concerned with managerial and organizational issues—the areas over which they have supervisory control. These readers will look for information on costs, profits, resources, personnel, timetables, and feasibility. Your summary must supply key information on the executive's **four E's—evaluation, economy, efficiency**, and **expediency**. Executive readers will expect you to reduce large, complex subjects into easy-to-read, easy-to-understand information that they can act on confidently.

Organization of an Executive Summary

An executive summary must be faithful to the report while giving the readers what they need. First read the report carefully, plan what you want to include, then draft and revise using valuable connective words (p. 413). Clearly, you cannot write an executive summary of your report until after you have written the report itself.

Basically, follow this organizational plan when you write an executive summary:

1. **Begin with the purpose and the scope of the report,** for example, to study new marketing strategies, to replace obsolete software, to relocate a branch store.
2. **Relate your purpose to a key problem.** Identify the source (history) and seriousness of the problem.

Figure 10.4   A final, effective summary of the article in Figure 10.2.

> Virtual reality offers benefits for law enforcement training that traditional methods cannot provide. This computer-generated technology simulates and re-creates real-life crime scenes without placing officers at risk. Thanks to virtual reality's three-dimensional world of sight, sound, and touch, officers enter the criminals' world to gain invaluable experience interacting with them. Because virtual reality has not been marketed for law enforcement use, administrators may not know about it. Yet it provides a cost-effective, realistic way to enhance training programs. The applications of virtual reality far exceed its military use of simulating battlefield conditions. Virtual reality allows administrators to give trainees hands-on experience in pursuit driving, firearms training, SWAT team assaults, incident re-creation, and crime location processing. Officers can investigate a crime without ever leaving the station. Although virtual reality is an emerging technology with limitations, it is quickly improving and rapidly expanding. Administrators need to incorporate it into their curriculum to give officers field-translatable experiences.

3. **Identify in nontechnical language the criteria used to solve the problem.** Be careful not to include too much information or too many details.
4. **Condense the findings of your report.** Relate what tests or surveys revealed.
5. **Stress conclusions and possible solutions.**
6. **Provide recommendations,** for example, buy, sell, hire more personnel, relocate, or choose among alternative solutions.

The order of information in an executive summary does not have to follow the exact order of the report itself. In fact, some executive summaries start with recommendations. Find out your boss's preference.

Evaluative Summaries

To write an evaluative summary, also called a **critique,** follow all the guidelines on pages 411–412. As with executive summaries, you will be expected to provide a commentary on the material, that is, give your opinion.

A misleading summary of the article in Figure 10.2.   Figure 10.5

A rookie police officer makes many mistakes in pursuing subjects. Training can cover many realistic situations, but young officers in the MTV Generation have short attention spans. Given the research so far on virtual reality, it holds little promise for law enforcement use. Virtual reality has too many limitations, but it works interestingly through gloves, helmets, and goggles, and with a position tracker users can see over their shoulders. It even has a joy stick (like those in an amusement park) and a crude device—a TFD—that simulates touch (nice to have in a horror movie). Instructors can gain much from virtual reality because they can better criticize their trainees. In the early 1980s, the DOD used virtual reality to duplicate battlefield conditions. The 2nd Armored Cavalry Regiment Offensive won the Iraqi War because of virtual reality. But companies manufacturing virtual reality technology are not interested in law enforcement applications, another indication of its limitations. The Los Angeles Sheriff's EVOC used a driving simulator—offering a 225-degree field of view but it can be ordered with a 360-degree field—but expressed their caution about it. There have been limited interactions in the use of virtual reality for firearms training, though floor plans might have helped SWAT teams. Witnesses may need to refresh their memories with virtual reality. Again drawbacks exist. Computers are not as fast as the human eye in processing information.

Nonessential introductory material

Distorts article, which advocates the benefits of virtual reality for law enforcement

Dwells on specific virtual reality equipment at the expense of the main advantages

Overlooks the significance of virtual reality for trainees

Reverses chronology of events; misrepresents the role of virtual reality

How relevant to law enforcement? Delete unit's name

Again, distorts intention of article

Delete specifications

One-sided; omits success of simulation

Focuses on limits rather than usefulness

Fails to attribute these benefits to virtual reality

Does not subordinate flaws

Figure 10.6   An executive summary.

A Report on Providing Better Training at Techtron Sites

Starts with purpose of report

Management commissioned this report to investigate ways to prepare for the OSHA audits scheduled between February and June 2006, at our seven regional Techtron plants. Most directly, this report focuses on our ability to complete Phase One of ISO 14001 certification.

Identifies problem and why it is important

Currently, the Techtron safety training programs are inadequate; they are neither comprehensive nor up-to-date. We lack necessary software to instruct employees about the EPA and OSHA regulations and requirements that apply to hazardous materials or procedures used in our company. Consequently, safety violations have occurred with lockouts, confined spaces, fall protection, and the "Right to Know Law" concerning labeling of chemicals.

Explains the solution tested

Exploring better ways to conduct our training sessions, we purchased a copy of the software program **EPA/OSHA Trainer**, regarded as the best on the market (available from EDI @ $600 per copy). The **Trainer** offers effective guidelines on developing safety meetings and giving demonstrations. It also includes instructions, written in clear, nontechnical language, on how to identify, collect, and document hazardous materials. Additionally, the **Trainer** supplies the full text of EPA/OSHA regulations, with updates issued quarterly.

Verifies effectiveness of solution

To test the effectiveness of the **Trainer** software, we scheduled an internal audit at our Hendersonville site last month. After progressing through the **Trainer** module, a core group of employees interviewed by management successfully completed all required regulatory training. Subsequently, employees who had undergone such training were able to instruct and monitor the performance of other employees in the program.

Ends by stressing action to be taken

To ensure the safety of our employees and to compete in a global marketplace, Techtron must pass the OSHA 14001 certification. Purchasing seven additional copies of the **EPA/OSHA Trainer** software (7 @ $600 = $4,200) is a wise and necessary investment.

Your instructors and employers may often ask you to summarize and assess what you have read. In school you may have to write a book report or compile a critical, annotated bibliography commenting on the usefulness of the material you found in those sources. On the job your employer may ask you to condense and judge the merits of a report, paying special attention to whether its recommendations should be followed, modified, or ignored. Your company or agency may also ask you to write short evaluative summaries of job applications, sales proposals, or conferences.

Characteristics of a Successful Evaluative Summary

To write a careful evaluative summary, follow these guidelines:

- Keep the summary short—5 to 10 percent of the length of the original.
- Blend your evaluations with your summary; do not save your evaluations for the end of the summary.
- Place each evaluation near the summarized points to which it applies so readers will see your remarks in context.
- Include a pertinent quotation from the original to emphasize your recommendation.
- Comment on both the content and the style of the original.

Evaluating the Content

Answer these questions on content for your readers:

1. How carefully is the subject researched? Is the material accurate and up-to-date? Are important details missing? Exactly what has the author left out? Where could the reader find the missing information? If the material is inaccurate, will the whole work be affected or just part of it?

2. Is the writer or speaker objective? Are conclusions supported by evidence? Is the writer or speaker following a particular theory, program, or school of thought? Is that fact made clear in the source? Has the author or speaker emphasized one point at the expense of others? What are the writer's qualifications and background?

3. Does the work achieve its goal? Is the topic too large to be adequately discussed in a single talk, article, or report? Is the work sketchy? Are there digressions, tangents, or irrelevant materials? Do the recommendations make sense?

4. Is the material relevant to your audience? How would the audience use it? Is the entire work relevant or just part of it? Why? Would the work be useful for all employees of your company or only for those working in certain areas? Why? What answers offered by the work would help to solve a specific problem you or others have encountered on the job?

Evaluating the Style

Answer these questions on style for the readers of your evaluative summary:

1. Is the material readable? Is it well written and easy to follow? Does it contain helpful headings, careful summaries, and appropriate examples?

2. What kind of vocabulary does the writer or speaker use? Are there many technical terms or jargon? Is it written for the layperson? Is the language precise or vague? Would readers have to skip certain sections that are too complicated?

3. What visuals are included? Charts? Graphs? Photographs? How are they used? Are they used effectively? Are there too many or too few?

Figure 10.7   An evaluative summary of an article.

Shelton, B. (1999). Building customer loyalty on the web. *EC World*. Retrieved May 7, 2002, from http://www.ecresources.com

According to this early, pioneering article, most e-businesses are not developing ways to "convert Web surfers into loyal customers." While pricing and convenience are factors, Shelton maintains that customer assistance is the most important determiner of repeat business. He identifies four significant ways for e-shops to personalize their services. The first is to offer more off-site help; surprisingly, some e-businesses offer none. Second, Shelton advocates better self-assistance through personalized service software. Many online shoppers need more than an FAQ menu and thus can benefit from layered support options. Third, decision support systems act as a "collaborative filter," making product suggestions and matching a customer's preference with a particular item or service. Finally, for Shelton, customer-care robots, programmed to understand and respond realistically to natural language, answer consumers' most relevant questions or, if there's a problem, switch them to a service representative. This readable and informative article offers online merchants practical advice on how to give customers the convenience and service of a fine retail store.

Figures 10.7, 10.8, and 10.9 contain evaluative summaries. Note how the writers' assessments are woven into the condensed versions of the originals. Figure 10.7 is a student's opinion of an article summarized for a class in e-commerce. Figure 10.8 is an evaluative summary in memo format collaboratively written by two employees who have just returned from a seminar. They have divided their labor, one writing the opening paragraph and the summary of "Techniques of Health Assessment" and the other doing the summaries of "Assessment of the Heart and Lungs" and "Assessment of the Abdomen." Together they drafted and revised the "Recommendations" and prepared the final copy of the memo.

Another kind of evaluative summary—a book review—is shown in Figure 10.9 (p. 429). Many journals and websites print book reviews to inform their professional audiences about the most recent studies in their fields. Reviews condense and assess books, reports, government studies, CD-ROMs, DVDs, films, and other materials. The short review in Figure 10.9 comments briefly on usefulness to the intended audience and on style, provides clarifying information, and explains how

A collaboratively written evaluative summary of a seminar.   Figure 10.8

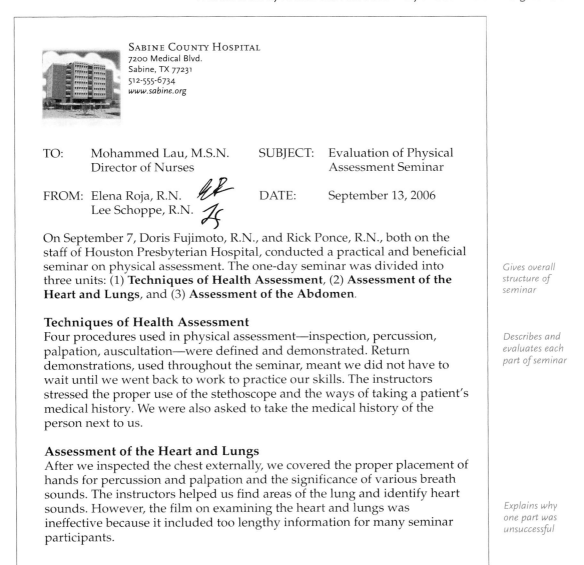

SABINE COUNTY HOSPITAL
7200 Medical Blvd.
Sabine, TX 77231
512-555-6734
www.sabine.org

TO: Mohammed Lau, M.S.N.   SUBJECT: Evaluation of Physical
       Director of Nurses   Assessment Seminar

FROM: Elena Roja, R.N.   DATE: September 13, 2006
       Lee Schoppe, R.N.

On September 7, Doris Fujimoto, R.N., and Rick Ponce, R.N., both on the
staff of Houston Presbyterian Hospital, conducted a practical and beneficial
seminar on physical assessment. The one-day seminar was divided into
three units: (1) **Techniques of Health Assessment**, (2) **Assessment of the
Heart and Lungs**, and (3) **Assessment of the Abdomen**.

Gives overall structure of seminar

Techniques of Health Assessment
Four procedures used in physical assessment—inspection, percussion,
palpation, auscultation—were defined and demonstrated. Return
demonstrations, used throughout the seminar, meant we did not have to
wait until we went back to work to practice our skills. The instructors
stressed the proper use of the stethoscope and the ways of taking a patient's
medical history. We were also asked to take the medical history of the
person next to us.

Describes and evaluates each part of seminar

Assessment of the Heart and Lungs
After we inspected the chest externally, we covered the proper placement of
hands for percussion and palpation and the significance of various breath
sounds. The instructors helped us find areas of the lung and identify heart
sounds. However, the film on examining the heart and lungs was
ineffective because it included too lengthy information for many seminar
participants.

Explains why one part was unsuccessful

Continued

Figure 10.8   (Continued)

2.

Assessment of the Abdomen
The instructors warned that the order of examination of the abdomen differs from that of the chest cavity. Auscultation, not percussion, follows inspection so that bowel sounds are not activated. The instructors then clearly identified how to detect bowel sounds and how to locate the abdomen and palpate organs.

Recommendations
We strongly recommend a seminar like this for all nurses whose expanding role in the health care system requires more physical assessments. Although the seminar covered a wealth of information, the instructors admitted that they discussed only basics. In the future, however, it would be better to offer follow-up seminars on specific body systems (chest cavity, abdomen, central nervous system) instead of combining topics because of the amount of information involved and the time required for demonstrations.

Ends with endorsement but offers suggestions for improving seminar

the book is developed. The Web contains numerous sites that run book reviews, including Amazon.com (*http://www.amazon.com/*), Real Books (*http://www.realbooks.com/*), Books on Line (*http://www.booksonline.co.uk*), Business Book Review.com (*http://www.businessbookreview.com/*), and eBookReviews.net (*http://www.ebookreviews.net*).

A book review includes the most important and useful—to a key audience—information about a book or report. Reviews are also important for the kinds of information that they do *not* include—details and irrelevant (for the audience) information that would only clog a summary. For example, the review in Figure 10.9 indicates that the book is an excellent guide to team building, but does not go into detailed descriptions of the author's recommended tips, strategies, and instruments.

Abstracts

Differences Between a Summary and an Abstract

The terms *summary* and *abstract* are often used interchangeably, resulting in some confusion. That problem arises because there are two distinct types of abstracts: *descriptive abstracts* and *informative abstracts*. The informative abstract is another name for a summary; the descriptive abstract is not. Why? An informative abstract

A book review.   Figure 10.9

Book Review

Team Troubleshooting: How to Find and Fix Team Problems
By ROBERT W. BARNER
Davies-Black Publishing, Palo Alto, Calif.
Representation: Anita Halton Associates, (949) 494-8564, 326 pages, $32.95

Overall Recommendation

DON'T BOTHER   BORROW   BUY   Engaging: 4   Innovative: 4   Usefulness: 5   Visual Aids: 4

Team building with at twist: While most books on the subject limit themselves to talk about getting a new team up and running or fixing a team after it breaks, Robert W. Barner deals with both and then goes a step farther. *Team Troubleshooting* promotes the concept of maintaining a healthy team through anticipating problems, performing regular team tune-ups and taking proactive measures to head off trouble before it begins. High points: strategies to foresee and develop plans for dealing with change, rather than becoming a victim of it; how-to tips to extend beyond the team itself to the problems of creating, maintaining and mending external relationships; ideas to cope with the fact that the team is not an isolated, independent entity, but is part of a bigger system and may be at the mercy of management and other forces.

The unusually user-friendly format makes the book truly serve as a guide.

Useful organization, clear chapter headings and cross-referencing help the reader find information quickly. Barner also does more than just name problems and offer quick fixes—he helps to assure accurate problem diagnosis by clearly describing both symptoms and underlying causes. Dozens of new instruments—not just the same tired old quizzes that appear in so many other teamwork books—lead both team leaders and members (and trainers or consultants involved in the "team" business) through exercises. They include scripting out scenario forecasts, identifying early warning signs of trouble, performing stakeholder analyses, and mapping relationships. It's been a long time since anything new has been said about teams—Barner's book deserves a space on the shelf of anyone truly interested in making a team work.
—*Jane Bozarth*

(or summary) gives readers conclusions and indicates the results or causes. Look at the summary in Figure 10.4. It explains why virtual reality should be included in law enforcement training: because virtual reality gives officers field-translatable training. Informative abstracts are found at the beginning of long reports. Descriptive abstracts do not give conclusions.

Figure 10.10   Abstract written from a table of contents.

Table of Contents	*Abstract*

Need for Genetic Counseling
    Definition of Genetic Counseling
    Statistics on Genetic Counseling
	Genetic counseling is a service for people with a history of hereditary disease. One in 17 births contains some defect; one-fourth of the patients in hospitals are victims of genetic diseases (including diabetes, mental retardation, and anemia). One of every 200 children born has chromosome abnormalities.

Purpose of Genetic Counseling	Genetic counseling offers advice to parents who may give birth to children with genetic diseases and assistance to those with children already afflicted.

The Counseling Process
    Evaluating the Needs of the
        Counselees
    Taking a Family History
    Estimating the Risks
    Counseling the Family
	The first step in counseling is to evaluate the needs of the parents. A family history is prepared and risks of future children being afflicted are evaluated. The life expectancy and possible methods of treatment of any afflicted child also can be determined. Alternatives are presented.

Determination of a Genetic Disorder
    Amniocentesis
    Karyotyping
    Fluorescent Banding
    Staining
	Four prenatal tests are used to determine if a genetic disorder is present: amniocentesis, karyotyping, fluorescent banding, and staining.

Advantages of Genetic Screening
    Lower Cost
    Increased Availability
	The development of these four relatively simple methods has lowered the cost of genetic counseling and increased its availability.

Reprinted by permission of Professor Mary Scotto.

All abstracts share two characteristics: the writer never uses "I" and avoids footnotes.

Writing the Informative Abstract

An informative abstract is not as long as an executive summary, which gives more supporting details. As a part of your course work or your job you will probably have to write informative abstracts for long reports (see Chapter 16).

One way to approach writing the abstract of a report is to think of it as a table of contents in sentence form. The table of contents is, in effect, the final outline; it is easily fleshed out into an abstract, as Figure 10.10 shows. On the left is a table of contents, and on the right is the abstract written from that outline.

This system works only if your table of contents is neither too detailed nor too skimpy. Starting off with a good outline of an article or a report provides the best beginning for your abstract. Make sure your sentences are complete and grammatical. Do not omit verbs, conjunctions, and articles. Proper subordination is essential.

You should expect to condense a whole paragraph of the original to a sentence, an individual sentence to a phrase, and a phrase to a single word.

Writing the Descriptive Abstract

A descriptive abstract is short, usually only a few sentences; it does not go into any detail or give conclusions. A descriptive abstract provides information on what topics a work discusses but not how or why they are discussed. Busy readers rely on a descriptive abstract to decide whether they want or need to consult the work itself. Here is a descriptive abstract of the article summarized in Figure 10.4.

> Virtual reality can be used to teach law enforcement officers firearms training, SWAT team assaults, incident re-creation, and crime location processing. This new training technology will be of interest to law enforcement administrators.

Figure 10.11 reproduces two descriptive abstracts from the reference work *Library & Information Science Abstracts* as well as two signed abstracts from the *Journal of Interactive Marketing*, a publication that includes abstracts as a way to help readers learn about research in this specialized discipline.

Writing Successful News Releases

A **news release**, sometimes called a **press release** or **media release**, is another type of on-the-job document that requires you to summarize key information for a variety of readers. Basically, a news release is an announcement (usually one page or a simple screen on the Web) about your company's or agency's specific product, services, or personnel. It is a crisp summary highlighting only the most important and relevant facts clearly and straightforwardly, as in the other summaries you have studied in this chapter. Such releases are frequently posted on a company's or agency's website (as well as sent in the mail or as a fax). They inform readers—the news media, potential and current customers, other agencies—of newsworthy events that promote the professional accomplishments of a company. Your company's image can be enhanced or tarnished by the release you write. What you summarize, therefore, has a tremendous impact on how your company will be seen. Double-check all your facts so you don't embarrass yourself or your company. The best releases project a professional, customer-centered, and quality-focused corporate or agency image.

Figures 10.12 and 10.13 contain sample news releases. The release shown in Figure 10.12 was distributed over the Web whereas the release in Figure 10.13 was distributed in hard-copy form. Both figures label the various parts of a news release, which are discussed on pages 434–438.

Subjects Appropriate for News Releases

News releases should be written only about newsworthy subjects, such as the following topics:

Figure 10.11   Descriptive abstracts of journal articles.

2002-01577

Mann, Charles C **Electronic paper turns the page.** *Technology Review* **104**(2): 42–48 (March 1, 2001) (ISSN: 1099-274X) In English.
Journal URL: http://www.techreview.com

Reports that the key to enabling electronic books to revolutionize the publishing industry is the development of electronic paper. Draws a parallel between the general availability of paper and the development of the first moveable-type printing press, noting that the technology to create the printing press existed for 100 years before the widespread use of ordinary paper provided the means to make the press practical. Notes that several companies are engaged in research and development of electronic paper, adding that at least one working prototype already exists. Indicates that the recent discovery of electrical conducting properties in plastic will enable researchers to overcome the issues of flexibility and cost that have slowed development in the past.

2002-01189

Ma, Wenfeng (yangpj@sun.ihep.ac.cn) [University of China, Beijing 100872, China] (China); Wang, Liqing **Toward the twenty-first century: research on the development of social science information services of university libraries in China.** *INSPEL: International Journal of Special Libraries* **33**(3): 150–158 (1999) (ISSN: 0019-0217) In English.
Journal URL: http://inspel.ifla.org

At the start of the 21st century, China's social sciences and higher education are experiencing a great innovation and development that is pressing university libraries to adapt themselves to the new situation and strengthen their social science information services. Discusses some major problems of the social science information services of Chinese academic libraries with respect to the goals, user needs for information, required behaviors, the processing and transmission of content, the social and economic benefits, and the theoretical research. Outlines some specific and positive proposals for addressing these problems.

Strategic and Ethical Considerations in Managing Digital Privacy

Ravi Sarathy and Christopher J. Robinson (August 2003), *Journal of Business Ethics*, 46(2), pp. 111–126.

Information about customers and prospects is readily available through a variety of digital sources. The questions a marketer must answer is how much of this available data should be used for commercial purposes and how much should remain privileged and off limits. In this paper the authors develop a model of the factors influencing privacy strategy. This model incorporates external, ethical, and firm-specific factors that impact customer privacy protection strategy formulation. The model is then applied to various scenarios to determine the firm's most likely customer privacy strategy. International implications of the model are also discussed.

Scovotti. (8, 13)

The Professional Service Encounter in the Age of the Internet: An Exploratory Study

Gillian Hogg, Angus Laing, and Dan Winkelman (2003), *The Journal of Services Marketing*, 17(5), pp. 476–495.

The Internet, by providing access to an unprecedented amount of healthcare-related information, is changing the balance of power in the relationship between healthcare consumers and professionals. Patients play a more active role in the relationship, interacting with healthcare professionals and other consumers to understand their illnesses. This situation changes the nature of the doctor/patient relationship—where the doctor becomes only one of the *advisors* in the service encounter. The implications of this research extend to other types of service encounters, where consumers may be engaging in virtual, parallel service encounters.

(Sherman)

1. **New products, services, or publications**

   - a new or improved model, line of equipment, or website
   - new or expanded technical or customer-friendly services
   - the entrance of your company (service or product) into a different and more productive market
   - the application of the latest technology in creating a product

2. **New policies and/or procedures**

   - acquisition of new technologies to lower production costs
   - changes in production to improve safety, delivery, accuracy
   - cooperation and collaboration between two agencies or branches

3. **Personnel changes**

   - appointments
   - promotions
   - employee recognition for winning an award
   - hiring additional staff
   - retirements

4. **New construction/developments**

   - plant or office openings
   - new satellite, branch, or overseas offices
   - expansion of an existing site

5. **Financial and business news**

   - company reorganizations—mergers, acquisitions
   - stock reports
   - quarterly earnings and dividends
   - sales figures
   - community service programs

6. **Special events**

   - training seminars
   - demonstrations of new equipment
   - charity benefits
   - visits of national speakers
   - dedications

News Releases About Bad News

While the topics above focus on a company's or organization's achievements—the positive contributions a firm or an agency makes to its consumers and its community—not all the news you may be asked to announce is pleasant. At times you may have to report on events that are difficult—product recalls, work stoppages or strikes, layoffs, limited availability or unavailability of parts, fires, branch or other closings, computer viruses, identity theft, higher prices, declining enrollments, or canceled events.

Even when you have to write releases about such unpleasant events, portray your company honestly in the most professional and conscientious light. Regardless of the news, be accurate, ethical, honest and straightforward, and available.

Topics That Do Not Warrant a News Release

Not every event or change at your company or agency will warrant a news release. Releases about events that have already happened are old, tired news. Keep in mind as well that things in the works may as yet be too new for you to announce. Below are some topics that hold little or no interest and about which you would *not* write a release.

1. **Well-known products or services.**

2. **Products or services still in the planning stages.** Not only would such news be premature, but releasing it ahead of time might meet with your boss's severe disapproval, not to mention your competition's delight.

3. **Controversial events or company problems.** Refrain from writing a news release on these subjects unless your boss instructs you to do so.

4. **A history of your department, division, or company.** Save remarks about your firm's history for the annual report to stake holders.

5. **An obviously padded tribute to your boss or to your company or to your customers.**

Organization and Style of a News Release

The following sections contain guidelines for organizing and writing the different parts of your news release. Note how these various parts flow together in the news releases in Figures 10.12 and 10.13.

The cardinal rule in writing a news release is to put the most important piece of news first. Don't bury it in the middle or wait until the end. Summarize the main event so readers get it at once. In fact, everything in a news release should be arranged in descending order of importance so that your first paragraph contains only the most significant fact and ideas. Think of your release as an inverted pyramid with the top summarizing only the most crucial points.

The Three Parts of a News Release

The Slug, or Headline.   One of the most crucial parts of your release is the headline, or **slug**. It should announce a specific subject for readers and draw them into it. Write a slug that entices or grabs your readers, but also one that informs them quickly and clearly. Note how the slugs in Figures 10.12 and 10.13 point readers to the main point in the first sentence and use key words to help readers track the subject.

A news release from the Web.   Figure 10.12

March 18, 2005   (404) 639-3286
Contact: CDC, Jennifer Marcone   http://bookstore.phf.org

Provides contact information

Local Content

Email Us
On-Line Publications
Image LIbrary
Press Kit
Press Releases
Daily Updates

Quick Jumps

Health Statistics
Health Topics A-Z
Global Health Odyssey

Press Release

CDC Releases New Interactive Website for *Health Information for International Travel* (The Yellow Book)

ATLANTA–The Centers for Disease Control and Prevention (CDC) unveiled a re-designed, interactive website of one of CDC's most widely disseminated publications, *Health Information for International al Travel,* commonly dubbed "The Yellow Book." The Yellow Book is considered by many health care providers, travel professionals, airlines, cruise lines, and humanitarian institutions to be the gold standard for health recommendations for international travel.

The Yellow Book and companion website **www.cdc.gov/travel/yb** are published biennially by CDC's Division of Global Migration and Quarantine as a reference for those who advise international travelers of health risks.

The key to the new, interactive website is the use of drop-down menus for all of the major subjects in the Yellow Book, including vaccination information, yellow fever requirements, malaria information, geographic distribution, and health hints. Users can obtain customized reports for individual travel plans and locate particular subjects or destinations in the text without having to search through unrelated topics.

"International travelers will find the interactive Yellow Book website to be very helpful," said CDC Director Jeffrey P. Koplan, MD, MPH. "The new features make it easier to find information about preventive measures travelers can take to protect their health."

The handy, interactive design of the Yellow Book website incorporated many comments and suggestions from the public and health care providers seeking more customized information in a user-friendly format. CDC encourages users to submit comments about the new website through the "comments section" on the site's homepage.

30

http://bookstore.phf.org

Slug emphasizes importance of topic

Lead answers who, when, how, what, and why

Body emphasizes benefits for audience

Quotation from expert endorses new design and features

Conclusion invites reader interaction

Signals end of release

Figure 10.13   A news release circulated in hard copy.

⊛ NEWS RELEASE

United States Department of Commerce • 1401 Constitution Avenue, NW •
Washington, DC 20230 • Web: http://www.commerce.gov

Release No. 0150.01

Cheryl Mendonsa
Cheryl.Mendonsa@technology.gov
202-482-8321

Marjorie Weisskohl
Marjorie.Weisskohl@technology.gov
202-482-0149

Slug

U.S. Department of Commerce Announces Website Focused on Resources for Tech-Based Economic Development (TBED)

Lead, or hook

Under Secretary of Commerce Phillip J. Bond today announced a new resource that will help communities working to encourage the growth of technology companies and build tech-based economies. A new website, the TBED Resource Center (http://www.tbedresourcecenter.org), offers users the chance to learn from others' experiences and benefit from the latest research on what it takes to create a tech-based economy.

Body

The TBED Resource Center categorizes and provides links to more than 1,300 research reports, strategic plans, best practices and impact analyses from state and federal government, university researchers, foundations. The website is a result of a cooperative project of the U.S. Department of Commerce's (DOC) Office of Technology Policy and State Science and Technology Institute, based in Westerville, Ohio.

Quote from authority

"This website will be an invaluable tool to anyone involved in economic development," said Under Secretary Bond. "Access to information on what has worked in various communities will help policymakers and business people make efficient use of valuable time and resources, and provide good ideas and contacts that others might find useful." Bond made the announcement via live telecast hosted by Commerce's Economic Development Administration and the National Association of Regional Councils.

Emphasizes benefits

The user-friendly search options allow for easy navigation with abundant topics spanning a wide field of interests. Users can search for reports based upon geography, topic, type, or keyword with the option of selecting multiple fields. Numerous international reports also are included, offering a globally diverse perspective in tech-based economic development.

Appropriate positive tone

Reports fall into one of the 35 topics, such as brain drain, education, entrepreneurship, innovation, research and development, and work force.

To keep current with TBED trends, the website is continually updated as new reports are released.

#

Signals end of release

Material reprinted from the United States Department of Commerce.

The Lead.   The first (and most significant) sentence of a news release is called the **lead**. It introduces and aptly summarizes your topic, sets the tone, and continues to keep the readers' attention. For that reason it is also called the **hook**. See how the leads in Figures 10.12 and 10.13 grab readers' attention. The best leads easily answer the basic questions *Who? What? When? Where? Why?*—the five W's—and *How?* (or *How much?*). Not every lead will answer all these questions, but the more of them you do answer, the better your chances will be of capturing your audience's attention. Here are some effective leads that answer these crucial questions:

---

   who   *when*
Massey Labs announced today that the FDA has approved the marketing
     what   *why*
of its vaccine—Viobal—to retard recurrent lesions of herpes simplex.

---

     who   *what*
Maryville Engineering, Inc., has been awarded a contract by Aerodynamics, Inc.,
   why
to develop an acoustical system to measure and monitor stress levels at the
       where   *when*
Knoxville aircraft plant, district manager Carmelita Stinn, P.E., announced today.

   Misleading leads that deviate substantially from the guidelines just discussed annoy readers and risk losing their interest. Resist the temptation to start off with a question or with folksy humor.

Feeble Humor: Slap, slap, scratch, scratch, itch. This is how millions of people will handle their mosquito problems this summer.
Boastful Start: If you thought 2006 was great, you ain't seen nothin' yet!
Undirected Question: Does the thought of hypothermia send chills up your spine?
Exaggeration: I bet you wonder how you ever did without the new Fourier scanner.

The Body.   What kinds of information should you give readers in the second and subsequent paragraphs of your release? If the five W's are answered in your lead, the following paragraphs fill in only the most necessary supporting details. Regard your lead as a summary of a summary. The body of your release then amplifies the *Why? How?*, and may also get into the *So what?*

But avoid filling your news release with unnecessary technical details, such as scientific formulas or intricate speculations. Instead, relate your product or service to your targeted audience's needs by emphasizing the benefits to them without loading your news release with hype.

Use quotations selectively and to clarify and highlight, not to apple-polish. Use a quotation only to report vital facts or to cite an authority. Do not turn your release into an interview with your employer or favorite customer.

Style and Tone

The style and tone of your news release need to be objective and take into account your audience's background. Keep your style simple and to the point. Here are some suggestions that will help you:

1. **Write concisely.**   Use easy-to-read paragraphs of three to five sentences, and keep your sentences short (under 20 words is ideal). Avoid long, convoluted sentences and fillers that start off with such phrases as "It has been noted that . . .".

2. **Raise your reader's interest level.**   Emphasize benefits to the reader with graphic, understandable language that applies to the reader's life. Avoid unfamiliar jargon—it's deadly. A news release summarizing the benefits of a hospital counseling center lost potential seminar participants by describing it in jargon: "Milford Hospital is pleased to offer an adventure-intensive counseling workshop that incorporates trust sequencing; high element activities; and quantifiable decision modules."

3. **Keep your tone upbeat, easygoing, and direct; stress the human side.**   But stay away from adjectives dripping with a pushy sell—"incomparable," "fantastic," "incredible." See Figures 10.12 and 10.13 with their emphasis on benefits to travelers and communities interested in technology-based economic development, respectively.

As with other types of summaries described in this chapter, news releases give readers essential, useful information quickly and concisely. They provide the "big picture," as Figures 10.12 and 10.13 illustrate. And by doing so, they capture the reader's interest and emphasize the goals and contributions of the agency at the same time.

Online Study Center
Access the summarizing material Revision Checklist online at college .hmco.com/pic/ kolin8e

 ## Revision Checklist

☐ Read and reread the original thoroughly to gain a clear understanding of the purpose and scope of the work.

☐ Underlined key transitional words, main points, significant findings, applications, solutions, conclusions, recommendations.

☐ Separated main points clearly from (a) minor ones, (b) background information, (c) illustrations, and (d) inconclusive findings.

Continued

Continued

☐ Excluded examples, explanations, and statistics from the summary or abstract.
☐ Deleted information not useful to audience—information too technical or irrelevant.
☐ Changed language of original to my own words so I am not guilty of plagiarism.
☐ Made sure that emphasis of summary matches emphasis in original.
☐ Determined that sequence of information in summary follows sequence of original.
☐ Added necessary connective words that accurately convey relationships between main points in original.
☐ Edited to eliminate wordiness and repetition from summary.
☐ Cited source of original correctly and completely.
☐ Avoided phrases that draw attention to the fact that I am writing a summary or abstract.
☐ Summarized material objectively without adding commentary (for informative summary).
☐ Commented on both content and style (in evaluative summary).
☐ Interspersed evaluative commentary throughout summary so that assessments appear near relevant points.
☐ Included a direct quotation to illustrate or reinforce my recommendation (for evaluative summary and news releases).
☐ Ensured that descriptive abstract is short and to the point and does not offer a judgment.
☐ Prepared news releases that project a professional image of my employer.
☐ Summarized only essential information in my news release.
☐ Arranged information from top down, with the most important first.
☐ Wrote clear, crisp slug and lead and a concise body.
☐ Sent news release on newsworthy topic to appropriate publications, organizations, and audiences.

Exercises

1. Summarize a chapter of a textbook you are now using for a course in your major field. Provide an accurate bibliographic reference for that chapter (author of the textbook, title of the chapter, title of the book, place of publication, publisher's name, date of publication, and page numbers of the chapter).

2. Summarize a lecture you heard recently. Limit your summary to one page. Identify in a bibliographic citation the speaker's name, date, and place of delivery.

3. Listen to a television network evening newscast and to a later news update on the same station. Select one major story covered on the evening news and indicate which details from it were omitted in the news update.

Online Study Center
Find additional summarizing material exercises at college.hmco.com/pic/kolin8e

4. Write a summary of the research paper on telecommuting (pp. 383–405) or the business report on non-native speakers of English in the work force (pp. 680–697).

5. Bring to class an article from *Reader's Digest* and the original material it condensed, usually an article in a journal or magazine published six months to a year earlier. In a paragraph or two indicate what the *Digest* article omits from the original. Also point out how the condensed version is written so that the omitted material is not missed and how the condensation does not misrepresent the main points of the article.

6. Assume that you are applying for a job and that the personnel manager asks you to summarize your qualifications for the job in two or three paragraphs. Write those paragraphs and indicate how your background and interests make you suited for the specific job. Mention the job by title at the beginning of your first paragraph.

7. Write a summary of one of the following articles.
   a. "Microwaves," in Chapter 1 on pages 38–40.
   b. "Security for Instant Messaging," below.

8. Write a descriptive abstract of the article you selected in Exercise 7.

Security for Instant Messaging
Eric Krapf

The term "killer app" has fallen out of favor, but if you're looking for a sure bet among trends emerging in corporate networking, you'd have to put instant messaging (IM) at or near the top of your list. Besides its inherent utility, it can be implemented quickly and learned easily by end users with little intervention by IT staff. That last point, of course, makes it a potential nightmare from a network security perspective.

Enterprise-oriented IM installations abound—Microsoft estimates that 30 percent of information workers have at least one public IM client on their desktops. But these consumer networks, dominated by AOL, Yahoo! and MSN, still aren't interoperable, so many users have more than one client.

Security Threats
The security threats from IM are straightforward. Since deployment isn't controlled, the enterprise can't keep a rein on how the systems are used. With the public IM networks, the individual employee registers for service. If the employee leaves the company, the firm has no (technology-based) way to prevent him or her from continuing to use the account, or from even continuing to represent him- or herself as still working for the company, noted Ryan Alexander, founder and COO of Omnipod, an enterprise IM service provider.

Furthermore, without additional tools, the company has no way of archiving IM messages for legal or regulatory purposes, or of monitoring and controlling the content of messages to filter for inappropriate communications.

Finally, there are the obvious holes that are opened up on the corporate network. Each of the IM networks uses a well-known port that must either be left open on the corporate firewall to allow traffic in, or closed, which, at least in theory, bans that service to end users.

Securing IM

Certainly the latter option has some appeal: 23 percent of all companies simply block all IM traffic, according to Microsoft. One down side to this strategy is that because workers find IM useful, blocking it isn't popular or necessarily even a good business move.

Another down side is that blocking might not work. "If [the IM] port has been blocked, all the popular clients today are designed to fall back to Port 80, the Web port, and that's usually open," explained Chris Williams, director of messaging management for NetIQ. The administrator would have to block individual URLs for the IM services to keep traffic from coming through Port 80.

Given IM's pervasiveness, enterprises can't think about security in a vacuum; it has to be part of a larger management structure. FaceTime Communications is probably the market leader here, with more than 100 large enterprise installations, including financial institutions like Citigroup and Bank of America, which face SEC requirements to archive all communications. Security vendor NetIQ also recently released a new product in this area, called imMarshal.

FaceTime's COO Mehdi Maghsoodnia explained some of the ways policies can be set: "We give you a layer of control all the way from completely blocking these clients and technologies to very detailed level of control, as in: From 8 to 5, you can do this, but you can't do it after 5, or you can do file transfers only three times a day."

Policies may regulate what types of files can and can't be transferred via IM systems, to limit the potential for introduction of viruses; some may even do virus scanning. Products also can examine message content much like existing e-mail spam filters; Net IQ's imMarshal scans for prohibited words and phrases, blocks them when they occur, and notifies the sender.

The IM management/security systems act as proxies for IM traffic going into the network; the traffic is allowed through the firewall but hits the FaceTime or NetIQ server, which imposes policies before letting traffic through. In a variation, Omnipod operates as a service to which enterprises subscribe.

Besides addressing security, this architecture puts the IM management/security vendors in a position to deal with the pesky problem of the lack of interoperability among networks. Right now, NetIQ can't address this, because imMarshal only handles the MSN client, although releases are expected for the other major clients this year.

FaceTime has partnerships with all three major networks, but ironically that has prevented it from making the networks interoperate: Until the three providers work out their IM business models, they're not interested in being interoperable—or in having their hardware partners do the job for them, Mehdi Maghsoodnia explained.

Omnipod, on the other hand, faces no such constraints, and bills itself as providing interoperability. The server, which sits in Omnipod's datacenter, takes in traffic from all three networks, applies policies, and then delivers them to Omnipod's client, called the Professional Online Desktop (POD). Customers open Port 443 on their firewall, and the traffic is encrypted and delivered. Enterprises pay a monthly fee starting at about $6 per desktop to give their users the Omnipod client, which replaces the consumer clients.

Conclusion

You'd think IM would be hot, but even the vendors that have made their name in IM are trying to expand their focus to other real-time applications such as voice and conferencing. And vendor representatives are surprisingly open about why: "IM as a standalone application gets commoditized pretty quickly," said Omnipod's Ryan Alexander.

Indeed, the tough thing about IM security and management isn't that it's technically hard to do; it's because adoption is happening so quickly that network managers are playing catch-up.

Source: From the April 2003 issue of *Business Communications Review,* p. 10, by Eric Krapf, managing editor of *Business Communications Review.*

9. Below are two sloppily written news releases that are poorly organized and, in a few instances, unethical. Reorganize and rewrite them according to the guidelines presented in this chapter.

   a. Friday   Alan Bowerstock

      Metropolitan State University is a four-year urban institution of higher education offering majors in many fields. Located two miles west of Taylorsville Tech Park, MSU currently boasts more than 7,000 undergraduate students, more than our rival, Central Tech.

      Among the many student services currently available at MSU is the Division of Career Placement; this division is located in the Student Services Building, Room 301, just across the hall from the Department for Greek Life.

      In the last year, the Division has assisted more than 2,000 MSU students to find part-time jobs. Full-time jobs, too.

      The goal of the Division is to help students earn money for their college expenses. The Division also wants to assist local businesses in contacting MSU qualified undergraduates.

      The MSU family is well represented on the homepage. Every department from the University has been encouraged to report on only its most favorable activities. The Division of Career Placement is also on the homepage.

      Counselors at the Division can help MSU students prepare a four- or five-line ad about their qualifications. The Division will run these ads in their homepage. The university will also run ads looking for job candidates from the state employment agency and the greater Taylorsville area.

b. For General Information   Frank Day

J.T. Bushart, CEO of Bonnetti and Blount Construction for the last three years, asserted today that the company is devoted to progress and change. Bushart came to B&B Engineering after several years working for Capitol City Engineering, a less progressive firm.

Bonnetti and Blount is a leading firm of contractors and has worked for both national and international corporations.

The firm specializes in construction projects that require special expertise because of their challenges in difficult terrains.

B&B has just been awarded a contract to work on the 10 million dollar renovation of two major Fairfax dams. The firm anticipates hiring more than 200 new workers. These new employees will work on the dams that present dangerous conditions to residents.

When completed, the two new dams will further assist residents of Fairfax and Hamilton Counties receive all the necessary irrigation and hydroelectric energy they need.

Engineering sketches and blueprints are in the works.

10. Write an appropriate news release on one of the following newsworthy topics to be included in your company's website.
   a. hiring a new webmaster
   b. premiering a new product or service
   c. acquiring a smaller firm whose products and services are very different from those of your company
   d. providing a service that enhances life in the community in which your employer's headquarters is located
   e. promoting an employee who has been with your company for at least five years
   f. offering highly competitive warranties on a new line of products

11. Write a news release on one of the following unpleasant topics while still projecting a positive image of your company.
   a. inconveniences because of recent construction
   b. a temporary power outage in a neighborhood or city

   c. a company/organization server is down
   d. a change in the hours of operation of a store or plant
   e. an increase in insurance premiums
   f. a reduction in number of times trash is picked up per week
   g. an order page is down on a frequently visited e-business site because of a computer virus
   h. a sports injury has benched a star quarterback on a local team for the next month

PART IV

Preparing Documents and Visuals

CHAPTER 11

Designing Clear Visuals

Experts estimate that as much as 80 percent of our learning comes through our sense of sight. The written word, of course, forms a large part of our visual information. In conjunction with words, though, **visuals** convey a large share of the facts we receive. Visuals are especially useful on the job because they help readers see what you are discussing.

Chapter 11 surveys the kinds of visuals you will encounter most frequently and shows you how to read, construct, and write about them. It also describes the types of visuals and visual configurations you can create and copy with graphics software packages. The impact and importance of visuals in document design is nowhere better illustrated than on the Internet, a "virtual library" where every successful webpage exploits graphics to capture attention.

Our discussion of visuals is not confined to just this chapter. They are important in preparing successful instructions, proposals, and written and oral reports and are covered in chapters on these topics.

Online Study Center

To expand your understanding of designing, take advantage of the ACE quizzes, sample documents, Web links, and exercises at college.hmco.com/pic/kolin8e

The Purpose of Visuals

Here are several reasons why you should use visuals. Each point is graphically reinforced in Figure 11.1.

1. *Visuals arouse readers' immediate interest.*   They catch the reader's eye quickly by setting important information apart and by giving relief from sentences and paragraphs. Note the eye-catching quality of the visual in Figure 11.1.

2. *Visuals increase readers' understanding by simplifying concepts.*   Visuals are especially important if you have to explain a technical process to a nonspecialist audience. They can make a complex set of numbers easier to comprehend, helping readers see percentages, trends, comparisons, and contrasts. Figure 11.1, for example, shows at a glance the growth of e-commerce.

3. *Visuals are especially important for non-native speakers of English and multicultural audiences.*   Given the growing international audience for many business

Figure 11.1   A line-and-bar chart depicting the growth of e-commerce compared to traditional businesses.

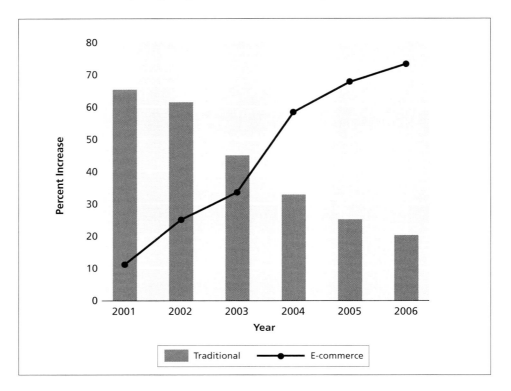

documents, visuals, if prepared carefully, can make your communication with them easier and clearer. Study the visuals in Terri Smith Ruckel's report in Figure 16.3.

4. *Visuals emphasize key relationships.*   Through their arrangement and form, visuals quickly show contrasts, similarities, growth rates, and downward and upward movements, as well as fluctuations in time, money, and space.

5. *Visuals condense and summarize a large quantity of information into a relatively small space.*   A visual allows you to streamline your message by saving words. It can record a great deal of statistical data in far less space than it would take to describe those facts in words alone. Note how in Figure 11.1 the growth rates of two different types of businesses are concisely expressed and documented.

6. *Visuals are highly persuasive.*   Visuals have sales appeal. They can convince readers to buy your product or service or to accept your point of view. A visual can graphically display, explain, and reinforce the benefits and opportunities of the plan you are advocating.

Choosing Effective Visuals

Select your visuals carefully. Special computer software programs allow you to select, create, and introduce visuals (see the Tech Note "Computer-Generated Visuals" below). The following suggestions will help you to choose effective visuals.

1. Use visuals only when they are relevant for your purpose and audience. Never include a visual simply as a decoration. A short report on fire drills, for example, does not need a picture of a fire station. Similarly, avoid any visual that is too technical for your readers or that includes more details than you need to show.

Tech Note

Computer-Generated Visuals

Whether you are copying an image from the Web, creating a custom-made graphic, or designing a graph to illustrate your data, computer-generated visuals are essential to enhance a document. Thanks to state-of-the-art computer hardware and software, incorporating crisp, effective visuals into your work is easy. High-resolution scanners, graphics software packages, and Web resources make it easy to incorporate images into any document. Laser printers will produce a high volume of photo-quality reproductions.

You can copy, create, store, retrieve, and edit visuals from a wide variety of sources with professional, easy-to-use software. These programs allow you to customize your visuals by altering their shape and size, rotating and cropping them, adding effects such as color and shadow, and correcting and updating them to suit your purpose and your audience's needs. Here are some of the resources available for copying and creating computer-generated visuals. Many of these will be discussed in greater detail throughout this chapter.

- **Scanning visuals**: You can copy an image for use as a visual by scanning it from a book or other hard copy. You actually get much better-quality images by scanning than you do with most images taken from the Web, since Web images are limited to about 72 to 100 dots per inch (dpi) and scanners now have much higher resolutions. Check to make sure the scanned images are not fuzzy. See the Tech Note "Scanners and Scanning" (pp. 453–454). As with downloading, always cite your source and obtain permission to reprint any of the images.
- **Downloading visuals from the Web**: The Internet is a key source of visuals that you can incorporate into your own papers, reports, or presentations. You copy these images by simply saving them to your hard disk or copying and pasting them into your document (see the Tech Note "Importing Visuals

Continued

Continued

from the Web" on pp. 455–456). Images copied from the Web can be saved in either GIF (graphic interchange format) or JPEG (Joint Photographic Experts Group) formats, which are methods of compressing images so that they take up less room on a website or your computer disk. But make sure that when you download images from online sources you always give them proper credit and that you request permission to reprint or publish them.

- **Graphs and charts**: Graphs and charts can be created in word processing programs, spreadsheets, graphics programs, and presentation software. There are also certain statistical programs, such as SPSS, that will help you create a variety of charts and graphs to record current data as well as to help you confidently project future trends based on those data. For further information, see the Tech Note "Computer-Generated Graphs and Charts" on pages 461–462.

- **Digital photographs**: Cameras, phones, and scanners allow you to edit and send photos via e-mail around the globe. See the Tech Note "Digital Photography" on pages 477–478.

- **Clip art**: Most word processors include clip art libraries, including cartoon-style images as well as photos, that you can insert into your document and use as visuals, for example, in pictographs. The section "Clip Art" on pages 485–486 gives you more information. Clip art is useful if you have to provide custom-made images. A clip art image in a design program can be the basis for a logo. You can also crop the image or superimpose text to create a unique visual.

- **Drawing programs**: Graphics software, such as CorelDRAW and JASC Paint Shop Pro, are designed to give you the tools to draw and design visuals that range from simple logos to complex diagrams and elaborate design elements. They provide you with custom shapes and clip art, color palettes, and drawing tools, and they include tutorials to help you learn the basics of creating your own visuals. Some of the most effective computer-generated logos and images can be created using varied fonts and geometric patterns found in these programs. Simple drawing tools allow you to create basic diagrams within text documents. These images can then be imported into documents, printed, or used in presentations or on websites.

- **Desktop publishing software**: Software such as Adobe PageMaker provides state-of-the-art tools to design newsletters, newspapers, and professional-looking print documents (text) and visuals. The ultimate resource in producing office documents, such programs allow you to format text, copy images from other online sources, merge them into your text, and add a variety of visual effects including font designs and shadowing.

Anna Gibson
Lori Brister

A visual used in conjunction with written work.   Figure 11.2

A PICTURE FROM THE INSIDE OUT

At the heart of the magnetic resonance imager is a large magnet that is big enough for you to lie inside. Look at the picture below. The **magnet** directs radio signals to surround sections of your body. When the signals pass through your body, they **resonate** (release a signal). Then your body's response is picked up by a receiver and sent to a computer. The computer analyzes the signal and converts it into a visual **image** of your tissues on a video screen.

1. The MR Imager surrounds your body with a harmless **magnetic** field and radio signals that safely pass through your body.

2. A receiver picks up and measures the radio signals that leave, or **resonate** from, your body.

3. The radio signals are turned into a computerized picture—or **image**—of your body's tissues.

Reprinted by permission of Krames Communications.

2. Use visuals in conjunction with—not as a substitute for—written work. Visuals do not take the place of words. In fact, you may need to explain information contained in a visual (see pp. 456–457). An illustration or a group of tables alone may not satisfy readers looking for summaries, evaluations, or conclusions. Note how the visual in conjunction with the description of a magnetic resonance imager (MRI) in Figure 11.2 makes the procedure easier to understand than if the writer had used only words or only a visual. This visual and verbal description is appropriately included in a brochure teaching patients about MRI procedures.

3. **Experiment with several visuals.**   Evaluate a variety of options before you select a particular visual. For instance, software such as PowerPoint (see pp. 712–715) allows you to represent statistical data in several ways. Preview a few different versions of a visual or even different types of visuals to determine which one would be best.

4. **Always use clear, easy-to-read, and relevant visuals.**   If readers have trouble understanding its function and arrangement, your visual probably is not appropriate and you need to change or revise it. If you download or scan a visual, make sure the copy is clear and readable and does not cut off any part of the original.

5. **Be prepared to revise and edit your visuals.**   Just as you draft, revise, and edit your written work to meet your audience's needs, create several versions of your visual to get it right. Expect to change shapes or proportions; experiment with different colors, shadings, labels, and various sizes. Avoid any visuals that may distract the reader or contradict your message. Make sure each visual is accurate and ethical, not unclear, distorted, or exaggerated. (See "Using Visuals Ethically" on pages 486–490.)

6. **Consider how your visuals will look on the page.**   Visuals should add to the overall appearance of your work, not detract from it. Don't cram visuals onto a page or allow them to spill over your text or margins. Many programs help you move your visuals directly into your word processor document so you can insert them properly. Go to pages 508–519 for advice on effective page layouts.

What *Not* to Do with a Visual

Here are some guidelines on what to avoid with visuals:

- Avoid visuals that include more details than your audience needs.
- Never use a visual that distracts from your work (for example, one that is too small, too large, does not use the right type of shading).
- Never use a visual that presents information that contradicts your work.
- Never distort a visual for emphasis or decoration.
- Be careful that you don't omit anything when you reproduce an existing visual.
- Never use visuals that discriminate or stereotype (for example, avoid pictures of a work force that excludes female employees).
- Don't use a visual that looks fuzzy, dotted, or streaked.

See how Figure 11.3 violates many of these rules. It divides the U.S. dollar bill into too many slices. Confronted with so many different wedges the reader would have trouble identifying, separating, comparing, and understanding the costs. It would be better to use a different visual to avoid so much clutter.

An ineffective visual: Too much information is crowded into one graphic.   Figure 11.3

What a U.S. dollar spent on food paid for in 2005.

About one-third went for food marketing labor costs.

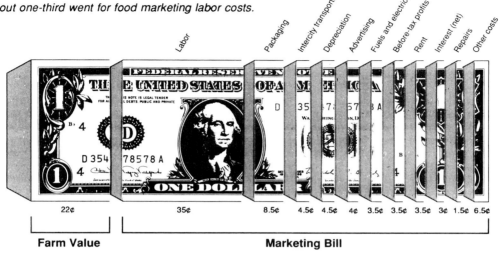

Farm Value   Marketing Bill

Scanners and Scanning

Scanners allow you to produce a digital copy of an image or a document to store and use on a computer. Using technology similar to that of a photocopier, a scanner captures an image and creates a digital reproduction that can then be altered or enhanced and printed, used as a visual in a document, or stored as a file in your computer. Scanners provide an efficient means of incorporating into your documents those visuals unavailable in digital form, such as older photographs, sketched diagrams, or pictures from books. For example, if you need to attach a diagram of a product to a document, but have only a hard copy, you can scan the image and use it within your document rather than attaching a hard copy. Scanning has begun to replace facsimiles in the business world to save time and money by transferring documents more efficiently. Unlike a fax, scanning allows you to attach the document to an e-mail message and send it directly. Scanning documents also preserves color images that may be distorted in faxing.

Using high-resolution digital imaging, with which scanners are equipped, you may produce high-quality replications of photographs. Using optical character

Continued

Continued

recognition (OCR) software, scanners can reproduce text on a word processing or spreadsheet program. This is particularly useful if you need to edit a document that is available only in hard copy, thus ensuring a virtually error-free transition of text from hard copy onto your computer.

Scanning helps companies to maintain an accurate, comprehensive, and searchable filing system that saves time, space, and money. Scanners contribute to a paperless office by capturing, storing, and cataloging documents, particularly useful for legal records and tax documents, which have to be stored for several years. Scanning these documents allows for quick retrieval and easy reproduction, and reduces the risk of losing paper copies.

Lori Brister
Anna Gibson

Inserting and Writing About Visuals: Some Guidelines

Using a visual requires more of you as a writer than simply inserting it into your written work. You need to *use visuals in conjunction with what you write*. The following guidelines will help you to (1) identify, (2) insert, (3) introduce, and (4) interpret visuals for your readers. By observing these guidelines, you can use visuals more effectively and efficiently.

Identify Visuals

Give each visual a number and caption (title) that indicates the subject or explains what the visual illustrates. An unidentified visual is meaningless. A caption helps your audience to interpret your visual—to see it with your purpose in mind. Inform your readers about what you want them to look for.

- Use a different typeface (bold) and size in your caption than what you use in the visual itself.
- Include key words about the function and the subject of your visual in a caption.
- Make sure any terms you cite in a caption are consistent with the units of measurement and the scope (years, months, seasons) of your visual.

Tables and figures should be numbered separately throughout the text—Table 1 or Figure 3.5, for example. (In the latter case, Figure 3.5 is the fifth figure to appear in Chapter 3.) Below are some examples of figure and table numbers and titles.

- Table 2. Paul Jordan's work schedule, January 15–23
- Figure 4.6. The proper way to apply for a small business loan
- Figure 12. Income Estimation Figures for North Point Technologies

Cite the Source for Visuals

If you use a visual that is not your own work, give credit to your source (newspaper, magazine, textbook, company, federal agency, individual, or website). If your paper or report is intended for publication, you must obtain permission to reproduce copyrighted visuals from the copyright holder.

Insert Visuals Appropriately

Many of the images you use will come from outside sources, including the Web. These will be digital images that you can incorporate directly into your document. See the Tech Note "Importing Visuals from the Web," below.

Here are some guidelines to help you incorporate the visuals in the most appropriate places for your readers.

- Never introduce a visual *before* a discussion of it; readers will wonder why it is there. Use a sentence or two to introduce your visuals.
- Always mention in the text of your paper or report that you are including a visual. Tell readers where it is found—"below," "on the following page," "to the right," "at the bottom of page 3."
- Place visuals as close as possible to the first mention of them in the text. Try not to put a visual more than one page after the discussion of it. Don't wait two or three pages to present it. By inserting a visual near the beginning of your discussion, you help readers understand your explanation better than if you place the visual near the end.
- Use an appropriate size for your visual. Don't make it too large or too small. Gauge size by how much data you are presenting and where the visual best fits into your discussion of it.
- If the visual is small enough, insert it directly in the text rather than on a separate page. If your visual occupies an entire page, place that page containing your visual on the facing page or immediately after the page on which the first reference to it appears.
- Center your visual and, if necessary, box it. Leave at least 1 inch of white space around it. Squeezing visuals toward the left or right margins looks unprofessional.
- Never collect all your visuals and put them in an appendix. Readers need to see them at those points in your discussion where they are most pertinent.

Tech Note

Importing Visuals from the Web

To incorporate visuals from the Internet in your report you will need to save the image to your hard disk or copy it into your computer's memory. Saving an image to your hard disk should only be done if you wish to store the image for future use, since otherwise it will clutter your hard drive. If you wish to use an image only once, copy it to your computer's temporary memory and paste it into the document.

Continued

Continued

When importing images from online sources, keep the following guidelines in mind:

- Be careful not to resize your image so that it becomes distorted. Images are limited to a certain size by the number of pixels (or dots) per inch (dpi). If you use your word processor's resize tool to make the image too large, it will become fuzzy and look unprofessional.
- When you copy images from the Web, your computer can store only one image at a time in its memory. Make sure you paste the image before you copy another, or it will be lost.
- Many websites will not allow you to copy their images. When you right-click on an image, a dialogue box will appear informing you that the image is protected and cannot be copied or saved. In order to obtain this image, you will need to e-mail the site's webmaster and request permission to use the visual.
- If you save an image to your hard drive for use in a document, give it an easy-to-remember file name, since your computer will automatically take the code word (often a combination of numbers and letters, as in a serial number) as the file name for the image. Save the file as a name you can easily recall.
- Be sure to format your visual so that the text wraps around it and does not become obscured by the image.

Lori Brister
Anna Gibson

Introduce Your Visuals

Refer to each visual by its number and, if necessary, mention the title as well. In introducing the visual, though, do not just insert a reference to it, such as "See Figure 3.4" or "Look at Table 1." Help readers to understand the relationships in your visual. Here are two ways of writing a lead-in sentence for a visual.

> Poor: Our store saw a dramatic rise in the shipment of electric ranges over the five-year period as opposed to the less impressive increase in washing machines. (See Figure 3.)

This sentence does not tie the visual (Figure 3) into the sentence where it belongs. The visual just trails insignificantly behind.

> Better: As Figure 3 shows, our store saw a dramatic rise in the shipment of electric ranges over the five-year period as opposed to the less impressive increase in washing machines.

Mentioning the visual in Figure 3 alerts readers to its presence and function in your work and helps them to better understand it.

Interpret Your Visuals

Give readers help in understanding your visual and in knowing what to look for. Let them know what is most significant about the visual. Do not expect the visual to explain itself. Inform readers what the numbers or images in your visual mean. What types of conclusions can you and your readers logically make after seeing the visual?

In a study on the benefits of vanpooling, one writer supplied the following visual, a table:

TABLE 1.   Travel Time (in minutes): Automobile Versus Vanpool

Private Automobile	Vanpool
25	32.5
30	39.0
35	45.5
40	52.0
45	58.5
50	65.0
55	71.5
60	78.0

Source: U.S. Department of Transportation. *Increased Transportation Efficiency Through Ridesharing: The Brokerage Approach* (Washington, D.C., DOT-OS—40096): 45.

Explaining the table, the writer called attention to it in the context of the report on transportation efficiency.

> Although, as Table 1 above suggests, the travel time in a vanpool may be as much as 30 percent longer than in a private automobile (to allow for pickups), the total trip time for the vanpool user can be about the same as with a private automobile because vanpools eliminate the need to search for parking spaces and to walk to the employment site entrance.[1]

Two Categories of Visuals

Visuals can be divided into two categories—tables and figures. A **table** arranges information—numbers and/or words—in parallel columns or rows for easy comparison of data. Anything that is not a table is considered a figure. **Figures** include graphs, circle charts, bar charts, organizational charts, flow charts, pictographs, maps, photographs, and drawings. Expect to use both in your work.

---

[1]James A. Devine, "Vanpooling: A New Economic Tool," *AIDC Journal.*

Tables

Tables are parallel columns or rows of information organized and arranged into categories to show changes in time, distance, cost, employment, or some other distinguishable or quantifiable variable in a compact space. Electronic spreadsheet programs heavily rely on tables to convey information, as in Table 11.1. Tables also summarize material for easy recall—causes of wars, provisions of a law, or differences between a common cold, flu, and pneumonia, as in Table 11.2. Observe how Table 11.3 (p. 460) also easily condenses much information and arranges it in quickly identifiable categories.

Parts of a Table

To use a table properly, you need to know the parts that constitute it. Refer to Table 11.3, which labels these parts, as you read the following:

- The main **column** is "Amount Needed to Satisfy Minimum Daily Requirement," and the **subcolumns** are the protein sources for which the table gives data.

TABLE 11.1   A Spreadsheet Table

	A	B	C	D	F	G	H
1	Acct#	Account Description	YTD	April	March	February	Janua
2							
3	**Employee Costs**						
4	110	Payroll	$171,465	$29,750	$28,547	$27,540	
5	120	IRS/FICA/Wk comp/State/SDI	$46,295	$8,032	$7,707	$7,435	
6	130	Commissions	$56,436	$9,520	$8,875	$9,825	
7	140	Retirement Plan	$20,575	$3,570	$3,425	$3,304	
8	150	Insurance	$9,000	$1,500	$1,500	$1,500	
9							
11	**Subcontractors & Services**						
12	201	Telecommunication Services	$2,616	$436	$436	$436	
13	202	Design Consultants	$875	$500	$375	$0	
14	203	Photo/Video Services	$535	$45	$325	$45	
15	250	Graphic Services	$2,957	$765	$95	$375	
16	251	Photo/Stats	$1,612	$568	$755	$0	
17	252	Typesetting	$1,453	$388	$325	$195	
18	253	Printing Services	$6,186	$951	$849	$325	
19	254	Legal & Accounting					
20							
21	**Supplies and Materials**						
22	301	Office Supplies	$875	$500	$732	$433	
23	302	Office Postage	$535	$45	$255	$325	
24	303	Office Equipment & Furniture	$2,957	$765	$78	$21	
25	304	Miscellaneous Supplies	$1,612	$568	$49	$36	
26							
27	**Facilities Overhead**						
28	405	Plant	$1,612	$568	$1,700	$1,700	

Sheet1 / Sheet2 / Sheet3

TABLE 11.2   Table Showing Differences Between a Common Cold, Influenza, and Pneumonia

Symptoms	Cold	Influenza	Pneumonia
Fever	Rare	Characteristic high (100.4–104°F); sudden onset, lasts 3 to 4 days	May or may not be high
Headache	Occasional	Prominent	Occasional
General aches and pains	Slight	Usual; often quite severe	Occasionally quite severe
Fatigue and weakness	Quite mild	Extreme; can last up to a month	May occur depending on type
Exhaustion	Never	May occur early and prominent	May occur depending on type
Runny, stuffy nose	Common	Sometimes	Not characteristic
Sneezing	Usual	Sometimes	Not characteristic
Sore throat	Common	Sometimes	Not characteristic
Chest discomfort, cough	Mild to moderate; hacking cough	Can become severe	Frequent and may be severe
Complications	Sinus and ear infections	Bronchitis, pneumonia; can be life-threatening	Widespread infections of other organs; can be life-threatening, especially in elderly and debilitated persons

Source: Jacquelyn G. Black, *Microbiology: Principles and Explorations.* Upper Saddle River, NJ: Prentice-Hall, 1996.

- The **stub** refers to the first vertical column on the left-hand side. The stub column heading is "Source." The stub lists the foods for which information is broken down in the subcolumns.
- A **rule** (or line) across the top of the table separates the headings from the body of the table.

Guidelines for Using Tables

When you include a table in your work, follow these guidelines.

- Number the tables according to the order in which they are discussed (Table 1, Table 2, Table 3).
- Include the table on the same page, where it is most appropriate. It is hard for readers to follow a table spread across different pages.

TABLE 11.3   Parts of a Table

Table number

TABLE 1 Efficiency of Some Protein Sources in Meeting an Adult's Minimum Daily Requirements				
Source	*Percent of Protein*	*Percent of Amino Acids*	*Amount Needed to Satisfy Minimum Daily Requirement*	
			(grams)	*(ounces)*
Cheese[a]	27	70	227	7.2
Corn	10	50	860	30.0
Eggs	11	97	403	14.1
Fish[a]	22	80	244	8.5
Kidney beans	23	40	468	16.4
Meat[a]	25	68	253	8.8
Milk	4	82	1,311	45.9[b]
Soybeans	34	60	210	7.3

← *Title*
← *Rule*
← *Column heading*
← *Subheading*

Stub

Source: Adapted from Cecie Starr and Ralph Taggart, *Biology: The Unity and Diversity of Life,* 4th ed. Belmont, CA: Wadsworth, 1987, p. 444. Copyright © 1987. Reprinted with permission of Brooks/Cole Publishing, a division of Thomson Learning.

← *Origin of data*

[a] = Average value
[b] = Equivalent of 6 cups

} *Footnotes*

- Give each table a concise and descriptive title to show exactly what is being represented or compared.
- Use words in the stub (a list of items about which information is given), but put numbers under column headings. The Source column in Table 11.3 is the stub.
- Supply footnotes (often indicated by small raised letters: [a], [b]) if something in the table needs to be qualified, for example, the number of cups of milk in Table 11.3. Then put that information below the table.
- List items in alphabetical, chronological, or other logical order.
- Situate your table vertically, not horizontally, on the page; it is easier to read that way.
- Arrange the data you want to compare vertically; it is easier to read down than across a series of rows.
- Place tables at the top (preferable) or bottom of the page and center them on the page rather than placing them up against the right or left margin.
- Don't use more than five or six columns; tables wider than that are more difficult for readers to use.
- Round off numbers in your columns to the nearest whole number to assist readers in following and retaining information.
- Always give credit to the source (the supplier of the statistical information) on which your table is based.

▋ Figures

As we saw, any visual that is not a table is classified as a figure. The types of figures we will examine next are

- line graphs
- circle, or pie, charts
- bar charts
- organizational charts
- flow charts
- pictographs
- maps
- photographs
- drawings

Line Graphs

Graphs transform numbers into pictures. They take statistical data presented in tables and put them into rising and falling lines, steep or gentle curves.

Functions of Line Graphs

Graphs vividly portray information that changes, such as

- sales
- costs
- trends
- distributions
- increases and decreases in, e.g., jobs, home building starts
- employment
- energy levels
- temperatures

Graphs not only describe past and current situations but also forecast trends.

Tech Note

Computer-Generated Graphs and Charts

You can easily generate charts, graphs, or tables by using the templates available in your word processing software, such as Microsoft Word, and by selecting Insert Chart or Insert Table. In fact, many of the visuals in this book, especially those in the long reports in Chapters 9 and 16, were created using such software. Graph and chart templates allow you to insert your raw numerical data

Continued

Continued

into the appropriate blanks and then add titles, labels for axes, and color-coded keys. Such software not only helps construct different visuals, including pie charts and flow charts, but it also allows writers to show visuals from different perspectives and emphases, such as shading, 3-D, exploded view, and many others. Spreadsheet programs, such as Microsoft Excel, also provide easy-to-use templates for creating graphs and charts using the numerical data you have entered into your spreadsheet. When using these software programs, avoid the temptation to make visuals too showy. Although dazzling graphics may look interesting, you don't want them to take over the report. Computer-generated graphs and charts should work with the writer's words, not overshadow them.

Graphs Versus Tables

Because graphs actually show change, they are more dramatic than tables. You will make the reader's job easier by using a graph rather than a table. Many financial websites and print publications—the *Wall Street Journal* and *USA Today*, for example—open with a graph for the benefit of busy readers who want a great deal of financial information summarized quickly.

A Simple Graph

Basically, a simple graph consists of two sides—a **vertical** or **y-axis** and a **horizontal** or **x-axis**—that intersect to form a right angle, as in Figure 11.4. The space between the two axes contains the picture made by the graph—in Figure 11.4 the amount of snowfall in Springfield between November 2007 and April 2008. The vertical line represents the **dependent variable** (the snowfall in inches), the horizontal line, the **independent variable** (time in months). The dependent variable is influenced most directly by the independent variable, which almost always is expressed in terms of time or distance. The vertical axis is read from bottom to top; the horizontal axis from left to right.

When a dependent variable occurs at a particular time on the independent variable (horizontal line), the place where the two points intersect, the **data point**, is marked, or plotted, on the graph. After all the points are plotted, a line is drawn to connect them; the resulting curve gives a picture of the overall pattern—snowfall in Springfield during the winter of 2007–2008.

Multiple-Line Graphs

The graph in Figure 11.4 contains only one line per category. But a graph can have multiple lines to show how a number of dependent variables (conditions, products) compare with each other.

The six-month sales figures for three salespeople can be seen in the graph in Figure 11.5. The graph contains a separate line for each of the three salespersons. At a glance readers can see how the three compare and how many dollars each salesperson generated per month. Note how the line representing each person is clearly differentiated from the others by symbols and colors. Each line is clearly tied to a **legend** (an explanatory key below the graph) specifying the three salespersons.

A simple line graph showing the amount of snowfall in Springfield from
November 2007 to April 2008.   Figure 11.4

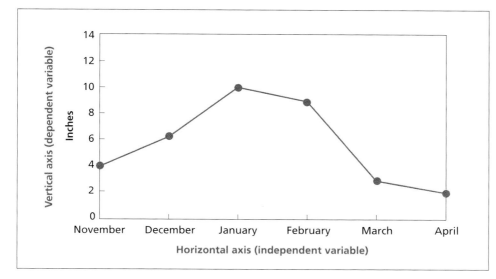

A multiple-line graph showing sales figures for the first six months of 2006 for
three salespeople.   Figure 11.5

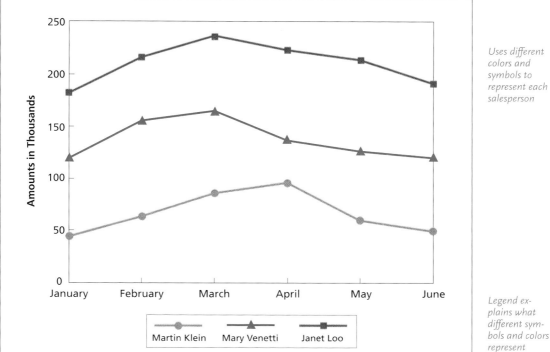

*Uses different
colors and
symbols to
represent each
salesperson*

*Legend ex-
plains what
different sym-
bols and colors
represent*

Figure 11.6   An area, or multiband, graph of Figure 11.5.

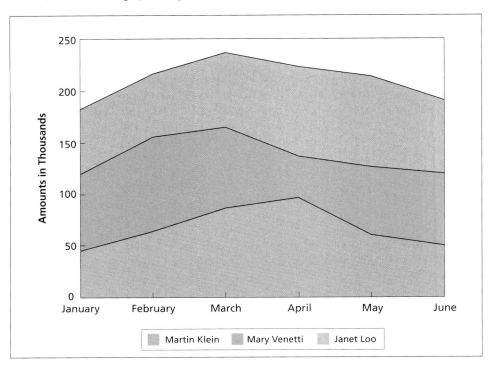

Figure 11.6 is another graphic representation of the information in Figure 11.5. The graph in Figure 11.6, known as an **area**, or **multiband, graph**, shows relationships among the three salespeople without providing the exact mathematical documentation of Figure 11.5. In the area graph in Figure 11.6 the spaces between the different curves are filled in, with colors keyed in the legend to identify the three salespersons.

Guidelines on Creating a Graph

1. Use no more than three lines in a multiple-line graph, so readers can interpret the graph more easily. If the lines run close together, use a legend to identify individual lines.
2. Label each line to identify what it represents for readers. Include a key, or legend, as in Figure 11.5.
3. Keep each line distinct in a multiple-line graph by using different colors, dots or dashes, or symbols. Note the different symbols in Figure 11.5.
4. Make sure you plot enough points to show a reasonable and ethical range of the data. Using only three or four points may distort the evidence.
5. Keep the scale consistent and realistic. If you start with hours, do not switch to days or vice versa. If you are recording annual rates or accounts, do not skip a year or two in the hope that you will save time or be more concise.

6. For some graphs there is no need to begin with a zero. This is called a **suppressed zero graph**, which automatically begins with a larger number when it would be impossible to start with zero. For others, you may not have to include numbers beyond seven or eight. Your subject and purpose will determine the rang of data you need to show.

Charts

Although charts and graphs may seem similar, there is a big difference between them. Graphs are usually more complex and plotted according to specific mathematical coordinates. Charts, on the other hand, do not display exact and complex mathematical data. Instead, they present an overall picture of how individual pieces of data (from a graph or table) fall into place to express relationships.

Among the most frequently used charts are (1) circle, or pie, charts, (2) bar charts, (3) organizational charts, and (4) flow charts.

Circle Charts

Circle charts are also known as **pie charts**, a name that descriptively points to their construction and interpretation. Tables are more technical and detailed than circle charts. Figure 11.7 shows an example of a pie chart used in a government document. A table or graph with a more detailed breakdown of, say, a city's budget would be much more appropriate for a technical audience (auditors, budget and city planners).

The full circle, or pie, represents the whole amount (100 percent or 360 degrees) of something: the entire budget of a company or a family, a population group, an area of land, the resources of an organization or institution. Each slice or wedge represents a percentage or portion of the whole.

A three-dimensional circle chart showing the breakdown by department of the proposed Midtown city budget for 2006.   Figure 11.7

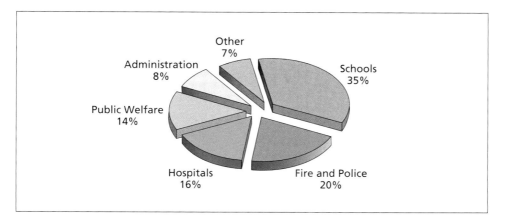

A circle chart effectively allows readers to see two things at once: the relationship of the parts to one another and the relationship of the parts to the whole.

Preparing a Circle Chart

Follow these seven rules to create and present your circle chart.

1. Keep your circle chart simple.   Don't try to illustrate technical statistical data in a pie chart. Pie charts are primarily used for general audiences.

2. Do not divide a circle, or pie, into too few or too many slices.   If you have only three wedges, use another visual to display them (a bar chart, for example, discussed below). If you have more than seven or eight wedges, you will divide the pie too narrowly, and overcrowding will destroy the dramatic effect. Instead, combine several slices of small percentages (2 percent, 3 percent, 4 percent) into one slice labeled "Other," "Miscellaneous," or "Related Items."

3. Make sure the individual slices total 100 percent, or 360 degrees.   For example, if you are constructing a circle chart to represent a family's budget, the breakdown percentages might be as follows:

Category	Percentage	Angle of slice
Housing	25%	90.9°
Food	22%	79.2°
Energy	20%	72.0°
Clothes	13%	46.8°
Health Care	12%	43.2°
Miscellaneous	8%	28.8°
Total	100%	360°

4. Put the largest slice first, at the 12 o'clock position, then move clockwise with proportionately smaller slices.   Schools occupy the largest slice in Figure 11.7 because they receive the biggest share of taxes.

5. Label each slice of the pie horizontally.   Key in the identifying term or quantity inside, but make sure the label is big enough to read. Do not put in a label upside down or slide it in vertically. If the individual slice of the pie is small, draw a connecting line from the slice to a label positioned outside the pie.

6. Shade, color, or cross-hatch slices of the pie to further separate and distinguish the parts.   Figure 11.7 effectively uses color. But be careful not to obscure labels and percentages; also make certain that adjacent slices can be distinguished readily from each other. Do not use the same color or similar colors for two slices.

7. Give percentages for each slice to further assist readers, as in Figure 11.7.

Bar Charts

A bar chart consists of a series of vertical or horizontal bars that indicate comparisons of statistical data. For instance, in Figure 11.8 vertical bars depict increases in numbers of working mothers. Figure 11.9 uses horizontal bars to depict the na-

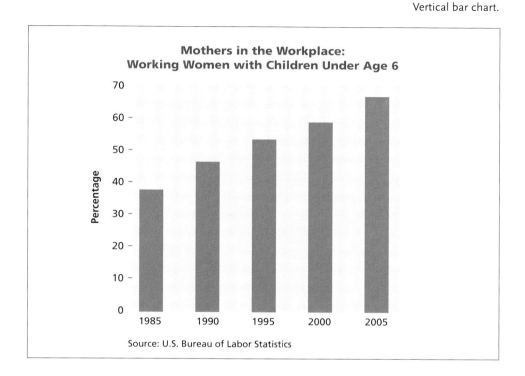

tion's top 20 metropolitan areas, based on building permits. The length of the bars is determined according to a scale that your computer software can easily compute.

Bar Charts, Graphs, and Tables—Which Should You Use?

When should you use a bar chart rather than a table or a line graph? Your audience will help you decide. If you are asked to present statistics on costs for the company accountant, use a table. Since it is limited to a few columns, however, a bar chart cannot convey as much information as a table or graph. However, if you are presenting the same information to a group of stockholders or to a diverse group of employees, a bar chart may be more relevant and persuasive.

Types of Bar Charts

There are three types of bar charts.

   1. Simple bar charts.   Figure 11.8 is the most basic form of bar chart. Each bar represents the percentage of working women with children under the age of 6, and the height of the bar corresponds to the number of percentage points for a given year. To read the chart effectively, note where the top of the bar is in relation to the vertical scale on the left. The chart compares one type of data (the percentage of working mothers) over a period of time (every five years from 1985 to 2005).

Figure 11.9   Horizontal bar chart.

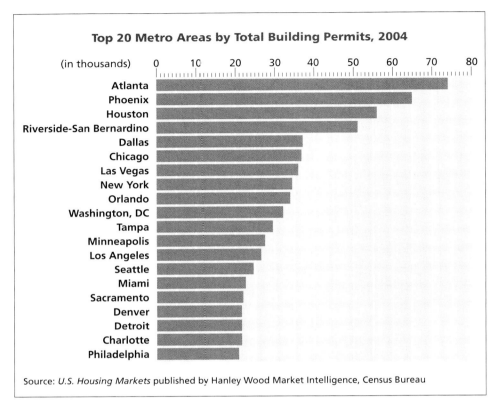

Top 20 Metro Areas by Total Building Permits, 2004

Source: *U.S. Housing Markets* published by Hanley Wood Market Intelligence, Census Bureau

2. Multiple-bar charts.   Figure 11.10 shows a variation of the simple, vertical bar chart. Four different colored bars are used for each year to represent the amount of money spent on different types of advertising in 2003, 2004, 2005, and 2006. A legend at the top of the chart explains what each bar stands for. But avoid using more than four bars in a group for any one year. More bars will make your chart crowded and difficult to read.

3. Segmented, or cross-hatched (divided), bar charts.   To show the different components that constitute a measured whole, use a segmented bar chart like the one in Figure 11.11. A single segmented bar lists the travel expenses of Weemco, a small firm, in October 2007. The entire bar equals the travel total—$137,000— which was spent in four areas: airfare, ground transportation, lodging, and meals. Each of these expenses is represented by a different type of shading on the single column. A group of segmented bars can be used to show multiple comparisons among many categories, as in Figure 11.12, which depicts energy consumption levels and types in five states.

A multiple-bar chart showing advertising expenditures by major media, 2003–2006.   Figure 11.10

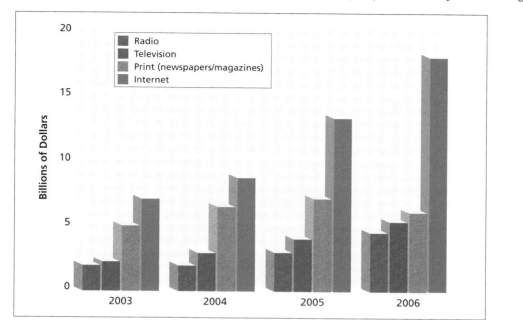

A segmented bar chart representing total travel expenditures for Weemco Communications for October 2007.   Figure 11.11

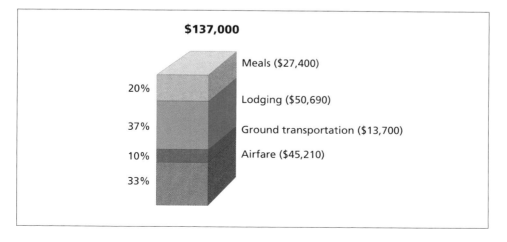

Organizational Charts

An **organizational chart** pictures the chain of command in a company or agency, with the lines of authority stretching down from the chief executive, manager, or administrator to assistant manager, department heads, or supervisors to the work force of employees. Figure 11.13 shows a hospital's organizational chart for its nursing services.

Organizational charts have these functions:

- to inform employees and customers about the makeup of a company
- to depict the various offices, departments, and units
- to show where people work in relationship to each other in a business
- to coordinate employee efforts in routing information to appropriate departments

Flow Charts

A **flow chart** displays the stages in which something is manufactured, is accomplished, develops, or operates. Flow charts are highly effective in showing the steps in following a procedure. They can also be used to plan the day's or week's activities.

A flow chart tells a story with arrows, boxes, and sometimes pictures. Boxes are connected by arrows to visualize the stages of a process. The presence and

Figure 11.12   A multiple-bar, segmented bar chart showing energy consumption by sector in five states that consumed the most energy in a given year.

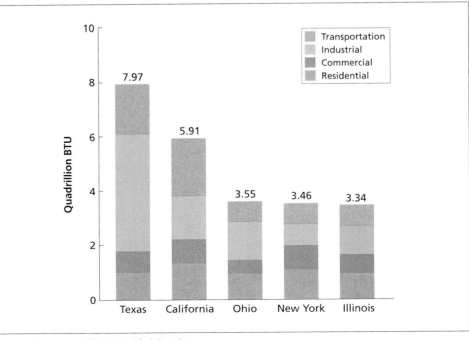

Source: U.S. Energy Information Administration.

direction of the arrows tell the reader the order and movement of events involved in the process. Flow charts often proceed from left to right and back again, as in the flow chart below, showing the steps to be taken before graduation.

Flow charts can also be constructed to read from top to bottom. Programming instructions frequently are written that way. See, for example, Figure 11.14 (p. 472),

An organizational chart representing critical care nursing services at Union General Hospital. Figure 11.13

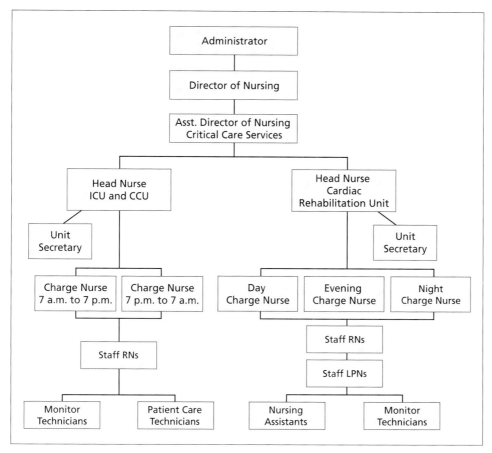

Figure 11.14   A programming flow chart showing steps in writing a research paper.

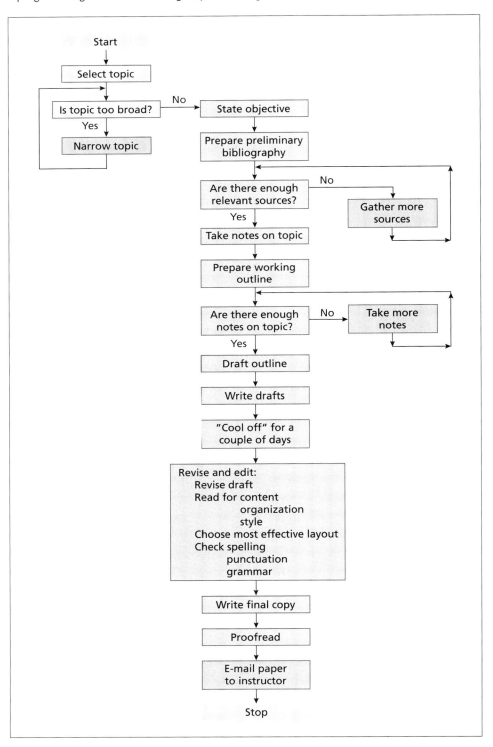

which uses a programming flow chart to show the steps a student must follow in writing a research paper.

A flow chart should clarify, not complicate, a process. Do not omit any important stages, but at the same time do not introduce unnecessary or unduly detailed information. Show at least three or four stages and make sure the various stages appear in the correct sequence.

Pictographs

Similar to a bar chart, a **pictograph** uses picture symbols (called **pictograms**) to represent differences in statistical data, as in Figure 11.15 below. A pictograph repeats the same symbol or icon to depict the quantity of items being measured. Each symbol stands for a specific number, quantity, or value. Pictographs are visually appealing and dramatic and are far more appropriate for a nontechnical than a technical audience.

A pictograph showing the growth of one state's retirement assets.   Figure 11.15

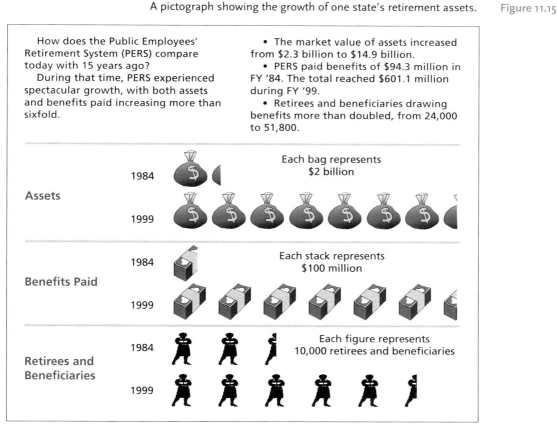

Source: PERS Member Newsletter, August 1999. Official Publication of the Public Employees' Retirement System of Mississippi. By permission of Public Employees' Retirement System.

Guidelines on Creating Pictographs

When you create a pictograph, follow these four guidelines:

1. Choose an appropriate, easily identifiable symbol for the topic.
2. Indicate the precise quantities each icon represents by placing numbers after or at the top of the visual.
3. Increase the number of symbols rather than their sizes because differences in sizes are often difficult to construct or interpret.
4. Avoid crowding too much information into a pictograph, such as the one in Figure 11.3, in which a U.S. dollar bill is divided into too many sections.

Maps

The maps you use on the job may range from highly sophisticated and detailed geographic tools to simple sketches such as the map in Figure 11.16, which shows the location of a town's water filter plants and pumping stations. This is a **large-scale map** that displays a good deal of social, economic, or physical data for a small area.

You may have to construct your own map, like the one in Figure 11.16, or scan one in a published source or one on the Internet. If you scan a map, be sure to obtain permission to use it from the copyright holder. Or you may use a map from MapQuest, as in Figure 11.17.

Figure 11.16   A map showing the location of Smithville Water Department's filter plants and pumping stations.

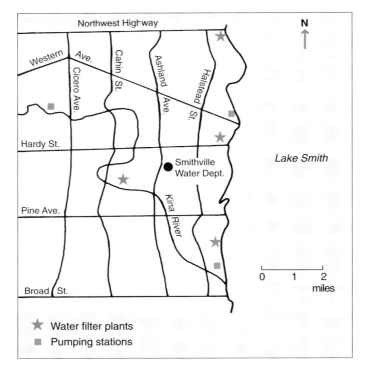

A large-scale map from MapQuest.   Figure 11.17

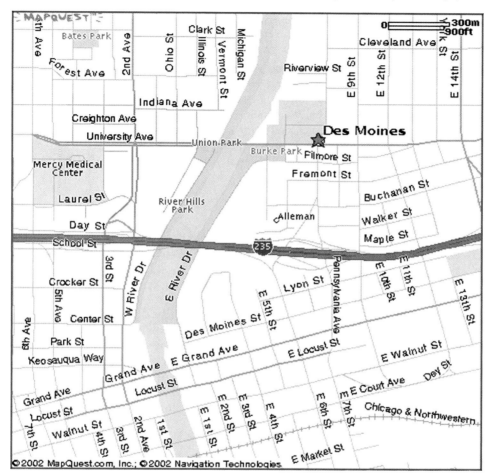

Provided by MapQuest.com. Reprinted with permission.

Tech Note

Using MapQuest

You can easily create detailed road maps, like the one in Figure 11.17, with MapQuest (*www.mapquest.com*). First you select a country, say, the United States, then below the map display area, you point and click on "Zoom in." Next point to the area on the map that you are interested in and click again; each time you point and click, a new map will be drawn that is more detailed

Continued

Continued

than the previous one and centered on the place you last pointed to. You just continue to point and click until you have the desired level of detail.

In addition to roads, MapQuest has a number of "Places of Interest" categories you can select to be displayed. As you are zooming in, you can go at any time to the bottom of the screen and select whatever categories of interesting places you want to add to your map. Categories include *Personal* (ones you add yourself), *Dining, Lodging, Entertainment, Education, Recreation, Shopping,* and *Health Care.* Each category has a selection of subcategories from which you can further choose so you will see displayed exactly what you need.

Guidelines for Creating a Map

Follow these steps when you create a map:

1. Always acknowledge your source if you did not construct the map yourself.
2. Use dots, lines, colors, symbols, and shading to indicate features. Markings should be clear and distinct.
3. If necessary, include a legend, or map key, explaining dotted lines, colors, shading, and symbols as in Figure 11.16.
4. Exclude features (rivers, elevations, county seats) that do not directly relate to your topic. For example, a map showing the crops grown in two adjacent counties need not show all the roads and highways in those counties. A map showing the presence of strip mining or features such as hills or valleys needs to indicate elevation, but a map depicting population or religious affiliation need not include topographical (physical) detail.
5. Indicate direction. Conventionally, maps show north, often by including an arrow and the letter N: $N\uparrow$.

Photographs

Correctly taken or scanned, photographs are an extremely helpful addition to job-related writing. A photograph's chief virtues are realism and clarity. A photo can

- show what an object looks like (Figure 11.18)
- demonstrate how to perform a certain procedure (Figure 11.19)
- compare relative sizes and shapes of objects (Figures 11.18 and 11.19)
- compare and contrast scenes or procedures (Figure 11.20)

Digital cameras allow you to supply professional-looking, customized photos with your written work. As with other cameras, you point and shoot with a digital camera. But unlike a traditional camera, the digital camera lets you review every photo you take before you print it. You can shoot a photo, take it in slow motion, and play it back, which allows you to scroll, zoom in, blow it up, adjust darkness or light, even change exposures.

A photo showing what a piece of equipment looks like.   Figure 11.18

Source: Corbis Royalty Free (*http://www.corbis.com*).

Digital Photography

There are many ways to take and manipulate digital pictures:

- Video cameras/camcorders have a digital camera option. These cameras can be hooked up to your computer to download, view, and send your photos.
- Camera phones, some as small as 2″ x 3″, are also equipped with digital cameras so you can take a photo on site and immediately e-mail it. Camera phones, though, have raised piracy and copyright concerns. It would be unethical to use a camera phone in certain environments.

Continued

Continued

■ You can download your pictures from a digital camera onto your PC and then adjust the color, sharpen the image/focus, enlarge or crop the picture, and save and print the photos. Since digital cameras use smart cards, you don't have to worry about taking film to be developed. You can send your photos as e-mail attachments, save them on a CD-ROM, upload them to a website, and, if you have a television connection, you can even view them on your TV.

Digitalized photography offers the following benefits in the global marketplace:

■ Shows conditions or sites right away so you can include a photo in an incident or credit report
■ Gives you more than one opportunity to take a picture—helps you select, highlight, and edit
■ Allows you to send photographs easily and quickly over the Internet
■ Gives you the opportunity to edit photographs for color, contrast, brightness, size, and red-eye

To achieve these goals, be careful when using a digital camera or camera phone that it is set to the correct photo-quality level. The poorer the quality, the more pictures your camera will hold. However, if you will be using photographs for a newsletter or company magazine or if you wish to print photographic-quality images, make sure your camera is set on a higher quality level.

Figure 11.19   A photo showing how to perform a procedure and comparing relative sizes and shapes of objects.

Source: Corbis Royalty Free (*http://www.corbis.com*).

Photos showing comparison/contrast: The top photo shows artwork prepared manually for a project without use of a computer, while the bottom photo shows artwork prepared and presented electronically using PowerPoint.

Figure 11.20

Source: © Stephen Frisch, Stock Boston.

Source: © Matthew Borkoski, Stock Boston.

Use special care when you take a photograph with either a traditional or a digital camera. The most important point to remember is that what you see and what the camera records might be two different sights. Before you take a photo, decide how much foreground and background image you need. Include only the details that are *necessary* and *relevant* for your purpose.

To get a graphic sense of the effects of taking a photo the right and wrong way, study the photographs in Figures 11.21 and 11.22. A clear and useful picture of a hydraulic truck (often called a "cherry picker") used to cut high branches can be seen in Figure 11.21. The photographer rightly placed the truck in the foreground, but included enough background information to indicate the truck's function. The worker in the bucket helps to show the truck in operation.

In Figure 11.22 everything merges because the shot was taken from the wrong angle. The reader has no sense of the parts of the truck, their size, or their function.

Observe the following five guidelines, many of which Figure 11.22 violates:

1. Focus your camera on the most important part of the image.
2. Select the correct angle. Choose a vantage point that will enable you to record essential information as graphically as possible.
3. Give the right amount of detail. Pictures that include clutter and irrelevant detail compete for the reader's attention and detract from or risk erasing the subject.

Figure 11.21   An effective photograph—truck in foreground, enough background information, and a worker to show the size and function of the truck.

Photograph by David Longmire.

Figure 11.22

A poor photograph—taken from the wrong angle so that everything merges and becomes confusing.

Photograph by David Longmire.

4. Take the picture from the right distance. If you need a shot of a three-story of-fice building, your picture may show only one or two stories if you are stand-ing too close to the building when you photograph it. Standing too far away from an object, however, means that the photograph will reduce the object's importance and record unnecessary details.
5. Watch your exposure—if there is overexposure, your photo will be too light; if there is underexposure, it will be too dark.

Drawings

Drawings can show where an object is located, how a tool or machine is put to-gether, or what signals are given or steps taken in a particular situation. A drawing can be simple, like the one in Figure 11.23, which shows readers exactly where to place smoke detectors in a house.

A more detailed drawing can reveal the interior of an object. Such sketches are called **cutaway drawings** because they show internal parts normally concealed from view. Figure 11.24 (p. 483) is a cutaway drawing of an antilock brake system.

Figure 11.23   A simple drawing showing where to place smoke detectors in a house.

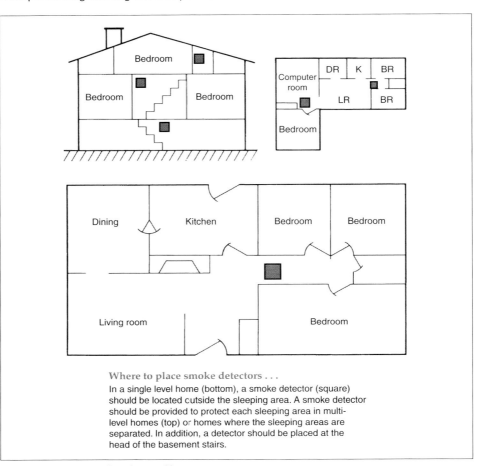

Where to place smoke detectors . . .
In a single level home (bottom), a smoke detector (square)
should be located outside the sleeping area. A smoke detector
should be provided to protect each sleeping area in multilevel homes (top) or homes where the sleeping areas are
separated. In addition, a detector should be placed at the
head of the basement stairs.

Reprinted by permission of *Southern Building.*

Another kind of sketch is an **exploded drawing**, which blows the entire object
(a notebook) up and apart as in Figure 11.25 (p. 484) to show how the individual
parts are arranged. An exploded drawing comes with most computers and uses **callouts,** or labels, to identify the components. The labels are often attached to the
drawing with arrows or lines. As the name suggests, the labels "call out" the parts
so that readers can identify them quickly.

Guidelines for Using a Drawing

1. Keep your drawing simple. Include only as much detail as your reader will need
   to understand what to do, be it to assemble or to operate a mechanism. Do not
   include any extra details.
2. Clearly label all parts so that your reader can identify and separate them.

Cutaway drawing of an antilock brake system.   Figure 11.24

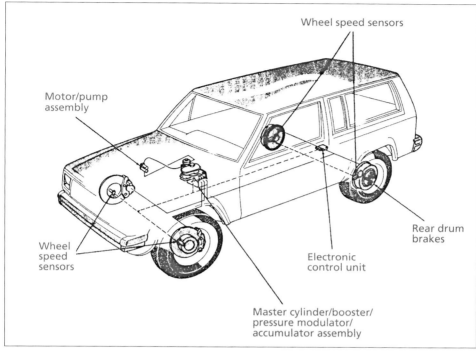

Source: Chilton Automotive Books. *Jeep Wagoneer/Comanche 1984–1996 Repair Manual.* Chilton is a registered trademark of Cahners Business Information, a Division of Reed Elsevier Inc. and has been licensed to W. G. Nichols, Inc. Reprinted with permission.

3. Decide on the most appropriate view of the object you want to illustrate—aerial, frontal, lateral, reverse, exterior, interior—and indicate in your title which view it is.

4. Keep the parts of the drawing proportionate unless you are purposely enlarging one section.

Visuals from the Internet

The Internet has an enormous impact on the types of visuals you can expect to use in the workplace. Photos, drawings, line art, animated images, clip art, logos, graphs, tables—all are found on the Web, and some websites may embed art from a cluster of other sites. (See the Tech Note "Computer-Generated Visuals" on pp. 449–450.) Companies as well as individuals create their own websites, most of which include both text and visual displays. Go to pages 521–523 for appropriate guidelines. There are several ways to find visuals on the Internet.

- Browse the Web for creative new ideas for graphics.
- Use search engines such as Scour.Net, Filez, and Webplaces: Clip art Searcher/Surf to locate graphics and images.

Figure 11.25   Exploded drawing of a notebook.

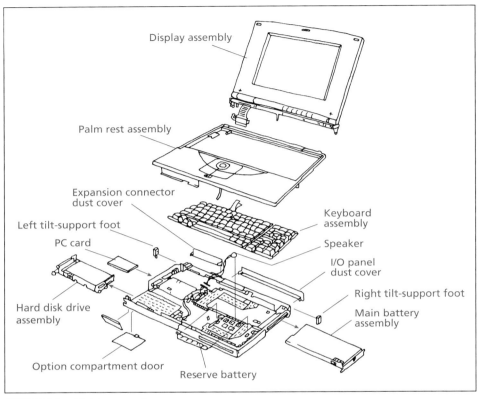

- Look at some of the "Top Sites" for examples and ideas of the Web's most ac-claimed work. A listing of those sites is at *http://scc.ntnu.edu.tw/~cta/top100/ _open.htm.*
- See the portfolios of artists online (*http://www.starvingartist.com/*) who sell their work for a fee.
- Consult the numerous online graphics magazines:
    —*Corel Magazine* (*http://www.corelmag.com/*)
    —*Design World* (*http://www.designworld-mag.com/*)
    —*Computer Graphics World* (*http://www.cgw.com/index2.htm*)
- Take advantage of royalty-free pictures and images available from these services:
    —*Corbis* (*http://www.corbis.com/*)
    —*Art I Need, Inc.* (*http://www.artineed.com*)
    —*Consulting First, Inc.* (*http://www.photosetc.com*)
    —*GraphX Kingdom* (*http://www.graphxkingdom.com*)

If you see a graphic image at a site that you want to use in a report or paper, it is fairly easy to download that image. But remember that because the images you save from the Web were placed there by someone else, you must reference your sources. If your work is to be published, or if you intend to put it on the Web yourself, you must obtain written permission from the copyright holders of any images you want to include. Electronic publications require you to follow the same ethical rules you do with print sources.

Clip Art

Clip art (or icons) refers to ready-to-use electronic images. These small cartoon-style representations and photographs, such as the ones shown in Figure 11.26, depict almost anything you can think of and pertain to almost every discipline—architecture, computer science, criminal justice, international marketing, sports, government, health care.

Many graphics packages come with comprehensive clip art libraries grouped under such useful headings as energy, government, leisure, health, money, the outdoors, food, technology, transportation. Microsoft Office includes a clip art library with links to a larger online database of free clip art. There are also free clip art and photo-illustration databases such as Yahoo Picture Gallery at *http://gallery.yahoo .com*. You can use clip art for a variety of projects.

When you use clip art, follow these guidelines:

1. **Use simple, easy-to-understand icons.** Select an image that conveys your idea quickly and directly. Avoid using an icon of an unfamiliar object or of a drawing or silhouette that might confuse your audience.

Examples of clip art.   Figure 11.26

2. **Use clip art functionally.** Do not insert clip art as decorations. Using too many will make your work look unprofessional. Each piece of clip art should contribute significantly to, not compete with, your message.
3. **Make sure the clip art is relevant for your audience and your message.** A clip art airplane does not belong in a technical report on fuel capacity or jet engine design.
4. **Make sure your clip art is professional.** Some clip art is humorous, even silly, which may not be appropriate for a professional business report or proposal.

Using Visuals Ethically

Make sure your visuals, whether you create or import them, are ethical. Like your words, your visuals should represent you, your company, and the data truthfully. Ethical visuals convey and interpret statistical information and other types of data, products and equipment, locations, and even individuals without misinterpretation. Your visuals should neither distort events and data nor mislead readers. Ethical visuals should be:

- accurate
- honest, fair
- complete
- appropriate

- easy to read
- clearly labeled
- uncluttered
- consistent with conventions

To ensure that your visuals are honest, accurate, and easy to read, avoid the following unethical practices no matter what type of visual you use.

Photos

- Do not distort a photo by omitting key details or by misrepresenting dimensions, angles, sizes, or surroundings or by superimposing one image over another. For example, taking or editing a photo up close without showing any background and with only four or five people standing in front of a speaker, but then writing that a large crowd attended a presentation, distorts the truth.
- Do not take a photo of your most expensive, top-of-the-line product/model but then place the cost of your lowest-priced product/model under it.
- Do not misrepresent location. For example, taking a photo in a "doctored" or off-site location, studio, or lab and then claiming it as an "actual" location shot is unethical.
- Never take a photo of an individual for business purposes (e.g., putting it in a newsletter, ad, on the Web) without his or her permission.
- Don't counterfeit or subtly alter a company's logo to sell, distribute, or promote an imitation as the real thing.

Graphs

- Don't distort a graph by plotting it in misleading or unequal intervals. For example, omitting certain years or dates to hide a decline in profits (contrast Figure 11.27, and its misleading interpretation, with the ethical revision in Figure 11.28).

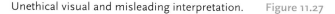
Unethical visual and misleading interpretation.   Figure 11.27

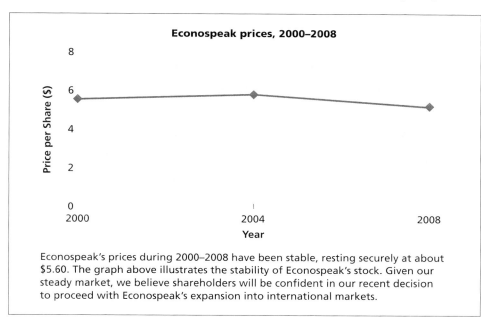

Econospeak prices, 2000–2008

Econospeak's prices during 2000–2008 have been stable, resting securely at about $5.60. The graph above illustrates the stability of Econospeak's stock. Given our steady market, we believe shareholders will be confident in our recent decision to proceed with Econospeak's expansion into international markets.

Ethical revision of Figure 11.27.   Figure 11.28

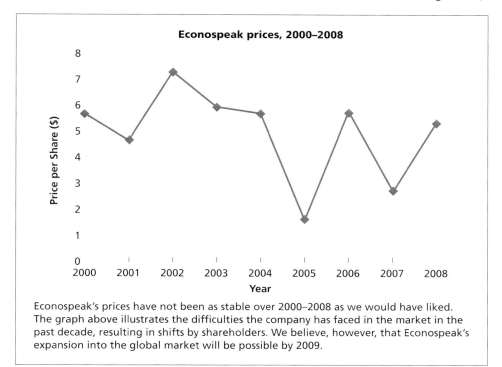

Econospeak prices, 2000–2008

Econospeak's prices have not been as stable over 2000–2008 as we would have liked. The graph above illustrates the difficulties the company has faced in the market in the past decade, resulting in shifts by shareholders. We believe, however, that Econospeak's expansion into the global market will be possible by 2009.

- Include information in correct chronological sequence along the horizontal axis.
- Don't switch the type of information usually given along the vertical axis with the horizontal axis.
- Don't project growth or increases without having reliable and valid reasons.
- Don't misrepresent data or trends by making increments along the vertical axis too limited, leaving a much smaller (and incomplete) area to represent. When data are plotted wrongly this way, readers are unethically led to misinterpret the numbers—to read that there was little loss in revenue, or no change in sales, for example. For instance, if the horizontal axis begins at $5 and advances to $6 a share, you leave only an intentionally small and misleading area to measure. If stocks fell below $5 a share, your graph would unethically not represent those declines.

Bar Charts

- Don't use color or shading to mislead or distort—for example, shading one bar to make it more prominent than the others.
- Make sure the height and width of each bar truthfully represents the data it purports to. That is, don't make one of the bars larger to maximize the profits, products, or sales in any one year.
- Show bars for every year (or other sales period) covered. Note how the unethical bar chart (and accompanying text) in Figure 11.29 violates the rule but the chart in Figure 11.30 faithfully represents the data.

Pie Charts

- Don't use 3-D to distort the thickness and unjustified emphasis of one slice of the circle to misleadingly deemphasize others.
- Don't conceal negative information (losses, expenses, etc.) by silently including the information in another category or slice or lumping it into a category marked "other" or "miscellaneous."
- Make sure percentages match the number and size of the wedges or slices of the pie chart. See Figures 11.31 and 11.32. Note how a larger expense for Guest Speakers (35% of budget) is unethically misrepresented in Figure 11.31 by using a smaller-sized wedge, while the expenses for Venue Rental are actually less than for Guest Speaker expenses but drawn larger to misrepresent costs.

Drawings

- Avoid any clutter that hides features.
- Label all parts correctly.
- Do not omit or shadow any necessary parts.
- Draw an object accurately. Tell readers if your drawing is the actual size of the object or equipment or if it is drawn to scale. Provide a scale.

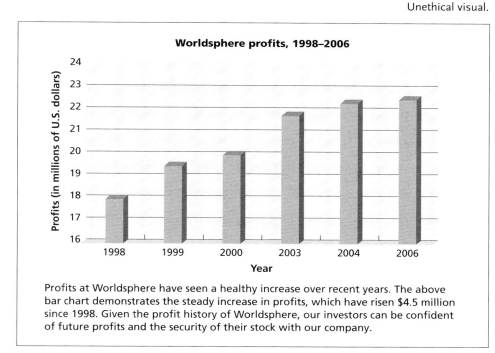

Profits at Worldsphere have seen a healthy increase over recent years. The above bar chart demonstrates the steady increase in profits, which have risen $4.5 million since 1998. Given the profit history of Worldsphere, our investors can be confident of future profits and the security of their stock with our company.

Although profits at Worldsphere have been volatile in the past eight years, we are now at our highest profit margin yet. The bar chart above shows the effects of market difficulties for the period 2000–2002, when the industry suffered major cutbacks. However, Worldsphere achieved a successful turnaround in 2003, with profits regaining strength due to revised marketing.

Figure 11.31   Unethical visual of pie chart.

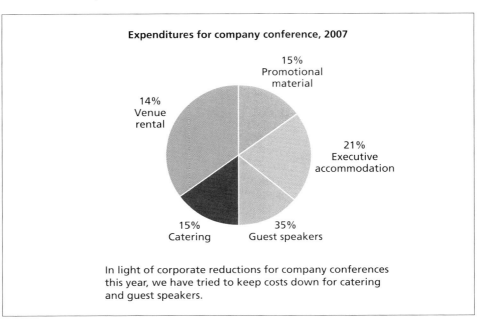

Expenditures for company conference, 2007

15%
Promotional
material

14%
Venue
rental

21%
Executive
accommodation

15%
Catering

35%
Guest speakers

In light of corporate reductions for company conferences
this year, we have tried to keep costs down for catering
and guest speakers.

Figure 11.32   Ethical revision of Figure 11.31.

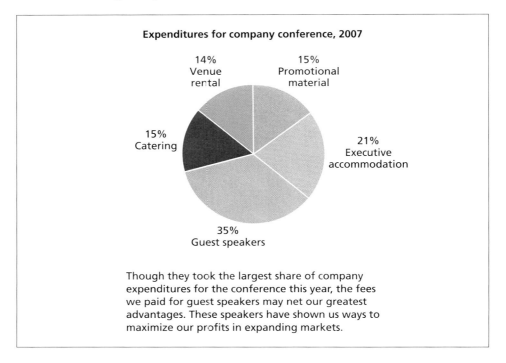

Expenditures for company conference, 2007

14%
Venue
rental

15%
Promotional
material

15%
Catering

21%
Executive
accommodation

35%
Guest speakers

Though they took the largest share of company
expenditures for the conference this year, the fees
we paid for guest speakers may net our greatest
advantages. These speakers have shown us ways to
maximize our profits in expanding markets.

Using Appropriate Visuals for International Audiences

Online Study Center

Locate designing globalization exercises at college.hmco.com/pic/kolin8e

Whether you are writing for an expanding international business community in South America or in China or for multicultural readers in the United States, you will have to prepare numerous documents that require visuals. These can range from instructions containing warning and caution statements and computer manuals explaining technical details to sales documents, reports, and online presentations. Clear, effective visuals and other graphic devices are crucial to the success of your website for the global marketplace.

Choose your visuals for international readers just as carefully as you do your words. Visuals should be designed to help international audiences understand your message clearly and without bias. Visuals and other graphics must be consistent with your message, not detract from or distort it. See page 695 of Terri Ruckel's report in Chapter 16 to learn more about communicating effectively with graphics for an international audience in the U.S. work force.

Keep in mind that visuals do not automatically transfer from one culture to another. They are not boilerplate images that have the same meaning for all readers across the globe. Like words, visuals—photos, clip art, designs, colors, and other graphic devices—may have one meaning or use in the United States and a radically different one in other countries. There are very few universal symbols aside from the jagged line indicating voltage, arms crossed in front of the throat to represent choking, or an ↑, showing the way to keep a package in an upright position. While the golden arches of McDonald's may be known around the globe, not every company achieves that level of a world brand. MasterCard has recently created a new symbol—a hand holding a card surrounded by a dotted circle—that it hopes will become a universal symbol signifying that merchants accept contactless payments.

Visuals reflect the national, ethnic, and racial traditions of a particular country. Since they are symbols of cultural identity and value, make sure you respect your readers' visual communication. To avoid confusing or offending an international audience, investigate the meaning and cultural significance of a visual before you include it. Consult a native speaker from your audience's country to see if your visuals are culturally acceptable; then follow up with your collaborative team and any graphic artists assigned to the project to assure every visual is acceptable.

To communicate appropriately and respectfully with international readers through visuals and other graphics, follow these guidelines:

1. Do not use any images that ethnically or racially stereotype your readers. A large clothing manufacturer was criticized by the Asian American community when it released T-shirts depicting two men with slanted eyes and rice paddy hats as laundromat owners. The verbal message on the T-shirt was as offensive as the stereotypical visuals: "Wong Brothers: Two Wongs Can Make It White." Similarly, depicting Native Americans through clip art images of red-faced chiefs is insulting. Rather than using an ethnic or racial pictogram, use neutral stick figures or clip art.

2. Be respectful of religious symbols and images.   A cross to a U.S. audience represents a church, first aid, or a hospital, and, when the cross is a large red one on a white background, the Red Cross. But the symbol for that humanitarian agency in Turkey and in other Muslim countries is the crescent. Portraying a smiling Buddha to sell products is considered disrespectful to residents in Southeast Asia.

3. Avoid using culturally insensitive or objectionable photographs.   What is acceptable and, in fact, expected in photographs in the United States may be taboo elsewhere in the world. For example, portraying men and women eating together at a business conference is unacceptable in Saudi Arabia; a photograph showing men and women swimming together in a hotel pool would go against local customs in China. Moreover, depicting individuals seated with one leg crossed over the other is regarded as a disrespectful gesture in many countries in the world.

4. Be cautious about importing images/photos with hand gestures in your work, especially in manuals or other instructional materials.   Many gestures are culture-specific; they do not necessarily mean the same thing in other countries that they do in the United States. Table 11.4 lists cultural differences around the globe for some common gestures.

5. Avoid any icons or clip art that international readers would misunderstand. Animal symbolism varies extensively from one country to another. In the United States, an owl can stand for wisdom, thrift, and memory, while in Japan, Romania, and some African countries it is a symbol for death. A blindfolded woman balanc-

TABLE 11.4   Different Cultural Meanings of Various Gestures

Gesture	*Meaning in the United States*	*Meaning in Other Countries*
OK sign Index finger joined to thumb in a circle	All right; agreement	Sexual insult in Brazil, Germany, Russia; sign for zero, worthlessness in France
Thumbs-up	A winning gesture; good job; approval	Offensive gesture in Muslim countries
Waving or holding out open palm	Stop	Obscene in Greece— equivalent to throwing garbage
Pointing with the index finger	This way; pay attention; turn the page	Rude, insulting in Japan; in Saudi Arabia used only for animals, not people
Nodding head up and down	Agreement, saying yes	Greek version of saying "no"; in China means "I understand," **not** "I agree"
Motioning with index finger	Signal to "come over here"	Insulting in China—instead, extend arm and wave to ask "come over"

ing a set of scales, the symbol for justice in the United States, is meaningless in this context for readers in Africa or East Asia. A computer programmer who used the symbol of a highway sign for Route 66 to convey an "IP router" failed to realize that this icon would confuse international audiences and perhaps some Americans as well. Similarly, a software program showing the icon of a mailbox (below)

for the designation "You Have Mail" confused readers in other countries who thought the icon represented a birdhouse. A better alternative would be an icon of an envelope.

6. Be careful using directional signs and shapes.   While road signs tend to be fairly recognizable throughout the world—for example, the octagon is the shape for the stop sign—there are country-specific signs and code books. For instance, a pennant on American highways, exclusively signaling a **No-passing zone,** may not have the same meaning in Nigeria or India. The symbol below points to a railroad crossing for American readers but would baffle an audience in the Czech Republic.

7. Don't offend non-native speakers of English by using culturally biased colors. Reconsider using red for warning or danger signals in instructions for Chinese readers, for whom that color is used for happiness and good fortune at weddings. Similarly, red represents another positive attribute in "La Red," the name of a network of Latina business women in California, or "Wear Red Day" sponsored by the American Heart Association in February to promote women's health. But in Indonesia red signifies anger, and a red sun in the Philippines evokes painful memories of World War II. Green may be the national color of the Irish Republic, but in China it stands for infertility or adultery. In the United States, orange is used as a background color for highway signs noting construction and for jackets worn by hunters. But this color has very different political overtones in Northern Ireland and in Holland. Rather than risk offending non-native speakers, try to use a variety of colors, rather than a single primary color. See also Chapter 5, page 178.

8. Don't confuse an international audience with punctuation and other writing symbols used in the United States.   Punctuation use and symbols vary widely around the globe. Not all cultures use a **?** to end a sentence asking a question, to represent the **Help** function in a computer program, or for an **FAQ** link on a website.

And an **!** does not symbolize an exclamation mark everywhere in the world. Spanish, for example, inverts these symbols at the start of questions or exclamations.

¿Quieres ir? (Do you want to go?)

¡Qué sorpresa! (What a surprise!)

In German, opening quotation marks are placed and inverted at the bottom of a line rather than above the letters, and the closing marks are inverted, too.

Er sagte: »Wir gehen am Dienstag.«

Elipses (**. . .**) and slashes **/** (and/or) are other punctuation symbols that may not be a part of the language your international audience reads and writes. Similarly, be careful about using the following graphic symbols, familiar to writers and speakers of U.S. English, but not necessarily to an international audience:

#	pound	&	ampersand (and)
©	copyright	*	asterisk
™	trademark	%	percentage

Include a glossary or a key to these symbols or any other graphics your reader may not understand or revise your sentences to avoid these symbols.

Using the graphic symbols and other visuals discussed in this chapter appropriately is vital to your success as a researcher, writer, and presenter in the global marketplace.

Conclusion

This chapter has introduced you to the types of visuals you can expect to use frequently in the world of work—and how to construct, label, insert, and introduce them in your writing. Following the guidelines here will make your documents persuasive and easier for your readers to follow. When using visuals, always keep in mind the importance of following the same ethical standards that you follow for your written work. You also need to be respectful of your audience's culture and the context in which your visual is found.

Online Study Center

Access the designing Revision Checklists online at college.hmco.com/pic/kolin8e

✔ Revision Checklist

☐ Located all places where a visual would help readers better understand my message.
☐ Used appropriate Internet images as a virtual library of visuals.

Continued

Continued

☐ Chose most effective visual (table, chart, graph, drawing, photograph) to represent information the audience needs.

☐ Experimented with different graphics software programs.

☐ Drafted and edited visual until it meets readers' needs.

☐ Verified statistical data that visual portrays.

☐ Made sure that visual does not simply repeat information in my written work.

☐ Selected right amount of technical detail to include in visual.

☐ Ensured that every visual is attractive, clear, complete, and relevant.

☐ Gave each visual a number, a title, and, where necessary, a legend and/or a callout.

☐ Numbered tables and figures consecutively.

☐ Inserted visual near the written description or commentary to which it pertains.

☐ Introduced and interpreted each visual in appropriate place in report or paper.

☐ Acknowledged sources for any copyrighted visuals and gave credit to individuals whose statistical data are the basis of a visual.

☐ Used and interpreted visuals ethically.

☐ Used visuals that respect the cultural traditions of international readers.

Glossary

By way of review, the following is a glossary of terms used in this chapter:

band graph   also called an **area graph**; graph in which the spaces between the curves are filled in.

bar chart   a visual using vertical or horizontal bars to measure different data in space or time; bars can also be segmented to show multiple percentages within one bar. Bar charts are used to show a variety of facts for easy comparison.

callouts   labels that identify the parts of an object in a visual.

captions   titles or headings for visuals.

circle chart   a visual shaped in a circle, or pie, whose slices represent the parts of the whole. Circle charts often portray budgets, expenditures, shares, and time allotments.

clip art   ready-made electronic icons, images, symbols, and pictures available in a computer library.

computer graphics   a variety of visuals generated by a computer; software (programs) and hardware (computer screens, scanners) create these visuals.

cross-hatching   the process of marking parts of a visual with parallel lines that cross each other obliquely; used to differentiate one bar or slice of a circle chart from another.

cutaway drawing   a sketch in which the exterior covering of an object has been removed to show an interior view.

data point   the intersection of the vertical and horizontal axes on a graph to plot the occurrence of statistical data.

definition   the distinctness of a photograph in outline and detail.

dependent variable   the element (cost, employment, energy) plotted along the vertical axis of a line graph and most directly influenced by the independent variable.

desktop publishing software   software that allows users to create professional-looking documents with both text and visuals.

digital photography   photographs taken with a camera or phone that uses a smart card instead of film; the "processing" takes place in your PC, and the photos are saved in files.

drawing software packages   computer graphics software that allows users to create visual representations of data either plotted for accuracy or drawn freehand (charts, graphs, general illustrations).

exploded drawing   a sketch of an entire object that has been blown up and apart to show the relationship of parts to one another.

figures   any visuals that are not tables—charts, drawings, graphs, pictographs, photographs, maps.

flow chart   a sketch with boxes and arrows revealing the stages in an activity or process.

graph   a picture that represents the relationship of an independent variable to one or more dependent variables; produces a line or curve to show movement in time or space. Graphs are used to depict data that change often—temperatures, rainfall, prices, employment, productions, and so forth.

importing visuals   transferring visuals from the Web to a document or hard drive.

independent variable   the element, plotted along the horizontal axis of a graph, that most directly and importantly affects the dependent variable; most often, the independent variable is time or distance.

large-scale map   a map that shows a great deal of detail, whether physical (elevations, rivers), economic (income levels), or social (population, religious affiliation).

legend   the explanation, or key, indicating what different colors, shadings, or symbols represent in a visual.

organizational chart   a visual showing the structure of an organization from the chief executive to the work force of employees. An organizational chart reveals the chain of command and areas of authority and responsibility.

pictograph   a visual showing differences in statistical data by means of pictures varying in size, number, or color.

pie chart   see **circle chart.**

scanning   the process of creating a digital reproduction of an image or document to store and use on a computer.

spreadsheet   an electronic table generated by a computer graphics package.

stub   the first column on the left side of a table; contains line captions listing those units to be discussed in the columns.

table   a visual in which statistical data or verbal descriptions are arranged in rows or columns.

template   a pattern used as a guide in creating a visual after a standard model, e.g., letterheads, résumé format.

Exercises

Online Study Center
Find additional designing exercises at college .hmco.com/pic/ kolin8e

1. Bring to class three or four website homepages that use especially effective visuals. In a short memo or e-mail (three or four paragraphs) to your instructor, indicate why and how each visual is appropriate for and convincing to a particular audience. What would each homepage look like without its visual?

2. Record the highest temperature reached in your town for the next five days. Then collect data on the highest temperature reached in three of the following cities—Boston, Chicago, Dallas, Denver, Los Angeles, Miami, New Orleans, New York, Philadelphia, Phoenix, Salt Lake City, San Francisco, Seattle—over the same five days. (You can get this information from a printed newspaper or on the Internet.) Prepare a table showing the differences for the five-day period.

3. Go to a supermarket and get the prices of four different brands of the same product (hair spray, aspirin, a soft drink, a box of cereal). Present your findings in the form of a table.

4. One government agency supplied the following statistics on the world production of oranges (including tangerines) in thousands of metric tons for the following countries during the years 2003–2006: Brazil, 2,005, 2,132, 2,760, 2,872; Israel, 909, 1,076, 1,148, 1,221; Italy, 1,669, 1,599, 1,766, 1,604; Japan, 2,424, 2,994, 2,885, 4,070; Mexico, 937, 1,405, 1,114, 1,270; Spain, 2,135, 2,005, 2,179, 2,642; and the United States, 7,658, 7,875, 7,889, 9,245. Prepare a table with that information and then write a paragraph in which you introduce and refer to the table and draw conclusions from it.

5. Keep a record for one week of the number of miles you walk, ride, or drive each day. Then prepare a line graph depicting that information.

6. Prepare a table to show the following statistical data: According to a 2000 census, the town of Ardmore had a population of 34,567. By a 2005 census the town's population had decreased by 4,500. In the 2000 census the town of Morrison had a population of 23,809, but by the 2005 census the population had increased by 3,689. The 2005 census figure for the town of Berkesville was 25,675, which was an increase of 2,768 from the 2000 census.

7. Prepare a line graph for the information in Exercise 6.

8. Prepare a bar graph for the information in Exercise 6.

9. Write a paragraph introducing and interpreting the following table.

Year	Soft Drink Companies	Bottling Plants	Per Capita Consumption (Gallons)
1940	750	750	10.3
1945	578	611	12.5
1950	457	466	18.6
1955	380	407	17.2
1960	231	292	15.9
1970	171	229	15.4
1975	118	197	16.0
1980	92	154	18.7
1985	54	102	21.1
1990	43	88	23.1
1995	45	82	25.3
2000	37	78	27.6
2005	34	72	30.1

10. Prepare a circle chart showing the breakdown of your budget for one week or one month.

11. According to a municipal study in 2007 the distribution of all companies classified in each enterprise industry in that city was as follows: minerals, 0.4%; selected services, 33.3%; retail trade, 36.7%; wholesale trade, 6.5%; manufacturing, 5.3%; and construction, 17.8%. Make a circle chart to represent the distribution and write a one- or two-paragraph interpretation to accompany (and explain the significance of) your visual.

12. Construct a segmented bar chart to represent the kinds and numbers of courses you took in a two-semester period or during your last year in high school.

13. Prepare a bar chart for the different brands of one of the products in Exercise 3. Write a paragraph introducing your illustration.

14. Find a pictograph in a math or business textbook, in a magazine (try *Newsweek* or *U.S. News & World Report*) online, or on a website from the Department of Labor Statistics. Make a bar graph from the information contained in the pictograph, and then write a paragraph introducing the bar graph and drawing conclusions from it.

15. Construct an organizational chart for a business or an agency you worked for recently. Include part-time and full-time employees, but indicate their titles or functions with different kinds of shapes or lines. Then attach the chart to a brief e-mail to your employer explaining why this kind of organizational chart should be distributed to all employees. Focus on the types of problems that could be avoided if employees had access to such a chart.

16. Prepare a flow chart for one of the following activities:
   a. jumping a "dead" car battery
   b. giving an injection
   c. making a reservation online
   d. painting a set of louvered doors
   e. checking your credit online
   f. putting out an electrical fire
   g. joining a chat group on the Internet
   h. preparing a visual using a graphics software package
   i. changing your e-mail account password
   j. sending e-mail notifications to a group

17. Draw an interior view of a piece of equipment you use in your major, and then identify the relevant parts using callouts.

18. Prepare a drawing of one of the following tools and include appropriate call-outs with your visual.

a. PDA	**f.** DVD player
b. iPod	**g.** ballpoint pen
c. pliers	**h.** soldering iron
d. stethoscope	**i.** high definition TV
e. swivel chair	**j.** pair of eyeglasses

19. Prepare appropriate visuals to illustrate the data listed below. In a paragraph immediately after the visual explain why the type of visual you selected is appropriate for this information.
   a. Life expectancy is increasing in the United States. This growth can be dramatically measured by comparing the number of teenagers with the number of older adults (over age 65) in the United States during the last few years and then projecting those figures. In 1970 there were approximately 28 million teenagers and 20 million older adults. By 1980 the number of teenagers climbed to 30 million and the number of older adults increased to 25 million. In 1990 there were 27 million teenagers and 31 million older adults. In 2000 the number of teenagers had leveled off to 23 million, but the number of older adults soared to more than 36 million.
   b. Researchers estimate that for every adult in the United States 3,985 cigarettes were purchased in 1985; 4,100 in 1990; 3,875 in 1995; 3,490 in 2000; and 2,910 in 2005.

20. Find a photograph that contains some irrelevant clutter. Write a letter to the marketing department of a company for which you presumably work that wants to use the photograph. Tell the department what to delete and why.

21. Following is a visual prepared to accompany a report on problems pilots have encountered with a particular model of jet engine. Redo the visual to make it easier to read and to organize information. Supply a paragraph to accompany your new visual.

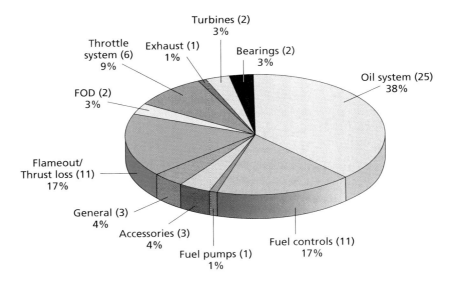

22. Make a simple line drawing of only the relevant portions of the photograph you found for Exercise 20. Explain in two paragraphs why the drawing works better than the photograph.

23. You work for a large manufacturer of industrial heat pumps and have been asked to help write a section of a report on the increased business your firm has been doing overseas. Based on the sales figures below for the years 2004, 2005, and 2006 (listed in that order) for each of the following countries, prepare two different yet complementary visuals. Also, supply a one-page description and interpretation of the statistics represented in your visuals. You may work collaboratively with one or more students in your class to prepare the visuals as well as to write the section of the report on international sales.

Argentina, 45, 53, 34; Australia, 78, 90, 115; Bolivia, 23, 43, 52; Brazil, 29, 34, 35; Canada, 116, 234, 256; Denmark, 65, 54, 87; England, 256, 345, 476; France, 198, 167, 345; Germany, 234, 398, 429; Holland, 65, 80, 89; Italy, 49, 52, 97; Japan, 67, 43, 29; New Zealand, 12, 69, 114; Norway, 33, 92, 104; Switzerland, 164, 266, 306; Sweden, 145, 217, 266; People's Republic of China, 7, 100, 296; Korea, 55, 43, 28.

In your written report, take into account trends, shifts in sales, and possible consequences for further marketing and conclude with a specific recommendation to your employer.

24. Find a misleading visual, either from a print or online source, and explain in an e-mail to your instructor why it is deceptive, incomplete, cluttered, inaccurate, and/or biased. Reconstruct the visual and provide a corrected, edited paragraph based upon information in the revised visual. Attach both versions of the visual to your e-mail to your instructor.

25. Explain why the following would be inappropriate in communicating with an international audience and how you would revise the document containing such visuals/graphics symbols:

   a. clip art showing a string tied around an index finger

   b. picture of a man with a sombrero on a website for Pronto Check Cashing Company

   c. clip art/drawing of a light bulb and logo "Smart Ideas" for a CPA firm

   d. clip art showing someone crossing the middle finger over the index finger (wishing sign)

   e. drawing of a cupid figure for a caterer

   f. a sales brochure showing a white and blue flag for a French audience.

CHAPTER 12

Designing Successful Documents and Websites

Online Study Center

To expand your understanding of designing, take advantage of the ACE quizzes, sample documents, Web links, and exercises at college.hmco.com/pic/kolin8e

The success of your document (letter, proposal, report) or website depends as much on how it looks as what it says. In designing print documents and websites, you need to project a positive, professional image of yourself, your company, your product. A report filled with nothing but thick paragraphs of type, with no visual clues to break them up or to make information stand out, is sure to intimidate readers and turn them away. They will conclude that your work is too complex and not worth their effort or time. And if there is one thing that the world of work especially dislikes it is someone who cannot get to the main point—the bottom line—quickly.

Websites and documents need to look user-friendly, signaling to your audience that your message is

- easy to read
- easy to follow and understand
- easy to recall

Don't bog your audience down in unbroken long paragraphs or crowded screens of information. Break material into smaller units that are visually appealing. You can help readers find key points at a glance through **chunking** (using smaller paragraphs) and using lists, boldface type, and bullets. That way they can find your ideas easily the first time through or on a second reading if they have to double back to check or verify a point.

Organizing Information Visually

Take a quick look at Figures 12.2 (p. 509) and 12.3 (pp. 510–512). The same information is contained in each figure. Which appeals more to you? Which do you think would be easier to read? As the two figures show, design or layout plays a crucial role in an audience's overall acceptance of your work. Information is organized (and perceived) visually as well as verbally. A document or website that looks logical and easy to read and that is clearly organized with the audience in mind will increase your credibility. If you offer your audience densely packed material, with few visual road signs to help them navigate through it, they will conclude that you are poorly organized and that your thinking is not very clear or direct.

Your company, too, will win or lose points because of your design choices. A visually appealing website or document will enhance a company's reputation and improve its sales. A poorly designed one will not. Consumers will think your firm is inflexible, hard to do business with, and uncaring about specific problems customers may have over a policy or a set of instructions. Your company can easily be perceived as not respecting the individuals it does business with or for being old-fashioned, hard-nosed, or just plain unprofessional.

Chapter 12 explains the tools you need and shows you how to design professional-looking, reader-friendly documents and websites.

Characteristics of Effective Design

As you read this chapter and apply its principles to your own work, make sure your documents and websites offer your audience the following qualities:

- visual appeal
- logical organization
- clarity
- accessibility
- variety
- relevance

By incorporating those characteristics into your documents and websites, you guarantee that your message will be well received.

Tools for Designing Print Documents

In the world of work, affordable and accessible PC and printer technology makes it easy for you to **design, illustrate, edit, format, store, retrieve, import**, and **print** documents. Thanks to this technology, you or your team can design almost any document discussed in *Successful Writing at Work*. In efforts similar to the collaborative writing process discussed in Chapter 3, people in business frequently use the flexibility in automation systems to collaborate on document design.

Three Basic Tools

The three categories of automation tools available for document design include

   1. Computer hardware.   Critical hardware components include the central processing unit (CPU) or microprocessor, the monitor, and the printer. The CPU houses the "brains" of the computer, while the monitor and the printer help you to visualize what is inside the CPU.

   2. Software.   Software tools are operating and program applications. The two primary operating systems are Mac OS and Windows, with Windows by far the more widely used of the two. The basic types of software include word processing, spreadsheet, database, graphics, and communications. Helpful software packages available for page design include

- word processing programs such as Microsoft Word and Corel WordPerfect
- desktop publishing programs such as QuarkXPress, Adobe PageMaker, and Microsoft Publisher (see Tech Note below.)
- graphics programs such as Adobe Photoshop, Macromedia Flash, and Microsoft PhotoDraw
- scanning software such as Caere OmniPage and Xerox Text Bridge

Word processing programs offer a variety of options that make document design fast and easy to develop and just as easy to change.

3. Printers and scanners. High-resolution laser printers are graphics-capable, letter-quality, and user-friendly. These printers offer high-quality text and graphics printing in striking color in a relatively short time. (See Marcus Weekley's memo on new multitask laser printers in Chapter 2, pages 52–54.)

Once documents (text or graphics) are placed in a scanner, the scanner makes a digital image, and the information is placed in a graphics file.

Tech Note

Desktop Publishing Programs

Word processing programs such as Microsoft Word and Corel WordPerfect have evolved into more and more powerful desktop publishing programs. Files created in word processing, database, and spreadsheet programs can be imported into sophisticated desktop publishing programs such as Adobe Page-Maker, Microsoft Publisher, and QuarkXPress, as can graphics created or edited in programs such as Adobe Photoshop, Macromedia Flash, Corel DRAW, and Microsoft PhotoDraw.

Desktop Publishing

Desktop publishing programs, sometimes referred to as **page layout software,** provide an inexpensive alternative to a professional print shop. Because desktop publishing software permits users to design page layouts, include visuals, and produce high-quality final copies, you can create printed documents right in your own home or office.

With desktop publishing you can

- delete, insert, and move entire blocks of text
- take advantage of numerous typefaces
- integrate various changes in typeface—such as bold, italics, and underlining

- vary type sizes
- justify margins
- change line spacing
- center words, titles, or lines of text
- break and number pages
- arrange text in multiple columns
- add headers and footers (printed words that appear at the top and bottom, respectively, of each page of text)
- blow up quotations (pull quotes)
- import graphics, such as drawings, photographs, and logos
- insert sidebars

Type

There are many different styles of type (see pp. 513–515). All computers come equipped with software that contains a large number of typefaces (anywhere from 100 to 1,000). For example, WordPerfect 12 features more than 1,000 high-quality fonts. Different fonts are also available over the Internet at such sites as *http://1001freefonts.com* and *http://www.fonts.com/*.

Templates

Desktop publishing software is equipped with predesigned **templates**. Templates are patterns and predesigned text columns, like those shown in Figure 12.1, that offer numerous page layout formats for reports, newsletters, brochures, and other marketing and communications documents. A template for a report, for example,

Examples of templates. Figure 12.1

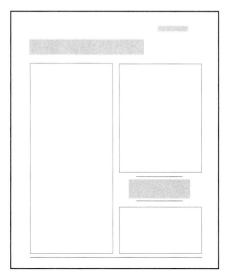
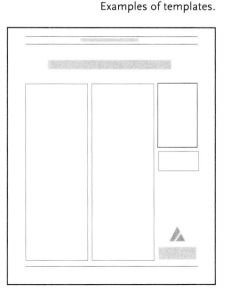

would contain all the headings and divisions you need. You can also create and save your own template for an original format you use frequently.

Graphics

A graphics program supplies shapes and lines that can be manipulated (skewed, enlarged) and offers options for sophisticated use of color and shading. With a drawing program you can create diagrams, charts, and illustrations that can be saved as electronic files and imported into word processing or desktop publishing documents.

You can move and place graphics anywhere in a document. Graphic design programs provide customized graphs, charts, tables, and expanded font (design) sizes and shapes.

Here are some types of graphics available to you.

1. Drawing tools.   Desktop publishing programs contain tools that allow you to create a variety of shapes, rules, borders, and arrows. Having drawn a box, circle, triangle, or whatever, you can use other tools to fill in or alter the appearance of the shape or to add words to it; then you can rearrange all the elements into a graphic that communicates quickly and effectively.

2. Icons.   Icons are symbols or visual representations of concepts or actions. The skull and crossbones on a container of poison is an icon that warns of danger. Many highway signs are icons that tell us quickly what to expect ahead: an S-curve, merging traffic, a hospital. *Graphic icons* are simply pictures that communicate directly. No matter what language we speak—and even if we cannot read—icons tell us at a glance which restroom to use or how to fasten the seat belt in an airplane. A nation's flag is an icon, and so are many religious symbols and most company logos.

Computer software often relies on icons to help us perform common actions without having to remember keyboard commands. Arrows in the scroll bars move us easily around a window; a file folder helps us group related documents; and a trash can holds files to be deleted later. Icons in the menu bar make it easy to print a file, open an address book, search for specific text, cut copy, or dial the phone. Examples of public service information icons are shown below:

3. Clip art.   Clip art is a library of simple drawings, often classified by themes, that can be imported (copied) from floppy disk, CD, or the Internet to your document. Some clip art software packages offer as many as 500,000 images, arranged into such diverse categories as animals, computers, holidays, famous people, food, and various technologies. Clip art is widely used to make business documents attractive and appealing. If the graphic is symbolic or represents something unique about the business, it can also be the basis for a company logo. Review pages 485–486.

4. Stock photos/stock art.   Assembled photos and art on a CD or the Internet can be imported, sometimes with a permissions fee, sometimes free with the purchase of the CD.

Before Choosing a Design

Before you begin designing a document, you need to know exactly what you are designing, for whom, and how. Think carefully about how your work will look on the page, what you want to achieve, and what your resources are. Here are questions to ask:

1. Who's your target audience? What do they have in common—gender, locality, educational level? How you reach and appeal to this group must be taken into consideration before you decide on a "look and feel" for your document. Print size, style, and so forth should be selected based on the audience's characteristics and needs.

2. What is the nature of your document—are you going to have to motivate the reader to look at it? Use an eye-catching cover page, attractive colors, and short paragraphs. Or is your document required reading for co-workers and therefore subject to "house style"? Are you designing a newsletter for a professional group that needs to comply with a set of guidelines about how it should be laid out to ensure that the design is consistent for every edition?

3. Find out how your document will be reproduced. Will it be set by a professional printer or is it an internal document that can be photocopied and distributed? This will affect the number and type of colors you use, the type of paper you use, and the size of the paper.

4. Think about how your document will fit into an envelope if it is to be distributed by mail. Will it need to be folded more than once? Will this make the document look untidy? Do you need larger envelopes or a smaller page size? Will the document be read by more than one reader or more than once? If so, the paper will need to be more sturdy.

5. Consider cost. Printing in color can be much more expensive than standard black-and-white printing. If you use color, try to stick to one or two colors throughout to keep the costs down. Talk to your employer about the costs of reproduction before you decide on anything.

▇ The ABCs of Print Document Design

The basic features of printed document design are

- page layout
- typography, or type design
- graphics

Each page of your document should integrate those three elements. The proper arrangement and balance of type, white space, and graphics involve the same level of preparation that you would spend on your research, drafting, revising, and editing. You need to create a document that cooperates with—not detracts from—your message. Just as you research your information, you have to research and experiment in order to adopt the most effective design for your document.

Page Layout

Each of your pages needs to coordinate space and text pleasingly. Too much or too little of one or the other can jeopardize the reader's acceptance of your message. To make sure you design an effective and attractive page layout, pay attention to the following elements:

1. White space.   White space, which refers to the open areas on the page that are free of text and visuals, can help you increase the impact of your message. If you attempt to pack too much information or too many design elements into a document, you may distract the reader from the message you really want to convey. White space can entice, comfort, and appeal to the reader's "psychology of space" by

- attracting the reader's attention
- assuring the reader that information is presented logically
- announcing that information is easy to follow
- assisting the reader to organize information visually
- allowing the reader to forecast and highlight important information

Compare Figures 12.2 and 12.3 again. Which document was designed by someone who understands the importance of white space?

2. Margins.   Use wide margins, usually 1 to 1½ inches, to "frame" your document with white space surrounding text and visuals. Most documents easily accommodate equal margins on all four sides, a technique that creates balance and prevents the document from looking cluttered or overcrowded. If your document requires binding, you may have to leave a wider left margin (2 inches).

3. Line length.   Most readers find a text line of 10 to 14 words, or 50 to 70 characters (depending on the type size you choose), comfortable and enjoyable reading. Line length, or "line measuring," depends, of course, on font type and size, number of columns, width of margins, and space between words. Never exceed your margin

A poorly designed document.   Figure 12.2

No title

The results for the recent cholesterol screening at our company's Health Fair were distributed to each employee last week. Many employees wanted to know more information about cholesterol in general, the different types of cholesterol, what the results mean, and the foods that are high or low in cholesterol.

Single-spacing makes document difficult to read

We hope the information provided below will help employees better answer their questions concerning cholesterol and our cholesterol screening program.

High cholesterol, along with high blood pressure and obesity, is one of the primary risk factors that may contribute to the development of coronary heart disease and may eventually lead to a heart attack or stroke. Cholesterol is a fatty, sticky substance found in the bloodstream. Excessive amounts of the bad type of cholesterol can deposit on the walls of the heart arteries. *This deposit is called plaque and over a long period of time plaque can narrow or even block the blood flow through the arteries.*

Lack of headings makes it hard for readers to organize material

Total cholesterol is divided into three parts—LDL (low-density lipoprotein), or bad cholesterol; HDL (high-density lipoprotein), or good cholesterol; and VLDL (very low-density lipoprotein), a much smaller component of cholesterol you don't have to worry about. Bad (LDL) cholesterol forms on the walls of your arteries and can cause a lot of damage. Good cholesterol, on the other hand, functions like a sponge, mopping up cholesterol and carrying it out of the bloodstream.

You should have received three cholesterol numbers. One is for your HDL, or good cholesterol, and the other is for your LDL, or bad cholesterol, reading. These two numbers are added to give you the third, or composite, level of your total cholesterol. You are doing fine.

Frequent font changes are confusing for readers

As you can see, a total cholesterol reading of below 200 is considered safe. Continue what you have been doing. If your reading falls in the moderate risk range of 200–239, you need to modify your diet, get more exercise, and have your cholesterol checked again in six months. *If your reading is above 240, see your doctor.* You may need to take cholesterol-lowering medication, if your doctor prescribes it. Reducing your total cholesterol by even as little as 25% can decrease your risk of a heart attack by 50%.

The Surgeon General recommends that your LDL, or bad, cholesterol should be below 130. And your HDL, or good, cholesterol needs to be at least above 36. Ideally, the ratio between the two numbers should not be greater than 5 to 1. That is, your HDL should be at least 20% of your LDL. The higher your HDL is, the better, of course. So even if you have a high LDL reading, if your HDL is correspondingly high you will be at less risk.

Lack of margins makes document look dense and complex

One of the easiest ways to decrease your cholesterol is to modify your diet. Cholesterol is found in foods that are high in saturated fat. *Saturated fat comes from animal sources and also from certain vegetable sources.* Foods high in bad cholesterol that you should restrict, or avoid, include whole milk, red meat, eggs, cheese, butter, shrimp, oils such as palm and coconut, and avocados. Generally, food groups low in cholesterol include fruits, vegetables, and whole grains (wheat breads, oatmeal, and certain cereals), lean meats (fish, chicken), and beans.

The goal of our cholesterol screening is to help each employee lower his or her cholesterol level and eventually reduce the risk of heart disease. **Besides the advice given above,** you can do the following: get regular aerobic exercise—bicycling, brisk walking, swimming, rowing—for at least 30 minutes 3–4 times a week. But get your doctor's approval first. *Eat foods low in cholesterol* but high in dietary fiber (beans, oatmeal, brown rice). Maintain a healthy weight for your frame to lower your body fat. Minimize stress, which can increase cholesterol. Learn relaxation techniques.

Inconsistent use of italics and boldfacing

Figure 12.3   An effectively designed document with the same text as Figure 12.2.

Title clearly set apart from text by caps and boldfacing

Text is double-spaced with generous margins, making it more readable

Cholesterol Screening

The results for the recent cholesterol screening at our company's Health Fair were distributed to each employee last week. Many employees wanted to know more information about cholesterol in general, the different types of cholesterol, what the results mean, and the foods that are high or low in cholesterol. We hope the information provided below will help employees better answer their questions concerning cholesterol and our cholesterol screening program.

Headings divide material into easy-to-follow units for readers

Determining Risk Factors

High cholesterol, along with high blood pressure and obesity, is one of the primary risk factors that may contribute to the development of coronary heart disease and may eventually lead to a heart attack or stroke. Cholesterol is a fatty, sticky substance found in the bloodstream. Excessive amounts of the bad type of cholesterol can deposit on the walls of the heart arteries. This deposit is called **plaque** and over a long period of time plaque can narrow or even block the blood flow through the arteries.

Separating Types of Cholesterol

Only key terms are boldfaced

Types of cholesterol are labeled with numbers

Total cholesterol is divided into three parts: (1) **LDL** (low-density lipoprotein), or bad cholesterol; (2) **HDL** (high-density lipoprotein), or good cholesterol; and (3) **VLDL** (very low-density lipoprotein), a much smaller component of cholesterol you don't have to worry about. Bad (LDL) cholesterol forms on the walls of your arteries and can cause a lot of damage. Good cholesterol, on the other hand, functions like a sponge, mopping up cholesterol and carrying it out of the bloodstream.

Continued

(Continued)   Figure 12.3

Understanding Your Cholesterol Results

You should have received three cholesterol numbers. One is for your **HDL** (or good cholesterol) and the other is for your **LDL** (or bad cholesterol) reading. These two numbers are added to give you the third, or composite, level of your total cholesterol.

Cholesterol levels can be classified as follows:

Minimal Risk	Moderate Risk	High Risk
below 200	200–239	above 240

Emphasizes range of risk categories by setting them apart

As you can see, a total cholesterol reading of below 200 is considered safe. You are doing fine. Continue what you have been doing. If your reading falls in the moderate risk range of 200–239, you need to modify your diet, get more exercise, and have your cholesterol checked again in six months. If your reading is above 240, see your doctor. You may need to take cholesterol-lowering medication, if your doctor prescribes it. Reducing your total cholesterol by even as little as 25% can decrease your risk of a heart attack by 50%.

Relationship Between Bad and Good Cholesterol

Includes more space between sections

The Surgeon General recommends that your **LDL**, or bad, cholesterol should be below 130. And your **HDL**, or good, cholesterol needs to be at least above 36. Ideally, the ratio between the two numbers should not be greater than 5 to 1. That is, your **HDL** should be at least 20% of your **LDL**. The higher your **HDL** is, the better, of course. So even if you have a high **LDL** reading, if your **HDL** is correspondingly high you will be at less risk.

Paragraphs are neither too long nor too short

Recognizing Food Sources of Cholesterol

One of the easiest ways to decrease your cholesterol is to modify your diet. Cholesterol is found in foods that are high in saturated fat. Saturated fat comes

2

Continued

Figure 12.3   (Continued)

from animal sources and also from certain vegetable sources. Foods high in bad cholesterol that you should restrict include:

A numbered list helps readers identify foods with bad cholesterol

1. whole milk
2. red meat
3. eggs
4. cheese
5. butter
6. shrimp
7. oils such as palm and coconut
8. avocados

Generally, food groups low in cholesterol include fruits, vegetables, and whole grains (wheat breads, oatmeal, and certain cereals), lean meats (fish, chicken), and beans.

Realizing It Is Up to You

The goals of our cholesterol screening program are to help each employee lower his or her cholesterol level and eventually reduce the risk of heart disease. Besides the advice given above, you can do the following:

Bulleted list serves as both summary and plan for future action

- Get regular aerobic exercise—bicycling, brisk walking, swimming, rowing—for at least 30 minutes 3–4 times a week. But get your doctor's approval first.
- Eat foods low in cholesterol but high in dietary fiber (beans, oatmeal, and brown rice).
- Maintain a healthy weight for your frame to lower your body fat.
- Minimize stress, which can increase cholesterol. Learn relaxation techniques.

3

The author is indebted to Sgt. Mannie E. Hall of the U.S. Army for creating this document.

settings. In the example below, note how the extra-long lines unsettle your reading and tax your eye movement; they signal rough going.

In order to succeed in the world of business, workers must learn to brush up on their networking skills. The network process has many benefits that you need to be aware of. These benefits range from finding a better job to accomplishing your job more easily and efficiently. Through networking you are able to expand the number of contacts who can help you. Networking means sharing news and opportunities. The Internet is the key to successful networking.

Conversely, do not print a document with too short or extremely uneven lines.

> In order to succeed in the world of
> business, workers must learn
> to brush up on their networking skills. The
> network process has many
> benefits you need to be
> aware of.

Readers will suspect your ideas are incomplete, superficial, or even simpleminded.

4. Columns. Document text usually is organized in either single-column or multicolumn formats. Memos, letters, and reports are usually formatted without columns, whereas documents that intersperse text and visuals (such as newsletters and magazines) work better in multicolumn formats.

Typography

Typeface
Readability of your text is crucial. Select a typeface, therefore, that ensures your text is

- legible
- attractive
- functional
- appropriate for your message
- complementary with accompanying graphics

The most familiar typefaces are Times Roman, Arial, and Helvetica, although other very useful typeface styles are available with WordPerfect, MS Word, and other software packages. Other typefaces include Script, Modern, Old Style, Decorative, and Traditional. Below are some examples of these typefaces.

Times Roman	Frutiger
Helvetica	Palatino
Alexa	**STENCIL**
Zapf Chancery	Arial

Type is also classified as having serif or sans serif fonts. **Serif fonts** appear to be the most readable in a body of the text. They are distinguished by tail features or cross-bars at the ends of the letters. These serifs add flair, arouse the reader's interest, and increase readability. Letter strokes are of varying widths and sometimes tapered.

Stone Serif	Sabon Roman
Courier	Janson Text
Times	Palatino

    Sans serif fonts are recommended for headings and subheadings. Having no tails or crossbars, sans serif fonts provide a clear, crisp, legible image ideal for short messages. But avoid sans serif fonts for text copy because they make it harder for readers to process information.

Futura	Stone Sans
Univers Oblique	Geneva
Gill Sans Extra Bold	TradeGothic

Type Size

Type size options are almost unlimited, depending again on your software package and printer capabilities. Type size is measured in units called **points**, 72 points to the inch. The bigger the point size, the larger the type. Most business and educational documents use from 10-point to 12-point type, although the range today varies from 6 to 72 points (and beyond). Newspaper classified ads are in small 6-point to 8-point type, while headlines are set in much larger, 30-point to 36-point type. The text in this book is set in 10-point type.

Times 7 point

Univers 10 point

Palatino 14 point

Frutiger 22 point

Stone Serif 36 point

Type Styles

Also known as **attributes**, these include boldface, italics, underlining, outline, shadow, small caps, and shading.

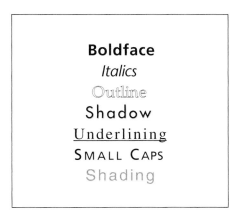

Boldface
Italics
Outline
Shadow
Underlining
SMALL CAPS
Shading

Line Spacing

The amount of white space between lines of your text also affects how your document will be perceived. Line spacing is sometimes referred to as **leading**. Leading is also measured in points, the same as type size. Standard line spacing should be 2 points more than type size, so 10-point type would use 12-point leading, 12-point type would use 14-point leading, and so on.

Justification

Sometimes referred to as alignment, justification consists of left, right, full, and center options. Left-justified (also called **unjustified** or **ragged right**) is the preferred method because it allows space between words in lines of text to remain constant. In fully justified alignment (both left *and* right) the word spacing varies from line to line. Left justification gives a document a less formal look than full justification. Narrow columns of text should be set left-justified to avoid awkward gaps between words and excessive hyphenation.

Our new website offers consumers a mall on the Internet. It gives shoppers access to our products and services and makes buying easy and fun. Our new website offers consumers a mall on the Internet. It gives shoppers access to our

Left-justified text

Our new website offers consumers a mall on the Internet. It gives shoppers access to our products and services and makes buying easy and fun. Our new website offers consumers a mall on the Internet. It gives shoppers access to our

Right-justified text

Our new website offers consumers a mall on the Internet. It gives shoppers access to our products and services and makes buying easy and fun. Our new website offers consumers a mall on the Internet. It gives shoppers access to our products and

Full-justified text

Our new website offers consumers a mall on the Internet. It gives shoppers access to our products and services and makes buying easy and fun. Our new website offers consumers a mall on the Internet. It gives shoppers access to our

Centered text

Heads and Subheads

Use brief descriptive words or phrases to introduce or summarize a document or a section or subsection within a document. Your headings, called **heads** and **subheads,** should be grammatically parallel and not wordy. Note how the headings below from a poorly organized proposal from the Acme Company are nonparallel.

- What Is the Problem?
- Describing What Acme Can Do to Solve the Problem

- It's a Matter of Time . . .
- Fees Acme Will Charge
- When You Need to Pay
- Finding Out Who's Who

Revised, the heads are parallel and easier for a reader to understand and follow.

- A Brief History of the Problem
- A Description of Acme Solutions
- A Timetable Acme Can Follow
- A Breakdown of Acme's Fees
- A Payment Plan
- A Listing of Acme's Staff

Heads and subheads immediately attract attention and quickly inform readers about the function, scope, purpose, or contents of the document or section. They help readers prioritize information, too, by emphasizing the main points they need to look for and remember. Additionally, heads and subheads introduce helpful white space to separate text and organize your document. The space around a heading is like an oasis for the reader, signaling both a rest and a new beginning.

Tech Note

Typeface and Type Style

Be consistent in differentiating between **typeface** and **type style**.

A **typeface** is a specific family of type, such as Times Roman or Helvetica. The word *typeface* is sometimes used synonymously with *font*, a slightly more specific term that refers to the family as well as the size of the type.

Type style, especially as used by software manufacturers, refers to attributes such as boldface, italics, shadowing, and other variations.

Subheads allow the reader to skim or review a document and its content in an outline type of format. Headings and subheadings follow an established order or hierarchy.

In designing a document with heads and subheads, follow these guidelines:

- Use larger type size for heads than for text; major heads should be larger than subheads. If your text is in 10-point type, your heads may be in 16-point type and your subheads in 12- or 14-point type. See Figure 12.3.
- Modify type to differentiate sections. For example, for heads and subheads use uppercase, bold type, underlining, and changes in font style or type.
- Establish a horizontal position for a head, such as centered or aligned left, and keep it consistent throughout the document.

Sixteen-Point Head
Subhead in 12 Point
Use larger type for heads than you do for text;
major headings should be larger than subheads.
If your text is in 10-point type, your heads may
be in 16-point type and your subheads in 12 or 14.

- Allow additional space, or leading, above a head to set it off from the preceding section. You may also want to allow additional space below a head.
- If you are using a color printer, consider using a second color for major headings.

Lists

Placing items in a list helps readers by dividing, organizing, and ranking information. Lists emphasize important points and contribute to an easy-to-read page design. Lists can be (a) numbered, (b) lettered, or (c) bulleted. Take a look at the memos, proposals, and reports in Chapters 4, 14, 15, and 16 that effectively use lists.

Captions

Used to accompany, explain, highlight, or reference pictures or other graphics (like charts and graphs), captions are titles that help a reader identify a visual and quickly explain the nature of the picture or other graphic. (Chapter 11 discusses using captions with visuals in a document.)

Graphics

Like other visuals, graphics work in conjunction with your words. A document without visuals or graphics may look boring, confusing, or unattractive. You will have to judge how and when a graphic can improve your message and convince your reader. The list below identifies some common graphics included in desktop publishing software packages.

1. **Clip art.** See page 507 and also pages 485–486 in Chapter 11.
2. **Boxes.** These lines isolate or highlight text or visuals. Tables 11.1, 11.2, and 11.3 in Chapter 11 use boxes.
3. **Rules.** These lines are classified as either vertical or horizontal. Vertical rules are used to separate columns of text, while horizontal rules separate sections introduced by subheads.
4. **Letterheads and logos.** A company's corporate image is represented and symbolized by its letterhead, usually consisting of a graphic, or icon, integrated with the company name. Often the company's street address, e-mail address, and website are included in the letterhead. Company letterhead conveys the

firm's message and expresses its character. Typically, logos and sometimes the entire letterhead are imported as graphics files. A letterhead/logo should creatively set one company apart from others. See Figures 6.4 and 6.10.

Using Color

Color is important in writing for the world of work. Nothing attracts attention and communicates more quickly and more powerfully than color. Color can set moods and create impressions. It may be one of the most important tools to increase sales, gain faster project approval, or provide a major advantage over competitors. Color helps to sell ideas 85 percent more effectively than black-and-white communications.

Color can be used in many ways to organize written information and therefore enhance readability. Color visually breaks up long segments of text and can tie important ideas together. For example, using colored boxes to identify special notes in the text helps readers locate important information quickly. Use color for borders and graphic accents, headings, titles, key words, Internet addresses, sidebars, rules, and boxes that link related facts, figures, or information. You can communicate your message far more effectively by using colorful charts and graphs.

Tech Note

Some Guidelines on Using Color

Here are some guidelines to follow when you use color in your documents:

- Match the most appropriate color with the object you want to display. Keep in mind that an object's perceived size is affected by color. Light colors make objects look larger; dark colors make objects appear smaller.
- Estimate how the color will look on the page—colors look different on the screen than they do on a sheet of paper. Print a sample page.
- Make sure text colors contrast sharply with background colors.
- Use no more than two or three colors on a page unless there are photographs, illustrations, or graphics.
- For graphs and charts, place similar colors close to one another to maximize differences.
- Too many bright colors overwhelm the eye, so use them sparingly to call attention to important elements.
- Select "cool" colors, such as blue, turquoise, purple, and magenta, for backgrounds. However, avoid light blue text, which is hard to read against a dark background.

See pages 536–539 for a discussion of using color on websites.

▌ Poor Document Design: What *Not* to Do

Up to this point we have introduced the various elements of effective document design. Now, in contrast, we'll look at what you need to avoid. By knowing what looks bad from a reader's point of view, you will be much better able to design a document that works well visually for your reader.

Figure 12.2, a poorly designed document, illustrates many of the following common mistakes in document design. But note how Figure 12.3, which contains the same information as Figure 12.2, incorporates many of the effective techniques just described. Avoid the following errors when you design your document.

1. **Insufficient white space.**   Narrow margins and limited space between headings and text are classic mistakes. Skimping on white space can frustrate your reader, who is eager to locate key parts of a document to identify and process them easily. A lack of white space between paragraphs or heads or around the borders of a document sends a negative message to your audience. Your work tells a reader, "Roll up your sleeves: This will be tough, unenjoyable reading."

2. **Inappropriate line length.**   Excessively long lines are hard to read and signal to your audience that your work is highly complex and unrewarding.

3. **Overuse of visuals.**   Too many visuals (boxes, rules, and clip art images) can create barriers and confusion and will crowd your pages. Establish a balance between text and visuals. Also, use visuals for a specific purpose, not just for decorations or to fill space. Review the guidelines on what to avoid when using visuals (see p. 452).

4. **Mixing typefaces.**   The large number of fonts available within desktop publishing packages makes it easy to use too many fonts in a document. Be aware of this temptation, as the result often looks amateurish and disorganized. Avoid using more than two type families on a page; generally, a serif typeface for body text and a sans serif for headings is a common and familiar formula.

5. **Using hard-to-read fonts for body copy.**   Some typefaces, such as Avant Garde, may look great in headlines, but are difficult to read in the text of your document.

6. **Using small type and tight leading.**   Most typefaces work best for body copy when sized between 9 and 11 points. Leave plenty of line space (leading) between each line, too. A good rule of thumb is to set leading two or three points larger than the body text size (e.g., 12-point leading with 10-point type).

7. **Too few or no heads and subheads.**   Without headings as useful guideposts your document will seem unorganized and illogical. As we saw in Figure 12.3, heads and subheads are typographical markers that signal starting points and major divisions; they thus provide helpful landmarks for readers charting their course through your document.

8. **Excessive spacing.**   Too much space distorts the document and its message. Leaving three or four spaces between consecutive lines of a text signals to readers that your ideas may be lightweight and not well researched. Also, including too

much space around a visual or around the borders of your text can call into question the overall professional status of your work.

To avoid such errors, follow these tips:

▪ Use only one space after a period, not the traditional two spaces.
▪ Don't indent the first line of text after a head or subhead.
▪ Avoid full justification on narrow columns.
▪ Eliminate excessive spacing in lists between the bullets, numbers, or symbols and the actual text entries.

9. **Misusing capitals, boldface, or italics.**   Printing an entire document with capitals (large or small) will make a document hard to read. (But printing heads or subheads in capitals will differentiate them from your text.) Similarly, avoid overusing boldface or italics. Do not underline text unless absolutely necessary. Not only will too many special effects make your work harder to read, but you will also lose the dramatic impact those attributes have to distinguish and emphasize key points that *do* deserve boldface or italic type.

Four Rules of Effective Page Design: A Wrap Up

The following four rules summarize the previous advice about effective document design; adhere to them and your printed work will be professional looking.

1. **Keep it simple.** Try not to overuse text effects and design styles in an effort to impress your audience; keep it simple so that you do not lose the purpose of the document in an over-the-top design.
2. **Be consistent.** Use your design layout and terminology consistently throughout your document. Repeat your design elements on each page, whether this is the fonts you use, the text alignment, or any colors and borders.
3. **Make it clear.** Make your message clear. While fancy designs may look good on paper, they do not always add to the clarity of your document.
4. **Less is more.** Limit the number of items on your page to a maximum of perhaps five, depending on your page size. An item can be a paragraph of text or a picture, as long as it provides a focal point on the page. Too much information on the page can make the document difficult to digest, and the information itself can be lost in the clutter.

Writing for and Designing Websites*

The Internet may be the most productive marketing tool ever invented, allowing an individual, a company, or an organization to gain access to a worldwide audience through a website. As the brief history of the Internet (see the Tech Note on pp. 523–525) shows, millions of individuals use the Internet as potential customers.

---

*Some of the material in this section comes from Michael Tracey, of Bay St. Louis, Mississippi, who designs websites and builds and upgrades computer hardware.

With the tremendous growth of e-commerce, businesses around the globe will increasingly rely on websites to announce, sell, and service their products and share information. The Internet presents your product or service in words and through graphics, sound, animation, video, and three-dimensional interactive virtual-reality applications. Recent technologies (e-tailing) are making it possible for one Web company to assist another in delivering a product or service.

In this section, we will look at writing for and designing a website. Surfing the Web, you will see at once that sites vary tremendously in length and parts. While there is a great deal of variation and idiosyncrasy in the design of websites, principles of good design practice still apply. Your website should target a varied audience and be appropriate in text, organization, and visuals for the product or service you want to sell.

The Web connects sets of information—pages—at millions of sites around the world. Some pages are quite long, while others take up just one computer screen. Websites can be personal (as we saw in Chapter 7), corporate, informational, and so forth. Regardless of where it originates, a website has to arouse a reader's interest; show the appeal of a product, service, or topic; demonstrate the application of the product, service, or topic; and include a call to action.

A website can consist of one screen or many screens. In fact, a website for a government agency such as E-Government, the U.S. Office of Management and Budget (*www.whitehouse.gov/omb/egov/*), can translate into hundreds of pages of printed text. The first page of a website—the **homepage**—is the thread that connects subsequent pages into a seamless presentation. The homepage should always provide a menu that allows easy navigation to the rest of the site. Also, each page should include a menu button that links directly back to the homepage, as illustrated below.

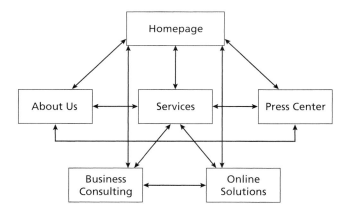

The homepage is often where visitors to a website will go first; if it catches their attention, they are likely to click onto your other pages. As you read the rest of this section, look at the sample homepages in Figures 12.5 through 12.10. Various programs are available to create a website, including Microsoft's FrontPage 2003, Macromedia's Dreamweaver MX 2004 and Studio MX 2004, HomeSite 5.5, Adobe's GoLive, Trellix, and several shareware programs.

In the following sections of this chapter, we'll discuss the differences between a website and a printed document, identify various parts or elements of a website, and help you to write for and design your own or your employer's website.

Tech Note

The Internet: Some Basic Facts

History of the Internet

1969: The Advanced Research Project Agency, part of the United States Department of Defense, is created. This computer network (ARPANET) was designed to safeguard military data stored on computers around the country. It involved four computers, located in California and Utah, linked together to conduct military research.

1972: The first e-mail program is created for ARPANET.

1972: The first computer-to-computer chat takes place at UCLA.

1973: The first international connections to the ARPANET are made at the University College of London, England.

1983: Networking switches from single, large, time-sharing computers connected to the Internet at each site to local network connections.

1990: ARPANET is officially discontinued.

1990: The first commercial provider of Internet dial-up access (The World) is launched.

1991: NREN (National Research and Education Network) is created. It was designed to connect K–12, colleges, universities, health care facilities, business, and manufacturing into a national public network using the Internet.

1994: First online shopping malls and Internet banks appear.

1995: First audio streaming technology and 24-hour Internet radio station are launched.

2003: The Recording Industry Association of America sues 261 people for distributing copyrighted music for free over Internet networks.

2004: The China Education and Research Network releases CERNET2, the largest "next-generation" Internet network in operation in the world, connects 25 universities in 20 Chinese cities at speeds of 1–10 Gbps, with plans to go commercial in 2006.

Source: Hobbes' Internet Timeline v. 8.0, *http://www.zakon.org/robert/internet/timeline/*, 2005.

Continued

Continued

Internet Uses

- Sending and receiving e-mail
- Reading updated news sources such as Yahoo! News, or CNN Online
- Tracking company activities on the stock and bond markets
- Accessing online discussion forums or newsgroups such as USENET or MSN Groups
- Conducting Internet research and looking for information using search engines
- Communicating via instant messaging, chat rooms, or message boards
- Keeping an online blog
- Transferring files over networks
- Shopping online and selling products via your own website
- Accessing online radio stations, video and music downloads, and interactive games
- Telecommuting by connecting to company networks

Internet Users

Overall: Almost 13 percent of the world's population has access to the Internet. In October 2005, 202 million U.S. citizens (about 69 percent of the population) were connected to the Internet—an increase of 111.5 percent from 2000. Worldwide, over 817 million people are connected to the Internet, with 26.7 percent of those living in North America. Universal McCann found that in 2004 8 to 10 percent of Americans ages 18 to 54 were online at any given time from 9 a.m. to 4 p.m.

Children: As many as 97.5 percent of U.S. children under 18 were online in 2005, according to a study by the University of Southern California's Center for the Digital Future. Twenty-three million U.S. children have Internet connections from home, and 10 percent of them have built their own website.

Shoppers: Internet shoppers grew from 15 million in 1990 to over 70 million in 2006. Online retail sales in the United States reached $65 billion in 2004 and are projected to rise to $117 billion by 2008. Thirty percent of U.S. Internet users who shop online spent an average of $585 each in 2004. By 2008, half of all U.S. Internet users will shop over the Internet. The Internet-based information industry accounted for more than 3 million jobs in 2004 in the United States, and the U.S. Department of Labor expects that number to rise by 54 thousand by 2012.

Continued

Continued

Some Web Statistics

- The Web contains billions of pages. Google, one of the Web's biggest and most popular search engines, indexes over 8 billion webpages.
- There are over 880 million images on the Web.
- In January 2005 there were over 46 million registered generic domains (including *.com*, *.org*, *.net*, and *.edu* domains) on the Internet. Of these, about 72 percent are .com sites; 11 percent are .net sites; and 7 percent are .org sites.
- The size of the "deep Web"—the Web content not accessed by most search engines—is 40 times the size of the easily accessible surface Web.
- E-mail accounts for the largest percentage of Internet activity at 46.33 percent.

Sources: http://www.clickz.com/stats/, http://www4.nas.edu/, www.zooknic.com, www.metamend.com, www.google.com, www.internetworldstats.com, http://www.centerformediaresearch.com/, http://www .consumerinternetbarometer.us/, http://www.libraryjournal.com/.

Web- versus Paper Pages

Writing and designing a website displayed on a computer screen requires the same emphasis on planning, drafting, formatting, and testing that traditional business documents printed on paper do. Since webpages include many of the same elements, the four keys to effective writing (from Chapter 1, pp. 8–17) apply to online content as much as they do to other business writing in print:

1. Identify your audience.
2. Establish your purpose.
3. Formulate your message.
4. Select your style and tone.

Yet, clearly, a website differs from a paper memo, letter, or report. Webpages include images, sometimes worked into Flash graphics animations or Java applets that fade one image into another or create blinking, movable elements. Additionally, websites are more colorful and their content is organized differently than in a print source. And they are not fixed on the screen. They can change, be edited, animated, and be available, to a far greater audience far more quickly, than any print source ever conceivably could be. Every website is really a work in progress—its design can change day to day. But in order to know how to write for a website you need to know how it differs from printed documents.

Web versus Print Readers

Webpages are read differently from the way print documents are. People do not generally read a website word for word hunting for information, carefully studying each sentence. They want to find information at a glance. On the average, Web readers will spend 10 to 20 seconds scanning a page. They will not waste their time scrolling in the hopes of finally finding what they need. They'll just click to another site. For that reason, Web articles, news stories, and features are shorter, more condensed, and more strategically arranged to give only essential information than those in print publications. Webpages are designed to be read quickly. Some experts advise using half the word count of a paper document for a website.

Keep in mind that text on the Web needs to be shorter because of the size of the screen. Text displayed on a screen will be harder to read than on a piece of paper. Lots of text, along with clip art and images, on a website squeezed onto a screen, coupled with the problem of glare on the computer screen, can lead to eyestrain and fatigue for a reader more quickly than in a print source.

Moreover, a Web audience may not necessarily read your entire website. In fact, they may not have even begun their search at your site. So you can't assume your Web audience, like one for a printed source, will read from the start to the finish of your site. Don't expect to write to build up a climax or to postpone key facts. Web readers may navigate through your pages in no determined order or even skip some of them to find the information they want. They can start with a home- or later page and then go to any other page on that site, to skim or to concentrate on. This flexibility on the part of Web readers makes the organization of each page— and your overall site—crucial factors to consider when you write for, edit, or design a website. As we will see, navigation and linkage of pages are important considerations (see pp. 547–548).

Finally, Web readers will expect navigational clues that readers of a print source do not. A Web audience will be looking for visual markers such as highlighted keywords to click on or bulleted lists, different colored text, commands such as *search, click here, go to, go back, contact us*, arrows and crosses, or addresses of other sites to visit. Note how these clues are incorporated into the websites in Figures 12.4–12.8.

Hyperlinks

What most sets a webpage apart from a printed document are **hyperlinks**. Called **links** for short, hyperlinks enable readers—with the click of a mouse—to jump from one section of a webpage to another, or from one website to another site. They are the pathway readers take on a journey through your website, and each is connected to the other, and to your homepage. Hyperlinks and menus provide readers with many choices and extraordinary mobility. Instead of thumbing through printed pages one page after another, with one section following another as an introduction at the beginning and a concluding section at the end, an online reader can virtually jump through the electronic pages of a website anywhere in the world.

Converting a Print Document into a Website: An Example

To illustrate how a print document differs from an online one, let's consider how the article "Virtual Reality: The Future of Law Enforcement," which appeared in Chapter 10, can be recreated for a Web audience. The print version had fourteen sections presented in the following order:

1. Introduction
2. Traditional Training Limitations

3. Training with Virtual Reality
4. What Is Virtual Reality?
5. How Does Virtual Reality Work?
6. Uses for Virtual Reality
7. Law Enforcement Training
8. Pursuit Driving
9. Firearms Training
10. High-Risk Incident Management
11. Incident Re-Creation
12. Crime Scene Processing
13. Is Virtual Reality Perfect?
14. Physical Limitations and Effects

Had that article been published as a website, the author might have presented the entire table of contents on a homepage, as in Figure 12.4, allowing readers to view the sections they wanted in the order they wanted. Instead of turning pages, they would click menu links.

A re-creation of the homepage for a website based on the virtual reality article.   Figure 12.4

Web address

VIRTUAL REALITY

- What Is Virtual Reality?
- How Does Virtual Reality Work?   Hyperlinks
- Uses for Virtual Reality
- Is Virtual Reality Virtually Perfect?   Uses appropri-ate visual
- Physical Limitations and Effects

VIRTUAL REALITY

THE FUTURE OF LAW ENFORCEMENT

Introduction

Traditional Training Limitations

Training with Virtual Reality

About this Website

Contact Information

A late night police pursuit of a suspected drunk driver winds through abandoned city streets. The short vehicle chase ends in a warehouse district where the suspect abandons his vehicle and continues on foot. The rookie patrol officer exits his vehicle and gives chase. . . **[More]**

LAW ENFORCEMENT

- Law Enforcement Training
- Pursuit Driving   Short chunk of text
- Firearms Training
- High-Risk Incident Management
- Incident Re-Creation
- Crime Scene Processing

The Web is an exciting medium to work in. But there are challenges to working on electronic content. In the following sections of this chapter, we'll discuss the different elements that make up webpages and some additional ways that webpages differ from paper pages. Understanding how webpages are constructed and read will help you to create your own or your employer's website.

Parts of a Webpage

Most webpages are created using hypertext markup language (HTML), which formats webpages the same way a word processor formats documents. More information about HTML and XHTML can be found in the Tech Note below. Websites also make use of many other tools to format pages (style sheets), organize content (frames), perform functions (scripts), or display animations (multimedia). This chapter cannot begin to cover all of the tools used in website creation. Instead, we will concentrate on those webpage elements that most concern business writers in the world of work.

Tech Note

HTML and XHTML

Currently, hypertext markup language (HTML) is in version 4.01, but extensible hypertext markup language (XHTML) is already positioned to succeed HTML. To learn more about HTML and XHTML, visit the following websites.

World Wide Web Consortium
(http://www.w3.org/MarkUp/)
The World Wide Web Consortium (W3C) develops specifications, guidelines, software, and tools for the Web. Its website includes guidelines on how to use HTML and XHTML.

Webmonkey
(http://hotwired.lycos.com/webmonkey/)
A comprehensive source of information for professional and amateur Web designers, Webmonkey offers articles and technical updates, as well as an archive of more than 200 features and tutorials.

The National Center for Supercomputing Applications
(http://archive.ncsa.uiuc.edu/General/Internet/WWW/HTMLPrimer.html)
The NCSA Beginner's Guide to HTML is a good starting point to understanding the hypertext markup language used on the World Wide Web.

Continued

Continued

Web Developer's Virtual Library
(*http://www.wdvl.com*)
A one-stop resource for Web developers, the Web Developer's Virtual Library includes HTML and XHTML tutorials, discussion forums, software reviews, advice on authorship, and resources.

HTML Dog
(*http://www.htmldog.com*)
As a guide and a resource for Web developers, HTML Dog provides HTML tutorials for beginning, intermediate, and advanced Web designers.

The World Wide Web Consortium, an international group of engineers and researchers, sets the standards for HTML and other Web languages. According to the consortium, a webpage is composed of three basic parts:

1. A line that describes the HTML version being used by the webpage. (This behind-the-scenes information is not displayed on the webpage.)
2. The "Head" section, which may include a declarative title that describes the purpose of the webpage, as well as descriptive keywords for search engines. Some webpages display the title as the main page heading. Other webpages use the title merely as a label or file name, and it is not displayed onscreen. Whether the human eye or a search engine is reading the title, it should describe the specific contents of the page, because it may appear in search engine results as the title of your site. "Homepage" does not tell a reader what a website is about, while "International Chamber of Commerce Homepage" does. For more information, see the Tech Note "Writing for Search Engines" (p. 541).
3. The "Body" of the webpage.

In most cases, you will be concerned only with the body of the webpage, because it contains almost all of the content elements delivered to the reader, including:

- Hyperlinks (for menus and other links)
- Headers (HTML's name for headlines, headings, and subheadings)
- Text paragraphs
- Lists
- Tables
- Color
- Images

Links and Menus

Links are the street signs of the Web. They can lead to another page within the same website, another website, a file that can be downloaded, or even an e-mail address or chat room. Internal links allow readers to navigate the content of a single website in any order they choose. External links allow readers to jump to completely different

Figure 12.5   Homepage of the International Chamber of Commerce.

*Site provides
internal links
and menus*

*Text uses brief
chunks*

*Headers are
clear, to the
point*

*Images break
up page*

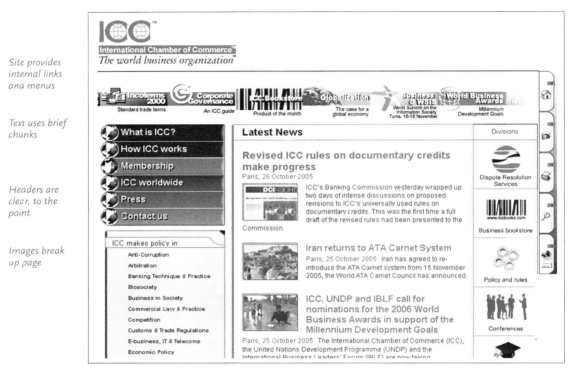

Reprinted with permission.

websites, linking your site to many others around the globe. Before you insert links, however, consider whether you really need the external information. When on-line readers click an external link, they may very well leave your website and not come back.

A *menu* on a webpage is nothing more than an organized and formatted list of internal links. Menu links typically jump to main sections of the website, whereas non-menu links may jump to specific nuggets of information within the site—or on another site. After clicking a few links, online readers may lose their bearings. Menus help them get back on track. As such, a site menu should appear in a consistent place on each of your webpages. If you've created a list of headers for your website, perhaps using your document's table of contents, you may already have the list you need to create a website menu.

As you can see in Figure 12.5, the International Chamber of Commerce uses several menus to frame the organization's homepage. Notice the differences in the

Homepage of the United States Postal Service.   Figure 12.6

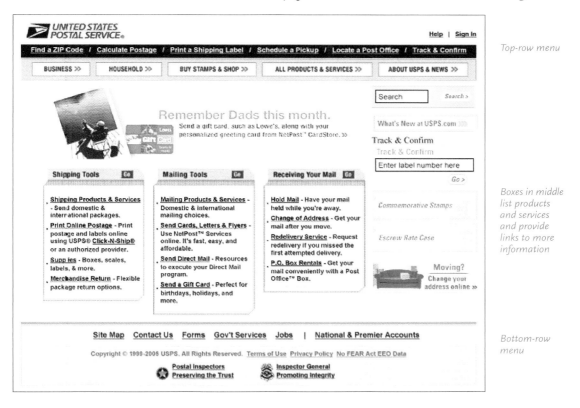

Top-row menu

Boxes in middle list products and services and provide links to more information

Bottom-row menu

menus. The top-row menu uses labeled icons that link to six topics. The left-column menu uses short descriptions that link to specific topics about the ICC. The right-column menu links to various divisions. Notice how the United States Postal Service homepage, in Figure 12.6, groups different items into menus. For example, the left-column menu links to shipping, while the top-row menus link to specific functions available on the site. The bottom-row menu lists helpful site navigation information, site map, contact information, jobs, and government services.

Headers

Headers function as headings in HTML and appear on a separate line from text paragraphs and other headers. HTML provides six levels of headers for organizing and labeling content. Just because there are six header sizes, however, doesn't mean you need to use all six on a page. Most webpages are limited to one or two different header sizes. Notice, in Figure 12.7 (on p. 537), how the website uses two different size headers. The left-column headers are large and highlighted with icons, whereas the second-column headers are smaller and are not highlighted.

Each header should be brief, especially those that are used as main headings. And, as we saw, website links and menus often link to headers. A header needs to be short in case it becomes the descriptive label for a link or a menu button. As a general rule, the larger the header, the shorter it should be—for several reasons. First, computer screen displays are small and a large header running from one side of your webpage to the other takes up a lot of valuable space. In Figure 12.5, note how the headers are limited to the center column. For the lead stories on the page, the headers are large; the datelines are smaller.

When organizing your webpage content into "chunks," decide how many headers and subheaders you need. In essence, you will be drafting a table of contents, or outline, for each webpage. Meanwhile, in a separate file, you may also want to be creating a table of contents—called a *site map*—for the entire website. If each webpage in your content is well organized, then it should be easy to create an overarching table of contents for the entire site. If your homepage has few or no text paragraphs on it, you may not need any headers. In Figure 12.6, for example, notice that the columns list links, such as "Hold Mail" and text descriptions of those links. No headers are used in the column, because each link has white space around it, and the underlined links also serve to separate the text into chunks.

Chunking Text

As in a print document, avoid using long, unbroken blocks of prose on a website. Instead, organize your Web text into briefer "chunks" or layers of text information, so readers can find key ideas at a glance. See the bad and good examples below. You can chunk your text in a variety of ways.

- Keep your paragraphs short. See how easy it is to find information in the short paragraphs in the websites in Figures 12.5 and 12.7.
- Put only one point per paragraph or chunk and make sure it contains only essential information right upfront. Don't make readers scroll or get them bogged down with background or supporting details.
- Use headings and titles to help readers scan information quickly.
- Make sure readers can scan your Web text quickly. Use and highlight only key terms or concepts.
- Break up different sections (or chunks) of text with white space.
- Present information in easy-to-read bulleted lists—like this one—to make it highly accessible to readers. Lists help readers locate information quickly in Figures 12.4, 12.7, and 12.10.

Note how hard it would be to read the example below of dense prose on a website, but how much easier the Web-friendly translation is because the writer chunked information into bite-size pieces.

Dense Text   According to a study conducted in 2005 by PricewaterhouseCoopers, the business world is moving more and more toward globalization. Fifty percent of the nation's fastest-growing private companies are exporting internationally, while 19 percent have sales or production working abroad. The report also found that 16.8 percent of the revenues of international marketers come from other countries. The rate of growth of international marketers is much higher than domestic marketers at 32 percent. In 2005, CEOs from over half (56 percent) of international marketers believe sales originating outside the country will be important to the growth of their companies. The findings of this recent study have far-reaching implications for the future of TELTech.

Chunked Example   A 2005 study by PricewaterhouseCoopers found **international markets** are becoming more important to the nation's fastest-growing companies because of:

- **Exports**—Half now export internationally
- **Sales**—19% have sales or production working abroad
- **Revenues**—16.8% of international marketers' revenues originate abroad
- **Growth**—International marketers grow 32% faster than domestic marketers. Fifty-six percent of CEOs agree on the importance of international sales.

Organizational Groupings

Organizational groupings should be simple and logical for your audience. For example, groupings and subgroupings may be organized around:

- Topic (e.g., technology, sales, marketing)
- Category (e.g., domestic sales, international sales)
- Brand names
- Product type (e.g., binders, notebooks, paper clips, staples)
- Chronology or reverse chronology (e.g., 2007 sales, 2006 sales)
- Events (convention, planning retreat, sales meeting)
- Number (1st employee meeting, 2nd employee meeting)
- Alphabet (Accounting, Advertising, Circulation, Design, Editorial, Marketing)

Headings

Once you have sorted your text into short paragraphs, bulleted lists, and other relevant groupings, write brief, descriptive headings that label those text passages for your reader. Use common words your audience, including international readers, will know. Not every paragraph needs a heading, but online documents need more headings and subheadings than almost any printed document you will write—for two reasons. First, most computer screens can display only one-third as much text as an $8\frac{1}{2}'' \times 11''$ piece of paper can. Second, headings and subheadings play a larger visual role on the computer screen, breaking up text sections with white space. As online readers scroll down the page to continue reading, they appreciate having a heading or subheading visible almost all of the time.

Lists

Lists can make your webpage successful. HTML provides four ways to list information:

- *Unordered lists*, which are indented with bullets, like this one. See the top left-column list of links in Figure 12.5 for an example of an unordered list.
- *Ordered lists*, which are indented and numbered sequentially.

- *Definition lists,* which, like dictionaries, pair listed items to terms and definitions. Refer again to the columns in Figure 12.6. These links function like a definition list, with link names followed by descriptions.
- *Nested lists,* which are similar to outlines. For example, an "A, B, C" ordered list may be nested within a "I, II, III" ordered list to create a formal outline. Using nested lists, an HTML author can combine unordered, ordered, and definition lists in a variety of ways—to create a list that best suits his or her purposes.

As with all webpage text, keep your lists brief, perhaps a few lines of text maximum. Employees attending a meeting might be written as an unordered list.

- Olivia Royka
- James Beauregard
- Jackie Hu

A series of procedures might call for an ordered list.

1. Before you install the version upgrade, please exit any other programs.
2. Double-click the version upgrade file "vx1.exe" on your desktop.
3. Follow the prompts provided by the installation software.
4. If you have questions, e-mail Technical Support at techsupport@nextdoor.com, or call extension 356.

A sales brochure of luggage product features and benefits might work well as a definition list. (In definition lists, the terms or features are typically bolded.)

Lightweight

- Easy to carry and use anywhere.

Durable

- Withstands repeated use.

Includes reflective yellow stripe

- Hard to lose at baggage claim.

The same sales brochure might also work as a nested list—combining an unordered (bulleted) list within a definition list—especially if there are multiple benefits to list with each feature.

Lightweight

- Easy to carry and use anywhere.
- Easy to place in overhead storage on airliners.

Durable

- Withstands repeated use.
- Looks new for years.

Includes reflective yellow strip

- Hard to lose at baggage claim.
- Added safety in dark, airport parking lots.

In Figure 12.10 (p. 549), notice the content links, which are listed as a definition list, with bold titles and text descriptions, and illustrated with icons. Note how only a few of the links are listed on the screen, and readers have to scroll down to see all thirteen links. How might that design be improved? Consider how any of the preceding lists might have been written in paragraph form—with no bullets, numbers, or letters to highlight the individual items on the list. Would the information have caught your attention as you scanned the page? Probably not. Lists break information into quickly digestible pieces. They are one of the simplest ways to organize information for readers.

Tables

As we saw in Chapter 11, pages 458–460, tables are widely used for organizing information on a page. The grid of a table is a fundamental visual design tool. Read through any newspaper or magazine and you will see that page elements—headlines, text, and images—are placed according to a grid of white spaces that appears as vertical columns and horizontal rows. This same grid design provides the foundation of most webpages, some of which use templates similar to those illustrated in Figure 12.1.

Tables are more versatile than almost any other Web design element. For example, a company logo, images, paragraphs of text, and a data table (with borders) can all be placed within a page layout table (without borders). Keep the following points in mind when designing a website using tables:

- Before designing your site, you need to ask the following questions:
  What content do you need to display on a homepage?
  What content should appear on secondary pages?
  How much text will be on each screen?
  How many menus will you need for your site and your audience?
  Where will your images be placed?
- Look at similar webpages or competitors' websites for ideas of suitable page designs.
- Consider how many columns and rows you want on each page. Many webpages use three- or four-column grids. In Figure 12.7 (p. 537), the FinAid page uses a three-column grid, with the first two columns devoted to short blurbs of textual content, and the third column offering interaction with the reader. Horizontal rows at the top and bottom list additional navigation links and visually frame the page. The global warming page for the EPA in Figure 12.8 (p. 538) uses a four-column format, but with different results. This site has one narrow menu column on the left, and three wider, center columns for presenting news story text and images.
- Consider the use of space between columns and rows of your layout table. Note how the large amounts of white space in Figure 12.7 make the site appear clean and friendly. The careful use of white space in Figure 12.8 also adds to the professional and informative appearance of the page.

Tech Note

The Basic Elements of HTML Tables

HTML can be used to create visible and invisible tables for webpage designs. The basic elements of HTML tables include

- **Columns and rows.** Rows can span across multiple columns, and columns can span across multiple rows. In other words, the grid is flexible. For example, if your table includes a title, the top row of the table may span all of the columns beneath it.
- **Cells.** Cells are the individual boxes where a column meets a row. Cells can have borders and *padding*, that is, defined space between the cell walls and the content of the cells. Page design tables may need a lot of cell padding or cell spacing to separate information and pictures from each other in order to minimize visual clutter on a page. If you are trying to squeeze some spreadsheet data onto the screen, however, the table's cells should probably not be padded. Cells can also be merged to create larger design areas within a table.
- **Borders.** For page layout, tables are usually displayed with invisible borders. In this case, the border width in the HTML coding is set to zero. However, tables can also be displayed with borders to create the look of a spreadsheet suitable for displaying data and other information, or to separate areas of a webpage, such as a menu or a heading. Borders can be displayed in any color, with thin or thick lines. As a general design rule, the less obtrusive the border, the better. What's important, after all, is the information within the cells, not the border separating them.
- **Alignment and size.** Tables can be aligned to the left, center, or even the right of a page, and they can be any size. However, do not make layout tables too wide, since users with smaller screens will have to do more scrolling on your site.

Color for Text and Background

As the section and Tech Note on using color on page 519 indicate, color is vital in catching a reader's eye and keeping his or her attention in a printed text. It is an even more significant component in cyberspace. Almost every element on a webpage could be displayed in color—text, headers, backgrounds, images, borders, and so on. That doesn't mean every element should be in color. Color can make any document more effective than a black-and-white version.

But color on many websites is often poorly used. Keep in mind that color is probably the most difficult design element to control. Be careful. A site with a wild

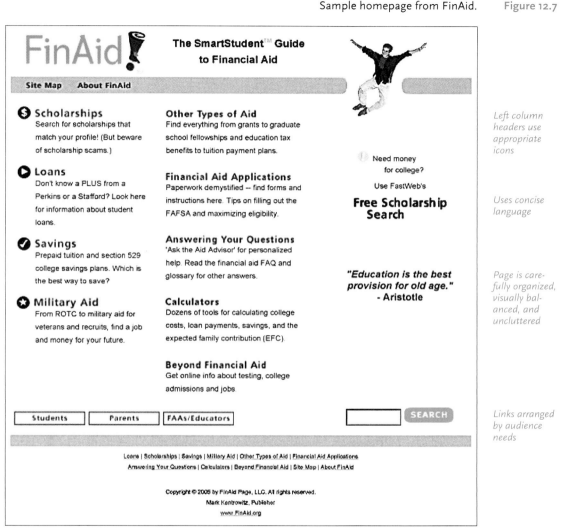

The SmartStudent™ Guide
to Financial Aid

Site Map   About FinAid

Scholarships
Search for scholarships that
match your profile! (But beware
of scholarship scams.)

Loans
Don't know a PLUS from a
Perkins or a Stafford? Look here
for information about student
loans.

Savings
Prepaid tuition and section 529
college savings plans. Which is
the best way to save?

Military Aid
From ROTC to military aid for
veterans and recruits, find a job
and money for your future.

Other Types of Aid
Find everything from grants to graduate
school fellowships and education tax
benefits to tuition payment plans.

Financial Aid Applications
Paperwork demystified — find forms and
instructions here. Tips on filling out the
FAFSA and maximizing eligibility.

Answering Your Questions
'Ask the Aid Advisor' for personalized
help. Read the financial aid FAQ and
glossary for other answers.

Calculators
Dozens of tools for calculating college
costs, loan payments, savings, and the
expected family contribution (EFC).

Beyond Financial Aid
Get online info about testing, college
admissions and jobs.

Need money
for college?

Use FastWeb's

**Free Scholarship
Search**

*"Education is the best
provision for old age."*
- Aristotle

Students   Parents   FAAs/Educators   SEARCH

Loans | Scholarships | Savings | Military Aid | Other Types of Aid | Financial Aid Applications
Answering Your Questions | Calculators | Beyond Financial Aid | Site Map | About FinAid

Copyright © 2005 by FinAid Page, LLC. All rights reserved.
Mark Kantrowitz, Publisher
www.FinAid.org

*Left column
headers use
appropriate
icons*

*Uses concise
language*

*Page is care-
fully organized,
visually bal-
anced, and
uncluttered*

*Links arranged
by audience
needs*

array of colors is as unattractive as one in only black and white. Always discuss the
use of color with your company's graphic designer and your boss.

Here are some suggestions for using color wisely on a website:

- Select colors that suit your audience and support the purpose of your website.
  Avoid dark backgrounds that reduce readability.
- Employ color only for emphasis—to draw attention to a menu, links, or up-
  dated content.

Figure 12.8   Examples of navigational links.

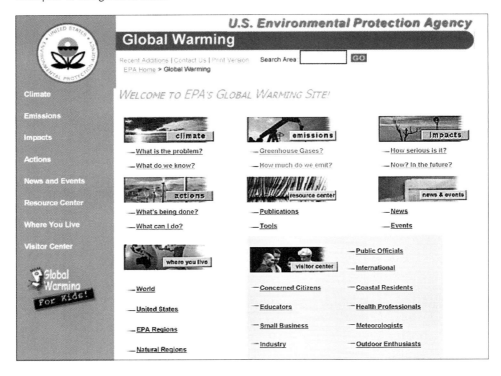

- Limit yourself to a few colors, and use those consistently. If you use dark blue headers on one page, they should be dark blue on all pages.
- Choose background colors very carefully to establish a sharp contrast between text and background. Readability should be your concern. Dark text on a dark background (purple, green, blue) is almost impossible to read. Similarly, avoid using light text (pastels, etc.) on a light screen background.
- Select appropriate text fonts and sizes. Avoid using fancy script, all italics, or mixing fonts and sizes. These will only detract from the attractiveness and functionality of your site and drive readers away.
- Take into account that colors and images may look different on different computer operating systems (Unix, Macintosh, Windows, Linux, etc.) and on different computer screens. Some screens, for example, are limited to fewer colors than are others.
- Steer clear of very dark backgrounds with light-colored text, since this combination makes a site difficult to read. Dark text on a light background is more effective, especially for large chunks of text.
- Note that the resolution, or sharpness, of a computer screen can drastically affect the way a webpage is displayed. Test a webpage by sending it to mem-

bers of your collaborative team so they can see how it appears on different computers.

You may also want to consult the following sites that provide helpful information on the use of color on a website:

- "Web Smart Color Spectrum Wheel," by Jemima Pereira (*http://www.ficml.org/jemimap/style/color/wheel.html*)
- "Colors on the Web" (color wizard or spin the color wheel), by Donald Johansson (*http://www.webwhirlers.com/colors/*)
- "Effective Color Contrast: Designing for Partial Sight & Color Deficiencies," by The Lighthouse (*http://www.lighthouse.org/color_contrast.htm#colorwheel*)
- "Considering the Color-Blind," by Chuck Newman (especially jump down to subsection of this article entitled "Design Guidelines") (*http://www.webtechniques.com/archives/2000/08/newman/*)

Images

As a visual medium, the Web depends on images to convey its message. And like color, getting the most effective images can be a very challenging design decision. Whether in print or online, effective use of images can make your business documents look striking and professional, while poor images will undermine the communication of your message.

Review Chapter 11 for specific guidelines on using images to enhance your documents. When you use images on a website, remember also to consider these three factors:

- **Color.** Try to use images that tie in with the color palette of your website, either by complementing or contrasting the background and other color elements on the page. If the image and background colors are too similar, the images won't stand out. If the colors are too different, the image may clash with the background.
- **File format.** Image files come in more than a dozen different formats, but only three are compatible with most Web browsers. As a business writer, you should know that different formats have different strengths and weaknesses. **GIF** (graphic interchange format) is used for images with fewer colors; **JPEG** (Joint Photographic Experts Group) is for photos and more complex images; and **PNG** (portable network graphics) is a newer format designed for line art and basic clip art. The file format you choose will be one of the main factors influencing the image file size.
- **File size.** As fast as they are, computers still need some time to process information. The larger the amount of information, the longer it takes for a file to load. Image files are notoriously large because images can be very complex. Before a website can be displayed on your screen, the information for that image has to travel—with the rest of the website information—from the computer where it is stored, across cables and/or telephone lines, and then be processed by your computer's hardware. As a general rule, a simple image

with less detail and a limited number of colors is smaller than a complex, full-color image.

Guidelines for Designing and Writing a Successful Homepage

A homepage has several functions. First of all, it has to catch visitors' attention. If it fails to do that, everything else is a waste of time; your visitors will click their mouse and be gone. Your next goal is to sell your company's product or service or to introduce your organization. That may seem backward, but unless you attract readers to your website, you cannot promote your product or service. Successful homepages accomplish both of these objectives clearly and effectively. For example, students applying for financial aid can find it a daunting process, but the design of the FinAid homepage, Figure 12.7, keeps things simple and upbeat. Even the image of the student "jumping for joy" contributes to the page's user-friendliness. Similarly, the EPA homepage on global warming in Figure 12.8 uses environmentally appropriate images to emphasize its purpose.

Designing a website requires you to follow many of the rules you read about earlier in this chapter for printed pages. (See pp. 508–519.) In addition, you should adhere to the following eight guidelines to create an effectively designed and written website that will capture your audience's attention.

1. **Make your site easy to find.**

   - Obtain a registered domain name for your site, which may require an initial fee and then a yearly charge. One major benefit of having a registered domain name is that it will remain consistent throughout the life of your site because your company or organization owns it. If your Internet provider goes out of business, you can easily transfer your site to another server without changing the name and, in the process, losing customers. A good place to start is the InterNIC website (*http://www.internic.net*), which provides updated information on Internet domain name registrations.
   - Submit your website to the various search engines and directories to make sure a broad audience knows about your site. The most notable search engines and directories include AltaVista, Excite, Google, Hotbot, Lycos, Northern Light, and Yahoo! (See page 329.)
   - Since there are hundreds of search engines and directories, you may want to take advantage of website submission services offered by companies such as Microsoft Small Business Services (*http://www.bcentral.com*) and Overture.com (*http://www.overture.com/d/home/*). For a subscription fee, these companies will promote your site to various search engines on an ongoing basis.

The following Tech Note describes how search engines read keywords.

Writing for Search Engines

Search engines do not "see" webpages the way visitors do. They do not see designed pages or colorful graphics. Instead, they only see the HTML (hypertext markup language) source code, which is the "skeleton" of a webpage.

Because search engines only see the source code of a page, you need to include the most important keywords related to your webpage in the most likely places for a search engine to find them—near the top of your webpage in a section called the "head." Since search engines read webpages from top to bottom, the keyword-containing text should appear in the "head" section and at the top of your page.

This holds true whether you are creating an electronic résumé (see pp. 263–266) or a company website. If your firm manufactures retractable awnings, you need to include the keywords *retractable* and *awnings* in the "head" tags and in the body text, thus proving definitively to the search engines that your page is indeed about "retractable awnings." Then, when a user visits a search engine to search for that keyword phrase, the likelihood of your site appearing toward the top of the rankings increases.

You will want to include your keyword phrase in the title, description, and keyword tags in the head section, and you want the title and description tags to be "selling" tools for your company. For instance, you might say "Discount Retractable Awnings" in your title tag to emphasize customer savings.

In the competitive online business world, the most important goal is to get your company's website in front of your customers. Knowing how search engines work can ensure that customers find your firm online.

For more information on how search engines function, see *http://www.searchengineworkshops.com/articles.html.*

Source: Adapted from "Knowing How to Build Web Sites Can Insure More Net Traffic," by Robin Noble, August 2002. Reprinted by permission of Robin Noble.

2. **Make your site easy to navigate.**

▪ Help your visitors find their way easily through your site with logical and effective use of navigation tools such as:

in-text hyperlinks	search engines
navigation bars	button links
indexes and menus	rollover icons
site maps and tables of contents	previous, next, and back links

Note how, in Figure 12.8, the EPA provides multiple navigation aids: menu buttons that are labeled and illustrated with images and that elaborate on the menu on the left-hand side.

- Don't overload your page with images. They take too long to load. Note how Figure 12.7 uses a single image, four smaller icons, and boxes at the bottom right. The carefully organized photos, images, and icons displayed in Figure 12.5 also make the site easy to navigate.
- Make sure all your pages are linked and that all the links work. A website that does not identify one of its links or that contains a broken link will drive readers/customers away.

3. **Make your site informative.**

- Provide all essential information on your homepage, including your company's name, address, e-mail, and phone numbers.
- Tell the visitor what products or services you offer. In Figure 12.6, note how the U.S. Postal Service promotes its many services on its homepage.
- Indicate what type of information may be obtained through the website, including links to your sales force, customer service, and technical support.
- Offer readers different types of interaction—FAQs, bulletin boards, animated product demonstrations, and free e-mail subscriptions.

4. **Make your site easy to read for both native and non-native English readers.**

- Put the most important point FIRST in the topic sentence.
- Get to the point right away.
- Write short paragraphs (chunks of content)—no more than three to four sentences long.
- Provide headings with keywords and bulleted lists to help readers locate information quickly.
- Use plain, concise English—concrete nouns, action verbs, and the like. This will allow your website to be accessible to global readers, who may have only a basic knowledge of English.
- Keep sentences short—use only active voice.
- Use plenty of white space but not after each sentence. Single-sentence paragraphs are harder to process.
- Include scannable terms and hyperlinks; highlight them to make them stand out
- Select fonts that are easy to read (review pp. 513–518 on typography). Use larger fonts than you would for a print document.

5. **Keep your site updated.**

- New information is vital for product and service company sites. Otherwise, readers have no reason to make return visits. Feature insider news updates about your business or preproduction information on products or services. Build in hyperlinks to product reviews, news articles, awards, books, journals, conferences, associations, or other businesses in your area.
- Revise the design of your site if your company offers a new product or service or a new promotional element on its homepage. Clearly, your site does not need a major design overhaul every week, but a new page alerts customers to new products and services.

- Indicate when the site was last updated, so readers will know your information is kept current.
- Periodically check your external links to make sure they work.

6. Use images and icons effectively.

- Arrange images and photos so they do not interfere with text or layout. Proportion is important for achieving a balance between different page elements. Note how the sizes of the images in Figure 12.5 are similar.
- Choose appropriate icons or images to illustrate menus and page sections. As with any textual document, images should serve a purpose. In Figure 12.8, note the striking photos that illustrate the sections of the webpage, reinforcing the site's organization.
- Be conservative in using animations or anything that might be viewed as a gimmick, because they may distract readers from other content on the page.
- Keep images proportional so that they are not too big or small for the page.
- Be conservative. Do not use images or elaborate watermarks for webpage backgrounds, since they can seriously detract from the text.

7. Encourage visitor interaction by soliciting feedback.

- Ask readers to e-mail you about your product, service, or website. And make sure a procedure for handling that feedback is developed within your organization.
- Include a feedback form or survey with specifically targeted questions (see pp. 304–305), including multiple-choice pull-down menus and comment boxes on your website to encourage visitors to leave useful comments.
- Conduct a usability test. Ask readers what you could do better or what they like about your website.

8. Make sure your website is ethical.

- Do not plagiarize from another Web (or print) source. If you include any information from another site, including quotations, visuals, or statistics, make sure you e-mail the author or webmaster for permission. If granted, acknowledge the source on your site.
- Validate the availability and accuracy of any websites you refer readers to.
- Never include broken links.
- Avoid biased, sexist language. Moreover do not offend an international audience by using terms or names that are insulting, stereotypical, or condescending. See pages 5–8.
- Never make false or exaggerated claims. Be honest and accurate. Earn your readers' trust.

Creating Storyboards for Websites

Creating a storyboard is a simple, preliminary step in designing websites. The term *storyboarding* originated in the film industry as a means for film directors to illustrate scenes in their films before actually shooting them. Storyboarding can be as simple as sketching what you want your webpage to look like. Acting as a map to your site, a storyboard allows you to visualize the graphic layout and content of each page, as well as plan the structure and navigation of the entire site before you put it on the Web. Storyboards help organize your company's site to ensure that it is as efficient as possible before the technical process of building the site begins. When you prepare a storyboard for a professional Web designer, you give the designer a clear concept of how you want the website to look and function and save your company time and money.

Here are some guidelines for developing a storyboard:

- Sketch pages of the site on a piece of paper and label them according to the various pages of the site, for example, Homepage, About Our Company, Contact Us, Place an Order, and so on.
- Beginning with the homepage, plan each page's graphics, content, information, and general layout. For instance, the homepage should include your company's logo, a brief introduction to the company, and information about the goods or services you offer.
- Organize basic design elements, such as fonts, backgrounds, frames, and color schemes, so that the website will appear professional and appeal to customers.
- Determine the size of and where to place columns, cells, images, text, highlighted areas, and other elements.
- Build in navigational menus and hyperlinks, making sure all links are positioned to make browsing and searching your website quick and effective. Include hyperlinks to your company's e-mail address so that readers can contact you.
- Ensure that the website is easy to navigate by drawing arrows on the storyboard between pages that should be linked together. Every page should be linked to the homepage.
- Some customers may find your company's website through a search engine or other link that opens a product page instead of your homepage. By including a menu on each page of your site, you ensure that customers can navigate from any point within the site. Without such mapped-in navigational devices you might omit them on a page and lose customers.
- When you have outlined the visual components of your website, begin to plan the textual content of each page. Include brief headings for your proposed content on your storyboard sketches to ensure that your site is organized and that information is presented in the best possible way.

See how the example of a storyboard below follows these guidelines.

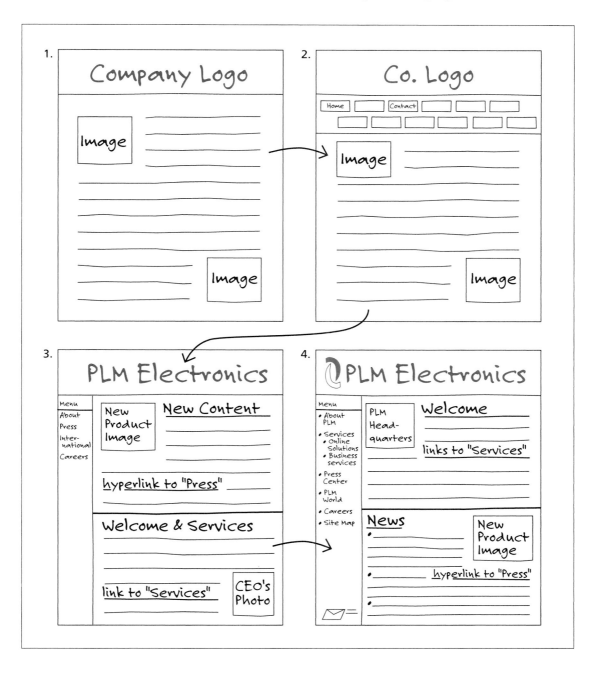

Effective and Ineffective Websites

There are millions of websites online. Some are outstanding communication tools for businesses and organizations, but not all websites are as effective as they might be. Perhaps you have visited a website to purchase a product, but found that it lacked necessary information, such as an 800 number or an array of menus. Perhaps you left that site and purchased the product elsewhere. If so, you can be fairly certain that your online experience was not what the company had intended.

Learning to identify effective and ineffective sites and explain the difference can help you to profit from the successes as well as the mistakes in webpage content, design, and function. When visiting any website, before you evaluate specific page elements, you may want to consider several strategic questions:

1. Does the website identify and target its audience? For example, are there specific menus for different types of customers?
2. What is the site's purpose? Is it clearly stated on the site? Is the purpose achieved?
3. What message does the website broadcast? Note that many business websites include multiple messages: the company image for investors, corporate culture for potential employees, products and services for customers, as well as contact information for vendors and distributors.
4. Are the style and tone of the website suitable for the products and services it promotes?

As you evaluate the site in more detail, prepare a list of webpage elements you think are most important to the site. Which elements are more effective? Which ones are less effective? The following Case Study will help you in evaluating your website.

Case Study: Evaluating the Effectiveness of Two Websites

It's a valuable exercise to evaluate the strengths and weaknesses of the websites you see and use. The following case study presents two websites for your analysis to give you an opportunity to do just that as you design or edit your own websites. Table 12.1 also compares the two websites side-by-side.

Compare Figures 12.9 and 12.10 (pp. 548–549). These two federal government websites target similar audiences and try to convey some of the same information. However, the sites go about it in different ways, with different results. What are your first impressions of the websites in Figures 12.9 and 12.10? If you were seeking information about the federal government, which site would you choose? Most of us would probably select the FirstGov website in Figure 12.10, because it appears better organized and easier to use. The National Contact Center site in Figure 12.9, in comparison, appears cluttered and disorganized, making it harder to find your way around.

TABLE 12.1   Comparing Two Government Websites

	www.info.gov (Figure 12.9)	*www.firstgov.com (Figure 12.10)*
Audience	Page includes wide assortment of links, but seems unsure of its intended audience. Needs to target its audience.	Content organized neatly into three audience segments: citizens, business, and government employees.
Purpose	Bills itself as the place to find information about federal programs. But admits that many topics aren't listed. Suggests readers go to another website.	"The Official Government Gateways . . ." bills itself as the place to find information about federal programs.
Message	"Here's some information. If you don't see what you want here, go elsewhere."	"This is an authoritative source of federal and state information."
Style/Tone	Friendly. Conversational, but the design seems perhaps too simplistic.	Professional and helpful. Comprehensive.
Interaction	Includes 800 number. Again, this leads readers away from the website.	Invites interaction with e-mail newsletters and online survey.
Navigation	▪ Poor organization. Note how top left menu duplicates other links on the page. ▪ Three columns of links are grouped into "Our Frequently Asked Questions" and "Useful Resources." These links, however, are presented in no particular order. ▪ More information describing the links is needed. ▪ Left column includes simple search engine, a site map, and links about the site. If this is a menu column, the "News and Notes" section is out of place here.	▪ Left column includes a search engine, plus an advanced search option, hierarchical menus, a topical drop-down menu, and four icon menu buttons. ▪ Four columns across the page group the links well. ▪ Rows across top and bottom of page clearly display links about the site.
Content	Mostly links, with no description of where they go or what information may be found there.	Comprehensive list of links. Short text blurbs provide descriptions of each column's links.
Design	▪ Cluttered. ▪ Type font is good, but clip art at the top makes site seem comical. ▪ Table borders are too heavy. Design makes them seem more important than the links in the table. ▪ Almost all of the text, including the links, is centered, so no text appears aligned with other text.	▪ Clean, symmetrical, four-column design. ▪ Balanced use of illustrative graphics, text, and bulleted lists. ▪ Conservative use of icons. ▪ Most of the text, including the links, is presented in a bulleted list, aligned left. This makes for a clean presentation.

Figure 12.9   A less effective website.

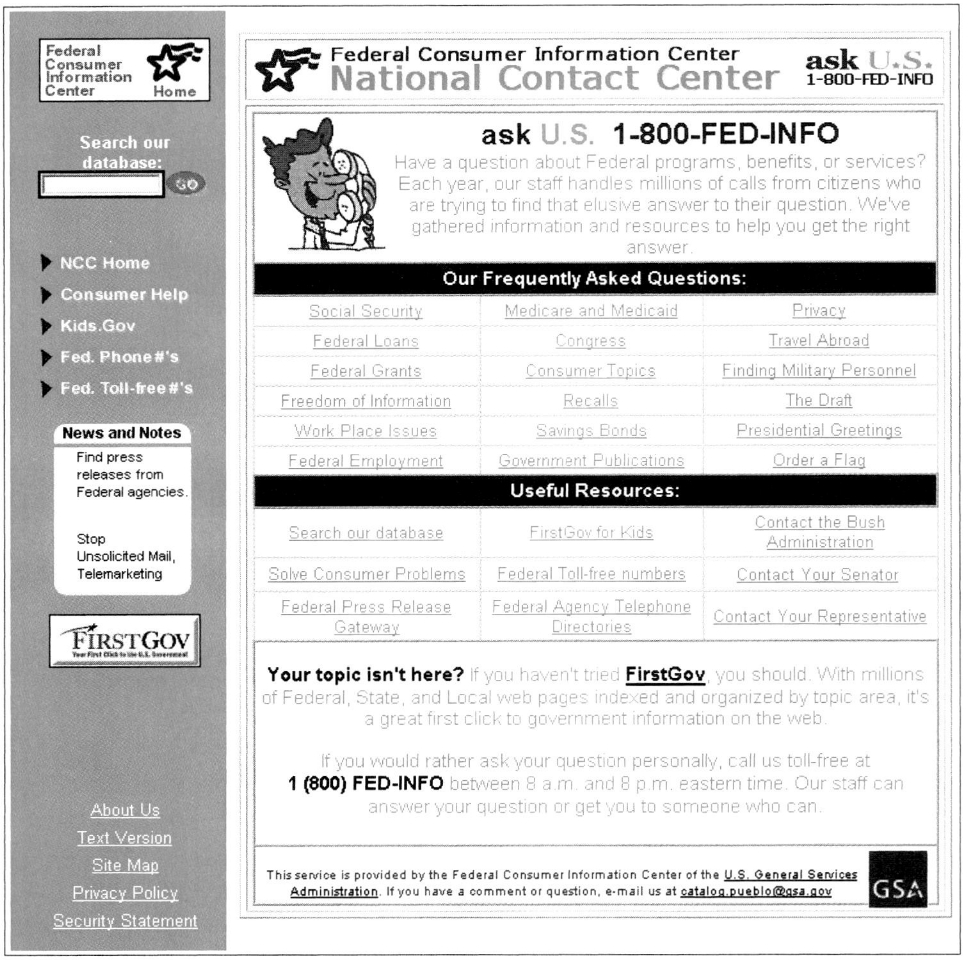

Overall, the National Contact Center is a less effective homepage because it presents too much information and does so in an unorganized way—with twenty-seven different links lumped into two general groupings. Online readers need and want more direction—textual descriptions and navigational tools—to find the information they seek. The FirstGov site, in contrast, sorts information by audience and by agency. It also provides solid navigational tools with multiple menus and links for readers.

A more effective website.   Figure 12.10

Final Thoughts on the Web

In the new global village, you need to be able to navigate as well as construct websites. Such knowledge is essential for you to communicate effectively with colleagues and customers around the world. While you will not be expected to have the technical proficiency of a webmaster, your employer will expect you to keep up with the latest looks and features of Web design. The last half of Chapter 12 has stressed principles and guidelines that pertain to almost every type of website—navigation, currency, user-friendliness (including for non-native, English-speaking audiences), visual attractiveness, and ethics in design and content—that will prepare you to write for the Web both now and into the future.

✔ Revision Checklist

Printed Documents

☐ Kept readers' busy schedules and reading time limits in mind when designing a document.

☐ Learned options of desktop publishing program.

☐ Arranged information in the most logical, easy-to-grasp order.

☐ Included only relevant visuals—clip art, icons, stock photos.

☐ Left adequate, eye-pleasing white space in text.

☐ Provided adequate margins to frame document.

☐ Justified margins, right, left, or center, depending on document and reader's needs.

☐ Maintained pleasing, easy-to-read line length.

☐ Kept line spacing consistent and easy on the readers' eyes.

☐ Chose appropriate typeface for message and document.

☐ Selected serif or sans serif font depending on message and readers' needs.

☐ Did not mix typefaces.

☐ Used effective type size, neither too small (under 10 point) nor too large (over 12 point), for body of text.

☐ Incorporated appropriate visual cues (for example, italics or boldface) for readers.

☐ Inserted heads and subheads to organize information for reader.

☐ Made all heads and subheads parallel and grammatically consistent.

☐ Supplied lists, bullets, numbers to divide information.

Web Navigation

☐ Made sure navigation is clear and logical, not overly complex.

☐ Grouped related items into menus but differentiated each function.

☐ Eliminated inconsistencies in the menus and page designs for better site organization.

☐ Provided identification for all pages either with headings or text that explains the purpose of each page.

☐ Tested all links to make sure they are functioning, including internal links and links to other websites so customers can easily navigate the site.

Web Content

☐ Ensured that the site is informative and content is current and periodically updated.

☐ Avoided too much technical detail on a page.

☐ Took precautions so that underlined text on the site is not mistaken for a link.

☐ Used headings, subheadings, and white space to break information into readable chunks.

Continued

Continued

☐ Highlighted lists with bullets, numbers, or letters.
☐ Provided ways for reader to interact with the site, whether for e-mail subscriptions or to provide feedback.

Web Design

☐ Used images that appear quickly on the screen.
☐ Employed similar designs for the homepage and secondary pages to make them look and feel coherent.
☐ Avoided clutter by aligning elements on a page.
☐ Did not crowd images and text on the same page.
☐ Used just the right number of meaningful images, making sure they were not too big or too small.
☐ Included memorable icons and other symbols in appropriate places on the page; tested them to determine why and how they contribute to the overall effect of the site.
☐ Offered menu buttons that are clear and appropriately differentiated from other elements on the page.
☐ Chose suitable colors that complement the purpose and organization of the website.
☐ Did not use background colors that obscured text.
☐ Avoided unnecessary animations such as flashing icons or blinking text that would interfere with message and annoy readers.

Exercises

Online Study Center

Access the designing Revision Checklists online at college.hmco .com/pic/kolin8e

Online Study Center

Find additional designing exercises at college .hmco.com/pic/ kolin8e

1. Find an example of an effectively designed document, according to the criteria discussed in this chapter. It could be a memo, a brochure, a newsletter, a report, a set of instructions, a section of a textbook, or a website. E-mail or write a short (one-page) memo to your instructor describing the document's design and explaining why it works. Attach a copy of the document or the website to your e-mail or memo.

2. Working with a team of three or four students, bring poorly designed documents to class. As a collaborative venture determine which of the documents the group submits is the hardest to follow, the most unappealing, and the least logically arranged. After selecting that document, collaboratively write a memo to your instructor on what is wrong with the design and what you would do to improve its appearance and organization.

3. Redesign (reformat; add headings, spacing, and visual clues; include relevant clip art; and so on) the document your group selected for Exercise 2 and submit it to your instructor.

4. Find an ineffectively designed document—a form, a set of instructions, a brochure, a section of a manual, a story in a newsletter—and assume that you are a document design consultant. Write a sales letter to the company or agency that prepared and distributed the document, offering to redesign it and any other documents they have. Stress your qualifications and include a sample of your work. You will have to be convincing and diplomatic—precisely and professionally persuading your readers that they need your services to improve their corporate image, customer relations, and sales or services.

5. Redesign one of the documents on pages 553–554 (on handwashing or detector placement) to make it conform to the guidelines specified in this chapter.

6. Locate two webpages that cover a similar product, service, industry, or other topic. Analyze some of the webpage elements each one uses, comparing each site's strengths and weaknesses. Write a one-page memo to your instructor explaining which is the more effective site.

7. Find a webpage that you feel is ineffective. Using the four keys to effective writing, as well as your knowledge of webpage elements, write a one-page assessment of the site, discussing three or four changes that would make it more effective. Attach a printed hard copy of the webpage to your assessment.

8. The homepage of the Stanley's Accounting Temps website below is not as effective as it could be. Review the coverage on effective and ineffective websites, page 546. Then write a one-page memo to your instructor specifying how Stanley's Accounting Temps might better address its online customers. Group your

STANLEY'S ACCOUNTING TEMPS

Let us help you save!

Welcome to our site!
You can learn more about
our firm and the services
we offer by clicking any
of the menu items at right.

- Accounting
- Book keeping
- Company History
- Tax plannign
- Job Opportunities
- Complaints
- Payroll solutions
- FAQs
- Other links

recommendations under the headings of content, design, and navigation. As a supporting document for your memo, design a new homepage for the company by sketching it on a piece of paper or creating it on the computer. (The Stanley's Accounting Temps homepage example was created using word processing software.)

9. As a collaborative exercise, find a business website that promotes a product or service. Your group will work as Web consultants proposing that the company redesign its site. Your presentation should include an evaluation of the existing site—general and specific elements—as well as a proposal for how you would improve the site.

WHY SHOULD YOU WASH YOUR HANDS?
Bacteria and viruses (germs) that cause illnesses are spread when you don't wash your hands.
If you don't wash your hands, you risk acquiring:
The common cold or flu
Gastrointestinal illnesses Shigella or hepatitis A
Respiratory illnesses
Should you wash your hands?
You need to wash your hands several times every day. Some important times to wash your hands are:
BEFORE
Preparing or eating food.
Treating a cut wound.
Tending to someone who is sick.
Inserting or removing contacts
After
Using the bathroom.
Changing a diaper or helping a child use the bathroom (don't forget the child's hands)
Handling raw meats/poultry/eggs
Touching pets, especially reptiles
Handling garbage
Sneezing or blowing your nose, or helping a child blow his/her nose
Touching any body fluids like blood or mucus
Being in contact with a sick person
Playing outside or with children and their toys
WHEN SHOULD YOU WASH YOUR HANDS?
There is a right way to wash your hands.
Follow these steps and you will help protect yourself and your family from illness.
Like any good habit, proper hand washing must be taught.
Take the time to teach it to your children and make sure they practice.

7

TTI's in the loop on effective detector placement

Ever sit in bumper-to-bumper traffic and wish they'd widen the roads so people could get through more quickly? Well, that costs a lot of money. Which is why transportation engineers who deal with traffic congestion and the problems it causes look for more cost-effective alternatives to get you where you're going—and faster.

TTI researchers recently completed a TxDOT/FHWA-sponsored study entitled *Effective Detector Placement for Computerized Traffic Management.* The research sought to expand and improve the use of inductance loop detectors (ILDs) to complement traffic signals, signal systems and other advanced traffic management systems. This is a cheaper congestion solution than building or widening a road.

An ILD is an electrical circuit containing a loop of copper wire embedded in the pavement. As a vehicle passes over the wire loop, it takes energy from the loop. If that change is large enough, a detection is recorded. Thus, we are able to collect data on the movement or presence of vehicles on the roadway. Advanced traffic management systems operate best with accurate information on how many vehicles are present and how fast they are traveling.

The primary goal of the recent project was to use loop detectors as an integral part of the congestion-reduction system. Traditional problems with ILDs were addressed—like crosstalk, or interference between two adjacent loops—and innovative new applications for ILDs in advanced traffic systems—like detecting wrong-way HOV-lane movements.

Other applications include using ILDs to move traffic more

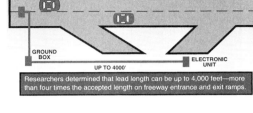

GROUND BOX

UP TO 4000'

ELECTRONIC UNIT

Researchers determined that lead length can be up to 4,000 feet—more than four times the accepted length on freeway entrance and exit ramps.

efficiently at diamond interchanges, at high-volume, high-speed approaches and on the freeway entrance ramps. The long-range contribution of the study is a set of guidelines for using ILDs in the situations listed above. As freeway management systems continue to evolve, the guidelines developed through the nine study reports will provide designers with practical information on the most effective placement of ILDs.

A major finding of the research deals with lead length, or the length of wire necessary to connect the loop to the detector electronic unit. The study showed that the loop can be placed more than 4,000 feet from the point of control—four times the currently accepted distance. This information will give traffic designers much more flexibility when integrating ILDs into their traffic system designs.

The researchers also made some important discoveries about using ILDs to measure speed. They found that the best speed trap is nine meters (two loops interconnected

with a timing device and spaced nine meters apart). They also determined that to get reasonably accurate and consistent speeds with an ILD, some things must be the same between a pair of loops: make, type or model of the detector units, sensitivity settings and loop configuration.

The findings from this research facilitate the use of loop detectors in managing traffic. And better management of driver frustration—just as important, even if less measurable than the congestion that causes it—is bound to follow.

Ultimately the three watchwords for this project were optimization, innovation, and implementation. Taking the tried-and-true and finding a better way to use it is, after all, the underlying building block for all engineering endeavors.

To order TTI Research Report 1392-9F, see the back page order form of this issue. For more information on loop detectors, contact Don Woods, 409/845-5792, FAX 409/845-6481 (E-mail: d-woods@tamu.edu).

Source: Texas Transportation Institute's *Researcher*; article author, Chris Pourteau. Reprinted with permission of the Texas Transportation Institute.

CHAPTER 13

Writing Instructions and Procedures

Clear and accurate instructions are essential to the world of work. Instructions tell—and frequently show—how to do something. They indicate how to perform a procedure (draw blood; change the oil in your car); operate a machine (a pH meter; a digital camera); construct, install, maintain, adjust, or repair a piece of equipment (an incubator; a scanner). Everyone from the consumer to the specialist uses and relies on carefully written and designed instructions.

Online Study Center

To expand your understanding of writing instructions and procedures, take advantage of the ACE quizzes, sample documents, Web links, and exercises at college.hmco.com/pic/kolin8e

Instructions and Your Job

As part of your job, you may be asked to write instructions, alone or with a group, for your co-workers as well as for the customers who use your company's services or products. When writing long, complex instructions, you certainly will be part of a team of engineers, programmers, document design experts, marketing specialists, and even attorneys. But whether the instructions are brief or lengthy, your employer stands to gain or lose much from the quality and the accuracy of the instructions you prepare.

While the purpose of writing instructions is to explain how to perform a task in a step-by-step manner, the purpose of writing procedures is slightly different. Often the two terms are incorrectly used interchangeably. **Procedures** (or policies) describe not a task to be completed, but a set of established rules of conduct to be followed within an organization, such as a business.

This chapter will first show you how to develop, write, illustrate, and design a variety of instructions, and then move into a discussion of writing procedures (pp. 582–585) about job-related duties.

Why Instructions Are Important

Perhaps no other type of occupational writing demands more from the writer than do instructions because so much is at stake—for both you and your reader. The reader has to understand what you write and perform the procedure as well. You

555

Tech Note

Online Instructions

Online instructions offer added benefits. Most computers have the ability to give you pictures and sounds, but those two features can be limited without additional hardware. With a sound card your computer can provide a much wider range of possibilities, including having someone actually talk you through the various steps of a procedure and alert you to special problem areas. If your computer also has a graphics card, you can speed up the display of images and take advantage of animation that shows the process being done. Such features—visuals and sound—further help instruction writers meet the precise needs of their readers who may need to perform a trial run before attempting a procedure or who may want to double-check a step before going on.

cannot afford to be unclear, inaccurate, or incomplete. Instructions are significant for many reasons, including safety, efficiency, and convenience.

Safety

Carefully written instructions get a job done without damage or injury. Poorly written instructions can be directly responsible for an injury to the person trying to follow them and may result in costly damage claims or even lawsuits. Notice how the product labels in your medicine chest inform users when, how, and why to take a medication safely. Without those instructions, consumers would be endangered by taking too much or too little medicine or by not administering it properly. To make sure your instructions are safe, they must be

- accurate
- consistent
- thorough
- clearly written
- carefully organized

Several U.S. agencies notify consumers about products that have been found to be unsafe. The U.S. Consumer Product Safety Commission is a useful source for such information; check out its website at *http://www.cpsc.gov*.

Efficiency

Well-written instructions help a business run smoothly and efficiently. No work would be done if employees did not have clear instructions to follow. For example, without the instructions on flextime (see Figure 13.11 on pp. 583–584) employees would not know when to work. Imagine how inefficient it would be for a business if employees had to stop their work each time they did not have or could not understand a set of instructions. Or, equally alarming, what if employees made a number of serious mistakes because of confusing directions, costing a business lost sales and increased expenses? Giving readers helpful tips to make their work easier will also increase their efficiency. See pages 572–574 for the use of notes.

Convenience

Clear, easy-to-follow instructions make a customer's job easier and less frustrating. In the customer's view, instructions reflect a product's quality and a service's quality and convenience. How many times have you heard complaints about a company because the instructions were hard to follow? Poorly written and illustrated instructions will cost your customers time and you their business. Instructions are also a vital part of "service after the sale." Owners' manuals, for example, help buyers to avoid a product breakdown (and the headache and expense of starting over) and to keep it in good working order.

The Variety of Instructions: A Brief Overview

Instructions vary in length, complexity, and format. Some instructions are one word long: *stop, lift, rotate, print, erase*. Others are a few sentences long: "Insert blank disk in external disk drive"; "Close tightly after using"; "Store in an upright position." Short instructions are appropriate for the numerous relatively nontechnical chores performed every day.

For more elaborate procedures, detailed instructions may be as long as a page or a book. When your firm purchases a new mainframe computer or a piece of earth-moving equipment, it will receive an instruction pamphlet or book containing many steps, cautionary statements, and diagrams. Many businesses prepare their own training manuals containing instructions for 200 or 300 different procedures.

Instructions can be given in a variety of formats, as Figures 13.1 through 13.4 show. They can be paragraphs (Figure 13.1), employ visuals to illustrate each step (Figure 13.2), or use a numbered list (Figures 13.3 and 13.4). You will have to determine which format is most appropriate for the kinds of instructions you write. For writing that affects policies or regulations, as in Figure 13.11 (on pp. 583–584), you will most often use a hard copy of a memo, which serves as a more permanent and legal notice than would an e-mail.

Assessing and Meeting Your Audience's Needs

Put yourself in the readers' position. In most instances you will not be available for readers to ask you questions when they do not understand something. Consequently, they will have to rely only on your written instructions. Your purpose in writing the instructions is to get the readers to perform the same steps you followed and, more important, to obtain the same results you did.

Do not assume that members of your audience have performed the procedure before or have operated the equipment as many times as you have. (If they had, there would be no need for your instructions.) No writer of instructions ever disappointed readers by making directions too clear or too easy to follow. Keep in

Figure 13.1   Instructions on how to repair a halyard.

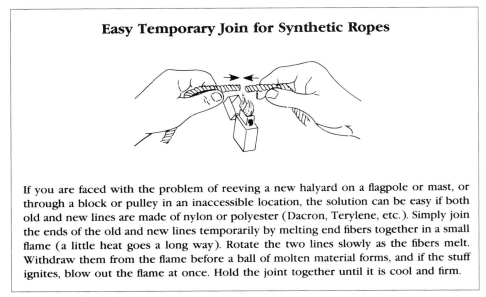

Easy Temporary Join for Synthetic Ropes

Directions written in clear, plain language

If you are faced with the problem of reeving a new halyard on a flagpole or mast, or through a block or pulley in an inaccessible location, the solution can be easy if both old and new lines are made of nylon or polyester (Dacron, Terylene, etc.). Simply join the ends of the old and new lines temporarily by melting end fibers together in a small flame (a little heat goes a long way). Rotate the two lines slowly as the fibers melt. Withdraw them from the flame before a ball of molten material forms, and if the stuff ignites, blow out the flame at once. Hold the joint together until it is cool and firm.

Source: R. I. Standish, *Parks.*

mind that your audience will often include non-native speakers of English, a world-wide audience of potential consumers.

Key Questions to Ask About Your Audience

To determine your audience's needs, ask yourself the following questions:

- How and why will my readers use my instructions? (Engineers have different expectations than do office personnel and customers.)
- What language skills do they possess—is English their first (native) language?
- How much do my readers already know about the product or procedure?
- How much background information will I have to supply?
- What steps will most likely cause readers trouble?
- How often will they use my instructions—every day or just as a refresher?
- Where will my audience most likely be following my instructions—in the workplace, outdoors, in a workshop or laboratory equipped with tools, or alone in their homes?
- What resources—such as special equipment or power sources—will my readers need to perform my instructions successfully?

Two Short Case Studies on Meeting Audience's Needs

The instructions contained in Figures 13.5 and 13.6 are addressed to two different audiences, each with separate needs. The Hercules memo in Figure 13.5 was sent to

Instructions that supply a visual with each step.   Figure 13.2

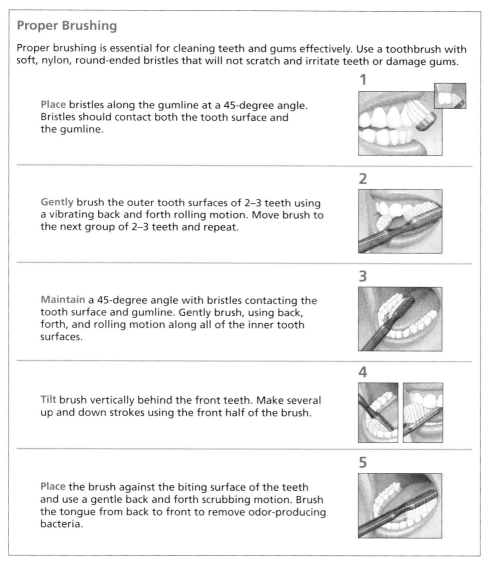

Proper Brushing

Proper brushing is essential for cleaning teeth and gums effectively. Use a toothbrush with soft, nylon, round-ended bristles that will not scratch and irritate teeth or damage gums.

1

Place bristles along the gumline at a 45-degree angle. Bristles should contact both the tooth surface and the gumline.

2

Gently brush the outer tooth surfaces of 2–3 teeth using a vibrating back and forth rolling motion. Move brush to the next group of 2–3 teeth and repeat.

3

Maintain a 45-degree angle with bristles contacting the tooth surface and gumline. Gently brush, using back, forth, and rolling motion along all of the inner tooth surfaces.

4

Tilt brush vertically behind the front teeth. Make several up and down strokes using the front half of the brush.

5

Place the brush against the biting surface of the teeth and use a gentle back and forth scrubbing motion. Brush the tongue from back to front to remove odor-producing bacteria.

Source: Reprinted by permission of American Dental Hygienists Association. Illustrations adapted and used courtesy of the John O. Butler Company, makers of *GUM* Healthcare products.

a technical audience—firefighters and supervisors—who needed instructions on a special process. Cliff Burgess's memo in Figure 13.6, on the other hand, went to all Burton employees, a more diverse, rather than technical, group of readers. His helpful instructions do not require a list of equipment or materials or a description of steps in a process. Instead, his memo consists of an introduction, three bulleted instructions, a conclusion, and a visual attachment.

Figure 13.3   Instructions given in a numbered list describing a sequence of steps.

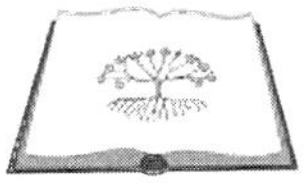

Source: Elkhart (Indiana) Public Library. Reprinted by permission of Brent Ferguson and Diana Gill.

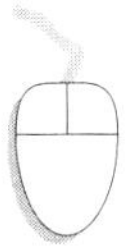

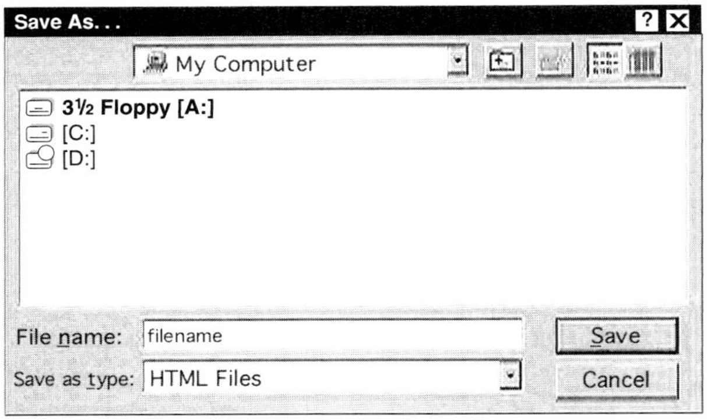

■ The Process of Writing Instructions

As we saw in Chapter 2, clear and concise writing evolves when you follow a process. To make sure your instructions are accurate and easy for your audience to perform, follow these steps.

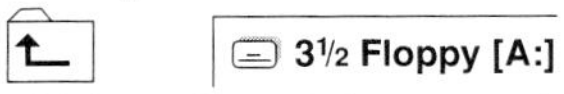

Plan Your Steps

Before writing, do some research to understand completely the job, process, or procedure that you are asking someone else to perform. Make sure you know

Instructions in a numbered list on how to assemble an outdoor grill.   Figure 13.4

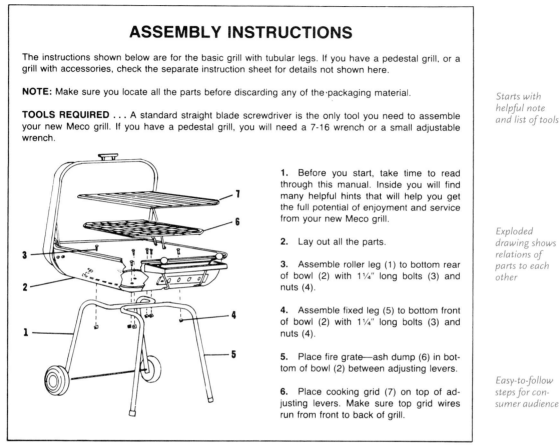

ASSEMBLY INSTRUCTIONS

The instructions shown below are for the basic grill with tubular legs. If you have a pedestal grill, or a grill with accessories, check the separate instruction sheet for details not shown here.

NOTE: Make sure you locate all the parts before discarding any of the·packaging material.

TOOLS REQUIRED ... A standard straight blade screwdriver is the only tool you need to assemble your new Meco grill. If you have a pedestal grill, you will need a 7-16 wrench or a small adjustable wrench.

Starts with helpful note and list of tools

1. Before you start, take time to read through this manual. Inside you will find many helpful hints that will help you get the full potential of enjoyment and service from your new Meco grill.

2. Lay out all the parts.

3. Assemble roller leg (1) to bottom rear of bowl (2) with 1¼" long bolts (3) and nuts (4).

Exploded drawing shows relations of parts to each other

4. Assemble fixed leg (5) to bottom front of bowl (2) with 1¼" long bolts (3) and nuts (4).

5. Place fire grate—ash dump (6) in bottom of bowl (2) between adjusting levers.

6. Place cooking grid (7) on top of adjusting levers. Make sure top grid wires run from front to back of grill.

Easy-to-follow steps for consumer audience

Source: Meco Assembly Instructions and Owners Manual, Metals Engineering Corp., P.O. Box 3005, Greenville, TN 37743. Reprinted by permission.

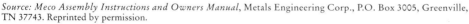

- the reason for doing something
- the parts or tools required
- the steps to follow to get the job done
- the results of the job
- the potential risks or dangers

If you are not absolutely sure about the process, ask an expert for a demonstration. Do some background reading and talk to or e-mail colleagues who may have written or followed a similar instruction.

Do a Trial Run

Actually perform the job (assembling, repairing, maintaining, dissecting) yourself or with all your writing team present. Go through a number of trial runs. Take notes

Figure 13.5   Instructions alerting a technical audience to special circumstances.

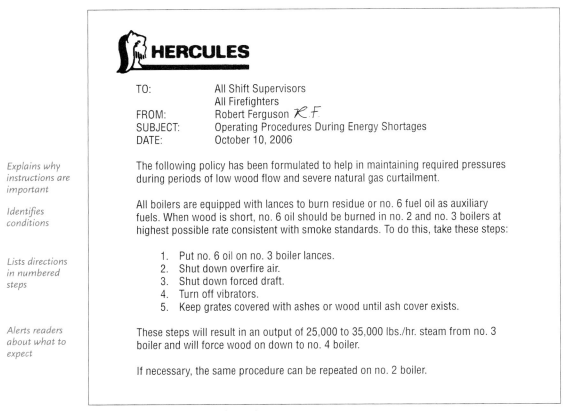

*Explains why
instructions are
important*

*Identifies
conditions*

*Lists directions
in numbered
steps*

*Alerts readers
about what to
expect*

Source: Reprinted by permission of Hercules, Inc.

as you go along and be sure to divide the job into simple, distinct steps for readers to follow. Don't give readers too much to do in any one step. Each step should be **complete, sequential, reliable, straightforward,** and **easy** for your audience to identify and perform.

Write and Test Your Draft

Transform your notes into a draft (or drafts) of the instructions you want readers to follow. Test your draft(s) by asking someone from the intended audience (consumers, technicians) who may never have performed the job to follow your instructions as you have written them. Observe where the individual runs into difficulty—cannot complete or seems to miss a step, gets a result different from yours.

An instructional memo listing safety precautions for a general audience.   Figure 13.6

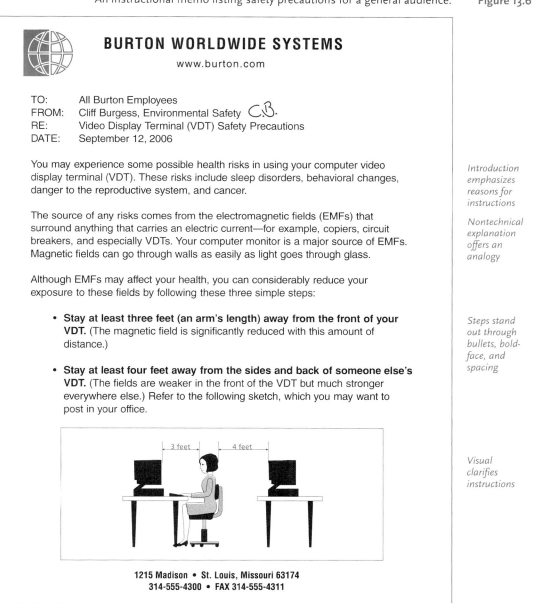

BURTON WORLDWIDE SYSTEMS

www.burton.com

TO: All Burton Employees
FROM: Cliff Burgess, Environmental Safety   C.B.
RE: Video Display Terminal (VDT) Safety Precautions
DATE: September 12, 2006

You may experience some possible health risks in using your computer video display terminal (VDT). These risks include sleep disorders, behavioral changes, danger to the reproductive system, and cancer.

The source of any risks comes from the electromagnetic fields (EMFs) that surround anything that carries an electric current—for example, copiers, circuit breakers, and especially VDTs. Your computer monitor is a major source of EMFs. Magnetic fields can go through walls as easily as light goes through glass.

Although EMFs may affect your health, you can considerably reduce your exposure to these fields by following these three simple steps:

- **Stay at least three feet (an arm's length) away from the front of your VDT.** (The magnetic field is significantly reduced with this amount of distance.)

- **Stay at least four feet away from the sides and back of someone else's VDT.** (The fields are weaker in the front of the VDT but much stronger everywhere else.) Refer to the following sketch, which you may want to post in your office.

3 feet   4 feet

1215 Madison • St. Louis, Missouri 63174
314-555-4300 • FAX 314-555-4311

Introduction emphasizes reasons for instructions

Nontechnical explanation offers an analogy

Steps stand out through bullets, bold-face, and spacing

Visual clarifies instructions

Continued

Figure 13.6   (Continued)

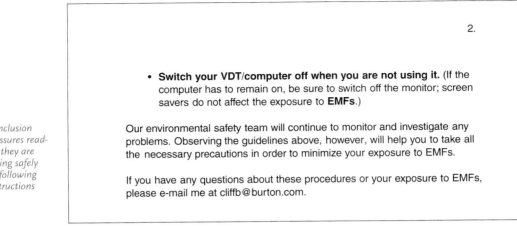

Conclusion reassures readers they are acting safely by following instructions

Source: Reprinted by permission.

Revise and Edit

Based on your observations and user feedback, revise your draft(s) and edit the final copy of the instructions that you will give to readers. Always consider whether your instructions would be easier to accomplish if you included visuals.

Analyzing the needs and the background of your audience will help you to choose appropriate words and details. A set of instructions accompanying a chemistry set would use different terminology, abbreviations, and level of detail than would a set of instructions a professor gives a class in organic chemistry.

General Audience: Place 8 drops of vinegar in a test tube with a piece of limestone about the size of a pea.

Specialized Audience: Place 8 gtts of CH_3COOH in a test tube and add 1 mg of CO_3.

The instructions for the general audience avoid the technical abbreviations and symbols the specialized audience requires. If your readers are puzzled by your directions, you defeat your reasons for writing them.

▌ Using the Right Style

To write instructions that readers can understand and turn into effective action, observe the following guidelines.

1. Use verbs in the present tense and imperative mood. Imperatives are commands that have deleted the pronoun *you*. Note how the instructions in Figures 13.1 through 13.4 contain imperatives—"Move the arrow" instead of "You move the arrow." In instructions, deleting the *you* is not discourteous, as it would be in a business letter or report. The command tells readers, "These steps work, so do them exactly as stated." Choose imperative (action) verbs such as those listed in Table 13.1.

TABLE 13.1   Some Helpful Imperative Verbs Used in Instructions

add	determine	increase	pick up	save	tighten
adjust	dig	insert	point	saw	tilt
apply	download	inspect	pour	scan	transect
blow	drag	lift	press	scroll	transfer
boot up	drain	load	prevent	set	trim
call up	drill	loosen	print	send	turn
change	drop	lower	pull	shift	twist
check	ease	lubricate	push	shut off	type
choose	eliminate	measure	raise	slide	unplug
clean	enter	mix	release	slip	use
click	flip	mount	remove	spread	ventilate
clip	flush	move	reply	squeeze	verify
close	forward	notify	review	start	wash
connect	freeze	oil	roll	switch	wear
create	group	open	rotate	tear	wind
cut	hold	paste	rub	thread	wipe
delete	include	peel	run	tie	wire

2. Write clear, short sentences in the active voice.   Keep sentences short and uncomplicated. Sentences under twenty words (preferably under fifteen) are easy to read. Note that the sentences in Figures 13.1 through 13.4 are, for the most part, under fifteen words.

3. Use precise terms for measurements, distances, and times.   Indefinite, vague directions leave users wondering whether they are doing the right thing. The following vague direction is better expressed through precise revision.

> Vague: Turn the distributor cap a little. (*How much is a little?*)
> Precise: Turn the distributor cap one quarter of a rotation.

4. Use connective words as signposts.   Connective words specify the exact order in which something is to be done (especially when your instructions are written in paragraphs). Words such as *first, then, before* help readers stay on course, reinforcing the sequence of the procedures.

5. Number each step when you present your instructions in a list.   You also can use bullets. Plenty of white space between steps also distinctly separates them for the reader.

Using Visuals Effectively

Readers welcome visuals in almost any set of instructions. Visuals are graphic and direct, helping readers to understand what they must do. A visual can

- simplify a process
- identify the location and size of a part
- show the relationships among components
- reinforce or even save words

- illustrate the "right" way and the "wrong" way
- increase readers' confidence
- help readers get a job done more quickly

The number and kinds of visuals you include will, of course, depend on the procedure or equipment you are explaining and your audience's background and needs. Some instructions may require only one or two visuals. The instructions in Figure 13.3 show users what they can expect to see on a screen as they download a visual. The shot of the screen clarifies the procedure and assists the reader. In Figure 13.2 each step is accompanied by a visual demonstrating a proper technique of brushing teeth.

Another frequently used visual in instructions is an exploded drawing, like the one in Figure 13.4, which helps consumers see how the various parts of the grill fit together, or the one in Figure 13.7, which labels and shows the relationship of the parts of an industrial extension cord.

Guidelines for Using Visuals in Instructions

Follow these guidelines to use visuals effectively in your instructions:

1. Place the visual next to the step it illustrates, not on another page or buried at the bottom of the page.

Figure 13.7   Exploded drawing showing how to assemble an industrial extension cord.

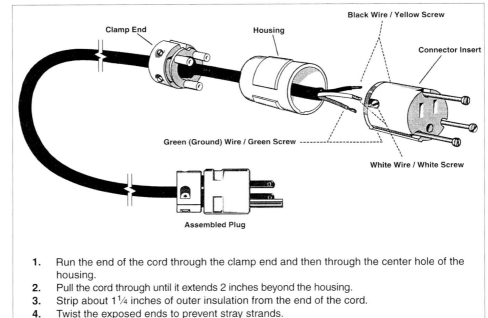

1. Run the end of the cord through the clamp end and then through the center hole of the housing.
2. Pull the cord through until it extends 2 inches beyond the housing.
3. Strip about 1¼ inches of outer insulation from the end of the cord.
4. Twist the exposed ends to prevent stray strands.

Source: Drawing courtesy of Sally Eddy and Georgia-Pacific Company.

2. Assign each visual a number (Figure 1, Figure 2) and refer to visuals by figure number in your instructions.
3. Make sure the visual looks like the object the user is trying to assemble, maintain, run, or repair. Don't use a photo of a different model.
4. Always inform readers if a part is missing or reduced in your visual.
5. Where necessary, label or number parts of the visual, as in Figure 13.4.
6. Set visuals off with white space so it is easy to find and examine them.

The Five Parts of Instructions

Except for very short instructions, such as those illustrated in Figures 13.1 through 13.4, or for instructions on policies and regulations (see Figure 13.11, pp. 583–584), a set of instructions generally contains five main parts: (1) an introduction; (2) a list of equipment and materials; (3) the actual steps to perform the process; (4) warnings, cautions, and notes; and (5) a conclusion (when necessary).

Introduction

The function of an introduction is to provide readers with enough *necessary* background information to understand why and how your instructions work. An introduction must make readers feel comfortable and well prepared before they turn to the actual steps.

What to Include in an Introduction

You can do one or all of the following in your introduction. Not every introduction to a set of instructions will contain facts in all four categories of information listed here. Some instructions will require less detail. You will have to judge how much background information to give readers for the specific instructions you write.

Refer to Figure 13.8 (p. 568), which is an introduction to a guide for nurses who have to know how to use an infusion pump.

1. State why the instructions are useful for a specific audience. Many instructions begin with introductions that stress safety, educational, or occupational benefits. Here is an introduction from a safety procedure describing protective lockout of equipment.

> The purpose of this procedure is to provide plant electrical technicians with a uniform method of locking out machinery or equipment. This will prevent the possibility of setting moving parts in motion, energizing electrical lines; or opening valves while repair, setup, or cleaning work is in progress.

Note how Figure 13.8 highlights the safety and convenience of the equipment for the nursing staff to meet their patients' needs.

2. Indicate how a particular machine, procedure, or process works. An introduction can briefly discuss the "theory of operation" to help readers understand why something works the way your instructions say it should. Such a discussion sometimes describes a scientific law or principle. An introduction to instructions on how to run an autoclave begins by explaining the function of the machine:

Figure 13.8   Introduction to a guide for using an infusion pump.

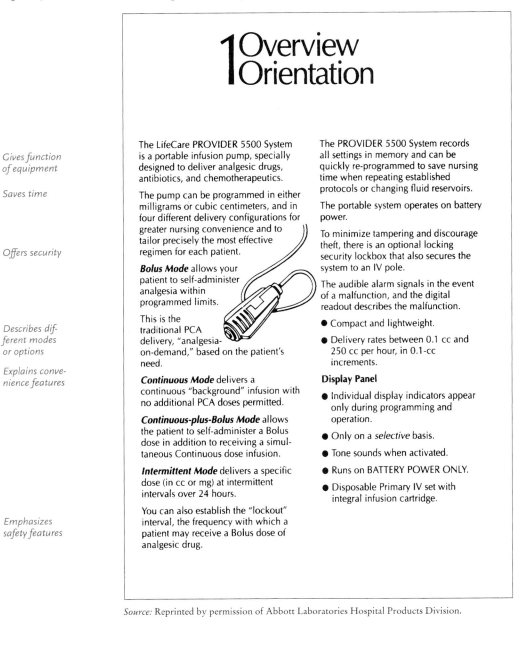

1 Overview Orientation

Gives function of equipment

Saves time

Offers security

Describes different modes or options

Explains convenience features

Emphasizes safety features

The LifeCare PROVIDER 5500 System is a portable infusion pump, specially designed to deliver analgesic drugs, antibiotics, and chemotherapeutics.

The pump can be programmed in either milligrams or cubic centimeters, and in four different delivery configurations for greater nursing convenience and to tailor precisely the most effective regimen for each patient.

Bolus Mode allows your patient to self-administer analgesia within programmed limits.

This is the traditional PCA delivery, "analgesia-on-demand," based on the patient's need.

Continuous Mode delivers a continuous "background" infusion with no additional PCA doses permitted.

Continuous-plus-Bolus Mode allows the patient to self-administer a Bolus dose in addition to receiving a simultaneous Continuous dose infusion.

Intermittent Mode delivers a specific dose (in cc or mg) at intermittent intervals over 24 hours.

You can also establish the "lockout" interval, the frequency with which a patient may receive a Bolus dose of analgesic drug.

The PROVIDER 5500 System records all settings in memory and can be quickly re-programmed to save nursing time when repeating established protocols or changing fluid reservoirs.

The portable system operates on battery power.

To minimize tampering and discourage theft, there is an optional locking security lockbox that also secures the system to an IV pole.

The audible alarm signals in the event of a malfunction, and the digital readout describes the malfunction.

- Compact and lightweight.
- Delivery rates between 0.1 cc and 250 cc per hour, in 0.1-cc increments.

Display Panel

- Individual display indicators appear only during programming and operation.
- Only on a *selective* basis.
- Tone sounds when activated.
- Runs on BATTERY POWER ONLY.
- Disposable Primary IV set with integral infusion cartridge.

Source: Reprinted by permission of Abbott Laboratories Hospital Products Division.

"These instructions will teach you how to operate an autoclave, which is used to sterilize surgical instruments through the live additive-free stream."

The introduction in Figure 13.8 describes the different modes of the infusion pump and the pump itself.

3. Point out any safety measures or precautions a reader may need to be aware of. By alerting readers early in your instructions, you help them to perform the procedure much more safely and efficiently. The introduction in Figure 13.8 cautions the nursing staff about an audible alarm signal in the event of a malfunction.

4. Stress any advantages or benefits the reader will gain by performing the instructions. Make the reader feel good about buying or using your product by explaining how it will make a job easier to perform, save the reader time and money, or allow the reader to accomplish a job with fewer mistakes or false starts. Nurses learn from the introduction in Figure 13.8 that the infusion pump is quickly programmed.

Note how the following introduction to a set of instructions on an auto dial/auto answer modem encourages the reader to learn how to operate this system.

Welcome to high-speed telecommunications and congratulations on choosing the Signalman EXPRESSi. You've made an excellent choice. The EXPRESSi is the ideal link between your computer and the ever-expanding world of information utilities, databases, electronic mail, bulletin boards, computer time sharing, and more.

The EXPRESSi can be used in the IBM Personal Computer. And because the EXPRESSi fits inside your PC, it saves valuable desk space and eliminates expensive, bulky cables.[1]

List of Equipment and Materials

Clearly, some instructions, as in Figure 13.1, do not need to inform readers of all equipment or materials they will need. But when you do, make your list complete and clear. Do not wait until the readers are actually performing one of the steps to tell them that a certain type of drill or a specific kind of chemical is required. They may have to stop what they are doing to find the equipment or material; moreover, the procedure may fail or present hazards if users do not have the right equipment at the right time. For example, if a Phillips screwdriver is essential to complete one step, specify that type of screwdriver under the heading "Equipment and Materials"; do not list just "screwdriver." See "Tools Required" in Figure 13.4.

Steps for Your Instructions

The heart of your instructions will consist of clearly distinguished steps that readers must follow to achieve the desired results. Figure 13.10 (pp. 575–581) contains a

---
[1]Courtesy of Anchor Automation, Inc., Chatsworth, CA.

model set of steps on how to set up a printer. Note how each step is precisely keyed to the visual, further helping readers perform the procedure. Refer to Figure 13.10 as you study this section. To make sure that you help your readers understand your steps, observe the following rules:

1. Put the steps in their correct order and number them.   If a step is out of order or is missing, the entire set of instructions can be wrong or, worse yet, dangerous. Double-check every step and number each step to indicate its correct place in the sequence of events you are describing.

2. Put only the right amount of information in each step.   Giving readers too little information can be as risky as giving them too much. Keep in mind that each step asks readers to perform a single task in the entire process. However, see the next rule for the exception.

3. Group closely related activities into one step.   Sometimes closely related actions belong in one step to help the reader coordinate activities and to emphasize their being done at the same time, in the same place, or with the same equipment. See how step 4 accomplishes this in Figure 13.9.

Instructions on how to use a fax machine are clearer when distinct steps are stated separately. The first set of instructions below incorrectly tells users how to transmit a fax by combining steps that must be performed separately. Step 2 asks users to pick up the phone and then dial the number—two separate actions. Step 3 asks users to press the button and return the handset, again two actions that cannot be performed simultaneously.

Incorrect:
1. Load the paper into the outgoing document slot, adjusting the paper guides to the appropriate width.
2. Pick up the telephone handset and listen for a dial tone. When you hear the dial tone, dial the number of the receiving fax machine.
3. When the receiving fax machine answers the ring, press the start button. After the transmission is completed, return the handset to its cradle.

Correct:
1. Load the paper into the outgoing document slot, adjusting the paper guides to the appropriate width.
2. Pick up the telephone handset and listen for a dial tone.
3. When you hear a dial tone, dial the number of the receiving fax machine.
4. When the receiving fax machine answers the ring, press the start button.
5. After the transmission is completed, return the handset to its cradle.

Don't divide an action into two steps if it has to be done in one. For example, instructions showing how to light a furnace would not list as two steps actions that must be performed simultaneously to avoid a possible explosion.

Incorrect:
1. Depress the lighting valve.
2. Hold a match to the pilot light.

Correct:
1. Depress the lighting valve while holding a match to the pilot light.

Similarly, do not separate two steps of a computer command that must be performed simultaneously.

Instructions (with visual) on how to connect a computer monitor.   Figure 13.9

Connecting the Monitor to the Computer

1 Make sure the monitor and computer are turned off. (See previous section on safety.)

2 Connect the power cord to the back of the display.

3 Plug the other end of the cable into a grounded outlet.

4 Connect the video cable on the monitor to the 15-pin video graphics connector on the rear panel of the computer, and tighten the fastening screws. (If you have an HP Pavilion computer, this port is marked in orange. For other computers, check your computer manual for the video port location.)

Note: *Don't force the cable into the connector; line it up carefully so you don't bend the pins.*

5 Connect the microphone cable to the computer's sound input. On HP computers, this port is yellow. The end of the cable is also yellow.

6 Connect the microphone cable to the monitor. The connector and the cable end are both yellow.

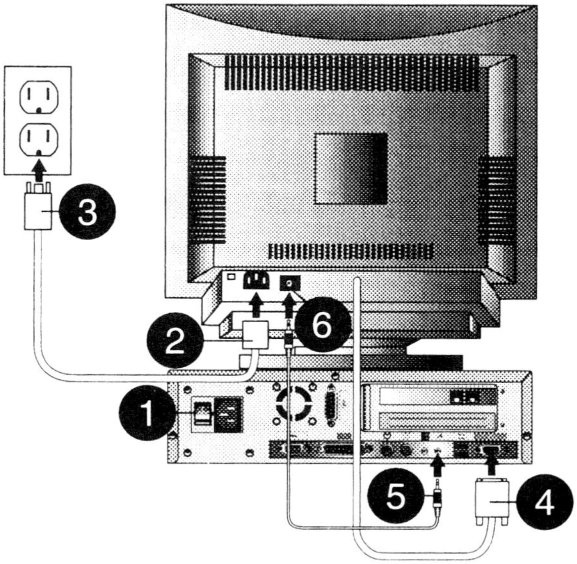

Steps clearly numbered and keyed to visual below

Describes what to look for

Gives readers a helpful hint

Visual placed on same page as directions to help reader follow steps

Source: Copyright © 1999 by Hewlett-Packard Company. Reprinted by permission.

Incorrect: 1. Press the CONTROL key.
             2. Press the ALT key.
  Correct: 1. While holding down the CONTROL key, press the ALT key.

4. Give the reader hints on how best to accomplish the procedure.   Obviously, you cannot do that for every step, but if there is a chance that the reader might run into difficulties you should provide assistance. Particular techniques on how to operate or service equipment also help readers: "If there is blood on the transducer diaphragm, dip the transducer in a blood solvent, such as hydrogen peroxide, Hemosol, etc." If readers have a choice of materials or procedures in a given step, you might want to list those that would give the best performance: "Several thin coats will give a better finish than one heavy coat."

5. State whether one step directly influences (or jeopardizes) the outcome of another.   Because all steps in a set of instructions are interrelated, you could not (and should not have to) tell readers how every step affects another. But stating specific relationships is particularly helpful when dangerous or highly intricate operations are involved. You will save the reader time, and you will stress the need for care. Forewarned is forearmed. Here is an example.

Step 2: Tighten fan belt. Failure to tighten the fan belt will cause it to loosen and come off when the lever is turned in step 5.

Do not wait until step 5 to tell readers that you hope they did a good job in tightening the fan belt in step 2. Information that comes after the fact is not helpful.

6. Where necessary, insert graphics to assist readers in carrying out the step.
For example, see the drawings of the printer in Figure 13.10 (pp. 575–581).

Warnings, Cautions, and Notes

At appropriate places in your instructions' steps you may have to stop the reader to issue a warning, a caution, or a note. These are found in Figure 13.9 and throughout Figure 13.10 (in particular, see step 4 in both figures).

Warnings
A warning tells readers that a step, if not prepared for or performed properly, can endanger their safety, as here.

> WARNING: UNPLUG MACHINE BEFORE REMOVING PLATEN GLASS.
>
> ADVERTENCIA: DESENCHUFE LA MAQUINA ANTES DE QUITAR EL VIDRIO.

Cautions
A caution tells a reader how to avoid a mistake that could damage equipment or to take certain precautions—"Wear protective goggles"; "Do not force the plug."

Caution: **Formatting erases all data on the disk**

Notes

A note adds a clarification, provides a helpful hint on how to do the step most efficiently, or lists different options.

At 20 degrees F, a battery uses about 68 percent of its power.

Guidelines on Using Warnings, Cautions, and Notes

1. **Do not regard warnings and cautions as optional.** They are vital for legal and safety reasons to protect lives and property. In fact, you and your company can be sued if you fail to notify the users of your product or service of potentially dangerous conditions that will or could result in injury or death.
2. **Put warnings and cautions in the right place.** Place them immediately before the step to which they pertain. If you insert a warning or caution statement too early, readers may forget it by the time they come to the step to which it applies. And if you put the notification too late, you almost certainly expose the reader to danger and the equipment to breakdown.
3. **Put warnings and cautions in a distinctive format.** Warnings and cautions should be graphically set apart from the rest of the instructions, as the triangle on page 572 illustrates. There should be no chance that readers will overlook them. Put such statements in capital letters, boldface type, boxes, different colors (red is especially effective for warnings if your readers are native speakers of English, but see page 493; yellow is often used for caution). Be careful, though, about using colors for non-native speakers of English. Use one or all of those devices. Make sure your audience understands an icon or a symbol, like a skull and crossbones, an exclamation point inside a triangle, or a traffic stoplight, often used to signal a warning, a hazard, or some other unsafe condition.
4. **Include enough explanation to help readers know what to watch out for and what precautions to take.** Do not just insert the word WARNING or CAUTION. Explain what the dangerous condition is and how to avoid it. Look at the examples of warnings and cautions in Figure 13.10.

5. **Do not include a warning or a caution just to emphasize a point.** Putting too many in your instructions will decrease the dramatic impact they should have on readers. Use them sparingly—only when absolutely necessary—so readers will not be tempted to ignore them.

6. **Use notes only when the procedure calls for them and they will help readers**, as in Figures 13.4 and 13.9.

Tech Note

Using Icons

You can use icons to draw readers' attention to warnings, cautions, notes, even tips. You can find a wide range of icons with any graphics software package you use. Once you select an icon, it is easy to paste it into any word processing document. But choose your icons carefully; use them only when they are functional and unambiguous for your intended audience. An icon of a trash can might ambiguously signal that material is to be thrown away as well as to be saved.

Conclusion

Not every set of instructions requires a conclusion. For short instructions containing a few simple steps, such as those in Figures 13.1 through 13.4, no conclusion is necessary. These instructions usefully end with the last step the reader must perform. For longer, more involved jobs, a conclusion can help readers finish the job with confidence and accuracy.

When they are necessary, conclusions can provide a succinct wrap-up of what the reader has done or end with a single sentence of congratulations, or reassure readers as the conclusion in Cliff Burgess's memo (Figure 13.6) does. A conclusion might also tell readers what to expect once a job is finished, describe the results of a test, or explain how a piece of equipment is supposed to operate.

Model of Full Set of Instructions

Study Figure 13.10, which is a set of instructions on setting up an Epson printer that includes the parts discussed in this chapter: an introduction; a list of materials; numbered steps; and warnings, cautions, and notes. Pay special attention to how the writer coordinates words with visuals to assist readers.

Complete set of instructions with steps, visuals, cautions, notes, warnings.   Figure 13.10

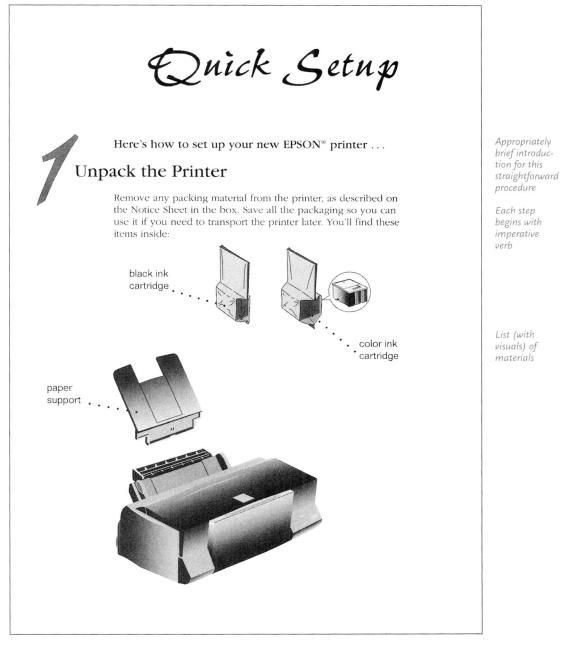

Quick Setup

1

Here's how to set up your new EPSON® printer . . .

Unpack the Printer

Remove any packing material from the printer, as described on the Notice Sheet in the box. Save all the packaging so you can use it if you need to transport the printer later. You'll find these items inside:

black ink cartridge

color ink cartridge

paper support

Appropriately brief introduction for this straightforward procedure

Each step begins with imperative verb

List (with visuals) of materials

Continued

Figure 13.10   (Continued)

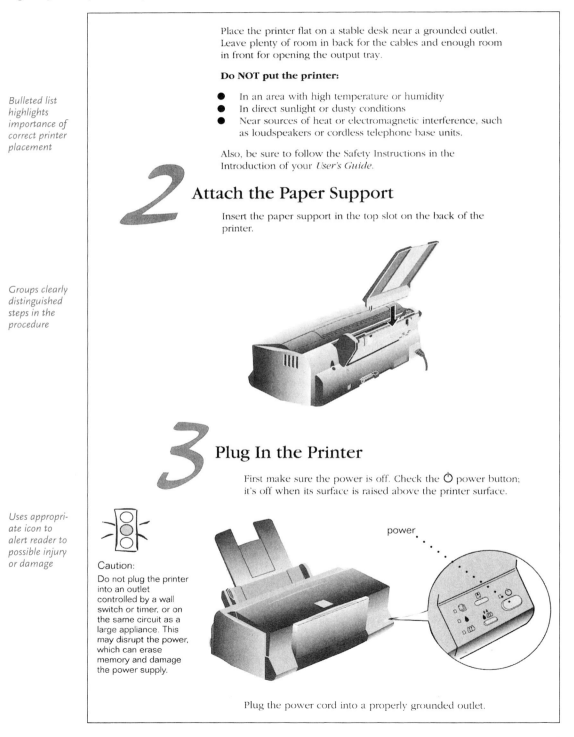

Bulleted list highlights importance of correct printer placement

Place the printer flat on a stable desk near a grounded outlet. Leave plenty of room in back for the cables and enough room in front for opening the output tray.

Do NOT put the printer:

- In an area with high temperature or humidity
- In direct sunlight or dusty conditions
- Near sources of heat or electromagnetic interference, such as loudspeakers or cordless telephone base units.

Also, be sure to follow the Safety Instructions in the Introduction of your *User's Guide.*

2 Attach the Paper Support

Insert the paper support in the top slot on the back of the printer.

Groups clearly distinguished steps in the procedure

3 Plug In the Printer

First make sure the power is off. Check the ⏻ power button; it's off when its surface is raised above the printer surface.

Uses appropriate icon to alert reader to possible injury or damage

Caution:

Do not plug the printer into an outlet controlled by a wall switch or timer, or on the same circuit as a large appliance. This may disrupt the power, which can erase memory and damage the power supply.

power

Plug the power cord into a properly grounded outlet.

Continued

(Continued)   Figure 13.10

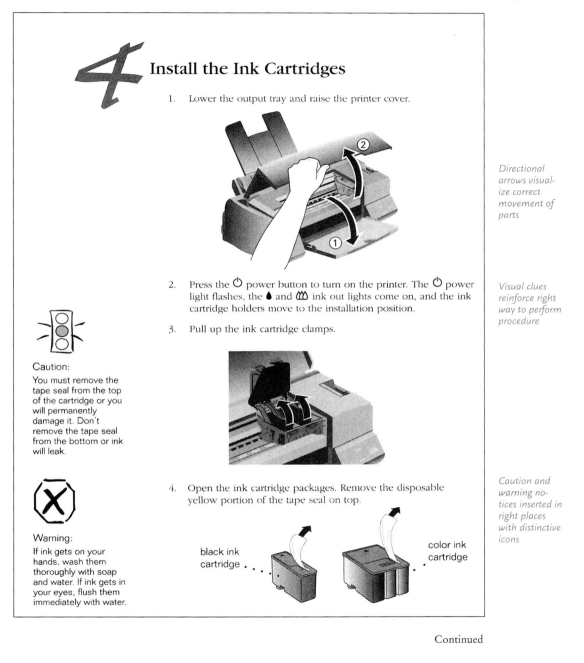

4 Install the Ink Cartridges

1. Lower the output tray and raise the printer cover.

Directional arrows visualize correct movement of parts

2. Press the ⏻ power button to turn on the printer. The ⏻ power light flashes, the ● and 𝕄 ink out lights come on, and the ink cartridge holders move to the installation position.

3. Pull up the ink cartridge clamps.

Visual clues reinforce right way to perform procedure

Caution:
You must remove the tape seal from the top of the cartridge or you will permanently damage it. Don't remove the tape seal from the bottom or ink will leak.

Warning:
If ink gets on your hands, wash them thoroughly with soap and water. If ink gets in your eyes, flush them immediately with water.

4. Open the ink cartridge packages. Remove the disposable yellow portion of the tape seal on top.

Caution and warning notices inserted in right places with distinctive icons

black ink cartridge

color ink cartridge

Continued

Figure 13.10   (Continued)

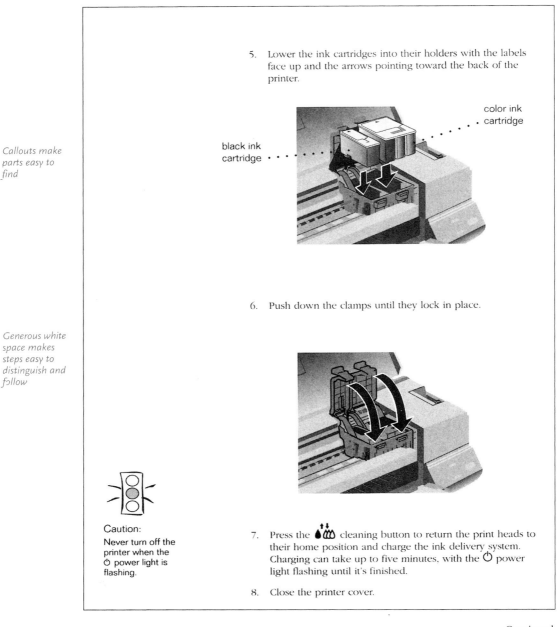

Callouts make parts easy to find

5. Lower the ink cartridges into their holders with the labels face up and the arrows pointing toward the back of the printer.

color ink cartridge

black ink cartridge

6. Push down the clamps until they lock in place.

Generous white space makes steps easy to distinguish and follow

Caution:
Never turn off the printer when the ⏻ power light is flashing.

7. Press the 🖤 cleaning button to return the print heads to their home position and charge the ink delivery system. Charging can take up to five minutes, with the ⏻ power light flashing until it's finished.

8. Close the printer cover.

Continued

5 Load the Paper

1. Slide the left edge guide all the way left and pull out the output tray extension.

Includes two visuals, one of them an exploded drawing, helpfully inserted between the steps to which they apply

2. Fan a stack of plain paper and then even the edges.

3. Load the stack with the printable surface face up. Push the paper against the right edge guide.

arrow
mark

Note:
Don't load paper above the arrow mark inside the left edge guide.

Helpful information to ensure best use of equipment

4. Slide the left edge guide back against the stack of paper.

Continued

Figure 13.10   (Continued)

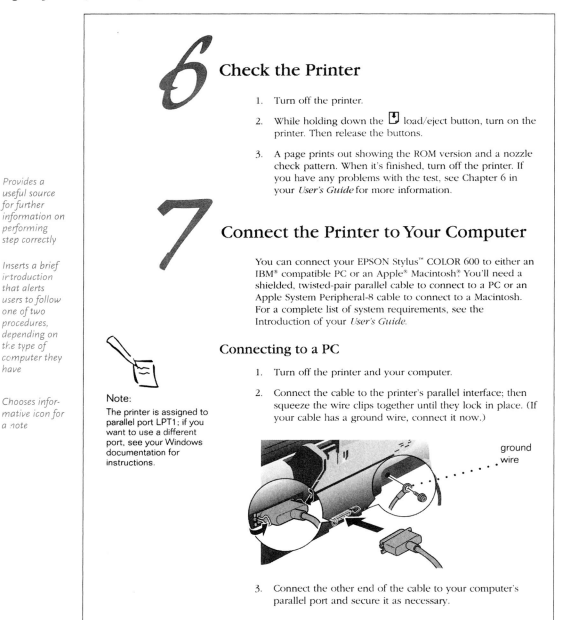

Provides a useful source for further information on performing step correctly

Inserts a brief introduction that alerts users to follow one of two procedures, depending on the type of computer they have

Chooses informative icon for a note

6 Check the Printer

1. Turn off the printer.

2. While holding down the load/eject button, turn on the printer. Then release the buttons.

3. A page prints out showing the ROM version and a nozzle check pattern. When it's finished, turn off the printer. If you have any problems with the test, see Chapter 6 in your *User's Guide* for more information.

7 Connect the Printer to Your Computer

You can connect your EPSON Stylus™ COLOR 600 to either an IBM® compatible PC or an Apple® Macintosh®. You'll need a shielded, twisted-pair parallel cable to connect to a PC or an Apple System Peripheral-8 cable to connect to a Macintosh. For a complete list of system requirements, see the Introduction of your *User's Guide*.

Connecting to a PC

1. Turn off the printer and your computer.

2. Connect the cable to the printer's parallel interface; then squeeze the wire clips together until they lock in place. (If your cable has a ground wire, connect it now.)

Note:
The printer is assigned to parallel port LPT1; if you want to use a different port, see your Windows documentation for instructions.

ground wire

3. Connect the other end of the cable to your computer's parallel port and secure it as necessary.

Continued

Connecting to a Macintosh

1. Turn off the printer and your Macintosh.

2. Connect one end of the cable to the serial connector on the back of the printer.

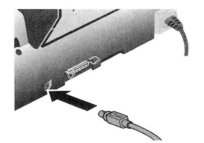

Note:
If you're using a PowerBook™ connect your printer to the modem port.

3. Connect the other end of the cable to either the modem port ✆ or the printer port 🖶 on your Macintosh.

8 Install the Printer Software

Now you need to install the printer software so you can control printing from your computer.

Functions as both a step—installing software—and a wrap-up

Installing on a PC

You can install the printer software for Windows 95 or Windows 3.1 from the EPSON printer software CD-ROM. If you don't have a CD-ROM drive, you can install the software using the EPSON printer software diskettes.

Installing from the CD-ROM

In addition to the printer driver and utilities, the CD-ROM contains EPSON Answers, a comprehensive online guide that includes:

EPSON ANSWERS
If you have a CD-ROM drive, you can run EPSON Answers, the on-screen guide to your new printer. It puts you on the right track quickly and easily.

▶ **How To** for step-by-step printer operating instructions
▶ **Color Guide** with practical color printing information
▶ **Problem Solver** to help you fix printer problems
▶ **Test Print** so you can check your print quality

Provides information for further troubleshooting and contact with manufacturer

Follow the instructions inside the CD-ROM case to install the software. To run EPSON Answers, click on its icon in the EPSON program group or folder.

Source: Reprinted by permission of Epson America.

Writing Procedures for Policies and Regulations

Up to this point, we have concentrated primarily on instructions dealing with how to put things together; how to install, repair, or use equipment; and how to alert readers to mechanical or even personal danger(s). But there is another similar type of writing that deals with guidelines for the world of work: procedures. These concern policies and regulations found in employee handbooks and other internal corporate communications, such as on websites, in memos, or in e-mail messages. (Note, however, that some companies do not disseminate policy via e-mail because it is perceived as less formal than hard copy and is not deletable.) Figure 13.11 shows an example of a company policy on flextime.

Some Examples of Procedures to Write

Procedures deal with a wide range of "how-to" activities within an organization, including the following:

- access a company file or database
- prepare for an audit
- apply for family leave
- dress professionally at work
- route information
- reserve a company vehicle or facility
- take advantage of telecommuting options
- prepare for and respond at a multinational conference
- file a work-related grievance
- request travel expense reimbursement
- operate updated corporate software
- fulfill promotion requirements

Policy procedures have a major impact on a company and its workers; they affect schedules, payrolls, acceptable and unacceptable behaviors at work, and a range of protocols governing the way an organization does business internally and externally.

Meeting the Needs of Your Marketplace

As with instructions, you will have to plan carefully for writing procedures. A mistake in business procedures can be as wide ranging and as costly as an error in a set of assembly instructions—perhaps more so since poorly written procedures can land a company and/or its employees in significant legal trouble.

To avoid such difficulties, spell out precisely what is expected of employees—how, when, where, and why they are to perform or adhere to a certain policy. Use the same strategies as for instructions discussed earlier in this chapter. Leave no chance for misunderstanding or ambiguity; be unqualifyingly straightforward and clear-cut. Determine what information employees need to comply with all the regulations you are specifying and supply it.

Instructions on a new scheduling policy.   **Figure 13.11**

WebTech. Inc.   **www.webtech.com**
4300 Ames Boulevard, Gunderson, CO 81230-0999   (303) 555-9721
                                                          FAX (303) 555-9876

TO: All Employees   DATE: March 20, 2006
FROM: Tequina Bowers T.B.   SUBJECT: Opting for a Flextime
         Human Resources   Schedule

Effective sixty days from now, on May 10, 2006, employees will have the
opportunity to go to a flextime schedule or to remain on their current 8-hour
fixed schedule. This memo explains the flextime option and establishes the
guidelines and rules you must follow if you choose this new schedule.

Notifies readers of new policy and states purpose of the memo

Flextime Defined

Flextime is based on a certain number of **core hours** and **flexible hours**. Our
company will be open twelve hours, from 6:00 a.m. to 6:00 p.m. weekdays, to
accommodate both fixed and flextime arrangements. During this 12-hour period,
all employees on flextime will be expected to work **eight and one-half consecutive
hours,** including a half-hour for lunch. All employees must work a **common core
time from 10:00 a.m. to 4:00 p.m.** but flextime employees will be free to choose
their own starting and quitting times. For instance, they might elect to arrive at
8:00 a.m. and leave at 4:30 p.m., or they may want to start at 9:30 a.m. and leave
at 6:00 p.m.

Spells out precisely how company defines flextime—uses boldface for most important information

Flextime Guidelines and Rules

Employees need to understand their individual responsibilities and adjust their
schedules accordingly. All employees must adhere strictly to the following
regulations and realize that flextime schedule privileges can be revoked for
violations.

Stresses employee responsibilities and consequences of violating rules

Continued

Figure 13.11   (Continued)

2.

Carefully out-
lines what is
and is not
acceptable
according to
new policy

What Flextime Employees Must Do

(1) Be present during core time, arriving and leaving the plant during their flexible work hours.
(2) Observe a minimum unpaid half-hour lunch break each working day.
(3) Cooperate with their supervisors to make sure coverage is provided for their departments from 6:00 a.m. to 6:00 p.m.
(4) Notify supervisors of absences.
(5) Attend monthly corporate meetings even though such meetings may be outside their chosen flextime schedules.
(6) Adhere to dress code during any time they are at work, regardless of their flextimes.
(7) Agree to work on a flextime schedule for a 6-month period.

Numbered
points make
policy easier to
understand,
follow, and
refer to in the
future

What Flextime Employees Can't Do

(1) Be tardy during core time.
(2) Switch, bank, borrow, or trade flextime hours with other employees without the approval of an immediate supervisor.
(3) File for overtime without a supervisor's approval.
(4) Self-schedule a vacation by expanding flextime hours.
(5) Switch back and forth between fixed time and flextime.

Stipulates
what new
policy will not
allow in sepa-
rate section of
memo

How Do You Sign Up for Flextime?

If you wish to begin a flextime schedule, first you need to obtain and complete a transfer of hours form from your supervisor. Next, you need to bring that signed form to Human Resources (Admin. 201) to participate officially in this program.

Explains steps
to begin flex-
time

I will be happy to talk to you about this new option and to answer any of your questions. Please call me at ext. 5121, e-mail me at **tbowers@webtech.com**, or come by my office in Admin. 201. Thank you.

Encourages
feedback and
questions

Many times procedure statements involve a change in the work environment. Help readers by including, whenever necessary, definitions, headings, some prefatory explanations, and an offer to help employees with any questions they may have. Always present a copy of the procedures to management to approve or to revise before sending them to employees.

Figure 13.11 shows a memo from a human resources director notifying employees how they can take advantage of a new flextime arrangement at work, including what they can and cannot do within the framework of flextime. Note how the writer divides her procedures document into an introduction explaining when flextime will go into effect and what choices employees have about it, a section that usefully defines and delineates the concept of flextime, and finally a section containing specific guidelines. These guidelines, while not sequential, function as a series of steps that employees have to follow, and ultimately these steps will affect the entire organization.

The various regulations about what employees cannot do in flextime might be seen as the equivalents of warning and caution statements discussed in this chapter's section "Warnings, Cautions, and Notes" (pp. 572–574). Observe, too, how the writer does not veer off to discuss benefits to the employer or to examine where and how often flextime has been used elsewhere. Finally, this example of procedural writing protects the employer legally by establishing the policies and rules by which an employee's scheduled work time is clearly defined, delineated, and evaluated.

Some Final Advice

Perhaps the most important piece of advice to leave you with is this: Do not take *anything* for granted when you have to write a set of instructions. It is wrong and on occasion dangerous to assume that your readers have performed the procedure before, that they will automatically supply missing or "obvious" information, or that they will easily anticipate your next step. No one ever complained that a set of instructions was too clear or too easy to follow.

Online Study Center

Access the writing instructions and procedures Revision Checklist online at college.hmco.com/pic/kolin8e

✔ Revision Checklist

☐ Analyzed my intended audience's background, especially why and how they will use my instructions.

☐ Tested my instructions to make sure they include all necessary steps in their proper sequence.

☐ Made sure all measurements, distances, times, and relationships are precise and correct.

☐ Avoided technical terms if my audience is not a group of specialists in my field.

☐ Used the imperative mood throughout my instructions.

☐ Wrote clear, short sentences.

☐ Chose effective visuals, labeled them, and placed them next to the step(s) to which they apply.

☐ Made my introduction proportionate to the length and complexity of my instructions and suitable for my readers' needs.

Continued

Continued

☐ Included necessary background, safety, and operational information in the introduction.

☐ Provided a complete list of tools and materials my audience needs to carry out the instructions.

☐ Put instructions in easy-to-follow steps and in the right order.

☐ Used numbers or bullets to label the steps and inserted connective words to indicate order.

☐ Used warnings, cautions, and notes where necessary and in a form that makes them easily seen and read.

☐ Supplied a conclusion that summarizes what readers should have done or reassures them that they have completed the job satisfactorily.

☐ Spelled out clearly responsibilities, benefits, restrictions, and consequences of any procedures for readers.

☐ Defined any terms readers may be unfamiliar with in procedures for policies and regulations.

☐ Gave a copy of procedures to administrators for their approval before distributing to employees.

Exercises

Online Study Center

Find additional writing instructions and procedures exercises at college.hmco.com/pic/kolin8e

1. Find a set of instructions that does not contain any visuals, but that you think should have some graphic material to make it clearer. Design those visuals yourself and indicate where they should appear in the instructions.

2. From a technical manual in your field or in an owner's manual, locate a set of instructions that you think is poorly written and illustrated. In a memo to your instructor, explain why the instructions are unclear, confusing, or badly formatted. Then revise the instructions to make them easier for the reader to carry out. Submit the original instructions with your revision.

3. Write a set of instructions in numbered steps (or in paragraph format) on one of the following relatively simple activities.
   a. tying a shoe
   b. using an ATM
   c. unlocking a door with a key
   d. sending a text file from a cell phone
   e. planting a tree or a shrub
   f. sewing a button on a shirt
   g. removing a stain from clothing
   h. pumping gas into a car
   i. creating a blog

    j. checking a book out of the library
    k. polishing a floor
    l. shifting gears in a car
    m. photocopying a page from a book

4. Write an appropriate introduction and conclusion for the set of instructions you wrote for Exercise 3.

5. Write a set of full instructions on one of the following more complex topics. Identify your audience. Include an appropriate introduction; a list of equipment and materials; numbered steps with necessary warnings, cautions, and notes; and an effective conclusion. Also include whatever visuals you think will help your audience.
    a. scanning a document
    b. changing a flat tire
    c. testing chlorine in a swimming pool
    d. shaving a patient for surgery
    e. changing the oil and oil filter in a car
    f. surveying a parcel of land
    g. pruning hedges
    h. jumping a dead car battery
    i. using the Heimlich maneuver to help a choking individual
    j. filleting a fish
    k. creating a logo for a letterhead
    l. taking someone's blood pressure
    m. downloading a homepage from the Web
    n. painting a car
    o. cooking a roast
    p. flossing a patient's teeth after cleaning
    q. creating a computer file

6. The following set of instructions is confusing, vague, and out of order. Rewrite the instructions to make them clear, easy to follow, and correct. Make sure that each step follows the guidelines outlined in this chapter.

Reupholstering a Piece of Furniture

(1) Although it might be difficult to match the worn material with the new material, you might as well try.
(2) If you cannot, remove the old material.
(3) Take out the padding.
(4) Take out all of the tacks before removing the old covering. You might want to save the old covering.
(5) Measure the new material with the old, if you are able to.
(6) Check the frame, springs, webbing, and padding.
(7) Put the new material over the old.
(8) Check to see if it matches.

(9) You must have the same size as before.
(10) Look at the padding inside. If it is lumpy, smooth it out.
(11) You will need to tack all the sides down. Space your tacks a good distance apart.
(12) When you spot wrinkles, remove the tacks.
(13) Caution: in step 11 directly above, do not drive your tacks all the way through. Leave some room.
(14) Work from the center to the edge in step 11 above.
(15) Put the new material over the old furniture.

P.S. Use strong cords whenever there are tacks. Put the cords under the nails so that they hold.

---

7. Write a set of procedures, similar to Figure 13.11, on one of the following policies or regulations at your school or job site:
    a. offering quality customer service over the phone or via the Web
    b. filing a claim for a personal injury on the job
    c. designing an employee's personal space—what is and is not allowed?
    d. using the Internet at work for personal use
    e. ensuring confidentiality at work (to practice professional ethics in the workplace)
    f. enrolling in mandatory courses to maintain a license or certificate
    g. playing music at the workplace
    h. going through an orientation procedure to begin a new job
    i. following an acceptable dress code

CHAPTER 14

Writing Winning Proposals

A proposal is a detailed plan of action that a writer submits to a reader or group of readers for approval. The readers are usually in a position of authority—supervisors, managers, department heads, boards of private foundations, military or civic leaders—to endorse or reject the writer's plan. Proposals are among the most important types of job-related writing. Their acceptance can lead to improved working conditions, better use of technology, a more efficient and economical business, additional jobs and business for a company, or a safer environment. We have already seen examples of persuasive writing such as sales letters, websites, and job application letters.

They are also among the most costly types of occupational writing, taking an enormous amount of time and personnel energy to prepare successfully. Preparation of a proposal, which is a much more complex document, requires a much greater investment in time and in talent and, therefore, in money.

Every proposal you write must exhibit a "can do" attitude, putting the reader and his or her company's needs at the center of your work. As you go through this chapter, keep in mind the slogan of Yates Engineering that has won millions of dollars of business through its reader-centered proposals: "On time . . . within budget . . . to your satisfaction." Time, budget, and your readers' satisfaction and convenience are among the most important ingredients of a winning proposal. Notice how the advertisement for Cingular in Figure 14.1 appeals to customers' desire for global access, technical expertise, and service.

Online Study Center

To expand your understanding of writing proposals, take advantage of the ACE quizzes, sample documents, Web links, and exercises at college.hmco.com/ pic/kolin8e

Writing Successful Proposals

Proposals are written for many purposes and many different audiences; for example:

- to your boss, seeking authorization to hire staff, change a procedure, or to purchase a new piece of equipment for the office (as Marcus Weekley did in Figure 2.5, requesting that his firm upgrade their laser printers).
- to potential customers, offering a product or a service (such as offering to supply a fire chief with special firefighting gear, or offering an office manager a line of ergonomically designed furniture).

Figure 14.1   An example of a "can-do" attitude.

Reprinted courtesy of Cingular.

- to a government agency, such as the Department of the Interior, seeking funds to conduct a research project (for instance, requesting money to study the mating and feeding habits of a particular species, or asking for funds to discover ways to detect environmental hazards more quickly).
- to foundations to raise funds for a nonprofit organization (for example, a small art gallery requesting funding from an arts foundation).

Depending on the job, proposals can vary greatly in size and in scope. A proposal to your employer could easily be conveyed in a page or two. A proposal to do a research project for a class assignment could also be successfully completed in a memo. To propose doing a small job for a prospective client—redecorating a waiting room in an accountant's office—a letter with information on costs, materials, and a timetable might suffice. The sales letters in Figures 6.3–6.5 (pp. 180–203) illustrate short proposals in letter format. But an extremely large and costly job—constructing a ten-story office building, for example—requires a detailed report hundreds of pages long with appendixes on engineering specifications, detailed budgets, and even résumés of all key personnel working on the project.

A discussion of long, elaborate proposals is beyond the scope of this chapter. But the principles and techniques of audience analysis, organization, and drafting that this chapter does cover apply equally well to any longer project you may have to prepare individually or as part of a team at work or school.

Proposals Are Persuasive Plans

Proposals, whether large or small, must be highly persuasive to succeed. Without your audience's approval, your plan will never go into effect, however accurate and important you think it is. Your enthusiasm is not enough to persuade readers; you have to supply hard evidence. Your proposal must convince readers that your plan will help them improve their businesses, make their jobs easier, save them money, enhance their image, improve customer satisfaction, or all of these. Stress the precise benefits and improvements your plan has for the reader.

Competition is fierce in the world of work, and a persuasive proposal frequently determines which company receives a contract. Demonstrate to your reader why your plan is better—more efficient, practical, economical—than a competitor's. In a sense, a proposal combines the persuasiveness of a sales letter (see Chapter 6), the documentation of a report (see Chapters 9 and 16), and the binding power of a contract, because if the reader accepts your proposal, he or she will expect you to live up to its terms to the letter.

A proposal is an argument (a plan) you must convince your reader to accept. You cannot write a successful proposal until you

1. fully understand your audience's needs/problems and why solving them is important to your audience's ongoing business
2. formulate a careful, detailed plan of action to address and solve these needs/problems
3. prove beyond doubt that you have the logic, time, technology, and personnel to solve the audience's precise problem
4. can match your timetable and budget with your reader's

These four goals are not only vital to your persuasive plan but, when incorporated within a proposal that your reader accepts, become part of a legally binding agreement.

Once accepted, proposals will require that you continue to be a highly persuasive writer and thorough researcher. When your plan is underway, you can expect to write progress reports (pp. 638–644), trip reports (pp. 644–651), and maybe even an incident report (depending on how the project develops).

Proposals Frequently Are Collaborative Efforts

Like many other types of business and technical writing, proposals often are the product of teamwork and sharing. Even a short in-house proposal is often researched and put together by more than one individual in the company or agency.

Often, individual employees will pull together information from their separate areas (such as graphics and design, finance, marketing, sales, transportation, and even legal) and put it into a proposal that each team member then reads and revises until the team agrees that the document is ready to be released.

Types of Proposals

Proposals are classified according to how they originate and where they are sent after they are written. Distinctions are made between *solicited* and *unsolicited* proposals based on how they originate and between *internal* and *external* proposals based on where they are sent. Depending on your audience and your purpose, you may write an internal solicited or unsolicited proposal, or you may write an external solicited or unsolicited proposal. Figure 14.2 provides a visual representation of the various types of proposals.

Figure 14.2   Types of proposals.

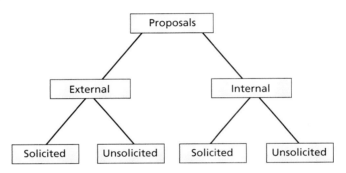

Requests for Proposals and Solicited Proposals

When a company has a particular problem to be solved or a job to be done, it will solicit, or invite, proposals. The company will notify you and other competitors by preparing a **request for proposals (RFP),** which is a set of instructions that specify the exact type of work to be done along with guidelines on how and when the company wants the work completed.

Some RFPs are long and full of legal requirements and conditions. Others, like the examples in Figures 14.3 and 14.4, are more concise. RFPs are sent to firms with track records in the area the company wants the work done. RFPs are also printed in trade publications and put on the Web (see Tech Note on page 599) to attract the highest number of qualified bidders for the job. The U.S. government publishes RFPs in the *Federal Register* or *Commerce Business Daily* (both are online), while private companies sometimes send their RFPs to *Business Daily*. No two RFPs are alike.

An RFP helps you to know what the customer wants. It is often extremely detailed and even tells you how the company wants the proposal prepared, for example, what information is to be included (on backgrounds, personnel, equipment, budgets), where it needs to appear, and how many copies of the proposal you have to submit. The list that follows is an example of the contents for an RFP for a government grant.

REQUEST FOR PROPOSALS

Mesa Community College is soliciting proposals to construct and to install fifty individual study carrels in its Holmes Memorial Library. These carrels must be highly serviceable and conform to all specification standards of the American Library Association (ALA). Proposals should include the precise measurements of the carrels to be installed, the specific acoustical and lighting benefits, Internet access, and the types and amount of storage space offered. Work on constructing and installing the carrels must be completed no later than the start of the Fall Semester, August 29, 2007. Proposals should include a schedule of when different phases of work will be completed and an itemized budget for labor, materials, equipment, and necessary tests to ensure high-quality acoustical performance. Contractors should detail their qualifications, including a description of similar recent work and a list of references. Proposals should be submitted in triplicate no later than March 1, 2007, to:

Mrs. Barbara Feldstein-Archer
Director of the Library
Mesa Community College
Mesa, CO 80932-0617
BFeldstein-archer@Mesa.edu

- Purpose of this RFA
- Research Objectives
- Mechanism of Support
- Funds Available
- Eligible Institutions
- Individuals Eligible to Become Principal Investigators
- Special Requirements
- Where to Send Inquiries
- Letter of Intent
- Submitting an Application
- Peer Review Process
- Review Criteria
- Receipt and Review Schedule
- Award Criteria
- Required Federal Citations

Your own proposal will be judged according to how well you fulfill the terms of the RFP. For that reason, follow the directions in the RFP exactly. Note that the solicited proposal in Figure 14.5 (pp. 596–598) directly refers to the terms of the

Figure 14.4   A sample of part of an RFP for a larger project.

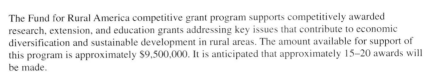

Fund for Rural America

The Fund for Rural America competitive grant program supports competitively awarded research, extension, and education grants addressing key issues that contribute to economic diversification and sustainable development in rural areas. The amount available for support of this program is approximately $9,500,000. It is anticipated that approximately 15–20 awards will be made.

Program Description

Preservation of the economic viability of rural communities will be the focus of the Fund for Rural America. The program focuses attention **on rural communities' twin challenges of rural community innovation and demographic change.** Challenges of an aging population, the arrival of new immigrant populations, youth retention, and work force development all are critical issues that impact the rural economy. **Rural communities may propose research, education, and extension/outreach projects that will create an understanding of these demographic forces and develop capacity to turn these challenges into economic promise.** Projects should facilitate the development of the capacity to translate on- and off-farm innovations into economic growth and community revitalization.

Rural Community Innovation

This program area seeks research, education, and extension proposals that will **help rural Americans address existing and new problems in innovative ways. The goals of this program area are to generate new knowledge and transfer that knowledge to assist rural communities to diversify their economies, to develop and maintain profitable farms, firms, and businesses, to build community capacity, to aid smart growth, to protect natural resources, and to increase family economic security.**

Projects are encouraged to combine multiple strategies for innovation such as the following:

- value-added agriculture as a rural development strategy (firm location, growth scenarios, economic players, variation by rural area and population, nature of markets);
- community implications of moving to a more bio-based economy (carbon sequestration credits, promoting locally based bio-based industries, linking bio-based materials to a diverse agriculture and community);
- impacts of land use development options (farmland preservation, farming on the urban fringe, rural-urban land use issues);
- policies and community institutions that help increase farm profitability among small and minority farmers;
- e-commerce applications for remote rural areas and minority populations, community information networks to support e-commerce and e-communities, and adapting e-commerce strategies for e-community planning and social capital development;
- network capabilities among producers, businesses, entrepreneurs, families, individuals, non-profit groups, community institutions, local government, and state and federal entities;

Continued

(Continued)   Figure 14.4

> **2.**
>
> - participatory development of economic blueprints, watershed futures, and land use forecasts; place-based methods that create quality jobs, prepare a quality labor force, support transitions from welfare, encourage successful entrepreneurship, and diversify local economies;
> - nature of new generation of computer-based planning tools (geospatial analysis, information stores, economic and land use blueprints) and ability to apply and tailor them for place-sensitive development.

RFP. You should even use the language (specialized terms, specifically stated needs) of the RFP in your proposal to convince readers that you understand their requirements and to get them to accept your plan. If you have any questions, by all means call the agency or company so you do not waste your time or theirs by including irrelevant or unnecessary details in your proposal.

Unsolicited Proposals

With an unsolicited proposal, you—not the reader—make the first move. Unlike a solicited proposal, in which the company to which you are submitting the proposal knows about the problem, your unsolicited proposal has to convince readers that (1) there is a problem and (2) you and your firm are the ones to solve it.

Doing that is not as difficult as it sounds. See how the writers of the unsolicited proposal in Figure 14.6 on pages 604–607 identify a relevant problem for their readers. If your readers accept your identification of the problem, you have greatly increased the chances of their accepting your plan to solve it. Just remember that you will have to prove that solving the problem carries major benefits for your reader.

Internal and External Proposals

An internal proposal is written to one or several decision maker(s) in your own organization who have to sign off or approve your plan. As you will see on pages 602–610, an internal proposal can deal with a variety of topics, including changing a policy or procedure, requesting additional personnel, or purchasing or updating equipment or software.

An external proposal, on the other hand, is sent to a decision maker outside your company. It might go to a potential client you have never worked for or to a previous or current client. An external proposal can also be sent to a government funding agency, such as the Department of Agriculture, in its request in Figure 14.4. External proposals tend to be more formal than internal ones.

Figure 14.5   An external solicited proposal in response to an RFP.

RJI

Reynolds Interiors • 250 Commerce Avenue S.W. • Portland, OR 97204-2129

January 20, 2006

Mr. Alfonso Herrara, Manager
General Purpose Appliances
Highway 11 South
Portland, OR 97222

Dear Mr. Herrara:

Begins with reference to RFP

In response to your RFP 7521 listed on your website for bids for an appropriate floor covering at your new showroom, Reynolds Interiors is pleased to submit the following proposal. We appreciated the opportunity to visit your facility in order to submit this proposal. After carefully reviewing your specifications for a floor covering and inspecting your new facility, we believe that **Armstrong Classic Corlon 900** is the most suitable choice. We are enclosing a sample of the Corlon 900 so you can see how carefully it is constructed.

Identifies best solution

Corlon's Advantages

Describes product's features that benefit reader

Guaranteed against defects for a full three years, **Corlon** is one of the most durable floor coverings manufactured by Armstrong. It is a heavy-duty commercial floor 0.085 inch thick for protection. Twenty-five percent of the material consists of interface backing; the other 75 percent is an inlaid wear layer that offers exceptionally high resistance to everyday traffic. Traffic tests conducted by the Independent Floor Covering Institute repeatedly proved the superiority of **Corlon's** construction and resistance.

Distinguishes product from competitors'

Another important feature of **Corlon** is the size of its rolls. Unlike other leading brands of similar commercial flooring—Remington or Treadmaster—**Corlon** comes in 12-foot-wide rather than

http://www.reynolds.com • 503-555-8733 • Fax: 503-555-1629

Continued

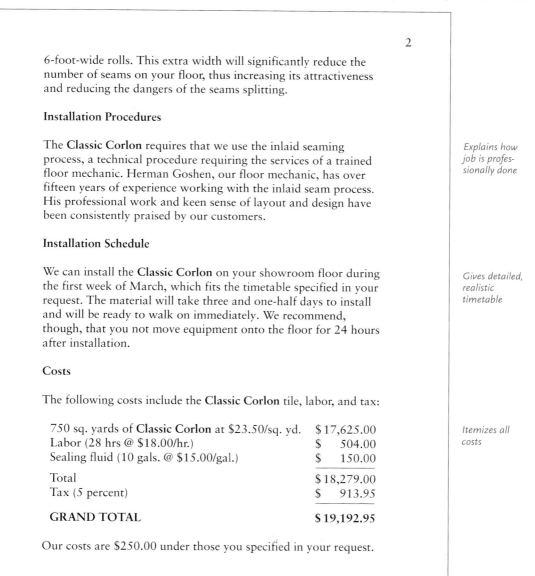

2

6-foot-wide rolls. This extra width will significantly reduce the number of seams on your floor, thus increasing its attractiveness and reducing the dangers of the seams splitting.

Installation Procedures

The **Classic Corlon** requires that we use the inlaid seaming process, a technical procedure requiring the services of a trained floor mechanic. Herman Goshen, our floor mechanic, has over fifteen years of experience working with the inlaid seam process. His professional work and keen sense of layout and design have been consistently praised by our customers.

Explains how job is professionally done

Installation Schedule

We can install the **Classic Corlon** on your showroom floor during the first week of March, which fits the timetable specified in your request. The material will take three and one-half days to install and will be ready to walk on immediately. We recommend, though, that you not move equipment onto the floor for 24 hours after installation.

Gives detailed, realistic timetable

Costs

The following costs include the **Classic Corlon** tile, labor, and tax:

750 sq. yards of **Classic Corlon** at $23.50/sq. yd.	$17,625.00
Labor (28 hrs @ $18.00/hr.)	$ 504.00
Sealing fluid (10 gals. @ $15.00/gal.)	$ 150.00
Total	$18,279.00
Tax (5 percent)	$ 913.95
GRAND TOTAL	**$19,192.95**

Itemizes all costs

Our costs are $250.00 under those you specified in your request.

Continued

Figure 14.5   (Continued)

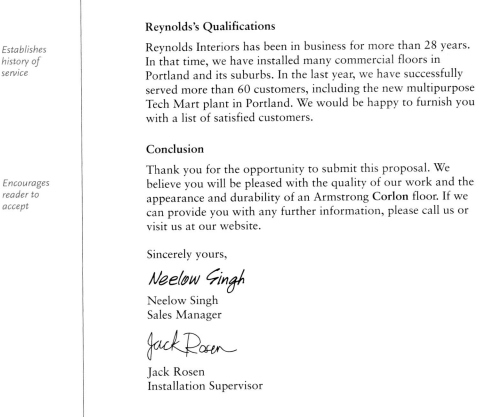

Establishes history of service

3

Reynolds's Qualifications

Reynolds Interiors has been in business for more than 28 years. In that time, we have installed many commercial floors in Portland and its suburbs. In the last year, we have successfully served more than 60 customers, including the new multipurpose Tech Mart plant in Portland. We would be happy to furnish you with a list of satisfied customers.

Encourages reader to accept

Conclusion

Thank you for the opportunity to submit this proposal. We believe you will be pleased with the quality of our work and the appearance and durability of an Armstrong **Corlon** floor. If we can provide you with any further information, please call us or visit us at our website.

Sincerely yours,

Neelow Singh

Neelow Singh
Sales Manager

Jack Rosen

Jack Rosen
Installation Supervisor

Guidelines for Writing a Successful Proposal

Regardless of the type of proposal you are called on to write, the following guidelines will help you persuade your audience to approve your plan. Refer to these guidelines and Figure 14.5 both before and while you formulate your plan.

   1. **Approach writing a proposal as a problem-solving activity.**   Everything in your proposal should relate to the problem, and the organization of your proposal should reflect your ability as a problem solver. Psychologically, make the readers feel confident that you have the knowledge and the experience they must use. Convince

Tech Note

Online RFPs

RFPs are not only sent out to firms and published in trade magazines, but they are often posted on numerous websites as well. The U.S. government, through its many departments and agencies, is an important source for RFPs. Fed Biz Opps claims that it offers "a comprehensive listing of government RFP's" (*http://www.fedbizopps.gov*). In addition, the *Federal Register,* published daily by the U.S. government, issues hundreds of legal regulations as well as requests for proposals from various government agencies. You can browse the *Federal Register* online via GPO access—*http://www.gpoaccess.gov.*

Following is a summary of a request for proposals from the Department of Transportation on Electronic Payment Systems.

DEPARTMENT OF TRANSPORTATION

Federal Transit Administration

Request for Proposals for an Operational Test of an Electronic Payment System for Transportation and Other Applications

AGENCY: Federal Transit Administration (FTA), DOT.

ACTION: Notice.

SUMMARY: The U.S. Department of Transportation (US DOT) announces a Request for Proposals from eligible applicants for an operational test of an electronic payment system for transit fare collection, parking payment, electronic toll collection and other applications. The US DOT is interested in identifying and evaluating issues associated with the establishment of partnerships between public transit service providers and other entities in the development and use of multiple-application electronic payment systems. The Department is specifically interested in an operational test of a payment system that includes a variety of applications, but must at a minimum include transit fare collection, parking payment and electronic toll collection.

DATES: Proposals shall be submitted by 4 p.m. EST on or before October 25.

CONTENTS OF PROPOSAL SHOULD FOLLOW THIS PLAN

I. Background
II. Visions, Goals, and Objectives
III. Project Development
    A. General
    B. Management Oversight
IV. Partnerships
V. National ITS Architecture

Continued

Continued

    VI.   Project Evaluation Activities
    VII.   Funding
    VIII. Schedule
    IX.   Proposals
        A. Technical Plan
        B. Management and Staffing Plan
        C. Financial Plan
    X.   Proposal Evaluation Criteria

ELIGIBILITY: Only public transit agencies and metropolitan planning organizations (MPOs) in the United States are eligible to submit proposals in response to this RFP.

Another source of RFPs on the Internet is *Commerce Business Daily* (*CBD*), which "lists notices of proposed government procurement actions, contract awards, sales of government property and other procurement information. A new edition of the *CBD* is issued every business day, and each edition contains approximately 500–1000 notices." The *CBD* website—*http://cbdnet.access.gpo .gov*—lists the government's requests for equipment, supplies, and a variety of services from assembling to maintaining equipment to fee-charging dredging. Here are a few of the agencies you can search in the *CBD* for RFPs:

- Department of Health and Human Services
- United States Department of Energy
- United States Department of Agriculture
- Defense Support Center and Agencies
- National Aeronautics and Space Administration
- Department of Justice and other law enforcement agencies

The Community of Science Web Server also lets you search the *Federal Register, Federally-Funded Research in the U.S.,* and *Funding Opportunities Database.*

your audience you know their needs and will meet them, as Neelow Singh and Jack Rosen do in Figure 14.5.

2. Regard your audience as skeptical readers. Even though you offer a plan that you think will benefit readers, do not be overconfident that they will automatically accept it as the best and only way to proceed. To determine the feasibility of your plan, readers will question everything you say. They will withhold their approval if your proposal contains errors, omissions, or inconsistencies or if it deviates from what they are looking for.

3. Research your proposal thoroughly. A winning proposal is *not* based only on a few well-meaning, general suggestions. All your good intentions and enthusiasm will not substitute for the hard facts readers will demand. Spell out your plan or procedure; give the nuts and bolts of how, when, and where the job will be done, as Figure 14.5 does. Concrete examples persuade readers; unsupported generalizations do not. You will have to do a lot of homework; for example, researching the problem, doing comparative shopping for the best prices, verifying schedules and timetables, interviewing customers and/or employees, making site visits, or visiting with individuals at your company or your client's company to make sure you are on the right track.

4. Scout out what your competitors are doing.   Closely related to guideline 3, assessing your competition is essential to write a winning proposal. Become familiar with your competitors' products or services, have a fair idea about their market costs, and be able to show how your company's work is better. As Chapter 8 emphasizes, you can accomplish all that by looking at your competitors' websites to

Tech Note

Document Design and Your Proposal

As we saw in Chapter 12, the overall design and layout of a document play a major role in the acceptance by an audience. This is especially true of a proposal—a key sales document for you and your company. Keep in mind that your proposal will be competing with many (perhaps 50 or 100) other proposals, and the first impression it makes will be visual. It should be attractive, logically organized, and reader friendly. If it is designed professionally and pleasingly, it will remain in the running. If not, your proposal may be rejected before your audience reads your first sentence.

Here are some guidelines to help you prepare an attractive and carefully designed proposal.

- Make sure you follow the RFP guidelines to the letter—in terms of spacing, title page, number of copies, appendixes, exhibits, and so on.
- Double-check to make sure it looks professional. Use good-quality paper and a sturdy binding.
- Organize your proposal into sections that help readers identify and follow the various parts of your proposal—for example, problem, solution, budget, timetable, personnel.
- Use plenty of clearly marked, logically ordered, and consistent headings (or, if necessary, subheadings) to separate sections of your proposal to help readers follow and understand your work easily, quickly, and clearly.
- Insert extra spacing between sections of your proposal so they stand out and show readers your work is organized.
- Use a professional-looking and easy-to-read font and type size. Stay away from script fonts and those with ornate designs. Do not try to cram more information in by resorting to an 8-point type.
- Include easy-to-follow indented lists, each item preceded by a bullet or an asterisk.

Continued

Continued

- Clearly label and insert all visuals in the most appropriate places in your proposal—see Figure 14.6 (pp. 604–607), which does an especially effective job.
- Put budgets in easy-to-read tables, not buried in a paragraph of prose. Make sure each item in a budget/timetable is identified and highlighted or relegated to a footnote or appendix.
- Keep paragraphs at five to six sentences. Heavy blocks of prose slow readers down and make them think your work is dense and hard to follow. Consider your readers' comfort level.
- Do not fail to include and label any supporting documents or materials that will not be a part of your proposal proper, for example, schedules, surveys, or samples (as in Figure 14.5).

see what is available. Examine print and online trade publications, too. Note how the writers in Figure 14.5 prove their product is superior.

5. Prove that your proposal is workable.   The bottom-line question from your reader is "Will this plan work?" Your proposal should be well thought out. It should contain no statements that say, "Let's see what happens if we do *X* or *Y*." Analyze and, when possible, test each part of your proposal in advance, to eliminate any quirks and to revise the proposal appropriately before readers evaluate it. What you propose should be consistent with the organization and capabilities of the company. It would be foolish to recommend, for example, that a small company with fifty employees triple its work force to accomplish your plan. Make sure you have the resources at hand to deliver the promises you make.

6. Be sure your proposal is financially realistic.   This point follows from guideline 5. "Is it worth the money?" is another bottom-line question you can expect from readers. Do not submit a proposal that would require an unnecessarily large amount of money to implement. For example, it would be unrealistic to recommend that your company spend $20,000 to solve a $2,000 problem. Note how Figure 14.5 stresses that the costs are under control. Above all, make readers believe that the benefits are worth the costs.

7. Package your proposal attractively.   Make sure your proposal is letter perfect, inviting, and easy to read (use headings, lists, different typefaces, graphics, and other visual devices discussed in Chapter 12 and in the Tech Note on design above). The format as well as the content of your proposal can determine whether it is accepted or rejected. Remember that readers, especially those unfamiliar with your work, will evaluate your proposal as evidence of the type of work you want to do for them.

Internal Proposals

The primary purpose of an internal proposal, such as the one shown in Figure 14.6, is to offer a realistic and constructive plan to help your company run its business more efficiently and economically.

On your job you may discover a better way of doing something or a more efficient way to correct a problem. You believe that your proposed change will save your employer time, money, or further trouble. (Note how Tina Escobar and Oliver Jabur in Figure 14.6 [pp. 604–607] identified and researched a more effective and less costly way for Community Federal Bank to conduct business and to satisfy its customers.)

Generally speaking, your proposal will be an informal, in-house message, so a brief (usually two- or three-page) memo should be appropriate. You decide to notify your department head, manager, or supervisor, or your employer may ask you for specific suggestions to solve a problem he or she has already identified. Mike Gonzalez's memo in Figure 4.3 (p. 123) responds to such a request from his employer.

Typical Topics for Internal Proposals

An internal proposal can be written about a variety of topics, such as

- purchasing new or more advanced technology to replace obsolete or inefficient computers, transducers, robots, and the like or upgrading equipment
- obtaining document security software and offering training sessions to show employees how to use it
- recruiting new employees, or retraining current ones on a new technique or process
- eliminating a dangerous condition or reducing an environmental risk to prevent accidents—for employees, customers, or the community at large
- improving communication within or between departments of a company or agency to save expenses or to increase jobs
- expanding work space or making it more efficient, private, ergonomically beneficial to employees, or more inviting to customers

As the list shows, internal proposals cover almost every activity or policy that can affect the day-to-day operation of a company or agency.

Following the Proper Chain of Command

Writing an internal proposal requires you to be aware of and sensitive to office politics. Meet first with your boss to see if she or he has already identified the problem or has suggestions on how to solve it. Then you might provide your boss with a draft and ask for revisions or feedback.

You cannot assume that your reader(s) will automatically agree with you that there is a problem or that your plan is the only way to tackle it. To be successful, write your internal proposal keeping in mind the needs and likes of your boss and others who may have to sign off on your proposal. Remember that your boss will expect you to be very convincing about both the problem you say exists and the changes you are advocating in the workplace under his or her supervision. Don't step on corporate toes. Similarly, you may need the approval of individuals in other offices, departments, or branches of your organization.

Figure 14.6   An internal unsolicited proposal.

COMMUNITY FEDERAL BANK

http://www.comfedbank.com

EQUAL HOUSING
LENDER

POWELL
617-584-5200

MONROE
781-413-6000

LANGSTON
508-796-3009

TO: Michael L. Sappington, Executive Vice President
Dorothy Woo, Langston Regional Manager

FROM: Tina Escobar, Oliver Jabur, ATM Services

DATE: June 11, 2007

RE: A proposal to install an ATM at the Mayfield Park branch

Clearly states why proposal is being sent

PURPOSE

We propose a cost-effective solution to what is a growing problem at the Mayfield Park branch in Langston: inefficient servicing of customer needs and rising personnel costs. We recommend that you approve the purchase and installation, within the next two to three months, of an ATM at Mayfield. Such action is consistent with Community's goals of expanding branch banking services and promoting our image as a self-serve yet customer-oriented institution.

Identifies problem by giving reader necessary background information

THE PROBLEM WITH CURRENT SERVICES AT MAYFIELD PARK

Currently, we employ four tellers at Mayfield. However, too much is being spent on personnel/salary for routine customer transactions. In fact, as determined by teller activity reports, nearly 25 percent of the four tellers' time each week is devoted to routine activities easily accommodated by ATMs. Outlined in the table below is a breakdown of teller activity for the month of May:

Provides easy-to-read table

Teller #	Total Transactions	Routine Transactions
1	6,205	1,551
2	5,989	1,383
3	6,345	1,522
4	6,072	1,518
	24,611	5,974

Divides problem into parts—volume, financial, personnel, customer service

Clearly, we are not fully using our tellers' sales abilities when they are kept busy with routine activities. To compound the problem, we expect business to increase by at least 25 percent at Mayfield in the next few months, as projected by this year's market survey. If we do not install

Continued

page 2

an ATM, we will need to hire a fifth teller, at an annual cost of $20,800 ($15,500 base pay plus approximately 30 percent for fringes), for the additional 6,000 transactions we project.

Most important, customer needs are not being met efficiently at Mayfield. Recent surveys done for Community Federal by Watson-Perry demonstrate that our customers are inconvenienced by not having an ATM at Mayfield. They are unhappy about long waits in line to do simple banking business, such as deposits, withdrawals, and loan payments, and about having to drive to other branches to do after-hours banking. Conversations we had with manager Rachael Harris-Koyoto at Mayfield confirm customers' complaints.

Verifies that problem is widespread

Ultimately, the lack of an ATM at Mayfield Park hurts Community's image. With ATMs available to Mayfield residents at local stores and at other banks, our institution risks having customers and potential customers go elsewhere for their banking needs. We not only miss the opportunity of selling them on our other services but also risk losing their business entirely.

Emphasizes possible future problems

A SOLUTION TO THE PROBLEM

Purchasing and installing an ATM at Mayfield Park will result in significant savings in personnel costs and time. We will

- Save money by not having to hire a fifth teller
- Allocate teller duties more efficiently and productively by assisting customers with questions and transactions not handled through an ATM, such as opening a new account; purchasing savings bonds, CDs, traveler's checks and foreign currency; and Internet banking.
- Increase time for tellers to cross-sell our services, including our line of nontraditional banking products—annuities, mutual funds, debit cards, and global market accounts
- Service customer retirement options by having tellers track IRAs, 401(k)s, 403(b)s, and Simples
- Improve customer satisfaction by giving them the option of meeting their banking needs electronically or through a teller
- Ease the stress on tellers at Mayfield Park

Relates solution to individual parts of the problem

It is feasible to install an ATM at Mayfield. This location does not pose the difficulties as at some older branches. Mayfield offers ample room to install a drive-up ATM in the stubbed-out fourth drive-up lane. It is away from the heavily congested area in front of the bank, yet it is

Shows problem can be solved and stresses how

Continued

Figure 14.6   (Continued)

easily accessible from the main driveway and the side drive facing
Commonwealth Avenue, as the photograph below shows.

Photo shows location has room for additional ATM

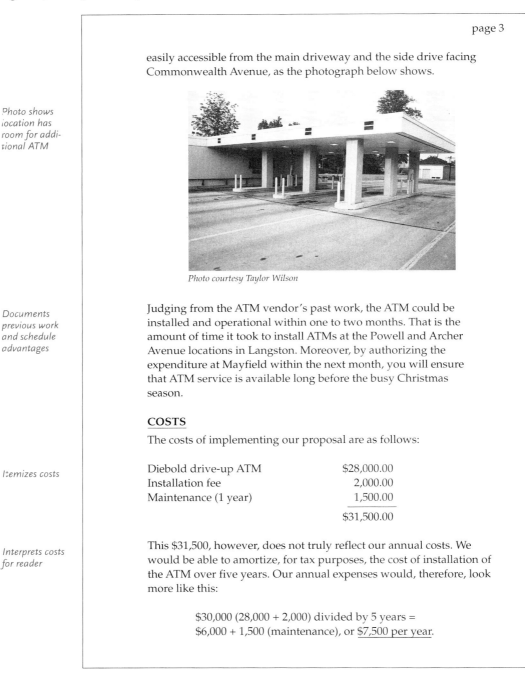

Photo courtesy Taylor Wilson

Documents previous work and schedule advantages

Judging from the ATM vendor's past work, the ATM could be
installed and operational within one to two months. That is the
amount of time it took to install ATMs at the Powell and Archer
Avenue locations in Langston. Moreover, by authorizing the
expenditure at Mayfield within the next month, you will ensure
that ATM service is available long before the busy Christmas
season.

COSTS

The costs of implementing our proposal are as follows:

Itemizes costs

Diebold drive-up ATM	$28,000.00
Installation fee	2,000.00
Maintenance (1 year)	1,500.00
	$31,500.00

Interprets costs for reader

This $31,500, however, does not truly reflect our annual costs. We
would be able to amortize, for tax purposes, the cost of installation of
the ATM over five years. Our annual expenses would, therefore, look
more like this:

$30,000 (28,000 + 2,000) divided by 5 years =
$6,000 + 1,500 (maintenance), or <u>$7,500 per year</u>.

Continued

page 4

Compared with the $20,800 a year the bank would have to expend
for a fifth teller position at Mayfield, the annual depreciated cost for
the ATM ($7,500) reduces by nearly two-thirds the amount of money
the bank will have to spend for much more efficient customer service.

CONCLUSION

Authorizing an ATM for the Mayfield Park branch is both feasible
and cost effective. Endorsement of this proposal will save our bank
more than $13,000 in teller services annually, reduce customer
complaints, and increase customer satisfaction and approval. We will
be happy to discuss this proposal with you anytime at your
convenience, and answer any questions you may have.

Shows change is cost-effective

Stresses benefits for reader and bank as a whole

Anticipating and Ethically Resolving Readers' Problems

When you prepare an internal proposal, you need to be aware of some difficulties and some ethical ways of handling them.

1. Realize that your reader may feel threatened by your plan.   After all, you are advocating a change. Be careful. Your plan may sound just right to you, but it may be seen by your boss as a piece of criticism leveled at him or her, your department, or the company as a whole. Some managers regard change as a challenge to their administration of an office or a department. Think about the long-term effect your proposed change will have on your boss's duties, responsibilities, or relationships with your co-workers or with his or her own superiors. Don't override your boss or attempt to undermine existing authority.

2. Take into account that your reader may have "pet projects" or predetermined ways of doing things.   Make every attempt to acknowledge them respectfully. You may even find a way to build on or complement such projects or procedures.

3. Keep in mind that your boss may have to take your proposal further up the organizational ladder for commentary and, eventually, approval.   Again, refer to Joycelyn Woolfolk's description in Figure 3.6 of the chain of command at her organization.

4. Consider the implications of your plan for other offices or sections in your company or for a branch or office overseas.   A change you propose for your department or office (transfers, new budgets or schedules, new hires, deploying existing staff) may have sweeping and potentially disruptive implications for another office or division in your company. If you work for an international firm, you also need to assess the implications of your proposal for co-workers from another cultural tradition.

5. Find out whether what you are proposing is within your company's budget. How much can your department, branch, or office spend (e.g., on hardware, software, updates)? Check with your boss, and always monitor the price of your company's stock to make sure any expenditures are likely to be approved.

6. Accept that even though you draft the proposal, it may not bear your name, or your name may be subordinate to your boss's name.   It is not uncommon in the world of work to write a document so another person can sign it. Writing a proposal may mean working as a team with your supervisor, whose name goes on the document, too, for notice and credit, as was pointed out in Figure 3.6.

7. Never submit an internal proposal that offers an idea you think will work but relies on someone else to supply the specific details on how it will work.   For example, do not write an internal proposal that says the finance, marketing, technical support, or human resources department can give the reader the necessary details about your proposal. That unfairly pushes the responsibility onto someone else.

Organization of an Internal Proposal

A short internal proposal follows a relatively straightforward plan of organization, from identifying the problem to solving it. Internal proposals usually contain four parts, as shown in Figure 14.6: **purpose, problem, solution,** and **conclusion**. Refer to Figure 14.6 with these four headings as you read the following discussion.

The Purpose of the Proposal

Begin your proposal with a brief statement of why you are writing to your supervisor: "I propose that. . . ." State why you think a specific change is necessary now. Then succinctly define the problem and emphasize that your plan, if approved by the reader, will solve that problem. Where necessary, stress the urgency to act—within the next week? month?

The Problem

In this section prove that a problem exists. Document its importance for your boss and your company; as a matter of fact, the more you show, with concrete evidence, how the problem affects the boss's work (and area of supervision), the more likely you are to persuade him or her to act.

Here are some guidelines for documenting the problem:

- Avoid vague (and unsupported) generalizations such as, "We're losing money each day with this procedure (piece of equipment)"; "Costs continue to escalate"; "The trouble occurs frequently in a number of places"; "Numerous complaints have come in"; "If something isn't done soon, more problems will result."
- Provide quantifiable details about the implications or consequences of the problem, such as the amount of money or time a company is actually losing per day, week, or month. Document the financial trouble so that you can show in the next section how your plan offers an efficient and workable solution.

- Indicate how many employees (or work-hours) are involved or how many customers are inconvenienced by a procedure or condition. Notice how Escobar and Jabur include such information in a table in their proposal in Figure 14.6.
- Verify how widespread a problem is or how frequently it occurs by citing specific occasions. Again, see how Escobar and Jabur cite evidence from the Watson-Perry survey and the interviews they conducted with the manager of the Mayfield branch.
- Relate the problem to an organization's image, corporate reputation, or influence (where appropriate). Pinpoint exactly how and where the problem lessens your company's effectiveness or hurts its standing in the market, as the writers do especially well in the first paragraph of Figure 14.6.

The Solution or Plan

In this section describe the change you propose and want approved. Tie your solution (the change) directly to the problem you have just documented. Each part of your plan should help eliminate the problem or should help increase the productivity, efficiency, or safety you think is possible.

Your reader will again expect to find factual evidence. Be specific. Do not give merely the outline of a plan or say that details can be worked out later. Supply details that answer the following questions: (1) Is the plan workable? and (2) Is it cost effective?

To get the reader to say yes to both questions, supply the facts you have gathered as a result of your research. Again, you might want to review page 298 of Chapter 8. For example, if you propose that your firm buy a new piece of equipment, do the necessary homework to locate the most efficient and cost-effective model available, as Tina Escobar and Oliver Jabur do in Figure 14.6.

- Supply the vendor's name, the costs, major conditions of service and training contracts, and warranties.
- Describe how your firm could use the equipment/technology to obtain better or quicker results.
- Document specific tasks the new equipment can perform more efficiently at a lower cost than the equipment now in use.

A **proposal to change a procedure** must address the following questions:

- How does the new (or revised) procedure work?
- How many employees or customers will be affected by it?
- When will/can it go into operation?
- How much will it cost the employer to change procedures?
- What delays or losses in business might be expected while the company switches from one procedure to another?
- What employees, equipment, technology, or locations are already available to accomplish the change?

As those questions indicate, your reader will be concerned about schedules, working conditions, employees, methods, locations, equipment, and the costs involved in your plan for change. The costs, in fact, will be of utmost importance. Make sure you supply a careful and accurate budget. Moreover, make those costs attractive by emphasizing how inexpensive they are compared to the cost of *not* making the change, as Escobar and Jabur do in the section labeled "**Costs**." Double-check your math.

It is also wise to raise alternative solutions, before the reader does, and to discuss their disadvantages. Notice how Tina Escobar and Oliver Jabur do that in Figure 14.6 by showing why installing an ATM is more feasible than hiring a fifth teller.

The Conclusion

Your conclusion should be short—a paragraph or two at the most. Remind readers that (a) the problem is ongoing and serious, (b) the reason for change is justified and beneficial to your organization, and (c) action needs to be taken. Reemphasize the most important benefits. Escobar and Jabur stress the savings that the bank will see by following their plan as well as the increase in customer satisfaction. Also indicate that you are willing to discuss your plan with the reader, a necessity in arguing for a corporate change at any level.

Sales Proposals

A sales proposal is the most common type of external proposal. Its purpose is to sell your company's products or services for a set fee. Whether short or long, a sales proposal is a marketing tool that includes a sales pitch as well as a detailed description of the work you propose to do. Figures 14.5 and 14.7 are sales proposals.

The Audience and Its Needs

Your audience will usually be one or more executives who have the power to approve or reject a proposal. Unlike readers of an internal proposal, your audience for a sales proposal may be even more skeptical since they may not know you or your work. Your proposal may also be evaluated by experts in other fields employed by your prospective customer. You can increase your chances of success by trying to anticipate their objections, questions, reasons for rejecting the plan as you propose it, and logic for accepting a competitor's proposal.

Make sure your proposal has a competitive edge. Readers will compare your plan with those they receive from other proposal writers. Your proposal has to convince readers that the product and the service your company offers are more reliable, economical, efficient, and timely than those of another company. Here is where your homework pays off.

The key to success is incorporating the "you attitude" throughout your proposal. Relate your product, service, or personnel to the reader's exact needs as stated in the RFP for a solicited proposal or through your own investigations for an unsolicited proposal. You cannot submit the same proposal for every job you want to win and expect to be awarded a contract. Different firms have different needs.

Typical Questions Readers Will Ask

The most important question the reader will raise about your work is, "How does this proposal meet our company's special requirements?" Some other fairly common questions readers will have as they evaluate your sales proposal include the following:

An unsolicited sales proposal.   Figure 14.7

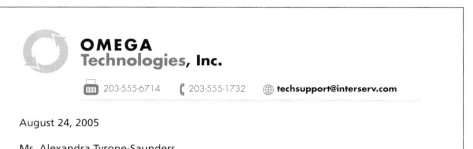

OMEGA Technologies, Inc.

203-555-6714   203-555-1732   **techsupport@interserv.com**

August 24, 2005

Ms. Alexandra Tyrone-Saunders
Vice President, Operations
Gemini Consultants, Inc.
Hartford, CT 06631-7106

Dear Ms. Tyrone-Saunders:

Thank you for allowing us to service your Webmax PCs last week. While we were working on the PCs, I saw several ways in which Omega Technologies might improve your communications system. Based on our assessment of Gemini's requirements for the most up-to-date automation available, we recommend that you purchase ten Lightstar 686 notebooks, one for each member of your sales staff. This latest generation of notebooks will provide your staff with a powerful and affordable system that will meet Gemini's needs well into the next decade.

PROBLEM AREAS

Each of your ten sales staff spends up to 60 minutes at the end of each business day entering orders he or she has accumulated in the field into the PCs at your office. That amounts to 50 overtime hours per week. This procedure is costly and inefficient, taking your staff away from their primary responsibility of serving your clients.

ADVANTAGES OF THE LIGHTSTAR 686 NOTEBOOK

Notebooks are essential complements to other computer systems. According to Felicia Gomez, writing for the Worldtech website (*http://www.worldtech.org*), the Lightstar 686 is "one of the best computer buys of the decade, a powerhouse that will amaze the most particular PC user." The description of Lightstar's features below will show you how its many advantages can help Gemini.

ADVANCED TECHNOLOGY

The Lightstar 686 is equipped with the following standard features:

- 1.8 GHz Pentium M745 processor
- 400 MHz system bus
- 512 MB of DDR SDRAM memory
- 60 GB hard drive
- 15-inch LCD panel monitor
- 128 MB graphics card
- 802.11 G wireless networking
- 56 K data and fax modem
- DVD/CD-RW combo drive

Begins by thanking Gemini for using Omega's services and suggests ways Omega can further help

Clearly identifies and quantifies the problem and why it is important to solve

Provides documented endorsement

Gives a detailed list of features and specifications

Continued

Figure 14.7   (Continued)

2.

Your Lightstar will allow you to fax, e-mail, and connect to the Web. Please visit our website (*http://www.omegatech.com*) for more details about Lightstar's technical specifications.

Details Light-star's many advantages, each clearly and persua-sively listed under easy-to-follow headings

Cost Effective

Your Lightstar 686 will cost far less than your PCs and offer equal or greater capability. Here are some of the bottom-line savings you can expect:

- costs $500.00 less than one of your PCs did two years ago
- provides software upgrades at no charge
- includes everything integrated into the system—monitor, CPU, software

Assured Security

Lightstar offers a unique protection system to ensure the security of your unit:

- an encryption system requiring a special password to log on and activate your notebook
- a special feature known as "call home" that will alert you to unauthorized use
- virus protection software

Efficient Accessibility and Customer Service

Because the Lightstar is compatible with your office network, your representatives can access all pertinent records at your main office while making sales calls. By having direct access to vital documentation, your staff can more efficiently verify, fulfill, and store information about customer orders. The Lightstar makes the virtual office a reality. And because your sales force would be carrying your office with them, you will enhance their telecommuting capabilities now and into the future.

Shows how Lightstar is compatible with Gemini's current tech-nology and is, therefore, easy to use

Power Supply Capabilities

Equipped with a lithium ion battery, the Lightstar 686 operates up to six hours without recharging, enabling your staff to make calls at any location for extended periods of time.

Portability

- weighs only 5.6 pounds
- slips easily into a briefcase
- comes with protective, dent-proof case

TRAINING AND SERVICE

Because all software can be preloaded, setup and installation can be brief—ten minutes. Since Lightstar is compatible with Gemini's network, your staff will need only minimal training to know how to use the Lightstar to upload sales orders or download product availability information. To help Gemini with any technical needs, our local tech representative, Ory Mawfic, is available to instruct your staff

Continued

3.

about the operation and to provide routine maintenance of the Lightstar. If a problem occurs, we offer customers the latest in remote diagnostics.

COSTS

Below is an estimated price list for one Lightstar 686 notebook with upgraded features:

- 2 GHz Pentium M 755 processor
- 80 GB hard drive
- Integrated 10/100 NIC (network interface)
- 1024 MB of DDR SDRAM memory
- Second lithium ion battery

Total purchase price: **$1,999.00**

You might also consider adding one or all of these options:

Pentium M processor 770 (2.13 GHz)	$469.00
External speakers	$38.00
USB 2-button optical mouse	$20.00
Total for options:	**$527.00**

OMEGA TECHNOLOGIES' REPUTATION

For the past 16 years Omega Technologies has provided state-of-the-art computer technology and fast, efficient service after the sale. A list of references is attached.

We appreciate your past confidence in choosing Omega Technologies and look forward to providing further service to Gemini. Please call me if you have any questions about the Lightstar or Omega Technologies. I would be happy to bring a few Lightstar 686's to Gemini for you and your sales staff to use for a few days.

If this proposal is acceptable, please sign and return a copy with this letter.

Sincerely yours,

Marion Copely
Marion Copely

I accept the proposal made by Omega Technologies, Inc.

_____

for Gemini Consultants, Inc.
Encl.

Spells out costs exactly, including any options Gemini might select

Uses boldface for bottom-line figures

Provides a short history of Omega and supplies references

Closes with reference to past and favorable business to encourage future sales

- Does the writer's firm understand our problem?
- Can the writer's firm deliver the services it promises?
- Can the job be completed on time?
- Is the budget reasonable and realistic (neither inflated nor too low)?
- What assurances does the writer offer that the job will be done exactly as proposed?
- How has the writer demonstrated his/her trustworthiness?

Answer each of those questions by demonstrating how your product or service is tailored to the customer's needs.

Organizing a Sales Proposal

Most sales proposals include the following elements: introduction, description of the proposed product or service, timetable, costs, qualifications of your company, and conclusion.

Introduction

The introduction to your sales proposal can be a single paragraph in a short sales proposal or several pages in a more complex one. Basically, your introduction should prepare readers for everything that follows in your proposal. The introduction itself may contain the following sections, which sometimes may be combined.

   1. Statement of purpose and subject of proposal.   Tell readers why you are writing and identify the specific subject of your work. If you are responding to an RFP, use specific code numbers or cite application dates, as the proposal in Figure 14.5 does. If your proposal is unsolicited, indicate how you learned of the problem, as Figure 14.7 does. Briefly define the solution you propose. Tell them exactly what you propose to do for them. Be clear about what your plan covers and, if there could be any doubt, what it does not.

   2. Background of the problem you propose to solve.   In a solicited proposal like Figure 14.5, this section is usually unnecessary, because the potential client has already identified the problem and wants to know how you would address it. In that case, just point out how your company would solve the problem, mentioning your superiority over your competitors (see the third paragraph of Figure 14.5).

   In an unsolicited proposal, you need to describe the problem in convincing detail, identifying the specific trouble areas. Depending on the type of proposal you submit, you may want to focus briefly on the dimensions of the problem—when it was first observed, who/what it most acutely affects, and the specific organizational/community context in which the problem is most troubling. However, if it is an external proposal to a current customer, such as the one in Figure 14.7, it would be unwise to point out previous problems your client may have had with your company's service or products. In Figure 14.7 note how the problems of the staff in the field are described mainly as a way to sell the advantages of the Lightstar 686 notebook.

Description of the Proposed Product or Service

This section is the heart of your proposal. Before spending their money, customers will demand hard, factual evidence of what you claim can and should be done. Here are some points that your proposal should cover.

1. Carefully show potential customers that your product or service is right for them. Stress particular benefits of your product or service most relevant to your reader. Blend sales talk with descriptions of hardware, as the sections "Advanced Technology" and "Cost Effective" do in Figure 14.7.

2. Describe your work in suitable detail. Specify what the product looks like, what it does, and how consistently and well it will perform in the readers' office, plant, hospital, or agency. You might include a brochure, picture, diagram, or, as the writer of the proposal in Figure 14.5 does, a sample of your product for customers to study. Note how in Figure 14.7 the reader is given an independent website to consult about the Lightstar's capabilities and endorsement.

3. Stress any special features, maintenance advantages, warranties, or service benefits. Convince readers that your product is the most up-to-date and efficient one they could select. Highlight features that show the quality, consistency, or security of your work. For a service, emphasize the procedures you use, the terms of the service, even the kinds of tools you use, especially any state-of-the-art equipment.

Timetable

A carefully planned timetable shows readers that you know your job and that you can accomplish it in the right amount of time. Your dates should match any listed in an RFP. Provide specific dates to indicate

- when the work will begin
- how the work will be divided into phases or stages
- when you will be finished
- whether any follow-up visits or services are involved

For proposals offering a service, specify how many times—an hour, a week, a month—customers can expect to receive your help; for example, spraying two times a month for an exterminating service.

Costs

Make your budget accurate, complete, and convincing. Don't underestimate costs in the hope that a low bid will win you the job. You may get the job but lose money doing it, because the customer will rightfully hold you to your unrealistic figures. Accepted by both parties, a proposal is a binding legal agreement. Neither should you inflate prices; competitors will beat you in the bidding.

Give customers more than merely the bottom-line cost. Show exactly what readers are getting for their money so they can determine if everything they need is included. Itemize costs for

- specific services
- equipment/materials

- labor (by the hour or by the job)
- transportation
- travel
- training

If something is not included or is considered optional, say so—additional hours of training, replacement of parts, upgrades, and the like.

If you anticipate a price increase, let the customer know how long current prices will stay in effect. That information may spur them to act favorably now.

Qualifications of Your Company

Emphasize your company's accomplishments and expertise in providing similar services and equipment. Mention the names of important local firms for whom you have worked that would be able to recommend you. But never misrepresent your qualifications or those of the individuals who work with or for you. Your prospective client may verify if you have in fact worked on similar jobs during the last five to six years.

Conclusion

This is the "call to action" section of your proposal. Encourage your reader to approve your plan by stressing major benefits of your plan. Offer to answer any questions the reader may have. Some proposals end by asking readers to sign and return a copy of the proposal indicating their acceptance, as the proposal in Figure 14.7 does. And build on any previous goodwill or business, as the last paragraph does in Figure 14.7, to further establish trust with your customer or client.

■ Proposals for Research Papers and Reports

You may have to write a proposal when your instructor asks you to submit a report or research paper, a topic for an independent study, or some other major term project.

Writing for Your Instructor

The principles guiding internal and sales proposals also apply to research proposals. As with internal and sales proposals, you will be writing to convince the reader—your instructor—to approve a major piece of work. But otherwise the goals of your instructor/reader will be considerably different from those of other proposal readers. An instructor will read your proposal to help you write the best possible paper or report and, in examining your proposal, will want to make sure of four things:

- that you have chosen a significant topic
- that you have a sufficiently restricted topic
- that you will investigate important sources of information about that topic
- that you can accomplish your work in the specified time

Your proposal gives your instructor an opportunity to spot omissions or inconsistencies and to provide helpful suggestions, as in Figure 14.8 (pp. 617–620).

To: Professor Leigh Felton-Parks
From: Barbara R. Shoemake B.R.S.
Date: February 4, 2005
Subject: Proposal for a report on the ethical and security issues involved in using e-mail

PURPOSE

For my term project I propose to research and write a report on the ethical and security issues involved in using e-mail in the workplace.

E-mail is the most frequently used form of business communication. It has been estimated that over 750 million e-mail users receive 15 billion messages per day, many for internal business communications. At West Technology, over 27,000 employees receive their company publications online through e-mail and listservs. Alexis Brown claims that "E-mail almost eclipses the reading rate of printed material" (*Public Relations Journal, http://www.prjournal.com* [Jan. 2005]: 25).

Despite its many advantages, e-mail presents major ethical and legal challenges. Using e-mail ethically can sometimes be a complicated issue for employees as well as their employers. E-mail privacy is at the heart of the controversy. Major legal battles have been waged over who can and should read an individual's e-mail at work. Similarly, court cases have been fought over companies using their employees' e-mail as evidence against them. More and more companies continue to reevaluate their standards for involvement in employees' e-mail rights, often requiring employees to sign an agreement to allow employers access to e-mail sent at the office. Likewise, a greater number of companies are demanding their employees attend training sessions regarding e-mail and Internet use at work. Understanding the ethical considerations and security drawbacks of e-mail is vital for managers evaluating their office's internal communications. My report will serve as a background report for those office managers.

PROBLEMS TO BE INVESTIGATED

At this preliminary stage of my research, I think my report will need to answer the following questions:

(1) How does e-mail differ from conventional communication methods (telephone, letters) and more recent technologies (instant messaging, blogs) in terms of confidentiality?

(2) Do employers have the right (or responsibility) to monitor employees' workplace e-mail or is this a violation of the employees' right to privacy?

(3) What can be done to establish a more secure e-mail system both to protect confidentiality and to ensure company security?

Concisely states purpose

Demonstrates importance of topic with statistics

Provides further detail about the scope and significance of the problem to be investigated

Identifies audience for whom paper is intended

Highlights questions the paper will explore

Continued

Figure 14.8   (Continued)

Shoemake 2

(4) What types of special training programs—on business communication, netiquette, document security software, virus alerts, and legal issues—are most necessary and effective for e-mail use?

Outlines tenta-tive organiza-tion of report

I propose, therefore, to divide the body of my paper according to the four key issues of confidentiality, monitoring, security, and training.

METHODS OF RESEARCH

I will survey recent literature dealing with e-mail and security and then attempt to do some primary research as well by interviewing a few local experts. Judging from the number of entries found on this general topic through the search engines Google, Lycos, MSN, Yahoo!, and AltaVista, e-mail is both a popular and significant topic. But in order to restrict my topic I narrowed my keyword search to concentrate on e-mail security and ethical issues as they affect managers, thus filtering out irrelevant search results. From a preliminary check of what is available from the holdings at McGovern Library and available to me online, I believe the following sources may be most useful.

Gives detailed lists of primary and secondary sources to be consulted, with rationale

Brown, Alexis. "A Study of E-Mail versus Printed Material." *Public Relations Journal* (Jan. 2005): 25. <http://www.prjournal.com>

Cowper, Jamie. "The Threat Within: Why Businesses Need to Manage and Monitor Employee E-Mail Usage." *Help Net Security* 14 Feb. 2005. 10 March 2005 <http://www.net-security.org/article.php?id=767>

Cruiz-Taylor, Deana. "Is It Corporate or Confidential or Both?: Security and Rights in Sending/Receiving Company E-Mail." *E-Commerce* 19.2 (2005): 14–19.

"E-Mail Policy." *E-Mail Policy.com.* 2004. 4 March 2005 <http://www.email-policy.com/>

Uses proper MLA style for documentation

Fetissov, Nikolai N. "Securing Electronic Mail in a Small Company." *SANS Institute White Paper* 12 (May 2005): 1–15.

Hernandez, Pedro, Mary Melka, and G. T. Kaplan. "The Legal Foundations for Monitoring Employee E-Mail." *Ethics and Commerce* 4 (February 2003): 7–12.

"Internet Mail Consortium." 29 Jan. 2005. 4 Feb. 2005 <http://www.imc.org/>

"Is Your E-Mail Safe?" *Business Technology* 9 (2003): 73–77.

Kangas, Erik. "The Case for Secure E-Mail." *LuxSci.* 2005. 3 March 2005 <http://luxsci.com/extranet/articles/email-security.html>

Continued

(Continued)   Figure 14.8

Shoemake 3

Klein, Karen E. "Writes and Wrongs of Online Security." *Business Week* 9 Dec. 2004. 6 April 2005 <http://www.businessweek.com/smallbiz/content/dec2004/sb2004129_5388_sb006.htm>

Klein, Penny. "2005—A Year for New Security Policies." *eSecurity Planet* 23 Jan. 2005. 5 Feb. 2005 <http://www.esecurityplanet.com/views/article.php/3463181>

Ricks, Shameeka. "Training Your Staff to Send Secure and Professional E-Mail." *Office Protocol and Systems* 17 (2003): 75–78.

Shih, Dong, and Hsiu-Sen Chiang. "E-Mail Viruses: How Organizations Can Protect Their E-Mails." *Online Information Review* 28.5 (2004): 356–66.

Shinder, Debbie. "E-Mail Spam: Is It a Security Issue?" *Windows Security* 22 July 2004. 11 Jan. 2005 <http://www.windowssecurity.com/articles/Email_Spam.html>

Singh, Ali. *E-Mail—Legal Issues: A Specially Commissioned Report.* London: Thorogood, 2004.

Spykerman, Mike. "Is E-Mail Monitoring Legal?" *Spydex.com.* 2004. 2 April 2005 <http://www.spydex.com/article-email-monitoring-legality.html>

Sunner, Mark. "The Role of E-Mail Security in Meeting Regulatory Requirements." *Help Net Security* 27 Jan. 2005. 4 March 2005 <http://www.net-security.org/article.php?id=762>

"Weblog: News from the Lab." [Weblog]. *F-Secure.* 6 March 2005 <http://www.f-secure.com/weblog/>

Zhang, Sherry. *E-Mail: Privacy, Ethics, and the Corporate World.* Boston: Business Publications, 2003.

Cites only most current and relevant sources

I also intend to interview two human resources managers in Springfield whose companies have offered employee seminars on e-mail security in the past year. My choices right now are Alice Phillips at Dodge & Spenser Systems and Faqua Azmar at General Dynamics. Because of possible schedule conflicts, I may have to interview two other individuals such as the business managers at Mercy Hospital and e-Tech, Inc.

Identifies need for additional interviews

Continued

Figure 14.8   (Continued)

Shoemake 4

Specifies schedule and how to meet it

SCHEDULE
I hope to complete my research by April 4 and my interviews by April 8. Then I will spend the following two weeks working on a draft, which I will submit by April 19, the date you specified. After receiving your comments on my draft, I will work on revisions and the final copy of my report and turn it in by May 13, the last day of class. I will submit two progress reports—one when I finish my research and another when I decide on the final organization of my paper—as you have instructed.

Offers contact information; requests feedback

REQUEST FOR APPROVAL
I ask that you approve my topic and my approach to it. I would appreciate any suggestions on how you think I might best proceed. My e-mail address is bshoemake@bsu.edu, if you prefer to send them to me online.

Thank you.

To prepare an effective proposal for a research project, you must do some preliminary research. You cannot pick any topic that comes to mind or guess about procedures, sources, or conclusions. As other proposal readers do, your instructor will want convincing and specific evidence for your choice of topic and your approach to it. Be prepared to cite key facts to show that you are familiar with the topic and that you can write about it confidently and knowledgeably.

Be very clear about the type of research you will do and what resources you intend to use. For example, you need to investigate your topic through the following sources before you write a research proposal for your instructors:

- Internet—list relevant websites you have consulted
- Search engines/databases—for a working bibliography
- Books and articles, online and print—but only those that bear directly on your topic
- Interviews—whether in person, over e-mail, instant messaging, blogs, and so on
- Proposed visits to relevant sites—laboratories, salt marshes, health care facilities, plants, offices, and so on

Review pages 300–314 of Chapter 8 on primary and secondary research methods.

Organization of a Proposal for a Research Paper

Your proposal for a school research project can be a memo or an e-mail divided into five sections, as illustrated in Figure 14.8: *introduction* (or purpose), *scope of the problem* or topic to be investigated, *methods or procedures, timetable,* and *re-*

quest for approval. However, be ready to reorder or expand these sections if your instructor wants you to follow a different organizational plan.

The Introduction

Keep your introduction short—a paragraph, maybe two, pinpointing the subject and purpose of your work.

> I propose to research and write a report about the "hot knife" laser used in treating port wine stains and other birthmarks.

> I intend to investigate the relationship that exists between office design and employees' need for "psychological space."

Then briefly indicate why the topic or the problem you propose to study is significant. In other words, be prepared to explain why you have chosen that topic and why research on it is relevant or worthwhile for a specific audience or course objective. Note how Barbara R. Shoemake in Figure 14.8 states how and why her report will be useful to office managers.

Supply your instructor/reader with a few background details about your topic, for example, the importance of using a laser as opposed to conventional ways of treating birthmarks or why psychological space plays a crucial role in employee productivity and morale. Prove that you have thought carefully about selecting a significant, relevant topic.

The Scope of the Problem or Topic to Be Investigated

The second section, which might be entitled "Problems to Be Investigated" or "Areas to Be Studied," shows how you propose to break the topic into meaningful units. Tell your reader what specific issues, points, or areas you hope to investigate. Doing that, you demonstrate how you will limit your topic.

Some instructors ask students to formulate a list of questions their research paper or report intends to answer. The topics included in such questions or in a list of areas or problems to be covered might later become major sections of your paper. Make sure the issues or questions do not overlap and that each relates directly to and supports your restricted topic. Note how the student in Figure 14.8 hopes to divide her study of e-mail into four distinct yet related areas.

Methods or Procedures

In the third section of your proposal inform your instructor how you expect to find the answers to the questions you raised in the previous section or how you intend to locate information about your list of subtopics. It's not enough to write, "I will gather appropriate information and analyze it." Specify what data you hope to include, where they are located, and how you intend to retrieve them.

Most students gather data from the Web and from literature published in print sources about their topics. (In fact, many research papers are based exclusively on literature searches.) The literature can include

- websites/sources
- books
- encyclopedias or other reference materials, such as statistical data found in manuals or almanacs, online and in print

- articles in professional journals in print and online
- newspapers, online and in print
- reviews

Inform your instructor what indexes, abstracts, or Internet searches you intend to use (review pp. 325–334) as part of your research. To document your preliminary work, provide your instructor with a list of appropriate titles on your topic following the style of documentation used for a Works Cited page (discussed on pp. 355–368).

In addition to online and print materials, you might collect information from primary research, including lab experiments, field tests, interviews with experts, questionnaires, or a combination of any of those sources.

Timetable/Schedule

Indicate when and in what order you expect to complete the different phases of your project. Your instructor needs that information to keep track of your progress and to make sure you will turn in an assignment on time. Specify tentative dates for completing your research, draft(s), revisions, and final copy.

Some instructors also ask students to turn in progress reports (see pp. 638–644) at regular intervals. If you are asked to do that, indicate when you will submit the progress reports, as Barbara R. Shoemake does in Figure 14.8.

Request for Approval

End your proposal with a request for approval of your topic and a plan of action. You might also invite suggestions from your instructor on how to restrict, research, organize, or write about your topic.

▎A Final Reminder

This chapter has given you some basic information and specific strategies for writing winning proposals. Keep in mind that a proposal presents a plan to a decision maker for his or her approval. To win that approval, your proposal must be (a) *realistic,* (b) *carefully researched,* (c) *highly persuasive,* and (d) *visually appealing and easy to follow.* Those essential characteristics apply to internal proposals in memo or e-mail format written to your employer, more formal sales proposals sent to a potential customer, and research proposals submitted to your instructor.

Online Study Center

Access the writing proposals Revision Checklist online at college .hmco.com/pic/ kolin8e

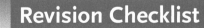 ## Revision Checklist

☐ Established and distinguished roles of collaborative team members involved in the preparation of the proposal.
☐ Researched appropriate sources for RFPs and followed their instructions.

Continued

Continued

- ☐ Identified a realistic problem, one that is restricted and relevant to my topic and my audience's needs.
- ☐ Tried effectively to convince audience that the problem exists and needs to be solved.
- ☐ Used headings, white space, lists, and professional-looking font to make proposal visually attractive and reader friendly.
- ☐ Incorporated quantifiable details demonstrating the scope and importance of the problem.
- ☐ Persuasively emphasized benefits of solving the problem according to the proposal; incorporated the "you attitude" throughout.
- ☐ Investigated and overcame competing alternatives or firms.
- ☐ Offered a solution that can be realistically implemented—that is, it is both appropriate and feasible for audience.
- ☐ Wrote clearly so audience can understand how and why my proposal would work.
- ☐ Researched background of problem.
- ☐ Used specific figures and concrete details to show how proposal saves time, money.
- ☐ Double-checked proposal to catch errors, omissions, and inconsistencies.
- ☐ Avoided exaggerations and underbidding.
- ☐ Presented information ethically.
- ☐ Organized proposal with appropriate headings for clarity and ease of reading.
- ☐ *For internal proposal:* Demonstrated how proposal benefits my company and my supervisor; took into account office politics in describing problem and solution; discussed proposal with co-workers or supervisors who may be affected.
- ☐ *For sales proposal:* Related my product or service to prospective customer's needs; showed a clear understanding of those needs.
- ☐ Prepared a comprehensive and realistic budget; accounted for all expenses; itemized costs of products and services in sales proposal.
- ☐ Provided a timetable with exact dates for implementing proposal.
- ☐ Cited other successful jobs and satisfied clients to show my company's track record.
- ☐ Concluded proposal with a summary of main benefits to readers and a call to action.
- ☐ Proved to my instructor that I researched the problem by supplying a list of possible references and sources for a proposal for a research report/paper.

Exercises

Online Study Center
Find additional writing proposals exercises at college.hmco.com/ pic/kolin8e

1. In two or three paragraphs identify and document a problem (in services, safety, communication, traffic, scheduling) you see in your office or your community. Make sure you give your reader—a civic official (head of a department) or

employer (section or department head; manager)—specific evidence that a problem does exist and that it needs to be corrected.

2. Write a short internal proposal, modeled after Figure 14.6, based on the problem you identified in Exercise 1.

3. Write a short internal proposal, similar to Tina Escobar and Oliver Jabur's in Figure 14.6, recommending to a company or a college a specific change in procedure, technology, training, safety, personnel, or policy. Make sure your team provides an appropriate audience (college administrator, department manager, or section chief) with specific evidence about the existence of the problem and your solution of it. Possible topics include
   a. providing more and safer parking/lighting
   b. forming a Usenet or listserv group
   c. purchasing new office or laboratory equipment or software
   d. hiring more faculty, student workers, or office help
   e. reorganizing or redesigning the school yearbook or company annual report or sales catalog or website
   f. changing the decor/furniture in a student or company lounge
   g. increasing the number of weekend, night, or online classes in your major
   h. adding more health-conscious offerings to the school or company cafeteria menu
   i. altering the programming on a campus radio station
   j. expanding distance learning offerings

4. Write an unsolicited sales proposal, similar to the one in Figure 14.7, on one of the following services or products you intend to sell or on a topic your instructor approves.
   a. providing exterminating service to a store or restaurant
   b. supplying a hospital with rental television sets for patients' rooms
   c. designing websites
   d. obtaining temporary office help or nursing care
   e. supplying landscaping and lawn care work
   f. testing for noise, air, or water pollution in your community or neighborhood
   g. furnishing transportation for students, employees, or members of a community group
   h. offering technical consulting service to save a company money
   i. digging a septic well for a small apartment complex
   j. supplying insurance coverage to a small firm (five to ten employees)
   k. cleaning the parking lot and outside walkways at a shopping center
   l. selling a piece of equipment to a business
   m. making a work area safer
   n. preparing a technology seminar or training program for employees
   o. increasing donations to a community or charitable fund
   p. offering discounted memberships at a fitness center

5. Write a solicited proposal for one of the topics listed in Exercise 4 or for a topic that your instructor approves. You might want to review Figure 14.5. Do this exercise as a collaborative effort.

6. Write an appropriate proposal—internal, solicited sales, or unsolicited sales—based on the information contained in one of the following three articles. Assume that you or your prospective customer's company or community faces a problem similar to one discussed in one of these articles. Use as much of the information in the article as you need and add any details of your own that you think are necessary. This exercise can be done as an individual or collaborative assignment.

(a) Multiuse Campuses: A Plan That Works

Gaylord Community School in Gaylord, Michigan, is a bustling center of activity from the first light of dawn to well after dusk. People of all ages come and go until late into the evening for a multitude of activities that include attending classes and meetings, catching up with friends, getting a flu shot, and seeing a play. That's because in addition to a high school, the campus also includes senior and day-care centers, classrooms for adult education, an auditorium for the performing arts, a community health care site, and even a space that can be booked for weddings and other special occasions.

In Big Lake, Minnesota, elementary, middle, and high school buildings are all situated on one centrally located campus that makes up the entire Big Lake School District. Also included in this innovative layout are a state-of-the-art theater, a community resource center, and a multipurpose athletic arena, all of which are used extensively by the entire community.

Both the Gaylord and Big Lake schools are models of a growing movement toward multiuse community campuses that serve as "anchor[s] in the civic life of our nation," according to U.S. Secretary of Education Richard W. Riley. I recently had the pleasure of visiting Secretary Riley in his office. Also present were AARP President Joe Perkins and National Retired Teachers Association Director Annette Norsman, both of whom are involved in many facets of education and lifelong learning.

We discussed many things, including our concerns about the current increase in the number of students caused by the Baby Boom echo (children of the Boomers) and how that population is going to further stress the already crumbling infrastructure of American schools. We also talked about the need for resources—to employ more teachers, bring technology into the classroom, strengthen educational curriculum and opportunities for all ages—and the pressing need to build and renovate schools. That led to a discussion about the necessity and benefit of involving the whole community in the design and use of new school facilities.

I always thought that it was a shame that the majority of schools are used only a third of the day, three fourths of the year, by only a fifth of the population. Considering that there will be more school construction over the next decade than at any time since the 1950s, it just makes sense to consider the intergenerational and community benefits of multiuse spaces, benefits that include everything from establishing better learning environments to getting more bang for the tax buck.

There are many additional bonuses for multiuse educational complexes: They create an exciting community hub, bring life and culture to a central area, and revitalize and nourish the neighborhood in which they are located.

It's a win-win situation for everyone involved.

(b) Self-Illuminating Exit Signs

The Marine Corps Development and Education Center (MCDEC), Quantico, Virginia, submitted a project recently, to replace incandescent illumination exit signs with self-illuminating exit signs for a cost of $97,238. The first-year savings were anticipated to be about $37,171 with an anticipated payback time of 2.6 years—an excellent prospect. The contractor bid much lower, however, and the actual payback will be about 1.5 years.

What are the benefits of these self-illuminating exit signs? The primary benefit is that virtually all operation and maintenance expense is eliminated for the life of the device, normally from 10 to 12 years. Power failures or other disturbances will not cause them to go out.

In new construction, expensive electrical circuits can be totally eliminated. In retrofits, the release of a dedicated circuit for other use may be of considerable benefit. Initial total cost of installing circuits and conventional devices approximately equals the cost of the self-illuminating signs. Installation labor and expense for the self-illuminating signs is about that of hanging a picture.

The amount of electricity saved varies and depends on whether your existing fixtures are fluorescent (13 to 26 watts) or incandescent (50 to 100 watts). Multiply the number of fixtures $\times$ wattage/fixture $\times$ hours operated/day $\times$ days/year = KWH/year savings. For example, assume:

$$400 \text{ incandescent fixtures}$$
$$\$0.08/\text{KWH } 0.05 \text{ KW/fixture}$$
$$24 \text{ hours/day } 365 \text{ day/year operation}$$
$$400 \times 0.1 \times 365 = 350400 \text{ KWH/year}$$
$$350400 \times 0.08 = \$28,032/\text{year for electricity}$$

Now add in savings achieved from:

- reducing labor to change bulbs
- avoiding bulb material, stocking, and storage costs
- avoiding transportation costs involved in bulb changes
- reusing existing bulbs

The above savings can be significant. For the MCDEC Quantico project, estimates of bulb change interval and savings were 700 hours (29 days) and $13,512/year when all factors were considered.

The cost of a self-illuminating sign depends on whether one or two faces are illuminated primarily and varies between different suppliers. Single-face prices will likely be $100 to $150 while double-face prices may be $250 to $330. The contractor at Quantico found better prices than these ranges indicate. The labor cost should be about $10 per sign.

If you can use an exit-sign system with high dependability, no maintenance, and zero operations cost in your retrofit on new construction projects, try a self-illuminating exit-sign system in your economic analysis today. "Isolite" signs, by Safety Light Corp., are listed as FSC (Fire Safety Code) Group 99, Part IV, Section A, Class 9905 signs and are available through GSA contract. Contact Gerald Harnett, Safety Light Corp., P.O. Box 266, Greenbelt, MD 20070 for more information.

Lt. James F. McCollum, CEG, USN. "Self-Illuminating Exit Signs Equal High Payback." *Navy Civil Engineer* (Summer 1983): 30–31.

(c) Wheelchair-Lift Switch Covers

In order to ensure year-round access to the Springfield Armory National Historic Site (Massachusetts) museum, Michael C. Trebbe designed the cover for switches on wheelchair lifts. During the extreme New England winters, the switch buttons would freeze, thus making the lift inoperable, which in turn required several hours to thaw. The installation of these covers prevented the freezing of the switch buttons and, therefore, allowed maintenance personnel to attend to matters such as snow removal.

The covers were made of materials found on site, which resulted in the covers being almost cost free. The covers can be quickly built, and they are mounted with the same mounting screws as the switch boxes so as to not destroy any original fabric (in the case of Springfield Armory NHS, brownstone). The materials used included:

- 1/8-in. by 4½-in. by 12-in. piece of rubber mat
- 3½-in. by 6½-in. piece of sheet metal
- three aluminum pop rivets
- primer for the sheet metal
- wheelchair symbol
- white paint for the symbol

The sheet metal is bent to a 90-degree angle at the 5½-inch point. The lowest two holes (see diagram) are drilled to mount the screws of the switch box, which also secure the cover. Triangular cutouts and other holes are drilled for the clearance of the housing screws on the rear of the switch box (see diagram).

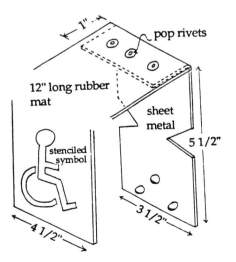

The handicap symbol is stenciled on the front of the piece of rubber mat using white paint.

Michael C. Trebbe, *Grist,* Vol. 36, No. 1 (Winter 1992). U.S. Department of the Interior, National Park Service.

7. Write a suitable research proposal on which the research paper on "The Advantage of Telecommuting in the Information Age" (pp. 383–405) could have been based.

8. Write a research proposal to your instructor seeking approval for a research-based long report. Do the necessary preliminary research to show that you have selected a suitable topic, narrowed it, and identified the sources of information you have to consult. List at least six relevant articles, two books, and two websites pertinent to your topic.

CHAPTER 15

Writing Effective Short Reports

This chapter shows you how to write short reports, also called informal or semiformal reports. A short report can be defined as an organized presentation of relevant data on any topic—money, travel, time, personnel, equipment, management—that a company or agency tracks in its day-to-day operations. Short reports are practical and to the point. They show that work is being done, and they also show your boss that you are alert, professional, and reliable. Short reports are written to co-workers, employers, vendors, and clients. When they are intended for individuals within your organization, short reports are most often sent as memos. But for clients you will send your reports out as letters.

Businesses cannot function without short written reports. Reports tell whether

- work is being completed
- schedules are being met
- costs have been contained
- sales projections are being met
- unexpected problems have been solved

You may write an occasional report in response to a specific request or question, or you may be required to write a daily or weekly report on routine activities.

Online Study Center

To expand your understanding of writing short reports, take advantage of the ACE quizzes, sample documents, Web links, and exercises at college.hmco.com/ pic/kolin8e

Types of Short Reports

To give you a sense of some of the topics you may be required to write about, here is a list of various types of short reports common in the business world.

appraisal report	inventory report	production report
audit report	investigative report	progress/activity report
budget report	justification report	recommendation report
construction report	laboratory report	research report
design report	manager's report	sales report
evaluation report	medicine/treatment	status report
experiment report	error report	survey report
feasibility report	operations report	test report
incident report	periodic report	trip/travel report

This chapter concentrates on the six most common types of reports you are likely to encounter in your professional work:

1. periodic reports
2. sales reports
3. progress reports
4. trip/travel reports
5. test reports
6. incident reports

The first five reports can be called **routine reports** because they give information about planned, ongoing, or recurring events. The sixth category, **incident reports**, are reports that describe events the writers did not anticipate—accidents, breakdowns, environmental mishaps, delivery delays, or work stoppages. All six, however, can be termed *short* reports because they deal with current happenings rather than long-range forecasts. Short reports focus on the "trees," not the "forest."

Tech Note

Creating Templates for Reports

You can use your word processor's template function to create professional-looking reports. Templates are predesigned formats for page layouts that specify style elements of a document, allowing you to automate designs for periodic, sales, progress, incident, and other types of reports. An existing template will format information to create a professional-looking report. Using templates, you reduce the risk of errors, omissions, and inconsistencies and ensure that you follow your company's style and format.

To create a specific report template, simply set the format options (such as font, margins, and line spacing) for a new document, typing place markers for your text (including headers, footnotes, and titles), importing custom visuals (such as a company logo), and saving the document as a template. When you need to create a new report using the template, simply open it, insert the content of your report, and save the document under a new file name as a standard word processing file. You can customize the formatting of any or all of the following style elements:

■ Headers, footnotes for a company address, titles, and dates
■ List formatting, such as bullet-point style, size, and indentation
■ Line spacing and text justification
■ Font style, size, and color
■ Standard graphics, for example, a flowchart or line divisions
■ Margin size, paragraph indentation, and columns

Continued

Continued

- Standard visual elements such as tables, which can also be filled with the data appropriate to your report
- Sidebars and box quotes
- Automatic table of contents based on the titles used in your report

But keep the following precautions in mind when using templates:

- Be sure to follow your company's style when creating templates, particularly those using a company logo.
- Double-check everything in the template to make sure it is appropriate for the type of report you're writing. Differences between reports will require visual adjustments.
- When creating a template with place markers to indicate the position of certain textual elements, insert them in boldface for emphasis. Using brackets (for example, **[type title here]** or **[body of text here]**) will highlight and thus emphasize these place holders.

Guidelines for Writing Short Reports

Although there are many kinds of short reports, they all are written for readers who need factual information so they can get a job accomplished. The following guidelines will help you write any short report successfully.

Do the Necessary Research

An effective short report needs the same careful planning that goes into other on-the-job writing. Your research may be as simple as instant messaging, e-mailing, or leaving a voice mail for a colleague or inspecting a piece of equipment. Or you may have to test or inspect a product or service or assess the relative merits of a group of competing products or services. Some frequent types of research you can expect to do on the job include:

- checking data in reference manuals or code books
- searching databases for recent discussions of a problem or procedure
- reading background information in professional and trade journals
- reviewing a client's file
- testing equipment
- performing an experiment or procedure
- conferring with colleagues, managers, vendors, or clients
- visiting and describing a site
- attending a conference

Follow these guidelines to do effective research for your short reports:

1. Take careful notes, either by hand, on your laptop, or on your PDA.
2. Record all necessary background information that helps readers understand why the report is being written.
3. Collect relevant factual data—dates, places, costs, technology, personnel, conditions.
4. Interview or consult key individuals whose comments and assessments are important to the success of your report. Don't leave essential viewpoints or people out of the loop.

Anticipate How an Audience Will Use Your Report

Consider how much your audience knows about your project and what types of information they need most. If your reader requests the report, he or she may be knowledgeable about your topic and approach. But you can't always assume readers will have such information or backgrounds. Employers, the largest audience for your reports, may not always know (or be interested in) the technical details of your work. Instead, they want bottom-line information—costs, personnel, organizational structure, problems, or delays. While co-workers may be familiar with your project, colleagues in other departments, consumers, or individuals outside your company (such as site inspectors or clients) may not. Accordingly, those readers may require more background information, definitions, and examples.

Tech Note

Using the Web to Write Short Reports

Many companies and government agencies provide the statistical raw data that go into various types of short reports—quarterly sales reports, employment figures, types and numbers of accidents/incidents, options for purchasing equipment. Downloading and incorporating information from these and other relevant sites gives readers the necessary documentation to accept a conclusion or recommendation.

Businesses also post progress reports. Large corporations such as General Motors or IBM help you see the progress of stocks and mutual funds, or find out what a company is making. Similarly, you can find other examples of progress reports on the Web ranging from how a building project is coming along to how a fund-raising goal is progressing, and ConsumerReports.org (*http://www.consumer-reports.org*) evaluates different brands or products.

Here are some sites that publish appropriate information for short reports:

Bureau of Transportation (*http://www.bts.gov*)
FAOSTAT Food and Agriculture Administration (*http://apps.fao.org*)
Federal Reserve (*http://www.federalreserve.gov*)

Continued

Continued

GM Buying Power
(*http://www.gmbuypower.com/app/gmbp/us/en/gmbp/gmbp/stage.html*)
Health Insurance Statistics (*http://www.census.gov/hhes/www/hlthins.html*)
IBM Research (*http://www.research.ibm.com*)
Lucent (*http://www.lucent.com*)
National Center for Educational Statistics (*http://nces.ed.gov*)
National Center for Health Statistics (*http://www.cdc.gov/nass*)
New York Stock Exchange (*http://www.nyse.com*)
Occupational Safety and Health Administration (*http://www.osha.gov*)
Statistics.com (*http://www.statistics.com*)
UNESCO Institute for Statistics (*http://www.uis.unesco.org*)
U.S. Department of Labor, Employment and Training Administration
(*http://www.doleta.gov*)

Maureen Curley

Be Objective and Ethical

Your readers will expect you to report the facts objectively and impartially—costs, sales, weather conditions, eyewitness accounts, observations, statistics, test measurements, and descriptions. Your reports should be truthful, accurate, and complete. Here are some guidelines.

- Avoid *guesswork.* If you don't know or have not yet found out, say so and indicate how you intend to find out.
- Do not substitute *impressions* or *unsupported personal opinions* for careful research.
- Provide a *straightforward* and *honest* account; don't exaggerate or minimize. Using biased, skewed, or incomplete data is unethical.

Your employer may also ask you to keep your report confidential and share the results with only key members of your organization. You may also want to review the section on ethics in business writing (pp. 26–33).

Organize Carefully

Organizing a short report effectively means that you include the right amount of information in the most appropriate places for your audience. Many times a simple chronological or sequential organization will be acceptable for your readers. As you organize your reports, help readers find information easily by using bullets or numbers, headings, and, where appropriate, visuals. Readers will expect your report to contain information on its purpose, findings, recommendations, and a conclusion, as described in the following sections.

Purpose

Always begin by telling readers why you are writing (your goal) and by alerting them to what you will discuss. Provide all necessary background information. For example, give your readers a summary of key events and details at the beginning to help them follow the remainder of the report quickly. When you establish the scope (or limits) of your report, you help readers zero in on specific times, places, procedures, or problems.

Findings

This should be the longest part of your report and contain the data you have collected—facts about prices, personnel, equipment, events, locations, incidents, the results of a survey, the status of a project, or tests. Gather the data from your research; personal observations; interviews; and/or conversations with co-workers, employers, or clients. Give readers the results, but do not overburden your reader.

Conclusion

Your conclusion tells readers what you think the data mean. A conclusion can summarize what has happened; review what actions were taken; or explain the outcome or results of a test, a visit, or a program.

Recommendations

A recommendation informs readers what specific actions you think your company or client should take—market a new product, hire more staff, institute safety measures, select among alternative plans or procedures, and so on. Recommendations must be *relevant, creditable,* and *reliable.* If they are not, your report could be responsible for sending your company down the wrong path. For example, if your budget recommendation report overestimates the amount of money left in the annual travel budget, your report might result in important business travel having to be canceled. Recommendations need to be based on the data you collected, the resources (budget) and schedule of your department and company, and the conclusions you have reached.

Note how the report in Figure 15.1 fails to help readers understand the organization and importance of the information. Note, too, how much harder it is for readers to wade through Figure 15.1, which does not include a visual, than to navigate Figure 15.2, the revised version of the report. Figure 15.2 (pp. 636–637, clearly illustrates effective report writing; it is an example of a periodic report. The reader is provided with information at regularly scheduled intervals—daily, weekly, bimonthly (twice a month).

The report in Figure 15.2, which was submitted to a police captain, carefully summarizes, organizes, and interprets the data collected over a three-month period from individual activity logs. Because of this report, Captain Alice Martin will be better able to plan future protection for the community and to recommend changes in police services.

Periodic Reports

Periodic reports, as their name signifies, provide readers with information at regularly scheduled intervals—daily, weekly, bimonthly (twice a month), monthly, quarterly. They help a company or agency keep track of the quantity and quality of the services it provides and the amount and types of work done by employees. Information in

An example of a poorly written, poorly organized, and poorly formatted short report.   Figure 15.1

To Serve and To Protect

GPD

Greenfield Police Department

Emergency 555-1000   **Administration** 555-1001   **Traffic** 555-1002

TO: Capt. Alice Martin
FROM: Sergeants Daniel Huxley, Jennifer Chavez,
            and Ivor Paz
SUBJECT: Crime rate
DATE: July 12, 2007

This report will let you know what happened this quarter as opposed to what happened last quarter as far as crimes are concerned in Greenfield. This report is based on statistics the department has given us over the quarter.

Here we'll let the facts speak for themselves. From Jan.–Mar. we saw 126 robberies while from Apr.–June we had 106. Home burglaries for this period: 43; last period: 36. 33 cars were stolen in the period before this one; now we have 40. Interestingly enough, last year at this time we had only 27 thefts. Four of them involved heirlooms.

Homicides were 9 this time versus 8 last quarter; assault and battery charges were 92 this time, 77 last time. Carrying a concealed weapon 11 (10 last quarter). We had 47 arrests (55 last quarter) for charges of possession of a controlled substance. Rape charges were 8, 1 less than last quarter. 319 citations this time for moving violations: speeding 158/98, and failing to observe the signals 165/102 last quarter. DUIs were good this quarter—only 45, or 23 fewer than last quarter.

Misdemeanors this time: disturbing peace 53; vagrancy/ public drunkenness 8; violating leash laws 32; violating city codes 39, including dumping trash. Last quarter the figures were 48, 59, 21, 43.

We believe this report is complete and up-to-date. We further hope that this report has given you all the facts you will need.

Poor format— some paragraphs indented, some not; margins too wide

Introduction doesn't tell reader anything about overall picture

Throws facts out without any sense of reader's needs

Irrelevant data

No analysis or guided commentary—just undigested numbers

Hard-to-follow comparisons and contrasts

Conclusion provides no summary or recommendation

Figure 15.2   A well-prepared quarterly report, revised from Figure 15.1.

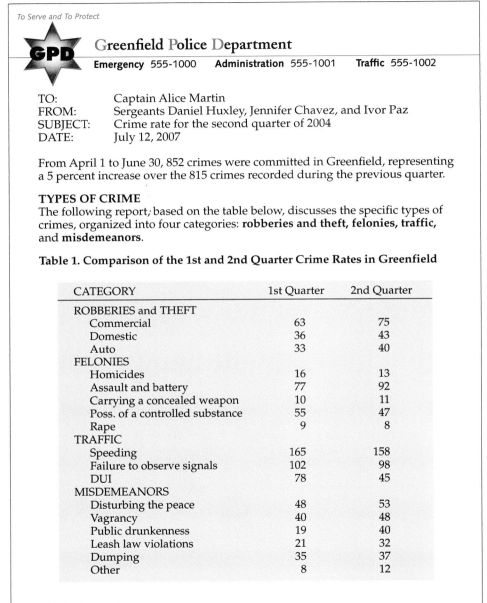

Begins with concise overview of report

Organizes crimes into categories and supplies easy-to-follow visual

Highlights visual

Provides essential background and statistical information and comparative analyses

To Serve and To Protect

Greenfield Police Department

GPD

Emergency 555-1000   **Administration** 555-1001   **Traffic** 555-1002

TO: Captain Alice Martin
FROM: Sergeants Daniel Huxley, Jennifer Chavez, and Ivor Paz
SUBJECT: Crime rate for the second quarter of 2004
DATE: July 12, 2007

From April 1 to June 30, 852 crimes were committed in Greenfield, representing a 5 percent increase over the 815 crimes recorded during the previous quarter.

TYPES OF CRIME
The following report, based on the table below, discusses the specific types of crimes, organized into four categories: **robberies and theft, felonies, traffic,** and **misdemeanors**.

Table 1. Comparison of the 1st and 2nd Quarter Crime Rates in Greenfield

CATEGORY	1st Quarter	2nd Quarter
ROBBERIES and THEFT		
Commercial	63	75
Domestic	36	43
Auto	33	40
FELONIES		
Homicides	16	13
Assault and battery	77	92
Carrying a concealed weapon	10	11
Poss. of a controlled substance	55	47
Rape	9	8
TRAFFIC		
Speeding	165	158
Failure to observe signals	102	98
DUI	78	45
MISDEMEANORS		
Disturbing the peace	48	53
Vagrancy	40	48
Public drunkenness	19	40
Leash law violations	21	32
Dumping	35	37
Other	8	12

Robberies and Theft
The greatest increase in crime was in robberies, 20 percent more than last quarter. Downtown merchants reported 75 burglaries, exceeding $985,000. The biggest theft occurred on May 21 at Weisenfarth's Jewelers when three armed robbers stole more than $97,000 in merchandise. (Suspects were

Continued

Page 2

apprehended two days later.) Home burglaries accounted for 43 crimes, though the thefts were not confined to any one residential area. We also had 40 car thefts reported and investigated.

Felonies
Homicides decreased slightly from last quarter—from 16 to 13. Charges for battery, however, increased—15 more than we had last quarter. Arrests for carrying a concealed weapon were nearly identical this quarter to last quarter's total. But the 47 arrests for possession of a controlled substance were appreciably down from the first quarter. Arrests for rape for this quarter also were less than last quarter's. Three of those rapes happened within one week (May 6–12) and have been attributed to the same suspect, now in custody.

Traffic
Traffic violations for this period were lower than last quarter's figures yet this quarter's citations for moving violations (335) represent a 5 percent increase over last quarter's (322). Most of the citations were issued for speeding (158) or for failing to observe signals (98). Officers issued 45 citations to motorists for DUI, an impressive decrease over the 78 DUIs issued last quarter. The new state penalty of withholding a driver's license for six months of anyone convicted of driving while under the influence appears to be an effective deterrent.

Misdemeanors
The largest number of arrests in this category were for disturbing the peace—53. Compared to last quarter, this is an increase of 10 percent. There were 88 charges for vagrancy and public drunkenness, an increase from the 59 charges from last quarter. We issued 32 citations for violations of leash laws, which represents a sizable increase over last quarter's 21 citations. Thirty-seven citations were issued for dumping trash at the Mason Reservoir.

CONCLUSION
Overall, while the crime rate has decreased in traffic (especially DUIs) and possession of controlled substances this quarter, we have seen a marked increase in arrests for robberies and battery.

Summarizes findings of report

RECOMMENDATIONS
To help deter robberies in the downtown area, we recommend the following:

- increasing surveillance units in the area
- offering merchants our workshop on safety and security precautions, as we did during the first quarter

Historically, battery arrests have risen during the second quarter. Our recommendations to counter that trend include:

- continuing to work closely with Neighborhood Watch Groups
- including more foot and bicycle patrols in the neighborhoods with the highest incidence of battery complaints

Lists specific actions/ changes department should make based on conclusion of report

periodic reports helps managers make schedules, order materials, assign personnel, budget funds, and, generally speaking, determine corporate needs.

Figure 15.2 provides essential police information clearly and concisely. As we saw, it summarizes, organizes, and interprets the data collected over a three-month period from individual activity logs. Because of this report, Captain Alice Martin will be better able to plan future protection for the community and to recommend changes in police services.

Sales Reports

Sales reports provide businesses with a necessary and ongoing record of accounts, online and mail purchases, losses, and profits over a specified period of time. They help businesses assess past performance and plan for the future. In doing that, they fulfill two functions: **financial** and **managerial**. As a financial record, sales reports list costs per unit, discounts or special reductions, and subtotals and totals. Like a spreadsheet, sales reports show gains and losses. They may also provide statistics for comparing two quarters' sales.

Sales reports are also a managerial tool because they help businesses make both short- and long-range plans. The restaurant manager's sales report illustrated in Figure 15.3 guides the owners in planning which popular entrées to highlight and which unpopular ones to change or delete. Note how the recommendations follow logically from the figures Sam Jelinek gives to Gina Smeltzer and Alfonso Zapatta, the owners of The Grill.

Progress Reports

A progress report informs readers about the status of an ongoing project. It lets them know how much and what type of work has been done by a particular date, by whom, how well, and how close the entire job is to being completed. A progress report emphasizes whether you are

- maintaining your schedule
- staying within your budget
- using the proper equipment
- making the right assignments
- identifying an unexpected problem or possible glitch
- providing adjustments in schedules, personnel, and so on
- completing the job efficiently, correctly, and according to codes

Almost any kind of ongoing work can be described in a progress report—research for a paper, construction of an apartment complex, preparation of a website, documentation of a patient's rehabilitation. These reports are often prepared at key phases, or milestones, in a project.

Audience and Length for a Progress Report

A progress report is intended for individuals who are not generally working alongside you but who need a record of your activities to coordinate them with other individuals' efforts and to learn about problems or changes in plans. For example,

A sales report to a manager.   **Figure 15.3**

Thegrill

Dayton, OH 43210 • (813) 555-4000 • (813) 555-4100 fax   www.Thegrill.com

TO: Gina Smeltzer   DATE: June 28, 2007
        Alfonso Zapatta, Owners
FROM: Sam Jelinek S J.   SUBJECT: Analysis of entrée sales,
        Manager   June 10–16 and June 17–23

As we agreed at our monthly meeting on June 4, here is my analysis of entrée sales for two weeks to assist us in our menu planning. Below is a record of entrée sales for the weeks of June 10–16 and June 17–23 that I have compiled into a table for easier comparisons.

Gives purpose and scope of report

	Portion size	June 10–16		June 17–23		2 weeks combined	
		Amount	Percentage	Amount	Percentage	Amount	Percentage
Cornish Hen	6 oz.	238	17	307	17	545	17
Stuffed Young Turkey	8 oz.	112	8	182	10	294	12
Broiled Salmon Steak	8 oz.	154	11	217	12	371	13
Brook Trout	12 oz.	182	13	252	14	434	9
Prime Rib	10 oz.	168	12	198	11	366	11
Lobster Tails	2–4 oz.	147	10	161	9	308	10
Delmonico Steak	10 oz.	56	4	70	4	126	4
Moroccan Chicken	6 oz.	343	25	413	23	756	24
		1,400	**100**	**1,800**	**100**	**3,200**	**100**

Organizes findings of the report in helpful table

Boldfaces totals

Recommendations

Based on the figures in the table above, I recommend that we do the following:

1. Order at least 100 more pounds of prime rib each two-week period to be eligible for further quantity discounts from the Northern Meat Company.
2. Delete the Delmonico steak entrée because of its low acceptance.
3. Introduce a new chicken or fish entrée to take the place of the Delmonico steak; I would suggest grilled lemon chicken to accommodate those patrons interested in tasty, low-fat, lower-cholesterol entrées.

Offers precise and relevant recommendations

Please give me your reactions within the next week. It shouldn't take more than a few days to implement these changes.

Requests authorization to implement recommendations

since supervisors (or non-native speakers of English who manage overseas offices) may not be in the field or branch office, they will rely on your progress report for much of their information. Customers, such as a contractor's clients, expect reports on how carefully their money is being spent, if schedules are being met, and whether there is a risk of going over the budget.

The length of the progress report will depend on your audience and on the complexity of the project. A short e-mail about organizing a time management workshop, such as that in Figure 15.4, might be all that is necessary. A report to an instructor about the progress a student is making on a research paper easily could be handled in a memo, such as Barbara Shoemake's progress report in Figure 15.5

Figure 15.4   A one-time progress report sent as an e-mail.

Reply   Save   Forward   Print   Delete

To:	\<ksands@multiplex.org\>
From:	\<pjavon@multiplex.org\>
Date:	Oct. 12, 2006 1:23:31 PM EDT
Subject:	Preparations for Time Management Workshop

Refers to reader's needs

As you requested last week, I e-mailed the managers of all departments in both our Trenton and Frankfurt, Germany, offices on Monday, October 9, to remind them of the time management workshop we will be offering on November 9 by teleconference.

Summarizes work done by citing specific dates, places, names, and means of collaboration

I have confirmed the date and the operation of the technical links and relays with Carmen Suarez in Technical Services and have also e-mailed Jürgen Weiss in Frankfurt to make sure things are in place there.

I have reserved the corporate conference center for November 9 and have ordered DTP copies of all the packets we will need. The packets going to Germany will be Jet-Expressed, overnight delivery, on November 5 so they will be in Frankfurt two days before the teleconference.

Assures reader that project is on schedule

By tomorrow, I will complete a list of all those employees scheduled to participate in the workshop and send it to you.

Plans are going according to schedule.

Philip Javon, Projects Coordinator
Trenton Branch
3800 S. Morris
Hershey, PA 12346
VOICE: 657-555-1719
\<Pjavon@multiplex.org\>

or her research paper described in the proposal in Chapter 14 (pp. 617–620). Similarly, Dale Brandt's assessment of the progress his construction company is making in renovating Dr. Burke's office is given in a two-page letter in Figure 15.6.

A progress report from a student to a teacher.   **Figure 15.5**

TO: Professor Leigh Felton-Parks
FROM: Barbara R. Shoemake *B.R.S.*
DATE: April 7, 2005
SUBJECT: First Progress Report on Research Paper

This is the first of two progress reports that you asked me to submit about my research paper on the ethical and security issues of using e-mail.

Clearly states purpose of the report

From March 8 until April 6, I gathered information from our library holdings, the Internet, and an interview. Of the nineteen references listed in my proposal, I found only twelve. Articles by Cruiz-Taylor ("Corporate or Confidential") and Hernandez et al. ("Legal Foundations for Monitoring Employee E-Mail") are not available in our library or on the Internet. Two of my Internet sites—"Internet Mail Consortium" and eSecurity Planet (for Klein)—are under construction. But eSecurity Planet will be open in the next few days. In the meantime, I'll try to replace "Internet Mail Consortium."

Provides up-date by citing individual references and actions taken

On February 23, I had an extended interview (1½ hours) with Faqua Azmar of General Dynamics, who gave me some seminar handouts as well as a copy of a report on e-mail protocols that she wrote for the Society of Midwest Business Communicators—materials I hope to incorporate in my report.

Details results of primary research

Because of an extended trip to Denver, Alice Phillips of Dodge & Spenser could not meet with me. At her suggestion, I am trying to schedule an interview with Robert Sims, the Documents Manager at Mid-Atlantic Power Company. Mr. Sims has given several seminars on e-mail security. Even if Ms. Phillips cannot meet with me, Ms. Azmar gave me enough information about a business manager's view of systems. However, not currently having the articles and websites listed above may slow, but not stop, my work.

Gives detailed descriptions of steps in the research process

Starting tomorrow, I will begin my paper and can submit a draft by April 27. You will receive my second progress report by April 20.

Concludes with next steps

Figure 15.6   The second of three progress reports from a contractor to a customer.

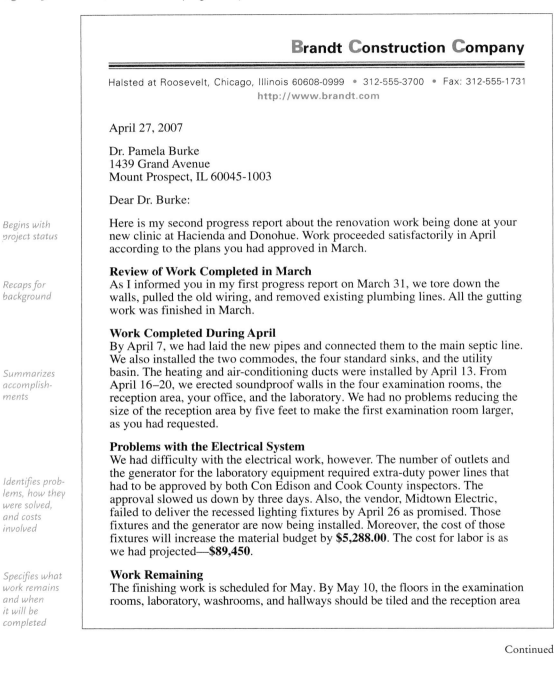

Brandt Construction Company

Halsted at Roosevelt, Chicago, Illinois 60608-0999 • 312-555-3700 • Fax: 312-555-1731
http://www.brandt.com

April 27, 2007

Dr. Pamela Burke
1439 Grand Avenue
Mount Prospect, IL 60045-1003

Dear Dr. Burke:

Begins with project status

Here is my second progress report about the renovation work being done at your new clinic at Hacienda and Donohue. Work proceeded satisfactorily in April according to the plans you had approved in March.

Review of Work Completed in March

Recaps for background

As I informed you in my first progress report on March 31, we tore down the walls, pulled the old wiring, and removed existing plumbing lines. All the gutting work was finished in March.

Work Completed During April

Summarizes accomplishments

By April 7, we had laid the new pipes and connected them to the main septic line. We also installed the two commodes, the four standard sinks, and the utility basin. The heating and air-conditioning ducts were installed by April 13. From April 16–20, we erected soundproof walls in the four examination rooms, the reception area, your office, and the laboratory. We had no problems reducing the size of the reception area by five feet to make the first examination room larger, as you had requested.

Problems with the Electrical System

Identifies problems, how they were solved, and costs involved

We had difficulty with the electrical work, however. The number of outlets and the generator for the laboratory equipment required extra-duty power lines that had to be approved by both Con Edison and Cook County inspectors. The approval slowed us down by three days. Also, the vendor, Midtown Electric, failed to deliver the recessed lighting fixtures by April 26 as promised. Those fixtures and the generator are now being installed. Moreover, the cost of those fixtures will increase the material budget by **$5,288.00**. The cost for labor is as we had projected—**$89,450**.

Work Remaining

Specifies what work remains and when it will be completed

The finishing work is scheduled for May. By May 10, the floors in the examination rooms, laboratory, washrooms, and hallways should be tiled and the reception area

Continued

page 2

and your office carpeted. By May 12, the reception area and your office should be paneled and the rest of the walls painted. If everything stays on schedule, touch-up work is scheduled for May 14–18. You should be able to move into your new clinic by May 21.

You will receive a third and final progress report by May 8. Thank you again for your business and the confidence you have placed in our company.

Sincerely yours,

Dale Brandt

Dale Brandt

Emphasizes successful completion of project

Promises to keep reader informed

Frequency of Progress Reports

Progress reports can be written daily, weekly, monthly, quarterly, or annually. Your specific job and your employer's needs will dictate how often you have to keep others informed of your progress. A single progress report is sufficient for Philip Javon's purpose in Figure 15.4. Barbara Shoemake was asked to submit two progress reports, the first of which is found in Figure 15.5. Contractor Brandt determined that three reports, spaced four to six weeks apart, would be necessary to keep Dr. Burke posted; Figure 15.6 is the second of those reports.

Parts of a Progress Report

Progress reports should contain information on (1) the work you have done, (2) the work you are currently doing, and (3) the work you will do.

How to Begin a Progress Report
In a brief introduction

- indicate why you are writing the report
- provide any necessary project titles or codes and specify dates
- help readers recall the job you are doing for them

If you are writing an initial progress report, supply background information in the opening. Philip Javon's first sentence in Figure 15.4, for example, quickly establishes his purpose by reminding Kathy Sands of their discussion last week. Similarly, Barbara Shoemake in the first paragraph in Figure 15.5 states the purpose and scope of her work for her instructor.

If you are submitting a subsequent progress report, inform your reader about where your previous report left off and where the current one begins. Make sure you clearly specify the period covered by each report. Note, too, how Dale Brandt's first paragraph in Figure 15.6 calls attention to the continuity of his work.

How to Continue a Progress Report

The body of the report should provide significant details about costs, materials, personnel, and times for the major stages of the project.

- Emphasize completed tasks, not false starts. If you report that the carpentry work or painting is finished, readers do not need an explanation of paint viscosity or geometrical patterns.
- Omit routine or well-known details ("I had to use the library when I wanted to read the back issues of *Safety News* that were not on the Web").
- Describe in the body of your report any snags you encountered that may affect the work in progress. See Dale Brandt's section on electrical problems in Figure 15.6. It is better for the reader to know about trouble early in the project, so appropriate changes or corrections can be made.

How to End a Progress Report

The conclusion should give a timetable for the completion of duties or submission of the next progress report. Give the date by which you expect work to be completed. Be realistic; do not promise to have a job done in less time than you know it will take. Readers will not expect miracles, only informed estimates. Even so, any conclusion must be tentative. Note that the good news Dale Brandt gives Dr. Burke about moving into her new clinic is qualified by the words "If everything stays on schedule." He is also well aware of the "you attitude" by thanking Dr. Burke again for her business.

Trip/Travel Reports

Reporting on the trips you take is an important professional responsibility. In documenting what you did and saw, trip reports keep readers informed about your efforts and how they affect ongoing or future business. Trip reports also should be written after you attend a convention or sales meeting or call on customers.

Questions Trip Reports Answer

Specifically, a trip report should answer the following questions for your readers:

- Where did you go?
- When did you go?
- Why did you go?
- Whom did you see?
- What did they tell you?
- What did you do about it?

For a business trip you are also likely to have to inform readers how much the trip cost and to supply them with receipts for all your expenses.

Common Types of Trip/Travel Reports

Trip reports can cover a wide range of activities and are called by different names to characterize those activities. Most likely, you will encounter the following three types of trip/travel reports:

1. Field trip reports.   These reports, often assigned in a course, are written after a visit to a laboratory, military installation, office complex, hospital, detention center, or other facility to show what you have learned about the operation of those places. You will be expected to describe how an institution is organized, the technical procedures and/or equipment it uses, pertinent ecological conditions, or the ratio of one group to another. The emphasis in these reports is on the educational value of the trip, as Mark Tourneur's report in Figure 15.7 (pp. 646–647) demonstrates.

2. Site inspection reports.   These reports inform managers about conditions at a branch office or plant, a customer's business, or on the advisability of relocating an office or other facility. After visiting the site, you will determine whether it meets your employer's (or customer's) needs.

Site inspection reports tell how equipment or production procedures are working or provide information about the physical plant, the environment (air, soil, water, vegetation), technology services, or financial operations.

Figure 15.8 (pp. 648–649), which begins with a recommendation, is a report written to a district manager interested in acquiring a new site for a fast-food restaurant.

3. Home health or social work visits.   Nurses, social workers, and probation officers report daily on their visits to patients and clients. Their reports describe clients' lifestyles, assess needs, and make recommendations. Figure 15.9 (pp. 650–651) is a report from a social worker to a county family services agency.

How to Gather Information for a Trip/Travel Report

Regardless of the kind of trip report you have to write, your assignment will be easier and your report better organized if you follow these suggestions.

1. Before you leave on the field trip, site inspection, or visit, be sure you are prepared as follows:
   a. Obtain all necessary names; street, e-mail, and website addresses; and relevant telephone, cell, and fax numbers.
   b. Check files for previous correspondence, case studies, or terms of contracts or agreements.
   c. Download work orders, instructions, or other documents pertinent to your visit, for example, websites and ads.
   d. Bring a laptop, PDA, or notebook with you.
   e. Locate a map of the area and get the directions you'll need beforehand (both maps and directions can be obtained easily at *http://www.mapquest.com* and similar websites).

Figure 15.7   A student's field trip report.

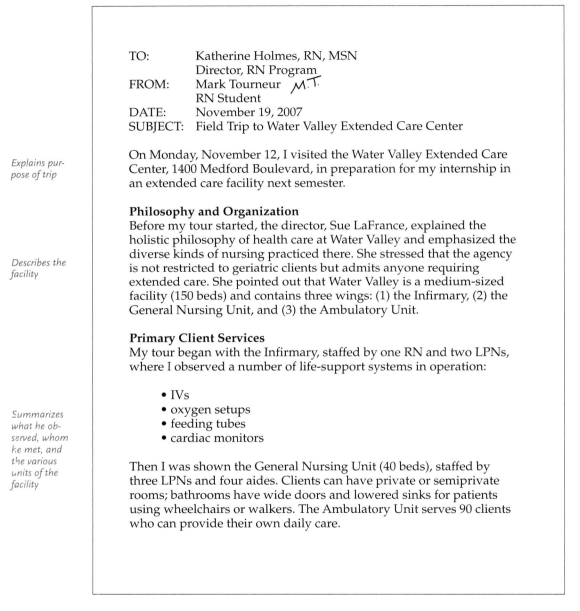

Explains purpose of trip

Describes the facility

Summarizes what he observed, whom he met, and the various units of the facility

TO: Katherine Holmes, RN, MSN
           Director, RN Program
FROM: Mark Tourneur   M.T.
           RN Student
DATE: November 19, 2007
SUBJECT: Field Trip to Water Valley Extended Care Center

On Monday, November 12, I visited the Water Valley Extended Care Center, 1400 Medford Boulevard, in preparation for my internship in an extended care facility next semester.

Philosophy and Organization
Before my tour started, the director, Sue LaFrance, explained the holistic philosophy of health care at Water Valley and emphasized the diverse kinds of nursing practiced there. She stressed that the agency is not restricted to geriatric clients but admits anyone requiring extended care. She pointed out that Water Valley is a medium-sized facility (150 beds) and contains three wings: (1) the Infirmary, (2) the General Nursing Unit, and (3) the Ambulatory Unit.

Primary Client Services
My tour began with the Infirmary, staffed by one RN and two LPNs, where I observed a number of life-support systems in operation:

- IVs
- oxygen setups
- feeding tubes
- cardiac monitors

Then I was shown the General Nursing Unit (40 beds), staffed by three LPNs and four aides. Clients can have private or semiprivate rooms; bathrooms have wide doors and lowered sinks for patients using wheelchairs or walkers. The Ambulatory Unit serves 90 clients who can provide their own daily care.

Continued

Additional Client Services
Dietetics
Before lunch in the main dining room, I was introduced to Jack Isoke, the dietitian, who explained the different menus he coordinates. The most common are low-sodium and ADA (American Diabetic Association) restricted-calorie. Staff members eat with the clients, reinforcing the holistic focus of the agency.

Pharmacy
After lunch, Kendra Tishner, the pharmacist, discussed the agency's procedures for ordering and delivering medications. She also described the client teaching she does and the in-service workshops she conducts.

Physical/Spiritual Therapy
I then observed clients in both recreational and physical therapy. Water Valley's full-time physical therapist, Tracy Cook, works with stroke and arthritic clients and helps those with broken bones regain the use of their limbs. In addition to a weight room, Water Valley has a small sauna that most of the clients use at least twice a week.

The clients' spiritual needs are not neglected, either. A small chapel is located just south of the Ambulatory Unit.

Benefits for My Internship
From my visit to Water Valley, I learned a great deal about the health care delivery system at an extended care facility. I was especially pleased to have been given so much information on emergency procedures, medication orders, and physical therapy programs. My forthcoming internship will be even more productive, since I now have firsthand knowledge about these various services.

-2-

Usefully provides subheads to organize his report

Documents conferences with staff

Concludes with the importance of the trip

Figure 15.8   A site inspection report using a map.

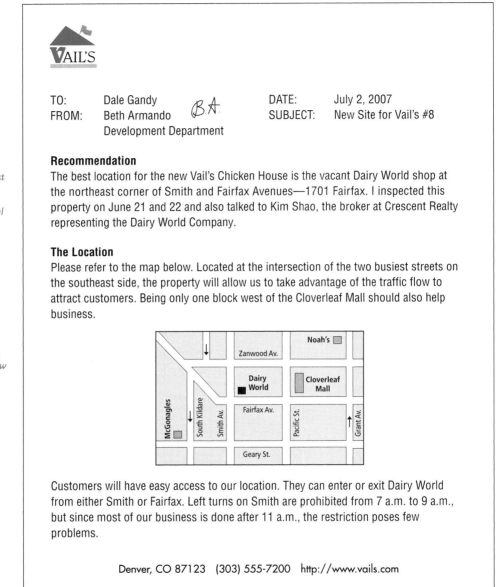

Continued

Dale Gandy
July 2, 2007
Page 2

Area Competition
Only two other fast-food establishments are in a one-mile vicinity. McGonagles, 1534 South Kildare, specializes in hamburgers; Noah's, 703 Zanwood, serves primarily seafood entrées. Their offerings will not directly compete with ours. The closest fast-food restaurant serving chicken is Johnson's, 1.8 miles away.

Parking Facilities
The parking lot has space for 45 cars, and the area at the south end of the property (38 feet $\times$ 37 feet) can accommodate 14–15 cars. The driveways and parking lot were paved with asphalt last March and appear to be in excellent condition. We will also be able to make use of the drive-up window on the north side of the building.

The Building
The building has 3,993 square feet of heated and cooled space. The air-conditioning and heating units were installed within the last fifteen months and seem to be in good working order; nine more months of transferable warranty remain on these units.

The only major changes we must make are in the kitchen. To prepare items on the Vail's menu, we would need to add three more exhaust fans (there is only one now) and expand the grill and cooking areas. The kitchen also has three relatively new sinks and ample storage space in the sixteen cabinets.

The restaurant has a seating capacity of up to 54 persons; 10 booths are covered with red vinyl and are comfortably padded. A color-coordinated serving counter could seat 8 to 10 patrons. The floor does not need to be retiled, but the walls will have to be painted to match Vail's color decor.

Assesses the location, condition of building, and identifies necessary alterations

Selects only the most relevant facts for audience's needs; does not overwhelm with petty details

Focuses on employer's needs

Figure 15.9   A social worker's visit report.

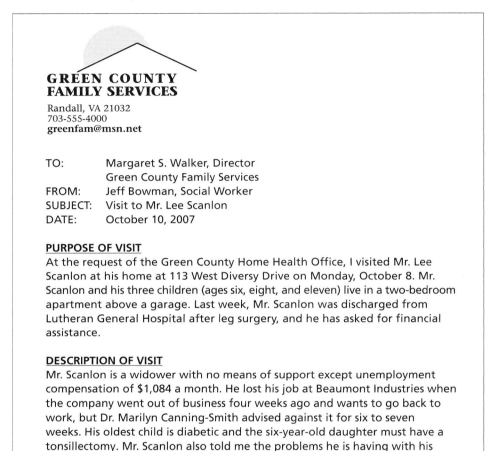

GREEN COUNTY FAMILY SERVICES

Randall, VA 21032
703-555-4000
greenfam@msn.net

TO: Margaret S. Walker, Director
           Green County Family Services
FROM: Jeff Bowman, Social Worker
SUBJECT: Visit to Mr. Lee Scanlon
DATE: October 10, 2007

PURPOSE OF VISIT

Starts with why, where, when, and with whom the visit was made

At the request of the Green County Home Health Office, I visited Mr. Lee Scanlon at his home at 113 West Diversy Drive on Monday, October 8. Mr. Scanlon and his three children (ages six, eight, and eleven) live in a two-bedroom apartment above a garage. Last week, Mr. Scanlon was discharged from Lutheran General Hospital after leg surgery, and he has asked for financial assistance.

DESCRIPTION OF VISIT

Lists information obtained from client, doctor, and owner

Mr. Scanlon is a widower with no means of support except unemployment compensation of $1,084 a month. He lost his job at Beaumont Industries when the company went out of business four weeks ago and wants to go back to work, but Dr. Marilyn Canning-Smith advised against it for six to seven weeks. His oldest child is diabetic and the six-year-old daughter must have a tonsillectomy. Mr. Scanlon also told me the problems he is having with his refrigerator; it "is off more than it is on," he said.

Mrs. Alice Gordon, the owner of the garage, informed me that Mr. Scanlon had paid last month's rent but not this month's. She also stressed how much the Scanlons need a new refrigerator and that she had often let them use hers to store their food.

Continued

Margaret S. Walker
October 10, 2007
Page 2

Here is a breakdown of Mr. Scanlon's monthly bills:

Expenses		Income
$ 550	rent	$1,084 unemployment compensation
150	utilities	
450	food	
120	drugs	
80	transportation	
$ 1,350		

Itemizes information to make it easy to follow and compare

ACTION TAKEN
To assist Mr. Scanlon, I have done the following:

1. Set up an appointment (10/19/07) for him to apply for food stamps.
2. Conferred with Blanche Derringo regarding Medicaid assistance.
3. Requested that the State Employment Commission help him to find a job as soon as he is well enough to work. My contact person is Wesley Sahara; his e-mail address is **wsahara@empcom.gov.**
4. Visited Robert Hong at the office of the Council of Churches to obtain food and money for utilities until federal assistance is available; he also will try to find the Scanlons another refrigerator.
5. Telephoned Sharon Muñoz at the Green County Health Department (555-1400) to have Mr. Scanlon's diabetic daughter receive insulin and syringes gratis.

Documents research done to assist client rather than giving reader recommendations to follow

---

    f. Bring a record of appointment times and locations, as well as the job titles of the people whom you expect to meet.

    g. Bring a camcorder, tape recorder, camera, or calculator, if necessary, to record important data.

2. When you return from your trip, keep the following hints in mind as you compile your report:

    a. Write your report promptly. If you put it off, you may forget important items.

    b. When a trip takes you to two or more widely separated places, note in your report when you arrived at each place and how long you stayed.

    c. Exclude irrelevant details, such as whether the trip was enjoyable, what you ate, or how delighted you were to meet people.

    d. Check to make sure you have listed names and calculated figures correctly. Mistakes in math make you look bad.

Test Reports

Much physical research (the discovery and documentation of facts) is communicated through short reports variously called **experiment, investigation, laboratory, operations,** or **research reports.** They all record the results of tests, whether the tests were conducted in a forest, computer center, laboratory, shopping mall, or soybean field. You may be asked to test an existing or new product or procedure or verify certain physical or environmental conditions for a class or employer.

Style

Objectivity and accuracy are essential ingredients in a test report. Readers want to know about your empirical research (the facts), not about your feelings (the "I"). Record your observations without bias or guesswork in a laboratory journal or log book and always document the results with precise measurements and in the standard symbols and abbreviations of your profession.

Questions Your Report Needs to Answer

Readers will expect your test report to supply the following information:

- why you performed the test—an explanation of the reasons, your goals, and who may have authorized you to perform the test
- how you performed the test—under what circumstances or controls you conducted the test; what procedures and equipment you used
- what the outcomes were—your conclusions
- what implications or recommendations follow from your test—what you learned, discovered, confirmed, or even disproved or rejected

When you sign the final copy of your report, you certify that things happened exactly when, how, and why you say they did.

Case Study: Two Sample Test Reports

Figure 15.10 is a relatively simple and short test report in memo format regarding sanitary conditions at a hospital psychiatric unit. The report follows a direct and useful pattern of organization:

- statement of purpose—*why?*
- findings—*what happened?*
- recommendations—*what next?*

Submitted by an infection control officer, the report does not provide elaborate details about the particular laboratory procedures used to determine whether bacteria were present; nor does it describe the pathogenic (disease-causing) properties of the bacteria. Such descriptions are unnecessary for the audience (the housekeeping department) to do its job.

A more complex example of a short test report is found in Figure 15.11 (pp. 654–656), which studies the effects of four light periods on the growth of paulownia

A test report with recommendations.   Figure 15.10

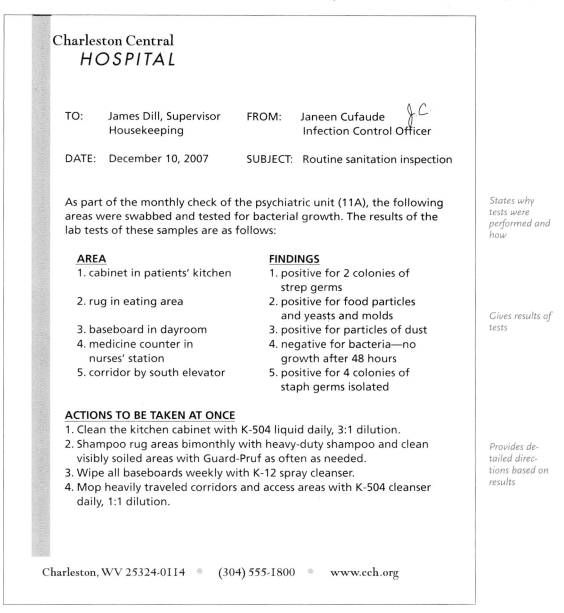

Charleston Central
HOSPITAL

TO: James Dill, Supervisor   FROM: Janeen Cufaude *J.C.*
       Housekeeping   Infection Control Officer

DATE: December 10, 2007   SUBJECT: Routine sanitation inspection

As part of the monthly check of the psychiatric unit (11A), the following areas were swabbed and tested for bacterial growth. The results of the lab tests of these samples are as follows:

AREA	FINDINGS
1. cabinet in patients' kitchen	1. positive for 2 colonies of strep germs
2. rug in eating area	2. positive for food particles and yeasts and molds
3. baseboard in dayroom	3. positive for particles of dust
4. medicine counter in nurses' station	4. negative for bacteria—no growth after 48 hours
5. corridor by south elevator	5. positive for 4 colonies of staph germs isolated

ACTIONS TO BE TAKEN AT ONCE
1. Clean the kitchen cabinet with K-504 liquid daily, 3:1 dilution.
2. Shampoo rug areas bimonthly with heavy-duty shampoo and clean visibly soiled areas with Guard-Pruf as often as needed.
3. Wipe all baseboards weekly with K-12 spray cleanser.
4. Mop heavily traveled corridors and access areas with K-504 cleanser daily, 1:1 dilution.

Charleston, WV 25324-0114   ●   (304) 555-1800   ●   www.cch.org

States why tests were performed and how

Gives results of tests

Provides detailed directions based on results

seedlings (a flowering tree cultivated in China). The report, published in a scientific journal, is addressed to specialists in forestry. Such a test report follows a different, more detailed pattern of organization than the report in Figure 15.10 and includes an **informative abstract,** an **introduction,** a **materials and methods section,** a **results and discussion section,** and a **list of references cited in the study.**

Figure 15.11   A short test report published in a scientific journal.

Paulownia Seedlings Respond to Increased Daylength

M. J. Immel, E. M. Tackett, and S. B. Carpenter

Abstract

Begins with informative abstract

Paulownia seedlings grown under four photoperiods were evaluated after a growing period of 97 days. Height growth and total dry weight production were both significantly increased in the 16- and 24-hour photoperiods.

Introduction

Gives background, purpose, and scope of study

Paulownia (*Paulownia tomentosa* [Thunb.] Steud.), a native of China, is a little known species in the United States. Recently, however, there has been increased interest in this species for surface mine reclamation (*1*).* Paulownia seems to be especially well adapted to harsh micro-climates of surface mines; it grows very rapidly and appears to be drought-resistant. In Kentucky and surrounding states, paulownia wood is actively sought by Japanese buyers and has brought prices comparable to black walnut (*2*).

This increased interest in paulownia has resulted in several attempts to direct seed it on surface mines, but little success has been achieved. The high light requirements and the extremely small size of paulownia seed (approximately 6,000 per gram) may be the limiting factors. Planting paulownia seedlings is preferred; but, because of their succulent nature, seedlings are usually produced and outplanted as container stock rather than bareroot seedlings. Daylength is an important factor in the production of vigorous container plants (*5*).

Our study compares the effects that four photoperiods—8, 12, 16, and 24 hours—had on the early growth of container-grown paulownia seedlings over a period of 97 days.

Materials and Methods

Describes steps taken: procedures, conditions, and equipment used

Seeds used in this study were stratified in a 1:1 mixture of peat moss and sand at 4°C for 2 years. Following cold storage, seeds were placed on a 1:1 potting soil–sand mix and mulched with cheesecloth. They were then placed under continuous light until germination occurred. Germination percentages were high, indicating paulownia seeds can survive long periods of storage with little loss of viability (*3*).

Thirty days after germination, 3- to 4-centimeter seedlings were transplanted into 8-quart plastic pots filled with an equal mixture of potting soil, sand, and peat moss.

* To save space, the References section has been omitted.

Continued

Page 2

Seventy-five seedlings were randomly assigned to each of the four treatments. Treatments were for 4 photoperiods—8, 12, 16, and 24 hours—and were replicated three times in 12 light chambers. Each chamber was 1.2- by 1.2-meters with an artificial light source 71 centimeters above the chamber floor.

The light source consisted of eight fluorescent lights: four 40-watt plant growth lamps alternated with four 40-watt cool white lamps. Light intensity averaged 550 foot-candles (1340μ einsteins/m^2/s) at the top of each pot and the temperature averaged 23°C ($\pm$2°C).

Uses technical terms and symbols audience expects

Seedlings were watered and fertilized after transplanting with a 6-gram 14-4-6 agriform container tablet. Beginning 1 month after transplanting, two seedlings were randomly selected and harvested from each chamber for a total of 24 trees. Height, root collar diameter, length of longest root, and oven-dry weight (at 65°C) were determined for each seedling. Harvests continued every week for 5 additional weeks.

Results and Discussion

Results indicate that early growth of paulownia is influenced by photoperiod, as shown in Table 1.

TABLE 1. Height Diameter, Root Length, Total Dry Weight, and R/S Ratio for Paulownia Seedlings Grown Under Four Photoperiods After 97 Days.

Photo period (hrs.)	Height (cm)	Diameter (cm)	Root length (cm)	Total dry weight (gm)	R/S ratio
8	13.1b	0.48	16.0	1.65c	0.18
12	17.8b	0.67	34.7	7.27b	0.32
16	27.3a	0.93	31.1	15.92a	0.39
24	29.2a	0.90	43.9	18.56a	0.33

Includes a visual to summarize results and then explains what happened

Expanding the photoperiod from 8 to either 16 or 24 hours increased height growth by 100 percent. Height growth in the 12-hour treatment also increased, but did not differ significantly from the 8-hour treatment. Heights under photoperiods of 8, 12, 16, and 24 hours were 13.1, 17.8, 27.3, and 29.2 centimeters, respectively.

Previous studies have also shown that photoperiod affects the growth of paulownia seedlings (4, 6). Sanderson (6), for example, found that paulownia seedlings grown under continuous light averaged 27.2 centimeters in height after 101 days compared with 29.2 centimeters for our 24-hour seedlings. Other corresponding photoperiods were equally comparable. Downs and Borthwick (4) also concluded that height growth of paulownia was affected by extending the photoperiod.

Cites related studies

Continued

Figure 15.11   (Continued)

Page 3

The greatest treatment differences were shown in total dry weight production. Refer again to Table 1. The mean weight of 1.65 grams for seedlings in the 8-hour treatment was significantly less than that of any of the other photoperiods. The 16- and 24-hour treatments did not differ significantly. In fact, they more than doubled the average weight for seedlings in the 12-hour treatment.

Provides accurate measurements in a clear, objective tone

Root-to-shoot ratio (R/S) indicates the relative proportion of growth allocated to roots versus shoots for the seedlings in each photoperiod. In this study, shoots were developing at nearly three times the rate of the roots for seedlings in the 12-, 16-, and 24-hour photoperiods.

The 0.18 R/S ratio for seedlings in the 8-hour treatment was much lower, indicating that relative growth of the shoot is approximately five times that of the root. The shorter photoperiod therefore decreased root development relative to shoot development as well as significantly reduced total dry weight production.

Although root collar diameter and root length did not significantly differ under the different photoperiods after 97 days, there was a trend for greater diameter and root growth with longer photoperiods.

Conclusions

Interprets the significance of the results

Results indicate that the growth of paulownia seedlings is affected by changes in the photoperiod. Increasing the photoperiod significantly increased height growth and total dry matter production. The distribution of dry matter (R/S ratio) was altered by increasing the photoperiod; the ratio was larger in the longer photoperiods. In contrast to earlier studies (4), we found paulownia seedlings subjected to extended photoperiods were still growing after 97 days.

To meet the needs of an expert audience, the writers of the report in Figure 15.11 had to include much more information than did Janeen Cufaude, the infection control officer who wrote the report in Figure 15.10, about the way the test was conducted and the types of scientific data the audience needs. The researchers did not have to define technical terms for their audience, and they could confidently use scientific symbols and formulas as well.

Incident Reports

The short reports discussed thus far in this chapter have dealt with routine work. They have described events that were anticipated or supervised. But every business or agency runs into unexpected trouble that delays routine work or results in personal injury. These circumstances need to be documented in an incident report. The audience for an incident (or accident) report can be within your organization or outside it. Employers, and on some occasions government inspectors, insurance agents, and attorneys, must be informed about those events that interfere with or threaten normal, safe operations.

Parts of an Incident Report

Include the following information in your incident report, which can be a memo or a specially prepared form with spaces for detailed comments. Because it can contain legally sensitive information, for which the reader needs a hard copy and paper trail, an incident report should not be sent as an e-mail. Note how Figure 15.12 includes precise and accurate information on these parts.

1. **Personal details.** Record titles, department, and employment identification numbers. Indicate if you or your fellow employees were working alone. For customers or victims, record home addresses, phone numbers, and places of employment. Insurance companies will also require policy numbers.

2. **Type of incident.** Briefly identify the incident—personal injury, fire, burglary, equipment failure. Identify any part(s) of the body precisely. "Eye injury" is not enough; "injury to the right eye, causing bleeding" is better. "Dislocated right shoulder" or "punctured left forearm" is descriptive and exact. A report on damaged equipment should list model numbers.

3. **Time and location of the incident.** Be precise. Include all relevant data.

4. **Description of what happened.** This section is the longest part of the report. Let readers know exactly what happened and why, how it occurred, who and what were involved, and what led up to the incident.

5. **What was done after the incident.** Describe the action you took to correct conditions, to get things back to normal, what was done to treat the injured, to make the environment safer, to speed a delivery, to repair damaged equipment.

6. **What caused the incident.** Make sure your explanation is consistent with your description of what happened. Pinpoint the trouble. In Figure 15.12, for example, the defective fisher joint is listed under the heading "Causes of Incident."

7. **Recommendations.** Recommendations about preventing the problem from recurring may involve calling a special safety meeting, asking for further training, adapting existing equipment, doing emergency planning, or modifying schedules.

When to Submit an Incident Report

An incident report is submitted when there is, for example,

- an accident—fire, automobile, physical injury
- a law enforcement offense
- an environmental danger, including a computer virus
- a machine breakdown
- a delivery delay
- a cost overrun
- a production slowdown

Figure 15.12 is an incident report about a train accident submitted by the engineer on duty.

Figure 15.12   An incident report in memo format.

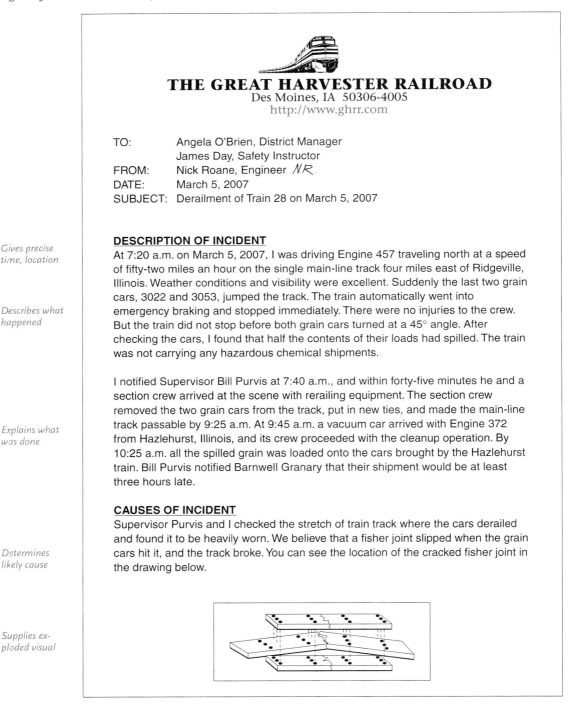

THE GREAT HARVESTER RAILROAD
Des Moines, IA 50306-4005
http://www.ghrr.com

TO: Angela O'Brien, District Manager
         James Day, Safety Instructor
FROM: Nick Roane, Engineer *NR*.
DATE: March 5, 2007
SUBJECT: Derailment of Train 28 on March 5, 2007

Gives precise time, location

DESCRIPTION OF INCIDENT
At 7:20 a.m. on March 5, 2007, I was driving Engine 457 traveling north at a speed of fifty-two miles an hour on the single main-line track four miles east of Ridgeville, Illinois. Weather conditions and visibility were excellent. Suddenly the last two grain cars, 3022 and 3053, jumped the track. The train automatically went into emergency braking and stopped immediately. There were no injuries to the crew. But the train did not stop before both grain cars turned at a 45° angle. After checking the cars, I found that half the contents of their loads had spilled. The train was not carrying any hazardous chemical shipments.

Describes what happened

I notified Supervisor Bill Purvis at 7:40 a.m., and within forty-five minutes he and a section crew arrived at the scene with rerailing equipment. The section crew removed the two grain cars from the track, put in new ties, and made the main-line track passable by 9:25 a.m. At 9:45 a.m. a vacuum car arrived with Engine 372 from Hazlehurst, Illinois, and its crew proceeded with the cleanup operation. By 10:25 a.m. all the spilled grain was loaded onto the cars brought by the Hazlehurst train. Bill Purvis notified Barnwell Granary that their shipment would be at least three hours late.

Explains what was done

CAUSES OF INCIDENT
Supervisor Purvis and I checked the stretch of train track where the cars derailed and found it to be heavily worn. We believe that a fisher joint slipped when the grain cars hit it, and the track broke. You can see the location of the cracked fisher joint in the drawing below.

Determines likely cause

Supplies exploded visual

Continued

Page 2

RECOMMENDATIONS
We made the following recommendations to the switch yard in Hazlehurst to be carried out immediately.
1. Check the section of track for ten miles on either side of Ridgeville for any signs of defective fisher joints.
2. Repair any defective joints at once.
3. Instruct all engineers to slow down to five to ten mph over this section of the track until the rail check is completed.

Offers recommendations to solve or prevent problem from recurring

Protecting Yourself Legally

An incident report can be used as legal evidence, and it then becomes part of a permanent legal record that can be used by law enforcement and attorneys in court to establish negligence and liability on your and your company's part. An incident report frequently concerns the two topics over which powerful legal battles are waged—health and property.

You have to be very careful about collecting and recording details. Make sure your report is not sketchy or incomplete. To avoid these errors, you may have to interview employees or bystanders; travel to the incident site; check manuals, code books, or other guides; consult safety experts; or research back records.

To ensure that what you write is legally proper, follow these guidelines.

1. Submit your report promptly. Any delay might be seen as a cover-up. Send your report to the appropriate parties immediately after you have gathered the necessary information found on page 657.

2. Be accurate, objective, and complete. Recount clearly what happened in the order it took place. Never omit or distort facts; the information may surface later, and you could be accused of a cover-up. Do not just write "I do not know" for an answer. If you are not sure, state why. Also be careful that there are no discrepancies in your report.

3. Give facts, not opinions. Provide a factual account of what actually happened, not a biased interpretation of events or one based on speculation or hearsay. Vague words such as "I guess," "I wonder," "apparently," "perhaps," or "possibly" weaken your objectivity. Stick to details you witnessed or that were seen by eyewitnesses. Identify witnesses or victims by giving names, addresses, places of employment, and so on. Keep in mind that stating what someone else saw is regarded as hearsay and therefore is not admissible in a court of law. State only what *you* saw or heard. When you describe what happened, avoid drawing uncalled-for conclusions. Consider the following statements of opinion and fact:

    Opinion: The patient seemed confused and caught himself in his IV tubing.
        Fact: The patient caught himself in his IV tubing.

    Opinion: The equipment was defective.
        Fact: The bolt was loose.

Be careful, too, about blaming someone. Statements such as "Baxter was incompetent" or "The company knew of the problem but did nothing about it" are libelous remarks.

    In law enforcement work, further identify suspects by their aliases and by any distinctive characteristics—for example, "jagged 4-inch scar on left forearm."

    4. Do not exceed your professional responsibilities.   Answer only those questions you are qualified to answer. Do not presume to speak as a detective, an inspector, a physician, or a supervisor. Do not represent yourself as an attorney or a claims adjuster in writing the report. And don't take sides.

Short Reports: Some Final Thoughts

To prepare successful short reports, keep in mind the rules of short report writing discussed in this chapter. Always take into account your readers' needs and expectations at every stage of your writing, document carefully what you write about, take accurate and complete notes, write objectively and ethically, present complicated data clearly and concisely, provide background and contexts where necessary, and include specific recommendations, where called for, based upon the facts. Remembering these basic rules will earn you praise and possibly promotions at work.

Online Study Center

Access the writing short reports Revision Checklist at college.hmco .com/pic/kolin8e

 ## Revision Checklist

    ☐ Had a clear sense of how my readers will use my report.
    ☐ Did appropriate research to give my audience enough information to help them make careful decisions.
    ☐ Provided significant information about costs, materials, personnel, and times so readers will know that my work consists of facts, not impressions.
    ☐ Double-checked all data—names, costs, figures, dates, places, and equipment models and numbers.

Continued

Continued

☐ Verified necessary statistics and trends so that my periodic and sales reports are thorough and accurate.

☐ Made sure all my comments and recommendations were ethical.

☐ Followed all agency or organization guidelines.

☐ Adhered to all legal requirements.

☐ Eliminated unnecessary details or those too technical for my audience.

☐ Kept report concise and to the point.

☐ Used headings whenever feasible to organize and categorize information.

☐ Supplied relevant visuals to help readers understand my message and crunch any numbers.

☐ Employed underlining, boldface, or italics to set headings apart or to emphasize key ideas.

☐ Began report with statement of purpose that clearly described the scope and significance of my work.

☐ Incorporated tables and other pertinent visuals to display data whenever appropriate.

☐ Explained clearly what the data mean.

☐ Determined that recommendations logically follow from the data and that recommendations are relevant and realistic.

Exercises

Online Study Center
Find additional writing short reports exercises at college.hmco .com/pic/kolin8e

1. Bring to class an example of a periodic report from your present or previous job or from any community, religious, or social organization to which you belong. In an accompanying memo to your instructor, indicate who the audience is and why such a report is necessary, stressing how it is organized, what kinds of factual data it contains, what visuals were used, and how it might be improved in content, organization, style, and design.

2. Assume that you are a manager of a large apartment complex (200 units). Write a periodic report based on the following information—26 units are vacant, 38 soon will be vacant, and 27 soon will be leased (by June 1). Also add a section of recommendations to your supervisor (the head of the real-estate management company for which you work) on how vacant apartments might be leased more quickly and perhaps at increased rents. Consider such important information as decorating, advertising, and installing a new security system.

3. Assume you work for a household appliance store. Prepare a sales report based on the information contained in the following table. Include a recommendation section for your manager.

Product	Number Sold	
	October	November
Kitchen Appliances		
Refrigerators	72	103
Dishwashers	27	14
Freezers	10	36
Electric Ranges	26	26
Gas Ranges	10	3
Microwave Ovens	31	46
Laundry Appliances		
Washers	50	75
Dryers	24	36
Air Treatment		
Room Air Conditioners	41	69
Dehumidifiers	7	2

4. Write a progress report on the wins, losses, and ties of your favorite sports team for last season. Address the report to the director of publicity for the team and stress how the director might use those facts for future publicity. As part of your report, indicate what might be an effective lead for a press release about the team's efforts.

5. Submit a progress report to your writing teacher on what you have learned in his or her course so far this term, which writing skills you want to develop in greater detail, and how you propose doing so. Mention specific memos, e-mail, letters, instructions, reports, or proposals you have written or will soon write.

6. Compose a site inspection report on any part of the college campus or plant, office, or store in which you work that might need remodeling, expansion, rewiring for computer use, or new or additional air-conditioning or heating work.

7. You and your collaborative team have been asked to write a short preliminary inspection report on the condition of a historic building for your state historical society. Inspecting the building, the home of a famous late-nineteenth-century governor, you discover the problems listed below. Include all these details in your report. Also supply recommendations for your readers—a director of the state historical society, a state architect, and four representatives of the subcommittee on finance from your state legislature. Design two appropriate visuals to include in your report.

   - The eight front columns are all in need of repair; two of them may have to be replaced.
   - The area below each bottom window casement needs to be excavated for waterproofing.

- The slate tile on the roof has deteriorated and needs immediate replacement.
- The front stairs show signs of mortar leaching and require attention at once.
- Sections of gutter on the northwest and northeast sides of the house must be changed; other gutters are in fair shape.
- Wood shutters need to be repainted; four of the twelve may even need to be replaced.
- All trees around the house need pruning; an old elm in the backyard shows signs of decay.
- The siding is in desperate need of preparation and painting.
- The brick near the front entrance is dirty and moss-covered.

8. Write a report to an instructor in your major about a field trip you have taken recently—to a museum, laboratory, health care agency, correctional facility, radio or television station, agricultural station, or office. Indicate why you took the trip, name the individuals you met on the trip, and stress what you learned and how that information will help you in course work or on your job.

9. Submit a test report on the purpose, procedures, results, conclusions, and recommendations of an experiment you conducted on one of the following subjects:

    a. soil
    b. Internet access
    c. water
    d. automobiles
    e. textiles/clothing
    f. animals
    g. recreational facilities
    h. computer hardware or software
    i. forests
    j. food
    k. air quality
    l. transportation
    m. blood
    n. noise levels

10. Write an incident report about a problem you encountered in your work or at home in the last year. Document the problem and provide a solution. Use the memo format in Figure 15.12.

11. Write an incident report about one of the following problems. Assume that it has happened to you. Supply relevant details and visuals in your report. Identify the audience for whom you are writing and the agency you are representing or trying to reach.

    a. After hydroplaning, your company car hits a tree and has a damaged front fender.
    b. You have been the victim of an electrical shock because an electrical tool was not grounded.
    c. You twist your back lifting a bulky package in the office or plant.
    d. Your boat capsizes while you are patrolling the lake.
    e. The crane you are operating breaks down and you lose a half-day's work.
    f. The vendor shipped the wrong replacement part for your computer, and you cannot complete a job without buying a more expensive software package.
    g. An electrical storm knocked out your computer; you lost 1,000 mailing addresses and will have to hire additional help to complete a mandatory mailing by the end of the week.
    h. A scammer has stolen some sensitive files (documents) about a new product or service your company had hoped to launch next month.

12. Choose one of the following descriptions of an incident and write a report based on it. The descriptions contain unnecessary details, vague words, insufficient information, unclear cause-and-effect relationships, or a combination of those errors. In writing your report, correct the errors by adding or deleting whatever information you believe is necessary. You may also want to rearrange the order in which information is listed. Use a memo format, like that in Figure 15.12, to write the report.

a. After sliding across the slippery road late at night, my car ran into another vehicle, one of those fancy imported cars. The driver of that car must have been asleep at the wheel. The paint and glass chips were all over. I was driving back from our regional meeting and wanted to report to the home office the next day. The accident will slow me down.

b. Whoever packed the glass mugs did not know what he or she was doing. The string was not the right type, nor was it tied correctly. The carton was too flimsy as well. It could have been better packed to hold all those mugs. Moreover, since the bus had to travel across some pretty rough country, the package would have broken anyhow. The best way to ship these kinds of goods is in specially marked and packed boxes. The value of the box contents was listed at $575.

CHAPTER 16

Writing Careful Long Reports

This chapter introduces you to long reports—how they differ from short reports, how they are written, and how they are organized. It is appropriate to discuss long reports in one of the last chapters of *Successful Writing at Work*. A major assignment in school and in the world of work, the long report gives you an opportunity to use and combine many of the writing skills and research strategies you have already learned. In business, a long report is the culmination of many weeks or months of hard work on an important company project.

The following skills will be most helpful to you as you prepare to study long reports; appropriate page numbers appear for those topics that have already been discussed.

- assessing and meeting your audience's multiple needs (pp. 8–13)
- gathering and summarizing information, especially from print and online sources, and conducting interviews (pp. 300–334; 412–428)
- generating, drafting, revising, and editing your ideas (pp. 41–69)
- reporting the results of your research accurately and concisely (pp. 57–65; 652–656)
- creating and introducing visuals (pp. 447–494)
- using an appropriate method of documentation (pp. 351–405)
- preparing an informative abstract (pp. 428–431)

Having improved those skills, you should be ready to write a successful long report. The writer of the long report in Figure 16.3 (pp. 680–697) uses all of the above skills in her work for RPM Technologies.

How a Long Report Differs from a Short Report

Both long and short reports are invaluable tools in the world of work. Basic differences exist, though, between the two types of reports. A short report is not a watered-down version of a long report; nor is a long report simply an expanded version of a short one. The two types of reports differ in scope, research, format, timetable, audience, and collaborative effort.

Online Study Center

To expand your understanding of writing long reports, take advantage of the ACE quizzes, sample documents, Web links, and exercises at college .hmco.com/pic/ kolin8e

The following section explains some of the key differences between these two reports. By understanding these differences, you will be better able to follow the rest of Chapter 16 as it covers the process of writing a long report and the organization and parts of such a report. A model long report (Figure 16.3) appears at the end of the chapter.

Scope

A long report is a major study that provides an in-depth view of a key problem or idea. For example, a long report written for a course assignment may be eight to twenty pages long; a report for a business or industry may be that long or, more likely, much longer, depending on the scope of the subject. The implications of a long report are wide-ranging for a business or industry—relocating a plant, adding a new network, changing a programming operation, or adapting the workplace for multinational employees, as in Figure 16.3.

Long reports examine a problem in detail, while short reports cover just one part of the problem. Unlike a short report, a long report may discuss not just one or two current events, but rather a continuing history of a problem or idea (and the background information necessary to understand it in perspective). For example, the short test report on paulownia in Figure 15.11 would be used with many other test reports in a long report for a group of environmentalists or a government agency on the value of planting those trees to prevent soil erosion.

The titles of some typical long reports further suggest their extensive (and in some cases exhaustive) coverage:

- *A Master Plan for the Recreation Needs of Dover Plains, New York*
- *The Transportation Problems in Kingford, Oregon, and the Use of Monorails*
- *Promoting More Effective E-Commerce and E-Tailing at TechWorld*
- *The Use of Virtual Reality Attractions in Theme Parks in Jersey City, New Jersey*
- *Public Policy Implications of Expanding Health Care Delivery Systems in Tate County*
- *Internet Medicine in Providing Health Care in Rural Areas: Ways to Serve Southern Montana*

Research

A long, comprehensive report requires much more extensive research than a short report does. Information can be gathered over time from primary and secondary research—Internet searches, listservs, books, articles, laboratory experiments, on-site visits and tests, interviews, and the writer's own observations. For a course report, you will have to do a great deal of research and possibly interviewing to track down the relevant background information and to discover what experts have said about the subject and what they propose should be done. For a report for class you will be asked to identify a major problem or topic while in business the topic and even your approach to it will more than likely be dictated to you by your boss and company policy.

Information gathered for many short reports can also help you prepare a long report. In fact, as the example of paulownia in Figure 15.11 (pp. 654–656) again shows, a long report can use the experimental data from a short report to arrive at a conclusion. Also for a long report, writers often supply one or more progress reports (one type of short report).

Tech Note

The Internet as "Virtual Library"

The Internet offers access both to primary research and to long reports published by scientists and mathematicians (*.sci*), university researchers (*.edu*), government agencies (*.gov*), the military (*.mil*), and every kind of organization (*.org*) and business (*.com*). You might want to review the sites found in Chapter 8. But keep in mind, too, that the U.S. government conducts or sponsors a great deal of research that you might find relevant for your reports. The government research is at the heart of science, technology, health care, and so on. Below is a short—very short—list of government and other relevant websites.

- *http://www.epa.gov* will lead you to press releases, test guidelines, and information about grants, contracts, and job opportunities at the Environmental Protection Agency.
- *http://www.osha.gov* is the website for the Occupational Safety and Health Administration, where you'll find information about OSHA standards, news releases and fact sheets, publications, technical information, and safety links.
- *nttp://www.astd.org* is the homepage of the American Society for Training and Development, which oversees research and maintains databases of information about employee training in business, industry, education, and government.
- *http://www.sba.gov* leads to the Small Business Administration's webpage, where you'll find guides on beginning a small business, the opportunity to include your business in the national register, and contact information for local SBA offices.
- *http://www.bls.gov* opens the official site of the Bureau of Labor Statistics. This organization compiles and maintains financial information such as charts on U.S. dollar inflation, growth or decline of the number of businesses, and wage increases.
- *http://www.gpoaccess.gov* is a service of the U.S. Government Printing Office that provides free electronic access to a variety of federal documents, including legislative, judicial, and executive resources.
- *http://www.archives.gov* is the National Archives and Records Administration, an independent federal agency that oversees the management of all federal records.

Continued

Continued

Other U.S. government agencies and departments that maintain websites you may want to consult include the following:

- Department of Agriculture (*http://www.usda.gov*)
- Department of Defense (*http://www.defenselink.gov*)
- Department of Energy (*http://www.energy.gov*)
- Department of the Interior (*http://www.doi.gov*)
- Federal Bureau of Investigation (*http://www.fbi.gov*)
- Department of Transportation (*http://www.dot.gov*)
- Supreme Court (*http://www.supremecourtus.gov*)
- U.S. Business Advisor (*http://www.business.gov*)
- U.S. Census Bureau (*http://www.census.gov*)
- U.S. Patent and Trademark Office (*http://www.uspto.gov*)
- The White House (*http://www.whitehouse.gov*)
- FirstGov (*http://www.firstgov.gov*)
- National Telecommunications and Information Administration (*http://www.ntia.doc.gov*)

Finally, preparing a proposal can lead to writing a long report. You might suggest a change to an employer, who then would ask you to write a long report containing the research necessary to implement that change. Your instructor may ask you to write a proposal on doing a long report for a class project, as Barbara Shoemake did in Figure 14.8.

Format

A long report is too detailed and complex to be adequately organized in a memo or letter format. The product of thorough research and analysis, the long report gives readers detailed discussions and interpretations of large quantities of data. To present the information in a logical and orderly fashion, the long report contains more parts, sections, headings, subheadings, documentation, and supplements (appendixes) than would ever be included in a short report. Look at the Table of Contents for Figure 16.3 (p. 682) to see at a glance the various divisions and parts of a long report.

Timetable

The two types of reports differ in the time it takes to prepare them. Writers of these two reports work under different expectations from their readers and under different deadlines. A long report explores with extensive documentation a subject involving personnel, locations, costs, safety, or equipment. Many times a long report is required by law, for example, investigating the feasibility of a project that will affect the ecosystem. A short report is often written as a matter of routine duty, with the writer sometimes given little or no advance notice. The long report, however, may take weeks or even months to write. When you prepare a long report for a class project, select a topic that really interests you, because you will spend a good portion of the term working on it. Below is a timetable for such a long report.

Gather Research Materials	Outline or Draft	Conferences for Revisions and Further Research	Revise and Prepare Figures	Proofread and Polish	Submit Long Report
4 weeks	3 weeks	1 week	3 weeks	1 week	Due Date

Audience

The audience for a long report is generally broader—and includes individuals higher up in an organization's hierarchy—than that for a short report. Your short report may be read by co-workers, a first-level supervisor, and possibly that person's immediate boss, but a long report is always intended for people in the top levels of management—presidents, vice presidents, superintendents, directors—who make executive, financial, and organizational decisions. These individuals are responsible for long-range planning, seeing the big picture, so to speak.

Collaborative Effort

Unlike many short reports, the long report in the world of business may not always be the work of one employee. Rather, it may be a collaborative effort, the product of a committee or group whose work is reviewed by a main editor to make sure that the final copy is consistently and accurately written. Individuals in many departments within a company—computer programming, document design, engineering, graphics, legal affairs, public relations, safety—may cooperate in planning, researching, drafting, revising, and editing a long report. Your instructor may ask you to work in a group in preparing your long report (review Chapter 3 on collaborative writing).

▎The Process of Writing a Long Report

As we just saw, writing a long report requires much time and effort. Since your work will be spread over many weeks, you need to see your report *not* as a series of static or isolated tasks but as an evolving project. Before you embark on that project, review the information on the writing process found in Chapter 2. You may also want to study the flow chart in Figure 11.14, which illustrates the different stages in writing a research paper. The following guidelines will help you to plan and write your long report.

   1. Identify a broad yet significant topic.   You'll have to do preliminary research—reading, online searching, compiling a questionnaire or survey, conferring with and interviewing experts—to get an overview of main problems, key ideas and individuals involved, and implications for your company and/or community.

   Note the kinds of research Terri Smith Ruckel did for her long report in Figure 16.3. As she did, expect to search a variety of print and Internet sources, to read and evaluate them, and to incorporate them in your work. You might want to review pages 300–334 in Chapter 8 to help you in your search for information.

2. Expect to confer regularly with your supervisor(s).   In these meetings, be prepared to ask pertinent and researched questions to pin down exactly what your boss wants. Focus your questions on the company's use of your report, how the company wants you to express certain ideas, and the amount of information it needs. Your supervisor may want you to submit an outline before you draft the report and may expect several more drafts for his or her and other executives' approval before you write the final version.

3. Revise your work often.   Be prepared to work on several outlines and drafts. Your revisions may sometimes be extensive, depending on what your boss, instructor, or collaborative team recommends. You may have to explore new sources and arrive at a new interpretation of those sources. Be sure to share major changes in your thinking with coauthors or the supervisor who assigned the project. As you narrow your purpose and scope, you may find yourself deleting information or modifying its place in your work. This shifting around as well as adding and deleting information will help you to arrive at a carefully organized report. At the later stages, you will be revising and editing your words, sentences, and paragraphs.

4. Keep the order flexible at first.   Even as you work on your drafts and revisions, keep in mind that a long report is not written in the order in which the parts will finally be assembled. You cannot write in "final" order—abstract to appendix. Instead, expect to write in "loose" order to reflect the process in which you gathered information and organized it for the final copy of the report. Usually, the body is written first, the introduction later so the authors can make sure they have not left anything out. The abstract, which appears very early in the report, is always written after all the facts have been recorded and the recommendations made or the conclusions drawn. The title page and the table of contents are always prepared last.

5. Prepare both a work calendar and a checklist.   Keep both posted where you do your work—above your desk or computer, or use your computer's built-in calendar program, if available—so you can track your progress. Make sure your collaborative team is following the same calendar and using the same checklist. The calendar should mark **milestones**, that is, dates by which each stage of your work must be completed. Match the dates on your calendar with the dates your instructor or employer may have given you to submit an outline, progress report(s), and the final copy. Your checklist should list the major parts of your report. As you complete each section, check it off. Before assembling the final copy of your report, use the checklist to make sure you have not omitted something.

▮ Parts of a Long Report

A long report may include some or all of the following twelve parts, which form three categories: *front matter* (letter of transmittal, title page, table of contents, list of illustrations, abstract); *report text* (introduction, body, conclusion, recommendations); and *back matter* (glossary, references cited, appendixes). The entire report may be placed in a clear plastic folder or other suitable cover.

Front Matter

As the name implies, the front matter of a long report consists of everything that precedes the actual text of the report. Such elements introduce, explain, and summarize to help the reader locate various parts of the report. Use lowercase roman numerals for front matter page numbers, not Arabic numbers.

Letter of Transmittal

This three- or four-paragraph (usually only one-page) letter states the purpose, scope, and major recommendation of the report. It highlights the main points of the report that your readers would be most interested in. If written to an instructor, the letter should additionally note that the report was done as a course assignment. Sometimes a letter of transmittal, which is not numbered, is bound with the report as part of it; most often it comes before the report, serving as a cover letter. Figure 16.1 is a sample letter of transmittal for a business report.

Title Page

Since MLA and APA have different formats for title pages, find out what your instructor prefers. Your employer may ask you to follow a company format. Basically, though, your title page should contain the following:

- the full title of your report; tell readers what your topic is and how you have restricted it in time, space, or method. Your title determines if and how you have done your work. Avoid titles that are vague, too short, or too long.

  Vague Title: A Report on the Internet: Some Findings

  Too Short: The Internet

  Too Long: A Report on the Internet: A Study of Dot-Com Companies, Their History, Appeal, Scope, Liabilities, and Their Relationship to Ongoing Work Dealing with Consumer Preferences and Protection Within the Last Five Years in the Midwest

- the name of the company or agency preparing the report
- the name(s) of the report writer(s)
- the date of the report
- any agency, order, or grant number
- the name of the firm for which the report was prepared

For a report for a class assignment, give your instructor's name and the specific course for which you prepared the report.

Make sure that your title page looks professional. Center your title and graphically subordinate any subtitles. Do not use abbreviations (e.g., *bldgs.* for *buildings, gov't* for *government, bus.* for *business*) or acronyms (e.g., *AMS* for *Association of Marketing Students; PTAs* for *Physical Therapist Assistants*).

Table of Contents

The table of contents lists the major headings and subheadings of your report and tells readers on which pages they can be found. Essentially, a table of contents shows

Figure 16.1   A letter of transmittal for a long report.

α

ALPHA CONSULTANTS

■   1400 Ridge   ■   Evanston, California 97214-1005   ■
■   805-555-9200   ■   FAX 805-555-0221   ■
www.alpha.com

August 3, 2007

Dr. K. G. Lowry, President
Coastal College
San Diego, CA 93219-2619

Dear Dr. Lowry:

Indicates why report was done

We are happy to offer you the enclosed report, **A Study to Determine New Directions in Women's Athletics at Coastal College**, which you commissioned us to prepare. The report contains our recommendations about strengthening existing sports programs and creating new ones at Coastal College.

Gives two key recommendations

Our recommendation is that Coastal should engage in more active recruitment to establish a more competitive women's baseball team, to offer additional athletic activities in women's track and field by August 2008, and to create a new interdisciplinary program between the Athletic Department and the Women's Studies Program.

Encourages response and questions

We hope that you find our report useful in meeting students' needs at Coastal College. If you have any questions or if you would like to discuss any of our recommendations, please call us.

Sincerely yours,

Barbara Gilchrist
Barbara Gilchrist

Lee T. Sidell
Lee T. Sidell

Encl. Report

how you organized your report. In Figure 16.2, for example, the reader can see how the report "A Study to Determine New Directions in Women's Athletics at Coastal College" is divided into four chief parts (Introduction, Discussion, Conclusion, and Recommendations). A table of contents emerges from many outlines and drafts. The items on those outlines frequently expand, shrink, and move around until you decide on the formal divisions and subdivisions of your report.

Tech Note

Automatically Formatting the Long Report

You can save a considerable amount of formatting time when writing your long report by using your word processing program's automatic formatting features. Automatic formatting can be applied either as you keyboard or after you've completed your report, by turning on the automatic formatting options and choosing which types of formats you'd like to apply to the report. You can

- automatically format the most basic parts of your paper
- apply bulleted or numbered lists
- automatically format the heading structure of your report by using your word processing program's tagging function
- create a table of contents via your tagged headers
- produce an index by tagging individual words

   It will take only a short time to familiarize yourself with your word processing program's autoformatting features, and by doing so you can reduce the cumbersome process of formatting each item individually. You should always carefully proofread your report to make sure that the autoformatting has been correctly applied.

Include front matter components in your table of contents, but never list the contents page itself, the letter of transmittal, or the title page in your table of contents. Never have just one subheading under a heading. You cannot divide a single topic by one.

Incorrect:	EXPANDING THE SPORTS PROGRAM
	Basketball
	BUILDING A NEW ARENA
	The West Side Location
Correct:	EXPANDING THE SPORTS PROGRAM
	Basketball
	Track and Field
	BUILDING A NEW ARENA
	The West Side Location
	Costs

Figure 16.2   A table of contents for a long report.

CONTENTS

Records key sections and subsections of report

Gives titles to documents in appendixes

List of Illustrations

This list of all the visuals indicates where they can be found in your report.

Abstract

As discussed in Chapter 10, an abstract presents a brief overview of the problem and conclusions; it summarizes the report. An informative abstract is far more helpful to readers of a report than is a descriptive one, which gives no conclusions or results.

Not every member of your audience will read your entire report, but almost everyone will read the abstract. For example, the president of the corporation or the director of an agency may use the abstract as the basis for approving the report and passing it on for distribution. Thus, the abstract may be the most important part of your report. See how the abstract Terri Smith Ruckel prepared for her readers on page 683 succinctly gives conclusions, or findings.

Abstracts may be placed at various points in long reports—on the title page, on a separate page, or as the first page of the report text.

Text of the Report

The text of a long report consists of an introduction, the body, conclusions, and sometimes recommendations.

Introduction

The introduction may constitute as much as 10 or 15 percent of your report, but it should not be any longer. If it were, the introduction would be disproportionate to the rest of your work, especially the body section. The introduction is essential because it tells readers why your report was written and thus helps them to understand and interpret everything that follows. See how Terri Smith Ruckel in Figure 16.3 emphasizes the importance of her reseach for her employer, RPM Technologies, on pages 684–687. Do not put your findings, conclusions, or recommendations in your introduction.

Do not regard the introduction as one undivided block of information. It includes the following related parts, which should be labeled with subheadings. Keep in mind, though, that your instructor or employer may ask you to list these parts in a different order.

1. Background. To understand why your topic is significant and hence worthy of study, readers need to know about its history. This history may include information on such topics as who was originally involved, when, and where; how someone was affected by the issue; what opinions have been expressed on the issue; what the implications of your study are. Note how the long report on multinational employees in the U.S. work force (Figure 16.3) provides useful background information on when, where, how, and why these employees entered the U.S. work force and the effect of world terrorism on such workers and their employers.

2. Problem. Identify the problem or issue that led you to write the report. Your problem needs to be significant to warrant a long report on it. Because the problem or topic you investigated will determine everything you write about in the report, your statement of it must be clear and precise. That statement may be restricted to a few sentences. Here is a problem statement from a report on how construction designs have not taken into account the requirements of disabled Americans.

> The construction industry has not satisfactorily met the needs for accessible workplaces and homes for all age and physical ability groups. The industry has relied on expensive and specialized plans to modify existing structures rather than creating universally designed spaces that are accessible to everyone.

3. Purpose statement.   The purpose statement, crucial to the success of the report, tells readers why you wrote the report and what you hope to accomplish or prove. It expresses the goal of all your research. In explaining why you gathered information about a particular problem or topic, indicate how such information might be useful to a specific audience, company, or group. Like the problem statement, the purpose statement does not have to be long or complex. A sentence or two will suffice. You might begin simply by saying, "The purpose of this report is . . .".

4. Scope.   This section informs readers about the specific limits—number and type of issues, time, money, locations, personnel, and so forth—you have placed on your investigation. You inform readers about what they will find in your report or what they won't through your statement about the scope of your work. The long report in Figure 16.3 concentrates on adapting the U.S. workplace to meet the communication and cultural needs of a work force of multinational employees, not trends in the international market—two completely different topics.

The Body

Also called the *discussion,* this section is the longest, possibly making up as much as 70 percent of your report. Everything in this and all the other sections of your report grows out of your purpose and how you have limited your scope. The body of your report should supply readers with statistical information, details about the environment, and physical descriptions, as well as the various interpretations and comments of the authorities whose work you consulted or individuals whom you have interviewed as part of your research. The body can also identify and describe the range of options you surveyed and earmark the most appropriate. (Follow consistently one of the methods of documentation discussed in Chapter 9.)
    The body of your report should do the following:

- be carefully organized to reveal a coherent and well-defined plan
- separate material into meaningful parts to identify the major issues as well as subissues in your report
- clearly relate the parts to each other
- use headings to help your reader identify major sections more quickly

Your organization should reflect the different headings (and even subheadings) included in your report. Use them throughout your report to make it easy to follow. Organizational headings will also enable someone skimming the report to find specific information quickly. The headings, of course, will be included in the table of contents. (Note how Figure 16.3 is carefully organized into sections.)

In addition to headings, use transitions to reveal the organization of the body of your report. At the beginning of each major section of the body, tell readers what they will find in that section and why. Summary sentences at the end of a section will tell readers where they have been and prepare them for any subsequent discussions. The report in Figure 16.3 does an effective job of providing internal summaries.

Conclusion(s)

The conclusion should tie everything together for readers by presenting the findings of your report. Findings, of course, will vary depending on the type of research you do. For a research report based on a study of sources located through various reference searches, the conclusion should summarize the main viewpoints of the authorities whose works you have cited. Perhaps your instructor will ask you to assess in your conclusion which resource materials were most thorough and helpful and why. For a marketing report done for a business, you must spell out the implications for your readers in terms of costs, personnel, products, location, and so forth.

Regardless of the type of research you do, your conclusions should do the following:

- be based on the information and documentation in the body of the report
- corroborate the evidence/information you gave in the body of your report
- grow out of the work you describe in the body of the report
- keep to the areas that your report covers, and not stray into areas it did not

In essence, to write an effective conclusion, you will have to summarize carefully a great deal of information accurately and concisely. Notice how the following conclusion of a long report on the Japanese tuna market clearly summarizes the market opportunities explained in the report.

Conclusion

The U.S. tuna industry has great potential to expand its role in the Japanese market. This market, currently 400,000 tons a year and growing rapidly, is already being supplied by imports that account for 35 percent of all sales. Our report indicates that not only will this market expand but its share of imports will continue to grow. The trend is alarming to Japanese tuna industry leaders, because this important market, close to a billion dollars a year, is increasingly subject to the influence of foreign imports. Decreasing catches by Japan's own tuna fleet as well as an increased preference for tuna by affluent Japanese consumers have contributed significantly to this trend.[1]

[1]Adapted from Sunee C. Sonu, *Japan's Tuna Market.* U.S. Department of Commerce, NOAA Technical Memorandum NMFS.

Recommendations

The most important part of the report, after the abstract, is the recommendation(s) section, which tells readers

- what should be done about the findings recorded in the conclusion
- how you want them to solve the problem your report has focused on
- what equipment to purchase, when to expand a market, how to expand a website, or whom to recruit and retain, as in Figure 16.3

The report on the Japanese tuna market mentioned above uses a numbered list to make its recommendations.

Recommendations

Based on our analysis of the Japanese tuna market, we recommend five marketing strategies for the U.S. tuna industry:

1. Farm greater supplies of bluefin tuna to export.

2. Market our own value-added products.

3. Sell fresh tuna directly to the Tokyo Central Wholesale Market.

4. Sell wholesale to other Japanese markets.

5. Advertise and supply to Japanese supermarket chains.[2]

---

[2]Adapted from Sonu, *Japan's Tuna Market.*

Back Matter

Included in the back matter of the report are all the supporting data that, if included in the text of the report, would bog the reader down in details and cloud the main points the report makes.

Glossary

The glossary is an alphabetical list of the specialized vocabulary used in the report and the definitions. A glossary might be unnecessary if your report does not use a highly technical vocabulary or if *all* members of your audience are familiar with the specialized terms you do use.

References Cited

Any sources cited in your report—websites, books, articles, television programs, interviews, reviews, audiovisuals—are usually listed in this section (see Chapter 9 on preparing a Works Cited or Reference list). Also, ask your instructor or employer how he or she wants information to be documented. Sometimes, in the world of work, employers prefer all information to be documented in footnotes or cited parenthetically in the text. Note that the long report in Figure 16.3 uses the American Psychological Association (APA) system of documentation. Although APA no longer recommends a table of contents or list of illustrations, these pages are supplied here as models for students who are asked to use them.

Appendix

An appendix contains supporting materials for the report—tables and charts too long to include in the discussion, sample questionnaires, budgets and cost estimates, correspondence about the preparation of the report, case histories, transcripts of telephone conversations. Group like items in an appendix, as the examples under "Appendixes" in Figure 16.2 show. (Note that the plural of *Appendix* is *Appendixes,* not *Appendices.*)

■ A Model Long Report

The following long report in Figure 16.3 was written by a senior training specialist, Terri Smith Ruckel, for her boss, the human resources director who commissioned it. Ruckel's main task was to demonstrate what U.S. businesses, and especially RPM, should do to meet the needs of multinational workers and thus promote diversity in the workplace. She gathered relevant data from both primary and secondary research, including journal articles, websites, personal interviews, government documents, and even in-house publications from newsletters and company records, all on the RPM intranet. Ruckel was also sensitive to 9/11 and later terrorist activities that affect both international workers and their employers.

Figure 16.3 contains all the parts of a long report discussed in this chapter except a glossary and an appendix. Intended for a general reader interested in learning more about the problems multinational workers face, Ruckel's report does not contain the technical terms and data that would require a glossary and an appendix. Note how her cover letter introduces her report and its significance for RPM Technologies and her abstract succinctly identifies the main points of her report.

Figure 16.3   A long report.

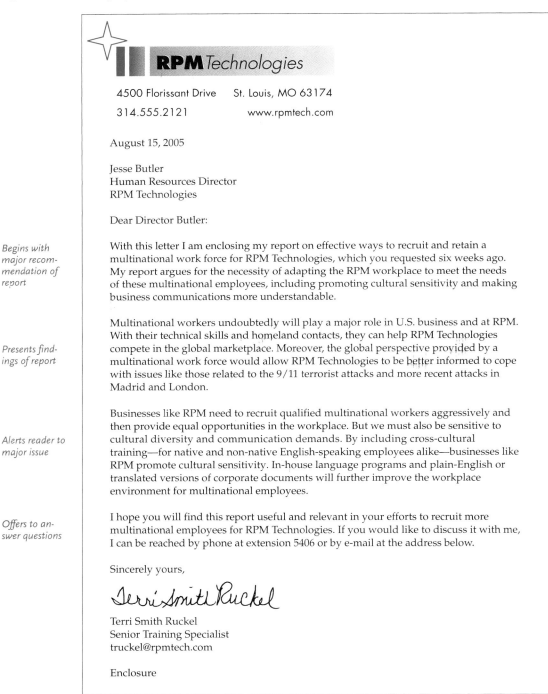

RPM Technologies

4500 Florissant Drive   St. Louis, MO 63174

314.555.2121   www.rpmtech.com

August 15, 2005

Jesse Butler
Human Resources Director
RPM Technologies

Dear Director Butler:

Begins with major recommendation of report

With this letter I am enclosing my report on effective ways to recruit and retain a multinational work force for RPM Technologies, which you requested six weeks ago. My report argues for the necessity of adapting the RPM workplace to meet the needs of these multinational employees, including promoting cultural sensitivity and making business communications more understandable.

Presents findings of report

Multinational workers undoubtedly will play a major role in U.S. business and at RPM. With their technical skills and homeland contacts, they can help RPM Technologies compete in the global marketplace. Moreover, the global perspective provided by a multinational work force would allow RPM Technologies to be better informed to cope with issues like those related to the 9/11 terrorist attacks and more recent attacks in Madrid and London.

Alerts reader to major issue

Businesses like RPM need to recruit qualified multinational workers aggressively and then provide equal opportunities in the workplace. But we must also be sensitive to cultural diversity and communication demands. By including cross-cultural training—for native and non-native English-speaking employees alike—businesses like RPM promote cultural sensitivity. In-house language programs and plain-English or translated versions of corporate documents will further improve the workplace environment for multinational employees.

Offers to answer questions

I hope you will find this report useful and relevant in your efforts to recruit more multinational employees for RPM Technologies. If you would like to discuss it with me, I can be reached by phone at extension 5406 or by e-mail at the address below.

Sincerely yours,

Terri Smith Ruckel

Terri Smith Ruckel
Senior Training Specialist
truckel@rpmtech.com

Enclosure

Adapting the RPM Workplace for Multinational Employees in the New Millennium

Terri Smith Ruckel
Senior Training Specialist
RPM Technologies

August 15, 2005

Prepared for

Jesse Butler
Human Resources Director

Title page is carefully formatted and uses boldface for the title

Identifies writer and job title

Date submitted

RPM executive who assigned the report

2

Table of Contents

*Major divisions
of report in all
capital letters*

*Subheadings
indicated by
different type-
face, indenta-
tions, and
italics*

*Page numbers
included for
major sections
of report*

3

List of Illustrations

Identifies each figure by title and page number

Abstract

This report investigates how U.S. businesses such as RPM must gain a competitive advantage in today's global marketplace by recruiting and retaining a multinational work force. This new wave of immigrants is in great demand for their technical skills, economic ties to their homeland, and as an invaluable resource in a post-9/11 world. Yet many companies like ours still operate by policies designed for native speakers of English. Instead, we need to adapt our company policies and workplace environment to meet the cultural, religious, social, and communication needs of these multinational workers. To do this, we need to promote cultural sensitivity training, both for multinationals and employees who are native speakers of English. Additionally, like other U.S. firms, RPM should adapt vacation schedules and daycare facilities for its multicultural work force. Equally important, RPM needs to ensure, either through translations or plain-English versions, that all documents can be easily understood by multinational workers. We might also offer non-native speakers of English in-house language instruction while providing foreign language training for employees who are native speakers of English.

Concise, informative abstract states purpose of report and why it is important

Uses helpful transitional words

4

Introduction

Gives convincing statistical evidence about the importance of topic

APA cites year of publication

Background

The U.S. work force is undergoing a remarkable revolution. The Bureau of Labor Statistics predicts that by 2012 the labor force in the U.S. will comprise 162 million workers who must fill an estimated 167 million jobs (2004). The most dramatic effect of filling this labor shortage will be in hiring increasing numbers of multinational employees, including those joining RPM. According to the U.S. Chamber of Commerce (2004), by 2025 the number of international residents in the United States will rise from 26 million to 42 million. This new wave of immigrants—Indians, Pakistanis, Hispanics, Asians, Caribs, and Eastern Europeans—will comprise 37 percent of the labor force by 2010 and continue to soar thereafter. Even in light of new immigration reforms mandated by the events of 9/11, immigration will average around 950,000 persons per year, confirming the United States as the most multiculturally diverse country in the global village (Pearson, 2003). This commissioned report explores the implications that this new work force will have on RPM and what we must do to accommodate these workers.

Explains why the report was written

Immigration: Then and Now

Although the United States has been seen as a nation of immigrants, the experiences of the current influx of new arrivals differ radically from those of their predecessors (Congressional Budget Office, 2004). The first great surge of immigration occurred in the late nineteenth and early twentieth centuries when nearly 9 million individuals entered the United States, mostly from the west and central European countries, as shown in Figure 1(a). Many of those citizens never went back to their homeland (Brown, 2004). But today's immigrants arrive from India, Pakistan, China, Mexico, Indonesia, the Philippines, and almost every other place around the globe, as Figure 1(b) reveals.

Contrasts immigration patterns and effects between an earlier period and now

Actively maintaining ties with their native countries, these new immigrants travel back and forth so regularly they have become global citizens, exercising an enormous influence on a business like RPM. Demographers Crane and Boaz claim, "Immigration [will] give America an economic edge in the global economy . . . most notably in the Silicon Valley and other high-tech centers. They provide business contacts with other markets, enhancing [a company's] ability to trade and invest profitably abroad" (2005).

Uses ellipses and brackets for quotes

High-Tech Immigrants

Undeniably, many immigrants today often possess advanced levels of technical expertise. A report by the Kaiser Foundation found that California's Silicon Valley has significantly benefited from the immigrants who have arrived with much needed technical training. Asian, Indian, Pakistani, and Middle Eastern scientists and engineers, who have relocated from a number of countries, now hold more than 40 percent of the region's technical positions

Describes new workers and documents their significance to businesses

5

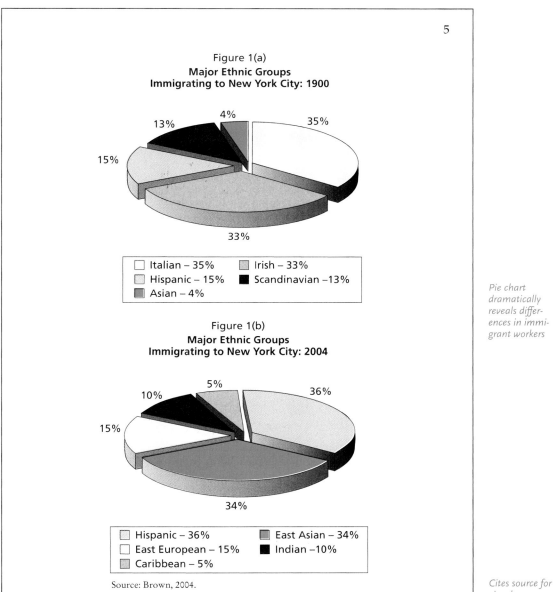

Figure 1(a)
**Major Ethnic Groups
Immigrating to New York City: 1900**

4%

13%

35%

15%

33%

☐ Italian – 35%   ▨ Irish – 33%
☐ Hispanic – 15%   ■ Scandinavian –13%
▨ Asian – 4%

Figure 1(b)
**Major Ethnic Groups
Immigrating to New York City: 2004**

5%

10%

36%

15%

34%

☐ Hispanic – 36%   ▨ East Asian – 34%
☐ East European – 15% ■ Indian –10%
▨ Caribbean – 5%

Source: Brown, 2004.

Pie chart dramatically reveals differences in immigrant workers

Cites source for visual

("Immigrants attain," 2004). Figure 2 indicates the countries of origin for Silicon Valley's immigrants and records each nationality's percentage.

Despite a business downturn following the events of 9/11 and other more recent terrorist activities in Madrid and London, information technology (IT) employers are enthusiastically searching for skilled international workers. The annual immigration limit, set at 65,000 by the controversial new H-1B

6

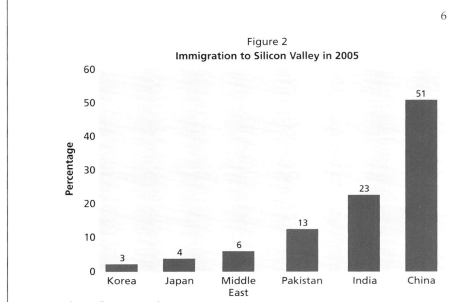

Figure 2
Immigration to Silicon Valley in 2005

Source: Fortune magazine.

guest worker visa, has been met on the very first day of a company's fiscal year by many IT firms (Frauenheim, 2004). Murali Krishna Devarakonda, president of the Immigrants Support Network in Silicon Valley, states why: "We contribute significantly to the research and development of a company's technology" (personal communication, July 21, 2005).

The Challenge to U.S. Businesses

As the U.S. population becomes more culturally diverse, RPM and many other U.S. corporations will be challenged to organize and to conduct business in new ways. E-commerce companies like RPM are striving to adapt their corporate policies and training programs to meet the communication needs of this new sector of multilingual consumers and employees (Adamson, 2005). Annuncio Software in Los Altos may set the pace for the rest of the U.S. corporate world. CEO Didier Moretti boasts about the high level of cultural diversity among employees: "The last time we counted, we had 18 languages represented in our work force. I think having a diversity of backgrounds is a big help. Both small and large businesses . . . need to think about hiring employees who can relate to customers in markets abroad" (cited in Hamilton, 2005, p. 37). As Devarakonda concluded, "It is a win-win situation. Multinational employees excel in the U.S. business culture, and employers profit from their expertise and contacts."

Problem

Meeting the cultural and communication demands of this important labor force poses serious challenges for U.S. employers like RPM. The traditional

7

workplace has to be transformed to honor the ways multinational employees communicate about business. Native English-speaking employees will also have to be better prepared to understand and appreciate their international co-workers. Unfortunately, many corporate policies and programs at RPM, and at other U.S. companies, have been created for native-born, English-speaking employees (Martin, 2005; Ray, 2005). Rather than rewarding multinational workers, such policies unintentionally punish them.

Purpose

The purpose of this report is to show that because of the increasing numbers of multicultural employees in the workplace, RPM must adapt its business environment for this essential and diverse work force.

Scope

This report explores cultural diversity in the U.S. workplace in the new millennium and suggests ways for RPM to compete successfully in the global village by providing equal employment opportunities for multinational workers, fostering cross-cultural literacy, and improving training in intercultural communication.

Discussion

Providing Equal Workplace Opportunities for Multinational Employees

Aggressive Recruitment of People from Diverse Cultures

A multilingual work force makes good business sense in our culturally diverse global market. But many firms such as RPM must be prepared to adapt or modify hiring policies and procedures to attract these multinational employees, beginning with rethinking our recruitment and retention policies. Routine visits to U.S. campuses by company recruiters or "specialized international recruiters" can help to identify and to recruit multinational job candidates (Hamilton, 2005, p. 35). We should even consider visiting universities abroad with distinguished technical programs to attract talented multinational employees. These searches should be combined with our websites and executive blogs to emphasize RPM's commitment to globalization. Working more cooperatively with the Immigration and Naturalization Service will unquestionably help us to retain the most qualified, professional staff.

Capitalizing on a diverse work force, RPM can more effectively increase its multicultural customer base in the global village. Logically, customers buy from the people they can relate to culturally. RPM can take a lead from Union Bank of California, a business that effectively serves a diverse West Coast population, especially its Asian and Hispanic customers. The bank has

Identifies a major problem and why it exists

Two separate, corroborating sources

Concisely states why the report was written

Informs reader that report will focus directly on RPM's needs

Organized into three main headings, each with subheadings

Emphasizes recruiting multinational workers and suggests how to do so

Identifies specific benefits for RPM

8

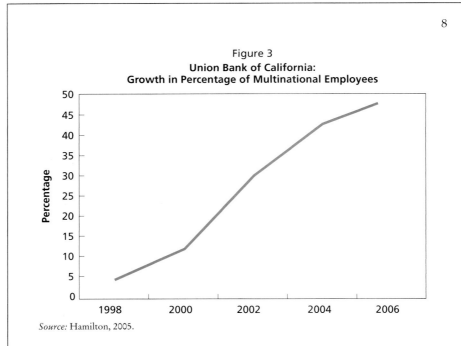

Figure 3
**Union Bank of California:
Growth in Percentage of Multinational Employees**

Source: Hamilton, 2005.

Tracks key information in a clear and concise graph

a successful recruitment history of hiring employees with language skills in Japanese, Vietnamese, Korean, and Spanish. In fact, Union Bank is ranked fourth overall as an employer of minorities ("*Fortune* magazine," 2004). Figure 3 above records the increase in the percentage of multinational employees hired by Union Bank.

Interview supports the need for recruitment

Another successful business, Darden Restaurants of Orlando, Florida, selected Richard Rivera, a Hispanic, to serve as president of Red Lobster, the nation's largest full-service seafood chain. Overseeing 680 restaurants nationwide, Rivera was the "most powerful minority in the restaurant industry" (R. Jackson, personal interview, June 24, 2004). Under Rivera's leadership, Red Lobster established an impressive history of hiring more international employees—totaling more than 35 percent of its work force by 2004—than it had in previous years. Rivera believes that management cannot properly respond to customers from different ethnic backgrounds if the majority of its employees is limited to native speakers of English. Closer to St. Louis, Whitney Abernathy—manager of Netshop, Inc.—found that contracts from Indonesia increased by 17 percent after she hired Jakarta native Safja Jacoef (personal communication, August 10, 2005).

Interview not included in APA Reference list

Commitment to Ethnic Representation

Many companies have strong mission statements on diversity and multinational employees in the workplace. The most progressive of these companies—

9

Toyota, Boeing, IBM, and Wal-Mart—promote multinationals as mentors and interpreters within the company. Such a proactive program, which we would do well to incorporate at RPM, recognizes the leadership abilities of multinational employees. "Glass ceilings," which in the past have prevented women and ethnic employees from moving up the corporate ladder, are being shattered. The recruitment and promotion of non-native speakers of English is vital for corporate success. Tesfaye Aklilu, vice president at United Technologies, astutely states

> In a global business environment, diversity is a business imperative. Diversity of cultures, ideas, perspectives, and values is the norm of the business environment in today's global enterprises. The exchange of ideas from different cultural perspectives gives a business additional, valuable information. Every employee can see his/her position from a global vantage point. ("Diversity at UTC," 2004)

Exemplifying other innovative corporations, Sodexho, ranked as the fiftieth-largest employer in the United States, created the position Vice President of Diversity to establish "an inclusive workplace." Holding that title, Rohini Anand, Ph.D., born in Calcutta, stressed a message RPM should heed: "Sodexho has a strong commitment to ensuring that diversity is not just a strategy or a program, but a way of doing business that guides our actions each and every day" ("Sodexho USA," 2004).

Promoting and Incorporating Cultural Awareness Within the Company

Cross-Cultural Training

Many of RPM's competitors are creating cultural awareness programs for international employees as well as native speakers. Employees find it easier to work with someone whose values and beliefs they understand, while employers benefit from effective on-the-job collaboration. Such a program could have prevented the problem last quarter when one of our non-native English-speaking employees was offended by a cultural misunderstanding ("RPM Second Quarter," 2005). We may want to model our cultural sharing programs after those at American Express, which has a work force representing 40 nations, or those at Extel Communications with its large percentage of Hispanic and Vietnamese employees. United Parcel Service (UPS) profitably pairs a native English-speaking employee with someone from another cultural group to improve on-the-job problem solving and communication. Jamie Allen, a UPS employee since 1995, found her work with Lekha Nfara-Kahn to be one of the most rewarding experiences of her job (cited in Adamson, 2005).

Although they need to encourage cultural sensitivity training, U.S. firms like RPM also need to be cautious about severing international workers' cultural ties—a delicate balance. When management actively promotes bonds

10

among employees from similar cultures, workers are less fearful about losing their identity and becoming "token" employees. The law firm of Latour and Lleras recommends that new multinationals join a "buddy system" to assist their transition to American culture while retaining their cultural identity (U.S. Visa News, 2005). Chase Manhattan Bank has long mobilized culturally similar groups by asking workers of identical cultural heritages to network with each other (Gabriel & Bentzman, 1999). Employees of Turkish backgrounds from Chase Manhattan's New York office go to lunch twice a month with Turkish-born employees from the Newark branches. Chase Manhattan hosts these luncheons and in return receives a bimonthly evaluation of the bank's Turkish and Middle Eastern policies (Hamilton, 2005, p. 36).

Cultural education must go both ways, though. Both sides have things to learn about doing business in a global environment. The U.S. business culture has conventions, too, and few international employees would want to ignore them, but they need to know what those conventions are (Adamson, 2005). A frequent problem with U.S. businesses such as RPM is that we assume everyone knows how we do things and how we think—it never occurs to us to explain ourselves. Problems often stem from easy-to-correct misunderstandings about business etiquette. For example, native speakers of English are typically comfortable within a space of 1.5 to 4 feet for general personal interactions in business. But workers from Taiwan or Japan, who prefer a greater conversational distance, feel uncomfortable if their desks are less than a few feet away from another employee's workspace (Johnson, 2005, p. 44; "Taiwanese business culture," 2004).

The Impact of World Terrorism

The terrorist attacks in New York, Afghanistan, Madrid, London, and elsewhere have had a profound impact on businesses with multinational employees. Thanks to their multinational work force, U.S. firms were able to familiarize themselves with different cultural values, codes, and responses and thereby gain valuable interpretations of policies and products. Equally significant, many of these multinational workers helped stamp out stereotypes that lead to prejudice. For example, Jameela Habib, a senior manager at E-Accounts, gave this moving testimony: "I was born in Damascus, and I celebrate my Syrian roots. Like all of my co-workers, I deplore terrorism and uplift the heroism of police, firefighters, and medical personnel around the world. I am honored to be a part of a company that brought relief to the victims of terrorism" (personal communication, April 9, 2005).

Promotion of Cultural Sensitivity

Company efforts to validate different cultures might also include the recognition of a non-Western ethnic group's holidays or memorable historical events. RPM has just begun to do this by hosting cultural events, including Cinco de Mayo and Chinese New Year celebrations. Techsure, Inc., an Illinois software firm, allows Muslim employees to alter their work schedules during

Relevant source on topic of immigration

Offers two examples RPM could follow

Another clear transitional sentence

Identifies key RPM problem

Gives cultural example

Relates world terrorism to business culture

Offers further benefit of multinational employees in the U.S. workplace

Gives precise ways RPM can incorporate cultural sensitivity into the workplace

11

Ramadan, Islam's holy month of fasting (M. Saradayan, personal communication, June 30, 2005). Many companies honor National Hispanic Heritage Month in September, which coincides with the independence celebrations of five Latin American countries (U.S. Department of Equal Employment Opportunity [USEEO], 2005). GRT Systems sends New Year's greetings at Waisak (the Buddhist Day of Enlightenment) to its Chinese employees and to Indian workers at Rama Dipawli. Chemeka Taylor, GRT's operations manager, wisely points out: "We send native-born employees Christmas cards; why shouldn't we honor our international work force, too?" (personal communication, May 10, 2005). Figure 4 (on page 12) provides a multicultural calendar that RPM needs to follow in developing cultural sensitivity policies.

Includes appropriate calendar of ethnic holidays

Successful U.S. firms have been sensitive to the needs of their English-speaking employees for years. Flexible scheduling, telecommuting options, daycare, and preventative health programs have become part of corporate benefit plans to take care of employees. Many of these options and benefits have already been in place at RPM. But an international work force presents additional cultural concerns for management to respond to with sensitivity. For example, company cafeterias might easily accommodate the dietary restrictions of vegetarian workers or those who abstain from certain foods, such as dairy products or meat. At Globtech, soybean and fish entrees are always available (Ray, 2005). Adding ethnic items at RPM would express our cultural awareness and respect for multinational employees.

Identifies current RPM programs and how they could be easily modified for multinational workers

Daycare raises critical issues for all working parents, native as well as non-native speakers of English. A discussion of daycare is also a key issue for RPM because we have provided such facilities at our high-tech park in San Luis Obispo, for which we have received much positive feedback over the past eight years ("RPM daycare facilities," 2004). By providing child care that reflects our workers' culturally diverse needs, RPM can give a multinational work force greater peace of mind and better enable them to do their jobs. DEJ Computers, for example, insists that at least two or three of its daycare workers must be fluent in Korean or Hindi (Parker, 2005). Another culturally sensitive employer, Angelica Nurseries, assisted its Hispanic work force by hiring bilingual daycare workers and by serving foods the children customarily eat at home (Gabriel & Bentzman).

Cites company publication showing research within the organization

Making Business Communication More Understandable for Multinational Employees

Third major section

Translation of Written Communications

All employees must be able to understand business communications affecting them. Among the essential documents causing trouble for multicultural readers are company handbooks, insurance and health care documents, policy changes, and OSHA and EPA safety regulations (Hamilton, 2005). To ensure

Turns to written communication and multinational workers

12

Figure 4
A Multicultural Calendar

December 2007

					1	2 Advent begins (Christian)
3	4	5 Hanukkah begins (Jewish) (ends Dec. 21)	6 Feast of St. Nicholas (some European countries)	7	8 Bodhi Day (Rohatsu- Buddhist)	9
10	11	12 Feast Day— Our Lady of Guadalupe (Hispanic Catholic)	13	14	15	16
17	18 Waqf al Arafa (Islam)	19	20 Id al Adha (Islam)	21	22	23 Emperor's Birthday (Japan)
24	25 Christmas (Christian)	26 Kwanzaa begins (Interfaith) (ends Jan. 1)	27	28 O-sho-ga-tsu (Japan) (eight-day festival)	29	30
31 New Year's Eve						

Some Information About December's Daily Observance

Dec. 5 Hanukkah: Eight-day celebration commemorating the rededication of the Temple of Jerusalem
Dec. 6 Feast of Saint Nicholas: Christmas celebration in Austria, Belgium, France, Germany, the Netherlands, Poland, Russia, and Switzerland
Dec. 8 Bodhi Day: Buddhists celebrate Prince Gautama's vow to attain enlightenment
Dec. 12 Feast of Our Lady of Guadalupe: (Mexico) Catholic Christian holiday honoring the appearance of the Virgin Mary near Mexico City in 1531
Dec. 18 Waqf al Arafa: Islamic observance day during Hajj when pilgrims pray for forgiveness and mercy
Dec. 20 Id al Adha: Islamic commemoration of Ibrahim's willingness to sacrifice his son Ismail for Allah
Dec. 25 Christmas: Christians celebrate the birth of Jesus
Dec. 26 Kwanzaa: African American and Pan-African celebration of family, community, and culture. Seven life virtues are presented.

Source: Johnson (2005): 45.

13

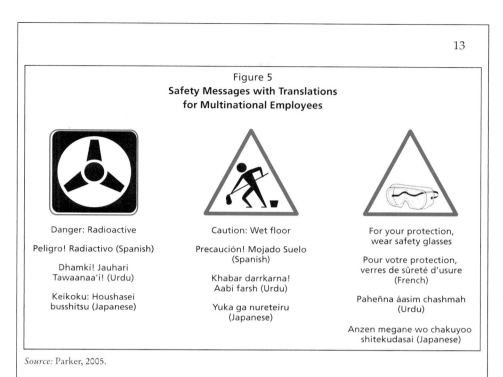

Figure 5
**Safety Messages with Translations
for Multinational Employees**

Danger: Radioactive

Peligro! Radiactivo (Spanish)

Dhamki! Jauhari
Tawaanaa'i! (Urdu)

Keikoku: Houshasei
busshitsu (Japanese)

Caution: Wet floor

Precaución! Mojado Suelo
(Spanish)

Khabar darrkarna!
Aabi farsh (Urdu)

Yuka ga nureteiru
(Japanese)

For your protection,
wear safety glasses

Pour votre protection,
verres de sûreté d'usure
(French)

Paheñna áasim chashmah
(Urdu)

Anzen megane wo chakuyoo
shitekudasai (Japanese)

Source: Parker, 2005.

*Cites examples
of safety visu-
als with trans-
lations into
multinational
workers' native
languages*

maximum understanding of these documents by a multinational work force, RPM will need to provide a translation or at least a plain-English version of them. To do this, RPM could solicit the help of employees who are fluent in the non-native English speakers' language as well as contract with professional translators to prepare appropriate documents.

*Offers practical
solution*

Workplace signs in particular, especially safety messages, must consider the language needs of international workers. In the best interest of corporate safety, RPM needs to have these signs translated into the languages represented by multinationals in the workplace and/or to post signs that use global symbols, such as those shown in Figure 5. Unquestionably, we need to avoid signs that workers might find hard or even impossible to decipher. For example, a large **P** for "parking" or a **?** for "questions are answered here" or an **H** for "hospital" might be unfamiliar to non-native speakers of English (Parker, 2005).

*Gives exam-
ples, and what
to avoid and
why*

Exchange of Language Learning

Providing English language instruction for employees also has obvious advantages for the RPM workplace in the new millennium. Should RPM elect not to provide in-house language training, the company should consider reimbursing employees for necessary courses, books, tapes, and software.

*Outlines spe-
cific benefits
for RPM*

14

Points to apt example

Moreover, we should make available an audio library of specific vocabulary and phrases commonly used on the job as well as multilingual dictionaries with relevant technical terms. Hiromi Naguchi, an e-marketing analyst at PowerUsers Networking, praised the English language training she received on her job. Although she had twelve years of English in the Osaka (Japan) schools, Naguchi developed her listening and speaking skills on the job, benefiting her employers, co-workers, and customers. As a result of her diligence, Naguchi was recognized as her company's "Most Valuable Employee for 2005" for her interpersonal skills (H. Naguchi, personal communication, June 9, 2005).

Argues that reader must consider both sides

Cites business survey to confirm the necessity of change at RPM

Identifies quote within a source

But language training has to be reciprocal—for native as well as non-native speakers—if communication is to succeed in the global marketplace. Sadly, most Americans do not know a foreign language and "fewer than 1 in 10 students at U.S. colleges major in [a] foreign language" (Cutshall, 2005, p. 20). Many international workers are bi- or even trilingual. In India and South Africa, for example, the average employee speaks three or more national languages every day to conduct business. A recent international survey of executive recruiters (2005) showed that being bilingual is critical to success in business ("Ease with languages"). According to this survey, 85 percent of European recruiters, 88 percent of Asian recruiters, and 95 percent of recruiters in Latin America stressed the importance of speaking at least two languages in the new global village. As Paul Reilly, CEO of Korn/Ferry International, emphasized, "Although English remains the dominant language of international business, multilingual executives clearly have a competitive advantage. This will only increase with the continued globalization of commerce" (cited in "Ease with languages," 2005). RPM executives might want to contract with one of the companies specializing in language instruction for business people found at *http://www.selfgrowth.com/foreignlanguage.html.*

Conclusions

Following the body, conclusion concisely summarizes the highlights of the report without repeating the documentation

To compete in the global marketplace, RPM, like other U.S. companies, must emphasize a cultural diversity in its corporate mission and in the workplace. Through its policies and programs, RPM must aggressively recruit and retain an increasing number of technologically educated and experienced multinational workers who are in great demand today and will be even more so in the next ten to twenty years. They can help us increase our international customer base and advance the state of our technology. But we need to ensure that the workplace is sensitive to their cultural, religious, and communication needs. Providing equal opportunities, diversity training and networking, and easy-to-understand business documents will keep RPM globally competitive in recruiting and retaining this essential group of workers. We

15

can expand only by making a commitment to learn about and respect other cultures and their ways of doing business.

Recommendations

By implementing the following recommendations, RPM Technologies can succeed in hiring and promoting the IT multinational professionals our company requires.

1. Recruit multinational workers more effectively through our website, international hiring specialists, and visits to campuses here and abroad, and work more closely with the Immigration and Naturalization Service (INS) to retain multinationals.
2. Create cultural sensitivity and networking groups comprising multinational and native English-speaking employees. Develop educational materials for employees who are native speakers of English about the cultures of their multinational co-workers.
3. Establish a mentoring program to identify leadership abilities in multinational employees.
4. Supply relevant translations and plain-English versions of company handbooks, manuals, and safety codes.
5. Reassess and adapt daycare facilities to meet the needs of children of multinational employees.

Provides specific, relevant recommendations, based on conclusions, to solve the problem at RPM

Numbered list format is easy to read for busy executives

Uses strong, active verbs to make recommendations

16

REFERENCES

Adamson, R. (2005, February). Challenges ahead for American business. *National Economics Review, 11*, 45–46.

Brown, P. (2004, December 20). History of U.S. immigration. Retrieved May 2, 2005, from http://immigration.ucn.edu

Chan, M. (2005). Incident report (RPM Technologies report number 14P-C). RPM Technologies.

Congressional Budget Office. (2004, November). A description of the immigrant population. Retrieved February 20, 2005, from http://www.cbo.gov/showdoc.cfm?index=6019&sequence=0

Crane, E. H., & Boaz, D. (Eds.). (2005). *Cato Handbook on Policy* (6th ed.). Washington, DC: Cato.

Cutshall, S. (2005, January). Why we need "the year of languages." *Educational Leadership, 62*(4), 20–23.

Diversity at UTC. (2004). *United Technologies Corporation.* Retrieved February 5, 2005, from http://www.utc.com/careers/diversity/index4.htm

Ease with languages gives executives advantage. (2005, February 3). *Business Edge.* Retrieved April 11, 2005, from http://www.businessedge.ca/article.cfm/newsID/8249.cfm

Foreign language training information. (2002). *SelfGrowth.com.* Retrieved July 16, 2002, from http://www.selfgrowth.com/foreignlanguage.html

Fortune magazine ranks Union Bank one of the best companies for minorities. (2004, June 23). *Union Bank of California.* Retrieved May 9, 2005, from http://www.uboc.com/about/main/0,3250,2485_11256_502261585,00.html

Frauenheim, E. (2004, October 1). H-1B visa limit for 2005 already reached. *C-Net News.* Retrieved February 20, 2005, from http://news.com.com/H-1B+visa+limit+for+2005+already+reached/2100-1022_3-5392917.html?tag=nl

Gabriel, B., & Bentzman, J. (1999, July). The 50 best companies for Latinas to work for in the U.S. *Latina Style, 50*, 1.

Hamilton, B. E. (2005, May 15). Diversity is the answer for today's workforce. *The New Business Journal, 10*(38), 35–37.

Immigrants attain the American dream in Silicon Valley. (2004, December 19). *The Taipei Times*, p. 12.

Johnson, V. M. (2005). Growing multinational diversity in business sparks changes. *Business Across the Nation, 23*(7), 43–48.

LaJoya, R. (Director). (2005, April). *Noticias por la gente* [Television program]. Miami's Extra TV. (Transcript available from Merganser Communications, 61 Woodlawn Street, Miami, FL 33166)

All entries listed alphabetically by author's last name, or (if no author) by first word of title

Date of publication included for every entry after author's name or title if author's name not given

Pages provided for print sources

17

Martin, P. (2005). Migration news. Retrieved July 20, 2005, from http://www.migration.ucdavis.edu

Parker, M. (2005, May). Immigration facts. Retrieved June 21, 2005, from http://immigration.org

Pearson, J. (2003, April). U.S. Population Expands as Europe's Levels Off. *New York City Sierra Club.* Retrieved March 4, 2005, from http://newyork.sierraclub.org/nyc/spring_03_4.htm

Ray, S. F. (2005, March 30). Serving up culture. Retrieved June 21, 2005, from http://www.culture.org

RPM daycare facilities rated high. (2004, January 15). *RPM News*, 31–32. (Also available on RPM intranet)

RPM second quarter activity report. (2005). *RPM Internal Reports.* Retrieved June 4, 2005, from RPM intranet.

Sodexho USA receives strategic examples of excellence in diversity award. (2004, August 11). *Sodexho USA.* Retrieved March 6, 2005, from http://www.sodexhousa.com/press%2Dreleases/pr81204.asp

Taiwanese business culture. (2004). *Executive Planet.* Retrieved May 27, 2005, from http://www.executiveplanet.com/business-culture-in/132438266669.html

U.S. Bureau of Labor Statistics. (2004). Tomorrow's jobs. Retrieved March 7, 2005, from http://www.bls.gov/oco/oco2003.htm

U.S. Chamber of Commerce. (2004, April). Chamber, labor leaders renew call for immigration reform. *USChamber.com.* Retrieved June 18, 2004, from http://www.uschamber.com/Press+Room/2004+Releases

U.S. Department of Equal Employment Opportunity. (2005). *Hispanic employment program report for 2005* (EEO Publication No. B56.2245). Washington, DC: U.S. Government Printing Office.

U.S. Visa News. (2005). Latour and Lleras immigration attorneys. Retrieved March 8, 2005, from http://www.usvisanews.com/relbuddy.shtml

Second and subsequent lines indented 5 spaces

APA requires access date as well as posting date in Web entries

Only the first word of title capitalized

Full Web addresses are given for verification and to make source easy to find

▮ Final Words of Advice About Long Reports

Perhaps no piece of writing you do on the job—or as a course assignment for your instructor—carries more weight than your work on a long report. The long report requires you to use all the researching, organizing, drafting, revising, and editing skills you have learned.

The preparation of a long report may appear at first to be formidable. But you can simplify your job and increase your chances for success by following these guidelines for scheduling, researching, and collaborating:

1. Plan and work early—do not postpone work on identifying, researching, and drafting until a deadline draws near.
2. Do a thorough search among Internet, print, and other resources.
3. Divide your workload into meaningful units—reassure yourself that you do not have to write the report or even an entire section of a report in a day or two.
4. Set up mini-deadlines for each phase of your work and then meet them.
5. If you are preparing the report as part of a team, confer often and carefully with others in your group.

Online Study Center

Access the writing long reports Revision Checklist online at college .hmco.com/pic/ kolin8e

✔ Revision Checklist

☐ Concentrated on a major problem—one with significant implications for my major, neighborhood, city, or employer.

☐ Identified, justified, and described the significance of the main problem as opposed to focusing on a minor side issue.

☐ Did sufficient research—in the library, on the Internet, through interviewing, from personal observation and/or testing—to convince my readers that I am knowledgeable about this problem, its scope and effects, and likely solution.

☐ Became familiar with key terms, major researchers in the field, major changes, trends, and accomplishments.

☐ Anticipated how various managers and other decision makers will use and profit from my report for their long-range planning.

☐ Made sure I understand what employer/teacher/reader is looking for.

☐ Followed company's/instructor's guidelines for the scope, format, and documentation of work.

☐ Followed company's/instructor's schedule for completing various stages of long report.

☐ Divided and labeled the parts of long report to make it easy for readers to follow and to show a careful plan of organization.

Continued

Continued

☐ Supplied an informative abstract that leaves no doubt in readers' minds about what report deals with and why.

☐ Designed attractive title page that contains all the basic information—title, date, for whom the report is written, my name.

☐ Gave readers all the necessary introductory information about background, problem, purpose of report, and scope. Made sure that introduction is neither too long nor too short.

☐ Included in body of report the weight of all my research—the facts, statistics, interview comments, and descriptions—that my readers need in order to know that I have done my homework on the topic well.

☐ Included subheadings to reflect the major divisions into which I have organized the research that forms the nucleus of the text.

☐ Wrapped up report in succinct conclusion. Told readers what the findings of my research are and accurately interpreted all data.

☐ Supplied a recommendations section (if required) that tells readers concretely how they can respond to the problem using the data. Offered recommendations that are realistic and practical and related directly to the research and topic. Ensured that recommendations are persuasive.

☐ Included in the final copy of report all the parts listed in table of contents.

☐ Supplied a one-page letter of transmittal or cover letter informing readers why the report was written and describing its scope and findings.

Exercises

1. Send an e-mail to your instructor on how one of the short reports in Chapter 15 could be useful to someone who has to write a long report.

2. Using the information contained in Figures 16.1 and 16.2, draft an introduction for the report "A Study to Determine New Directions in Women's Athletics at Coastal College." Add any details you think will be relevant.

3. What kinds of research did Terri Smith Ruckel do to write the long report in Figure 16.3? As part of your answer, include the titles of any specific reference works you think the writer may have consulted. (You may want to review Chapter 9.)

4. Study Figure 16.3 and answer the following questions based on it.
   a. Why can the abstract be termed informative rather than descriptive?
   b. How has the writer successfully limited the scope of the report?
   c. Where does the writer use internal summaries especially well?
   d. Where and how has the writer adapted her technical information for her audience (a general reader)?
   e. What visual devices does the writer use to separate parts of the report and divisions within each part?

Online Study Center
Find additional writing long reports exercises at college.hmco.com/pic/kolin8e

    f. How does the writer introduce, summarize, and draw conclusions from the expert opinions she cites in order to substantiate the main points?

    g. What are the ways in which the writer documents information she has gathered?

    h. What functions does the conclusion serve for readers? Cite specific examples from the report.

    i. How do the recommendations follow from the material presented in the report? How are they both distinct and interrelated?

5. Come to class prepared to discuss at least two major problems that would be suitable topics for a long report. Consider an important community problem—traffic, crime, air and water pollution, housing, transportation—or a problem at your college. Then write a letter to a consulting firm or other appropriate agency or business, requesting a study of the problem and a report.

6. Write a report outline for one of the problems you decided on in Exercise 5. Use major headings and include the kinds of information discussed in the setion on front matter in this chapter (pp. 671–675).

7. Have your instructor look at and approve the outline you prepared for Exercise 6. Then write a long report based on the outline, either individually or as part of a collaborative writing team.

CHAPTER 17

Making Successful Presentations at Work

Almost every job requires employees to have and to use carefully developed speaking skills. In fact, to get hired, you have to be a persuasive speaker at your job interview. And to advance up the corporate ladder, you will have to continue to be a confident, well-prepared, and persuasive speaker. The goal of this chapter is to help you be a more successful speaker.

Online Study Center

To expand your understanding of making presentations, take advantage of the ACE quizzes, sample documents, Web links, and exercises at college.hmco.com/pic/kolin8e

Types of Presentations

On the job you will have numerous presentation responsibilities that will vary in the amount of preparation they require, the time they last, and the audience and the occasion for which they are intended. Here are some frequent types of presentations you can expect to make as part of your job:

- sales appeals to prospective customers
- evaluations of products or policies
- progress reports to your boss and clients
- reports to superiors about your job accomplishments
- justifications of your position or even your department
- appeals and/or explanations before elected officials
- presentations at professional conferences
- explanation of a procedure, decision, or plan before a community/civic group (chamber of commerce or local PTA)

Whatever type of presentation you are asked to deliver, this chapter gives you practical advice on how to become a better, more assured communicator in both informal briefings, including on the telephone, and formal presentations.

Informal Briefings

If you have ever given a book report or explained laboratory results in front of a class, you have given an informal briefing. Such semiformal reports are a routine part of many jobs. Here are some of the typical informal briefings you may be asked to deliver at work:

- a status report on your current project
- an update or end-of-shift report, like those nurses and police officers give
- an explanation of a policy to co-workers
- a report on a conference you attended
- a demonstration of new equipment or software
- a follow-up session on equipment or procedures
- a summary of a meeting you attended

Such presentations are usually short (one to seven minutes, perhaps), and you won't always be given advance notice. When the boss tells you to "say a few words about the new website" (or the new programming procedure), you will not be expected to give a lengthy formal speech.

Guidelines for Preparing Informal Briefings

Follow these guidelines when you have to make an informal briefing.

- Make your comments brief and to the point.
- Keyboard a few bulleted items you plan to cover.
- Highlight key phrases and terms you need to stress.
- Include in your notes only the major points you want to mention.
- Arrange your points in chronological order or from cause to effect.

Figure 17.1 is an informal outline with key facts used by an employee who is introducing Diana J. Rizzo, a visiting speaker, to a monthly meeting of safety directors.

Using Telephones and Cell Phones Effectively

Using a telephone or cell phone is an essential part of workplace communication. You represent your company over the telephone, and *how* you say something can be as crucial as *what* you say. Your voice and your attitude symbolize your employer's service or product for the person on the other end of the line.

Here are some basic rules of telephone etiquette that can help you succeed at work:

1. Answer calls on the second or, at the latest, third ring.
2. Never tie up a company phone with personal business. One large bank put it this way: "To a customer a busy signal is almost the same as a locked door."
3. Avoid shouting, whispering, mumbling. Sound friendly, eager to help. Keep a smile in your voice. Never chew gum or try to start or finish your lunch while on the phone. Don't slur your words.
4. Answer courteously. Identify yourself, your title, your department. "Hello, this is John Loo, assistant programmer at Northwest Megalink." Ask how you can assist the caller. "How may I help you?" Responses like "thank you," "please," and "you're welcome" epitomize customer service.
5. Eliminate disturbing background noises—radios, televisions, printers, and beepers.
6. Never put someone on hold unless you ask his or her permission. It is rude to say "Hold on. I'll look it up," and then drop the phone on your desk.

Some notes for an informal briefing to introduce an engineer to a group of safety directors.   Figure 17.1

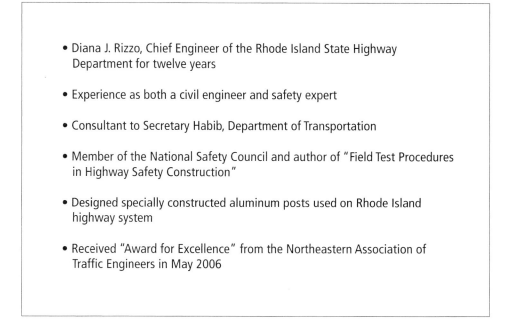

- Diana J. Rizzo, Chief Engineer of the Rhode Island State Highway Department for twelve years

- Experience as both a civil engineer and safety expert

- Consultant to Secretary Habib, Department of Transportation

- Member of the National Safety Council and author of "Field Test Procedures in Highway Safety Construction"

- Designed specially constructed aluminum posts used on Rhode Island highway system

- Received "Award for Excellence" from the Northeastern Association of Traffic Engineers in May 2006

7. If you make a call, prepare for it. Have copies of any correspondence, reports, price lists in front of you. Pull up relevant documents on your computer so they are in front of you as you speak. After a polite opening, identify yourself and your purpose: "Good morning, Ms. Agawa, this is Seetha Salinas at Web-World returning your call to give you the information you asked about."

8. Check your voice mail every day, just as you would your e-mail. In not doing so, you may miss making a sale or attending a conference.

9. Never give intricate instructions over the phone. E-mail, fax, or snail mail such documents and use a telephone call to follow up and see if the individual has any questions that you can answer or any further concerns that you need to clear up.

10. If you record a message to greet callers when you are not available, make it friendly and helpful, not gruff and rude—"I'm not in. Leave your message at the tone."

Cell Phone Courtesy

When you use a cell phone, follow all the rules of telephone courtesy just discussed in addition to heeding these guidelines:

1. Do not use your personal cell phone (or beeper) at work.

2. Silence the ringer on any cell phone during a conference; sales meeting; business breakfast, lunch, or dinner; or at any event where it would be heard as intrusive and disturbing. Instead, use the cell phone vibrator option to notify you of a call.

3. When you use a cell phone for business-related calls, select a professional-sounding ring tone. "The Charge of the Light Brigade" or a melody from a cartoon is not appropriate.

4. Turn cell phones off when you come to class; enter a hospital (where they can interfere with life-support equipment); or attend a religious service, legal hearing (courtroom), or professional conference.

5. Never allow a ringing cell phone to interrupt a meeting with a customer. The immediate effect is to make you and your company look like you are not totally focused on the customer's needs.

6. It is unethical to charge personal long-distance calls to your company cell phone number without authorization from your boss, or to allow a co-worker, friend, or family member to use your company cell phone.

7. Always make sure your cell phone is charged and working. It's embarrassing to lose contact with your boss or a client in the middle of a conversation.

Formal Presentations

Whereas an informal briefing is likely to be short, generally conversational, and intended for a limited number of people, a formal presentation is much longer, far less conversational, and may be intended for a wider audience. It involves much more preparation.

Avoid speaking "off the cuff." The professional speechmaker may be comfortable with this approach, but for most of us, the worst way to make a presentation is to speak without any preparation whatsoever. You only fool yourself if you think you will have all the necessary details and explanations in the back of your head. Once you start talking, generally everything does not fall into place smoothly. Without preparation, you are likely to confuse important points or forget them entirely. Mark Twain's advice is apt here: "It takes three weeks to prepare a good impromptu speech."

Expect to spend several days preparing your presentation. You cannot just dash it off. You will need time to

- research the subject
- interview key resource individuals
- prepare, time, and sequence visuals
- coordinate your talk with presentations by co-workers or your boss
- rehearse your presentation

Many of us are uncomfortable in front of an audience because we feel frightened or embarrassed. Much of that anxiety can be eased if you know what to expect. The two areas you should investigate thoroughly before you begin to prepare your presentation are (1) who will be in your audience and (2) why they are there.

Analyzing Your Audience

The more you learn about your audience, the better prepared you will be to give them what they need. Just as you do for your written work, for your oral presentation you will have to do some research about the audience, emphasizing the "you attitude" and establishing your own credibility.

Consider Your Audience as a Group of Listeners, Not Readers

While audience analysis pertains both to readers of your work and to listeners of your presentation, there are several fundamental differences between these two groups. Unlike a reader of your report, the audience for your presentation

- is a captive audience
- may have only one chance to get your message
- has less time to digest what you say
- has a shorter attention span
- can't always go back to review what you said or jump ahead to get a preview
- is more easily distracted—by interruptions, chairs being moved, people coughing, and so on
- cannot absorb as many of the technical details as you would include in a written report

Take all of these differences into account as you plan your presentation and assess who constitutes your audience.

Who Is Your Audience?

Here are five key questions to ask when analyzing your audience.

1. **How much do they know about your topic?**

   - consumers with little or no technical knowledge
   - technical individuals who understand terms, jargon, and background
   - business managers looking only for the bottom line

2. **What unites them as a group?**

   - members of the same profession
   - customers using the same products
   - employees of the company you work for

3. **What is their interest level in your topic?**

   - highly motivated
   - uninterested in your topic—only there because attendance is mandatory
   - neutral—waiting to be informed, entertained, or persuaded
   - worried—looking for comforting explanations
   - mildly skeptical
   - uncooperative and antagonistic, likely to challenge you

4. **What do you want them to do after hearing your presentation?**

   - buy a product or service
   - adopt a plan
   - change a schedule
   - learn more about your topic
   - sign a petition

5. **What questions are they likely to raise?**

- about money
- about personnel
- about locations

Special Considerations for a Multinational Audience

Online Study Center

Locate making presentations globalization exercises at college.hmco.com/pic/kolin8e

Given the international make-up of audiences at many business presentations, you may have to address a group of listeners whose native language is not English or even make a presentation before individuals in a country other than your own. Consider your audience's particular cultural taboos and protocols. Do they accept your looking at them directly, or do they frown on eye contact? Will they expect you to stand in one place, or will they be comfortable if you move about the room while you speak?

As you prepare a talk before a multinational audience, keep the following points in mind:

1. Brush up on your audience's culture, especially accepted ways they communicate with each other (see pp. 165–184).
2. Find out what constitutes an appropriate length for a talk before your audience. (German listeners might be accustomed to hearing someone read a thirty- to forty-page paper, while members from another culture would regard that practice as improper.)
3. Be especially careful about introducing humor—avoid anything that is based on nationality, dialect, religion, or race.
4. Think twice about injecting anything autobiographical into your speech. Some cultures regard such intimacy as an invasion of privacy.
5. Steer clear of politics; you risk losing your audience's confidence.
6. Choose visuals with universally understood icons.

▊ The Parts of Formal Presentations

As you read this section, refer to Marilyn Claire Ford's PowerPoint presentation in Figures 17.2 and 17.3. Note how effectively she used the PowerPoint format (see pp. 712–715) to convince a potential client, GTP Systems, to purchase a service contract provided by World Tech, her employer. Her talk consists of seven slides that contain relevant images and concise text.

The Introduction

The most important part of a presentation is your introduction, which should capture the audience's attention by answering these questions: (1) Who are you? (2) What are your qualifications? (3) What specific topic are you speaking about? and (4) How is the topic relevant to us?

Your first and most immediate goal is to establish rapport with your audience, win their confidence, and elicit their cooperation. Since your audience is probably at their most attentive during the first few minutes of your presentation, they will

Marilyn Claire Ford's presentation—slide sorter view.   Figure 17.2

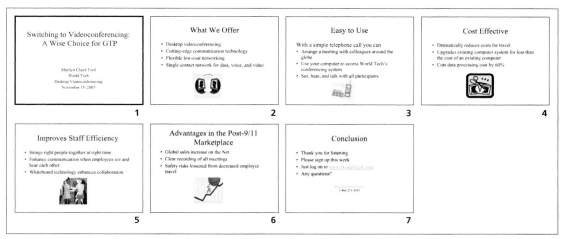

Note: PowerPoint slide sorter view shows slides reduced in size.

pay close attention to everything about you and what you say. Seize the moment and build momentum.

An effective introduction should be proportional to the length of your presentation. A ten-minute speech requires no more than a sixty-second introduction; a twenty-minute speech needs no more than a two- or three-minute introduction. Note how Marilyn Claire Ford in slides 1 and 2 introduces herself, her company, and its benefits for GTP.

How to Begin

You can begin by introducing yourself, emphasizing your professional qualifications and interests. (A self-introduction is unnecessary if someone else has introduced you or if you know everyone in the room.)

Give Listeners a Road Map

Give listeners a "road map" at the beginning of your presentation so that they will know where you are, where you are going, and what they have to look forward to or to recall. Indicate what your topic is and how you have organized what you have to say about it.

> My presentation today on Digital Business software will last about 20 minutes and is divided into three parts. First, I will outline briefly recent software changes. Second, I will give a detailed review of how those changes directly affect our company. Third, I will show how our company can profitably implement those changes. At the end of my presentation, there will be time for your questions and comments.

The most informative presentations are the easiest to follow. Restrict your topic to ensure that you will be able to organize it carefully and sensibly—for example, a tasty diet under 1,000 calories a day or a course in learning Java or another software package.

Figure 17.3   A sample PowerPoint presentation.

Introduces speaker, provides reason for presentation

Switching to Videoconferencing: A Wise Choice for GTP

Marilyn Claire Ford
World Tech
Desktop Videoconferencing
November 15, 2005

Succinctly lists benefits her company offers

What We Offer

- Desktop videoconferencing
- Cutting-edge communication technology
- Flexible low-cost networking
- Single contact network for data, voice, and video

First of four slides that make up the body of the presentation

Develops first key sales feature

Easy to Use

With a simple telephone call you can
- Arrange a meeting with colleagues around the globe
- Use your computer to access World Tech's conferencing system
- See, hear, and talk with all participants

Continued

(Continued)   *Figure 17.3*

Cost Effective

- Dramatically reduces costs for travel
- Upgrades existing computer system for less than the cost of an existing computer
- Cuts data processing cost by 60%

Key second point gives only essential facts

Appropriate icon emphasizing "cutting" costs

Improves Staff Efficiency

- Brings right people together at right time
- Enhances communication when employees see and hear each other
- Whiteboard technology enhances collaboration

Third crucial sales feature appropriately mentions specific technology

Icon shows bringing staff together

Advantages in the Post-9/11 Marketplace

- Global sales increase on the Net
- Clear recording of all meetings
- Safety risks lessened from decreased employee travel

Addresses security as last point in list of advantages

Figure 17.3   (Continued)

Conclusion

Issues a call to action, makes contact easy through website, e-mail, and telephone

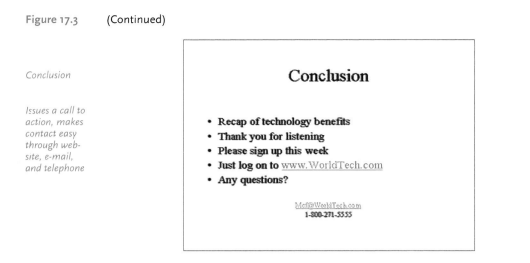

Capture the Audience's Attention

Use any of the following strategies to get your audience to "bite the hook."

- Ask a question. "Did you know that every thirty minutes a foreign-owned business opens in China?"
- Start with a quotation. Winston Churchill said, "We get things to make a living but we give things to have a life." (Consult *Bartlett's Familiar Quotations* online at *http://www.bartleby.com.*)
- Give an interesting statistic. "In 2007, two million heart attack victims will live to tell about it." (Go to the *World Almanac and Book of Facts* to find something relevant to your presentation topic.)
- Relate an anecdote or story. Be sure it is relevant and in good taste; make your audience feel at ease and friendly toward you by establishing a bond with them.

Be careful about using humor in a business talk. It could backfire—the audience may not get the point or may even be offended by it.

The Body

The body is the longest part of your presentation, just as it is in a long report. Make it persuasive and relevant to your audience by (1) explaining a process, (2) describing a condition, (3) solving a problem, (4) arguing a case, or (5) doing all of these. See how the body of Marilyn Claire Ford's presentation in Figure 17.3 is organized around the customer benefits of GTP's switching to desktop videoconferencing. In slides 3–6 she outlines how easy, economical, and efficient such technology is to use in a post-9/11 economy.

To get the right perspective, recall your own experiences as a member of an audience. How often did you feel bored or angry because a speaker tried to overload you with details or could not stick to the point?

Ways to Organize the Body

Here are a few helpful ways you can present and organize information in the body of your presentation. In writing a report, design your document to help readers visually, supplying headings, underscoring, bullets, necessary white space, and headers and footers. In a speech, switch from those purely visual devices to aural ones, such as the following:

1. **Give signals (directions) to show where you are going or where you have been.** Enumerate your points: *first, second, third.* Emphasize cause-and-effect relationships with *subsequently, therefore, furthermore.* When you tell a story, follow a chronological sequence and fill your speech with signposts: *before, following, next, then.*

2. **Comment on your own material.** Tell the audience if some point is especially significant, memorable, or relevant. "This next fact is the most important thing I'll say today."

3. **Provide internal summaries.** Spending a few seconds to recap what you have just covered will reassure your audience and you as well.

> We have already discussed the difficulties in establishing a menu repertory, or the list of items that the food service manager wants to appear on the menu. Now we will turn to ways of determining which items should appear on a menu and why.

4. **Anticipate any objections or qualifications your audience is likely to have.** Address the issues with relevant facts about costs, personnel, and/or equipment in your presentation.

The Conclusion

Plan your conclusion as carefully as you do your introduction. Stopping with a screeching halt is as bad as trailing off in a fading monotone. Never stop abruptly after you cover the main points in the body of your presentation. An effective conclusion should leave the audience feeling that you and they have come full circle and accomplished what you promised. Notice how Marilyn Claire Ford ends her presentation by persuading GTP Systems that they will gain a competitive edge, the point with which she began (see pp. 708–709).

What to Put in a Conclusion

A conclusion should contain something memorable. Never introduce a new subject or simply repeat your introduction. A conclusion can contain the following:

- a fresh restatement of your three or four main points
- a call to action, just as in a sales letter—to buy, to note, to agree, to volunteer
- a final emphasis on a key statistic (for example, "The installation of the stainless steel heating tanks has, as we have seen, saved our firm 32 percent in utility costs, since we no longer have to run the heating system all day.")

End your presentation, as Marilyn Claire Ford does in slide 7, with a concise summary of the main points and urge listeners to invest company money in your product or service—for example, World Tech Desktop Videoconferencing system.

Mean It When You Say, "Finally"

When you tell your audience you are concluding, make sure you mean it. Saying, "In conclusion," and then talking for another ten minutes frustrates listeners and makes them less receptive to your message.

Presentation Software

As Marilyn Claire Ford's presentation in Figures 17.2 and 17.3 demonstrates, more and more business talks use PowerPoint, Corel Presentation, and other presentation software. Using these graphics packages is a crucial skill your employer will expect you to have. These software packages enable you to create an electronic slide show with concise text and carefully chosen visuals that can be created on any computer that has Windows 98, 2000, or XP. They allow you to plan, write, and create your slides with visuals all at once. Presentations stored on disks can be shown on your laptop for a small group or projected from your computer to any available flat, illuminated surface for larger audiences.

Presentation Software Capabilities

With PowerPoint, Corel, and other presentation software, you can

- format and edit text or graphics
- revise and update text and visuals
- create hyperlinks
- give audiences an outline of your presentation
- send an image to customers
- share with a collaborative team for their commentary
- import visuals, photos, digital art, clip art
- incorporate a variety of shapes and symbols—arrows, cylinders, pyramids, flow charts, pictograms
- offer animation, sound bites, movie/video clips
- design and insert logos and letterheads
- develop overhead and onscreen transparencies
- reuse your presentation anytime

Presentation software will also help you as a speaker. For instance, you can keyboard your notes so that they scroll at the bottom of your computer screen. These notes are not projected for the audience, but they are available if you need to glance at them. You also can print parts of your presentation or your entire program in color or gray scale (black and white) to reinforce your presentation with professional-looking handouts.

Editing with your presentation software allows you to customize any text or visual. You can copy, move, alter, and delete text, graphics, or sound bites. For example, you could edit the number of categories (bars, lines of a graph, items in a table) of an imported visual for a consumer audience that does not need much detail, or you could change the levels and positions of an organizational chart to suit your agency's needs. You can also change the color or texture of a background, saving you time and effort in recreating a visual.

Map your presentation before you actually create your slides. First, identify the large topics you want to cover, as Marilyn Claire Ford did in presenting information to save GTP time and money, increase staff efficiency, and help the company compete in a post-9/11 economy. Then organize your topics logically and persuasively. Divide your presentation into major topics that best accomplish your objective—whether to inform, to persuade, or to document. Include only those supporting details that relate directly to your topic and to your audience's needs. These key points should help you determine the number of slides and visuals you use. But don't overwhelm audiences with too much information. Note that Marilyn Claire Ford needs only seven slides in Figure 17.3. Also choose your visuals carefully. Resist the temptation to dazzle your audience with electronic special effects. Your goal is not to create a glitzy show but to represent your company professionally.

Be prepared technologically as well as organizationally. Find and eliminate any bugs at the rehearsal stage. Call in advance to confirm the room and any equipment you may need. Allow extra time for the setup. Save and preview your presentation often in the format in which you will be giving it. If possible, bring your own computer to the meeting and set up the projector and your laptop together in advance. If you are not using your laptop, make sure your software is compatible with the equipment you will use. Be sure any websites you use are (1) valid and (2) actually connected to the Internet. This is what Marilyn Claire Ford does in slide 7 of her presentation. Have backup transparencies and handouts available if your computer malfunctions before or during the presentation.

Guidelines on Using Presentation Software Effectively

Here are some tips to ensure that the design, organization, and delivery of your presentation go smoothly. Refer to Figure 17.3 as you study them.

Readability

- Make sure each slide is easy to read—clear and uncluttered
- Use a type size that is crisp and easy to see, even from a distance. For a small presentation on your laptop, use 30-point type or larger. Increase your type size for headings, as in Figure 17.3. If you use a projector, be sure everyone in the room can read your slides clearly.
- Choose a font that enhances readability—single block is best (see pp. 513–518). Keep your type style and size consistent. Don't switch from one font to another.
- Avoid ornate or script type, and do not put everything in boldface or in all capital letters. See how Marilyn Claire Ford boldfaces only her headings in Figure 17.3.

Text

- Keep text short and simple. Use easy-to-recall names, words, and phrases. Your audience will not have the time to read long, complex messages.

- Use bulleted lists instead of unbroken paragraphs. But put no more than five bulleted lines on a slide and limit each line to seven or eight words. Don't squeeze words on a line. Include no more than forty to forty-five words per slide.
- Double-space between bulleted items and leave generous margins on all sides of every slide.
- Title each slide—using a question, a statement, or key name or phrase.

Sequencing Slides

- Keep your slides in the correct order in which you need to show them.
- Limit your presentation to twelve slides, maximum.
- Keep the same transition (cover left or straight right) from slide to slide to avoid visual confusion.
- Spend about two to three minutes per slide, but don't read each slide verbatim. Summarize key ideas or concisely expand them while looking at your audience, not the slide.
- Adjust your presentation to fit your time limit. Time your slides so your audience can read them. Never continue to show a slide after you have moved on to a new topic.
- Determine if you will take questions between slides or only after your presentation has been completed. If you invite audience participation and interaction, build in extra time between your slides.
- Don't show blank screens to transition from one point to another.

Background/Color

- Find a pleasant contrasting background to make your text easy to read. Extremely light or dark backgrounds make it harder to decipher your message. Stay away from stark backgrounds, such as using cold white images on a black screen.
- Use the same background for each slide.
- Avoid shadowing your text for "decorative" visual effect.
- Include color when it is professionally appropriate, but use color sparingly. Don't turn each slide into a sizzling neon sign.

Graphics

- Keep graphics clear, simple, and positioned appropriately on the slide.
- Be sure visuals do not cover or shadow text.
- Show only those visuals that support your main points. Not every slide requires a visual. Slides 1 and 7 in Figure 17.3 do not use visuals.
- Include no more than one graphic per slide; otherwise, your text will be more difficult to read.
- Import visuals from identified sources rather than designing new ones.
- Include easy-to-follow graphs and charts instead of complicated tables, elaborate flow charts, or busy diagrams.
- Use clip art sparingly. Remember: Less is more. Clip art must be functional, not distracting. Each icon in Figure 17.3 is functional.

- Incorporate animation, sound effects, or movie/video clips only when they are persuasive, relevant, and undeniably professional.
- Don't bother with borders; they do not make a slide clearer.

Quality Check

- Be sure your spelling, grammar, names, dates, costs, and sources are correct.
- Double-check all math.
- Don't show a slide if you aren't going to discuss it in your presentation.

Noncomputerized Presentations

Visuals are important in all workplace presentations. Refer to pages 506–507 of Chapter 12 for specific guidelines on constructing and incorporating visuals. You can expect to incorporate visuals in a variety of other media besides PowerPoint presentations. There will be situations where you may have to use a conventional chalkboard, a flip chart (where large pieces of white paper are anchored on an easel and flipped over like pages in a notebook or tablet), or an overhead projector where you make your transparencies on sheets of clear plastic. You will almost surely be asked to prepare handouts that include visuals accompanying a presentation and distribute them either before or during your talk.

Regardless of the medium you use, make sure your visuals are

- visible
- easy to understand
- self-explanatory
- relevant
- correct

Getting the Most from Your Noncomputerized Visuals

The following practical suggestions will help you get the most from your visuals when time and space may prohibit using computer setups.

1. **Do not set up your visuals before you begin speaking.** The audience will be wondering how you are going to use them and so will not give you their full attention. When you are finished with a visual, put it away so that your audience will not be distracted by it or tempted to study it instead of listening to you.

2. **Firmly anchor any maps or illustrations.** Having a map roll up or a picture fall off an easel during a presentation is embarrassing.

3. **Never obstruct the audience's view by standing in front of your visuals.** Use a pointer or a laser pointer (a pen-sized tool that projects a bright red spot up to 150 feet) to direct audience attention to your visual.

4. **Avoid crowding too many images onto one visual that you transfer to a projector or onto one pasteboard.** Use different screens or pasteboards instead.

5. Do not put a lot of writing on a visual.   Elaborate labels or wordy descriptions defeat your reason for using the visual. Your audience will spend more time trying to decipher the writing than attempting to understand the visual itself. If any writing must appear on one of your visuals, enlarge it so your audience can read it quickly and easily.

6. Be especially cautious with a slide projector.   Check beforehand to make sure all your slides are in the order in which you are going to discuss them and that they are right side up. Most important, make sure the projector is in good working order. Practice changing from one transparency to another. And test your tape recorder if you are using one as part of your presentation.

Rehearsing Your Presentation

Don't skip rehearsing your talk thinking it will save you time. It will actually help you become more familiar with your topic and overall message, building your confidence. Rehearsing will also help you to acquire more natural speech rhythms—pitch, pauses, and pacing. Here are some strategies to use as you rehearse your speech.

- Know your topic and the various parts of your talk.
- Practice in the room where you will make your presentation, if possible.
- Speak in front of a full-length mirror for at least one rehearsal to see how an audience might view you.
- Talk into a tape recorder to determine whether you sound friendly or frantic, poised or pressured. You can also catch and correct yourself if you are speaking too quickly or too slowly. A rate of about 120 to 140 words a minute is easy for an audience to follow.
- Time yourself so that you will not exceed your allotted time or fall far short of your audience's expectations.
- Practice with the presentation software, visuals, equipment, or projector that you intend to use in your speech for valuable hands-on experience.
- Monitor the type of gestures (neither too many nor too few) you can use for clarity and emphasis in your talk.
- Videotape your final rehearsal and show it to a colleague or instructor for feedback.

Delivering Your Presentation

A poor delivery can ruin a good presentation. You will be evaluated by your style of presentation just as you are in your written work. When you speak before an audience, you will be evaluated on the image you project: how you look, how you talk, and how you move (your body language). Do you mumble into your notes, never looking at the audience? Do you clutch the lectern as if to keep it in place? Do you shift nervously from one foot to the other? All those actions betray your nervousness and detract from your presentation.

In business presentations, it is crucial to make a good first impression. Research shows that people decide what they think of you in the first two or three minutes of your presentation. The way you dress is crucial but so is your body language. In fact, 75 percent of your audience's impressions are influenced by your body language. The nonverbal signals you send affect how your audience will regard your leadership abilities, your sales performance, even your sincerity. Pay attention to gestures, movement of your hands, how you stand, and so on. No matter how many hours you have worked to get your message ready, if your nonverbal presentation is misleading or inappropriate, the impact of what you say will be lost.

The following suggestions on how to deliver a presentation will help you to be a well-prepared, poised speaker.

Settling Your Nerves Before You Speak

Being nervous before your presentation is normal—a faster heartbeat, sweaty palms, shaking. But don't let your nerves stand in your way of delivering a highly successful talk. Here are some ways you can calm yourself before you deliver your presentation and get some healthy doses of confidence.

- Give yourself plenty of time to get there. The more you have to rush, the more anxious you will be.
- Don't bring anything with you that is likely to spill, such as coffee or a soft drink.
- Avoid caffeine for a few hours before your talk if it makes you jittery.
- Take some deep breaths and then hold your breath while you count to ten. Then exhale. This will slow your heart rate and lower your blood pressure.
- Remind yourself that you have spent hours preparing. Your hard work will pull you through.
- Try to chat with one or two members of the audience ahead of time and relax. See your audience as friends—people who can help your career.

To get helpful experience in making presentations, consider joining Toastmasters International, an educational organization that has transformed many frightened speakers into accomplished speech makers. Members of Toastmasters meet at least once a month to listen to and evaluate one another's speeches. From feedback and strategic training, you will grow to be a more confident public speaker. The Toastmasters website is *http://www.toastmasters.org.*

Finally, you could try a panic control method advocated by Don Greene in his book *Fight Your Fear and Win* (New York: Broadway Books, 2002): "Picture the person you would most like to emulate, someone whose confidence or style you admire," and then combine his or her grace, speaking voice, and persuasion with your own qualifications for a successful, less-stressed presentation.

Making Your Presentation

Everyone is nervous before a talk. Accept that fact and even allow a few seconds for "panic time." Then put your nervous energy to work for you. Chances are, your audience will have no idea how anxious you are; they cannot see the butterflies in your stomach. Again, see your audience as friends, not enemies. Remember to do the following:

1. **Establish eye contact with your listeners.**   Look at as many people in your audience as possible to establish a relationship with them. Never bury your head in notes or keep your eyes fixed on a computer screen or keyboard. You will signal your lack of interest in the audience or your fear of public speaking. Some timid speakers think that if they look only at some fixed place or object in the back of the room, the audience will regard this as eye contact. But that kind of cover-up does not work. In a small PowerPoint presentation, try to establish rapport with each person in the room.

2. **Adjust to audience feedback.**   Watch your listeners' reactions and respond appropriately—nodding to agree, pausing a moment, paraphrasing to clarify a confusing point. Know your material well so that if someone asks you a question or wants you to return to a point, you are not fumbling through your notes or trying feverishly to locate the right screen.

3. **Use a friendly, confident tone.**   Speak in a natural, pleasant voice, but avoid verbal tics ("you know," "I mean") and fillers ("um," "ah," "er") repeated several times each minute. Such nervous habits will make your audience nervous and your speech less effective. Use pauses instead.

4. **Vary the rate of your delivery.**   Use your natural speaking voice. Vary your rate and inflection to help you emphasize key points and make transitions. Talk slowly enough for your audience to understand you, yet quickly enough so that you don't sound as if you are belaboring or emphasizing each word.

5. **Adjust your volume appropriately.**   Talking in a monotone, never raising or lowering your voice, will lull your audience to sleep or at least inattention! Talk loudly enough for everyone to hear, but be careful if you are using a microphone. Your voice will be amplified, so if you speak loudly, you will boom rather than project. Every word with a *b*, *p*, or *d* will sound like an explosive in your listener's ear. Watch out for the other extreme—speaking so softly that only the first two rows can hear you.

6. **Watch your posture.**   Don't shift from one foot to another. But do not slouch or look wooden either. If you stand motionless, looking as if rigor mortis has set in, your speech will be judged cold and lifeless, no matter how lively your words are. Be natural yet dynamic; move, and let your body react to what you are saying. Smile, nod your head, move your arms, refer to an object on the screen by touching it, or use a pointer to emphasize something on an overhead projector.

7. **Use appropriate body language.**   Be natural and consistent. Do not startle an audience by suddenly pounding on the lectern or desk for emphasis. Avoid gestures that will distract or alienate your audience. For example, don't fold your arms as you talk, a gesture that signals you are unreceptive (closed) to your audience's reactions. Also, avoid the nervous habits that can divert the audience's attention: clicking a ballpoint pen, scratching your head, rubbing your nose, twirling your hair,

pushing up your glasses, fumbling with your notes, tapping your foot, or drumming your fingers on a desk. Nor do you have to remain still or step with robotlike movements. The remote control for a PowerPoint presentation allows you to casually walk around the room as you click and change screens.

8. Dress professionally. Do not wear clothes or clanking jewelry (such as necklace or bracelet charms) that call attention to themselves. Be conservative and dress formally. Wear clothes that are the business norm—know your company's dress code. Women should wear a businesslike dress or suit; men should wear a dark business suit, white shirt, and a tasteful tie.

When You Have Finished

Don't just sit down before your computer, walk back to your place on the platform or in the audience, or, worse yet, march out of the room. Thank your listeners for their attention and stay at the lectern or at your laptop for audience applause or questions, as Marilyn Claire Ford did in Figure 17.3. If appropriate, give the person who introduced you a chance to thank you while you are still in front of the group.

If a question-and-answer session is to follow your speech, anticipate questions your audience is likely to ask. But it's a good idea to give your audience a time limit. For example, you might say, "I'll be happy to answer your questions now before we break for lunch in ten minutes." By setting limits, you reduce the chances of a lengthy debate with members of the audience, and you also can politely leave after your time elapses.

Evaluating Presentations

A large portion of this chapter has given you information on how to construct and deliver a formal presentation. As a way of reviewing that advice, study Figure 17.4—an evaluation form similar to those used by instructors in communications classes. Note that the form gives equal emphasis to the speaker's performance or delivery and to the organization, content, and sequence of the presentation.

Figure 17.4   An evaluation form for an oral presentation.

Name of speaker _____ Date of presentation _____

Title of presentation _____ Length of presentation _____

PART I: THE SPEAKER (circle the appropriate number)

1. Appearance:	1 sloppy	2	3	4	5 well groomed
2. Eye contact:	1 poor	2	3	4	5 effective
3. Voice:	1 monotonous	2	3	4	5 varied
4. Posture:	1 poor	2	3	4	5 natural
5. Gestures:	1 disturbing	2	3	4	5 appropriate
6. Self-confidence:	1 nervous	2	3	4	5 poised

PART II: THE PRESENTATION (circle the appropriate number: 1 = poor;
5 = superior)

1. Speaker's knowledge of the subject—carefully researched; factual errors;
missing details:

    1   2   3   4   5

2. Relevance of the topic for audience—suitable for this group:

    1   2   3   4   5

3. The speaker's language—too technical; filled with clichés or slang
expressions; or crisp and descriptive:

    1   2   3   4   5

4. The speaker's slides and/or other visuals—easy to read, large, relevant,
carefully timed and ordered:

    1   2   3   4   5

5. Presentation easy to follow—speaker gave the audience signs where
he or she had been and where he or she was going:

    1   2   3   4   5

6. Presentation fit time limit; included appropriate number of slides:

    1   2   3   4   5

7. Speaker's conclusion—clearly identified major points:

    1   2   3   4   5

✔ Revision Checklist

- ☐ Anticipated audience's background, interest, or even potential resistance, and questions about message of both informal and formal presentations.
- ☐ Used effective telephone/cell phone etiquette.
- ☐ Prepared introduction to provide "road map" of presentation and to arouse audience interest.
- ☐ Started with interesting and relevant statistics, a question, an anecdote, or similar "hook" to capture audience attention.
- ☐ Limited body of presentation to main points.
- ☐ Sequenced main points logically and made connections among them.
- ☐ Used supporting examples and illustrations appropriate to audience.
- ☐ Made sure conclusion contains summary of main points of my presentation and/or specific call for action.
- ☐ Prepared outline and identified and corrected any weak or redundant areas.
- ☐ Designed visuals that are clear, easy to read, and relevant for audience.
- ☐ Experimented successfully with presentation software and applications before including it in a presentation.
- ☐ Rehearsed presentation thoroughly to become familiar with its organization and visuals.
- ☐ Monitored volume, tone, and rate to vary delivery and emphasize major points.
- ☐ Rehearsed gestures to make them relevant and nonintrusive.
- ☐ Timed presentation, complete with visuals, to run close to allotted time.

Exercises

Online Study Center
Access the making presentations Revision Checklist online at college.hmco.com/pic/kolin8e

Online Study Center
Find additional making presentations exercises at college.hmco.com/pic/kolin8e

1. Prepare a three- to five-minute presentation explaining how a piece of equipment that you use on your job works. If the equipment is small enough, bring it with you to class. If it is too large, prepare an appropriate visual or two for use in your talk.

2. You have just been asked to talk about the students at your school or the employees where you work. Narrow the topic and submit an outline to your instructor, showing how you have limited the topic and gathered and organized evidence. Use two or three appropriate visuals (tables, photographs, maps, charts, icons, or even videos) to give a PowerPoint presentation. Follow the format of the presentation in Figure 17.3.

3. Prepare a ten-minute presentation on a controversial topic that you would present before a civic group—the PTA, the local chapter of an organization, a post of the Veterans of Foreign Wars, a synagogue, a mosque, or a church club.

4. Using the information contained in the report on telecommuting in Chapter 9 (pp. 383–405) or the long report on multinational workers in Chapter 16 (pp. 680–697), prepare a short presentation (five to seven minutes) for your class.

5. Using the evaluation form in Figure 17.4, evaluate a speaker—a speech class student, a local politician, or a co-worker delivering a report at work. Specify the time, place, and occasion of the speech. Pay special attention to any visuals the speaker uses.

6. Deliver a formal presentation (fifteen to twenty minutes) on the various uses and advantages of the Internet for individuals in your chosen career field. Restrict your topic and divide it into four key issues or parts, as Marilyn Claire Ford did in Figure 17.3. Use at least three visuals with your talk. Submit an outline to your instructor.

A Writer's Brief Guide to Paragraphs, Sentences, and Words

To write successfully, you must know how to create effective paragraphs, write and punctuate clear sentences, and use words correctly. This guide succinctly explains some of the basic elements of clear and accurate writing.

Paragraphs

Writing a Well-Developed Paragraph

A paragraph is the basic building block for any piece of writing. It is (1) a group of related sentences (2) arranged in a logical order (3) supplying readers with detailed, appropriate information (4) on a single important topic.

A paragraph expresses one central idea, with each sentence contributing to the overall meaning of that idea. The paragraph does that by means of a *topic sentence*, which states the central idea, and *supporting information*, which explains the topic sentence.

Supply a Topic Sentence

The topic sentence is the most important sentence in your paragraph. Carefully worded and restricted, it helps you to generate and control your information. An effective topic sentence also helps readers grasp your main idea quickly. As you draft your paragraphs, pay close attention to the following three guidelines.

1. Make sure you provide a topic sentence. In their rush to supply readers with facts, some writers forget or neglect to include a topic sentence. The following paragraph, with no topic sentence, shows how fragmented such writing can be.

No topic sentence: Sensors found on each machine detect wind speed and direction and other important details such as ice loading and potential metal fatigue. The information is fed into a small computer (microprocessor) in the nacelle (or engine housing). The microprocessor automatically keeps the blades turned into the wind, starts and stops the machine, and changes the pitch of the tips of the blades to increase power under varying wind conditions. Should any part of the wind turbine suffer damage or malfunction, the microprocessor will immediately shut the machine down.

Only when a suitable topic sentence is added—"The MOD-2 wind turbine is programmed to run completely by computer"—can readers understand what the technical details have in common.

723

2. Put your topic sentence first.   Place your topic sentence at the beginning—not the middle or end—of your paragraph because the first sentence occupies an emphatic position. Burying the key idea in the middle or near the end of the paragraph makes it harder for readers to comprehend your purpose or act on your information.

3. Be sure your topic sentence is focused.   If restricted, a topic sentence discusses only one central idea. A broad or unrestricted topic sentence leads to a shaky, incomplete paragraph for two reasons.

- The paragraph will not contain enough information to support the topic sentence.
- A broad topic sentence will not summarize or forecast specific information in the paragraph.

The following example of a carefully constructed paragraph contains a clear topic sentence in an appropriate position (highlighted in color) and adequate supporting details.

> Fat is an important part of everyone's diet. It is nutritionally present in the basic food groups we eat—meat and poultry, dairy products, and oils—to aid growth or development. The fats and fatty acids present in those foods ensure proper metabolism, thus helping to turn what we eat into the energy we need. Those same fats and fatty acids also act as carriers for important vitamins like A, D, E, and K. Another important role of fat is that it keeps us from feeling hungry by delaying digestion. Fat also enhances the flavor of the food we eat, making it more enjoyable.

Three Characteristics of an Effective Paragraph

Effective paragraphs have **unity**, **coherence**, and **completeness**.

Unity

A unified paragraph sticks to one topic without wandering. Every sentence, every detail, **supports**, **explains**, or **proves** the central idea. A unified paragraph includes only relevant information and excludes unnecessary or irrelevant comments.

Coherence

In a coherent paragraph all sentences flow smoothly and logically to and from each other like the links of a chain. Use the following three techniques to achieve coherence.

1. Use transitional words and phrases.   Some useful connective, transitional words, along with the relationships they express, are listed in Table A.1.

> Paragraph with connective words: Advertising a product on the radio has many advantages over using television. *For one thing*, radio rates are much cheaper. *For example*, a one-time 60-second spot on television can cost $750. *For that money*, advertisers can purchase nine 30-second spots on the radio. *Equally attractive* are the low production costs for radio advertising. *In contrast*, television advertising often includes extra costs for models and voice-overs. *Another* advantage radio offers advertisers is immediate scheduling. *Often* the ad appears during the same week a contract is

TABLE A.1   Transitional, or Connective, Words and Phrases

Addition	again additionally along with also and as well as	besides first, second, third furthermore in addition many	moreover next together with too what's more
Cause/effect	accordingly and so as a result because of	consequently due to hence if	on account of since therefore thus
Comparison/ contrast	but conversely equally however	in contrast in the same way likewise on the contrary	on the other hand similarly still yet
Conclusion	all in all altogether as we saw at last finally	in brief in conclusion in short in summary lastly	on the whole to conclude to put into perspective to summarize to wrap up
Condition	although depending even though	granted that if of course	provided that to be sure unless
Emphasis	above all after all again as a matter of fact as I said	for emphasis indeed in fact in other words obviously	of course surely to repeat to stress unquestionably
Illustration	for example for instance in effect	in other words in particular specifically	that is, to demonstrate to illustrate
Place	across from adjacent to alongside of at this point behind	below beyond here in front of next to	over there under where wherever
Time	afterward at length at the same time at times beforehand currently during earlier	formerly hereafter later meanwhile next now once presently	previously soon simultaneously subsequently then until when while

signed. *On the other hand*, television stations are *frequently* booked up months in advance, so it may be a long time *before* an ad appears. *Furthermore*, radio gives advertisers a greater opportunity to reach potential buyers. *After all*, radio follows listeners everywhere—in their homes, at work, and in their cars. *Although* television is very popular, it cannot do that.

2. Use pronouns and demonstrative adjectives.   Words like *he, she, him, her, they*, and so on contribute to paragraph coherence and increase the flow of sentences.

Paragraph with pronouns: Traffic studies are an important tool for store owners looking for a new location. These studies are relatively inexpensive and highly accurate. They can tell owners how much traffic passes by a particular location at a particular time and why. Moreover, they can help owners to determine what particular characteristics the individuals have in common. Because of their helpfulness, these studies can save owners time and money and possibly prevent financial ruin.

3. Use parallel (coordinated) grammatical structures.   Parallelism means using the same *kind of* word, phrase, clause, or sentence to express related concepts.

Orientation sessions accomplish four useful goals for trainees. First, they introduce trainees to key personnel in accounting, data processing, maintenance, and security. Second, they give trainees experience logging into the database system, selecting appropriate menus, editing core documents, and getting off the system. Third, they explain to trainees the company policies affecting the way supplies are ordered, used, and stored. Fourth, they help trainees understand their responsibilities in such sensitive areas as computer security and use.

Parallelism is at work on a number of levels in the paragraph above, among them

- The four sentences about the four goals start in the same way grammatically ("... they introduce/give/explain/help ...") to help readers categorize the information.
- Within individual sentences, the repetition of *present participles* (logg*ing*, select*ing*, edit*ing*, gett*ing*) and of *past participles* (order*ed*, us*ed*, stor*ed*) helps the writer to coordinate information.
- Transitional words—*first, second, third, fourth*—provide a clear-cut sequence.

Completeness

A complete paragraph provides readers with sufficient information to **clarify, analyze, support, defend,** or **prove** the central idea expressed in the topic sentence. The reader feels satisfied that the writer has given necessary details.

Skimpy paragraph: Farmers can turn their crops and farm wastes into useful, cost-effective fuels. Much grown on the farm can be converted to energy. This energy can have many uses and save farmers a lot of money in operating expenses.

Fully developed paragraph: Farm crops and wastes can be turned into fuels to save farmers on their operating costs. Alcohol can be distilled from grain, sugar beets, potatoes, even blighted crops. Converted to gasohol (90 percent gasoline,

10 percent alcohol), this fuel can run such farm equipment as irrigation pumps, feed grinders, and tractors. Similarly, through a biomass digestion system, farmers can produce methane from animal or crop wastes as a natural gas for heating and cooking. Finally, cellulose pellets, derived from plant materials, become solid fuel that can save farmers money in heating barns.

Sentences

Constructing and Punctuating Sentences

The way you construct and punctuate your sentences can determine whether you succeed or fail in the world of work. Your sentences reveal a lot about you. They tell readers how clearly or how poorly you can convey a message. And any message is only as effective and as thoughtful as the sentences of which it is made.

What Makes a Sentence

A sentence is a complete thought, expressed by a subject and a verb that can make sense standing alone.

    subject   verb

    Websites   sell   products.

The Difference Between Phrases and Clauses

The first step toward success in writing sentences is learning to recognize the difference between phrases and clauses. A **phrase** is a group of words that does not contain a subject and a verb; phrases cannot make sense standing alone. Phrases cannot be sentences.

in the park	No subject:	Who is in the park?
	No verb:	What was done in the park?
for every patient in intensive care	No subject:	Who did something for every patient?
	No verb:	What was done for the patients?

A **clause** does contain a subject and a verb, but *not every clause is a sentence.* Only **independent** (or **main**) **clauses** can stand alone as sentences. Here is an example of an independent clause that is a complete sentence.

    subject verb   object

    The president closed the college.

A **dependent** (or **subordinate**) **clause** also contains a subject and a verb, but it does not make complete sense and cannot stand alone. Why? A dependent clause contains a subordinating conjunction—*after, although, as, because, before, even though, if, since, unless, when, where, whereas, while*—at the beginning of the clause. Such conjunctions subordinate the clause in which they appear and make the clause dependent for meaning and completion on an independent clause.

After
Before
Because } the president closed the college
Even though
Unless

"After the president closed the college" is not a complete thought but a dependent clause that leaves us in suspense. It needs to be completed with an independent clause telling us what happened "after."

dependent clause	independent clause		
	subject	verb	phrase
After the president closed the college,	we	played	in the snow.

Avoiding Sentence Fragments

An incomplete sentence is called a **fragment**. Fragments can be phrases or dependent clauses. They either lack a verb or a subject or have broken away from an independent clause. A fragment is isolated: It needs an overhaul to supply missing parts to turn it into an independent clause or to glue it back to an independent clause to have it make sense.

To avoid writing fragments, follow these rules. *Note that incorrect examples are preceded by a minus sign, correct revisions by a plus sign.*

 1. **Do not use a subordinate clause as a sentence.**   Even though it contains a subject and a verb, a subordinate clause standing alone is still a fragment. To avoid this kind of sentence fragment, simply join the two clauses (the independent clause and the dependent clause containing a subordinating conjunction) with a comma—*not* a period or semicolon.

  – Unless we agreed to the plan. (What would happen?)
  – Unless we agreed to the plan; the project manager would discontinue the operation. (A semicolon cannot set off the subordinate clause.)
  + Unless we agreed to the plan, the project manager would discontinue the operation.
  – Because safety precautions were taken. (What happened?)
  + Because safety precautions were taken, ten construction workers escaped injury.

Sometimes subordinate clauses appear at the end of a sentence. They may be introduced by a subordinate conjunction, an adverb, or a relative pronoun (*that, which, who*). Do not separate these clauses from the preceding independent clause with a period, thus turning them into fragments.

  – An all-volunteer fire department posed some problems. Especially for residents in the western part of town.
  + An all-volunteer fire department posed some problems, especially for residents in the western part of town. (The word *especially* qualifies posed, referred to in the independent clause.)

 2. **Every sentence must have a subject telling the reader who does the action.**

  – Being extra careful not to spill the solution. (Who?)
  + The technician was being extra careful not to spill the solution.

3. Every sentence must have a complete verb.   Watch especially for verbs ending in *-ing*. They need another verb (some form of *to be*) to make them complete.

   – The machine running in the computer department. (Did what?)

You can change that fragment into a sentence by supplying the correct form of the verb.

   + The machine *is running* in the computer department.
   + The machine *runs* in the computer department.

Or you can revise the entire sentence, adding a new thought.

   + The machine running in the computer department processes all new accounts.

4. Do not detach prepositional phrases (beginning with *at, by, for, from, in, to, with*, and so forth) **from independent clauses.**   Such phrases are not complete thoughts and cannot stand alone. Correct the error by leaving the phrases attached to the sentence to which they belong.

   – By three o'clock the next day. (What was to happen?)
   + The supervisor wanted our reports by three o'clock the next day.

Avoiding Comma Splices

Fragments occur when you use only bits and pieces of complete sentences. Another common error that some writers commit involves just the reverse kind of action. They weakly and wrongly join two complete sentences (independent clauses) with a comma as if those two sentences were really only one sentence. Such an error is called a **comma splice**. Here is an example.

   – Gasoline prices have risen by 10 percent in the last mont<u>h, </u>we will drive the car less often.

Two independent clauses (complete sentences) exist:

   + Gasoline prices have risen by 10 percent in the last month.
   + We will drive the car less often.

A comma alone lacks the power to separate independent clauses.
   As the preceding example shows, many pronouns—*I, he, she, it, we, they*—are used as the subjects of independent clauses. A comma splice will result if you place a comma instead of a semicolon between two independent clauses where the second clause opens with a pronoun.

   – Maria approved the pla<u>n, </u>she liked its cost-effective approach.
   + Maria approved the pla<u>n; </u>she liked its cost-effective approach.

However, relative pronouns (*who, whom, which, that*) are preceded by a comma, not a period or a semicolon, when they introduce subordinate clauses.

   – She approved the plan. Which had the cost-effective approach.
   + She approved the plan, which had the cost-effective approach.

Four Ways to Correct Comma Splices

1. Remove the comma separating two independent clauses and replace it with a period.   Then capitalize the first letter of the first word of the new sentence.

+ Gasoline prices have risen by 10 percent in the last month. We will drive the car less often.

2. Insert a coordinating conjunction (*and, but, or, nor, so, for, yet*) after the comma.   Together, the conjunction and the comma properly separate the two independent clauses.

+ Gasoline prices have risen by 10 percent in the last month, and so we will drive the car less often.

3. Rewrite the sentence (*if it makes sense to do so*).   Turn the first independent clause into a dependent clause by adding a subordinate conjunction; then insert a comma and add the second independent clause.

+ Because gasoline prices have risen by 10 percent in the last month, we will drive the car less often.

4. Delete the comma and insert a semicolon.

+ Gasoline prices have risen by 10 percent in the last month; we will drive the car less often.

Of the four ways to correct the comma splice, sentences 3 and 4 are equally suitable, but sentence 3 reads more smoothly and so is the better choice.

The semicolon is an effective and forceful punctuation mark when two independent clauses are closely related, that is, when they announce contrasting or parallel views, as the two following examples reveal.

+ The union favored the new legislation; the company opposed it. (contrasting views)
+ Night classes help the college and the community; students can take more credit hours to advance their careers. (parallel views)

How *Not* to Correct Comma Splices

Some writers mistakenly try to correct comma splices by inserting a conjunctive adverb (*also, consequently, furthermore, however, moreover, nevertheless, then, therefore*) after the comma.

– Gasoline prices have risen by 10 percent in the last month, consequently we will drive the car less often.

Because the conjunctive adverb (*consequently*) is not as powerful as the coordinating conjunction (*and, but, for*), the error is not eliminated. If you use a conjunctive adverb—*consequently, however, nevertheless*—you still must insert a semicolon or a period before it, as the following examples show.

+ Gasoline prices have risen by 10 percent in the last month; consequently, we will drive the car less often.
+ Gasoline prices have risen by 10 percent in the last month. Consequently, we will drive the car less often.

Avoiding Run-On Sentences

A **run-on sentence** is the opposite of a sentence fragment. The fragment gives the reader too little information, the run-on too much. A run-on sentence forces readers to digest two or more grammatically complete sentences without the proper punctuation to separate them.

Run-on   The Internet is unquestionably a major source of information and students and other researchers are right to call it a virtual library this library is not like the collections of books and magazines that are carefully shelved always waiting for students to check and recheck them too often a website disappears or changes considerably and without a backup file or a hard copy the researcher has no document to quote from and no exact citation to prove that he or she consulted an authentic source.

Revised   The Internet is unquestionably a major source of information. Students and other researchers are right to call it a virtual library, although this library is not like the collections of books and magazines that are carefully shelved, waiting for students to check and recheck them out. But too often a website disappears, is under construction, or changes considerably. Without a backup file or a hard copy of the site, the researcher has no document to quote from and no exact citation to prove that he or she consulted an authentic source.

As the revision above shows, you can repair a run-on sentence by (1) dividing it into separate, correctly punctuated sentences and (2) by adding coordinating conjunctions (*and, but, yet, so, or, nor*) between clauses.

Making Subjects and Verbs Agree in Your Sentences

A subject and a verb must agree in number. A singular subject takes a singular verb, whereas a plural subject requires a plural verb.

Singular Subject	Plural Subjects
the engineer calculates	engineers calculate
a report analyzes	reports analyze
a policy changes	policies change

You can avoid subject-verb agreement errors by following several simple rules.

1. Disregard any words that come between the subject and its verb.

Faulty: The customer who ordered three parts want them shipped this afternoon.
Correct: The <u>customer</u> who ordered three parts <u>wants</u> them shipped this afternoon.

2. A compound subject (two parts connected by *and*) **takes a plural verb.**

Faulty: The engineering department and the safety committee prefers to develop new guidelines.
Correct: The engineering department and the safety committee prefer to develop new guidelines.

3. When a compound subject contains *neither . . . nor* or *either . . . or*, the verb agrees with the subject closest to it.

Faulty: Either the residents or the manager are going to file the complaint.
Correct: Either the residents or the manager is going to file the complaint.
Correct: Either the manager or the residents are going to file the complaint.

4. Use a singular verb after collective nouns (like *committee, crew, department, group, organization, staff, team*) **when the group functions as a single unit.**

Correct: The crew was available to repair the machine.
Correct: The committee asks that all recommendations be submitted by Friday.

but

Correct: The staff were unable to agree on the best model.
            (The staff acted as individuals, not a unit, so a plural verb is required.)

5. Use a singular verb with indefinite pronouns (such as *anyone, anybody, each, everyone, everything, no one, somebody, something*).

Each of the programmer<u>s</u> has completed the seminar.
Somebody usually volunteer<u>s</u> for that duty.

Similarly, when *all, most, more*, or *part* is the subject, it requires a singular verb.

Most of the money is allocated.
Part of the equipment was salvageable.

6. Words like *scissors* and *pants* are plural when they are the true subject.

Faulty: A pair of trousers were available in his size. (*Pair* is the singular subject.)
Correct: The trousers were on sale.

7. Some foreign plurals (*curricula, data, media, phenomena, strata, syllabi*) **always take a plural verb.**

The data conclusively <u>prove</u> my point.
The media <u>are</u> usually the first to point out a politician's weak points.

8. Use a singular verb with fractions.

Three-fourths of her research proposal was finished.

Writing Sentences That Say What You Mean

Your sentences should say exactly what you mean, without doubletalk, misplaced humor, or nonsense. Sentences are composed of words and word groups that influence each other.

Writing Logical Sentences

Sentences should not contradict themselves or make outlandish claims. The following examples contain errors in logic; note how easily the suggested revisions solve the problem.

Illogical: Steel roll-away shutters make it possible for the sun to be shaded in the summer and to have it shine in the winter. (The sun is far too large to shade; the writer meant that a room or a house, much smaller than the sun, could be shaded with the shutters.)

Revision: Steel roll-away shutters make it possible for owners to shade their living rooms in the summer and to admit sunshine during the winter.

Using Contextually Appropriate Words

Sentences should use the combination of words most appropriate for the subject.

Inappropriate: The members of the Nuclear Regulatory Commission saw fear radiated on the faces of the residents. (The word *radiated* is obviously ill advised in this context; use a neutral term.)

Revision: The members of the Nuclear Regulatory Commission saw fear reflected on the faces of the residents.

Writing Sentences with Well-Placed Modifiers

A **modifier** is a word, phrase, or clause that describes, limits, or qualifies the meaning of another word or word group. A modifier can consist of one word (a *green* car), a prepositional phrase (the man *in the telephone booth*), a relative clause (the woman *who won the marathon*), or an *-ing* or *-ed* phrase (*walking three miles a day*, the student was in good shape; *seated in the first row*, we saw everything on stage).

A **dangling modifier** is one that cannot logically modify any word in the sentence.

– When answering the question, his calculator fell off the table.

One way to correct the error is to insert the right subject after the *-ing* phrase.

+ When answering the question, he knocked his calculator off the table.

You can also turn the phrase into a subordinate clause.

+ When he answered the question, his calculator fell off the table.
+ His calculator fell off the table as he answered the question.

A **misplaced modifier** illogically modifies the wrong word or words in the sentence. The result is often comical.

– Hiding in the corner, growling and snarling, our guide spotted the frightened cub. (Is our guide growling and snarling in the corner?)
– All travel requests must be submitted by employees in red ink. (Are the employees covered in red ink?)

The problem with both of those examples is word order. The modifiers are misplaced because they are attached to the wrong words in the sentence. Correct the error by moving the modifier to where it belongs.

+ Hiding in the corner, growling and snarling, the frightened cub was spotted by our guide.
+ All travel requests by employees must be submitted in red ink.

Misplacing a relative clause (introduced by relative pronouns like *who, whom, that, which*) can also lead to problems with modification.

   − The salesperson recorded the merchandise for the customer that the store had discounted. (The merchandise was discounted, not the customer.)

   − The salesperson recorded the merchandise that the store had discounted for the customer. (The salesperson recorded for the customer; the store did not discount for the customer.)

   + The salesperson recorded for the customer the merchandise that the store had discounted.

Always place the relative clause immediately after the word it modifies.

Correct Use of Pronoun References in Sentences

Sentences will be vague if they contain a faulty use of pronouns. When you use a pronoun whose **antecedent** (the person, place, or object the pronoun refers to) is unclear, you risk confusing your reader.

> Unclear: After the plants are clean, we separate the stems from the roots and place them in the sun to dry. (Is it the stems or the roots that lie in the sun?)
>
> Revision: After the plants are clean, we separate the stems from the roots and place the stems in the sun to dry.
>
> Unclear: The park ranger was pleased to see the workers planting new trees and installing new benches. This will attract more tourists. (The trees or the benches or both?)
>
> Revision: The park ranger was pleased to see the workers planting new trees and installing new benches, because the new trees and benches will attract more tourists.

▉ Words

Spelling Words Correctly

Your written work will be judged in part on how well you spell. A misspelled word may seem like a small matter, but on an employment application, e-mail, incident report, letter, or short or long report it stands out to your discredit. A spelling mistake will look careless or, even worse, uneducated to a client or a supervisor. Readers will inevitably question your other skills if your spelling is incorrect.

The Benefits and Pitfalls of Spell Checkers

Computer **spell checkers** can be handy for flagging potential problem words. But beware! Spell checkers recognize only those words that have been listed in them. A proper name or infrequently used word may be flagged as an error even though the word is spelled correctly. Moreover, a spell checker will not differentiate between such homonyms as *too* and *two* or *there* and *their*. A spell checker identifies only misspelled words, not misused words. In short, do not rely exclusively on spell checkers to solve all your spelling and word-choice problems.

Consulting a Dictionary

Always have a dictionary handy. Two online dictionaries to consult are *Merriam-Webster On-Line* at *http://www.m-w.com* and *The American Heritage Dictionary of the English Language* at *http://www.bartleby.com/61/*.

Using Apostrophes Correctly

Apostrophes cause some writers special problems. Basically, apostrophes are used for four reasons: (1) contractions, (2) possessives, (3) plurals, and (4) abbreviations. The guidelines below will help you to sort out those uses.

1. In a **contraction**, the apostrophe takes the place of the missing letter or letters: *I've = I have; doesn't = does not; he's = he is; it's = it is.* (*Its* is a possessive pronoun (the dog and *its* bone), not a contraction. There is no such form as *its'*.)

2. To form a **possessive**, follow these rules.

a. If a singular or plural noun does not end in an *-s*, add *'s* to show possession.

Mary's locker	the woman's jacket
children's books	the women's jackets
the staff's dedication	the company's policy

b. If a singular noun ends in *-s*, add *'s* to show possession.

the class's project	the boss's schedule

c. If a plural noun ends in *-s*, add just the *'* to indicate possession.

employees' benefits	computers' speed
lawyers' fees	stores' rates

d. If a proper name ends in *-s*, add *'s* to form the possessive.

Jones's account	Keats's poetry
the Williams's house	James's contract

e. If it is a compound noun, add an *'* or *'s* to the end of the word.

brother-in-law's business	Ms. Allison Jones-Wyatt's order

f. To indicate shared possession, add just *'s* to the last name.

Warner and Kline's Computer Shop	Juan and Anne's major

g. To indicate separate possession, add *'s* to each name.

Juan's and Tia's transcripts	Shakespeare's and Byron's poetry

3. To form the plural of numbers and capital letters used as nouns, including abbreviations without periods, just add *s*. To avoid misreading some capital letters, however, you may need to add the apostrophe.

during the 1980s	all perfect 10s
their SATs	several local YMCAs
the 3 Rs	straight A's

4. For abbreviations with periods and for lowercase letters used as nouns, form the plural by adding *'s*.

his *p*'s and *q*'s	Ph.D.'s

Using Hyphens Properly

Use a hyphen (- as opposed to a dash —) for

- **compound words**
  four-part lecture   heavy-duty machine   hand-held PC

- **most words beginning with** *self*
  self-starting   self-defense   self-regulating   self-governing

- **fractions used as adjectives**
  at the three-quarter level   two-thirds majority   three-dimensional drawing

Using Ellipses

See pages 341–342.

Using Numerals Versus Words

Write out numbers as words rather than numerals

- **to begin a sentence**

  Nineteen ninety-nine was the first year of our recruitment drive.

- **to list the first number when two numbers are used together**

  The company needed eleven 9-foot slabs.

But use numerals, not words,

- **with abbreviations, percentages, symbols, units of measurement, dates**

  17%   11:30 a.m.   70 ml
  Dec. 3, 2003 $250.00   50 K

- **for page references**

  pp. 56–59

- **for large numbers**

  3,000,000   23,750   1,714

Use both numerals and words when you want to be as precise as possible in a contract or a proposal.

  We agreed to pay the vendor an extra twenty-five dollars ($25.00) per hour to finish the job by the 18th of May.

For information on conventions of writing and using numbers for an international audience, see Chapter 5.

Matching the Right Word with the Right Meaning

The words in the following list frequently are mistaken for one another. Some are true homonyms; others are just similar in spelling, pronunciation, or usage. The part of speech is given after each word. Use the right word in the right context.

accept (v) to receive, to acknowledge: *We accept your proposal.*
except (prep) excluding, but: *Everyone attended the meeting except Neelou.*

advice (n) a recommendation: *I should have taken Xi's advice.*
advise (v) to counsel: *Our lawyers advised us not to sign the contract.*

affect (v) to change, to influence: *Does the detour on Route 22 affect your travel plans?*
effect (n) a result: *What was the effect of the new procedure?*
effect (v) to bring about: *We will try to effect a change in company policy.*

all ready (adj) two-word phrase *all + ready*; to be finished; to be prepared: *We are all ready for the inspector's visit.*
already (adv) previously, before a given time: *Our webmaster had already constructed the sites.*

ascent (n) move upward: *We watched the space shuttle's ascent.*
assent (n) agreement: *She won the teacher's assent.*
assent (v) to agree: *The committee asked the company to assent to the new terms.*

attain (v) to achieve, to reach: *We attained our sales goal this month.*
obtain (v) to get, to receive: *You can obtain a job application on their website.*

cite (v) to document: *Please cite several examples to support your claim.*
site (n) place, location: *They want to build a parking lot on the site of the old theater.*
sight (n) vision: *His sight improved with bifocals.*

coarse (a) rough: *The sandpaper felt coarse.*
course (n) subject of study: *Sharonda took a course in calculus this fall.*

complement (v) to add to, enhance: *Her graphs and charts complemented my proposal.*
compliment (v) to praise: *The customer complimented us on our courteous staff.*

continually (adv) frequently and regularly: *This answering machine continually disconnects the caller in the middle of the message.*
continuously (adv) constantly: *The air conditioning is on continuously during the summer.*

council (n) government body: *The council voted to increase salaries for all city employees.*
counsel (n) advice: *She gave the trainee pertinent counsel.*

discreet (adj) showing respect, being tactful: *The manager was discreet in answering the complaint letter.*
discrete (adj) separate, distinct: *Put those figures into discrete categories for processing.*

dual (adj) double: *A clock-radio serves a dual purpose.*
duel (n) a fight, a battle: *The argument almost turned into a duel.*

eminent (adj) prominent, highly esteemed: *Dr. Felicia Rollins is the most eminent neurologist in our community.*
imminent (adj) about to happen: *A hostile takeover of that company is imminent.*

fair (n) convention, exhibition: *The technological fair featured a DVD-CD home theater with five satellite speakers.*
fair (adj) honest: *Their price was fair.*
fare (n) cost for a trip: *She was able to get a discount on a round-trip fare.*
fare (n) food: *They ate East Asian fare.*

foreword (n) preface, introduction to a book: *The foreword outlined the author's goals and objectives in her research study.*
forward (adv) toward a time or place; in advance: *We moved the time of the visit forward on the calendar so we could meet the overseas manager.*
forward (v) to send ahead: *We forwarded her e-mail to her new server.*

imply (v) to suggest: *The supervisor implied that the mechanics had taken too long for their lunch break.*
infer (v) to draw a conclusion: *We can infer from these sales figures that the new advertising campaign is working.*

it's (pronoun + verb) contraction of *it* and *is*: *Do you think it's too early to tell?*
its (adj) possessive form of *it*: *That old printer is on its last legs.*

knew (v) (past tense of *know*): *She knew the new regulations.*
new (a) never used before: *The subwoofer was new.*

lay/laid/laid (v) to put down: *Lay aside that project for now. He laid aside the project. He had already laid aside the project twice before.*
lie/lay/lain (v) to recline: *I think I'll lie down for a while. He lay there for only two minutes before the firefighter rescued him. She has lain out in the sun too often.*

lose (v) to misplace, to fail to win: *Be careful not to lose my calculator. I hope I don't lose my seat on the planning board.*
loose (adj) not tight: *The printer ribbon was too loose.*

miner (n) individual who works in a mine: *His uncle was a miner in West Virginia.*
minor (n) someone under legal age: *The law forbids the sale of tobacco to minors.*

pare (v) to cut back: *Sandoval pared the skin from the apple.*
pair (n) a couple: *They offered a pair of resolutions.*
pear (n) a fruit: *Alphonso ate a pear with lunch.*

passed (v) went by (past tense of *pass*): *He passed me in the hall without recognizing me.*
past (n) time gone by: *We've never used their services in the past.*

personal (adj) private: *The manager closes the door when she discusses personal matters with one of her staff.*
personnel (n) staff of employees: *All personnel must participate in the 401(k) retirement program.*

perspective (n) view: *From the customer's perspective, we are an honest and courteous company.*

prospective (adj) expected, likely to happen or become: *E-mail the prospective budget to district managers.*

plain (adj) simple, not fancy: *He ate plain food.*
plane (n) airplane: *The plane for Dallas leaves in an hour.*
plane (v) to make smooth: *The carpenter planed the wood.*

precede (v) to go before: *A slide show will precede the open discussion.*
proceed (v) to carry on, to go ahead: *Proceed as if we had never received that letter.*

principal (adj) main, chief: *Sales of new software constitute their principal source of revenue.*
principal (n) the head of a school: *She was a high school principal before she entered the business world.*
principal (n) money owed: *The principal on that loan totaled $32,800.*
principle (n) a policy, a belief: *Sales reps should operate on the principle that the customer is always right.*

quiet (adj) silent, not loud: *He liked to spend a quiet afternoon surfing the Net.*
quite (adv) to a degree: *The officer was quite encouraged by the recruit's performance.*

stationary (adj) not moving: *Miguel rides a stationary bicycle for an hour every morning.*
stationery (n) writing supplies, such as paper and envelopes: *Please stop off at the stationery store and buy some more address labels.*

than (conj) as opposed to (used in comparisons): *He is a faster keyboarder than his predecessor.*
then (adv) at that time: *First she called the vendor; then she summarized their conversation in an e-mail to her boss.*

their (adj) possessive form of *they*: *All the lab technicians took their vacations during June and July.*
there (adv) in that place: *Please put the printer in there.*
they're (pronoun + verb) contraction of *they* and *are*: *They're our two best customer service representatives.*

who's (pronoun + verb) contraction of *who* and *is*: *Who's up next for a promotion?*
whose (adj) possessive form of *who*: *Whose idea was that in the first place?*

you're (pronoun + verb) contraction of *you* and *are*: *You're going to like their decision.*
your (adj) possessive form of *you*: *They agree with your ideas.*

▌ Proofreading Marks

Mark	Example	Corrected
⌒o	Correct a typu.	Correct a typo.
r⌒/m⌒/⌒o	Correct nore than one typu.	Correct more than one typo.
t	Insert a leter.	Insert a letter.
or words	Insert a word.	Insert a word or words.
⨺	Make a a deletion.	Make a deletion.
⨺	Deletʄe and close up space.	Delete and close up space.
⌒	Close up ex tra space.	Close up extra space.
#	Insertproper spacing.	Insert proper spacing.
#/⌒	Closeup and insert space.	Close up and insert space.
eq #	Regularize proper spacing.	Regularize proper spacing.
tr	Transpose inidcated letters.	Transpose letters indicated.
tr	Transpose as words indicated.	Transpose words as indicated.
tr	Reorder shown as words several.	Reorder several words as shown.
⎡ ⎡	Move text to left.	Move text to left.
⎤ ⎤	Move text to right.	Move text to right.
¶ ⎣	Indent for paragraph.	Indent for paragraph.
no ¶ ⎡	No paragraph indent.	No paragraph indent.
// //	Align type vertically.	Align type vertically.
run in	Run back turnover lines.	Run back turnover lines.
	Break line when it runs far too long.	Break line when it runs far too long.
◯	Insert period here.	Insert period here.
⌃	Commas commas everywhere.	Commas, commas everywhere.
⌄	Its in need of an apostrophe.	It's in need of an apostrophe.
⌄/⌄	Add quotation marks, he begged.	"Add quotation marks," he begged.
;	Add a semicolon don't hesitate.	Add a semicolon; don't hesitate.
:	She advised "You need a colon."	She advised: "You need a colon."
?	How about a question mark.	How about a question mark?
(/)	Add parentheses as they say.	Add parentheses (as they say).
lc	Sometimes you want Lowercase.	Sometimes you want lowercase.
caps	Sometimes you want upperCASE.	Sometimes you want UPPERCASE.
ital	Add italics instantly.	Add italics *instantly*.
bf	Add boldface if necessary.	Add **boldface** if necessary.
wf	Fix a wrong font letter.	Fix a wrong font letter.
sp	Spell out all 3 terms.	Spell out all three terms.
⌄	Change x to a subscript.	Change $_x$ to a subscript.
⌄	Change y to a superscript.	Change ^{y} to a superscript.
stet	Let stand as is.	Let stand as is. (To retract a change already marked.)

INDEX